Regulation and Consumer Protection

Second Edition—Second Printing

Kenneth J. Meier and E. Thomas Garman

Contributing Authors:

James L. Brown
Mary L. Carsky
Mary Ellen R. Fise
Alexander Grant
Ramona K. Z. Heck
Gong-Soog Hong
Lael Keiser
Carol B. Meeks
Sharon Olmstead

S. Lee Richardson
Evan J. Ringquist
Mark Silbergeld
Samuel A. Simon
Kevin B. Smith
Joseph Stewart, Jr.
Judith Lee Stone
Clark D. Thomas
Jing J. Xiao

DAME
Publications, Inc.
Houston, Texas

D1418354

Cover Design: Shelley Bates

© DAME PUBLICATIONS, INC.—1995

ISBN 0-87393-331-1
Second Printing

Printed in the United States of America

Table of Contents at a Glance

Table of Contents

Chapter 3   Regulating Occupations 41

Chapter 8　　　　Workplace Safety and Health Regulation 197

Chapter 11   Consumer Product Safety Regulation 277

Preface

Regulation is essential to modern society. Without rules for acceptable behavior in relationships with other individuals, any complex society would rapidly collapse. Regulation provides a framework that defines acceptable behavior for individuals in a variety of situations. People in business must be concerned with the quality of products they produce, the safety of the workplace, and any pollution that results as a by-product. Other citizens also find their lives regulated: Restrictions are placed on how fast they can drive, what kind of products they can buy, even where they can live.

The Changing Environment of Regulation and Consumer Protection

In the last two decades we have seen a wave of regulatory reform. The 1960s and 1970s saw an explosion of regulatory functions at the federal level with new agencies created to regulate the environment, workplace safety, product safety, and automobiles among others. The 1980s saw a backlash against regulation with the market-oriented reforms of the Reagan administration. If anything regulation and consumer protection have emerged from these reforms stronger than before. Those who dream of an unregulated society are further from realizing that dream than they were 15 years ago.

American politics recently shifted to the Republicans who have promised to reduce the size and power of the federal government. The first Congress in forty years controlled by Republicans is expected to challenge and change the regulatory consumer protection environment. The golden age for critics of Big Federal Government Regulation may have arrived.

Expectations of the new Congress include attempts to cut taxes; slash budgets; narrow missions of regulatory agencies; place new constraints on regulatory authority; consolidate agencies; demand new risk assessments, impact analyses and cost-benefit analyses before agencies are permitted to issue regulations; eliminate programs; increase waivers from federal rules to state and local government; eliminate cost shifting to state and local governments; abolish unfunded mandates (requirements of the federal government that cause state and local government to increase spending to be in compliance); and make greater use of devolution (sending federal programs to states, localities and the private sector).

The constituency that seeks to protect consumers through more government will be seriously challenged to retain gains already achieved, especially as the role of the federal government is reduced. Alternative ways of protecting consumers (i.e., information, education, self-regulation) are likely to receive increased emphasis in the years ahead. No doubt, the remainder of the 1990s will be interesting to students of regulation and consumer protection.

How and Why This Book Was Written

Regulation and Consumer Protection is intended to document the scope and coverage of regulation and consumer protection in the United States. The growth in regulation and consumer protection plus the unique aspects of each area mean that one or two persons simply cannot serve as an authority across all policy areas. We have invited experts in these fields to write about the areas that they know best.

To provide some coherence, a conceptual framework is provided in Chapter 2. The framework essentially combines the viewpoints of those who feel regulatory policies are determined by the social and economic environment and those who feel that bureaucracies are permitted the freedom to set policies without restriction. The economic and technological environment, along with the macropolitical forces, sets the general parameters for regulatory policy. These elements provide both opportunities to make policy and restrictions on such activities. Within the context of these forces, specific policies are established by bureaucracies in interaction with their policy environments. Internal agency factors can be used to explain the specific policies an agency follows among those permitted by the environment.

Goals of *Regulation and Consumer Protection*

In this study of regulation and consumer protection, we have attempted to do three things. First, we have not felt bound by disciplinary restrictions but rather seek to use the valuable information provided by all perspectives on regulation and consumer protection. The result is a multidisciplinary view of public policy. At times concepts and approaches are taken from history, economics, law, consumer science, organization theory, and political science. Guiding this multidisciplinary approach, however, is the belief that regulation is a political process. We have emphasized political rather than economic or legal explanations for regulation and consumer protection.

The second and third goals of this study are sometimes in conflict. One goal is to explain regulatory and consumer protection policy outcomes. The other goal is to suggest specific changes in public policy. Although positivist tradition holds that empirical analysis should be separated from value judgments, in regulatory and consumer protection policy this rarely occurs. Most regulatory analysis has either normative objectives or was instigated by normative concerns. This is as it should be. Social sciences, as Herbert Simon (1969) argued, are sciences of the artificial, concerned as much with how things might be as how they actually are.

Accordingly, this book will not ignore normative issues, nor does it expect the reader to do so. Regulatory and consumer protection policy determines who benefits from government intervention into the marketplace, a topic with few people who can claim neutrality. Rather than disguise normative presentations as empirical arguments, as much of the literature does, this book will make its normative contentions explicit. Although normative and empirical arguments cannot always be separated, some effort has been made to do so by keeping the normative arguments in separate sections and labeling them as such.

Useful Features of This Book

Features of the book that enhance readability and usefulness include employing four levels of headings, putting key terms and concepts in bold print, placing discussion footnotes at the bottom of the page where each reference is cited, locating all references in a single appendix, placing all case citations in a separate appendix, and including a detailed index. An *Instructor's Manual With Test Bank* is also available from the publisher. Arranged according to chapters, it contains a list of key terms and concepts, review questions, chapter outlines (all in a large-font format suitable for making transparencies), and over 1,000 true-false and multiple-choice questions. The "test bank" portion is available from Dame Publications (713-995-1000) on computer disk.

Expressions of Appreciation

The genesis of this project lies with Tom Garman who convinced Ken Meier that *Regulation: Politics, Bureaucracy and Economics* needed to be updated and expanded. Tom was right. Coordinating the work of twenty people and fitting it within a single conceptual framework, however, was not an easy task. As is tradition in political science and now for the first time in consumer affairs, all remaining errors of omission or commission are the responsibility of Paul Sabatier.

This book would not have been possible without the help of many people. We especially want to thank the wonderful authors—people who are rich in real-life regulatory and consumer protection experiences and possess substantial higher-level thinking powers—the experts who generously contributed their authoritative views to *Regulation and Consumer Protection*:

> ***James L. Brown**, Director of the Center for Consumer Affairs and Associate Professor, The University of Wisconsin-Milwaukee
>
> ***Mary L. Carsky**, Associate Professor of Marketing, The University of Hartford
>
> ***Mary Ellen R. Fise**, Product Safety Director, Consumer Federation of America
>
> ***Alexander Grant**, Associate Commissioner for Consumer Affairs, Food and Drug Administration
>
> ***Ramona K. Z. Heck**, Associate Professor and J. Thomas Clark Professor of Entrepreneurship and Personal Enterprise, Cornell University
>
> ***Gong-Soog Hong**, Assistant Professor of Consumer Sciences, Purdue University
>
> ***Lael Keiser**, PhD candidate in Political Science, University of Wisconsin-Milwaukee

*Carol B. Meeks, Professor and Head, Department of Housing and Consumer Economics, University of Georgia

*Sharon Olmstead, Consumer Affairs Specialist, Office of Consumer Affairs, Food and Drug Administration

*S. Lee Richardson, G. Maxwell Armor Eminent Scholar and Professor of Marketing, University of Baltimore

*Evan J. Ringquist, Assistant Professor of Political Science, Florida State University

*Mark Silbergeld, Director, Washington Office of Consumers Union, Washington, DC

*Samuel A. Simon, President, Issues Dynamics, Inc., Washington, DC

*Kevin B. Smith, Assistant Professor of Political Science, University of Nebraska-Lincoln

*Joseph Stewart, Jr., Professor of Government and Politics, University of Texas at Dallas

*Judith Lee Stone, President, Advocates for Highway and Auto Safety

*Clark D. Thomas, PhD candidate in Political Economy, University of Texas at Dallas

*Jing J. Xiao, Assistant Professor of Consumer Economics, University of Rhode Island

Thanks also goes to individuals who patiently facilitated the logistics of this project, Debbie Elkins and Mary Rupe. Also, Elizabeth DeMerchant was extremely helpful with the review questions in the **Instructor's Manual With Test Bank**. Finally, both Meier and Garman are grateful to their spouses for their continued support for yet another book writing project that again took away some shared time, but we all hope that these efforts will contribute to people learning more about regulation and consumer protection so they can help create a better society.

KJM and ETG

ABOUT THE AUTHORS

KENNETH J. MEIER

Kenneth J. Meier is a professor of political science at the University of Wisconsin-Milwaukee. Part of the famed South Dakota connection in political science, he received his BA from the University of South Dakota. His doctorate is from the Maxwell School of Citizenship and Public Affairs at Syracuse University. He previously taught at Rice University, the University of Oklahoma, and the University of Wisconsin-Madison and is currently the editor of the *American Journal of Political Science*. Unlike Garman, Meier tries to avoid working for a living but he occasionally picks up some nonacademic experience. He was a member and chair of the Oklahoma State Ethics and Merit Commission where he gained experience enforcing merit system laws in a patronage state. He was a member of both the Governor's Task Force on Professional and Occupational Discipline and the Insurance Commissioner's Task on Property and Casualty Insurance (Wisconsin).

Professor Meier has wide ranging research interests, considering almost any topic relevant for a political scientist. He has published on bureaucracy, minority politics, education policy, insurance regulation, alcohol and drug policy, abortion and family planning policy, agriculture, traffic safety policy, infant mortality, and several other areas. *The Political Economy of Regulation: The Case of Insurance* (SUNY 1987) was awarded the Clarence Kulp award by the American Risk and Insurance Association and both *The Politics of Hispanic Education* (SUNY 1991) and *Race, Class, and Education* (Wisconsin 1989) won the Gustavus Myers Award. His most recent books are *Politics and the Bureaucracy* 3rd ed. (Wadsworth 1993) and *The Politics of Sin: Drugs, Alcohol and Public Policy* (M.E. Sharpe 1994). He has served as president of three different sections of the American Political Science Association (Public Policy, Public Administration, and State Politics and Policy).

Meier does not consult and wonders how Garman can do all that consulting and still have time to write so much. Instead he performs the role of satirical gadfly for the political science profession. Among his contributions are: organizing and participating on the "Contributions of Elvis Presley to Political Science" panel, coauthoring with Joe Stewart, "Rotisserie Political Science," presenting "Get Your Tongue Out of My Mouth 'Cause I'm Kissing You Goodbye: The Politics of Ideas" at the "Country Music and Political Science" panel, as well as authoring a number of underground cult classics that shall remain nameless owing to the nation's libel laws.

Meier teaches graduate classes in research methods, public policy, and political institutions. He enjoys teaching undergraduates but the University's Vice Chancellor for Risk Management will not let him. Meier lives with the love of his life, Diane Jones Meier, in a turn of the century home near Lake Michigan where his hobbies are stripping paint and trying to find the perfect California zinfandel.

E. THOMAS GARMAN

E. Thomas Garman is a professor of consumer affairs at Virginia Polytechnic Institute and State University in Blacksburg, Virginia. He received his bachelor's and master's degrees in business administration from the University of Denver and his doctorate in economic education from Texas Tech University. Garman's experience includes work for a United States Senator in Washington, retail sales management in Colorado, economic development project management in West Africa, and teaching for thirty years in eight different states. He has taught fifteen summer workshops, including seven "Consumer Issues in Washington" classes taught in the nation's capital, for ten different universities. Garman is a professor who truly enjoys teaching. In 1994, Garman received the Stewart Lee Consumer Education Award from the American Council on Consumer Interests in recognition of his lifetime achievements in the field; in 1995 Garman was elected a "Fellow" by the same organization.

Professor Garman has authored or co-authored over one hundred refereed articles and proceedings publications as well as twelve books, including the currently available *Consumer Economic Issues in America* (Dame Publications), and *The Consumer's World* (McGraw Hill), and *Personal Finance* (Houghton Mifflin). His current writing project is *Consumer Protection: Issues and Perspectives*. He has made over seventy major speeches to professional groups in twenty-three states and four foreign countries. Garman is a past president of one state professional association, the Consumer Education and Information Association of Virginia, and two national organizations, the Association for Financial Counseling and Planning Education and the American Council on Consumer Interests.

Garman has been a consultant to over forty corporations, trade associations and government agencies. He recently completed appointed terms of service for the National Advertising Review Board, the Consumer Advisory Council of the Board of Governors of the Federal Reserve System, and the National Advisory Council on Financial Planning for the International Board of Standards and Practices for Certified Financial Planners. Garman currently serves as a consumer advisory council member for Bell Atlantic-Virginia; as an arbitrator for the Municipal Securities Rulemaking Board and the New York Stock Exchange; as a consultant for American Express Company, Educational Testing Service, and the U.S. Navy; as a member of the National Advisory Committee for "Money Over Fifty Program" of the American Association of Retired Persons; and as a member of the board of directors of the Consumer Credit Counseling Service of Western Virginia.

Meier has the nerve to suggest that Garman overworks. Ha! Meier is like the "pot calling the kettle black" since he edits and publishes a 300-page prestigious professional journal *every* three months, has already authored fifteen books, and keeps two big toes in government work. And, he has accomplished this at a younger age than the more mature Garman. Meier's co-author teaches both graduate and undergraduate courses in consumer affairs.

Garman has two grown children, and lives with his loving partner in life, his registered dietitian-wife Lucy, who for many years has helped him clarify his thoughts on a great number of consumer issues over their nightly candlelit, evening meals together. The Garmans—both workaholics who enjoy low-fat gourmet dining and overseas travel—live in their home located on Gap Mountain overlooking the rural valleys near Newport, Virginia.

Chapter 1
Myths of Regulation and Consumer Protection

Kenneth J. Meier

WHAT IS REGULATION?

Regulation is any attempt by the government to control the behavior of citizens, corporations, or subgovernments. In a sense, regulation is nothing more than the government's effort to limit the choices available to individuals within society (Mitnik, 1980). Such limits may or may not be designed to protect consumers. Despite the simple definition, regulation can take numerous forms (see Daly and Brady, 1976).

First, the most commonly perceived form of regulation is price regulation. **Price regulation** means that a government regulator determines the minimum, maximum, or range of prices that an individual can charge for a good or service. State public utility commissions, for example, set the price that utility companies charge for a kilowatt hour of electricity. Some states, but not all, regulate the price of insurance. Numerous other state boards at one time set the price of haircuts, dry cleaning services, and even funerals. In the last twenty years, federal regulatory agencies have become less involved in price regulation (the primary exception is health care); state and local governments, however, continue to regulate prices in many industries.

Second, **franchising** or **licensing** is a process by which regulatory agencies permit or deny an individual the right to do business in a specified occupation or industry. To operate a television station, for example, an individual must receive a license from the Federal Communications Commission. To open a bank, a person must obtain the necessary charter from either the Office of the Comptroller of the Currency or from a state banking commission. To drive a taxi, a person must get a permit from local government. Along with licenses come regulations. Acceptance of a license to conduct a certain business normally implies that the government has an interest in how that business is operated.

Third, **standard setting** is a form of government regulation in which the government establishes standards for a product or a production process. Standards may be either **performance standards** or **engineering standards**. When the U.S. Department of Agriculture (USDA) requires that hot dogs contain no more than a certain percentage of foreign matter, it is setting a performance standard. USDA's concern is the level of foreign matter, not how any excess foreign matter is removed. On the other hand, when the Occupational Safety and Health Administration (OSHA) requires that factory workers be exposed to no more than two parts per million of cotton dust particles, it often tells the business how to meet this standard. An engineering standard specifies both the goal and the means.

Fourth, government can regulate by the **direct allocation of resources**. Under energy policies that grew out of the energy crisis of 1974, the federal government directly allocated crude oil to various refiners and to various end products. After these oil regulations expired, direct allocation of resources by government was fairly uncommon in the United States. Indirect allocation, however, has become more frequent with the development of tradable emissions permits as a part of national environmental policy.

Fifth, government can regulate by providing **operating subsidies**. Such subsidies can be direct as they were when the Civil Aeronautics Board granted subsidies to airlines to encourage them to serve small cities or when the Agricultural Stabilization and Conservation Service offers loans and subsidies to farmers not to plant crops. Subsidies can also be indirect; the national gasoline tax is an indirect subsidy of the trucking industry because proceeds from the tax are used to improve the roads used by the trucking industry. Even though subsidies look like a direct benefit rather than regulation, they become regulation when they are used for the purpose of changing the behavior of the individuals who receive the benefit.

Sixth, government can regulate to **promote fair competition**. Free markets are so essential to the American economic system that certain regulatory agencies are created simply to monitor the marketplace for fairness. Regulations against deceptive advertising by the Federal Trade Commission and antitrust regulation are two prominent examples.

As the various types of regulation illustrate, not all regulation is coercive. Much regulation is done through inducements offered by the government or its agencies. The objective of regulation, however, is the same—to change the behavior of individual citizens, corporations, or governments.

THE REGULATORY EXPLOSION OF THE 1960S AND 1970S

Forty years ago regulation was a fairly minor part of the federal government. The major political issues were redistributive issues such as medicare and tax reform or were foreign policy issues. Regulation was rarely on the national agenda, and little was being done to study the impact of regulation on society.

That situation has changed dramatically. According to the Center for the Study of American Business, regulation became a major growth industry in the 1960s and 1970s. The number of federal regulatory agencies increased from 28 in 1960 to 56 in 1980 (Penoyer, 1981:3). A series of major regulatory agencies were created in these two decades. The National Highway Traffic Safety Administration was established in 1966 to regulate both automobile and highway safety. The Environmental Protection Agency was created in 1970 to coordinate the federal efforts to protect the environment. To eliminate harmful and hazardous products from the marketplace, Congress formed the Consumer

Product Safety Commission in 1972. Equal employment opportunity was placed under the jurisdiction of the Equal Employment Opportunity Commission in 1964. Workplace health and safety were delegated to the new Occupational Safety and Health Administration in 1971. Nor was the federal government alone in creating regulatory agencies. State governments created a variety of consumer protection agencies and were required by federal law to establish agencies to regulate air and water pollution.

Other indicators of the growth in regulation also exist. The funds budgeted for the federal regulatory agencies tripled in real dollars between 1970 and 1980 (Penoyer, 1981:5). The number of regulatory employees increased to almost 90,000 by 1980. Because this figure included only federal employees, it was a significant underestimate because many federal regulatory programs are implemented by state and local governments (e.g., environmental protection, workplace safety, equal opportunity). The regulatory critics' favorite indicator of regulatory activity, the size of the *Federal Register*, increased from 14,479 pages in 1960 to 65,603 pages in 1977.

Not only was regulation growing, but the form of regulation had also changed. Early regulation was generally termed "**economic regulation**"; a regulatory agency regulated the price, entry, exit, and service of an industry. The Interstate Commerce Commission, for example, granted licenses to truckers, set the price that truckers could charge, and established their routes. Economic regulation had a negative reputation; it was characterized as regulation in the interests of the regulated industry only (see Stigler, 1971; Bernstein, 1955).

The regulatory activities of the 1960s and 1970s were different from this earlier form of regulation. Rather than prices, it focused on consumer issues of safety, health, employment fairness, and a variety of other noneconomic questions. The new regulation was termed "**social regulation**." Although social regulation dates back to at least nineteenth-century efforts to limit water pollution discharges, during the last two decades it became the predominant form.

Social regulation differed greatly in its approach to regulation. Economic regulation was often undertaken because the industry requested it (e.g., the Federal Communications Commission, the Civil Aeronautics Board) and often protected the regulated industry from the ill-effects of competition. Social regulation, on the other hand, was rarely demanded by the regulated industry and was more likely to be forced on it by a Congress that responded to consumers or other nonindustry groups.

Regulation became an issue on the political agenda. First placed there by various consumer and public interest groups pressing for additional regulation, it was later opposed by business organizations that felt that the effort had gone too far. Regulation became salient enough to be an issue in both the 1976 and 1980 presidential election campaigns. Regulatory reform occupied the attention of both Congress and the president. After the 1980 election, significant changes were made in regulatory policy by the Reagan administration. At the most general level, the rapid increase in the volume of regulation was slowed. No new regulatory agencies were created. Staffing for regulatory agencies, which had leveled off in 1978 at approximately 90,000, was reduced by 11 percent by 1983 (*Regulation*, 1982:9), and the expenditures by the regulatory agencies were reduced both in real dollars and in 1970 constant dollars.

Although the Reagan administration stopped the growth in regulation, it did not make any significant cutbacks in regulatory structure. For the most part, laws were left unchanged. The initial efforts to rewrite environmental protection statutes, for example, were abandoned in the face of strong congressional opposition. Gradually regulatory agencies reasserted themselves. Under prodding by Congress and consumer groups, regulation again became popular. Much to his chagrin, President Bush was even designated the "Regulatory President" by *National Journal*.

A more favorable political climate for regulation and consumer protection developed with the advent of the Clinton administration. The era of "regulatory reform," however, also changed the regulatory process. Regulation and consumer protection proposals now focus more on alternatives and the use of information and incentives to shape behavior.

THE MYTHS ABOUT REGULATION

The study of regulation and consumer protection is clouded by several myths. These myths are widely accepted by politicians, students of the regulatory process, and even the general public. Because these myths are inaccurate or only partially accurate, they limit serious regulatory reform. Reformers often respond to the myths rather than the true shortcomings of regulation. Four prominent myths should be noted.

Regulation is Ineffective—False

Regulation is often charged with failing to achieve its goals. When the savings and loan industry collapsed in the 1980s, the Federal Home Loan Bank Board was blamed with ineffective regulation. Major industrial accidents are frequently blamed on the Occupational Safety and Health Administration (OSHA) which is then denounced for regulating without improving the safety of industrial workplaces. The Food and Drug Administration (FDA) is condemned for not approving drugs that would benefit the American public and at the same time failing to eliminate drugs that pose a major risk to health.

To be sure, regulatory agencies have their share of failures. Failures are to be expected, however, given the high standards set for regulatory agencies, the almost impossible goals set for them by Congress, and the limited resources given to the agencies. The Consumer Product Safety Commission, for example, is charged with regulating 10,000 consumer products produced by 2 million firms with approximately 600 employees. Such a task is simply not possible. In addition, many regulatory tasks require activity at the cutting edge of science. In 1972 the Environmental Protection Agency (EPA) was tasked with cleaning up water and permitting "zero discharges" of untreated waste into the nation's waterways by 1984. In retrospect, the task was impossible. (Yet to be fair the regulation did lead to major improvements in environmental technology.)

Less visible than failures are the successes of regulatory agencies. The Consumer Product Safety Commission's regulations on childproof caps and baby cribs are credited with significant reductions in accidents and deaths. Air and water are significantly cleaner now than when the EPA was created. The Federal Trade Commission's optometrist rule resulted in greater competition and a lowering of the prices of eyeglasses. No person with less than $100,000 on deposit in a federally insured account at a depository institution has ever lost money despite the failure of many such institutions.

Regulatory agencies are like all other large scale bureaucracies; they have some successes, and they have some failures. Because they are public sector organizations open to public view, their failures receive more attention than their successes. Because successes prevent problems, they are often obscured from public view. Failures such as a major bank collapse or an airline crash are always newsworthy.

The myth of regulatory failure is perhaps the most detrimental to reforming regulation. Citizens can benefit from efforts to reform the regulatory process if such an effort is informed by an understanding of regulation's strengths and weaknesses. Reforms triggered by the belief that all regulation is ineffective will do more harm than good.

Regulation is Out of Control—False

A second myth is that regulation is no longer under the control of the American people or their elected representatives. Faceless bureaucrats without authorization from Congress or the president are imposing their own political values on the American public. EPA bureaucrats tried to ban automobile traffic in downtown Los Angeles. The National Highway Traffic Safety Administration (NHTSA) attempted to require that no car be able to start without a seatbelt. Academic researchers must file long reports about the protection of human subjects to conduct research. The Office of Education proposed that all father-son and mother-daughter functions be banned as sexually discriminatory.

Although some of these actions and others might appear to be irrational or to impose hardships on the American public, they do not indicate that regulatory agencies are out of control. In many cases, the actions of regulatory agencies reflect the guidance that Congress, the president, or individuals in the area give to them. The Los Angeles traffic rule was proposed because the EPA was required by Congress to establish a plan for each air quality region to meet national pollution standards; the plan illustrated a point—without significant changes in traditional transportation methods, Los Angeles would not attain the national goals. NHTSA vigorously pursued passive restraints because Congress urged it to do so.

No better illustration that regulatory agencies are not out of control exists than the Reagan administration. Regulators appointed by Reagan were able to change the regulatory priorities of many regulatory agencies. OSHA became a pro-industry regulator. The FDA approved a record number of new drugs for the pharmaceutical industry in 1981 and 1982. The NHTSA withdrew some 20 rules governing automobile safety to assist the auto industry.

President Reagan had little problem in asserting control over the regulatory agencies. Clearly, if regulatory agencies were out of control, this would not have been possible. Regulatory agency resistance to President Clinton has been virtually nonexistent, although this is expected to change with the new Republican Congress. Regulatory agencies in reality are highly responsive to the pressures of the political system. When a critic charges that a regulatory agency is out of control, the critic may really be stating that the regulatory agency is responding to political values different from those of the critic.

Regulatory Agencies Are Captured—False

A charge heard frequently among public interest groups and in the past by a variety of scholars is that regulatory agencies are **captured** by the industry that they regulate. The charge was initially presented by Samuel Huntington (1952) in a study of the Interstate Commerce Commission (ICC). Later such individuals as Marver Bernstein, George Stigler, and Sam Peltzman expanded on the idea.

In some cases, this charge has an element of truth. The Federal Communications Commission (FCC) was created at the request of the industry and regulated in many cases to protect it (Sabatier, 1976). Similar conclusions can be drawn about the Civil Aeronautics Board and the airline industry (but see Brown 1987). On the other hand, many regulatory agencies are definitely not captured by the industry. The Environmental Protection Agency has a strong reputation for independence from the industry. Arguments could be made that federal bank regulators, the Occupational Safety and Health Administration, and the Food and Drug Administration frequently act contrary to industry demands.

In fact, the relationship between a regulatory agency and the industry or industries it regulates is an important political question and one that will concern us throughout this book. Agencies vary a great deal in their relationship with the regulated; some are close, and some are distant. One purpose of this book is to find out what variables affect the relationship between the regulator and the regulated.

The Purpose of Regulation is Efficiency—False

A large volume of regulatory analysis by economists has evaluated regulation against the standard of **economic efficiency**. Much of this literature claims to be empirical rather than normative; that is, it claims that the goal of regulation is efficiency and that it is simply examining regulation against this standard. Judged against the absolute efficiency standard, regulatory agencies often come up short.

Unfortunately for this approach, however, efficiency is rarely ever the prime goal of regulation and, in some cases, is not even a secondary goal. The idea that efficiency is the prime goal of regulation is taken from economic public interest theory; it contends that because a perfectly competitive market allocates goods and services efficiently, regulation should be undertaken only when the market fails (see Stokey and Zeckhauser, 1978 for an excellent summary of this position). Monopoly, imperfect information, and externalities are situations where the market operates less than efficiently; regulation should correct these problems.

Regulation in the real world is often undertaken for political reasons rather than for economic reasons. The Interstate Commerce Commission was created to counter the economic power of the railroads; the Food and Drug Administration was established to make the consumption of food and drugs safer; environmental protection statutes were adopted to restrict the efficient operation of the unregulated market; The Civil Aeronautics Board was established to protect the airlines from competition. Although one might dispute whether or not these goals are the primary reasons why each of these regulators was created, one rarely ever finds efficiency mentioned in the legislative history of these agencies' statutes. In fact, the economic concept of efficiency was fairly undeveloped at the time the early regulatory agencies were created. Only when economists began serious studies of regulation after World War II was the concept of efficiency in regulation stressed.

Arguing that efficiency is the goal of regulation is essentially a normative argument; it is an argument that efficiency should be the goal of regulation. To be sure, agencies can have more than one goal, and regulatory objectives should be accomplished in the most efficient way possible. But when efficiency conflicts with other goals, efficiency is often a second priority.

Banning harmful products, for example, may not be the most efficient way to protect consumers. Letting injured consumers sue for damages may well be the least costly way to compensate injured consumers. A product ban, however, makes enforcement easier, can prevent injuries before they occur, and does not rely on the vagaries of the tort system for correcting ills. In short, an efficient process might not be effective and vice versa. In such cases efficiency can be no more than a secondary goal.

The argument for efficiency as a regulatory goal also concerns the locus of regulatory decisions. Efficiency advocates usually demonstrate that if a business must be regulated, incentives (e.g., effluent fees, injury taxes, and so on) are preferable to traditional regulation. Incentive systems may well be more efficient, but they also shift the decision locus from government agencies to private business. Whether government or industry makes decisions concerning regulatory compliance will clearly affect the type of decisions made.

Efficiency is often a useful concept and plays a role in current regulatory and consumer protection policy. It is not the primary goal of regulation or consumer protection, however, and treating it as such results in a distorted point of view. If regulatory agencies are judged by a standard they do not have, they are bound to fall short.

THE REALITY OF THE STUDY OF REGULATION AND CONSUMER PROTECTION

Numerous ways exist to study regulation and consumer protection. Legal approaches focus on the law and such legal concepts as due process and fairness. Economic approaches are centered on efficiency and the role of regulation in correcting market failures. Historical approaches set regulation within the broader forces in society. The approach in this book, though decidedly political, has some distinct differences from traditional political science as well as from the preceding approaches given. These differences are important. Using a **political perspective** in the study of regulation and consumer protection, as this book does, recognizes that (1) the subject is complex, (2) it can be examined using a multidisciplinary approach, and (3) **normative judgments** are inherently part of regulation and consumer protection.

Regulation is Complex

Simple generalizations about regulation and consumer protection will almost always be wrong. Regulation and regulatory agencies vary significantly on many dimensions.

Some agencies are fairly effective; others are not. Some policy areas are controlled by the regulatory agency; others are not. Some agencies are known for expertise, cohesion, and dynamic leadership; others are not.

With so much variation, simple explanations of regulatory and consumer protection policy are rarely possible. The conceptual framework used to explain regulation in this book (see Chapter 2) is fairly complex. Regulatory policy is the product of a regulatory agency operating in an environment that places demands on it. Both factors within the agency (e.g., expertise, leadership) and factors in the environment will affect public policy. Among the other actors involved in regulatory policy are legislators, the chief executive, the courts, interest groups, state governments, journalists, and other bureaucrats.

Regulatory policy actors interact in a political, economic, and technological environment. These environmental forces place demands on the regulatory system, provide it with opportunities to act, and limit the scope of its actions. The relative impact of each factor varies from area to area. Understanding the complex relationship between the various actors and the environmental forces will enable a person to explain why a specific regulatory policy exists as it does.

Studying Regulation Requires a Multidisciplinary Focus

Regulation and consumer protection has been fruitfully studied by a wide variety of disciplines because regulation contains facets amenable to study in different ways. Determining the relationship between market concentration and competition in antitrust is an economic exercise. Assessing the procedural requirements necessary for rulemaking is a legal question. Discovering the reasons why an agency was created is a political and historical question. Determining the impact of these regulations is the realm of consumer science.

This study of regulation will borrow from such disciplines as law, economics, history, organization theory, consumer science, and political science. Although the general focus is on politics, each of the other disciplines has useful contributions to make. Law can be used to analyze the role that the judiciary plays in regulatory policy, an especially important factor in an area such as antitrust. Economics allows us to assess the role economic forces play in shaping policy responses; banking regulation, for example, responds to economic forces that set interest rates. Organization theory illuminates the processes within the bureaucracy such as how organizational ideologies develop and how they affect policy decisions. Consumer science focuses on the impact of these decisions and what difference the policy makes.

Of the various disciplines, perhaps as much attention is given to history as to any other. The political forces present at the creation of a regulatory agency often persist. Agency personnel take decision cues from the organization's history. Interest groups active at the creation will probably remain active. If Congress has historically resolved disputes in a regulatory area, it will be expected to resolve future disputes. The history of a regulatory agency contains the explanations for many present decisions.

Above all, however, regulation is a political process involving political actors seeking political ends. Economic and legal arguments are often used to define the problem in such a way that a given outcome occurs. Such activity is a political effort. Economics, law, history, and a variety of sciences can provide the justification for many public policies; only politics, however, can explain why the policies are what they are.

Most Regulatory Analysis Contains Normative Judgments

This study has two goals that are sometimes in conflict. One goal is to explain regulatory policy outcomes. The other goal is to suggest specific changes in regulatory policy. Although positivist tradition holds that empirical analysis should be separated from value judgments, in regulatory and consumer protection policy this rarely occurs. Most regulatory analysis has either normative objectives or was instigated by normative concerns. This is as it should be. Social sciences, as Herbert Simon (1969) argued, are sciences of the artificial, concerned as much with how things might be as how they actually are.

Accordingly, this book will not ignore normative issues, nor does it expect the reader to do so. Regulatory and consumer protection policy determines who benefits from government intervention into the marketplace, a topic on which few people can claim neutrality. Rather than disguise normative presentations as empirical arguments, as much of the literature does, this book will make its normative contentions explicit. Although normative and empirical arguments cannot always be separated, some effort has been made to do so by keeping the normative arguments in separate sections and labeling them as such.

Chapter 2
The Policy Process

Kenneth J. Meier

Michael J. Licari [1]

The study of regulatory and consumer protection policymaking is dominated by two perspectives (Weingast and Moran, 1983). One view holds that regulatory agencies are vested with vast discretion and are the major force in determining policy. Among the agency characteristics that affect policy outputs are professional values, policy expertise, bureaucratic entrepreneurs, and agency structure (e.g., see Wilson, 1980; Katzman, 1980; Eisner, 1991). A second view suggests that regulatory agencies are dominated by their environment. Interest groups, presidents, legislative committees, economic forces, and technological change are among the determinants of policy (e.g., see Stigler, 1971; Lowi, 1969; Mazmanian and Sabatier, 1980; Wood and Waterman, 1994). Both views are essentially incomplete. Regulatory and consumer protection policy is a product of both regulatory bureaucracies and environmental forces. This chapter develops an outline of the policy process that integrates both these explanations. Although the conceptual framework developed is moderately complex, so is public policy. Little is gained by introducing simple views of policy that are not linked to the real world.

REGULATORY POLICY OUTPUTS

The study of regulation and consumer protection is important because it is part of the policy process that allocates values among members of society. It is, as Lasswell (1936) described **politics**, a determination of "Who gets what, when and how." In short, what is important about regulatory policy from a political perspective is, Who benefits from regulation? — and who loses.

Although much literature has focused on who benefits from regulation, this focus has been muddled by relying on the concept of the **public interest**. Bernstein's (1955) theory that regulatory agencies in the long run were captured by the regulated industries contrasted reality with an ideal standard of regulation in the public interest (see also Stigler, 1971; Peltzman, 1976). Unfortunately, defining the public interest in regulatory policy has been as elusive as it has been in other areas of politics (see Schubert, 1960). Even the most self-serving appeal by a regulated group is now phrased as a quest for the public interest.

[1]

Put footnote in about me

In a perceptive essay, Paul Sabatier (1977) proposed an alternative to the public interest theory of regulation; regulatory policy can be arrayed on a continuum from **self-regulation** (regulation in the interests of the regulated) to **aggressive regulation** (regulation of one individual in the interests of another).[1] Sabatier's thesis can be divided into two separate dimensions: (1) the degree to which regulation benefits the regulated industry, and (2) the degree to which it benefits nonregulated individuals such as consumers. These are two separate dimensions rather than poles on a single continuum.

As Figure 2.1 reveals, the two dimensions of **beneficiaries** produce four extreme types of regulation. Cell 1 contains policies designed to benefit the regulated but not the nonregulated, the traditional "**captured**" regulation. Regulation by state occupational regulators designed to protect the status and incomes of professionals is a classic example of cell 1 regulation. Cell 3 contains those policies whereby an industry is regulated for the benefit of another party. Occupational safety and health regulation, for example, restricts industry behavior in an attempt to benefit workers; most consumer protection policies discussed in this book fall in this cell. Cell 4 contains those policies that benefit both the regulated and some portion of the nonregulated. Bank regulation and deposit insurance following the Great Depression benefitted both depositors by guaranteeing the safety of their funds and the banks by encouraging the use of banks. A similar though somewhat more controversial argument could be made about bank regulation and deposit insurance today. Finally, cell 2 includes policies that benefit no one. Current antitrust policy concerning price discrimination under the Robinson-Patman Act appears to harm both businesses that wish to compete and consumers. This policy is designed to prevent large business from cutting prices to draw consumers away from small business.

Although who benefits from regulatory policy is not always easy to discover, the question provides a focal point for comparing unlike policies. This text will examine two aspects of regulatory and consumer protection policy—what is the current set of policies, and who benefits from them? The conceptual framework in this chapter permits us to explain why regulatory agencies act as they do and why policies benefit whom they do.

SUBSYSTEM POLITICS

Although regulatory and consumer protection policies can be produced directly by legislatures, the chief executive, or the courts, in general, regulatory policy is implemented via bureaucracy. Typically, broad areas of regulatory discretion are granted to a regulatory agency by these political institutions of government. The Interstate Commerce Commission, for example, is charged with regulating interstate commerce with only a vague goal (the "public interest") as a guide. The policymaking activities of bureaucratic agencies can best be understood by examining the subsystem in which these agencies operate.

---

[1] I have taken some liberties with Sabatier's (1977) work here, but he is used to that by now. His intent was to distinguish between managerial and policing types of regulation. His work results in three types of regulation, along a single dimension rather than four types along two.

Figure 2.1   Dimensions of regulatory policy

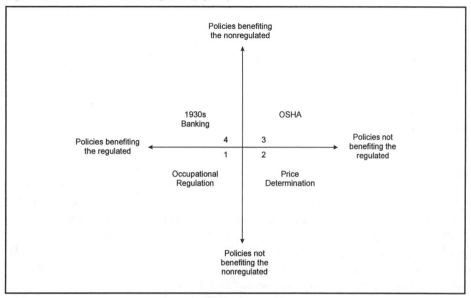

That public policy is made in semiautonomous subsystems composed of government bureaus, congressional committees, and interest groups has been a basic tenet of political analysis since the 1950s (see Freeman, 1965; McConnell, 1966). Subsystems exist because the American political system fragments political power (Long, 1962). With its division of federal authority into three branches—executive, legislative, and judicial—each operating with constraints on the other two, political power at the national level is fragmented among numerous political actors. Power is further divided by the federal system and informally kept that way by broker political parties that seek electoral success rather than unified political government. As a result, political power is rarely concentrated enough to dominate the policy process.

The fragmentation is exacerbated by the numerous **policy issues** that compete for attention on the policy agenda. Major political institutions must constantly jump from crisis to crisis—health care reform today, gasoline user fees tomorrow, Bosnia next week. Power in a given issue area flows to those who retain a continuing interest in it. In American politics a continuing interest usually means the permanent bureaucracy, specialized congressional committees, and the interest groups affected by the issue.

Policy subsystems can operate in a relatively independent fashion from the major political institutions if the members of the policy subsystem can satisfy each others' needs. The **bureaucracy** makes policy. It issues the permits, exceptions, and punishments; but to do so it needs resources and legislative authority. Congressional committees can provide the funds and authority needed by the bureau to operate, but the committee members need to be reelected. Reelection requires political support and campaign contributions. The interest groups affiliated with the regulated industry need the outputs that the bureaucracy is creating, especially if the outputs are favorable; and they have the political resources to commit to members of congressional committees. In combination, the members of the subsystem can often supply the needs of the other members. If all the needs of the subsystem members are satisfied, then subsystem members make no major demands on the macropolitical system. In turn, the subsystem is given autonomy.

Subsystems Are Not Homogeneous

Although subsystems have been fruitfully applied to numerous areas of political research (see Ripley and Franklin, 1991), subsystems are not the homogeneous **"iron triangles"** (made up of the executive agencies, the legislative committees, and the organized special-interest groups) that they are portrayed to be (see Heclo, 1978; Sabatier, 1988). There are six reasons why subsystems are not homogeneous.

First, interest groups, even industry groups, rarely agree completely about regulatory policy. Dissension among airline companies permitted deregulation of airline fares in the 1970s (Brown, 1987); broadcasting interests are fragmented into several groups with vastly different goals, including groups representing networks, independent stations, religious broadcasters, ultrahigh frequency (UHF) stations, frequency modulation (FM) stations, and countless others (Krasnow, Longley, and Terry, 1982). The insurance industry is divided into property/casualty companies versus life/health companies, direct writers versus agents, stock companies versus mutuals, etc.

Second, interest groups other than industry groups actively participate in the regulatory subsystem. Consumer groups are active in the auto safety, drug regulation, and several other consumer products subsystems; labor unions are active in safety regulation and sometimes in environmental regulation. Rarely do industry groups have the opportunity to operate without opposition.

Third, subsystems are often divided among several different subcommittees each with different policy objectives. Environmental protection programs, for example, are under the jurisdiction of seven committees in the House and five in the Senate (Kenski and Kenski, 1984:111). Even with only a single committee involved in a subsystem, policy conflict occurs (Johnson, 1993). Conflicting positions by the Commerce Committees at different times during the 1970s resulted in a series of policy changes by the Federal Trade Commission (Weingast and Moran, 1982).

Fourth, a variety of other actors penetrate the subsystem to urge policy actions, including journalists and scholars who generate important information on policy options. Such issues as acid rain, pesticide regulation, drug safety, and others were placed on the agenda by such actors.

 Fifth, one subsystem will sometimes overlap one or more other subsystems, thus adding additional actors to the political battles and creating greater conflict. Environmental protection subsystems collided with energy subsystems following the Arab oil embargo of 1974; insurance subsystems and automobile regulation subsystems came into conflict following the Reagan administration's relaxation of automobile safety regulations.

Sixth, the subsystems concept ignores the vital role of state and local government officials in the regulatory process. In many areas, federal regulatory programs are implemented by state governments; environmental protection and workplace health and safety are prominent examples. In a variety of other areas such as consumer protection, antitrust, and equal employment opportunity policies, both the federal government and state governments operate programs. Often the policy goals of state regulators can differ significantly from those of federal regulators (see Hedge, Menzel, and Williams, 1988), resulting in policy outputs different from those intended by the federal government (Wood and Waterman, 1994). This conflict can result in either more vigorous regulation or less vigorous regulation depending on state objectives. California's aggressive mobile source air pollution regulation in the 1960s and 1970s, for example, often preceded federal efforts and set the agenda for the 1991 Clean Air Act amendments, but state-run workplace safety programs often lag behind federal-run programs.

Other Aspects of the Subsystem — Expand this ✳✳✳

In Figure 2.2 an expanded version of the subsystem is shown that includes **other** (e.g., **nonindustry) interest groups**, **significant others** (e.g., researchers, journalists), and **state governments** in addition to the "iron triangle." The lines may be thought of as information highways where any of the six actors can interact with any of the others. Paul Sabatier (1988) argues that policy subsystems can best be viewed as opposing advocacy coalitions; a coalition of industry and its allies (members of Congress, other groups, and so on) is opposed by other interest groups and their allies. Under such a conceptualization, the traditional iron triangle becomes a special case of a policy subsystem with only one advocacy coalition.

[margin note: more on this...]

[margin note:]
- *nature of an AC*
- *core beliefs*
- *how AC's interact*
- *time context (changing nature of policy subsystem).*

Figure 2.2   The regulatory policy system

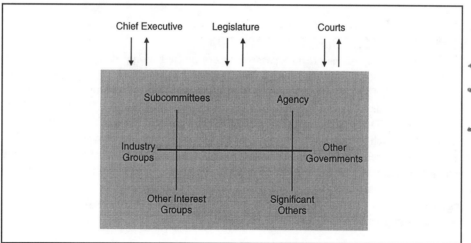

Among the most important aspects of policy subsystems is how open the subsystems are to outside influences via the chief executive, the legislature, and other nonsubsystem actors. Policy subsystems are perceived as fairly consensual, and in areas of **distributive**

politics—health care research, agricultural policy, and educational aid—they are (Ripley and Franklin, 1991; but see Johnson, 1993). The distribution of tangible benefits paid for by general tax revenues ties the members of the subsystems closely together. Consensual subsystems resolve policy issues internally and can present a unified front to the larger political system. As a result, consensual subsystems are usually allowed to operate without outside interference.

Regulatory subsystems are not as consensual as those in distributive policy and, therefore, are more likely to be affected by outside influences for three reasons.

First, regulatory policy restricts choice so that an industry is likely to see regulation as a mixed blessing. Regulated industries may defend their regulator when it is attacked by other **political actors** (e.g., the airlines and the Civil Aeronautics Board (CAB) circa 1976), but they are slower to come to the defense and less committed when they do so.

Second, members of Congress are likely to be less committed to a regulatory subsystem than to a distributive subsystem. Unlike other policies, regulation often imposes direct costs. A member of Congress from a rural district will receive far more credit from constituents if he or she is on the soil conservation subcommittee distributing benefits than if he or she is on the environmental committee limiting pesticide use.

Third, regulatory subsystems are likely to have more nonindustry groups that want to participate in the subsystem. The Federal Communications Commission (FCC), for example, cannot operate in a consensual, autonomous subsystem because numerous interests other than the television industry are also interested in regulating television. Politicians, the movie industry, cable operators, the phone company, and many others see television as important to their interests; accordingly, they will seek to participate in FCC decisions.

REGULATORY AGENCIES: INSIDE THE BLACK BOX

Government agencies are not passive actors pushed along at the whim of other subsystem members. They shape as well as respond to pressures from the subsystem (Rourke, 1984). The U.S. Department of Agriculture (USDA), for example, played a role in creating and developing the American Farm Bureau; Farm Bureau members, in turn, assisted the USDA in crop regulation. The Environmental Protection Agency funds academic research on pollution; such research is then used in debates over environmental protection. In a sense, both agencies helped create a portion of the subsystem. If bureaus can take an active role in structuring their environments, they need not passively respond to subsystem pressures. They can actively seek to influence the forces impinging on regulatory policy. To understand the policy actions of regulatory agencies, two variables—goals and resources—must be discussed.

Agency Goals

Every regulatory agency has goals including policy goals that agency employees wish to attain. Environmental Protection Agency employees seek cleaner air and water; FDA personnel pursue safe and effective drugs. Although this contention may seem trivial, many treatments of bureaucracy either assume an organization's sole goal is to survive or assume that the bureaucrats' goal is to maximize their income (e.g., see Niskanen, 1971). Both approaches provide a misleading view of regulatory agencies.

Ascribing regulatory policy goals to bureaucrats is consistent with motivation theory (e.g., Maslow, 1970) and empirical evidence. Employees work for the Office of Civil Rights because they believe in racial equality (Romzek and Hendricks, 1982). Individuals work for OSHA because they desire to improve workplace safety (Kelman, 1980). In the long run, most agency employees become advocates of the agency and its goals (Downs, 1967). Those interested in higher incomes or in the goals of the regulated industry will probably leave the agency.

Having policy goals does not mean that bureaucrats would not like to see their organization survive, all things being equal. Survival, after all, is necessary to obtain most policy goals. In some cases, the former Civil Aeronautics Board bureaucrats, for example, were content to accomplish policy objectives that eliminated the agency. In sum then, regulators regulate because they wish to attain policy goals; without understanding that regulators are goal-seeking and without determining what those goals are, regulatory behavior will appear random to the outside observer.

Also important in terms of regulatory goals is the potential for goal conflict within an agency. Such lack of consensus might result from several different conflicts within the organization: central staff versus field personnel, professionals versus administrators, one profession versus another profession, career staff versus political appointees. The last source of conflict is especially important. Career staff are more likely to identify with the agency and be strongly committed to its programs (Heclo, 1977). Political appointees are more likely to see themselves as the president's representative (Wood and Waterman, 1994; Welborn, 1977) and, therefore, hold different views.

Resources

In pursuit of policy goals, regulatory agencies have access to five resources: (1) expertise, (2) cohesion, (3) legislative authority, (4) policy salience, and (5) leadership.[2] Access to such resources determines the value of the agency's participation to other subsystem members. The greater a regulatory agency's resources, the more likely the agency will be able to resist industry pressures for regulation solely in the interests of the industry.

EXPERTISE

Bureaucratic organizations are designed to develop and store knowledge. To a degree greater than legislatures or courts, bureaucracies can divide tasks and gain knowledge via specialization (Rourke, 1984:16). An EPA employee, for example, could spend an entire

---

[2]The section on bureaucratic variables relies heavily on Rourke (1984) and Sabatier (1977). The most applicable parts of the writings of each are used. In some cases, the impact of the variables reflects my interpretation of their work rather than their interpretation.

career dealing with the intricacies of regulating a single pesticide. As part of specialization, American government bureaucracies recruit skilled technocrats as employees, and the agencies become professionalized. A professionalized agency often adopts the values of the predominant profession; the values of safety and health professionals in the Occupational Safety and Health Administration, for example, are the reason why OSHA relies on engineering standards (Kelman, 1980).

Professionalization and specialization permit an agency to develop independent sources of knowledge so that the agency need not rely on the industry (or others) for its information. Although the levels of professionalism and specialization in regulatory agencies cannot rival those of such agencies as the National Institutes of Health, they are a factor. The Nobel laureate Glenn Seaborg's appointment to head the Atomic Energy Commission (AEC; now the Nuclear Regulatory Commission) increased the AEC's reputation for expertise. Similarly, the creation of a separate research arm for the Environmental Protection Agency provided the EPA with expertise it could use in its political battles (Davies and Davies, 1975).

Professionalism does not mean that an agency is dominated by a single profession. At times one or more professions may be struggling for control of the agency. In the Federal Trade Commission (FTC), for example, economists and lawyers have long fought over control of the FTC's antitrust functions. The professional conflict, in fact, has major policy implications. Lawyers prefer cases that can be quickly brought to trial like Robinson-Patman cases. Economists, depending on their ideology, favor either major structural monopoly cases that will significantly increase competition or cases against collusion.

COHESION

A second resource permitting the agency to affect public policy is the cohesiveness of the bureau's personnel. If agency personnel are united in pursuit of their goals, coalitions opposed to agency actions will need to develop their own sources of information to challenge agency decisions. A cohesive agency is far more difficult to resist than an agency that engages in public disputes over policy direction. **Cohesion**, in turn, is a function of an agency's goals and its ability to socialize members to accept these goals. Some public agencies such as the Marine Corps or the Forest Service even go so far as to create an organizational ideology for their members. Although no regulatory agency engages in the same degree of socialization that the Marine Corps does, they do seek consciously or unconsciously to influence the values of employees. Bureaucrats in the Environmental Protection Agency, for example, show much greater concern for environmental protection than for compliance costs. The Office of Education in the 1960s was a zealous advocate of school desegregation.

LEGISLATIVE AUTHORITY

All regulatory agencies must have legislative authority to operate, but all grants of legislative authority are not equal (see Sabatier, 1977:424-431).[3] Five important differences in legislative authority exist and contribute to agency resources.

First, **policy goals** as expressed in legislation can be specific or vague. At times, Congress has specified agricultural price support levels exactly, leaving little discretion for Agriculture Department regulators. In contrast, the Interstate Commerce Commission regulates interstate commerce with the general goal that regulation should be in the public interest. The vaguer the legislative expression of goals, the greater the agency's ability to set regulatory policy. Specific policy goals should be correlated with regulation in the interests of whichever group has the best access to Congress. Consequently, specific goals are associated both with the regulation in the interests of the regulated (e.g., agriculture) and with regulation for the benefit of the nonregulated (e.g., environmental protection).

Second, legislative delegations vary in the **scope of authority** they grant. Some agencies have jurisdiction over everyone (e.g., EPA). Other agencies might be denied jurisdiction over portions of their industry; OSHA's law, for example, exempts small farms. An agency with limited authority cannot affect the behavior of those outside its jurisdiction. The greater the limitations and restrictions on a regulatory agency, the more likely such an agency will regulate in the interest of the regulated industry.

Third, legislative delegations vary in the **sanctions** permitted to an agency. Bank regulators possess a wide variety of sanctions that can greatly influence the profits and viability of financial institutions. In contrast, the Equal Employment Opportunity Commission (EEOC) has no sanctions and must rely on court action to extract compliance. The greater the range of sanctions available to a regulatory agency, the more likely the agency will regulate in the interests of the nonregulated.

Fourth, regulatory agencies differ in their **organizational structure**. The two most common structural forms are the department regulatory agency (an agency headed by one person within a larger executive department) and the independent regulatory commission (a multimember board that reports directly to the legislature). Although the different structures do not appear related to performance (see Meier, 1980; Welborn, 1977), often independent regulatory commissions are subjected to other restraints. At the state level, regulatory commissions are often by law composed of members of the regulated industry. When selection restrictions such as this occur, regulation in the interests of the regulated is a given.

Fifth, legislative grants of authority often specify **agency procedures**. The FTC must follow the lengthy formal rulemaking process to issue rules, and the Consumer Product Safety Commission was initially handicapped with a cumbersome "offeror" procedure. Other agencies such as the EEOC and the antitrust regulators are limited further because

---

[3]The analysis of legislative authority follows that of Sabatier (1977). I have added the category of procedure and shortened his discussion of structure.

they must use the courts to set policy and resolve disputes. The more restrictive an agency's procedures are, the less likely the agency will be able to regulate the industry closely.

POLITICAL SALIENCE

The **salience** of a regulatory issue (e.g., its perceived importance by the public) can be used as a resource in the agency's regulatory battles. Regulatory issues vary greatly in salience. Nuclear plant regulation after the Three Mile Island accident was a highly salient issue to political elites and the general public. State regulation of barbers, on the other hand, is rarely salient. Not only does salience vary across issue areas, it also varies across time within an issue area. Banking regulation was not salient in 1972 but it certainly was in 1982.

According to William Gormley (1986a), salience determines the willingness of political elites to intervene in the regulatory process. When issues become salient, the rewards for successful intervention are greater for elected officials. In salient issue areas, therefore, regulators will find their actions closely watched by political elites whereas in nonsalient areas regulatory discretion is likely to go unchecked. A lack of salience should be to the advantage of the regulated industry because it will have little opposition to its demands.

LEADERSHIP

The final regulatory resource is the agency's **leadership**. Unlike the career bureaucracy, which is fairly stable, leadership positions turn over frequently. Two elements of leadership are important—quality and the leader's goals. Quality of leadership is a nebulous resource that, though difficult to define, is clearly a factor. The leadership abilities of Alfred Kahn as Civil Aeronautics Board chairperson were instrumental in deregulating airlines; the absence of strong leadership in Federal Trade Commission Chairman Paul Rand Dixon was often cited as a reason for poor performance by the pre-1969 FTC.

Essential to understanding the impact of leadership are the policy goals of regulatory agency heads. Through the leadership of Caspar Weinberger, Miles Kirkpatrick, and Michael Pertschuk, the Federal Trade Commission became less tied to the interests of the regulated industry and more interested in consumer issues. The appointment of Reese Taylor to head the Interstate Commerce Commission in 1981 signaled an end to the rapid movement toward deregulation of the trucking industry.

Leadership is especially important because the agency head is the focal point for interaction with the subsystem. In such interactions, the agency head is constrained by the expertise, cohesion, legislative authority, issue salience, and policy goals of the agency. An agency head who acts in opposition to the values and normal policy activities of the career staff risks political opposition from within the agency. Anne Burford's effort to alter environmental policy in the 1980s and the response of the EPA career staff is a classic example of this.

Agency Discretion: A Recapitulation

Regulatory agencies, therefore, exercise some discretion in regulatory policy. This discretion is not limitless, however. The amount of discretion accorded an agency is a function of its resources (expertise, cohesion, legislative authority, policy salience, and leadership) and the tolerances of other actors in the political system. Each actor has a zone of acceptance (see Simon, 1957); and if agency decisions fall within that zone, no action will be taken. Because regulatory policy is more important to subsystem actors, the zone of acceptance for subsystem actors is probably narrower than that for macropolitical system actors (e.g., the president). Consequently, subsystem actors will be more active.

As long as the regulatory subsystem produces policies within the zone of acceptance of Congress, the president, and the courts, then these actors will permit the subsystem some autonomy. Actions outside the zone of acceptance will bring attempts to intervene. The size of the zones of acceptance should vary with both salience and complexity (see Gormley, 1986a). Salience increases the benefits of successful intervention to a political actor, and complexity increases the costs of intervention. All things being equal, therefore, political actors will be more likely to intervene in policies that are salient but not complex (Gormley, 1986a).

THE ORGANIZATION OF INTERESTS

Many regulatory analysts view interest groups, especially those from the regulated industry, as dominating the regulatory process. Bernstein (1955; see also Huntington, 1952) presented the "**capture**" theory of regulation. As the only political force in the agency's environment with any stability, the industry eventually forced the agency to accommodate its needs. The agency was captured and henceforth tried to regulate in the interests of the industry. George Stigler (1971), Sam Peltzman (1976), and Anthony Downs (1967) generalized this theory. They contended that regulatory policy reflects the interests and the power of the concerned groups. Because this usually means only industry groups, policy should be responsive to the industry. Although versions of the capture theory have remained popular, they have been devastated by the empirical literature (see Meier and Plumlee, 1978; Mitnik, 1980; Quirk, 1981; Meier, 1988). The theory's most telling weakness is that in numerous cases regulatory agencies regulate the industry vigorously even though only industry groups are well organized (e.g., airline safety, banking, and pharmaceuticals). Clearly interest group pressures are mediated and mitigated by other external pressures (e.g., from political elites) and internal pressures within the agency (expertise, cohesion, professionalism, leadership, and so on).

Interest groups form part of the advocacy coalitions that seek to influence regulatory policy (Sabatier, 1988). These coalitions include bureaucrats, legislators, state and local government officials, researchers, journalists, and members of other subsystems in addition to interest groups. The value of both industry groups and nonindustry groups to advocacy coalitions is a function of the resources that the interest groups possess. These resources can be used either to persuade an agency to accept favored policy options or to convince political elites to intervene in the subsystem. Several resources merit discussion.

Size of Interest Group

An interest group's **size** can be measured by its membership or its budget (Stigler, 1971; Zeigler and Peak, 1972). A great many members confer legitimacy on an interest group because interest groups claim to represent people and large membership figures legitimate that claim. In a crude sense, membership also means voters, and these individual voters can approach a legislator as constituents rather than as lobbyists. Studies show that legislators are more responsive to constituents than other petitioners (Ornstein and Elder, 1978:88). For an interest group representing an industry, size has another aspect; the greater the size of the industry, the more important the industry is economically. Economic importance, especially in times of recession, is a powerful asset when petitioning policymakers worried about inflation and unemployment. Automakers, for example, were able to use the specter of widespread unemployment to convince policy-makers to delay pollution controls in the 1970s. All things being equal, therefore, a large group such as bankers in theory are more likely to affect a regulatory policy than a small group like manufacturers of lawn mowers.[4]

Resources of Interest Group

Although size implies resources, those resources must still be mobilized and applied to public policy efforts. Consumers, for example, have massive resources but have only partially mobilized them (see Berry, 1977). Some businesses are notorious for devoting few resources to public sector efforts. General Motors, for example, did not employ a full-time government lobbyist until 1969 (see Ornstein and Elder, 1978:168). Groups must procure not only skilled analysts and lobbyists but also campaign contributions through a political action committee (PAC) A lack of committed resources often explains why large corporations can be outmaneuvered by smaller public interest groups (e.g., the Clean Air Act or see Ornstein and Elder, 1978).

Dispersion of Interest Group

Interest groups have an advantage if they are widely dispersed throughout the country rather than concentrated in a single geographic area. Dispersed groups can argue that they represent national rather than local interests. Dispersion also permits a group to appeal to many different members of Congress as constituents. Even though a major element of the economy, the steel industry was unable to get fast antidumping relief in the 1980s because the industry was regionally concentrated. In contrast, the savings and loan industry, a dispersed and locally controlled industry, was able to persuade Congress to pass the Garn-St Germain Depository Institutions Act of 1982 and later to delay closing many insolvent

---

[4]This hypothesis generally lacks empirical support. See the studies by Meier (1988), Ringquist (1993), Brown (1987) and Ornstein and Elder (1978).

institutions. Although many variables other than dispersion accounted for the differences between the steel industry and savings associations, dispersion was a definite advantage.

Cohesion of Interest Group

Analysts of interest groups have long argued that the most effective lobby tactic is to provide technical and political information to allies (Zeigier and Peak, 1972; Milbrath, 1963). The value of information increases dramatically if it is the only information available. Cohesion among an interest's members is, therefore, a vital resource. If all automakers (including foreign manufacturers) would contend that achieving 32 miles per gallon for their entire sales fleet was impossible, they might have a good chance of convincing the EPA or Congress to ease such a requirement. Dissension, on the other hand, destroys the value of information. United Airlines' willingness to support airline deregulation in 1978 weakened the economic arguments of the other major airlines (Brown, 1987).

For those interest groups that rely on votes to persuade, cohesion is also important. Without cohesion, a group threatening electoral sanctions has little credibility. Organized labor's support for the Occupational Safety and Health Administration, for example, is backed by the unions' voting power. Evidence that union endorsements do not result in massive vote shifts, however, limits this resource (see Abramson, Aldrich, and Rohde, 1983).

Intensity of Commitment of Interest Group

In distributive policy areas such as agriculture, health research, or education, interest groups are intensely committed to policy options. In general, few interest groups, especially industry groups, are intensely committed to regulatory agencies. Threats to deregulate an industry may be the only way to get intensity from an industry group and then only if the industry benefits from the regulation (e.g., trucking and the ICC).

Although they are rare, interest groups intensely committed to a regulatory agency or its goals do exist. Such nonindustry groups as auto safety advocates at the national level or Mothers Against Drunk Drivers (MADD) at the local level are two recent examples. Intensity translates into greater effort, which, depending on the agency's position relative to the group, could be a cost or a benefit to the regulator.

Prestige of Interest Group

Francis Rourke (1984:102) argues that the prestige of an interest group's members is a valuable asset. Physicians, according to Rourke, make better clientele than do convicts. For most regulatory agencies, however, the prestige of interest group members varies little. All industry groups are usually comprised of producers with a vested interest in the regulation. Most nonindustry groups are likely to be professional consumer organizations. To be sure, a lobbyist from Chase Manhattan Bank may have slightly more prestige than one for the Land O'Lakes dairy cooperative, but these differences are relatively small. Prestige of interest group supporters, therefore, is unlikely to be an important variable in determining regulatory policy.

The Breadth of the Interest Group's Coalition

On specific regulatory issues, especially those before Congress, coalitional breadth becomes an important variable. **Coalitional breadth** is the number of different interests supporting a position.[5] A broad coalition links the regulated industry with interests outside the industry. In 1983 the American Bankers Association was able to attract the American Association of Retired Persons to its fight against tax withholding of savings account interest. Automobile companies coalesced with the United Auto Workers on a delay of Clean Air Act provisions in 1977 (Ornstein and Elder, 1978); consumer groups and insurance companies both opposed the National Highway Traffic Safety Administration's 2.5 mile per hour bumper impact regulation (versus 5 miles per hour). Broad coalitions permit the coalition to argue it is seeking a broad public interest rather than a narrow self-interest; as a result, more political elites can be approached.

Interest groups, therefore, are more likely to intervene successfully in the regulatory process if they are large groups with resources and if they are dispersed, cohesive, intense, and a member of a broad coalition, everything else being equal. To the extent that the interest group's opposition lacks these qualities, it is doubly strong. Even so, these resources are not sufficient for an interest group to dominate a regulator. The pharmaceutical industry has many of these characteristics, yet their dissatisfaction with the Food and Drug Administration indicates that they clearly do not dominate the FDA (Quirk, 1980). Interest group power is only one of the variables that in combination produce regulatory policy.

For nonindustry groups such as consumer groups, the resources just mentioned often must be supplemented by another-standing (see Berry, 1984:199; Melnick, 1983:10). Because regulations affect consumers indirectly, consumers may lack legal standing to intervene in the formal regulatory process. For example, the Federal Communications Commission held that the United Church of Christ lacked standing to challenge the license of television station KLBT. The church wanted the license revoked because KLBT had neither minority employees nor minority program content. The U.S. Court of Appeals (*United Church of Christ* v. *FCC* 1966) reversed the FCC decision. Without standing, a nonindustry group is forced to abandon the administrative arena and fight its battles in political jurisdictions.

Interest group resources, then, are important in both pressing positions within the subsystem and in persuading political elites to intervene. The ability of an interest group to attain specific policy outcomes, in part, is determined by the political power of the interest group and its allies versus that of its opposition. The struggle between these advocacy coalitions occurs within the context of the macropolitical system, the next topic for discussion.

---

[5] I am indebted to Robert Healy, a lobbyist for Atlantic Richfield, for pointing out the need for broad coalitions.

THE POLITICAL ENVIRONMENT

Although policy subsystems have been perceived as autonomous with the ability to operate independently from the larger political system, subsystems can be opened to the influence of political elites. Regulatory subsystems are especially permeable to political forces. Because regulatory subsystems generally impose costs rather than dispense benefits (Rourke, 1984:53), regulatory subsystems lack the cohesion that other policy subsystems possess. The three main political actors in the environment of federal regulatory subsystems are Congress, the presidency, and the courts.[6] Each has the resources to intervene in the regulatory system if it desires.

Congress

Regulatory agencies, especially independent regulatory commissions, are often perceived as congressional rather than executive agencies. Members of subcommittees that oversee regulatory agencies have always been heavily involved in regulatory policy. In the past, subcommittees operated with little interference from the entire Congress, but recent evidence indicates that norms such as deference to committees, specialization, and seniority that led to committee dominance have broken down. Deference to committees in the present Congress is far less than it was in the 1950s, and members of Congress are more likely to amend or reject a committee bill (Patterson, 1978:160). Specialization, the conceded way to get ahead in Congress, has become less valued as members devote themselves to constituency service and, therefore, to more general roles. The impact of changes in congressional norms is that individual members of Congress are more likely to be interested in the actions of a regulatory agency (especially if the agency regulates a constituent) and, therefore, more likely to intervene in the regulatory policy process.

Members of Congress have numerous avenues of influence if they seek to intervene in a regulatory subsystem. The most common methods are appropriations, legislation, hearings, legislative vetoes, and informal contact. Each has been used in the regulatory process to express displeasure to a regulatory agency or to encourage it to pursue a different path.

APPROPRIATIONS

Congress controls the purse strings of regulatory agencies through both the authorization and the appropriation process. Although across-the-board budget cuts are fairly blunt instruments, members of Congress have been creative in using the budget process to influence regulatory agencies. A prominent example is the use of **authorization riders**. When passing legislation that authorizes funds for an agency, amendments or riders are added that restrict agency actions. In the late 1970s and early 1980s, several members of Congress used this procedure to express displeasure with the Federal Trade

---

[6]The discussion in this section is limited to the federal level although the same forces apply at the state level.

Commission's consumer activism (Pertschuk, 1982). An authorization rider, for example, prohibited the FTC from pursuing its deceptive advertising case against children's cereal manufacturers. The appropriations process can also be used to assist an agency. Kemp (1982a) found that major airline crashes resulted in the appropriation of additional funds to the Federal Aviation Administration. The budget process, therefore, can be an effective method for members of Congress to attain specific regulatory goals.

LEGISLATION

Through the legislative process, Congress can issue instructions to regulatory agencies. Much regulatory legislation, especially the initial enabling legislation, is often vague, thus, vesting a great deal of discretion with the agency. In some cases, however, enabling legislation has been specific about goals and the timetables for achieving them (e.g., the Clean Air Act or the Clean Water Act).

Legislative actions can be used to alter agency procedures, change a single agency decision, or alter the agency's fundamental goals. The Magnuson-Moss Act of 1974, for example, required the Federal Trade Commission to use formal hearings in its rulemaking process; the end result was major delays in issuing regulations (West, 1982). An example of Congress's intervening to change one decision is the FTC's initial attempt to regulate cigarette advertising (Fritschler, 1975). Responding to tobacco companies' appeals, Congress limited the FTC's actions in this area by substituting their own. Finally, the Airline Deregulation Act of 1978 fundamentally changed the goals of the Civil Aeronautics Board by deregulating the industry.

CONGRESSIONAL HEARINGS

Part of the **congressional oversight process** includes hearings designed to determine what an agency has been doing or how new policy problems should be solved. In 1982, Senator Jake Garn's hearings on the savings and loan industry provided a forum for the S&Ls to plead their case for additional powers successfully. The Senate Judiciary Committee hearings on airline deregulation, on the other hand, encouraged the Civil Aeronautics Board to continue its experimentation with deregulation under Chairman Alfred Kahn (Brown, 1987). Similarly, hearings can be used to punish. Hearings in 1982 on implementation of the hazardous waste superfund law provided a forum to criticize agency actions and resulted in a contempt citation for EPA head Anne Burford for not supplying enforcement information. Eventually, Burford resigned under pressure.

Although hearings often result in legislation, they have an impact over and above any legislative activity. During hearings or in the committee report, specific instructions may be given to the agency about **legislative intent** (see Kirst, 1969). In addition, the simple fact that hearings are held cannot but affect an administrator's decision-making process. Hearings or the potential of hearings let the regulator know that actions will be subjected to public scrutiny. The anticipation of review may be as great a prod toward responsiveness to members of Congress as the actual hearings.

Hearings also enable Congress to influence regulation by participating in the appointment process. High-level agency personnel are subject to confirmation hearings. In such hearings, members of Congress can express policy positions or even refuse to confirm nominees. In 1983, Congress delayed approving President Reagan's ICC nominees, Paul Lamboley and Jane Holt, for policy reasons. To avoid such problems, presidents sometimes invite legislators to participate in selecting regulatory nominees (see Greenwald, 1977:229).

THE LEGISLATIVE VETO

In past years the **legislative veto** was a popular method among members of Congress for controlling bureaucratic action. According to the Congressional Research Service, legislative veto provisions were placed in over two hundred pieces of legislation (Norton, 1976). The legislative veto operated as follows. Congress delegated the authority to make rules regarding some industry or activity to a regulatory agency. After these rules were issued but before they went into effect, the rules were sent to Congress. Congress, then, could veto these rules by voting to reject them. Although the veto process appears simple, in practice there were numerous types of veto. Some legislation provided veto by one house of Congress; others by both houses. Some vetoes required Congress to vote no whereas other rules were vetoed if Congress failed to vote yes. The Federal Trade Commission in 1982 had its used car dealers rule vetoed (a fairly modest rule that required used car dealers to specify if certain parts of the car were in working order or had not been checked). In fact, the anticipation of a veto may well have been the reason that the FTC used car rule was so modest. Legislative vetoes were popular among members of Congress; Representative Elliot Levitas of Georgia proposed that all regulations be subject to legislative veto provisions, and his proposal attracted numerous cosponsors. The bandwagon for the legislative veto stalled when Supreme Court declared one house legislative vetoes unconstitutional in an immigration case (*INS* v. *Chadha*, 1983).

INFORMAL CONTACT

Informal contact is just that—any informal contact between a member of Congress and a regulatory agency. Informal contact exists and in all likelihood affects the direction of regulatory policy, but it is generally hidden from public view and, therefore, difficult to study. If informal contact in regulation resembles that in other policy areas (and there is no reason to think it does not), then the contact normally results from a constituent complaint and seeks an exception from current regulatory policy (see McCubbins and Schwartz, 1984). For example, a constituent might complain to a member of Congress that OSHA failed to understand how an industry operates. A call to OSHA from the member will likely increase the speed of a decision although not necessarily change its content.

In sum, then, a member of Congress has numerous ways to intervene in regulatory policy. **Subsystem members** (e.g., member of the oversight and appropriations subcommittees) intervene frequently; other legislators are less active. Some interventions require the support of a majority of members (e.g., legislation, budgets) whereas others can be done by the individual member (hearings, informal contact). Because the avenues exist, the only question is whether or not the individual member has the resources and skills to intervene successfully.

The Presidency

The president is the political actor least likely to intervene in a regulatory policy subsystem. The press of foreign policy and major domestic issues means that presidents rarely have the time to focus on regulation, a fairly small portion of the overall federal government (Welborn, 1977:146). Despite this situation and the historical avoidance of regulation, recent presidents have been involved in regulatory policy. Gerald Ford became an early advocate of deregulation. Jimmy Carter was perhaps the most active president in regulatory policy, recruiting consumer advocates to government posts and sponsoring numerous deregulation initiatives. Ronald Reagan stressed regulation in his campaign and established an institutionalized review process through the Office of Management and Budget. George Bush declared a regulatory moratorium in 1992.

Presidents can exercise influence in four ways: (1) appointments, (2) oversight, (3) leadership, and (4) budgeting (see Wilson, 1980; F. J. Thompson, 1982; Wood and Waterman, 1994).

PRESIDENTIAL APPOINTMENTS

Through the appointment process, the president can name the head of every regulatory agency. In larger agencies such as the EPA, he can name several top administrators. Although, in theory, this power is limited in regulatory commissions with multimember boards and overlapping terms, in practice, it is not. The president can designate the commission chairperson who normally exercises the most power (see Welborn, 1977:132), and early resignations often provide the opportunity to appoint a commission majority (Scher, 1960; Greenwald, 1977:229).

The appointment power, even though subject in most cases to senatorial confirmation, provides the president with a major vehicle for influencing regulation. By appointing regulators who share his general political views, a president can change a key actor in the subsystem and influence the general direction of agency policy. Reagan's appointment of James Miller III to replace Michael Pertschuk as head of the Federal Trade Commission, for example, limited the consumer activism of the FTC. Similarly, Reagan's replacement of Darius Gaskins with Reese Taylor slowed the movement of trucking deregulation at the Interstate Commerce Commission. With agencies headed by one person, the impact can be even more dramatic. The appointment of Anne Burford as head of the Environmental Protection Agency resulted in major internal struggles over policy and the reduced credibility of the agency (Wood, 1988; Wood and Waterman, 1994).

Appointments only offer the potential to influence regulation. If regulatory appointments are used as **patronage rewards** (e.g., many state public utility commissions before 1970; Anderson, 1980) rather than for policy reasons, then the president will exercise little influence over the direction of regulatory policy (see Kemp, 1983). Careful presidential appointments to regulatory agencies have been a recent phenomenon.

PRESIDENTIAL LEADERSHIP

Simply because a person is president, that person's public policy views become legitimate. As a result even without direct contact, the president may influence a regulator to pursue given policy options. Reagan's general position on regulation as well as his criticism of the Occupational Safety and Health Administration provided enough incentive for Thorne Auchter to reduce the enforcement activities of OSHA; under Auchter the volume of fines dropped by 49 percent from 1980 to 1981. Similar arguments could be made about President Carter and consumer protection agencies. Carter's pro-consumer views were pursued by several regulatory agencies.

A president's powers are not limited to persuasion. A president bent on influencing regulation has direct powers that allow it. When the then-Department of Health, Education, and Welfare proposed banning father-son and mother-daughter school functions as discrimination on the basis of sex, President Ford "vetoed" the regulation. Similarly when several Carter appointees attempted to promulgate new regulations on the last day of the Carter administration, President Reagan held up these regulations so that they could be evaluated by his people. The informal elements of presidential leadership are undergirded by the president's formal powers.

The formal powers of the president are not without limit. Presidential actions must conform to legal and constitutional restrictions. When the Reagan administration's National Highway Traffic Safety Administration abolished the 5 mile per hour bumper standard, for example, the Courts rejected the rule withdrawal. Because NHTSA did not follow the procedures for promulgating a rule when they withdrew the rule, the action was illegal (*Motor Vehicle Manufacturers* v. *State Farm*, 1983).

BUDGETS

Just as budgets can be used by Congress to guide regulatory policy, so can they be used by the president. All "dependent" (those that are housed in departments and report to the president) regulatory agencies and many independent regulatory commissions (those that report simultaneous to Congress and the president) request funds via the executive budget. For an agency such as the Occupational Safety and Health Administration or the Agricultural Marketing Service, this means presidential appointees both in the executive department (in this case, the Department of Labor and the Department of Agriculture) and in the Office of Management and Budget (OMB) must pass on the budget request. The president or his agents, therefore, have ample opportunity to eliminate or add funds for a specific program or for the entire agency. Agencies favored by the administration may be given generous budgets so that they may pursue their objectives with greater vigor. Agencies out of favor may be limited in funds and, thus, prevented from taking aggressive actions opposed by the White House (see Kemp, 1982b; Stewart, et al., 1982). Perhaps the most effective use of the budget to influence regulatory policy was Reagan's fiscal year 1982 budget that dramatically cut regulatory agency budgets (Wood, 1988).

OVERSIGHT

The management reforms of recent presidents (program budgeting, zero-base budgeting, cost-benefit analysis, and so on) can be viewed as efforts to increase the president's oversight capabilities. Although all presidents, by definition, exercise oversight over all federal agencies, regulatory agencies are targets of specific review mechanisms. President Ford required inflation impact statements for major regulations and subjected regulations to review by the Council on Wage and Price Stability (COWPS). President Carter created the Regulatory Analysis Review Group (RARG) to review major regulations. Similarly, President Reagan had formal regulatory oversight through the Office of Information and Regulatory Affairs (OIRA) in OMB, and required all major rules be subjected to cost-benefit analysis by OMB. The cost benefit process was continued by Presidents Bush and Clinton. Under President Bush, the related Council on Competitiveness, headed by Vice President Quayle, was perceived as a way to provide business with better access to the regulatory process (Novak 1993, 1802). The Clinton process has not operated long enough to evaluate.

The existence of regulatory oversight in and of itself plays a role in influencing regulation. Regulators know that others will be looking at a regulation and its supporting analysis. The subsystem, therefore, is by definition open to outside influences. The rational regulator will seek to anticipate this oversight and be sufficiently responsive to avoid reversal (see Friedrich, 1940 on anticipated reactions). Even if the oversight organization cannot achieve its goals via anticipated reaction, it still has the option of formal intervention. At the very least, these oversight mechanisms can delay the promulgation of a regulation.

In sum, the president has at his disposal four avenues to intervene in regulatory policy. Given the weaknesses of regulatory subsystems, the president should be able to win many of these interventions. Moe (1982), for example, examined presidential influence on three regulatory agencies the National Labor Relations Board, the Securities and Exchange Commission, and the Federal Trade Commission. He found that the policy outputs of these regulatory agencies varied systematically across presidential administrations. Implied in these findings is the conclusion that presidents can and do influence the actions of regulatory agencies. Studies by Wood (1988, 1990, 1992) and Wood and Waterman (1994) document presidential impact in several agencies across an extended period of time.

The key variables, therefore, are the president's interest in regulation and his willingness to expend his political resources to intervene. No federal regulatory agency, not even the Board of Governors of the Federal Reserve, can resist the pressures of a president who devoted full time and all presidential resources to that pressure. Even the modest efforts of Presidents Carter and Reagan have contributed to major changes in regulatory policy.

Courts

In recent years courts, especially the federal court system, have been active in regulatory policy (see Melnick, 1983). Regulation has attracted numerous lawyers and as a result has turned much of the regulatory process into legal battles. Disputes that cannot be resolved between the various advocacy coalitions in a subsystem quite naturally end up in court. Initially, courts were hostile to the concept of regulation; the Interstate Commerce Commission, for example, lost 15 of the first 16 cases that it took to the Supreme Court (Belonzi, D'Antonio, and Helfand, 1977:42). Over the past hundred years, the courts' position has moderated and stabilized to a more neutral role. Courts offer relief to regulatory "victims" under two general criteria: (1) procedural violations, and (2) substantive wrongs.

PROCEDURE

An entire legal profession has grown up around regulatory agency procedure. **Administrative law** concerns the procedures that must be followed so that persons (and corporations are considered as persons) are not deprived of life, liberty, or property without due process of law. Because regulation by definition limits the choices of individuals, it, in a legal sense, deprives persons of full use of property. The Administrative Procedure Act of 1946 supplemented by agency enabling statutes specifies proper regulatory procedures for most agencies (West, 1995).

Due process in administrative law is most detailed concerning adjudications—the determination of whether or not an individual has violated a government regulation. In such a case, a person must be given notice of the actions being considered and must be granted the right to be heard on the issue, the right to submit evidence on his or her behalf, the right to confront and challenge evidence against him or her, and the right to a decision by an impartial arbitrator. In addition, if found in violation, the person has some limited right to appeal. Although some agencies have more elaborate procedures, these are the basic procedural protections in administrative law (see Heffron with McFeeley, 1983:268 ff.; Cooper, 1988:143 ff.; West, 1995).

Agencies are fairly adept at the practice of administrative law; after all, they have many years of experience. As a result, procedural challenges to agency decisions are unlikely to succeed. Studies have shown that some agencies win 90 percent of their cases in court (see Canon and Giles, 1972; Crowley, 1987; Sheehan, 1990). Despite agency dominance in the courts, some challenges on procedural matters do succeed and do result in policy change. The United Church of Christ sued the Federal Communications Commission over the ruling that the church did not have standing to challenge the television license of another party (*United Church of Christ* v. *FCC*, 1966). The Church of Christ was granted standing by the Court of Appeals and used the implied threat of this standing to negotiate greater minority hiring and minority program content in exchange for dropping the challenge (see Krasnow, Langley, and Terry, 1982). In general, courts have extended standing to a wide variety of individuals who wish to participate in the regulatory process (Melnick, 1983:10; West, 1995).

SUBSTANCE

Courts have hesitated to address substantive regulatory issues. Because judges are generalists and bureaucrats are not, courts tend to defer to bureaucratic expertise. Individuals challenging regulations bear the costs of this deference because the burden of proof lies with the challenger, not with the regulator.

Despite this deference, one challenge has always been acceptable in a court of law—that the regulator has overstepped legislative intent. If the citizen can demonstrate that a regulation is contrary to statute or exceeds the authority that Congress delegated, then the court may void the regulatory action. Because many regulatory statutes are exceedingly general, urging regulation in the public interest, convenience, or necessity, overstepping legislative intent is difficult to do and equally difficult to prove. In addition, the agency need only demonstrate that its decision is supported by substantial evidence. This criterion is weaker than either the civil (preponderance of the evidence) or the criminal (beyond a reasonable doubt) standards for a factual decision. This vests greater discretion with the regulator.

For a brief period of time the Supreme Court and Courts of Appeals decisions suggested that the courts were willing to go beyond the "legislative intent" criteria (Shapiro 1982; Melnick, 1983:11; West, 1995). Courts were asking not only whether decision X was made correctly but also whether it was the correct decision. In a case involving the Occupational Safety and Health Administration regulation limiting workplace exposure to benzene (*Industrial Union Department* v. *American Petroleum Institute*, 1980), the Supreme Court voided the rule because OSHA did not produce sufficient evidence to support a conclusion that the specific standard would provide greater benefits. The Court later ruled that this did not mean regulation must provide more benefits than costs (see *American Textile Manufacturers* v. *Donavan*, 1981) and has backed away from such rigorous standards (West, 1995).

Courts have been criticized as ineffective checks on bureaucratic action because they are too slow, too passive, and too costly and because they lack appropriate remedies (Meier, 1993). Accepting this conclusion overlooks the obvious. Although courts cannot dominate the regulatory process, they can profoundly influence it. Over the last 50 years agency procedures have become heavily judicialized, thus slowing the process of regulation. Courts, by invoking their jurisdiction, can be of assistance to those who would benefit from delay. Most major health standards issued by OSHA, for example, were challenged in court. Although OSHA has won most of these cases, in each case the regulation's effective date was delayed pending the court decision. The regulated industry benefits from this delay because it postpones the day when expenditures must be made to comply with the regulation. As the myriad of lawsuits under the **National Environmental Policy Act** (NEPA) reveals, however, delay can also be used by the forces for greater regulation if delay penalizes the industry.

In sum, then, courts are a neutral weapon in the politics of regulation. They offer a resource to those participants who would benefit from delaying changes in the status quo. Although courts offer a chance of reversing a regulatory decision, they usually only grant a delay. A delay, however, can be used to marshal other political resources to combat the regulation.

THE GENERAL ENVIRONMENT

The **regulatory policy system** made up of the regulatory subsystem and the set of immediate political forces that play on it is set in a broader environment that affects both components (see Figure 2.3). Numerous forces in the environment influence regulation and the politics of regulation—history, political culture, public opinion, the legal system, public philosophy, and so on. Many of these influences are remote and indirect. Two environmental factors, however, directly impact on regulatory policy and limit the options of the regulators—economics and technology. Economics and technology structure the decisions that can be made by regulators and political elites. They limit the choices available to each decision-maker, and they also create opportunities for politicians and subsystem members to exploit.

Figure 2.3   The environment of regulatory policy

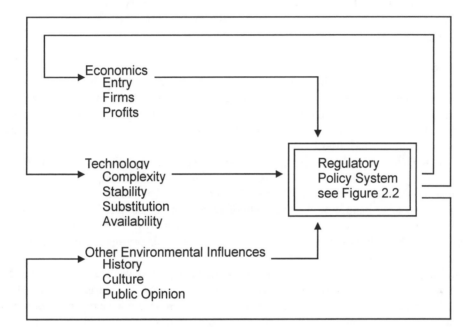

Economics

The key economic variables in the general environment are ease of entry, number of firms, and profitability.

EASE OF ENTRY

Both ease of entry and number of firms relate to the market structure of an industry. **Ease of entry** is defined as the difficulty in starting a new firm in the industry. For example, entry into the railroad industry is difficult because large capital investments are necessary to construct track and purchase equipment. In other areas such as the establishment of a genetic research firm, the barrier to entry is expertise. Not included as barriers to entry in this framework are political barriers to entry. For example, numerous professions use state-granted licensing powers to restrict entry to their profession. This is a political barrier to entry, not an economic one.

Ease of entry is a key variable in regulation because it determines the potential of adding new firms to the industry. Adding more firms to an industry may increase its competitiveness. When an industry is competitive, a regulator has more options available, including efforts to deregulate. For example, the trucking industry has some 35,000 licensed carriers, and entry is reasonably easy. Deregulating and the benefits of spirited competition are more likely in trucking than in the railroad industry, where only a handful of viable long-haul railroads exist. The greater the ease of entry, therefore, the less likely that regulation will be in the interests of the regulated.

NUMBER OF FIRMS

The number of firms in an industry affects the regulator's options in two ways. Similar to the case of ease of entry, the greater the number of firms in an industry, the more likely it is that the actions of one or more firms cannot affect price or overall supply. In situations similar to this, a semi-free market exists that may optimally allocate goods among their best uses.

In addition, the existence of numerous firms means that the failure of a single firm is less likely to be noticed. The failure of Braniff in 1982, for example, subjected the airline deregulation efforts to the scrutiny of political elites. The economic failure of a law firm, on the other hand, would be unlikely to generate much interest from the state bar association. Because failures are a sign in a capitalist economy that weak firms are being eliminated, the ability to absorb some failures permits a regulatory agency to preside over a healthier industry.

Failures are especially important from a policy perspective when a firm is so large that its failure creates negative externalities for others. The Bank of America, for example, is so integrated with the rest of the economy that its failure would have repercussions for thousands of other firms. In such a case, regulatory options are restricted.

PROFITABILITY

Industries vary a great deal in their return on investment. The television industry, for example, in some years had a return on investment of over 100 percent (Strickland, 1980:272) whereas the savings and loan industry had a negative return on investment for 1982 (see Carron, 1982). Although industries with low profits may demand regulation, a low profit structure limits the type of regulation that a regulator can undertake. From the 1950s to the 1970s, for example, dry cleaning was a declining industry as the result of innovations in clothes and fabrics. Efforts to regulate workplace safety in this environment were futile because any additional costs usually bankrupted the cleaners, and efforts to set prices were unsuccessful because profit-conscious (e.g., desperate) cleaners were always willing to undercut regulated prices to gain a larger share of the market (see Meier and Plumlee, 1979).

In an industry with ample profits, the regulators do not need to be as concerned about imposing costs on the industry. In the television industry, for example, imposing public service costs would be reasonably easy (if the FCC were so inclined) from an economic perspective because profits are large enough to absorb the costs. Many of those profits are, in fact, monopoly profits resulting from a government license. In sum, therefore, higher profits create the potential for regulation in the interests of the nonregulated. Whether this potential is realized, however, is a function of numerous other subsystem and environmental variables.

FEEDBACK

Although economic factors influence the direction of regulatory policy, they clearly do not determine it. One need only take a look at any economic analysis of regulation in the past 20 years to see that economic factors do not determine policy (see MacAvoy, 1979). In fact, more often the other argument is seen—that policy affects economics.

What occurs is a simple feedback mechanism. Much regulatory policy is an output into the environment. Much of this policy is intended to affect the economic system, and much of it does. The large profits in the television industry may be attributed to early FCC decisions about the allocation of very high frequency (VHF) and ultrahigh frequency (UHF) stations (see Krasnow, Langley, and Terry, 1982). Utility regulation before the energy crisis allowed sufficient return on investment to attract the necessary capital for expansion (Anderson, 1980). Industries frequently complain about the costs that regulation imposes on them, a clear indication that policy feeds back to affect economic factors in the environment. → thus time is important to study

Technology

Technology encompasses the production technology of the industry. In large part, technology determines the economics of the industry; complex technologies create barriers to entry and thus determine if a market is competitive or not. The elements of production technology relevant here are complexity, stability, and substitutability. Similar to economic factors, each of these limits the options available to the regulator and influences the direction of regulatory policy.

COMPLEXITY

Complexity is the closeness of the industry's technology to the scientific state of the art. Industries engaged in genetic engineering or computers, for example, have technologies that are very close to, if not actually at, the state of the art in genetic research and computer design. Barbers, on the other hand, have very uncomplex technologies that are readily apparent to the layperson.

Technological complexity discourages close regulation. The more complex an industry is, the more likely it will not be easily understood by the regulator without large research budgets. This complexity should yield regulatory policy that reflects deference on the part of the regulator because ill-advised regulation may be harmful to the industry. Regulation may even evolve toward self-regulation. Industries with simple technologies, on the other hand, can be subjected to greater scrutiny and more restrictive regulation.

STABILITY

The stability of an industry's technology is the rate of change in the basic technology of production. Some industries' technologies are slow to change; the trucking industry, for example, has had little change in its basic technology over the past 50 years. Similarly, the American railroad industry has not adopted even the elementary technologies of other nations' railroads. Other industries have rapidly changing technologies. The banking industry, for example, although not an industry known for technological complexity, underwent rapid changes in the 1970s and 1980s as the result of computerization. Broadcast communication is now entering an era of high instability with the introduction of direct satellite broadcasting, low-power television, microwave distribution systems, and innovations in cable capacity.

The greater the instability of an industry's technology, the more opportunities the regulator has to change how the industry is regulated. Computerization and innovation in the securities industry, for example, made bank deregulation a feasible political proposition. Although instability provides opportunities, this does not mean that the opportunities will be taken. Industry may well mount large campaigns to restrict the introduction of new technology that might disrupt the status quo (Krasnow, Longley, and Terry, 1982).

SUBSTITUTABILITY

Substitutability is the extent that substitutes are available for the industry's products or services. Are there alternative technologies available in the industry or in other industries that would permit someone to offer a comparable good or service? For example, rail passenger service can easily be replaced and was by intercity airline service and private automobiles. In the 1980s the spread of computer technology and access to international money markets allowed nonbank institutions such as brokerage firms, credit card companies, and major retailers to offer services previously available only through banks.

The greater the availability of alternative technologies, the more discretion the regulator has in implementing public policy and the less likely regulation will be used to benefit the industry. In fact, this may create the impetus to act. Alternative investment instruments for small investors offered by money market funds, for example, created the pressure to permit depository institutions to offer similar instruments. Again, the availability of alternative technology only provides the opportunity for action; it does not guarantee it. In fact, political pressures may well close off options as the FCC did for a period of time when microwave long-distance calls became a reality.

AVAILABILITY

A fourth aspect of technology is not part of the production technology of the industry. The **availability of a technology** refers to whether or not a technology is available to achieve a regulatory goal. For example, if Congress decreed that by 2000 all U.S. automobiles would achieve fuel efficiency of 85 miles per gallon of gasoline, the technology to attain this may not be available. On the other hand, the technology for producing cable systems with 200 channels is feasible. The availability of a technology to achieve regulatory goals is a key issue in the regulation of the environment, energy production, automobile safety, worker health and safety, and other areas. If the feasibility of reaching a policy goal can be challenged, the industry has the potential to win regulatory battles. In anticipation of such challenges, the regulator may well push less vigorous regulation. Nothing detracts from the reputation of a regulator more than promulgating a standard that is impossible to achieve.

FEEDBACK — *Stress this more; new regs can change entire nature of Subsystem.*

Similar to the case of the economic environment, regulatory policy also feeds back to the technological environment and influences its development. Regulatory policy may encourage new technology as the Environmental Protection Agency has done with its bubble concept. Regulation may also restrict the development or the adoption of technology; the FCC restricted the development of cable TV for many years; the ICC restricted innovations in railroad cars designed to improve efficiency (Fellmuth, 1970); and OSHA's reliance on engineering standards rather than performance standards is likely restricting development of new safety techniques.

SUMMARY

This chapter presented an outline of the regulatory process that will be used to analyze regulatory and consumer protection policy in the remaining chapters. Policy can be characterized by who benefits from the regulation; two dimensions of beneficiaries exist: (1) the regulated industry, and (2) the nonregulated. Each are separate dimensions because policy can benefit both the regulated and the nonregulated, and it can also benefit no one.

To determine who benefits from policy, the locus of regulatory decision making must be determined. Essentially, the locus of regulatory decision making means whether or not regulatory policy is set within the regulatory subsystem with little guidance by macropolitical forces. Subsystems can be either relatively autonomous, or affected by a large number of interventions on the part of Congress, the president, and other political elites. The key variables in determining the autonomy of the subsystem are the regulatory issue's salience and complexity. Issues that are complex and issues that are not salient are generally left to the subsystem. Issues that are simple and issues that are salient attract political intervention.

If a subsystem is semiautonomous, then the key question is whether or not the regulatory bureaucracy dominates the subsystem or if the bureaucracy is reduced to a more passive role of mediating disputes among the active interests. A subsystem is likely to be under greater control of the regulatory bureaucracy if the bureaucracy has political resources such as expertise, cohesion, strong legislative authority, and good leadership. If the bureaucracy lacks these resources, regulatory policy is likely to be determined by the interplay of the various advocacy coalitions.

In a subsystem with the bureaucracy as the dominant actor, who benefits from regulation is determined by a variety of factors. If the regulatory agency operates under specific goals, has **universal authority** (e.g., no limitations on its range of authority), has effective sanctions, and is not limited by procedural restrictions, regulation is likely to be in the interests of the nonregulated. Agencies with vague goals, limited authority, few sanctions, and weak procedures are more likely to regulate in the interests of the regulated. If the issue area is salient but not salient enough to limit subsystem autonomy, regulation is more likely to reflect the interests of the nonregulated. In addition, the policy goals of the regulatory agency staff and leadership are extremely important. To the extent that regulators identify with the industry rather than with regulation, regulation will benefit the regulated industry.

In a subsystem where the bureaucracy plays a lesser role, policy is determined by the interplay between the advocacy coalitions. In general, two major coalitions will exist, one representing the interests of the regulated industry and one opposed to those interests. Which coalition gains the upper hand depends on a series of variables. Coalitions that are large, resource rich, dispersed, cohesive, intense, and broad have advantages over those that lack these characteristics. Because advocacy coalitions include bureaucrats, legislators, legislative staff, state and local government officials, researchers, and journalists as well as interest groups, these variables must be applied to the advocacy coalitions as a whole, not to the interest groups.

In an advocacy-coalition-dominated subsystem, the direction of regulation is a function of two variables. The first is obvious; the goals of the dominant advocacy coalition are the primary factor. If the industry advocacy coalition overwhelms all others, regulation will be in the interests of the industry. If the nonindustry coalition overwhelms the industry coalition, regulation will be in the interests of the nonregulated. When the coalitions are relatively balanced, regulation will be balanced. The second important variable in such subsystems is the cohesion of the regulatory industry because the degree of cohesion affects the power of the industry advocacy coalition. When the industry lacks cohesion, regulation in the interests of the nonregulated is more likely.

In regulatory areas where subsystems lack autonomy, Congress and the president play a greater role. Congress has access to legislation, appropriations, oversight, and informal contacts to influence the actions of regulatory subsystems. The president can affect regulatory policy via appointments, budgeting, leadership, and oversight. Courts perform a generally neutral role, but they can be used by other political actors to delay and to attempt to change regulatory outcomes.

The political forces take place within an economic and technological environment that creates opportunities for some actors and places restraints on others. This environment can also influence the direction of regulatory policy by strengthening the hand of those seeking greater regulation or those wanting to permit the industry to regulate itself. In economic terms, when entry to the industry is easy, when the number of firms is large, and when profits are generally high, regulation in the interests of the nonregulated is more likely. In technological terms, when industry technologies are simple, when technologies are changing, and when substitutes exist, regulation will likely be in the interests of the nonregulated.

In any area of regulation, having all the variables point in the same direction will be unlikely. In some cases, the environment might favor regulation in the interests of the regulated whereas the political and bureaucratic forces suggest regulation in the interests of the nonregulated. The hypotheses presented in this chapter, therefore, should all be qualified with this caveat: all other things being equal. In cases when all other things are not equal, the interplay of the various forces on regulation can be observed to determine the relative influence of each variable.

Chapter 3
Regulating Occupations

Joseph Stewart, Jr. and Clark D. Thomas[1]

Determining if a person is qualified to practice law, medicine, plumbing, or well drilling—**occupational regulation**—is a function generally left to the state or, sometimes, local governments. There are no national government sponsored or sanctioned exams for electricians, barbers, or tree surgeons. Federal law even prohibits the development of a federal bar exam.

The number of regulated occupations is large. Every state in the union regulates accountants, architects, attorneys, barbers, chiropractors, cosmetologists, dental hygienists, dentists, insurance agents, nurses—registered and practical, optometrists, osteopaths, pharmacists, physical therapists, physicians and surgeons, podiatrists, real estate agents, and elementary and secondary school teachers. These 20 occupations are the tip of the iceberg. Occupations ranging from securities agent to TV technician are regulated in some states. A list of 58 occupations and the number of states that regulate them is found in Table 3.1 (Bianco, 1993).

Approximately 1,100 different occupations are regulated through licensure, certification, or registration somewhere in the United States (Brinegar and Schmitt, 1992), a 37.5 percent increase since 1982. Approximately 600 of these occupations involve licensing, but fewer than 60 are regulated by more than half the states. Some states are very active in regulating occupations or professions; California, for example, has 29 boards and commissions overseeing everything from physicians to acupuncturists. Others limit their efforts to the larger professions, such as physicians, pharmacists, and attorneys (Schneider, 1987).

---

[1]Joseph Stewart, Jr. is a professor of government and politics in the School of Social Sciences as the University of Texas at Dallas. His primary area of interest is in civil rights policy and minority politics, but he also maintains a teaching and research interest in regulatory politics and policy. He has published in all political science journals that are typeset and right justified.

Clark D. Thomas is a PhD candidate in political economy at the University of Texas at Dallas. His previous publications have appeared in the *Texas Journal of Political Studies* and the *Southern Methodist University Law Review*. His current research focuses on the concept of agenda control in the policy-making process and its utility in explaining education reform efforts.

Table 3.1   Number of States That Regulate Certain Occupations

Abstractor	5*	Acupuncturist	26
Aerial Duster	2	Emergency Med Tech	51*
Auctioneer	24	Audiologist	42
Boiler Inspector	10	Chauffeur	7
Collection Agent	14	General Contractor	25
Specialty Contractor	4	Well Driller	19
Driving Instructor	16	Electrician	37*
Elevator Inspector	7	Funeral Director	51*
Employment Agency	12*	Engineer	51*
Forester	14	Geologist	16
Guide (Fishing/Hunting)	22	Hearing Aid Dealer	51*
Landscape Architect	44	Librarian	37*
Marriage Counselor	27	Medical Lab Technician	10
Lay Midwife	6	Nurse-Midwife	16
Milk Sampler/Tester	36	Mine Foreman	9
Painter	2	Naturopath	7
Nursing Home Administrator	51*	Occupational Therapist	47*
Occupational Therapy Assistant	42*	Optician	23
Pesticide Applicator	51*	Pharmacist Assistant	4
Physical Therapy Assistant	30	Physician Assistant	51*
Plumber	37	Polygraph Examiner	29
Private Detective	35*	Psychologist	51*
TV Technician	4	Radiologic Technician	27
Sanitarian	18	School Bus Driver	7
Harbor Pilot	12	Social Worker	51*
Soil Tester/Classifier	6	Surveyor	50
Tree Surgeon	4	Tattoo Artist	4
Veterinarian	51*	Watchman/Guard	34*
Weather Modifier	3	Weighmaster	7

* Includes District of Columbia

Source: Bianco, 1993

WHY REGULATE OCCUPATIONS?

Occupational regulation has usually been justified by economists in terms of "**public interest theory**" (see Stigler, 1971). We dub this "**economic public interest theory**" to avoid confusing it with the **public interest theory of political scientists**. Economic public interest theory holds that government regulation is justified only by **market failure**. In the practice of occupations, markets fail because of (1) consumer ignorance (politely termed, asymmetrical information) or (2) negative externalities (for which there is no polite term).

Consumer ignorance is a market failure because in a perfectly competitive market both the buyer and the seller have perfect information about the good or service being sold. In the case of medicine, for example, the consumer lacks information. The consumer cannot judge a priori whether or not "Dr. Farmer" is a competent physician. In fact, even after the treatment the consumer may be at a disadvantage because so many factors other than a physician's treatment have an impact on the consumer's health. In addition, the consumer is in a poor position to determine how much of Dr. Farmer's services he or she needs. Is the recommended X-ray, medicine, biopsy, or surgery required, or are less radical, equally effective alternatives available?

Faced with a lack of information, a consumer would normally engage in an **agency relationship** with a third party. For example, consumers often employ a stock broker to advise them on how to cope with the complexities of the securities market. But in the case of medical treatment, the consumer has little alternative but to trust Dr. Farmer to tell him or her whether or not and, if so, how much medical treatment is needed (Shapiro, 1986).

An **agent** is supposed to act in the interest of the consumer by suggesting how much of the service the consumer should buy from the agent. The potential problem is obvious. Dr. Farmer, the agent, has an incentive to recommend more services than the consumer needs because these services will be purchased from Dr. Farmer, the seller. Regulation, in economic public interest theory, is therefore needed to prevent an excessive demand for the product.

Closely related to the problem of over demand for a service is the problem of **poor quality service**. Because the consumer does not have the skills or knowledge to prejudge the quality of a service, it is possible that an unscrupulous person will sell the consumer a poor or dangerous good or service. A dentist might do long-run damage to a patient's teeth, or an abstractor might miss a lien on a property sold to a consumer. When the value of the good or service is small or when the consumer engages in repeat purchases (e.g., haircuts), the problem is not serious. Still, poor quality service is a reason why economic public interest theory suggests that occupational regulation might be needed.

Another reason that almost all economists accept as a justification for regulation is the occurrence of negative externalities from the consumption of a service (see Friedman, 1962). A **negative externality** results if, by consuming a good or service, the consumer creates a danger or a threat of a danger to a third party. For example, a person who hires an incompetent architect endangers all those who will use the building. A person who employs an incompetent plumber puts at risk the health of others in the community through the spread of disease. In cases where negative externalities are probable, economic public interest theory justifies state intervention to protect the health, welfare, and interests of the public.

THE ENVIRONMENT OF OCCUPATIONAL REGULATION

Most state regulated occupations have characteristics conducive to competitive markets. The number of practitioners is large, and economic barriers to entry are small (profits vary by occupation). The technology of these occupations varies, but generally the technology is complex (barbers are an exception) and changing (for white-collar but not blue-collar professions), and substitutes almost always exist.

THE PROCESS OF OCCUPATIONAL REGULATION

Generalizing from the regulation of 1100 different occupations is difficult, but some patterns exist. Usually, the initial demand for regulation comes not from consumers but from the practitioners of the occupation. Even though it is the practitioners who seek regulation, the argument for regulation is couched in terms of economic public interest theory. For example, the state, it is argued, needs to regulate doctors to protect citizens from incompetent doctors. Its sole goal is to protect the public's interest.

Regulatory Commissions

Responding to these demands, legislators create a **regulatory commission**. In many cases, the commission is composed of **practitioners** from the regulated occupation. After all, the claim is, who can judge the competence of a doctor (or nurse, plumber, electrician, polygraph examiner, etc.) but a fellow practitioner. Regulation is needed because citizens are not competent to judge the skills of the practitioner in the first place. Shimberg (1982) notes that most regulatory board members are practitioners of the occupation that they regulate.

Sometimes the law goes even further in delegating power of the state to the occupation. In some states, the state medical association and the state dental association actually appoint the regulatory board for their respective professions (Akers, 1968:472). In a majority of the states the governor appoints regulators from a list of nominees provided by the state association (for dentists, physicians, and pharmacists). The occupation, therefore, not only demands regulation but tries to select who the regulators will be. Nonmedical occupations are usually not as successful in restricting how regulators are selected, but state law often requires that a regulator be a member in good standing of the profession that he or she will regulate.

Until the early 1980s, a majority of state occupational regulatory commissions were generally small agencies with a great deal of autonomy. While their numbers are declining, these agencies still exist in several states. To try to prevent partisan political forces from affecting the agency, often the major control over the regulatory body, the budget, is taken away from the legislature. Many state regulatory commissions are funded solely from the **licensing fees** collected from the occupation's practitioners. Sometimes these agencies are so small that they share office space with the occupational association whose members they regulate.

Now, less state regulation of occupations is done in small commissions controlled exclusively by the regulated occupation. Over 35 states such as Florida and California have a large Department of Occupational Licensing (the name varies) that consolidates the licensing functions for several occupations (Brinegar and Schmitt, 1992). New York regulates the occupations with **career civil servants**. California requires that some members of the regulatory board be **public members** who do not practice the occupation (see Shimberg et al., 1973).

Large or Small Agency?

The choice between numerous small regulatory commissions and a single, large regulatory agency has political implications. Occupations prefer to be regulated by a small commission (see Sprecher, 1967; Carey and Doherty, 1967; Connors, 1967). A small commission composed of practitioners and funded by license fees is more likely to be controlled by the occupation and run in the occupation's interest.

A large consolidated agency is more likely to engage in vigorous regulation for three reasons:

First, no single occupation can control the agency; every occupation must compete with all others for attention. In such an agency, for example, physicians will be less likely to be able to use the powers of the regulatory agency to make life miserable for chiropractors. The claims of one occupation will be challenged by the claims of other occupations.

Second, political elites are more likely to pay attention to the activities of such an agency because they decide on the agency's budget. Exposing the agency to political interests provides an avenue for nonoccupational interests to affect the agency.

Third, the consolidated agency is likely to attract a higher-quality employee. A small regulatory commission (some have only one or two employees) provides no opportunities for advancement for a job well done. In fact, if the employee is not a member of the regulated profession, he or she may be prevented from holding certain posts in a small agency. A consolidated agency, on the other hand, will attract individuals with a general interest in regulation. Individuals who perform well will have promotion opportunities within the agency. With rewards for good performance, performance should improve (if our economist brethren are correct). The result is the potential for more consumer-oriented regulation. It is no wonder, then, that regulated professions prefer the small commission (Meier and Plumlee, 1979).

THE REGULATORY SUBSYSTEM

At the risk of overgeneralizing, a typical regulatory subsystem for state occupational regulation can be described in terms of several key variables. Because occupational regulation is usually not a salient issue, regulatory issues are normally resolved within the subsystem (see Gormley, 1983). The subsystem is fairly unusual, however; in most cases it is composed of only the agency and the regulated interest.

The agency is usually a multimember body composed of members of the regulated occupation and employs not more than a few full-time employees. Although the boards may possess some expertise, they cannot be characterized as cohesive, nor do they develop aggressive leadership. In terms of legislative authority, these agencies usually have vague goals, cover the entire profession, have weak or rarely used sanctions, and have elaborate procedures to protect the rights of the practitioners.

For all intents and purposes the subsystem usually has only one advocacy coalition (Sabatier, 1988), the coalition dominated by the occupation. A second advocacy coalition is possible when one occupation conflicts with another, when a member of the macropolitical system seeks to intervene, or when a well-organized consumer movement exists. In general, however, the regulated and the regulator operate in isolation.

Three Regulatory Options

In theory, a state regulatory agency has three options in regulating an occupation: (1) registration, (2) certification, and (3) licensing. In actuality, legislation usually specifies the type of regulation to be employed. An occupation that seeks regulation in its own self-interest will likely prefer licensing over the other two options.

REGISTRATION

Under **registration**, everyone who practices an occupation must register that fact with the agency. Registration occurs without restriction. Anyone who wishes to register may; there are no barriers to entry. The agency may place restrictions on the type and quality of service that is offered or on any other aspect of practicing the occupation. In general, however, agencies that only register occupations rarely ever restrict them to a significant degree. This need not be the case; even under a registration system, the regulatory agency can receive complaints about the providers of service. It could hold hearings on complaints and suspend registration if circumstances merit. An example of regulation by registration is California's regulation of television repair personnel.

CERTIFICATION

Under **certification**, a regulatory agency gives an exam or examines the credentials of individuals wishing to practice an occupation. If the individual passes the exam and meets other necessary criteria, that individual is certified as a practitioner of that occupation. In many states, accountants are certified (Connors, 1967).

Under such a system, any individual wanting to practice a certified occupation can still do so without certification; that person, however, cannot hold himself or herself out as a "certified" member of the profession. For example, anyone who wishes can prepare tax returns and do other work that is normally done by a certified public accountant (CPA). The practice of accounting is not restricted to CPAs. The only restriction on those accountants who are not CPAs is that they may not represent themselves to the public as such (some states place additional restrictions on noncertified accountants).

Certification has some advantages for consumers if done correctly. A consumer has the option of purchasing services from an individual who is certified as competent by the regulatory agency. If a consumer feels the price of such service is too expensive, he or she still has the option of bearing a greater risk and purchasing the service from a noncertified practitioner. This procedure allows those who wish to purchase lower-quality services to do so. Although few people seek low-quality brain surgery, many do want low-quality legal and accounting services (as evidenced by the demand for do-it-yourself divorce kits and tax preparation services).

LICENSING

Licensing is the most restrictive form of regulation. Under licensing, an individual wishing to practice an occupation sits for an examination or has his or her credentials evaluated. If the person meets all the qualifications, he or she is licensed to practice. Individuals who are not licensed to practice are prohibited from doing so. For some occupations, practicing without a license may be a felony. Most current regulation is done through licensing. Physicians, attorneys, barbers, cosmetologists, and dry cleaners are only a few of the occupations that are licensed.

The categories of registration, certification, and licensing are not mutually exclusive. A regulator can combine elements of the three. For example, in all states lawyers are licensed; in some states they also may be certified in a specialty such as tax law. Although this does not prevent other attorneys from practicing tax law, they may not represent themselves, as certified tax experts. Similarly, physicians are both licensed to the general practice of medicine and certified as specialists.

POTENTIAL HARMS OF REGULATION

Whenever any group of individuals is given the coercive power of the state and asked to regulate themselves, potential for abuse exists. Adam Smith (1937) best summarized this position over 200 years ago: "People of the same trade seldom meet together, even for merriment or diversion, but the conversation ends in a conspiracy against the public or in some contrivance to raise prices." Smith was concerned with **guilds**, private associations that performed functions similar to state regulatory agencies. Allowing individuals to regulate themselves exposes them to the temptations of greed, the major motivating force that Smith held dear. If they did not seek to enrich themselves, then Smith and the economists he begot would be greatly disappointed.

Adam Smith's viewpoint has been adopted by Milton Friedman and the Chicago school of economics. Friedman (1962) and others (Rottenberg, 1980; Lott, 1987) charge that occupational regulation results in a multitude of evils.

First, it restricts the free flow of labor from one occupation to another. By creating barriers to entry such as examinations, education, apprentice programs, and so on, regulation prevents labor from flowing freely to those occupations with the greatest returns.

Second, as supply is restricted or even reduced and demand remains static or increases, prices for the occupational service must rise. Consumers will pay more for a service than they would in a free market.

Third, as a result of restricted entry and high prices, members of the regulated occupation will receive economic rents, that is, returns that are not justified in terms of skills, experience, or true scarcity.

Fourth, regulation will have little impact on the quality of service provided. Members of an occupation that already receive high incomes from provision of services have no incentive to offer greater-quality service and, thus, invest more resources in producing the same income.

The charges raised by Friedman merit closer investigation. If he is correct, little justification exists for regulating occupations in the current manner. His proposed reform, complete deregulation, would then be a reasonable policy option. Before we examine the systematic research on Friedman's charges, one contemporary example, American medicine, is examined in depth. Friedman feels that AMA-imposed restrictions on entry have such deleterious consequences that the nation would be better served if medicine were deregulated and the licensing of physicians abandoned.

REGULATING MEDICINE: A CONTEMPORARY EXAMPLE

At the time that the American Medical Association (AMA) was founded (1847), medical doctors (MDs) were only one of a variety of medical practitioners using the designation "doctor." Medical practice at the time was primitive by modern standards. Amputation and bleeding were common cures for a variety of ailments. Surgery was done by barbers.

Goals of the American Medical Association

Within this context, the AMA had some laudable goals. It sought (1) to require a uniform course of study for premedical students and (2) to elevate and standardize the requirements of medical education (see Kessel, 1959; 1970). The first step in this process was political effort to convince state legislatures to license physicians. From 1847 to 1900 this effort was fought successfully, and medical examining boards were created in all the states. These medical boards were, of course, composed of physicians.

With control over the practice of medicine established through state regulation, the medical profession pursued its education goals. Although the attempt to raise the educational standards of medical schools was portrayed as an effort to protect the public's health, historians (Shryock, 1967) have discovered that the AMA's concern was the number of physicians. The AMA tied standards to the health issue by arguing that many physicians were poorly educated and that the nation only had resources to produce a limited number of quality physicians. The public would be better off with fewer, better-trained physicians.

Medical Education

In 1904 the United States had 160 medical schools. Many were **proprietary schools**. Because proprietary schools increased the income of their owners by accepting more students, they had an incentive to increase the size of their enrollments and to produce physicians as fast as possible. This, according to the AMA, led to the evils they wished to eradicate.

In 1906 the AMA Council on Medicine Education examined the medical schools of the United States and found that only 80 met their idea of what a medical school should be (see Kessel, 1959; 1970). Furthermore, 32 schools were completely unacceptable. Using such information to restrict the supply of doctors was not feasible because the AMA might be perceived as seeking economic gain for physicians at the expense of the public.

Restricting Supply

To solve this credibility problem the AMA convinced the Carnegie Foundation for the Advancement of Teaching to examine medical schools. The Carnegie Foundation agreed and hired Abraham Flexner to do so. Flexner was assisted in this effort by the staff of the AMA and had access to the AMA's 1906 data. The Flexner report on medical education came to conclusions that could have been written by the AMA. Flexner concluded that too many doctors diluted the quality of medical care. The public would be better served by fewer, better-trained doctors. Accordingly, many of the current medical schools should be closed. Those that remained open should restrict their admissions and adopt the uniform curriculum recommended by the AMA.

Armed with the Flexner report and control over the state medical examining boards, the American Medical Association proceeded to restrict entry to the medical profession (Kessel, 1970). State medical boards required that a person graduate from a Class A medical school before he or she would be allowed to take the state medical exam. A **Class A medical school** was one approved by the American Medical Association or the American Association of Medical Colleges. The schools on both lists were identical.

Moving one step backward in the licensing process, the AMA asserted control over the internship process. Serving an internship with a hospital was a prerequisite to licensing. Hospitals, at least those controlled by physicians, required that a student graduate from a Class A medical school to receive an internship.

In combination, these two factors restricted entry to the medical profession. A graduate of a nonaccredited medical school would have difficulty finding an internship at an approved hospital. Without an internship, the student could not sit for the medical exam. Even with an internship at another hospital, the student might not be allowed to take the state exam because he or she failed to graduate from a Class A medical school.

Impacts

The impact of these policies on medical education was striking. Faced with a system that refused to accept their graduates, proprietary medical schools closed. From 160 U.S. medical schools in 1904, the number dropped to 85 in 1920 and 76 in 1930 (Frech,

1974:124). Schools with AMA approval restricted admissions dramatically. In 1905, 26,000 students enrolled in medical schools, and 4,606 students graduated. By 1920 enrollments had been cut to 14,000 with 3,047 graduates, all at a time when the war in Europe should have increased demand for medical services.

The impact of these cutbacks was so effective that the 1905 level for students was not reached again until 1955 (Frech, 1974:124). Major increases in medical enrollments did not occur until the health care explosion of the 1960s that was inspired by the federal government.

As interesting as the restriction on entry was the process by which medical schools restricted entry—**discrimination**. Medical schools limited enrollments to white Christian males. The seeds of this policy were found in the Flexner report; Flexner (1910:180) concluded "an essentially untrained negro wearing an MD degree is dangerous...the practice of the negro doctor will be limited to his own race."

The impact of the Flexner "reforms" on black medical education was devastating. Five of the seven black medical schools were closed (Kessel, 1970:270). In 1920 the 3,409 black doctors represented 2.7 percent of the total. That was the high water mark for black physicians for many years. In 1970, even after a decade of affirmative action, the proportion of the nation's doctors who were black was roughly one-half (1.4 percent) that found fifty years earlier (Frech, 1974:125). By 1993, this figure had risen to only 3.3 percent (U.S. Department of Commerce, 1993). In 1948, one-third of all medical schools refused to admit black students, and as late as 1965, five medical schools were still segregated (Strelnick and Young, 1980:2).

Discrimination was also practiced against women wanting to study medicine. In 1910, 8,810 women were practicing physicians, 6.5 percent of the total (Kessel, 1970:270). The proportion of women dropped dramatically with the implementation of the Flexner report and did not reach this proportion again until the 1970s (Strelnick, 1983:7). Similarly, Jews were systematically excluded from medical school. Admissions to City College of New York, for example, were 58 percent Jewish in 1925 but dropped to 16 percent by 1936 (Frech, 1974:126). Discrimination against Jews perhaps also explains the imposition of citizenship requirements in the 1930s as large numbers of Jewish doctors fled Nazi Germany (Gellhorn, 1976).

The economic impact of this restriction on entry was as dramatic as the racial impacts. Physicians engaged in **price discrimination** (Kessel, 1959) by adjusting their fees to the income level of the patient. As part of this desire to set prices arbitrarily without outside intervention, the medical community opposed innovations in health care delivery that were not based on individual fee-for-service medicine. Prepaid health care plans were opposed by local medical societies, and doctors who participated in them were ostracized and denied hospital privileges (see Kessel, 1959:33-41). This opposition to innovation extended to national policy as well. The AMA opposed free medical care and Medicaid (Kessel, 1959:39). They engaged in a series of state level battles with chiropractors, podiatrists, osteopaths, and midwives to restrict and even eliminate these professions (Akers, 1968).

Medicine, in effect, became a closed society as far as consumers were concerned. It was not unknown, for example, that a doctor testifying for a patient in a malpractice suit would have future difficulties in using hospital facilities (Kessel, 1970). All this restriction did not result in health care superior to that of other, less restrictive nations. Infant mortality rates and average life spans, although crude measures of heath, reflect lower health quality in the U.S. than in several European countries.

Slow Quality Improvements in Medicine

Perhaps one reason why quality did not improve faster was the notorious **grandfather clause**. By not examining current doctors, any impact of improvements on quality could only be incremental. Only recently, has the issue of mandating continuing medical education for continued licensing been seriously considered. As late as 1970, Kessel (275) was able to marvel at the incongruency that we require drivers to take periodic reexaminations but do not impose the same requirement on physicians. Since then, however, 23 states, while still not requiring reexamination, have begun requiring some form of continuing medical education as a prerequisite for reregistering licenses (Langsley, 1991).

Unfortunately, there is little evidence that continuing education has any impact in altering medical practices. There could be a variety of reasons for this lack of impact. First, it may be attributable to the failure of physicians to take courses related to their practice (Davis et al., 1990). Second, the state may fail to audit compliance. For example, for the first eleven years that Michigan mandated continuing legal education, physicians had merely to sign a statement saying they were in compliance to be deemed so (Stross and DeKornfeld, 1990). Third, when Michigan began auditing compliance, it found that over one-half of the continuing medical education hours were taken out of state, suggesting that the opportunity to combine business with pleasure, while getting away from a practice, was not lost on these physicians (Gruppen et al., 1986).

Summary of Medical Regulation

The example of medicine illustrates how a profession uses regulation that was proposed in the public interest for its own benefit. The situation in medicine was dramatically altered in the 1960s, when the federal government became active in health policy. With the implementation of Medicare and Medicaid as well as federal programs to expand health care, health resources, and health planning, control of the profession by the AMA was weakened. Health policy became too important to be left solely in the hands of doctors (although they still retain the preponderant influence). Four indicators of the federal effort were: (1) the increase in medical schools to 141, (2) the increase in medical students to a number in excess of 72,000 in 1990 (U.S. Department of Commerce, 1993), (3) the growing number of women and minorities in medicine, and (4) the increase in efforts to encourage and monitor provider quality.

THE IMPACT OF OCCUPATIONAL REGULATION

Although the case study of the medical profession illustrates the potential ill effects of occupational regulation, it remains a single case. The study of occupational regulation has gone far beyond the study of physicians and has examined the impact of such regulation in a variety of contexts. Five major impacts of occupational regulation have been examined: (1) barriers to entry, (2) the existence of economic rents, (3) impact on price, (4) impact on quality, and (5) the general impact of regulation. Each is discussed in turn.

Impact: Three Barriers to Entry May be Created

Occupational regulation has been charged with creating **barriers to entry** (Friedman, 1962; Lott, 1987) that restrict the free flow of labor, thus reducing supply and leading to increases in price. Without a doubt, regulation does create barriers to entry by limiting the number of persons who practice an occupation. A barrier to entry, however, is not by definition bad. If a barrier to entry prevents an incompetent person from selling a service and, thus, raises the overall quality of services to the consumer, it constitutes a reasonable barrier to entry. Barriers to entry that lack any redeeming benefits for consumers, however, must be considered unreasonable barriers that benefit only the producers. Three potential barriers to entry are associated with regulation: (1) nonsense requirements, (2) examinations, (4) and lack of reciprocity.

NONSENSE REQUIREMENTS

State regulatory laws often establish licensing requirements that are unrelated to effective performance, e.g., **nonsense requirements**. Gellhorn (1976) takes great relish in listing a variety of such requirements. In some states, for example, photographers have had to pass a venereal disease test, boxers to take loyalty oaths, and barbers, in California, to present evidence of knowledge of basic anatomy. During the big Red scare of the 1950s, several professions required oaths that individuals were not Communists. All these requirements plus the general requirements that a person be of good moral character and a citizen of the United States (or the state of registration) are unreasonable barriers to entry. To be sure, some people may be concerned about a horde of Communist plumbers taking over the country, but any requirements that are unrelated to the effective performance of the service being licensed are unreasonable.

EXAMINATIONS THAT MAY LACK VALIDITY

Examinations are, of course, by definition barriers to entry. Even a completely valid exam restricts entry because the applicant must invest time and money to travel to where the exam is being given. Such a restriction, however, is reasonable when the exam is valid. Examination validity is a question that should be raised about all occupational exams. Registered nurses, a profession that requires judgment based on a variety of situational variables, for many years reduced their exam to a series of multiple choice questions. Cosmetology exams in California have traditionally allocated a portion of the credit on the exam to the applicant's personality, and the beautician exam administered by the District of Columbia Board of Cosmetology includes finger waves, popular in the 1930s, and pin curls, popular in the 1950s (Crovitz, 1992). Plumbing exams in Oklahoma graded applicants on their ability to join two pieces of iron pipe long after copper and plastic pipe eliminated any need for this skill. Only five percent of electricians pass the Oklahoma exam on the first try, primarily because the exam covers topics not normally part of an electrician's job. In each of these cases, the validity of the exam is open to question.

Some research on occupational licensing has directly addressed exam validity. Dorsey (1980), in a study of cosmetology exams, finds that scores on the written portion of the exam were related to formal education and race, but only marginally related (correlation = .25) to the skills portion of the exam. Because a great many applicants failed the written portion of the exam, Dorsey concluded that it was used as a barrier to entry. Butter (1976) offers evidence of significant differences in pass rates on exams that license physicians which have the effect of limiting the entry of practitioners lacking U.S. citizenship.

Other studies have shown that the failure rate on exams is positively related to the per capita income of the profession (Holen, 1977; Leffler, 1978; Pfeffer, 1974). In states where the income for lawyers, dentists, doctors, accountants, pharmacists, and barbers was higher, more applicants failed entry exams. Maurizi (1974) discovered that the failure rate on exams was higher when the number of applicants taking the exam was large, and Young (1988) found that before the implementation of a nationally standardized exam the failure rate of aspiring CPAs was greater when state unemployment rates were high. If exams are used as an unreasonable barrier to entry, one would expect to find this sort of impact. By failing larger numbers of applicants, the occupation restricts supply and generates a higher income for current practitioners.

LIMITED RECIPROCITY AMONG STATES

Occupations limit entry not only by restrictive examinations but also by limiting reciprocity among states. A barber licensed in Alabama, for example, cannot simply move to Oklahoma and expect to cut hair. For the most part, this barber is expected to meet all the requirements of licensing in Oklahoma and must pass the Oklahoma barber's exam. Although the U.S. Constitution's full faith and credit clause requires states to recognize the acts of other states, this does not apply to occupational licensing. In some cases, such as attorneys, where the practice of law varies from state to state, a state has an interest in limiting practice to individuals licensed by that particular state. For most occupations, including dentists, nurses, barbers, electricians, and so on, the lack of reciprocity is absurd. Good dental practice should be the same in Ohio as it is in Colorado.

DISCRIMINATION AGAINST NONSTATE RESIDENTS Discrimination against nonstate residents usually starts with the examination procedure. Boulier (1980), for example, found that out-of-state students were four times as likely to fail bar exams as in-state students. A consistent finding of the research literature is that reciprocity restrictions limit the interstate mobility of licensed occupations. Doctors, for example, face fewer restrictions on reciprocity than dentists and lawyers and are more likely to move to another state to practice (Holen, 1977; Pashigian, 1979; 1980).

EFFECT ON MOBILITY AND INCOME Despite the impact of reciprocity on mobility, it does not appear that restrictive practices have a consistent impact on income. The restrictiveness of state reciprocity standards is unrelated to the income of professionals (e.g., attorneys), but does have some impact in raising the income of non-professionals. (e.g., barbers, electricians; see Kleiner et al., 1982).

UNREASONABLE RESTRICTIONS ON THE FREE FLOW OF LABOR Overall, regulation appears to erect barriers to entry, and some of these barriers are unreasonable restrictions on the free flow of labor. In 1973, for example, all 2,149 applicants for contractor licenses in Florida failed the exam (Elzinga, 1980:119). Despite the barriers to entry, however, some question exists as to whether or not these barriers are successful in restricting the number of person licensed in a given occupation. Despite the massive and well-documented effort of the AMA to restrict the number of physicians, the federal government was able to override these restrictions in the 1970s. The number of doctors increased by 116,000 from 1970 to 1979, a growth rate 37 percent faster than the population. Even though many state bar exams are clear attempts to limit the number of attorneys, the number of lawyers practicing the United Stated doubled between 1970 and 1980, reached 753,000 in 1992 and is expected to be as high as 850,000 by 2005 (Julin, 1980; U.S. Department of Commerce, 1993:405,408). Arguing that the nation currently faces a critical shortage of lawyers would be difficult. For all their efforts, then, occupations have been less than completely successful in restricting supply.

A PRO-CONSUMER ARGUMENT THAT SUPPLY RESTRICTIONS ARE BENEFICIAL The entire area of barriers to entry is further complicated by a perverse argument presented by economist Hayne Leland (1979; 1980). Leland argues that all efforts to restrict supply are beneficial to the consumer. He reasons that any effort to increase barriers to entry will limit the quantity of an occupational service that is supplied. Any decline in supply will result in a corresponding increase in the price of a service. An increase in price for a service will rationally attract the attention of more individuals who will want to enter the occupation. If the price rises high enough, the quality as well as the quantity of applicants will increase because individuals with opportunities for high incomes elsewhere will be attracted to the restricted occupation. Even if applicants are licensed on a random basis, according to Leland, the overall quality of service will rise because the market will attract better-quality applicants. Although Leland's argument fits well in economic theory, the process he describes is clearly not efficient. More effective ways exist to improve the quality of services offered to consumers. But he is correct in noting that restrictive licensing may have as one of its by-products a gradual improvement in quality.

Impact: The Existence of Economic Rents

According to economic theory, monopoly will produce a return on investment in excess of the return that could be expected in a competitive market. In terms of occupations, restricting entry should produce incomes higher than can be justified by the education, skills, hours, and so on, of the practitioners. Economists call these excess returns **rents**. Economic rents must be distinguished from income. The existence of rents, for example, does not imply higher incomes because individuals may have preferences for leisure that exceed their preferences for higher incomes. Similarly, high incomes can exist without economic rents if the members of an occupation are willing to work longer hours or invest more in capital.

Milton Friedman (Friedman and Kuznets, 1945), in some of his original work, found that medical doctors earned economic rents that he attributed to the restrictive practices of the AMA. The existence of rents from occupational regulation has generally been assumed (see Rottenberg, 1980:8) even though many self-regulated occupations take actions that dissipate economic rents. For example, many occupations, when they achieve self-regulation, immediately increase the educational requirements or the apprenticeship requirements to gain entry. Similarly, many occupations require continuing education. Such actions require practitioners to invest more heavily in human capital. Thus, economic rents disappear, to be replaced by a return on investment in education (see Weingast, 1980:83).

Because economic rents are difficult to determine empirically, only a few studies have examined economic rents and occupational regulation. Keith Leffler (1978) reexamined Friedman's work on doctors and found that Friedman was able to find economic rents because he used an unrealistically low discount rate (4 percent) in his calculations. When rates more consistent with recent economic theory were used, Leffler found that physicians received no rents at all until the passage of Medicare and Medicaid. In 1973, Leffler estimated the economic rents to physicians at $15,000. An extrapolation of this trend to 1993 would place current rents in the neighborhood of $40,000 to $50,000. Again, however, these rents were created by federal government actions, not by the economic regulation of physicians. In addition, the rapid increase in physicians since 1973 may have dissipated these rents.

For the important questions of regulation, the existence of rents may be irrelevant. For example, an occupation could receive rents from regulation at the same time that regulation results in improvements in the quality of service. Similarly, an absence of rents says nothing about the quality of service to consumers. An occupation can dissipate the rents due from restricted entry by poor administration, bad luck, or technological change. Oklahoma dry cleaners, for example, were unable to sustain high prices despite price-fixing powers when wash-and-wear fabrics were introduced. The massive drop in demand rendered any regulatory actions to correct the situation meaningless (see Plott, 1965; Meier and Plumlee, 1979). Other examples abound. Barbers, for example, do not appear to be getting excessively wealthy despite the major restrictions on entry and the power to set prices in some states. Perhaps the decline in the demand for their skills as surgeons and a rise in preference for new wave hair styles (neither factor under their control) have dissipated any rents they could expect to earn.

Impact: Prices Rise

The heart of the economic argument against occupational regulation is that it raises the price of the services provided. Four aspects of regulation are assumed to decrease supply and, therefore, to **increase prices**: (1) restrictions on reciprocity, (2) restriction on advertising, (3) restriction in input substitution, and (4) the general overall restrictive nature of regulation. Each of these is discussed in turn.

PRICE AND RECIPROCITY RESTRICTIONS

By restricting the free flowing of labor within an occupation, lack of **reciprocity** (a reciprocal agreement between states to permit relatively easy licensing or certification of occupations based upon similar standards) allows state-to-state variations in supply and demand to persist. Unfortunately, economic theory is not at all that clear about what happens in a specific area when geographic restrictions are created. In states with inadequate supply, allowing full reciprocity will reduce the price of a service. Concomitant with the decrease will be an increase in price in that state that loses occupational members. In actuality, very little research has been done on the effect of reciprocity restrictions on price, and that research reaches conflicting conclusions. Shepard (1978), for example, presents evidence that geographic restrictions on dentists increase the price of dental services by 12 to 15 percent. Boulier (1980:92), on the other hand, finds that lack of reciprocity increases the price of dental services by only 1 percent. Further research in this area is necessary, but the difficulty in gathering comparable price data for occupational services makes such research difficult.

PRICE AND RESTRICTIONS ON ADVERTISING

Advertising's impact on prices is subject to some dispute. If the services being sold are fairly similar, and if a firm advertises lower prices, demand for that firm's services will increase. Other firms will then have to match the lower prices to retain their share of the market. The retail market for gasoline in a community follows this pattern. A more political theory of advertising, however, argues that advertising stimulates the consumer to purchase more services, perhaps even more than are needed. This greater demand will raise prices if supply is held constant, and the consumer pays for the passed-through costs of advertising. The prescription drug industry with its high advertising costs is cited as an example (Leffler, 1981).

Advertising is one area of occupational regulation that has interested the federal government. The Federal Trade Commission issued more competitive rules for optometrists, including advertising, and pressured other professional groups to eliminate such restrictions. The U.S. Supreme Court in *Bates* v. *Arizona* (1977) struck down provisions that prevented attorneys from advertising. The Supreme Court has also dealt harshly with a symptom of nonadvertising, the collusive setting of fees (Goldfarb v. Virginia, 1975).

The initial evidence on advertising and price was very positive. In a classic study of the eyeglass industry, Benham (1972) found that states that permitted advertising price information had prices 25 to 40 percent lower than states that did not. A 1980 Federal Trade Commission report found that state advertising restrictions contributed to average prices of eyeglasses that were 33 percent higher than in states which allowed price advertising (AARP, 1986). The price of routine legal work dropped as much as 50 percent after advertising was permitted and legal clinics began to advertise prices (Muris and McChesney, 1979). Other evidence, however, shows negative consequences for advertising. Leffler (1981) discovers that large quantities of advertising speeded the use of prescription drugs, but it also retarded the substitution of identical, but cheaper drugs.

Advertising is an area of occupational regulation that is currently undergoing a great deal of change. Barriers to advertising occupational services are dropping rapidly. As more occupations advertise, more data will accumulate on the relationship between advertising and price.

PRICE AND RESTRICTIONS ON INPUT SUBSTITUTION

Input substitution occurs when a practitioner of an occupation substitutes a cheaper input for a more expensive one. For example, a dentist who uses a hygienist to clean teeth rather than do it himself or herself is engaging in input substitution. If restrictions are placed on input substitution, then the most efficient use of resources is prevented. In theory, a producer should substitute one input for another until each input generates a marginal return equal to its marginal cost. Restrictions on input substitution, therefore, should result in price increases.

Much occupational regulation concerns input substitution. For example, many states restrict the number of hygienists that any single dentist can hire (DeVany et al., 1982:378). Bar association rules against joint practice prohibit lawyers from combining forces with accountants or from working under the direction of a nonattorney manager. Input substitution restriction often goes beyond the organization of the occupation in question to prevent other occupations from serving as substitutes. Virtually every state in the United States, for example, places restrictions on nurse practitioners and physician's assistants that prevent them from engaging in the practice of medicine independently of a physician (Dolan, 1980:229).

The empirical research on input substitution is meager, but it does underscore the theoretical problem. One study finds that restrictions on the use of dental assistants and hygienists resulted in an overuse of dental time on routine matters (DeVany et al., 1982). Another study reveals that states not restricting the practice of opticians (the cheapest input in dispensing glasses) had lower eyeglass prices (Benham and Benham, 1975). Similarly, states with commercial eyeglass dispensers also had lower prices (Maurizi et al., 1981; AARP, 1986). Although the volume of empirical evidence is small, it is all consistent with the conclusion that restrictions on input substitution result in higher prices.

PRICE AND GENERAL RESTRICTIONS ON LICENSING

Several studies examine the general impact of occupational regulation on prices. A study of the price of title opinions in Northern Virginia after the Goldfarb decision reveals that the price had fallen by 50 percent (Wood, 1978). A study of wages in the construction industry finds that licensing increased the wages of electricians and plumbers (Perloff, 1980); but because this study used laborers (an occupation that has a much lower skill level) as the base of comparison, the findings are subject to question. W.D. White (1980) finds no impact of licensing on the level of nurses salaries for 1960 and 1970, but in another study he finds that requiring a college degree for registered nurses increased wages by 16 percent (W.D. White, 1978). The Federal Trade Commission, in its study of the TV repair industry, reports that prices were higher in a state that regulated the industry (Louisiana) than in a state that used registration (California) or an area with no regulation (Washington D.C., see Phelan, 1974). Plott (1965) finds no differences in dry cleaning prices between Oklahoma (a regulation state) and Kansas (a nonregulation state). Pfeffer (1974) could not find any income differences attributable to regulation for plumbers, insurance agents, and real estate agents.

The general impact of licensing on price is an area that does not reveal consistent findings. Several studies claim to show an increase in prices, and several other studies find no price impact. In addition, many studies have serious methodological flaws resulting from an inappropriate research design and inappropriate statistical techniques. The only supportable conclusion in this area is that the general impact of licensing on prices is indeterminate.

In sum, the impact of occupational regulation on price is fairly complex. Restrictions on advertising appear to result in increased prices (with the exception of prescription drugs). Similar impact is found for input substitution limitations, although the volume of evidence is small. Restrictions on reciprocity, however, limit the interstate flow of occupational members, but have not shown a consistent impact on price. Licensing, in general, often does not appear to affect the price of a service. The evidence indicates that prices for a service are probably affected only when restrictions on advertising underscore collusive price agreements and when one occupation (optometrists, dentists) restricts the use of another occupation (opticians, hygienists). As these are the areas that have received the greatest federal attention, we should expect that price impacts of occupational regulation will be lessened in the future.

Impact: Does Quality of Service Increase?

Occupational regulation is often justified as a quality control mechanism; it should protect consumers from harmful services. If the quality of service increases under regulation, some of the ill-effects of regulation such as price increases may well be justified.

Poor quality of service can result from two different sources (Blair and Kasserman, 1980:189). First, some poor quality of service might exist because occupational members vary in the skills that they possess. Such variation is addressed by licensing exams. Second, poor quality of service might exist because some practitioners are tempted to increase their incomes by delivering a larger volume of lower-quality service. If greed is a motivating factor in reducing service quality, the elements of regulation that restrict entry and, theoretically, raise prices will eliminate much of this motivation by raising the incomes of all practitioners (see also Beales, 1980).

Assessing the impact of regulation on **service quality** is a difficult undertaking. Quality is an elusive concept to measure. One cannot simply rely on outputs because the quality of service may not be reflected in the outputs. A lawyer, for example, can provide an exceptional defense and still have his or her client convicted. A doctor may perform brilliant surgery and lose the patient. In fact, a reputation for skill may well attract the most difficult cases so that the best surgeons or the best lawyers may not have the best overall results (Elzinga, 1980). Similarly, good outputs can be achieved in spite of some occupational treatment; many medical patients of the nineteenth century recovered despite being bled.

Another problem with studying quality under regulation is that little quality-oriented regulation appears to take place. In 1991, for example, 3,034 disciplinary actions were taken by medical boards in the U.S. in contrast to the up to 300,000 injuries or deaths a recent consumer group study estimates are the result of medical negligence each year (Cordes, 1993). Most of those disciplinary actions involved drug use or failure to meet continuing education requirements, not quality of care. For the 1992-1993 "bar year" (May 1-April 30), 9,079 grievances were filed with the Texas Bar Association, resulting in 354 disciplinary actions. For the following year, the comparable figures are 8,783 grievances and 655 disciplinary actions. While still not Draconian, this increase in disciplinary actions is reflective of heightened regulatory oversight.

To be sure, occasionally vigorous regulation appears; the California contractors board in one year suspended 729 licenses and revoked 447 others (Shimberg et al., 1973). But, "vigorous" should be thought of in context. One economist argues "that, compared to per capita criminal sentencing in the United States, medical disciplinary actions (per physician) appear to be fairly common" (Svorny, 1987:502). In general, however, quality control is more often a symbolic goal of occupational regulation rather than an actual goal.

Even when quality-oriented regulation occurs, because it is at the state level, the opportunity exists for miscreants to move to another state and resume their activities. A most extreme example is Dr. Alan Fields, a Michigan osteopath and "part-time drug peddler" (Wallis, 1986:57) who was licensed in 14 states before his incarceration. Even within a state, given the lack of implementation resources, it is possible for unscrupulous medical personnel to flout the law. For example, in 1993 a doctor in New York was tried for murder for allowing a patient to bleed to death after surgery. His license had first been suspended nine years earlier, but he had simply moved to another part of the state, assumed a new name, lied about prior disciplinary problems, and began practicing medicine again (Wolfe, 1994).

A few studies on quality have been conducted. After the deregulation of advertising for attorneys, a California study showed that the quality of routine legal services did not decline, even with large reductions in price (Muris and McChesney, 1979). Also in California, the number of complaints against contractors increased after the industry became regulated. Although complaint increases might indicate a decline in service, in fact, the increase in complaints simply reflected an easier process for filing complaints (Maurizi, 1980). The Federal Trade Commission's television repair study found that the amount of unnecessary repairs declined when the state of California engaged in output monitoring. California used the well-known device of taking television sets to various repair shops and reporting the costs and the amount of unnecessary repairs (Phelan, 1974). States that have stringent requirements for the practice of dentistry (e.g., as shown by high examination failure rates) also receive better dental care (lower dental malpractice rates and better dental health; Holen, 1977).

The relationship between regulation and quality is difficult to discern. No evidence exists that quality actually declines under regulation, and some regulatory efforts appear to improve the quality of service. Many of these results, however, may be a function of measurement error. A study of medical malpractice (an indicator of poor quality of service) found that the practice of doctors who lost malpractice cases did not drop in volume (Haug, 1980:63). Until more precise measures of quality are available, therefore, the relationship between quality and regulation must be viewed as indeterminant.

Miscellaneous Impacts

Regulation of occupations has two other impacts that are relatively important. First, occupational regulation restricts consumer choice. Second, it is associated with discrimination against women and minorities.

OCCUPATIONAL REGULATION RESTRICTS CONSUMER CHOICE

A consumer is not allowed to seek out an independent practicing paramedic for example, to treat a routine illness. Neither is a consumer allowed to find an independent dental hygienist to clean teeth. Both of these examples indicate a market for "lower-quality" occupational services. To be sure, a patient would be irrational to seek out an incompetent brain surgeon, but in many cases of health care a high level of skills is neither necessary nor justified in terms of cost. If low-quality health care were available, perhaps more health care services would be purchased and the overall quality of health care would improve. Similarly, low-cost/low-quality legal services would encourage more consumers to draft wills and other routine legal actions.

Much occupational regulation is designed to limit consumer choice. Every state prohibits paramedics from establishing practices independently from physicians (Dolan, 1980). The American Medical Association has conducted campaigns against midwives (also chiropractors, podiatrists, osteopaths, naturopaths, and so on) despite the evidence from European countries that the use of midwives is associated with lower number of infant deaths (Kessel, 1970). The full-time care of a less trained midwife may be more healthy than the sporadic attention of a highly trained obstetrician.

WOMEN AND MINORITIES ARE DISCRIMINATED AGAINST

Occupational regulation is also associated with **discrimination** against women and minorities. Freeman (1980) found that occupational regulation was associated with limiting black access to jobs in the South. The AMA and its post-Flexner discrimination against women, blacks, and Jews is well documented (Kessel, 1959; 1970; Frech, 1974). Blacks are twice as likely to fail bar exams as white applicants (Freeman, 1980:72-73). Exam scores for cosmetologists in Missouri and Illinois were found to be correlated with race (Dorsey, 1980). In 1967 the state of Florida did not have a single black optician, and Montgomery County, Alabama, had only one black plumber (who was licensed through a loophole in the law). As recently as 1967, the state of Oklahoma restricted the practice of dental hygiene to females only (Shimberg et al., 1973).

In the past, discrimination in the regulation of occupations has been overwhelming. Minorities have been less able to overcome the barriers to entry that are erected by state regulation. This lack of access is clearly not a function of variables other than race because many of the occupations regulated are trades that require little formal education. Clearly, discrimination has been one of the consequences of occupational self-regulation.

IMPACTS OF OCCUPATIONAL REGULATION

Several impacts of occupational regulation, therefore, have been identified. First, occupational regulation creates barriers to entry, but there is some question as to how successful those barriers are in limiting the number of practitioners. Second, the evidence indicates that occupational regulation has some role in increasing the price of regulated services. Third, regulation does not create economic rents for the occupation regulated; or if it does, the actual regulatory process and its actions dissipate these rents. Fourth, the relationship between regulation of occupations and service quality is not clear. Fifth, occupational regulation unnecessarily limits consumer choice. Sixth, the process of regulating occupations results in discrimination against minorities and discrimination on the basis of sex and race.

THE POLITICS OF OCCUPATIONAL REGULATION

Although occupational regulation has been condemned as nothing but regulation in the economic interest of the regulated (Rottenberg, 1980; Friedman, 1962), once again economists are guilty of making silly statements. Too many examples of regulation that do not benefit the regulated occupation exist for this conclusion to be tenable. For example, funeral directors are required by Federal Trade Commission regulations to disclose prices and avoid other questionable business practices. The California regulation of contractors created a complaint process that made the filing of complaints easier (Maurizi, 1980), and allowed punitive actions to be taken against contractors who engage in unfair business practices (Shimberg et al., 1973). Generic drug laws have been enacted by several states over the opposition of the pharmacists (Meyer, 1982). Prohibitions against advertising in the health and legal professions have been struck down, and competition has been encouraged. Numerous state agencies have required midcareer education courses for a variety of professionals (Berry, 1982).

Although no systematic evidence exists, sufficient cases suggest that not all occupational regulation is in the interests of the regulated. Such a situation could occur in one of two ways. Either the regulatory agency seeks to regulate in the self-interest of the occupation but makes major mistakes in the process, or consumers have been able to exert sufficient political pressure to attain some of their objectives. With the rise in organized consumer groups in the 1970s and 1980s, the latter hypothesis is tenable.

Without our being overly cynical, the possibility also exists that the occupation's interest and the public's interest might coincide. In an occupation with an unfavorable public image (used-car sales, medicine in the nineteenth century, chiropractic), vigorous regulation might improve the profession's public image. Such regulation may well serve the needs of individual practitioners because self-regulation may be undertaken for status reasons as well as economic reasons. The ability to regulate one's own practice is often seen as the first step to becoming a "profession" (Benham, 1980).

A Consumer Orientation in State Regulation

Before we take up the political forces in occupational regulation, some discussion of what is meant by a **"consumer orientation in state regulation"** is necessary. Consumer interests are more likely to be served if the regulatory agency is concerned with service quality rather than focusing its efforts on entry restrictions, legal actions against individuals who practice without a license, advertising restrictions, and price-fixing. Several aspects of regulation might indicate that consumer interests are considered in occupational regulation. **Continuing education requirements** for professionals are an attempt to keep practitioners current with new skills in the profession and reflect a concern for consumers (a regulated profession has no real interest in keeping current because this entails opportunity costs and dissipates potential economic rents). Other indicators of a consumer orientation might be **consumer representation** on the regulatory board, a large consolidated agency where civil servants do the regulating, a large percentage of disciplinary actions for quality reasons, and the use of experimental output monitoring (e.g., TV repair).

Consumer Versus Occupational Interests

A study of state occupational regulation reveals that the direction of regulation (consumer v. occupational interests) is function of four variables (Meier, 1983a).

SIZE OF OCCUPATION

First, the size of the occupation in question plays a role in whether or not the occupation is regulated and in the content of the regulation. Size means votes, and votes mean political resources (see Stigler, 1971; Rourke, 1984; Schneider, 1987). Because occupations are likely to form associations, occupational groups tend to be fairly cohesive. Mobilization is not a problem; the group needs only to turn numbers into public policy advocates. The larger the occupation, the more likely that the occupation will be regulated by a state, and the more likely that regulation will be in the interests of the regulated occupation.

CONSUMER SOPHISTICATION

With the advent of the consumer movement, occupational interest groups no longer have the political field all to themselves. One restraint on occupational groups is consumer sophistication, the second variable. As a consumer becomes better educated, he or she becomes more aware of the potential ills in the marketplace. In addition, with education comes an increase in political skills and increased willingness to use them (Verba and Nie, 1972). States with high education levels, therefore, have more potent consumer orientation in occupational regulation (Graddy and Nichol, 1989).

CONTACT AMONG CONSUMERS

Sophistication is not the only factor that facilitates or limits the mobilization of consumer interests in this area. The third important factor is **contact**. Without contact with others who have suffered similar problems, the consumer may believe that the poor service he or she received was only a rare occurrence. As contact among consumers increases, consumer consciousness is raised; and consumers can be mobilized as a political force. One variable that indicates this increase contact is urbanization. In fact, states that are more highly urbanized are more likely to regulate with consumer interests in mind (but see Graddy and Nichol, 1989). Urbanization does not affect producer mobilization because contact among producer groups is likely to be high, regardless of the degree of urbanization.

COMPETITIVE PARTY SYSTEM

A fourth factor affecting the direction of occupational regulation is a **competitive party system**. It is essential to consumer-oriented regulation. In a state dominated by one party, legislators of the majority party face a political environment where they can choose between consumer and producer interests. Because producers are likely to have far greater resources and be much better organized, the dominant party legislators will rationally seek an alliance with the producers (in this case, the occupation). Consumers will be ignored by the majority party, and any links between the minority party and consumers will produce no impact on public policy.

In a competitive party state, where both the Democratic and Republican party have a good chance of winning elections, the occupational interest groups cannot forge an alliance with one party for risk of serious defeat. The rational occupational group, therefore, plays both sides of the fence, making contributions and offering political support to both Democrats and Republicans (just as major economic interest groups contribute to both parties at the national level). Producer resources to both parties, therefore, are in a relative balance. Competitive elections and a balance of political resources mean that the rational politician looks elsewhere for an electoral edge. A marginal contribution that would be of little value in a noncompetitive state could well provide the margin of victory in a competitive state. The rational politician, therefore, will make appeals to consumers to gain their votes to win the election. This does not mean that the politician will become a consumer advocate, but rather that his or her producer orientation will be tempered with some effort to accommodate consumer interests. The result is a balancing of these interests.

This balancing of interests occurs in numerous legislative districts simultaneously. In some districts, producer interests will be dominant, and the candidates in these districts will temper their pro-producer orientation only slightly. In other districts, there will be few or no producer interests, and candidates in these districts will side with consumer interests. The end result in a competitive state is a legislature that considers consumer interests in regulation (see Weingast, 1980). Consumer interests do not necessarily win, but they are considered.

REFORMING OCCUPATIONAL REGULATION

Benjamin Shimberg (1973), a perceptive student of occupational regulation, has noted that there are no simple solutions to the evils of occupational regulation because the status quo is a reflection of the political power of the groups involved. The ability to advocate a reasonable solution to a public problem, however, is one step toward changing the political distribution of power. In a state with competitive political system, this may be sufficient to get consideration of reform.

Similar to regulation in general, the reforms proposed for occupational regulation are a function of what the reformer perceives the problem to be. Those who believe the ills of occupational regulation stem from barriers to entry and restrictions on competition generally favor less regulation. Those who believe that insufficient concern is paid to service quality advocate more regulation or procedures to change the direction of current regulation.

Complete Deregulation

Milton Friedman (1962) has argued that the solution to the evils of occupational regulation is **complete deregulation**. This position corresponds to his view that barriers to entry and increased prices are the problems to be solved. Friedman, in fact, disputes the public interest reasons for regulation. He does not feel that consumer ignorance is a major problem because ways exist to gather information about the quality of a particular service. When a consumer purchases a service numerous times, experience provides a pool of information on quality. For one-time purchases, the suggestions of friends and relatives often provide some information. Although the consumer may not know as much about the service as the seller, Friedman contends that it is paternalistic to assume the state is a better judge than the individual. Friedman also discounts the impact of externalities. For many occupations (barbers, cosmetologists, abstractors), few externalities exist. In occupations where potential externalities exist (e.g., health care, engineering), peer judgements on referrals and legal remedies if harm occurs limit their impact. Friedman is so convinced that the harmful effects of regulation outweigh any gains that could be made that he advocates complete deregulation even for the medical profession.

Certification

A less radical free market approach to reforming occupational regulation is to replace **licensing** with **certification**. Although licensing restricts the practice of an occupation to only those individuals who are licensed, certification allows noncertified persons to practice. The advantage of certification over licensing is that the two processes are theoretically equal in terms of quality control. Just as a licensed professional is deemed competent, so is a certified one. In terms of consumer choice, however, certification is a far superior option. The consumer who wishes to purchase a low-quality service is allowed to make such purchases from uncertified practitioners. The consumer in this case assumes a greater risk that the service will not be satisfactory, but this risk is compensated by a lower price. Consumers who desire high-quality services still have that option.

All-Comers Examinations

An **all-comers examination** system simply opens up licensing exams or certification exams to any individual who wishes to take them. Often experience or educational requirements are barriers to entry. Under an all-comers system, any individual who wanted to take a state bar exam to practice law would be allowed to sit for the exam; and if the individual passed the exam, he or she would be allowed to practice law.

Two benefits are attributed to all-comers exams. First, they eliminate rigidity in a learning process that usually specifies the exact training a person must have and recognize that on-the-job experience may be as valuable as classroom experience and vice versa. Second, such a system places a great deal of pressure on examiners to design valid exams. Without a doubt, a current set of occupational exams leaves much to be desired (see Shimberg et al., 1973). Often covering techniques no longer used, examining in areas of little use to the practitioner, or giving credit for personality and appearance, the current exams are unlikely to pass any **validity tests**. Allowing all-comers exams would force an occupation to address the question of exam validity, and either changes would be made, or the occupation's reputation would plummet.

Legal Remedies

The lawyer's approach to deregulation couples elimination of regulation with a greater reliance on the legal system. Any damages imposed on a consumer by a practitioner could be pursued under tort law. Jurisdictions with small claims courts permit even minor disputes to be decided in court. Such a system could even be turned into an administrative process with reduced restrictions on evidence and testimony before expert hearing examiners.

To the extent that increased use of legal remedies constitutes an improvement over the current system of regulation, it must be coupled with deregulation and reforms of the legal system. Deregulation is necessary to eliminate many costs of regulation. Without freedom to enter and exit an occupation, increased use of legal remedies offers no improvement over the current system. In addition, without restructuring the legal process to avoid the problems of high cost, slow process, and uncertain remedies, this reform also offers little improvement. Without these changes use of the legal system merely contributes to the well-being of the legal profession.

Institutional Licensure

One option presented in the health field is **institutional licensure** (Hershey, 1969). Licensing restrictions often prevent a hospital from allocating its personnel to their most effective role. Unlike an individual consumer, a hospital is not subject to the two major ills of an unregulated labor force—consumer ignorance and externalities. A hospital staff is highly trained and, as a unit, competent to judge the skills and qualifications of its personnel. Even if mistakes are made initially, observation over time will reveal errors in the personnel process.

The proposed reform, therefore, is to license hospitals, clinics, health maintenance organizations, and other systems to deliver health care. A licensed institution is then freed from conforming to any other state laws on occupational licensing. If such a hospital feels that licensed practical nurses can perform a function normally done by registered nurses, then it can act accordingly. Paramedics could be substituted for physicians in a variety of routine medical situations, thus freeing the more expensive resource for more difficult tasks.

The equivalent of institutional licensure occurs in some large legal firms. Legal research is often done by paralegals rather than attorneys; in many cases, secretaries fill out the legal forms involved in divorces, wills, and similar routine matters. Attorneys still retain some functions for themselves exclusively (appearing in court), but such restrictions protect the status of the professional rather than serve the consumer interest.

Sunset Legislation

Sunset legislation is a favorite tool of reformers, so its advocacy for occupational regulation comes as no surprise. Under a sunset law, a regulatory agency is authorized for a set period of time, say, ten years. Once every ten years, if the legislature does not pass a law reauthorizing the agency, it will cease to exist; that is, the sun will "set" on it. Sunset legislation recognizes that many agencies continue to exist out of inertia, without any assessment of whether or not they are still needed. Sunset merely reverses the presumption so that the continued existence of the agency has to be justified rather than assumed.

Several states have tried sunset legislation and have applied it to agencies engaged in occupational regulation. One study examines the impact of sunset legislation on occupational regulators in 15 states for 1977 to 1978 (Martin, 1980). In these states, 54 of the 182 regulatory agencies reviewed by legislative staff were recommended for termination. The fact that over 30 percent of the agencies were recommended for termination illustrates that numerous regulatory agencies exist for which little justification can be made. Unfortunately, the record of legislatures is less admirable. Of these 54 agencies, only 21 were terminated. Still, eliminating 11 percent of the occupational regulatory commissions should be deemed a success given the general practice of evaluating their performance.

In another study, Texas reviewed 38 occupational licensing agencies during the 1979 and 1981 legislative sessions (Slaughter, 1986). Reorganization was recommended in 21 cases, but adopted in only six instances. Three agencies were abolished, one had its functions transferred to another agency, and two were merged so that representatives of both agencies were included in a common board. Since Slaughter's analysis there has been a dramatic use of the sunset law in Texas. Due to conflict among dental professionals, the State Board of Dental Examiners was allowed to lapse during the last quarter of 1994. No new dentists could be licensed, nor could dentists moving to Texas from other states use reciprocity, until the legislature took action to implement the state's Dental Practices Act (Jennings, 1994).

Other substantive recommendations reducing the autonomy of certain agencies were adopted at a rate of 61.5 percent, suggesting that sunset evaluation does have some effect on regulatory boards. Slaughter (1986) also identified variables that resulted in differences in adoption rates of reforms across agencies. Larger boards, with more members and greater constituencies, were more likely to survive sunset review with fewer changes. Also, occupational groups with larger political action committee (PAC) contributions saw fewer changes in their regulatory agencies. Thus, regulatory reform through sunset evaluation is subject to political pressures and an agency's survival may depend on more on its influence and constituency support than its serving the public interest.

Public Representation

If a major problem with occupational regulation is that consumer interests are rarely considered, then one possible solution is to require **consumer representatives** or **public representatives** on the regulatory boards. California, for example, requires public members on many of its regulatory boards, including a voting majority on 15 boards (Schutz, 1983:506). Two problems exist with this type of reform.

First, where public representation is used in states other than California, however, it is generally only used halfheartedly. Rarely are consumers given a majority on the board—usually one or, at most, two seats. For example, most states now require at least one public member on medical licensing boards; 24 have two; and 12 have 3 or more. Only California's board has 7 non-physician members (AARP, 1987). This voting disadvantage means that, on serious disagreements, the regulated occupation usually has a voting majority.

Second, public members on a regulatory board may be no different from general consumers; they can probably be overwhelmed by professional expertise (Gormley, 1986b). In fact, DeVries (1986) finds evidence of board members being intimidated by the authority and expertise of practitioner members of boards. As one regulator said, "after we spend some time educating a public member, he or she votes correctly" (quoted in Shimberg et al., 1973).

Although the effort to include public members on regulatory boards continues, there is little evidence that these citizens have had an impact. Schutz (1983) finds no significant changes in policy outputs two years after California increased public representation on its licensing boards. Schneider (1987) also finds no effect from public membership on four measures of board performance in Missouri. Lammers (1985) found that public members on boards regulating nursing home administrators affected the extensiveness of continuing education requirements, but the effect was opposite what one might expect. A higher proportion of public members on the boards resulted in a reduction in such standards. Graddy and Nichol (1990) found that having public members on health occupational licensing boards had a small, positive effect on the likelihood of such boards taking serious disciplinary actions.

Another study finds that public members prefer to sit only on boards with purely advisory responsibilities while practitioners prefer those with quasi-judicial powers (Chesney, 1984). Citizen members tend to be reluctant to participate in proceedings than can become highly antagonistic with outcomes that have an impact on specific individuals.

While this evidence suggests that the inclusion of public members is unlikely to result in major changes in the way these boards do business, the reform does have some advantages. Graddy and Nichol (1989) consider the impact of public membership on legislative action, suggesting that more public members should result in legislative reforms of licensing requirements. They argue that public members will be a more accessible lobbying point for public interest groups and that they will lobby legislators themselves seeking reforms that they believe will enhance consumer protection. This study finds that increased citizen membership does result in a reduction of nonsense requirements in the licensing of three medical fields: chiropractic, registered nursing, and licensed practical nurses. Finally, the simple presence of public members widens the scope of the conflict by including nonoccupational members in the decision-making process. Such a member should have greater access to news media so that the most self-serving policies would not be considered by the board. This is a small check, to be sure, but still a check.

A Department of Occupational Regulation and Consumer Affairs

A major structural reform of occupational regulation is to consolidate all regulatory commissions into a single regulatory department, called a Department of Occupational Regulation and Consumer Affairs, or Department of Regulation and Consumer Affairs, or

Department of Occupational Licensing. An example of such a department is shown in Figure 3.1. If regulation is then done by career civil servants rather than by autonomous occupational boards, greater pressure for consumer interests will be present. Regulated occupations will have to compete with each other for the attention of the regulator, thus expanding the scope of the conflict so that regulatory decisions are made in the open. An open process in a department with sufficient resources means that consumer interests will be given more weight.

The role that bureaucratic ambition can play in this process cannot be overemphasized. In a small, occupation-dominated regulatory commission, positions are unattractive to talented individuals. There is little hope for promotion into a position of authority, and salaries are likely to be low (not even considering the psychological costs of regulating barbers for their own self-interest). In a large regulatory department, however, good performance is more likely to be rewarded with promotions and increases in pay. Good performance, that is, performance recognized by others in the department, is not likely to be pro-producer performance. The head of a major multi-occupational regulatory agency is unlikely to care that any given employee is able to please the polygraph examiners because the agency head does not identify with polygraph examiners. The agency head identifies with regulation and, therefore, is far more likely to notice that an employee has battled entrenched interests for the consumer's well-being.

Interstate Coordination

Occupational regulation is an extremely complex activity and varies in form and scope from state to state. As shown earlier in Table 3.1, some occupations are regulated in all states, others in only a few. Why is it necessary to regulate acupuncturists in 26 states, but not in the other 24? Even when an occupation is regulated in all states, and even where reciprocity is not granted, **malpractitioners** have had no difficulty moving from one venue to another.

This is a situation which seems to beg for interstate coordination or communication. Some tentative efforts along these lines have been launched. In 1980, state licensing officials, with staff support from the Council of State Governments, created the National Clearinghouse on Licensure, Enforcement and Regulation (CLEAR). CLEAR facilitates communication through conferences, training programs, newsletters, and maintaining a library. Specifically related to the health professions, Congress has authorized the construction of a National Practitioner Data Bank to collect data on malpractice and disciplinary actions against personnel in almost 30 fields, but implementation problems have rendered this legislation useless to this point.

A Composite Reform

In actuality, the most effective reform of occupational regulation, political feasibility aside, may well be a combination of the preceding reforms.

ELIMINATE STATE-SANCTIONED LICENSING

First, states might consider eliminating any state-sanctioned licensing, relying on certification to maintain quality controls, without restricting consumer choice.

Figure 3.1   Department of Occupational Regulation and Consumer Affairs

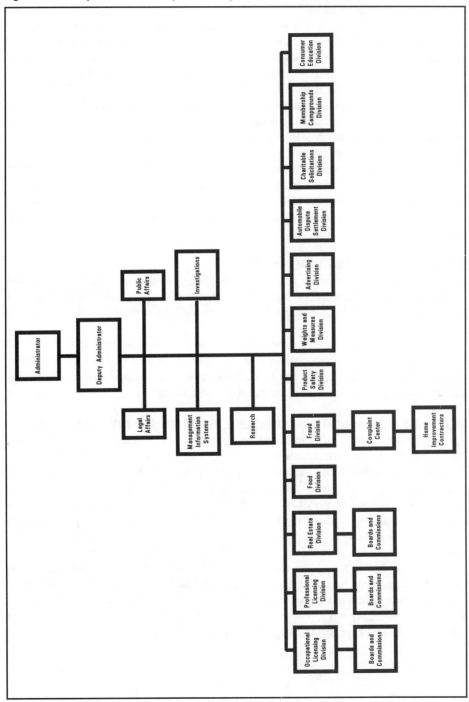

PERMIT INSTITUTIONAL LICENSURE

Second, any occupation that is primarily employed by members of another occupation should not be certified. Certifying or licensing dental hygienists, occupational therapy assistants, physician's assistants, and other similar occupations is a perversion of the governmental process. The employer of all these professionals is in all cases competent to judge the skills of these personnel. If the employing person is not competent to judge these skills, then that person is not competent to practice his or her occupation. Licensing employees only creates barriers to entry that are unrelated to quality performance. This does not mean that some state might not wish to certify health or legal paraprofessionals; such an action is rational if the state also permits an independent practice by these **paraprofessionals**. A state with the consumer interest foremost in mind will indeed permit such practices. In combination, then, this creates a policy of institutional certification. Any certified practitioner who employs paraprofessionals is free to hire any individuals that he or she desires (bearing in mind liability for malpractice). Any paraprofessional who wishes an independent practice may sit for examinations and be certified to so do.

OPEN CERTIFICATION EXAMS TO ALL COMERS

Third, exams for certification in all fields should be open to all comers. If the exams are valid measures of the skills needed to provide competent service, unqualified individuals will not pass the exams. If the exams are not valid indicators of occupational skill, they should not be given in the first place.

In combination, the preceding three reforms seek to increase consumer choice. Should not the consumer be free to seek occupational services that are tailored to his or her needs? An individual with a routine will does not need the service of a prestigious major law firm. That individual may be better off with a competent paraprofessional.

AN INTEGRATED DEPARTMENT OF OCCUPATIONAL REGULATION AND CONSUMER AFFAIRS

Fourth, this freedom of market choices should be supplemented with an integrated Department of Occupational Regulation and Consumer Affairs that is responsible for all occupational regulation. Such a department should be staffed with career civil servants who administer all regulations and exams. If occupational advisory boards are necessary, they should be part-time and advisory only. This department should be given regulatory authority to receive consumer complaints about all regulated occupations. It should have a separate administrative hearing unit where complaints, once investigated, can be adjudicated. The department should have the authority to issue subpoenas, to issue cease-and-desist orders, to enforce such orders without court action, and to suspend certification of individuals who violate state regulations. Such a department also needs broad investigatory powers. The use of output monitoring where services are surreptitiously purchased by the department and evaluated for quality, unnecessary work, and unnecessary cost should be encouraged. Frequent use of such techniques will have an inhibiting effect on unethical actions.

FUND DEPARTMENTAL INFORMATION PROVISION FUNCTIONS

Fifth, the Department of Occupational Regulation and Consumer Affairs must be funded to perform its information provision functions. The problem with most occupational services is that consumers have less information than the producers. The department's role should be to negate this information gap. The most important element of this information function is educating consumers as to what certification means. Armed with such information, consumers can then decide whether or not they want to purchase services from uncertified practitioners. Concomitant with this role is publicity about how to complain about poor quality service.

In combination, the greater reliance on the market plus an enhanced consumer affairs agency focusing on product quality should result in more concern for consumer interests. To be sure, the political feasibility of these reforms is questionable given that they attack entrenched interests. Given the current status of occupational regulation in most states, however, even small parts of this proposed reform cannot help but improve the situation.

CONCLUSION

Although the large number of regulatory agencies has prevented the detailed analysis of specific policies found in other chapters, an effort to tie the chapter to the regulatory process described in Chapter 2 is still beneficial. The literature consistently finds that occupational regulation is intended to benefit the regulated. Although the nonregulated can indirectly benefit from educational barriers to entry and other regulations, the prime beneficiary is the regulated.

The key variables presented in Table 3.2 explain why the regulated benefit, occupational regulation, is not salient; the public is little concerned about this issue. In addition, judging the qualifications of podiatrists, electricians, or morticians can be fairly complex; consumption may be determined by factors other than qualifications or price. These factors suggest that occupational regulation will be determined within the subsystem.

The regulatory bureaucracies are not able to dominate this subsystem because they have few resources. The agency might develop moderate-to-strong expertise because the regulators are drawn from the regulated occupation, but that is the only agency resource. Cohesion is rare; and leadership, unlikely. Goals tend to be vague, sanctions are weak or not used, and selection procedures usually force the governor to select regulators from the regulated profession.

This weak regulatory agency operates in a subsystem with a well-organized advocacy coalition representing the regulated. In fact, the agency was probably created at its request. A nonregulated advocacy coalition is unlikely to be found. Consumer groups are likely to be pressing far more salient issues at the state level. The subsystem's policy outputs, therefore, should favor the regulated.

Neither the macropolitical actors nor the environment is likely to counter proregulated policies. Macroactors, in general, will see no incentives to intervene. Even though most professions have many practitioners, few economic barriers to entry, some degree of instability, and many substitutes, the design of the subsystem will normally prevent these environmental forces from being transformed into proconsumer regulation. The situation is not predetermined, however. Where agency norms encourage a consumer orientation, a consumer-oriented policy is possible. In most state regulatory commissions, however,

Table 3.2   A Summary of Occupational Regulation

Economics	
Firms	Many
Entry	Easy
Profits	Vary
Technology	
Complexity	High
Stability	Low/High
Substitutes	High
Subsystem	
Bureaucratic control	Weak
Industry coalition	Strong
Nonindustry coalition	Weak
Bureaucratic resources:	
Expertise	Moderate/High Low
Cohesion	Low
Leadership	Low
Legislative authority:	
Goals	General
Coverage	All
Sanctions	Poor
Procedures	Poor
Involvement of Macropolitical Actors	
Legislature	Weak
Governor	Weak
Courts	Weak

small agencies with close ties to the regulated occupation prevent the development of such an organizational ideology. In large consolidated regulatory agencies, consumers are more likely to be heard.

The political process also plays an important role in opening these subsystems. In states with competitive party systems that must be responsive to a wide range of interests and a well-organized consumer movement, occupational regulation is less producer-oriented. The political resources of a regulatory agency (as opposed to the regulated occupation) are fairly small and, therefore, sensitive to political pressures. The low salience of occupational regulation in most states, however, means that political actors will generally ignore occupational regulation, thus permitting the occupation and the agency to form a symbiotic relationship that is mutually beneficial.

Chapter 4
Antitrust Policy Regulation

Kenneth J. Meier

Antitrust is both a regulatory policy and an alternative to regulation. One portion of antitrust law provides the rules for "fair competition" and, thus, is similar to other regulatory policies that restrict individual choice. Another portion of antitrust is directed at monopolies and, therefore, is proposed by some as an alternative to regulation (e.g., Kohlmeier, 1969).

Because antitrust is a hybrid policy covering most of the economy rather than specific industries, this chapter is organized differently from the others. Commonly used variables such as technology, profits, number of firms, and so on, vary by industry and are used in judicial determinations of antitrust decisions. Because many industries are involved, an extended discussion of these specific environmental variables will not be included. Rather, this chapter will briefly introduce the regulatory subsystem, note the economic underpinnings of antitrust, and discuss the laws and political goals of antitrust. With this introductory base, the five major areas of antitrust policy: (1) monopoly, (2) collusion, (3) mergers, (4) price discrimination, and (5) exclusionary practices will be discussed. Finally, an extended discussion of the merits of antitrust will conclude the chapter.

THE SUBSYSTEM

This examination of the subsystem of antitrust policy regulation includes an overview of the agencies involved and the advocacy coalitions involved.

The Agencies

Antitrust regulation is handled in a variety of different ways. The Antitrust Division of the Department of Justice has authority over both the civil and criminal aspects of antitrust law. Under the criminal provisions of the law, the Antitrust Division has grand jury powers to investigate possible violations of antitrust laws. If violations are found, the division files suit in a federal district court. Federal district court tries the case on its merits with appeals on questions of law to the Circuit Court of Appeals and the Supreme Court. In most criminal cases, the Antitrust Division negotiates a plea rather than going through the lengthy process of a trial. Some 87 percent of all cases won by the division result from no contest pleas by the industry. No contest pleas are often attractive to the defendant because private parties can file civil suits under the law (discussed later).

Under its **civil authority**, the Antitrust Division can sue a firm for the damages that it caused by violating the antitrust laws. Often the government files both civil and criminal suits because the government can appeal a civil suit lost in district court but cannot appeal a criminal case it has lost. Again, civil suits are usually settled by a consent decree whereby the company does not admit any guilt but agrees to avoid certain behavior in the future. Some 90 percent of all civil cases are resolved through consent decrees (Posner, 1970:375). In 1993 the Antitrust Division had a budget of $62.5 million and 444 employees (about 40% less than in 1985).

The Antitrust Division shares its civil authority with the Federal Trade Commission. Unlike the Antitrust Division's procedures, the FTC's procedures are **administrative**. Antitrust cases are tried before an administrative law judge. If a violation is found, the administrative law judge can issue a **cease and desist order** (the administrative equivalent of an injunction). The decision of the administrative law judge can be appealed to the full Federal Trade Commission and from there to the courts on questions of law. The FTC can also negotiate **consent orders** whereby a company does not admit guilt but agrees not to commit certain acts in the future.

A major advantage of the FTC over the Antitrust Division is that the FTC has the authority to issue rules. These **trade regulation rules** have the force of law and can be issued by following the rulemaking procedures of the Magnuson-Moss Act. In theory, this permits the FTC to be preventative rather than waiting for violations to occur. In fiscal year 1993 the FTC's budget was $87.6 million with 938 employees (or 28% less than in 1985).

Both the Antitrust Division and the FTC have some resources at their disposal. Neither agency has developed a reputation for expertise because antitrust lawyers do not make government a career. The normal career pattern for an antitrust lawyer is a few years in government and then a private practice in antitrust law (Weaver, 1977; Katzman, 1980). Recently, the agencies have developed some economic expertise so that overall expertise must be rated as moderate (Eisner, 1991). With the exception of a few aggressive antitrust heads such as Thurman Arnold and William Baxter, leadership has been average. Consistent with these variables, cohesion in the Antitrust Division is low; in the FTC, cohesion is higher, but this is a function of its consumer protection functions. Despite this, the Antitrust Division is quite clearly the lead agency on antitrust.

A potential agency resource is the salience of antitrust. Antitrust is a sporadically salient issue. The merger of large corporations, for example, often makes headlines for weeks. At other times, antitrust policy is rarely noticed. Legislative authority, on the other hand, is weak for a regulatory agency. Legislative goals are vague and in conflict (discussed later). Coverage is limited because the agencies share antitrust authority with several other regulators. Mergers in banking, for example, are handled by the national bank regulators; the Interstate Commerce Commission oversees mergers in transportation; the Federal Communications Commission has some antitrust powers in broadcasting. Sanctions are strong but rarely used. Procedures are a key weakness; both agencies must ultimately rely on the courts to enforce their policy decisions; such a reliance makes enforcement slow and uncertain.

The government provisions for antitrust enforcement are buttressed by the ability of individuals to file private antitrust suits against corporations. If, for example, firm A contends that firm B has engaged in unfair competitive practices that are prohibited by the antitrust laws, A may sue B. If illegal activity is found, the court determines damages and orders B to pay A three times the amount of the damages. Criminal guilt established by a Justice Department suit is prima facie evidence in all private antitrust suits.

Advocacy Coalitions

Because a business is interested in antitrust law only when the law is applied to it, the advocacy coalitions do not break down into the normal regulated-nonregulated coalitions. Two broad shifting advocacy coalitions do exist, however. One advocacy coalition might be termed the **proantitrust coalition**. This coalition favors the vigorous prosecution of all antitrust laws. Members of this coalition often share populist roots with the early advocates of trustbusting. Among the recent individuals active in this coalition are Ralph Nader, former Senator Howard Metzenbaum, former Senator Phillip Hart, and the small business community. The members of the antitrust bar might also be included in this coalition because they directly benefit from vigorous antitrust activity.

A second advocacy coalition might be termed the **Chicago school antitrust critics**. This coalition is supported by substantial scholarship by University of Chicago economists and their disciples that argues antitrust enforcement is counterproductive. Individuals such as Robert Bork and Richard Posner are prominent critics as was former Assistant Attorney General William Baxter. Although large business supports this advocacy coalition, the support is usually sporadic.

ECONOMIC PREMISES OF ANTITRUST

Economists' support for antitrust policy is based on their **models of pure competition** (Posner, 1976:8-22). In a purely competitive situation, a market is made up of numerous sellers and numerous buyers so that no single buyer or seller can affect the price of a good by his or her actions. In addition, each seller offers identical products so that no buyer prefers the product of one seller over that of another. Producers and sellers have perfect information, and entry and exit from the market are costless. Under such conditions, price is set by supply and demand; and production is adjusted until marginal cost is equal to marginal revenue. Sellers do not make economic profits (as opposed to return on capital), and buyers benefit from low prices.

According to neoclassical economics (see Armentano, 1982:19), deviations from perfect competition allow sellers to exploit buyers. In the most obvious case, **monopoly**, the one seller can limit the production of a good and, thus, raise the price that buyers pay. Consumers are injured because they pay more for a good than they would under conditions of pure competition.

In situations where the number of sellers is limited (e.g., **oligopoly**) monopoly-like ill-effects are possible through collusion among the sellers or restrictive marketing practices. The assumptions of neoclassical economics, therefore, imply that the market failures resulting from lack of competition can be remedied by introducing more competition. If monopolies and oligopolies are broken up, the benefits of competition can accrue to the consumer. This position is termed the **structuralist view of antitrust** (Eisner, 1991). Antitrust, therefore, can be an alternative to economic regulation (instead of regulation to hold monopoly prices down, use competition to achieve this) and at the same time be regulation in that the policies are designed to limit behavior detrimental to competition.

The Chicago school critique in a nutshell argues if the entry of new firms is unrestricted, then neither oligopoly nor monopoly is inefficient per se. Firms grow because they are efficient producers; if they were not, they would lose market share to other firms or new entrants. **Bigness** in this view is good. Only collusion among firms remains a problem and antitrust should focus on preventing collusion.

A LEGAL HISTORY OF ANTITRUST

The origins of antitrust are grounded in the populist movement of the nineteenth century. Following the withdrawal of greenbacks from circulation after the Civil War, the nation experienced a major period of deflation. Deflation contributed to the economic woes of debtors, especially farmers who were hurt by low prices and the chronic post-Civil-War recession. Faced with expensive loan payments, low agricultural prices, and high transportation costs, farmers manifested this discontent in the agrarian politics of the day. Farmers were joined by small businessmen and other individuals dislocated by the growth of large corporations. The unfavorable economic conditions of many stood in vivid contrast to the flaunting of wealth by the rich (Johnson, 1965:302). As a result, part of the blame for the situation was laid at the feet of the large industrial corporations of the day—the railroads and the new trusts such as Standard Oil.

The discontent was translated into political action by the disadvantaged groups. Both the Democratic and the Republican parties included planks in their 1888 platforms calling for federal antitrust legislation (Kintner, 1964:12). By 1890, 17 states had passed legislation against trusts. In Congress, Senator John Sherman articulated this distrust in the legislation that bears his name. Sherman sought to prohibit business practices that tended to "advance the cost to the consumer" (in the original bill, see Thorelli, 1955:164 ff). The intent of the act was clearly to redistribute some of the benefits of the marketplace from producers to consumers; productive efficiency is little discussed in the legislative debates over the act.[1] As Sherman was quoted on the Senate floor, "If we will not endure a King as a political power, we should not endure a King over the production, transportation, and sale of the necessaries of life."

---

[1]The Sherman Act passed both Houses of Congress with only one dissenting vote. The vagueness of the law plus the unanimity may indicate the Sherman Act was intended to be an exercise in symbolic politics.

Specifically, the Sherman Act was aimed at industrial trusts, an invention of John D. Rockefeller's Standard Oil. In an **industrial trust**, the stock of individual companies was transferred to the directors of a trust, who then operated the companies. If enough companies joined the trust, control over the market can be established.

What the Sherman Antitrust Act Accomplished

The Sherman Antitrust Act of 1890 did two things. First, it prohibited contracts, combinations, and conspiracies in restraint of trade; and, second, it declared that **acts of monopolizing** were illegal (Van Cise, 1982:11-12). To its ardent supporters, the Sherman Act must have been a disappointment. First, the act was technically obsolete because it was aimed at trusts that were quickly replaced by a more efficient method of controlling an industry, the **holding company**. Second, in the first major court case, the Supreme Court (discussed later) held that manufacturing was not **commerce** and, therefore, exempted much of industry from the Sherman Act. Third, perhaps the most effective use of the Sherman Act was by business against labor unions as courts determined that unions were combinations in restraint of trade.

As a result, the Sherman Act did not prevent the cartelization of major portions of American industry from 1897 to 1904. Some 70 major industries merged into monopolies or near monopolies. Between 1897 and 1904, 4,227 firms merged into 257 combinations that established "**trusts**" in over 300 different industries. "Trusts" were created in oil (Standard Oil), cigarettes (American Tobacco), steel (U.S. Steel), farm machinery (International Harvester), biscuits (Nabisco), and other areas (Markham, 1965:157). Obscured in history is the fact that many trusts such as those in leather, rope, buttons, glue, wallpaper, starch, and salt failed to survive (McCraw, 1981:33).

Additional Proposals for Changing Antitrust Laws

In response to the problems of the Sherman Act, almost everyone proposed changes in the antitrust laws. The platforms of Taft, Roosevelt, and Wilson in 1912 all had proposals. Labor unions opposed the Sherman Act because it was used to break up unions; in fact, the Supreme Court held that unions could be sued for treble damages as the result of strikes (*Loewe* v. *Lawler*, 1908). Small business opposed the Sherman Act because it questioned their own efforts to work out cooperative arrangements. Big business opposed the act because the "rule of reason" guidelines for court action were so vague that what constituted illegal behavior was unclear (Johnson, 1965:315).

The House of Representatives under the leadership of Representative Clayton listed several business practices that were to be considered illegal while the Senate pursued the idea of creating an agency with general powers to regulate antitrust. The debates over the reforms illustrated that reformers had multiple goals. Louis Brandeis, an economic adviser to Wilson, testified before Congress that antitrust should be used to protect small business from the evil practices of large business (McCraw, 1981:44). Business organizations, on the other hand, favored the creation of a federal agency to make government antitrust policy predictable; an agency could then advise business on the legality of their proposed actions (see Kolko, 1963:262). Congress eventually followed both strategies. The Clayton

Antitrust Act listed a series of behaviors that would be illegal while the Federal Trade Commission Act created the Federal Trade Commission to regulate **"unfair competition."**

Major Amendments to Antitrust Law

Three major amendments to the antitrust laws were enacted in 1938, 1950, and 1976 in response to political pressures to control big business. In 1938 the **Robinson-Patman Act** was passed to prohibit price discrimination in response to demands for legislative action against the large chain stores. By purchasing in bulk, large chain stores could undercut the prices of local stores and drive them out of business. The Robinson-Patman Act prohibited price discrimination by sellers that might lead to monopoly (Kintner, 1964:59).

In 1950 the **Celler-Kefauver Act** was passed to close some loopholes in the Clayton Act with respect to mergers. Section 7 of the Clayton Act dealt with mergers but had three weaknesses. First, it prohibited monopolizing mergers only via the purchase of stock and not by the purchase of assets. Second, courts had interpreted Clayton as applying only to horizontal mergers (see later). Third, the government had to prove that the effect of the merger would be to injure the public by lessening competition (Audretsch, 1983:4-5). The result of these weaknesses was little prosecution; the FTC filed 58 merger suits from 1914 to 1950 but lost 48 of them; the Justice Department in the same time period lost 10 of 20 (Markham, 1965:167-168). The Celler-Kefauver Act essentially applied the law to acquisitions of assets and stated that mergers were illegal if they might lead to monopoly or a lessening of competition.

The **Hart-Scott-Rodino Antitrust Improvements Act** of 1976 significantly increased penalties for antitrust violations. It also required that companies notify the government before merging with another firm. Finally it permitted state Attorneys General to sue on behalf of consumers damaged by antitrust violations.

Exemptions from Antitrust Laws

In several other legislative actions, Congress has from time to time exempted portions of the economy from the antitrust laws. The Capper-Volstead Act exempts agricultural cooperatives and federal marketing orders from antitrust. The Webb-Pomerene Act of 1918 exempts export trade associations from antitrust. The Clayton Act exempts labor unions from the provisions of the law. Government enterprises such as the post office have not been subjected to antitrust. Several price-setting functions of private organizations that are regulated by federal or state governments have traditionally been exempt from antitrust by law (e.g., insurance). Finally, in a 1922 court case that would probably be overruled if challenged, professional baseball holds an exemption as a **"sport."**[2]

---

[2]A 1993 federal district court narrowed this ruling when it held that the exemption only applied to players' contracts. Several members of Congress have also expressed interest in repealing this exemption.

MONOPOLY

The most visible portion of antitrust law and the most important initially was the Sherman Act's consideration of monopolies. Section 2 of the Sherman Act provides that every "person who shall monopolize, or attempt to monopolize, or combine or conspire with any other person or persons, to monopolize any part of the trade or commerce among the several States, or with foreign nations, shall be deemed guilty of a misdemeanor" (now a felony). Before discussing the judicial interpretation of section 2, we should note that the act prohibits "**monopolizing**," not the possession of a monopoly. In other words, the mere possession of a monopoly was not declared illegal, only the process of attempting to or intending to monopolize. In addition, the statute does not discuss the size of the market that must be subject to monopolization. Whether the market to be monopolized is defined as a national market, a regional market, or a local market may determine guilt or innocence in an antitrust case.

The Initial Failures of Antitrust Policy

The first monopoly case at the Supreme Court, *U.S.* v. *E.C. Knight* (1895), involved the sugar trust. The American Sugar Refining Company acquired E.C. Knight and several other sugar refining companies to gain control over 98 percent of the market. In a decision that virtually destroyed the Sherman Act, the Supreme Court held that American Sugar was in **manufacturing**, not commerce, and that the act prevented monopolizing in commerce, not in manufacturing. Because the law did not apply to the Sugar Trust, a decision on the merits, therefore, was not necessary.

The E.C. Knight case was devastating for any attempt to use antitrust powers against the "trusts" of the day. If commerce did not include manufacturing, then most of the great industrial trusts of the day were exempt. The period following the E.C. Knight case saw thousands of mergers and the creation of monopolies in some 70 industries.[3]

Not until 1904 did the U.S. government win its first monopoly case, *Northern Securities* v. *U.S.* (1904). Northern Securities was a holding company formed as the result of a business rivalry between three major railroads, James J. Hill's Great Northern, J.P. Morgan's Northern Pacific, and E.H. Harriman's Union Pacific. Although all three railroads covered the Northwest from St. Paul to Seattle, they had not vigorously competed against each other for at least 20 years (Meyer, 1906:227). Hill and Morgan jointly purchased the Burlington line, which linked St. Paul with Chicago. Perceiving that he was being squeezed out of an important market, Harriman began purchasing Northern Pacific stock in an effort to gain control of Morgan's railroad.

---

[3] There is some question as to whether the government could have won the E. C. Knight case on the merits. Armentano (1982: 51) presents evidence that the sugar trust did not wield monopoly power. During the history of the trust, the trust did not reduce output or increase prices. In fact, the evidence shows that prices fell from 9 cents a pound in 1880 to 5.3 cents in 1895. Because the sugar trust had no efficiencies of scale, the trust eventually collapsed by itself. By 1927, American Sugar held only 25 percent of the U.S. market.

Northern Securities was designed as an effort to prevent Harriman's control over the lines. Incorporated in New Jersey, it served as a holding company to control the stock of the Great Northern and the Northern Pacific. The Supreme Court found that railroads were clearly in commerce and under the Sherman Act. Because the holding company "combined" two previously independent and "competitive" railroads, it was declared illegal.

Busting the Trusts

Encouraged by the victory in Northern Securities, the government filed numerous antitrust suits under both Roosevelt and Taft.[4] Two of these cases against the oil trust and the tobacco trust became the cornerstone of American antitrust policy. Significantly, these cases were the last major cases that the government won in court and that empowered it to break up large companies into their component parts.

STANDARD OIL

In the 1860s, John D. Rockefeller, with several partners, entered the oil refining business in Cleveland, Ohio. By 1870, Rockefeller interests controlled no more than 4 percent of the oil refining market. The oil refining industry at the time was intensely competitive; prices for kerosene fell from 30 cents a gallon in 1869 to 10 cents in 1880 (see Tarbell, 1950). Standard Oil survived and prospered in this environment because the company invented many of the efficiencies in oil refining and was able to take advantage of the large economies of scale in oil refining (see McCraw, 1981:8). By 1874, Rockefeller interests controlled 25 percent of refining; and by 1880 they controlled in excess of 80 percent.

To ensure long-run profits and environmental stability, Standard Oil began a **vertical integration** effort. To ensure a market for the product, Standard Oil integrated forward into transportation and wholesaling. To provide itself with plentiful supplies of crude oil, the company integrated backward into transportation of crude and exploration. Fully integrated, Standard Oil was a formidable and ruthless competitor. It was able to extract large volume rebates from railroads (such rebates were probably rational for the railroads because the rates exceeded their variable costs and could be justified for volume reasons). In addition, Standard charged prices lower than other firms, which resulted in numerous bankruptcies.[5]

In an effort to manage the far-flung Rockefeller interests, a legal trust was created with the assets of 39 companies assigned to the trust. When the Ohio courts declared the

---

[4]Although Roosevelt has the reputation as the great trustbuster, historians agree that Taft was far more aggressive in this area, filing approximately twice as many antitrust suits as Roosevelt (see Kolko, 1963).

[5]There is some question about the legality of the competitive methods of John D. Rockefeller. Traditionally, Standard Oil is portrayed as a massive giant that used rebates and predatory pricing to drive others from the market. Armentano (1982: 61-64), however, argues that Standard Oil was simply an aggressive competitor and that because it was more efficient, less efficient firms were driven out of business. Regardless of the economic merits of Standard Oil's actions, such actions are bound to make numerous enemies and result in numerous petitions for government intervention.

trust arrangement illegal, a holding company, Standard Oil of New Jersey, was created to manage the companies. This holding company was challenged by the government.

In *Standard Oil* v. *U.S.* (1911), the Supreme Court stated that the important question was not the monopoly position of Standard but whether Standard had attained that position by other than normal business practices; that is, was Standard Oil guilty of monopolization? The Court held that Standard's practices of local price wars, dummy corporations, preferential railroad rates, and coercion of suppliers did not constitute normal business practices. Standard Oil, therefore, was found guilty of monopolizing, and the remedy was to break Standard Oil into 33 separate companies (most organized on a geographic basis).

In weighing the methods of attaining a monopoly, the Court enunciated a "rule of reason" approach to determine whether or not monopolies were legal under antitrust law. Under the **rule of reason**, monopolies were legal if they resulted from efficiency or government grants. Monopolies that resulted from the control of scarce inputs or from business combinations may or may not be legal depending on the methods used (see Strickland, 1980).

AMERICAN TOBACCO

The American Tobacco Company was the result of a merger instigated by James Duke, who pioneered aggressive advertising in the cigarette industry. By both advertising and the use of new tobacco-rolling machines, American Tobacco controlled 93 percent of the cigarette market by 1899. Duke then used this market power to move into the smoking tobacco, chewing tobacco, snuff, and cigar industries, gaining sizable market shares in all except cigars (which had few economies of scale in manufacturing; see McCraw, 1981).

Using the rule of reason, the Supreme court found American Tobacco guilty of monopolizing (*U.S.* v. *American Tobacco*, 1911). Specifically mentioned in terms of **"unreasonable tactics"** were mergers to avoid competition, use of monopoly power in cigarettes to monopolize other tobacco markets, vertical integration to create barriers to entry, purchases of tobacco plants for the sole purpose of closing them, and agreements with independent tobacco producers not to compete against each other. Like Standard Oil, American Tobacco was found guilty as the result of the tactics it used to gain a dominant position rather than for any monopolistic behavior after a dominant position was achieved. American Tobacco was split into three companies.[6]

The End of Trustbusting

For all practical purposes, the Standard Oil and the American Tobacco cases marked the end of what objective observers would term effective antitrust. **Effective antitrust**, if the goal of antitrust policy is the introduction of efficiency by increasing the number of competitors in a market, requires that the government both win antitrust cases and

---

[6]The remedy did not solve the problem of collusion, for the three firms continued to collude and restrict competition in the cigarette industry, eventually being convicted for such behavior in 1930 (see Posner, 1976: 86)

achieve some breakup of the monopoly upon victory. Since 1911, the government has generally failed to do so. Other ordered breakups (either by court order or consent decree) such as International Harvester (1918), Corn Products (1919), Kodak (1920), Pullman (1947), Grinnel (1968), IBM (1956), United Fruit (1958), and MCI (1962), resulted in trivial spin-offs from the losing company (see Posner, 1976:86-87) or in spin-offs that actually helped the company (e.g., AT&T, 1984). In addition, the government often wins monopoly cases and fails to get a remedy that includes any breakup.

The end of trustbusting did not result from a rationally established policy but rather from a series of court decisions that showed that **"intent to monopolize"** under section 2 was difficult to demonstrate. In addition, the large cost of major antitrust suits (see later) in quest of uncertain remedies meant that few major antitrust suits were filed. As two students of the antitrust bureaucracy have concluded (Weaver, 1977; Katzman, 1980), ambitious antitrust lawyers are unlikely to file suits with uncertain outcomes that require major investments in time and energy.

U.S. STEEL

In 1920 the Supreme Court decided the antitrust suit against U.S. Steel (*U.S.* v. *U.S. Steel*, 1920). At one time in its history, U.S. Steel was clearly guilty under the Sherman Antitrust Act of monopolizing and engaging in monopolistic behavior. U.S. Steel was formed in 1901 by merging ten independent steel producers and one ore and transportation company. One requirement of the U.S. Steel merger was that Andrew Carnegie, the head of Carnegie Steel, would retire from the industry. Carnegie Steel was one of the more innovative and competitive steel producers of the nineteenth century and was the reason why previous attempts at forming a steel cartel failed (see Kolko, 1963).

With Carnegie out of the way, J.P. Morgan and others involved in U.S. Steel engaged in monopolistic behavior. Using its 66 percent of the market, U.S. Steel was able to increase steel prices by 50 percent in 1901 (Parsons and Ray, 1975:186). In addition, U.S. Steel sponsored a series of dinners, meeting with other steel producers in an effort to restrain price competition.

By 1920, however, the threat of U.S. Steel was less imposing. The monopolizing behavior had occurred years earlier. In addition, U.S. Steel had become a conservative, uninnovative firm; its market share dropped to 50 percent by 1920. The Supreme Court held that U.S. Steel's share of the market was insufficient for monopoly power and that even that share was achieved through normal business practices. (Given the long-run performance of U.S. Steel's dropping to less than 20 percent of the market, the Court was probably correct on the first point; it was clearly in error on the second point; see Armentano, 1982:98-99 for an alternative view.)

ALCOA

The next major opportunity to establish antitrust policy came in *U.S.* v. *Aluminum Company of America* (1945). Alcoa first established dominance over the aluminum market by government-granted patents. Charles Hall developed the first practical method of reducing alumina into aluminum via electrolytic reduction. With a **patent monopoly** until 1909, Alcoa integrated backward into ownership of bauxite, conversion of bauxite into alumina, and ownership of the large electrical plants necessary for converting alumina into aluminum. It also integrated forward into the fabrication of aluminum goods. In fact, Alcoa through market development created most of the demand for aluminum.

Aluminum reduction is subject to large **economies of scale**, and Alcoa used these economies of scale to control 90 percent of the market (10 percent came from imports). Economies of scale were so great that Alcoa supplied the entire nation's demand from a single plant as late as 1938 (Greer, 1983:152). Because four of the Supreme Court justices had participated in the suit before appeal to the Supreme Court was made, the Alcoa case was decided by a special panel of appeals court judges.

The establishment of monopoly rested with the market definition. If the market for aluminum consisted of all aluminum sold to companies other than Alcoa, then Alcoa had only 33 percent of the market. If the market was defined as the amount sold to Alcoa and everyone else, then Alcoa had 64 percent of the market. If only the market for virgin aluminum was considered (omitting scrap), then Alcoa held 90 percent of the market. The court accepted the 90 percent definition and examined Alcoa for monopolizing behavior.

Essentially, the monopolistic behavior that Alcoa was found guilty of was continued expansion of output to meet demand. The court reasoned that by expanding, Alcoa preempted other companies from entering the market. Although this was monopolizing in the court's terms, it was very unmonopolylike behavior. The identifying characteristic of monopolies is **restriction of output** to raise prices. Alcoa increased output and cut prices.

The remedy in Alcoa was more bizarre than the decision. Alcoa was not broken up. Rather, Alcoa was prohibited from purchasing the surplus aluminum plants that the government planned to sell after World War II. Eventually, these plants were sold to Reynolds and Kaiser, leaving a market of Alcoa with 50 percent, Reynolds with 30 percent, and Kaiser with 20 percent. In the 1950s the government also assisted the entry of Anaconda, Harvey, and Ormet with loans, cheap government electricity, and access to government supplies of raw materials (Greer, 1983:153).

From the completion of the Alcoa case until 1969, the monopoly area of antitrust was fairly quiet. To be sure, cases involving United Shoe, Du Pont, and Grinnel were tried; but no new law was established; and the total impact of these cases was minimal. Not until antitrust became advocated by individuals with such disparate views as conservative economists and Ralph Nader did the U.S. government take new action in the area.

The New Attack and the Surrender

On the last day of the Johnson administration, an antitrust suit was filed against International Business Machines. When the market was defined as mainframe computer systems, IBM controlled 70 percent of the U.S. market, with Control Data the only other major manufacturer with more than a few percent. IBM was charged with **bundling** (selling computers, software, and support for one price), price cutting, and selling paper machines (e.g., computers that they had not produced yet).

THE IBM CASE

IBM's share of the market, in fact, could be explained by IBM's aggressive marketing. IBM clearly was not a leader in computer technology; that title went to Remington Rand, RCA, Philco, Data General, Honeywell, Burroughs, General Electric, and countless other companies. What IBM did especially well was produce machines similar to the breakthroughs very quickly and sell service and reliability (Fisher, McKie, and Mancke, 1983:95-96). Its market position was based on marketing skill and little else (in its earlier days IBM dominated the punch card tabulating market the same way).

The IBM case set records for futility. Filed in 1969, the case went to trial in 1975. In 1978 the government ended its case, and IBM began its defense. In 1982, Assistant Attorney General William Baxter dropped the case because it lacked "merit."

THE AT&T CASE

The other major case involved the 1974 suit against American Telephone and Telegraph (AT&T). AT&T controlled 83 percent of the telephone market. Unlike IBM, AT&T was clearly guilty of monopolizing behavior in originally establishing its monopoly. AT&T aggressively protected its patents and extended their life with additional patents based on trivial changes. Refusing to connect its lines with other phone company lines, AT&T also discriminated against non-Bell equipment. The early history of AT&T has substantial evidence of monopolizing behavior (see Cohen, 1992).

Charges of decades-old violations of the Sherman Act, however, were not likely to be upheld in the 1980s. The government charged 83 instances of monopolizing behavior (MacAvoy and Robinson, 1983). In essence, these boiled down to two charges that (1) AT&T used long-distance profits to subsidize local service and (2) AT&T refused access to its lines by long-distance competitors. In both cases, the charges were weak because the **cross subsidization** was ordered by the Federal Communications Commission and state regulatory commissions and the connecting problem had been resolved in favor of the other competitors.

As the case progressed, AT&T discovered that it would be better off losing than winning (see MacAvoy and Robinson, 1983). AT&T agreed to a consent decree dissolving the company. The 22 local telephone monopolies would be consolidated into 7 regional companies, and the long lines division (long distance), Bell Labs, and Western Electric would form the new AT&T. Although the regional monopolies would remain regulated, AT&T would be free to enter any new nonregulated fields that it wished. Containing the most profitable portions of the system, the new AT&T accounted for over half of the telephone system's revenues (MacAvoy and Robinson, 1983:21). The projected result was a rapid rise in local telephone costs and large profits for the new AT&T. The implementation of the consent decree by federal Judge Harold Green, however, resulted in continued cross subsidies and permitted AT&T less freedom than it had envisioned.

THE CEREAL MAKERS' CASE

Also with the advent of the Reagan administration, the FTC dropped its shared monopoly case against the cereal makers, closed its case against the big four automakers, and dropped a long running case against eight large oil companies. Monopoly antitrust ceased to be a public policy.

An Evaluation of Monopoly Antitrust

The status of monopoly antitrust law under section 2 of the Sherman Act is unclear. The courts have not clearly defined what **monopoly power** is. They have stated that 90 percent of the market is a monopoly but that 50 percent of the market is not. Exactly where the line is, is unclear. In addition, possession of monopoly power by itself is not illegal; rather, to be found guilty the company must have committed acts of monopolization. Monopoly that results from superior products, business acumen, or historical accident is acceptable.

MONOPOLY ANTITRUST LAW HAS SERIOUS FAILINGS

From both political and economic perspectives, monopoly antitrust law has serious failings. First, the existence of section 2 and the threat of monopoly prosecution may lead to inefficiencies. Corporations may become passive and fail to exploit new developments and new markets. IBM, for example, ignored the microcomputer market until after its antitrust suit was dropped. Within one year after the suit was dropped, the IBM personal computer was the largest-selling microcomputer in the United States. Similar arguments have been made about Bell Labs, reputed to be one of the best research labs in the world. With the threat of antitrust over the heads of such corporations, they have little incentive to innovate; and the end loser is the consumer.

MONOPOLIES OCCUR NATURALLY

Similar criticisms can be heard from historians and economists. McCraw (1981), for example, argues that monopolies occur naturally in what he calls center firms where some part of the production process is subject to large economics of scale. In industries without such economies, attempts at monopolization inevitably fail. Breaking up monopolies, according to McCraw, results in losses of productive efficiency and higher prices to consumers. Dominick Armentano (1982) presents similar arguments from an economic perspective. Armentano argues that most major "trusts" got to be monopolies because they were aggressive competitors and that they continued to compete by cutting prices and expanding output after market control was established. When they failed to compete (e.g., U.S. Steel), these firms lost market shares to more aggressive competitors. Armentano argues that antitrust law with its emphasis on intent actually punishes firms that are aggressive competitors.

ANTITRUST LAW HAS HAD LITTLE IMPACT ON ECONOMIC CONCENTRATION

Second, antitrust law really has not had any impact on economic concentration. Rational firms today diversify into conglomerates rather than seek monopoly control of a single market. Such action is outside the scope of antitrust, and, as a result, **aggregate concentration** has increased. In 1929 the 100 largest firms (less than one-tenth of 1 percent of the total number of firms) controlled 39.7 percent of the nation's assets. In

1978 the 100 largest firms controlled 45.5 percent of the nation's assets. For the 200 largest firms, the figures are 47.7 percent and 58.3 percent respectively.

Even within industries, monopolies continue to exist. Western Electric, Kellogg, Kodak, IBM, Campbell Soup, Caterpillar, Gillette, Hershey, and Coca-Cola, control substantial portions of their respective markets. If the goal of section 2 is to prevent economic concentration, it has failed dismally.

WHY ANTITRUST POLICY HAS HAD LITTLE IMPACT ON ECONOMIC CONCENTRATION

Why antitrust policy has had little impact on economic concentration is fairly clear—poor remedies and difficulty proving **intent**. Failure to achieve **competitive remedies** is the major administrative failure of antitrust policy. As Posner (1976:82-83) argues, the government has shown a great deal of ability in winning cases but losing remedies; that is, firms were found guilty but not punished. Of the 118 monopoly cases from 1890 to 1974, the government either won in litigation or signed a consent decree in 81 percent of the cases. The government was able to get a substantial divestiture, however, in only 23 percent of the cases. Since 1940 the government's winning percentage has increased (84 percent), but the proportion of substantial divestitures has decreased (15 percent). Antitrust cannot have much impact on economic concentration if monopolizing companies are left intact.

In addition, under the rule of reason, the government must prove intent to monopolize; and such proof is fairly difficult. The case law is vague about what specific conduct is prohibited, and proving conspiracy is a difficult undertaking.

ANTITRUST LAW IS SLOW AND EXPENSIVE

Third, antitrust law is slow and expensive. Antitrust cases drag on for years. Filed in 1938, Alcoa was resolved in 1945; U.S. Steel was filed in 1911 and resolved in 1920. Filed in 1969, the IBM case covered some 8,000 exhibits, 104,400 pages of transcript, 473 court days, and then was dropped without a decision in 1982 (Fisher, McKie, and Mancke, 1983:x). Carried to completion, the IBM case may well have continued to 1990 with appeals. The massive investment of resources in monopolization cases with little to show in results clearly indicates that allocating resources to monopoly antitrust is inefficient.

PROPOSALS FOR REFORMING MONOPOLY ANTITRUST LAW

Three proposals for reforming monopoly antitrust law exist and deserve brief mention. First, the individuals who believe in the goals of monopoly antitrust law advocate procedural reforms to avoid long court proceedings. Specifically, they advocate administratively narrowing the issues so that only the disputed core is taken to court (see Posner, 1976), and they advocate time limits on trials. Second, liberals who favor antitrust law (such as former Senator Phillip Hart) have proposed that the law be rewritten to outlaw monopoly per se and to require divestiture when the government wins. Third, still others feel that monopoly antitrust should be abolished (see further on) and other forms of regulation or policy substituted.

COLLUSION

Section 1 of the **Sherman Antitrust Act** states: "Every contract, combination in the form of trust or otherwise, or conspiracy, in restraint of trade or commerce...is hereby declared to be illegal." Clearly, Congress did not intend section 1 to be taken literally, for almost every contract restrains trade or commerce in some way. Even simple partnerships restrain trade because two persons join forces as partners instead of competing.

Under section 1, two things must be demonstrated. First, an **agreement** exists (e.g., a contract, combination, or conspiracy); and second, the **agreement restrains trade**. Under court-interpreted law, some agreements such as agreements to fix prices are illegal per se; and the government or the filing party need only prove an agreement exists. In other types of agreements such as trade associations, a "rule of reason" applies.

The courts have characterized restraints of trade as of two types: (1) ancillary, and (2) nonancillary. An **ancillary restraint of trade** is one that serves a legitimate business function. For example, if A sells a business to B, B might stipulate that A cannot engage in the same business for a period of years. Because B buys both the business and the goodwill of A's business, such a restraint has a legitimate business function and, therefore, is an ancillary restraint. A **nonancillary restraint of trade** has no legitimate business function except to limit competition (e.g., deciding to divide up the market into regions and not compete with each other) and is illegal.

Price-Fixing and Collusion

The Supreme Court enunciated the basic principles of **collusion** in *Addyston Pipe* v. *U.S.* (1899). Six iron pipe manufacturers, including Addyston, divided a portion of the United States into regions and agreed not to compete with each other in the regions. Establishing a system of prearranged bids, manufacturers did not bid competitively against each other. The winning bidder paid a bonus, which was then split among the other firms.

The pipe manufacturers defended their conspiracy, contending that the prices charged were reasonable, and some evidence indicates that they were (see Armentano, 1982:140). The Court refused to apply the rule of reason to price-fixing and held that price-fixing was an ancillary restraint and was illegal **per se**.

The Court has been fairly consistent in the area of price-fixing. In *U.S.* v. *Trenton Potteries* (1927), 23 bathroom fixtures companies were found guilty of price-fixing, and their defense of reasonable prices was disallowed. In *U.S.* v. *Socony-Vacuum* (1940), indirect price-fixing was declared illegal. The major gasoline companies in the Midwest, including Socony-Vacuum (now Mobil), agreed to purchase any surplus gasoline refined by independent refineries so that prices would not fall. The Court found that this was merely an indirect form of price-fixing and, therefore, illegal.

The classic price-fixing case of all time was the Electrical Equipment Case (*Philadelphia* v. *Westinghouse* [1961]). Sometime in the 1920s or 1930s, the electrical equipment manufacturers as part of their trade association began to share price and bid information. By the 1950s the conspiracy included almost the entire $7-billion-a-year market, covering equipment ranging from turbine generators to electrical meters. The conspiracy was elaborate with code names, calls from pay phones, information passed in plain envelopes, clandestine meetings, and secret agreements (see Walton and Cleveland, 1964).

Some 29 companies and 44 individuals were indicted, with 7 executives serving jail terms and a total of nearly $2 million in fines. Despite conclusive evidence of conspiracy (even though corporate chief executives denied they knew about the conspiracy), the conspiracy might not have been successful. Cheating by members of the conspiracy was common, and some competition still existed.

Briefly important in terms of law was *Illinois Brick* v. *Illinois* (1977). The case involved companies fixing prices on materials sold to another set of companies, which then passed along the costs of the price-fixing to downstream purchasers. The Supreme Court held that downstream purchasers did not have **standing to sue**. What Illinois Brick meant was that consumers could not use antitrust law to combat price-fixing unless they were the direct (first) purchasers of the price-fixed product. In 1989 the court reversed this position in *California* v. *ARC American Corporation* which in turn encouraged a more aggressive stance by state attorneys-general in antitrust law (Abrams and Constantine, 1991). Some significant victories have been won in this area in airiine fare pricing and legal textbooks.

Although empirical data are difficult to find, the Sherman Act does not seem to have deterred price-fixing among major corporations. In the 1970s alone, the following corporations were either found guilty of price-fixing, pleaded no contest, or signed consent decrees: Allied Chemical, Bethlehem Steel, Combustion Engineering, Dean Foods, Du Pont, FMC, Flintkote, Gulf Oil, ITT, International Paper, Purolator, R.J. Reynolds, and Rockwell International. Both the Carter and Reagan Antitrust Divisions made price-fixing a major priority. Focusing on highway construction and electrical equipment, this effort resulted in 147 jail terms and $47 million in fines by 1984 (Anderson, Thomas, and Ma, 1983:52).

Trade Information Agreements

Trade information agreements among corporations are a gray area of Sherman law. In *American Column and Lumber* v. *U.S.* (1921), known as the Hardwoods Case, the hardwood flooring trade association gathered information from its members on the prices they charged for various products as well as on production and stock estimates. These figures were then sent to all association members, who adjusted their prices to conform with other prices in the industry. The Supreme Court held that such behavior was illegal.

Similar findings were presented in *U.S.* v. *Container Corporation of America* (1969), when cardboard box manufacturers exchanged price and cost information. **Trade associations** are not illegal per se, however; they may gather and disseminate information. They may share data on past transactions if those data are aggregated, they can set up rules for ethical behavior in the trade, and they can promote the industry (Van Cise, 1982:31).

Innovations in Antitrust Law in the 1970s

As part of its revitalization, the Federal Trade Commission in the 1970s established or tried to establish new legal precedents in this area of law. Its first battle, against professional associations, was successful; its second, against the cereal manufacturers' "shared monopoly," was not; its third, against gasoline additive makers, was reversed in court.

Professional associations such as bar associations, medical associations, and optometry associations have traditionally been exempt from antitrust law as **"learned professions."** The courts in a series of cases and the FTC by administrative procedures have gradually eliminated this exemption. In *Goldfarb* v. *Virginia Bar Association* (1975), the Supreme Court held that the establishment of **minimum fees** by bar associations was price-fixing. Using Goldfarb, the FTC and the Justice Department signed agreements or convinced medical associations, accounting associations, architects, civil engineers, and mechanical engineers to drop their fee schedules. The FTC issued a rule banning the practice by optometrists.

In another new area of law, the FTC addressed the problem of **conscious parallelism**, whereby firms raise or lower prices following an industry price leader. In such cases, no agreement exists, but the result is similar to price-fixing. The FTC filed suit against the three largest cereal manufacturers, Kellogg, General Foods and General Mills, alleging that they were a **"shared monopoly."** Specifically, the cereal manufacturers were charged with controlling supermarket shelf space, not competing on the basis of price, and proliferating cereals to keep other cereals off the shelves. In 1982 this attempt to set precedent was abandoned when the FTC, under James Miller III, dropped the case.

In 1983 the FTC found manufacturers of lead-based gasoline additives guilty of conscious parallelism. From 1974 to 1979, the four firms controlling this market raised the price of lead additives by 100 percent despite a declining demand for the product. Twenty of the 24 price increases occurred for all 4 firms on the same day with the exact same price increase. Du Pont and the other firms found guilty appealed this case, and the federal court of appeals reversed the FTC. The FTC did not appeal its loss.

Summary and Evaluation of Collusion

The law on collusion is divisible into two parts. Certain activities are illegal per se such as price-fixing or market divisions, and a demonstration of an agreement is sufficient to establish guilt. Other activities such as information sharing or trade associations are illegal only if they serve no legitimate business function and restrain trade.

Antitrust law on collusion is probably the least controversial part of antitrust law. Posner (1976), for example, is willing to repeal all antitrust legislation except section 1 of the Sherman Act. Strickland (1980:123) feels the law has been a success and has prevented the formation of the formal cartels that are so dominant in European markets (see also Posner, 1976:39).

PRICE-FIXING CARTELS

Whether or not the lack of formal **price-fixing cartels** in the United States is a function of the Sherman Act, however, is open to question. European cartels have one crucial ingredient that U.S. cartel attempts have lacked, government support. Without clear government support, Armentano (1982) argues that price-collusion cartels are inherently unstable.

For a successful cartel, Armentano (1982:134) argues that eight conditions must be met:

- First, demand for the good must be inelastic so that consumers are forced to absorb higher prices (there are no substitute goods).
- Second, demand must be stable; declines in demand, as demonstrated by OPEC, will cause conspirators to cheat and undercut prices.
- Third, the cartel must agree on output quotas as well as prices.
- Fourth, each firm must have relatively equal costs, or the high cost firms will realize lower profits and be tempted to cheat on the cartel.
- Fifth, importation of the cartelized good must be limited.
- Sixth, the conspirators must trust each other.
- Seventh, the product must be fairly homogeneous so that the agreement can be enforced.
- Eighth, if the goods must be transported, the price of transportation must be factored into the cartel price.

Armentano's conditions suggest that price-fixing cartels will rarely succeed. In fact, he argues that all the price-fixing cartels in the United States eventually failed to work on their own without any assist from the antitrust laws. Only where the cartel had the support of government (e.g., bar associations with the powers of the state) did the cartels successfully fix prices. The lack of cartels in the United States, therefore, may be less a function of the Sherman Act than a lack of explicit government support for cartels.[7]

PENALTIES ARE SO TRIVIAL THAT THEY DO NOT DISCOURAGE PRICE-FIXING

Even among those who consider section 1 a success, the law comes in for some criticism. First, section 1 of the Sherman Act is a weak deterrent to collusion. Whether they are successful or not, a great many attempts at price-fixing take place. Posner (1970) documented 365 such cases before 1969, and hundreds more have been filed since then. The law fails to deter price-fixing because the penalties for violating the law are trivial compared to the potential profits. Posner (1976:32) found that the average price-fixing fine in the 1960s was 0.21 percent of the sales involved in the conspiracy. As low as this figure is, it represents a 150 percent increase from the 1950s, when the average fine was 0.08 percent. Prison sentences are even less of a deterrent. Of the 33 cases that resulted in prison sentences from 1890 to 1974, the average sentence was only a few months. Although the number of jail sentences has increased dramatically under recent prosecution

---

[7]The United States does have cartels that operate. Agricultural cooperatives are classic cartels that set output quotas and prices (see chapter 6). In this case, however, the government sanctions the cartels, exempts them from antitrust law, and enforces the cartel agreements in court.

of individuals for rigging bids in highway construction, the average sentence was still only about 12 months in 1990. A rational businessperson could conclude that the gains from price-fixing far exceed the penalties if caught.

PRIVATE ANTITRUST LAWSUITS HAVE THE THREAT OF TREBLE DAMAGES

Private antitrust suits with the threat of treble damages, in fact, may be a greater deterrent to collusion than government prosecution. Whether private antitrust suits have a deterrent effort or whether they just add to the already overcrowded courts by encouraging suits is not clear. Many observers of antitrust law have suggested that the treble damages portion of antitrust law encourages too many private suits (Schwartz, 1981).

DIFFICULT BURDEN OF PROOF

A second criticism against section 1 of the Sherman Act is that the reliance on conspiracy and combination places a difficult **burden of proof** on the individual charging price-fixing. Posner (1976) advocates going to a behavior-based standard; suits would be filed if the pricing behavior in an industry followed a pattern that would be expected if price-fixing were occurring. Posner essentially argues that one should not have to prove intent and agreement, only result.

MERGERS

A **merger** is the consolidation of two or more independent firms into a single unit. Mergers were basically outside antitrust law until the passage of the Celler-Kefauver Act of 1950. Celler-Kefauver, which amended the Clayton Act, prohibited the acquisition of stock of one firm by another firm or the merger of two firms where "the effect of such acquisition may be substantially to lessen competition or to tend to create a monopoly."

Three types of mergers are possible: (1) horizontal, (2) vertical, and (3) conglomerate. A **horizontal merger** is a merger between two competitors in the same market; a merger of Mobil Oil with Exxon, for example, would be a horizontal merger. A **vertical merger** is a merger between a company and either a supplier or a distributor; a merger of a textile manufacturer with a garment manufacturer would be a vertical merger. A **conglomerate merger** is a merger between two firms that do not compete in the same markets and do not buy or sell to each other. If Getty Oil purchased the Texas Rangers baseball team, for example, that would be a conglomerate merger.

Mergers in History

American business has witnessed three eras of great merger activity. The first from 1897 to 1904 was a period of horizontal mergers and the creation of "**trusts**." Some 2,864 mergers involving over 4,000 firms took place, resulting in the creation of near monopolies in 70 different industries (Nelson, 1959). The era of horizontal mergers ended with the recession of 1904 and the government victory in the Northern Securities case.

The second era of mergers from 1916 to 1929 might be termed the oligopoly mergers. Essentially, small firms merged into larger firms so that they could compete with the major firms in the industry. Bethlehem Steel, for example, merged out of several smaller firms to compete with U.S. Steel. From 1925 through 1929, 5,382 firms merged (Markham, 1955:180). This era of mergers was effectively ended by the Great Depression.

The third merger period began in 1945 and continues to the present day. The contemporary merger period, however, differs from earlier ones in that most mergers are conglomerate mergers. Conglomerate mergers are essentially a way for corporations to grow and to spread their risks by engaging in a variety of different industries. From 1960 to 1970 the Federal Trade Commission recorded an average of 2,500 mergers a year. From 1970 to 1980 the merger pace tapered off but did not cease (Greer, 1983:169); by 1981 the annual merger rate again exceeded 2,400 (Brownstein, 1983d:1538) heralding a second wave of horizontal mergers (see below).

Horizontal Mergers

The **Celler-Kefauver Act** most directly addressed horizontal mergers because mergers are illegal only if the merger substantially lessens competition or tends to create a monopoly. When two competitors merge, competition by definition decreases. As a result, the courts initially dealt harshly with horizontal mergers.

BETHLEHEM STEEL

Bethlehem Steel's purchase of Youngstown Sheet and Tube was the first horizontal merger challenged under the Celler-Kefauver Act. Bethlehem and Youngstown together controlled 21 percent of the market and would have been the number two steel producer after U.S. Steel with 30 percent. Bethlehem defended the purchase, arguing that it did not have any plants in the center of the country and, therefore, did not compete in Youngstown's market area. The district court held that Bethlehem could have entered the Chicago market by building a plant there and ruled, therefore, that the merger would lessen competition and could not take place (*U.S.* v. *Bethlehem Steel Corporation*, 1958). Later Bethlehem vindicated the court's reasoning by opening a plant in the Chicago area.

BROWN SHOE

Because Bethlehem Steel did not appeal its case, the first case to reach the Supreme Court was *Brown Shoe Company* v. *U.S.* (1962). The Brown Shoe case involved both horizontal and vertical merger aspects. Brown Shoe Company was the fourth largest shoe manufacturer with 4 percent of the market and, in addition, had some 1,200 retail shoe stores (6 percent of the market). Brown purchased Kinney, the eighth largest shoe retailer with 1.2 percent of the market.

Clearly, the shoe manufacturing and retailing market at that time was not concentrated. The Supreme Court ruled that one need only show that a merger would probably lessen competition. Although 1.2 percent of the market nationwide was not much, the Court found that in some cities these two firms would control over 20 percent of the retail market in women's shoes. In rejecting the Brown-Kinney merger, the Court suggested two defenses under the Celler-Kefauver Act. First, one of the firms was failing economically, and, therefore, a merger would not lessen competition. Second, the merger combined two small firms into a larger, more effective competitor.

BANKS AND GROCERY STORES

Because the Brown Shoe case contained both horizontal and vertical merger elements, its impact on horizontal mergers was not totally clear. In *U.S.* v. *Philadelphia National Bank* (1963), the Court rejected the merger of two Philadelphia banks that would have given the new bank 30 percent of the Philadelphia market. The banks argued that they merged to compete more effectively with the financial center banks in New York.

In *U.S.* v. *Von's Grocery* (1966), the Court held illegal a merger between two reasonably small firms. Von's Grocery with 4.3 percent of the Los Angeles market merged with Shopping Bag Food Stores with 3.2 percent of the market. After the merger only Safeway with 8 percent had a larger market share. Even though Von's and Shopping Bag were rarely in the same neighborhoods, the Supreme Court prevented this merger under the Celler-Kefauver Act.

In 1974 the court backed away form the rigid use of **market percentages**. In *U.S.* v. *General Dynamics* the court approved a merger that would have increased the four firm concentration ratio of coal in Illinois from 43% to 63%. The court held that factors could be considered other than market percentages in determining competitive impact. The General Dynamics case, thus, created some flexibility in horizontal merger cases.

Under the Court rulings in *Brown Shoe* and *Von's Grocery*, most mergers except for the very smallest are subject to challenge under the antitrust laws. The Justice Department and the FTC have used **informal guidelines** to determine whether or not to challenge horizontal mergers. Before 1981 the **four-firm concentration** figure was used. If a merger increased the concentration of the industry to over 60 percent, it was closely examined for a potential challenge. In 1982 (and adjusted slightly in 1984) the antitrust bureaucrats adopted the **Herfindahl index** (the sum of the squares of the market shares of the firms). If the merger increased the Herfindahl index above 1000, the merger was studied more closely.

Under Assistant Attorney General William Baxter and the FTC antitrust head Timothy Muris, the flexibility of the General Dynamics cases and the application of the Herfindahl index resulted in a series of megamergers in the oil industry. Because the oil industry is relatively unconcentrated (no company has more than 8.1 percent of U.S. reserves), mergers do not raise the Herfindahl index above 1000. The oil industry consolidation began when Mobil attempted to buy Marathon Oil, which avoided the merger by combining with U.S. Steel. The proposed Mobil takeover received no objection from the FTC in 1981. The oil industry responded with a series of record-setting mergers: Du Pont purchased Conoco (a vertical merger) for $7.4 billion, Kuwait Petroleum Corp. acquired Santa Fe International ($2.5 billion), the French oil company Elf Aquitaine bought Texasgulf ($2.8 billion), Occidental Petroleum merged with Cities Service ($4 billion), Texaco took over Getty Oil ($10.1 billion), Mobil grabbed Superior Oil ($5.7 billion), and Socal acquired Gulf ($13.2 billion). Although some of these mergers required minor divestitures to gain FTC approval, then-FTC antitrust head Timothy J. Muris told

Congress that "no merger between competing oil companies is likely to be challenged based on its effect on the overall crude oil market" (Corrigan, 1984:602).

Although the Reagan antitrust bureaucracy was consistent in using the Herfindahl index (mergers between Coca-Cola and Dr. Pepper and Pepsi and Seven-Up were challenged), the results of their policy were not consistent in terms of competition. Heilmann, the brewing company, was prevented from acquiring additional beer companies that would enable it to compete with the two giants, Miller and Budweiser. In the steel industry, an industry with low profits and excess capacity, a merger between the number three and number four producers was accepted (LTV and Republic) but not a merger between numbers one and seven (U.S. Steel and National Steel). Many analysts felt that the steel mergers would improve productive efficiency and the oil mergers would not (Wines, 1984:605-606).

In both cases, oil and steel, policy was set by the bureaucracy when it exercised discretion to not challenge the mergers. The policy also generated some congressional hearings and legislative proposals to limit mergers in the oil industry, but no action was taken.

Vertical Mergers

The status of vertical mergers under antitrust law is less clear. A vertical merger is illegal if the merger closes substantial markets to competitors. For example, if Ford Motor Company purchased Firestone Tires, Ford probably would purchase its tires from Firestone. Thus, a large portion of the tire market would be foreclosed to other tire manufacturers. Under such circumstances, a vertical merger would lessen competition.

In general, however, a vertical merger lessens competition only if the market share of one of the firms is substantial (*Brown Shoe Company* v. *U.S.*, 1962). A vertical merger is unlikely to be challenged, therefore, unless the market for one firm or the other is concentrated or one firm holds a dominant market share. Without such horizontal aspects, most vertical mergers will not be challenged, and the number of vertical merger challenges have been very few (Greer, 1983:182).

Conglomerate Mergers

In a pure conglomerate merger where the companies do not compete with each other in any markets, showing a lessening of competition is extremely difficult. In general, the merger laws have had little effect on conglomerate mergers. Only those mergers that can somehow be linked to competing markets, even in an obscure way, are subject to challenge.

In *FTC* v. *Consolidated Foods* (1965), the Courts used the logic of vertical mergers to void a conglomerate merger. Consolidated Foods, a large food wholesaler and retailer, purchased Gentry, a manufacturer of dehydrated onion and garlic. Consolidated Foods asked firms from which it purchased who used dehydrated onion and garlic to purchase from Gentry. Gentry's market share increased from 32 to 35 percent. The Court held that this merger foreclosed markets (via reciprocal buying) and was, therefore, illegal.

The precedent-setting "**potential competitor**" doctrine was established by the FTC in *FTC* v. *Proctor & Gamble* (1967). Procter & Gamble, a major producer of household products, purchased Clorox, which controlled approximately 50 percent of the liquid bleach market. Although Procter & Gamble did not market any liquid bleaches, they did account for 54 percent of packaged detergent sales and did market dry bleaches. The FTC argued that the merger was anticompetitive because Procter & Gamble was a potential liquid bleach manufacturer. The Supreme Court agreed with the FTC.

In an attempt to challenge a pure conglomerate merger, the Justice Department filed suit when ITT acquired Grinnel, the major manufacturer of automatic sprinkler devices. The Justice Department contended that aggregate concentration alone lessened competition given the trend toward aggregate concentration in the economy. The federal district court refused to set new law by condemning a merger on the ground of aggregate concentration alone (*U.S.* v. *ITT*, 1970). The case was settled by consent decree after the district court decision, and the Supreme Court was denied a chance to rule on this issue. With the reduced concern for mergers in general, conglomerate mergers are generally safe.

Summary and Evaluation of Mergers

The **Celler-Kefauver Act** prohibits mergers if the "effect of such acquisition may be substantially to lessen competition or tend to create a monopoly." Under the act, all but the very smallest horizontal mergers are illegal. Vertical mergers are legal unless they foreclose markets, which usually means that one of the firms competes in a market that is somewhat concentrated. Conglomerate mergers are generally legal unless the government can prove that one firm is a potential competitor of the other.

Allyn Strickland (1980:152) feels that the Celler-Kefauver Act can be termed a success because it has eliminated the **horizontal mergers** to monopoly that once plagued the country. Strickland, however, is overly optimistic. The period of horizontal mergers to monopoly ended in 1904 and may well have ended for economic reasons rather than antitrust reasons. Armentano (1982) presents evidence that large, near-monopoly firms have consistently lost market shares to smaller, more aggressive competitors. Only when government has protected the monopoly or the monopoly firm has remained an innovator has market power been maintained. Armentano would not credit antitrust policy for any of the reduction in horizontal mergers. The reduction occurred because horizontal mergers are an inefficient use of capital.

Success or not, antitrust merger policy has five serious shortcomings:

First, the policy has been ineffective in slowing down the number of mergers in the economy. Aggregate concentration in U.S. industry has increased by 10 percentage points for the 200 largest firms from 1928 to the present. In 1988 a record $264 billion in mergers occurred (Moore, 1993a:2667). What the policy did was shift the focus of mergers from horizontal mergers to conglomerate mergers. Elzinga (1969:294) found that 60 percent of pre-1950 mergers were horizontal whereas only 25 percent were horizontal during the 1950s and 12 percent in the early 1960s. If aggregate concentration is a concern, therefore, antitrust has been ineffective in preventing such concentration.

Second, antitrust policy is subject to **bureaucratic inertia**. A merger is acceptable unless challenged by the FTC or the Justice Department. One problem with bureaucratic discretion in this area is that sometimes the discretion is abused (the ITT and Hartford Insurance merger during the Nixon administration) and sometimes mergers that clearly would not pass court scrutiny are accepted by the agencies (the FTC did not object to the Texaco-Getty or the Socal-Gulf mergers in 1984). From 1950 to 1977 only 27.6 percent of all horizontal mergers were challenged (Mueller, 1979). Under the Reagan administration's antitrust leaders William Baxter and Timothy Muris, vertical and conglomerate mergers were not challenged, and only those horizontal mergers in highly concentrated industries were opposed (Wines, 1982e:1204). This policy variation has a direct impact on the number of mergers; Yantek and Gartrell (1988) found mergers increase as both the president and Congress become more conservative.

Third, the law is **unpredictable** and **inconsistent**. How large (in terms of market size) a horizontal merger can be is not clear, and this uncertainty is heightened by variation in the agencies' willingness to challenge mergers (variation that appears to correlate with presidential administrations; see Wood and Anderson, 1993). In vertical and conglomerate mergers, the law is even more unpredictable. What constitutes a "potential competitor" is not clear because almost every business is the potential competitor of every other business. The proportion of a market that must be foreclosed by a vertical merger is also not clear.

Fourth, as is true of the monopoly area, the merger area is another one where the government frequently loses the remedy when it wins the case. Elzinga (1969) found that in 39 cases won by the government, the government was able to get the merger disallowed in only 10 cases. Even court victories, therefore, do not contribute to more competitors.

Fifth, some economists feel that merger policy is not efficient. In a major study of costs and benefits of the Celler-Kefauver Act, Audretsch (1983) found that horizontal merger suits often cost more than the benefits that were gained (especially when the remedy failed). The only positive benefit was that these cases often had a redistributive effect within the industry.

PRICE DISCRIMINATION

Price discrimination occurs when a firm charges more than one price for a good sold to other firms. The **Clayton Act** only prevents **predatory price discrimination**. The Robinson-Patman Act prohibits price discrimination where the effect may be "to lessen competition or tend to create a monopoly" or "to injure, destroy or prevent competition." Price discrimination is an area of the law that pits small business against large business. The pressure for the Robinson-Patman Act was from small businesses that found themselves at a competitive disadvantage with big business. Congress in 1936 in essence modified the Clayton Act to protect competitors as well as competition. The conflict between the two business sectors can be seen from the issues that evolved in price discrimination.

Retail Price Maintenance or Fair-Trade Pricing

If one business, say, a large retail chain, can sell goods at a price less than another business, say, a locally owned store, then competitive pressures suggest that the second business will fail. To prevent large businesses from undercutting the prices of small business, the first policy mechanism to enhance competition in part by protecting small business was fair-trade pricing. Under **fair-trade pricing** or **resale price maintenance**, the manufacturer set a suggested retail price for a good and expected that all firms would sell at that price.

The Supreme Court held that fair-trade pricing was illegal as early as 1911 (*Miles Medical Co.* v. *John Park*). The same pressure that resulted in the Robinson-Patman Act also produced the Miller-Tydings Act of 1937, which exempted fair-trade pricing from antitrust. Unfortunately, for small business, fair-trade pricing is impossible to enforce. Manufacturer M probably does not care what price chain store C sells M's goods for at retail. In fact, the lower the price C charges for the goods, the greater the demand, and the more goods C will buy from M. M is unlikely to alienate a good customer like C over a minor matter, particularly one that does not affect the profits of M such as fair-trade pricing. Fair-trade pricing's exemption from the antitrust laws was eventually repealed by the Consumer Goods Pricing Act of 1975.

Recently resale price maintenance has been the subject of some debate. Both the FTC and the Antitrust Division have proposed that resale price maintenance be subjected to a "rule of reason" test rather than be illegal per se.

Five arguments for a change in policy have been presented. First, a rule of reason approach would make resale price maintenance consistent with the law on exclusionary practices (see later; Areeda, 1984:20; Easterbrook, 1984:23). Second, because resale price maintenance will be effective only in rare circumstances (e.g., when there are few manufacturers, few dealers, homogeneous products, and a way to enforce it), resale price maintenance is not worth worrying about (Easterbrook, 1984:25). Third, resale price maintenance can be competitive behavior if it permits a manufacturer to sell a different mix of goods or services (Easterbrook, 1984:26). Fourth, the manufacturer might have an essential interest in the resale price to protect the **"status"** of a good (Pitofsky, 1984:28). Fifth, without resale price maintenance, a store that provides services as well as sales (e.g., advice about computers, repairs, and so on) is exploited by discounters who merely sell the good (Miller, 1984:31).

Both antitrust agencies accepted these arguments and de-emphasized cases involving retail price maintenance. Such cases averaged about ten a year prior to 1981. From 1981 to 1983 neither the Antitrust Division nor the FTC filed a single resale price maintenance case. After a brief attempt by some advocates in the mid 1980s to revive resale price maintenance as a competitive policy, the area returned to the doldrums.

Price Discrimination

The classic price discrimination case is *FTC* v. *Morton Salt* (1948). Morton Salt priced its salt on the volume ordered. The basic price for less than carload lots was $1.60 per case; for carload lots, $1.50; for more than 5,000 cases per year, $1.40; and for more than 50,000 cases per year, $1.35. Only four major chains qualified for the lowest prices, but almost every store through group purchases paid less than the $1.60 price. The Supreme Court recognized Congress' intent to protect small business and noted that the higher prices paid by small business might lead to monopoly. Morton Salt, therefore, was guilty of price discrimination.

The **Robinson-Patman Act** has actually been used to limit competition. A good example is *Utah Pie* v. *Continental Baking* (1967). Utah Pie had a monopoly in the frozen pie market in Utah. Moving into this market from California, Continental Baking charged lower prices than Utah and lower prices than it charged in California. The judicial question is, Was Utah Pie injured? In general, the courts find injury whenever a competitor must significantly drop prices to meet competition. The court found that Utah Pie was injured despite the fact that Utah Pie had a monopoly (and, therefore, may have charged monopoly prices) before Continental moved in.

The courts have generally permitted three defenses in price discrimination suits. First, one can underprice competitors if the prices are justified by lower costs. This defense is rare because businesses hesitate to reveal this amount of financial information to competitors and because cost accounting lacks the precision to handle such concepts as marginal cost. Second, an acceptable defense is changing conditions such as a going-out-of-business sale. Third, dropping prices in order to meet the prices of a competitor is also acceptable.

Evaluation of Price Discrimination

Robinson-Patman law is a complex, involved field. Legal textbooks are written about the area, and individuals spend their entire lives practicing Robinson-Patman law. Although the law is complex from a legal perspective, it is not from a policy perspective. Robinson-Patman, by outlawing price discrimination and making the defenses for price discrimination difficult, is essentially anticompetitive. Consumers benefit from competitive markets where price competition is vigorous. Prices fall, inefficient businesses fail, and efficient businesses survive. The goal of protecting small business is inconsistent with the goal of benefiting individual consumers. How are consumers injured if a large department store sells goods at prices lower than a local store? How were the people of Utah injured when Continental Baking sold frozen pies at less than their prices in California?

If one policy goal is to protect small business, clearly more effective ways exist to do so without having consumers bear the cost. Tax incentives, loan programs, and preferential awarding of contracts are three possible ways. Price cutting is an essential element of a market system that works. Rather than establish barriers that increase costs to consumers without compensating benefits, the government should be advocating the interests of consumers. The general public and individual consumers would be better served if the Robinson-Patman Act were repealed.

EXCLUSIONARY PRACTICES

Exclusionary practices are practices that attempt to exclude individuals from a market. **Section 3** of the Clayton Act prohibits selling goods or charging prices "on the condition...that...purchaser thereof shall not use or deal in the goods...of a competitor...where the effect of such...may be to substantially lessen competition or tend to create a monopoly in any line of commerce." As in the Robinson-Patman area, exclusionary practices are a grievance that one business files against another. Consumer interests are only indirectly involved. Three common exclusionary practices will be discussed in this section: (1) tying agreements, (2) exclusive dealing agreements, and (3) exclusive distributorships. Other types of "exclusionary practices," including boycotts, predatory price cutting, and vertical mergers (see Posner, 1976:171), will not be discussed in this section because they were included elsewhere in the chapter or are of minor importance.

Tying Agreements

A **tying agreement** is an agreement that requires an individual who purchases one good from a company to purchase a second good. If a copy machine corporation refused to rent or sell copy machines to a business unless the business also purchased paper from the company, this would be a tying agreement. In actual practice, thousands of goods are tied because common sense requires tying. When a consumer purchases a new automobile, the purchase of tires is tied to the automobile (rationally because the automobile does not work without them). Shirts come with buttons, shoes come with shoelaces, tennis rackets usually come with strings, and so forth.

Tying agreements become a problem only when one of the goods involved is monopolized or the company exerts some monopoly power. When the selling firm lacks monopoly power, the buyer can simply go elsewhere for a nontied good. Butterball Turkeys, for example, has recently tied some of its turkeys to a premixed stuffing. Because Butterball lacks market power, individuals who wish turkeys without premade stuffing can simply buy other turkeys. Only if Butterball had a monopoly on the frozen turkey market would this form of tying be a problem to the consumer.

Unfortunately, the law on tying agreements is not so simple. **Complexity** results because the law is intended to protect businesses from each other rather than to protect consumers. *International Salt* v. *U.S.* (1947) established that a tying agreement was illegal if the seller possessed sufficient market power and presented no reasonable justification for the tying. International Salt had a patent on salt-dispensing machines used in food processing. Companies that used International Salt machines had to purchase their salt from International Salt. The Supreme Court held that International Salt had market power in the salt machines business and that tying the sale of salt to the use of machines served no purpose other than to foreclose the market.

The Court has also rejected tying the rental of good movies to bad ones when selling them to television (*U.S.* v. *Loew's Inc.*, 1962), but accepted tying morning and afternoon newspaper advertisements (*Times-Picayune Publishing Co.* v. *U.S.*).

The Court has suggested two defenses to tying agreements when the state of the market indicates tying is harmful. First, tying might be justified if the tied goods are **inputs** and certain quality inputs are required to maintain the quality of the tied good. Although the Supreme Court suggested the quality inputs defense, the Circuit Court rejected such a defense when Chicken Delight required franchises to purchase both chicken and cooking equipment from Chicken Delight (*Siegel* v. *Chicken Delight, Inc.*, 1971).

Second, the Court has accepted tying as a method of protecting the quality of service in a new industry. In *U.S.* v. *Jerrold Electronics* (1961), the Court upheld Jerrold's practices in the cable TV industry. Jerrold only sold cable systems that included the equipment, installation, layout, and maintenance. The Court accepted tying in this case to protect a new industry but hinted that the acceptance was temporary until the industry reached maturity.

Exclusive Dealing Agreements

Exclusive dealing agreements are agreements between a supplier and a distributor whereby the distributor agrees not to handle products of the supplier's competitors. Justifications for exclusive dealing agreements include a guarantee of a steady supply of a good, the ability to reduce inventory by stocking fewer brands, and the pledge of advertising or other services. Exclusive dealing agreements are illegal if they foreclose a significant market and, thus, lessen competition.

In the Standard Stations case (*Standard Oil of California* v. *U.S.*, 1949), Standard Oil of California required that its dealers purchase all their gasoline from Standard and in some instances purchase their batteries, tires, and other parts as well. (The case concerned the independent dealers marketing Standard products, not the stations owned by Standard.) The Supreme Court held that Standard's share of the market (6.7 percent) effectively foreclosed a $58 million market from competitors and, therefore, was illegal. If the size of the market was substantial, no evidence of market power was necessary in exclusive dealing.

Exclusive dealing is not a concise area of the law. Exclusive dealing is allowed if the market share is small or the dollar value of the market is small. In *Tampa Electric Co.* v. *Nashville Coal Co.* (1961), the Court accepted exclusive dealing when the market share was only 1 percent and the seller provided additional services to the dealer.

Exclusive Distributorships

An **exclusive distributorship** is a grant by a supplier to a distributor that the distributor will be the sole distributor in a geographic area. Beverage companies, for example, usually only use a single distributor in any geographic area. The distributor, in practice, is granted a local monopoly in the distribution of goods from the supplier.

The Supreme Court addressed the issue of exclusive distributorships in *Packard Motor Car Co.* v. *Webster* (1957). In an effort to protect the largest Packard dealer in Baltimore, Packard did not renew two other Baltimore dealerships, including Webster. The Circuit Court (affirmed by the Supreme Court) held that this was a reasonable restraint of trade. Exclusive dealerships could be used to promote the brand or to protect individual dealers.

Although the Packard case upheld the right of companies to select their distributors, it did not address the issue of whether or not the company could place restrictions on the resale of the product (e.g., limit it to a geographic area or to specific customers). This issue was addressed twice. In *U.S.* v. *Arnold, Schwinn & Co.* (1969), the Supreme Court held that product resale restrictions on an independent dealer were illegal per se. Eight years later, the Court modified this position in *Continental TV* v. *GTE Sylvania* (1977). GTE marketed television sets through independent dealers who were limited to specified geographic areas (but could also sell other brands). Continental opened another store outside its geographic area, and GTE canceled its dealership. Adopting a "rule of reason" standard, the Court held that such restrictions were permissible to increase brand promotion and, thus, interbrand competition.

Evaluation of Exclusionary Practices

From a public policy perspective, exclusionary agreements law is relatively unimportant. The law basically deals with relationships between businesses and has little direct impact on the consumer. Tying agreements are illegal if the seller exerts substantial market power in a tied good. Exclusive dealing agreements are illegal except when the dollar value of the market is small. Exclusive distributorships are legal, and restrictions on distributors are governed by a rule of reason.

The most interesting question of all in this area is, Why should there be any laws at all? Buyers do not lack information; tying agreements, exclusive dealing agreements, and exclusive distributorships are contracts that one business voluntarily enters into with another. If terms are unfavorable, the business may terminate the relationship. If the selling company makes unreasonable demands or ties goods unreasonably, then that company will lose business to others. Exclusionary practices law is an attempt to address the power differences between larger businesses (suppliers) and small ones (distributors). Perhaps government should not be involved in economic relationships between consenting adults.

From the perspective of consumers, exclusionary agreements are irrelevant. Whether goods are offered to consumers via exclusive dealerships or not probably has little impact on price or variety of goods as long as the market for the goods was not concentrated beforehand. If problems exist, they are problems of market concentration rather than problems of exclusionary agreements. Policies designed to limit concentration will be more likely to benefit the consumer in this regard than exclusionary practices law.

ANTITRUST LAW AS PUBLIC POLICY

Antitrust law is frequently discussed in legal terms; that is, What is the law? Is the law consistent? What should the law be? Antitrust law has been subjected to a fair amount of economic analysis by people like Posner, Armentano, Elzinga, Bork, and Audretsch. What is generally lacking from the literature is any analysis of antitrust law from a political perspective. This final section will add to the political analysis in the preceding sections and examine antitrust as a public policy from a political perspective.

Five Proposed Goals of Antitrust Policy

A major problem with antitrust policy is that it attempts to attain several goals simultaneously. Multiple goals are a characteristic of many public policies, but rarely are the policy goals as inherently contradictory as they are in antitrust policy. An examination of legislative debates and subsequent implementation reveals at least five proposed goals for antitrust policy.

ECONOMIC DECONCENTRATION

First, one **antitrust goal** is clearly **economic deconcentration**. The problem addressed by the Fifty-first Congress was the problem of trusts, which, by nature of their size, stifled competition. According to Senator Sherman, "The popular mind is agitated with...the inequality of condition, of wealth, and opportunity that has grown within a single generation out of the concentration of capital into vast combinations" (cited in Van Cise, 1982:23). Again, Sherman stated, "If we will not endure a King as a political power, we should not endure a King over the production, transportation and sale of the necessaries of life." Conspiracies alone were not sufficient to pass the Sherman Act, but conspiracies to set prices along with economic concentration were.

POLITICAL DEMOCRACY

The economic deconcentration goal is as much a political goal as an economic goal. By deciding where to locate rail lines and the rates to charge, railroads could decide if cities were to flourish or die. Trusts were seen by the muckrakers and cartoonists of the day as exacting political concessions from politicians. Deconcentration is linked, therefore, to arguments for political democracy as well as for economic democracy (see Van Cise, 1982). Large business, according to the argument, undermines the competitive marketplace and perverts the political process. This suggests a second goal for antitrust, political democracy.

ECONOMIC EFFICIENCY

A third proposed goal for antitrust is economic efficiency. Monopolies, according to traditional microeconomic theory (see Armentano, 1982), restrict output and set prices higher than the competitive market price. Such a process is inefficient. This antitrust goal is embraced by most economists. Posner (1976:20), for example, states that for the Sherman Act "the dominant legislative intent has been to promote some approximation to the economist's ideal of competition, viewed as a means toward the end of maximizing efficiency."

Efficiency was the goal, and competition was the means. Efficiency as a goal of antitrust policy is clearly correct; when individuals argue, as Bork (1978) does, that efficiency is the *only* goal, they are clearly incorrect. Efficiency as an economic concept was hardly developed at the time of the Sherman Act (see Brozen, 1982). The debates over the Sherman Act (or over the Robinson-Patman Act or the Celler-Kefauver Act for that matter) do not reveal a solid grasp of microeconomics and an understanding of the economic concept of efficiency. Until the 1920s the discipline of economics itself was not supportive of the logic that antitrust could improve competition (DiLorenzo and High, 1988). To argue that efficiency is the sole goal of antitrust, therefore, is to argue that the goal of antitrust policy should be efficiency.

ADVANCING CONSUMER WELFARE

Fourth, consumer welfare has been proposed as an antitrust goal. The most persuasive arguments on this point are made by Bork (1978:20): "[D]elegation [of legislative authority to the judiciary in the **Sherman Act**] was confined by the policy of advancing consumer welfare." Bork argues that only consumer welfare can be justified as a goal of antitrust policy from the legislative intent of the Sherman Act. Bork then, however, makes an economic leap of faith to equate "consumer welfare" with efficiency.

To be sure, consumer welfare does increase from the results of allocative and productive efficiency. As prices drop as the result of efficiency, consumers benefit. Consumer welfare, however, should not be defined in such narrow economic terms. Consumers have interests in things other than low prices. Consumer welfare is enhanced by expanding consumer choice, a prospect not likely if monopoly production of a homogeneous good is the end result of efficiency. Consumer welfare is also enhanced by the responsiveness of the market to individual consumer demands—again, something less likely in a concentrated, yet efficient market because large firms produce efficiencies often by eliminating service (e.g., chain hardware stores). Consumer welfare is clearly a goal of antitrust policy, and it encompasses more than mere efficiency.

ASSISTING SMALL BUSINESS

Fifth, antitrust policy has the goal of assisting small business (Van Cise, 1982). The arguments of Brandeis for the **Clayton Act** refer to the necessities of protecting small business from the evils of large business (McCraw, 1981). The **Robinson-Patman Act** was passed in response to pressures of small businesses that sought to limit the national chain stores. Interpreting the law under exclusionary practices and price discrimination as anything other than an effort to protect small business is difficult.

Are the Goals of Antitrust Policy Consistent?

Is it possible to treat the five antitrust goals as consistent? In the eyes of various persons, the goals of antitrust policy can be seen as complementary.[8] According to this view, the base problem is that industry is concentrated (either by trusts, monopolies, or collusion).

The *economic side* of this argument holds that concentration results in inefficiency because it violates the assumptions of neoclassical microeconomic theory. Inefficiency, in turn, results in a drop in consumer welfare (broadly defined).

The *political side* of the argument holds that economic concentration is easily translated into political power and that the political power is used for abusive purposes. Securing preferential treatment from legislators, influencing court decisions by determining appointments (e.g., the number of railroad lawyers serving on the Supreme Court from 1880 to 1930 far exceeds the number one would expect by chance alone), or buying Senate seats are three possibilities. Political abuses, in turn, result in a decline in consumer welfare as the political process is used to protect large business.

The *small business branch* of the argument holds that concentration tends to drive small businesspeople out of business. With the decline in the number of small businesses,

---

[8]By making this argument, using a model of goals, we do not mean to imply that any one person holds all the views expressed here. What is presented is a combination of views from a variety of different individuals and should not be attributed an any single individual.

consumers lose some of the benefits they were receiving in terms of special service, responsiveness, and even price competition. Brandeis' arguments about the inherent goodness of small business are relevant here.

All the antitrust goals, therefore, could be compatible in a theoretical ideal. In the real world, however, they are not. The relationship between concentration and efficiency has been directly and competently challenged by Armentano (1982). In many cases, concentrated industries with large, almost monopolistic firms are more efficient than a series of small firms (see McCraw, 1981).[9] If efficiency is unrelated to concentration, then efficiency conflicts with the goal of helping small business. Exclusionary practices and price discrimination are competitive devices, yet they are harmful to small business. Efficiency and protection of small business may not be consistent. Similar logic contrasts the goals of political democracy with those of efficiency and small business. If efficiency leads to concentration, then efficiency can contribute to political abuses by concentrated industries. Posner, Brozen, Bork, and others rejected this conflict; and this rejection will be discussed later on. What Posner and the others argue is that small business is far more likely to abuse the political system with truckers fixing prices, agricultural coops getting preferential price supports, and textile makers gaining import tariffs. Although Posner's argument that small business has far more influence on government than big business is open to question, he does show how the goal of protecting small business might conflict with the political abuse goal. With little effort, all the goals of antitrust can be shown to conflict with each other.

The debate of antitrust goals and objectives is more than an academic dispute. The general Chicago school philosophy that antitrust should focus perhaps exclusively on collusion was accepted by the antitrust bureaucracy (Eisner, 1991) and vigorously endorsed by the Reagan administration (Wood and Anderson, 1993). Because antitrust cases take some time to develop and because staffs shrunk during the 1980s, the ability to redirect policy remains in doubt even for an advocate of aggressive enforcement such as Clinton appointee Anne K. Bingaman (Moore, 1993b).

Antitrust Has Failed to Attain Its Goals

Comparing antitrust policy to its goals reveals a policy that must be considered a failure. There are five aspects to this conclusion.

First, if the **goal** of **antitrust policy** is to prevent economic concentration, it has clearly failed. As noted earlier, the aggregate concentration of American industry has increased since 1929 even though the increase is not dramatic. The concentration ratios

---

[9]What Armentano (1982) argues is that the microeconomic ideal of perfect competition never exists in the real world. As a result, seeking such an ideal often diverts us from realizing that efficient structures can exist that do not follow the ideal. By rejecting the model of perfect competition as an ideal against which public policy is to be measured, Armentano implicitly calls into question much of the economic arguments in other areas of regulation. A single phone company, for example, might be more efficient than a series of competing phone systems. A system of government regulation might provide more consumer benefits than the market might ever hope to attain. The implications of Armentano's arguments are important for the study of regulation; unfortunately he does not pursue them.

within individual industries have varied. Some industries have become more concentrated whereas other industries have become less concentrated (see Brozen, 1982:24). Between 1935 and 1972, for example, the top four firms in the beer industry increased their market share from 11 percent to 50 percent (with substantial increases since 1972 to at least 70 percent). The top four firms in meat-packing, on the other hand, dropped from 56 percent of the market to 20 percent. One result that is clear, however, is that antitrust policy has not led to a significant deconcentration of industry.

Second, has antitrust policy resulted in **improvements in efficiency**? Armentano (1982) marshals convincing evidence that the large industrial firms of the early twentieth century achieved and held large market shares because they were more efficient than other firms. Breaking up such efficient firms resulted in smaller, less efficient firms. In addition, the antitrust actions under the Robinson-Patman Act and the Clayton Act's provisions on exclusionary practices are designed to limit competition and the resulting efficiencies. The conclusion of economic analysis (e.g., Armentano, 1982; Brozen, 1982; Posner, 1976; Bork, 1978) is that antitrust law has not led to greater efficiency.

Third, has antitrust law contributed to **greater political and economic democracy**? Is our government less subject to the abuses of big business than it was in the nineteenth century? This is a fairly complex question, and an answer will be attempted later. The weight of the scholarly literature in political science, however, does not indicate that government has become any less responsive to the pressures of large business (see Lowi, 1969).

Fourth, has antitrust policy aided **small business**? No systematic evidence has been gathered on this question, and, therefore, no unequivocal answer is possible. Price discrimination cases clearly benefit small business at the expense of others. Exclusionary practices suits probably do likewise. If antitrust policy meets any goal, it probably meets this one.

Fifth, are consumers better off with antitrust policy than they would be without it? **Probably not**. Some evidence exists that antitrust policy sanctions inefficiencies in the market. Other evidence indicates that it has had no impact on economic concentration, and, as a result, the choices available to consumers are being limited. The brands of beer, the types of American-made automobiles, the variation in grocery stores, and the choices in countless other areas have decreased. Maintaining that consumers have benefitted from antitrust policy would be difficult.

Market Concentration Aside, Should We Worry About Bigness?

The economic revisionists (e.g., Bork, Brozen, Armentano, Posner) argue that the goal of antitrust policy ought to be economic efficiency and that we should accept big business for the benefits it yields. They argue that firms grow to large proportions and retain a large market share over time because they serve the needs of the market better than small firms. Firms such as IBM or Campbell's Soup face no lack of potential competitors, but retain their market share only if they have achieved superior efficiencies somewhere in the process. Firms that are not competitive, such as U.S. Steel, which dropped from 65 percent of the market to less than 15 percent, or International Harvester, which dropped from a near monopoly to near bankruptcy, will be punished by the market. Armentano

(1982:121) concludes: "All of the corporations [e.g. Standard Oil, American Tobacco, Alcoa] examined in these classic cases had expanded outputs, reduced prices, and engaged in important technological innovation, entirely consistent with competitive behavior and efficient performance."

Brozen (1982) goes so far as to argue that bigness is a positive good. He presents data that show large businesses are more productive, pay higher wages, and raise prices more slowly than do small businesses. Other evidence not presented by Brozen indicates that large businesses are generally safer places to work, although this may be a function of visibility to OSHA or to labor union pressure.[10]

As to the political influence of big business, Brozen pooh-poohs it. He correctly notes that definitive studies of the relationship between government influence and the size of business do not exist. To support his argument that large business is not influential, he cites two case studies of political scientists (one from 1961 and one from 1969), argues that big oil companies have not been successful in pressing their demands on government, argues that local drugstores are more protected than large pharmaceutical companies, and then quotes Posner. Posner (1976:18) states "it is therefore unclear whether on balance concentrated, or monopolistic, industries will obtain greater help from the political process than unconcentrated, or competitive industries. This theoretical indeterminacy is mirrored in the empirical works, where we observe many unconcentrated industries—agriculture, trucking, local broadcasting, banking, medicine, to name a few enjoying governmental protection against competition."

RESPONSES TO THE ECONOMIC AND POLITICAL ARGUMENTS FOR LARGE BUSINESS

Both the economic and the political arguments for large business merit some response.

MARKET PUNISHMENT IS SLOW AND UNCERTAIN   First, in terms of economics, to realize that a monopolistic firm will lose its market percentage if it fails to compete effectively is gratifying but not satisfying. A noncompetitive firm will lose its market share in the long run, but that long run is fairly long. U.S. Steel began its existence in 1901 with a market share of 66 percent. In its corporate history, U.S. Steel has been characterized by conservative, risk-avoiding management, has failed to innovate, has sought the protection of import duties, and has clearly not been competitive. Despite all this, U.S. Steel still controls one-sixth of the steel market in the United States and is the largest steel producer in the country. At the same time that it was pressing for import duties against "unfair" foreign competition, rather than modernize to compete, U.S. Steel purchased Marathon Oil (later divested). Market punishment for large firms that are not competitive appears to be very slow and somewhat uncertain.

---

[10]Small business, on the other hand, is more innovative and more likely to create new jobs.

LARGE BUSINESSES HAVE DISTINCT ADVANTAGES   Second, the argument that government is not more responsive to large business is difficult to maintain. Large businesses have inherent advantages in the process of lobbying governments. Among the variables that scholars of interest groups feel are important in affecting the policy process are size, resources, and cohesion (see Zeigler and Peak, 1972; Rourke, 1984). Size in either employment or sales translates into power resources such as votes that are valued in the political process. Resources, especially with the laws that now permit corporations to set up political action committees, are essential in gaining access to policymakers. Cohesion is important because it can be used to argue that there is only one side to the issue. Lack of cohesion is less a problem for businesses in concentrated industries because there are fewer firms to coordinate.

The advantages can be translated into political results. Large corporations can argue that they need protection because if they are allowed to fail, it will have a major disruptive impact on the economy. Both Chrysler and Penn Central Railroad were given loan guarantees after making this argument. Continental of Illinois, the seventh largest bank in the nation, was kept open with an influx of federal money in May 1984, the same week that First Continental Bank of Del City, Oklahoma (a much smaller bank), was allowed to fold. Large businesses inherently make larger demands on government. Surely no small business has ever abused the political system in the manner of ITT in the 1970s. Direct bribes of legislators, a proposed under-writing of the Republican National Convention, and a condemning connection with coups and electoral manipulation in Chile make the local drug stores' efforts at fair trade laws seem pretty mild.

The noncompetitive practices in agriculture that Posner notes are true, but he fails to realize that these practices are also the work of large corporations. Clearly, the most protected and heavily subsidized portion of agriculture is dairy farming; and with the milk scandals of the 1970s, it may also be the most corrupt. The massive campaign contributions and political influence are not the result of small dairy farmers from Wisconsin lobbying their member of Congress but the result of giant agricultural cooperatives committed to noncompetitive public policies. Five dairy cooperatives received more than $100 million in subsidies in 1983 (Wines, 1983h:2668); each had sales in excess of $1 billion, hardly the size of a small business.

Small business is less worrisome in politics because small business simply lacks the resources or the need to make the same types of demands on government as large business. The domestic shoe industry would love to have "**domestic content**" legislation (that is, legislation requiring that a certain percentage of the shoe contain materials made in the United States) for all shoes sold in the United States, but they lack the resources to convert such a demand. To argue that large businesses are not as effective as small business in politics is to ignore reality. The Business Roundtable and direct business lobbying in recent years have had an impact on the restriction of the powers of the FTC, the failure to establish an Agency for Consumer Advocacy, and the limitation of payments to outside intervenors in the regulatory process.

In addition to political concerns about the influence of large businesses in politics, their impact on the economy is also worthy of concern. The concern, however, is not as some present it that the Fortune 500 companies will eventually own the entire economy;

that is clearly not a threat. Large corporations, like all large bureaucracies, are **risk-averse** and are unlikely to take the economic risks necessary to dominate the entire economic market. In every decade, new product lines develop as the result of risk-taking by entrepreneurs in small and marginal firms. The success of the personal computer market can be attributed to Apple and other small firms, not to the industry giants (IBM's dominance in the personal computer market was short lived).

ECONOMIC ARGUMENTS AGAINST LARGE CORPORATIONS

There are four economic arguments against large corporations.

LARGE CORPORATIONS ARE QUITE BUREAUCRATIC AND NOT VERY INNOVATIVE First, large corporations by definition are more bureaucratic than small corporations. Because they need to oversee the work of more individuals, large corporations will have more levels of control and more levels of supervision (see Downs, 1967). As bureaucratized organizations, they will devote a greater portion of their resources to nonproductive activities and rely on cumbersome **committee decision patterns** (see Wright, 1978). Such large organizations are slow to respond to changes in the environment. IBM, for example, would not have entered the computer business at all were it not for a separate unit under Thomas Watson, Jr. (Fisher, McKie, and Mancke, 1983). In sum, theoretical reasons exist why large corporations are likely to be slower to change, to invest more resources in control than production, and to be less innovative.

LARGE CORPORATIONS CAN WEATHER MISTAKES Second, large corporations can weather mistakes much more easily than can small ones. A small corporation is unlikely to be able to survive a major error in product line innovation as General Motors did with the X-car. Despite introducing a car that performed poorly compared to other models and despite known safety problems, General Motors was able to survive and flourish (GM Knew, 1983). Similarly, Eli Lilly knowingly failed to disclose information about deaths attributed to Oraflex in Europe when applying for distribution of the drug in the United States (Oraflex Linked, 1983:26). Economic mistakes by small corporations simply do not compare in magnitude to those of large corporations, and small corporations are more likely to bear the penalties of such mistakes.

LARGE CORPORATIONS SUBSIDIZE INEFFICIENT UNITS WITHIN Third, large conglomerates have the ability to avoid the brutality of a competitive marketplace. Inefficient units in a conglomerate can be subsidized with the profits of other units. ITT, for example, for a long time held onto its less profitable subsidiaries such as Continental Baking and Sheraton Hotels, subsidizing them with profits elsewhere in the firm (Pauly with lpsen, 1984:50). Although such a process is not economically rational, such behavior might occur when size rather than profits is the dominant concern of management or when the unit has some other value to top management (Chrysler, for example, sold off a profitable defense unit to funnel money into its money-losing car production).

LARGE CORPORATIONS CAN FORCE THE ENVIRONMENT TO ADAPT TO THEM Fourth, large corporations often have the option of not responding to environmental pressures and may be large enough to force the environment to adapt to them in the short run (see Azumi and Hage, 1972). This applies in both economic and political situations. Rather than respond to the competitive pressures of Japanese automakers, a large corporation can seek to change the environment by pressing for import quotas and domestic content (efforts that work even better if labor can be convinced to lead the fight, a lesson learned from the Clean Air Act Amendments in 1977; see Ornstein and Elder, 1978). With enough skill, political solutions can be substituted for economic solutions as long as governments can be persuaded to impose such solutions.

ARGUMENTS ABOUT LARGE CORPORATIONS ARE POLITICAL   The arguments against large corporations (which economists confuse with arguments against concentration in specific industries) are not so irrational as economists paint them. Although some of the arguments have an economic base, they are essentially political arguments about the distribution of power in society. Advocating that government avoid action in this area is the same as advocating that the current distribution of power is optimal. Such arguments, despite their reliance on economic analysis, are essentially political.

Proposals to Reform Antitrust Policy

The goal of antitrust policy should be to improve consumer welfare, broadly defined. The policy should permit the consumer the widest choice of goods, at the lowest prices, with the types of quality and supporting services that are desired. Using this as the goal of antitrust policy suggests that several changes should be made.

First, the only area of antitrust policy that clearly leads to gains in consumer welfare is the **section 1 Sherman Act** prohibition against collusion. Price-fixing is detrimental to consumer interests; and judged by the number of cases prosecuted, substantial price-fixing occurs in our economy (see Bork, 1978). The resources of the antitrust agencies should be committed to this area. Indeed price-fixing cases are now the predominant enforcement process (Eisner, 1991).

Second, if the political decisions of this country indicate that small business is somehow especially meritorious, then policies should be undertaken to encourage small business. Such action should be direct, open, and handled through the Small Business Administration. Antitrust law, when used to protect small business from competition, can be harmful to consumers. The Clayton Act and the Robinson-Patman Act should be repealed.

Third, **section 2** of the **Sherman Act** and all antitrust laws other than section 1 of the Sherman Act should also be repealed. Section 2 has occasionally been used to break up effective, efficient firms and to saddle similar firms with costly antitrust suits. If economic bigness and concentration are major concerns of people, then the United States should adopt a policy on economic concentration. Allowing the courts to guess at what Senators Sherman, Edmunds, or Hoar intended under the Sherman Act is an inefficient method of dealing with the problems of concentration.

An economic concentration policy might take the following form. First, the market will be allowed to determine the optimal size of firms; the government will not file any suits to break up firms in an industry. Second, once an industry becomes concentrated (say, with a Herfindahl index of over 1000 or a four-firm concentration figure of 60+ percent), then all government policies designed to assist that industry will be repealed. A concentrated industry would be denied the protection of any tariffs or import quotas. Competition from foreign manufacturers appears to be a reasonable way of ensuring that large firms remain competitive. If goods can be produced more cheaply in other countries, we should import them and produce goods where the United States maintains a competitive advantage. In addition, once an industry becomes concentrated, all special tax systems or tax expenditures for this industry would be automatically repealed. This process should greatly simplify the tax code in the process. Third, if such a concentrated firm wishes to acquire another firm, either vertical, horizontal or conglomerate, it should absorb the **full costs** of such an acquisition, including the full cost of money borrowed (e.g., no tax deductions for interest payments).

The preceding brief outline of a concentration policy is not the only one nor may it even be the best one. The point of the argument is that if economic concentration is a concern, then the issue should be addressed directly. If the consensus of the governmental process is to encourage corporate growth, then corporate growth should be encouraged. If the consensus is to limit corporate growth, then measures to limit corporate growth should be instituted. If the consensus is to do neither, then concentration should be determined by the market. The question of economic concentration is as much a political question as an economic question, and it should be addressed in the political process. This is a far more reasonable way to consider economic concentration than the current system of antitrust laws.

SUMMARY

Who benefits from antitrust policy? The only clear beneficiary of antitrust policy is small business. The total benefit, however, is marginal; antitrust is unable to insulate these firms from the penalties of the marketplace. Antitrust policy imposes some costs on large business and consumers. Costs and benefits are generally minor because antitrust policy has failed to attain its goals.

In terms of the variables discussed in Chapter 2, why does antitrust policy benefit no one? (see Table 4.1.) The general environment has had little impact on the direction of antitrust policy. Technology (see McCraw, 1981) should influence antitrust policy if some large firms are more efficient than small firms, but it does not. Economics, especially the number of firms and the profit level in an industry, should be related to antitrust policy. The courts' emphasis on intent, however, has generally removed such structural economic factors from antitrust policy.

The explanation for the state of antitrust policy lies in the political environment and in bureaucratic motivations. Antitrust policy is sometimes salient so that changes in the law have been enacted in response to political demands. The Populists of the 1890s, the labor unions and businesses in 1914, and the small businesses of 1938 all pressed Congress for relief from some type of oppression. Broadening the scope of antitrust can be attributed to Congress. Presidents, in turn, have emphasized and de-emphasized antitrust. The Nixon, Ford, and Carter administrations increased antitrust activity; the Reagan administration dropped many of these suits. President Clinton's antitrust head Anne Bingaman has been more assertive on mergers but has yet to redirect overall policy. Presidential encouragement appears important in stimulating antitrust activities. Through the appointment process, presidents can have a major impact on the direction of antitrust policy.

Table 4.1   A Summary of Antitrust Policy

Economics	
Ease of entry	Vary
Number of firms	Varies
Profits	Vary
Technology	
Complexity	Varies
Stability	Varies
Substitutes	Vary
Subsystem	
Bureaucracy	Moderate
Industry coalition	Weak
Nonindustry coalition (critics)	Moderate
Bureaucratic resources:	
Expertise	Moderate
Cohesion	Low/High
Leadership	Moderate
Legislative authority:	
Goals	Vague
Coverage	Limited
Sanctions	Weak
Procedures	Weak
Involvement of Macropolitical Actors	
Congress	Moderate
President	Moderate
Courts	High

These political forces are tempered by the bureaucracy. Although antitrust bureaucracies are fairly responsive to presidential initiatives, they also reflect the norms of the economics and legal professions. Trial experience is important to these bureaucrats, especially experience where the attorney can demonstrate his or her talents (Weaver, 1977;

Katzman, 1980). As a result, price-fixing cases now dominate antitrust policy because they generate simple cases and fit the predominant economic philosophy.

Bureaucracies have been allowed discretion in antitrust because it is a complex, legalistic area. The bureaucracy, however, has failed to dominate the subsystem because the bureaucracies have only moderate expertise and lack cohesion and often leadership. With vague goals and procedures that require court action for enforcement, the bureaucracy must respond to, rather than resist, the pressures from the political environment. The lack of strong advocacy coalitions, however, means that at times there will be no environmental pressures.

Finally, the courts remain a major policy force in this area. Antitrust policy is implemented through the courts; even the FTC usually ends up in court after its administrative procedures are exhausted. Case-by-case resolution means that application is uneven and policy is inconsistent.

In total, antitrust policy may be a symbolic policy. Antitrust evokes strong images of Teddy Roosevelt busting trusts. Despite the inability of antitrust policy to produce economic deconcentration, antitrust advocates often retain this idealized goal. In practice, however, the policy rarely benefits the general public, individual consumers, or anyone other than antitrust lawyers and an occasional small business.

Chapter 5
The Revitalization of the Federal Trade Commission

Mark Silbergeld[1]

No agency better illustrates the "swing of the regulatory pendulum" than the Federal Trade Commission (FTC). Rising from the ashes of a devastated agency in 1969, the FTC became the most aggressive advocate of consumer protection in the federal government by 1977. It also became the major target for the forces opposing consumer protection and the major battle ground after the defeat of the proposed Agency for Consumer Advocacy in 1978. By the early 1980s, however, it was frozen in a state of virtual regulatory cryogenesis imposed by two Reagan-appointed chairmen. Then, in 1989, a Bush-appointed moderate started a process of slow thaw. It remains to be seen whether the pendulum will ever swing back more than half way.

THE SUBSYSTEM

This examination of the subsystem of the Federal Trade Commission includes an examination of the agency, its advocacy coalitions, and its environment.

The Agency

The Federal Trade Commission is an independent commission charged with regulating unfair and deceptive trade practices; it also has antitrust functions, and these were covered

---

[1]Mark Silbergeld is the director of the Washington office of Consumers Union, a nonprofit consumer organization. Consumers Union publishes *Consumer Reports*, a monthly magazine with approximately 5 million members. He received his law degree from Washington University. Before joining Consumers Union, Silbergeld worked as an attorney for the Federal Trade Commission as well as for consumer advocate Ralph Nader's national Public Interest Research Group. Silbergeld has extensive experience in a wide range of policy issues, including international trade, federal trade regulation, and federal consumer health and safety regulation. He frequently testifies before committees of the United States Congress and participates in federal administrative proceedings.

in the previous chapter. The Federal Trade Commission has jurisdiction over virtually all industries for the purpose of ensuring against **unfair and deceptive practices** in the marketplace. The agency is headed by a chairman appointed by the president and confirmed by the U.S. Senate for a seven-year term. There are four other commissioners appointed and confirmed by the same process and a majority of three is required to take formal legal action against a company or a prevalent business practice. The activities of concern in this chapter are housed in the FTC's **Bureau of Consumer Protection** (Hinich and Staelin, 1980: 76). The FTC's budget in fiscal year 1994 was almost $96 million. The agency in fiscal year 1994 had only about 950 employees, as contrasted with 1,300 in fiscal year 1986.

The FTC of the 1970s attracted many young consumer activists as employees. Reflecting the values of these persons, the agency developed a high level of cohesion and a consensus for vigorous regulation. It undertook initiatives that had social as well as traditional FTC-regulation aspects, such as the effects on children and family purchasing decisions of advertising during **children's television programming**. These activities were cut short abruptly by the agency's Senate oversight committee (sometimes called a "watchdog committee") in 1980. The FTC leadership during the eight-year Reagan administration shelved all such "cutting-edge" activity, focusing its consumer protection resources instead on hard-core fraud and deception and the competitive aspects of marketing restraints, especially with respect to professional services. It also launched early initiatives to limit its own authority over advertising and marketing practices, but the same Senate committee that had stalled the social initiatives of the 1970s refused to squash the FTC's basic legal powers. During this era, the agency also gained the enmity of many state consumer protection authorities, often to the point of open warfare. During the Bush administration and carrying into the early Clinton era, the agency made no further efforts to clip its own wings, but seldom found a majority among the five commissioners to take bold or controversial actions. This period did see a mending of the FTC's fences with state officials.

Advocacy Coalitions

Because the FTC regulates many different industries, the industry advocacy coalition varies from issue to issue. The business interests that have most effectively in the past decade resisted the reinstitution of a more vigorous FTC are the large national advertisers and the advertising agencies. Their case before Congress for limiting FTC's power over advertising practices has been assisted by the National Association of Manufacturers and the U.S. Chamber of Commerce.

Advocacy coalitions calling for more vigorous FTC action also vary from issue to issue. These often include such national organizations as the Center for Science in the Public Interest (which would like more FTC focus on **nutritional claims in advertising**), the American Association of Retired Persons, Consumer Federation of America, Consumers Union, and the National Consumers League. The National Association of Attorneys General and various state attorneys general also have frequently demanded bolder FTC action.

Environment

Because the FTC regulates a variety of industries, the economic and technological environment cannot be described in detail. Some industries have numerous firms and relatively easy entry (e.g., used-car dealers, commercial firms that purchase portfolios of consumer debt). Others have few firms with high barriers to entry (e.g., cereal manufacturers, soft drink manufacturers). Some affected businesses have complex and unstable technologies (e.g., oil companies) whereas others do not (e.g., funeral directors). Each FTC issue takes place in a slightly different economic and technological environment.

The Early Performance of the FTC

In the 1960s the FTC was among the least effective regulatory agencies in the federal government. Its reputation for ineffectiveness dated back to the 1920s, when its close ties to business were established. In fact, the famous court case Humphrey's Executor v. U.S. (1935), concerned Franklin Roosevelt's effort to remove William Humphrey, a notoriously probusiness commissioner, from the FTC, and it established the principle that independent regulatory commissions were to be independent of presidential control. Even Congress recognized the FTC's orientation. In 1938 the FTC rather than the FDA was given authority over drug advertising under the belief that the FTC would be more sympathetic to advertisers (see earlier).

In 1969, a group of law students under the auspices of Ralph Nader (they were termed "**Nader's Raiders**") released a highly critical report on the Federal Trade Commission (see Cox, et al., 1969). The Commission and its employees were characterized as incompetent, lacking commitment, and often absent. The Commission had poor personnel practices, failed to set priorities for agency action, and did not even have any full-time staff assigned to monitor deceptive advertising on television. Blaming Federal Trade Commission Chairman Paul Rand Dixon for these problems, the study charged Dixon preferred mediocre attorneys from southern law schools to those from prestigious eastern schools. The Nader report suggested that the best thing Dixon could do for the FTC would be to resign (Feldman, 1976: 68).

The Nader report, written in part by President Nixon's future son-in-law Edward Cox, received widespread publicity. In response, Nixon asked the American Bar Association (ABA) to conduct a similar evaluation of the FTC. In September 1969 the ABA released its report with findings similar to those of the Nader report. The FTC was termed "a failure on many counts" with "many instances of incompetence in the agency, particularly in senior staff positions" (Report of the ABA, 1969).

The Revitalization of the FTC

Nixon then appointed Caspar Weinberger to head the FTC. Although Weinberger remained at the Federal Trade Commission for only seven months, he had a lasting impact on the agency. Weinberger reorganized the FTC, ostensibly for efficiency reasons but probably to justify his firing many senior people in the agency (Clarkson and Muris, 1981: 4). The two FTC bureaus, **Competition and Consumer Protection**, were then staffed with aggressive consumer advocates. With a massive turnover in agency personnel, Weinberger was able to generate some enthusiasm for consumer protection and a cohesive spirit in the agency (Nadel, 1971: 40). A total of 18 of the top 31 FTC staff members were discharged in the Weinberger "reorganization" as were one-third of the mid-level and lower level staff (Clarkson and Muris, 1981: 4).

Weinberger's successor, Miles Kirkpatrick, the head of the American Bar Association committee that had reported to Nixon on the FTC, continued these policies. The Federal Trade Commission became known as the place for consumer activists to work. Congress encouraged the FTC in this regard; in hearing after hearing, members of Congress urged FTC commissioners to be aggressive in pursuit of consumer protection (see Pertschuk, 1982). Perhaps the most forceful effort of Congress on the FTC's behalf was the Magnuson-Moss Act of 1974. The **Magnuson-Moss Act** set standards for warranties and also granted the FTC authority to issue **industry-wide rules**. In addition, the Supreme Court augmented the FTC's powers when it held that the FTC could act if advertising were **unfair** (a less strict standard to prove than the charge of deception on which the FTC usually relied; see FTC v. Sperry and Hutchinson, 1972).

The FTC pursued its congressional mandate aggressively. In 1975 after the passage of Magnuson-Moss, the FTC announced 13 proposed rules (LaBarbera, 1977: 6). Unlike past FTC efforts that were designed not to offend anyone, the post-Magnuson-Moss efforts affected powerful economic interests. Professional regulation programs were targeted at price fixing by doctors, optometrists, and dentists. A major study of television advertising directed at children (the **"kidvid"** study) was started. An antitrust suit was filed against the major oil companies, and a similar suit was filed against cereal manufacturers, using the unique charge that the four largest cereal producers were a **shared monopoly** (see Chapter 4).

The FTC issued a series of rules affecting major industries. In 1975 rules governing the **holder-in-due-course of a note** (e.g., the person who purchases a loan) and mail-order businesses were issued. In 1978 the FTC issued rules covering franchises, vocational schools, and eyeglasses. The year 1979 saw rules on octane posting for gasoline, R-values for insulation, and energy efficiency ratings for appliances. In all these cases, rules established regulation where none had existed and did so in the interests of the consumer. The FTC eyeglasses rule, for example, eliminated restrictions on advertising eyeglasses and required that optometrists give patents a copy of their prescription so that they could shop around for the best deal. The rule was widely conceded to have reduced eyeglass prices. Perhaps equally important was the effort to make sure that the consumer viewpoint was presented in the rulemaking process. Under Chairman Michael Pertschuk (the former staff director of the Senate committee, chaired by Senator Warren Magnuson, that watchdogged the FTC), the FTC began to **reimburse the expenses** of consumer groups which participated in rulemaking proceedings.

The Anticonsumer Backlash

Rarely in the history of bureaucracy has so small an agency provoked the ire of as many powerful interests in as short a time as the FTC did from 1974 to 1977. The quick rise of opposition to the FTC's consumer activities was the function of three variables.

First, the industry-wide rules changed dramatically the way businesses had to deal with the FTC. No longer was business subjected to a case-by-case adjudication before being penalized. And even worse from the business perspective, the ability to rely on the FTC for a favorable decision (as was the case in the 1960s) no longer existed. Several industries were subjected to real federal regulation for the first time. Second, the Commerce Committees of the House and Senate changed significantly between 1972 and 1977. Both committees went from being very liberal to being more conservative with the large turnover in the members of Congress (Weingast and Moran, 1982). No longer could the FTC rely on the protection of senators like Warren Magnuson. Third, Carter's FTC chairperson, Michael Pertschuk, was an aggressive consumer advocate who, in hindsight, concedes that he did not read well the shift in the political attitudes of the Congress. His actions and statements did not calm the fears of businesses and members of Congress concerned about the FTC (Gottron, 1982: 81).

The effort to reign in the FTC centered in Congress. Industries concerned about the FTC quite naturally took their complaints to their member of Congress and sought relief. So strong was the disagreement concerning the FTC and what to do about it that Congress was unable to pass legislation authorizing the agency's budget from 1977 to 1980. The agency was funded via **continuing resolutions**. A major effort to restrict the FTC in 1979 failed, not because the legislators could not agree to limit the FTC but because they had a dispute over the use of the legislative veto (see Chapter 2). Led by Representative Elliot Levitas, the House tried to subject FTC's rules to a **legislative veto**. Senate opposition to the proposed veto killed a bill that would have significantly limited the FTC.

The 1980 session of Congress saw a formidable coalition of interests seeking restrictions on the FTC. Included in the coalition were the American Medical Association (AMA), the American Bar Association (both concerned about FTC efforts to encourage competition in these areas), the insurance industry (an FTC investigation), the television industry advertisers (kidvid), automobile dealers (the used-car rule), drug manufacturers (an over-the-counter advertising study), Sunkist (the target of an antitrust suit), and Formica (the FTC had petitioned to eliminate Formica as a trademark). These forces were led by the Chamber of Commerce and the National Association of Manufacturers. The professional associations alone contributed over $1 million in 1980 to congressional campaigns (Wines, 1982b: 993).

Opposed by consumer groups, the FTC, and the Carter White House, the anti-FTC coalition was able to pass a bill euphemistically called the Federal Trade Commission Improvements Act. The 1980 bill was far more moderate than the 1979 effort and led Pertschuk to conclude that the agency had weathered the attack (Pertschuk, 1982). The act effectively ended the FTC's insurance investigation, limited the use of funding for intervenors (e.g., consumer groups), restricted the kidvid study to questions of deception rather than questions of unfairness, required the FTC to engage in a form of cost-benefit analysis before issuing rules, prohibited the FTC from petitioning the Patents and Trademarks Office to repeal trademarks, and subjected FTC rules to a two-house legislative veto. Although the FTC was limited, the end result was a compromise that no one liked. It was denounced by FTC supporter Howard Metzenbaum as well as by FTC critic Jesse Helms (*Congressional Quarterly Almanac*, 1980: 236).

The Reagan Federal Trade Commission

Unlike regulatory agencies that are not independent commissions, the FTC changed its policy gradually after the election of Ronald Reagan. In part, this reflected the president's limited ability to appoint new commissioners. Economist James Miller III, briefly the head of the regulatory relief task force at the powerful Office of Management and Budget, was named to chair the FTC in September, 1981. Pertschuk remained on as a commissioner.

Under Miller, the FTC made a series of decisions to indicate it was retreating from its aggressive consumer protection policies. Miller recruited numerous economists to the FTC so that he could rely on others with similar views to implement policy (Wines, 1982b: 992). Included among the personnel was Timothy J. Muris, a longtime FTC critic, to head the Bureau of Consumer Protection. During 1981 the FTC terminated its study of over-the-counter drug advertising, dropped its study of the automobile industry that it had begun in 1976, withdrew its shared monopoly case against the cereal manufacturers, and closed down the famous kidvid study (see Kosters, 1982: 15-18). Approximately one-fourth of the FTC's pending cases were dropped by the Miller FTC in 1981 alone (Wines, 1982b: 993).

As an illustration of the reliance of the Miller FTC on different remedies for market ills, the **survival suit case** is exemplary. The case involved hundreds of "survival suits" that had been sold to the government and private buyers to protect persons involved in ocean accidents. The suits leaked, and repairs would have cost no more than a few cents per suit. The FTC decided in December 1981 not to order a recall of the suits. The reasoning was that the free market would handle the problem because the relatives of drowning victims would sue the manufacturer for damages. After an investigation by the House Energy and Commerce Subcommittee on Oversight and Investigations publicized this case, the manufacturer voluntarily recalled the survival suits (Wines, 1983c: 223).

The Congressional Fight Continues

The congressional fight over the FTC did not end in 1980. Those who failed to achieve their goals continued to press their cases. Some of this battle centered on the legislative veto. In 1982 the FTC issued its long awaited **used-car rule**. The rule, a watered-down version of earlier proposals, basically required used-car dealers to disclose any major defects in a vehicle if known and to disclose any warranties on the vehicle. In overwhelming votes in both houses of Congress, the rule was vetoed May 26, 1982. This marked the first use of the legislative veto against a regulation issued by an independent regulatory commission (*Congressional Quarterly Almanac*, 1982: 346).

Another rule, this one concerning practices of funeral directors, was submitted to Congress by the FTC in late 1982. The rule survived a veto when it was not brought to a vote in either house. The legal status of the used-car rule remained in doubt. Consumers Union challenged the veto as unconstitutional; but before the Supreme Court heard this challenge, the veto was declared unconstitutional in INS v. Chadha (see Chapter 2).

The 1982 fight over reauthorizing the FTC involved many of the same political forces as the first fight. The move against the FTC was headed by Senator Robert Kasten, then the chairman of the Commerce Subcommittee on Consumers. Kasten introduced legislation that placed 14 specific restrictions on the FTC. The major limitations were to restrict the FTC's jurisdiction to **deceptive advertising** (as opposed to unfair advertising), to exempt agricultural cooperatives from the FTC's control, and to eliminate FTC jurisdiction over professions.

The motivations behind the coalition supporting the Kasten bill were fairly obvious. In March 1982 the FTC won a Supreme Court case upholding its regulation of physicians; the FTC prohibited this instance of **price-fixing** (setting minimum fee schedules) and voided state prohibitions of advertising (AMA v. FTC, 1982). To build support for their cause, the American Medical Association along with the organizations for dentists and optometrists contributed $832,000 to members of Congress, including $300,000 to members of the Commerce Committees.

The FTC did not wage its lobby efforts alone in 1982; business organizations that benefitted from the FTC's pro-consumer stance defended the organization. Leading the coalition was the American Nurses Association, which favored greater FTC control over the actions of physicians. Also part of the coalition were the National Association of Chain Drug Stores (which profited from generic drug sales and the ability to advertise prices for eyeglasses and drugs), and the American Association of Retired Persons. Perhaps most important was the Washington Business Group on Health, an organization representing 200 of the Fortune 500 companies. This organization supported the FTC because it felt the FTC was playing a role in holding down health care costs (which all these businesses were paying for in employee benefits). These business and professional groups were joined by the FTC's consumer group allies.

Although FTC opponents were successful in attaching restrictions to the FTC authorization, the FTC proponents were able to win the battle by a parliamentary ploy. By striking the FTC authorization from an omnibus authorization bill covering several agencies, the restrictions were not enacted. In the end of the session rush, the FTC was funded by continuing resolution.

The 1982 election with its Democratic landslide provided some relief for the FTC. Seven new Democrats were added to the House Commerce Committee, and Senator Ernest Hollings replaced Senator Wendell Ford as the ranking Democrat on the Senate Committee. Hollings was a general supporter of the FTC whereas Ford had been a strong critic (Wines, 1983c: 221). In this environment, the AMA and others who wanted additional limits on the FTC found fewer supporters for their position. The National Association of Manufacturers still wanted to limit FTC rules and remedies but decided to sit out the fight over regulation of the professions. As a result, the AMA struck a compromise with the FTC whereby the FTC could regulate only those activities of the professions that were not actively regulated by the states. Because state level regulation of professions does not actively regulate anything (see Chapter 3), this compromise was widely viewed as an FTC victory (Wines, 1983d: 859). As a portent of challenges to come, however, the American Bar Association at its 1983 annual meeting passed a resolution to seek an exemption from the FTC's jurisdiction (Wines, 1983e: 1832).

The deadlock over restrictions on FTC authority was not to end in the then-foreseeable future. The FTC has continued to operate on the basis of annual continuing resolutions, as the Senate and the House have remained deadlocked over the agency's "**unfairness**" authority as applied to advertising. However, the prospects for a further weakened FTC are not as great as they once were.

The FTC After Miller

Since James Miller's succession to the chairmanship of the FTC in 1981, the Federal Trade Commission has not been the aggressive regulator it was during the Pertschuk era and has not engaged in excursions into **social issues territory**. Miller left the FTC in October, 1985, to become Director of the Office of Management and Budget. His successor, Daniel Oliver, took office in 1986. He was a little-know federal official in the Department of Education with no specific FTC-related background or expertise, a cultivated similarity in appearance, speech and political philosophy to conservative journalist William F. Buckley and a seemingly greater interest in foreign and national cultural affairs than in trade regulation. If anything, the agency undertook even fewer initiatives under Oliver than it had under Miller. His departure in 1989 left little legacy except further stagnation.

Oliver was, in turn, succeeded by an appointee of President Reagan's successor, George Bush. The new Chairman, Janet D. Steiger, came to the FTC with a reputation as the hard-nosed chairman of the U.S. Postal Rate Commission. At the outset, though tactfully refraining from direct criticism of her predecessors, she declared the FTC back in the business of consumer protection. Perhaps bowing to the ever-vigilant Senate Commerce Committee, she promised to exercise self restraint. But, she noted, "self restraint isn't a euphemism for comatose." The chairman often spoke of a more aggressive consumer protection policy and the agency under her aegis came to be viewed as more active, certainly a marked departure from the approach of the Miller-Oliver regimes. Still, this was a middle of the road approach. The biggest issue of the Steiger era has been **delay** among the five commissioners in dealing with staff recommendations for action. This was in great part a symptom of **ideological deadlock**, marked by a search of Chairman Steiger on any given issue for two additional votes among the other four commissioners to take positive action. Finally, in 1994, the commissioners adopted a **deadlines policy** with self-imposed limits on how long the commissioners would allow themselves to decide on staff recommendations for action. Still, the actions taken could not generally be described as more than run of the mill consumer protection—important without a doubt, but never bold enough to strike controversy. Most characteristic was the agency's failure in June, 1994, to gain three votes among the commissioners in support of a staff recommendation to sue the R.J. Reynolds Tobacco Co. over its "Joe Camel" ads, a long-running series of ads featuring prolifically-smoking cartoon camels which consumers advocates strongly argue and studies tend to confirm are aimed at underage smokers. The FTC was virtually the only federal agency with jurisdiction over tobacco products not to challenge that industry.

Summary and Conclusion

The Federal Trade Commission has seen many incarnations over the years. Ranging from its tradition of being an industry bedfellow during the 1960s, to a liberal champion of consumer protection in the 1970s, and virtual inactivity in the 1980s, the regulatory ability of the FTC has truly spanned a wide spectrum. The future of the FTC remains to be written and will bear the stamp of many influences. Figure 5.1 depicts those influences that are likely to most affect the efficacy of the Federal Trade Commission.

Figure 5.1   Influences Affecting the Efficacy of the Federal Trade Commission

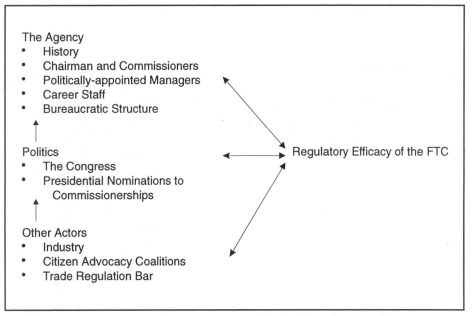

Table 5.1 provides a summary of Federal Trade Commission regulation. As the chapter outlines, perhaps one of the most important influences over the regulatory ability of the FTC is the impact of macropolitical actors. The president sets the tone for the goals and policy of the agency through nominations to commissionerships. Even more importantly, the actions of Congress can serve to limit the agency's pursuit of its statutory goals. History has shown that the actions of these actors has the power to make or break agency programs and acts as a barometer for the climate towards consumer protection regulation.

Of course, these macropolitical actors are affected from forces within the subsystem. Since the FTC serves as a regulator of many industry practices, it follows that as the FTC cracks down on industry practices these interests act to stem the tide of sweeping reforms. A whisper in the ear of Congress has gone a long way to check the activity of the FTC. Other distinct forces have included nonindustry groups and citizen advocacy coalitions

Table 5.1   A Summary of the Federal Trade Commission

Economics

Ease of entry	NA
Number of firms	Many
Profits	NA

Technology

Complexity	Moderate
Stability	Very
Substitutes	High

Subsystem

Bureau control	Moderate
Industry coalition	Strong
Nonindustry coalition	Moderate
Bureaucratic resources:	
Expertise	Moderate
Cohesion	High
Leadership	Varies
Legislative authority:	
Goals	General
Coverage	Most
Sanctions	Moderate
Procedures	Moderate

Impact of Macropolitical Actors

Congress	Strong
President	Strong
Courts	Moderate

who have traditionally stood by the FTC in its aim to adequately protect consumers in the marketplace and/or demanded its strengthened vitality.

The importance of these actors and influences on the bureaucratic process and resources of the agency should in no way be underestimated. As these forces have lobbied for or against an active FTC, they have affected the leadership and expertise that the agency attracts. It has been argued that in the period leading up to its revitalization in the late 1960s that FTC employees lacked commitment and were in many cases mediocre if not incompetent in their ability to fulfill their consumer protection mandate. This situation was reversed in the 1970s when after the turnaround in the agency's mission and leadership the FTC started to attract consumer activists and those highly committed to spurring the agency into action. The agency's goals have only been as good as the will of its employees to pursue it. In fiscal 1994, for example, the FTC brought 33 law-enforcement actions, the highest number of cases since 1980.

The future of the agency's regulatory policy remains to be seen. In 1994, the Clinton administration faced the prospect of two vacancies in commissionerships; Christine Anne Varney and Robert Pitofsky were named to these positions. Janet Steiger's moderate tenure as chairman of the FTC is slated to end in 1995. Her expected replacement as chair, former FTC Commissioner and Bureau of Consumer Protection Director Robert Pitofsky, a distinguished antitrust professor and academic administrator since he left the FTC, will have the opportunity to guide the many forces driving the Federal Trade Commission into the next century.

Chapter 6
Regulating Agriculture

Kenneth J. Meier

Agricultural regulation is a microcosm of regulation in the entire economy. Parts of agriculture are highly regulated to the point of resembling **government-sanctioned cartels** (e.g., tobacco) whereas other parts operate almost completely free from government regulation (e.g., poultry). Within agriculture all six methods of regulation noted in Chapter 1: (1) price setting, (2) licensing, (3) standard setting, (4) direct allocation of resources, (5) subsidies, and (6) promotion of competition—are used. Regulation sets prices either by putting a floor under prices (e.g., wheat and feed grains) or by specifying wholesale prices (milk). The equivalent of licensing exists when producers are granted **allotments** to grow and sell a certain amount of product or plant on a given acreage (e.g., tobacco, some marketing orders). Standards are set for such things as oranges marketed as fresh or almonds produced for domestic consumption. Direct allocation of resources is used when the government builds soil conservation projects for individual farms. Subsidies in the form of **target price supports** provide income to numerous farmers. To promote "fair" competition, farmers are urged to form cooperatives and market their products directly.

This chapter examines a variety of economic regulatory policies that affect animal and plant production, the traditional core of agriculture. Other regulatory policies that affect agriculture such as environmental protection and food-processing safety are discussed elsewhere. After an overview of the industry is presented, the economic, technical, and political environment will be examined, followed by an analysis of economic regulatory policies affecting agriculture.

THE INDUSTRY

As is true of financial institutions, agriculture is not one industry, but several. The production of fresh oranges, for example, is an industry totally separate from the production of eggs or the growing of wheat. Farms and the types of commodities produced on them are determined in part by natural conditions such as soil characteristics and weather and by the preferences of individual farmers. As a result, some agricultural industries can serve as substitutes for each other (e.g., soybeans and peanuts grow under similar conditions), but complete **substitutability** is not possible. Orange groves cannot be turned into wheat farms without great difficulty and would have only a marginal chance of success.

The Agricultural Sector

Despite the tremendous variety of production within the industry, a general description of the agriculture sector is possible. The United States has approximately 2.1 million farms (Economic Research Service[ERS] 1993, 16). The number of farms is declining at the rate of about 1.4 percent per year. Although this rate of decline (for the 1990s) was less than the rate for the 1960s (2.7 percent), it was higher than the decline during the 1970s (1.1 percent). Concomitant with the decline in the number of farms has been an increase in the size of individual farms. Although farm size varies dramatically depending on what is produced on the farm, the average size of farms has doubled to 466 acres since 1950.

In 1991 agriculture had sales of $190 billion and assets of $842 billion, dwarfing the size of most other industries in the United States (ERS 1993, 14). Sales within the industry, however, are not equally distributed. Some 42,000 farms (approximately 2 percent of the total) with sales of over $500,000 produced 43 percent of the total farm output. The smallest 59 percent of the farms (over 1.2 million farms) produced only 5 percent of the farm output (ERS 1993, 69).

Economist J. B. Penn (1981: 36) divides American **farms** into three categories. The largest category includes farms with less than $5,000 in sales; this 44 percent is characterized by off-farm income that greatly exceeds on-farm income. Penn refers to these farms as **rural residences** rather than farms. One-third of all farms are classified as **small farms** with sales between $5,000 and $40,000; these farms provide a marginal existence for full-time farmers. Finally, the largest 22 percent of farms, those with sales in excess of $40,000, are termed **primary farms** and account for three-fourths of farm output.

Individual Industries in Agriculture

Agriculture produces in excess of 300 products, and describing each of these industries is beyond the scope of this chapter. This section will briefly note several farm industries that fall into four general categories of regulation.

First, the **major regulated crops**—wheat (4.1 percent of total farm sales), feed grains (11.4 percent), cotton (3.3 percent), and soybeans and other oil crops (7.5 percent)—are the most visible regulated agricultural products. These crops are regulated by price support programs and occasionally by an effort to restrict the acreage planted. All these crops are not regulated equally, however, with wheat permitted high price supports whereas soybeans are supported below their market price.

Second, three **minor crops** are heavily regulated to the point of being produced by government-sponsored cartels. Tobacco (1.7 percent of total farm sales), peanuts (0.7 percent), and sugar (both beet and cane 1.2 percent) are supported by government payments to processors and producer associations, which, in turn, pass these benefits through to individual producers. These arrangements have the economic characteristics of cartels with high prices and production limitations. As an example, tobacco can be grown only on land authorized to grow tobacco; the crop can be sold only in government-sponsored warehouses. Prices are maintained by the government's bidding the support price for all lots of tobacco (see Gardner, 1981a: 22).

Each **cartel crop** has some unique characteristics. Tobacco is highly labor-intensive; allotments to grow tobacco are restrictive and profitable. Peanuts are a crop with little economic value because for most uses soybeans can be substituted for peanuts, and soybeans are generally cheaper. Sugar is protected at well above world market rates by import quotas to prevent cheap foreign sugar from driving domestic sugar producers out of business.

Third, the **market-order controlled crops** include fruits, nuts, vegetables, and milk. A **marketing order** (see further on) is a government-sanctioned agreement among producers to provide for orderly marketing of a product and may include a variety of supply reduction mechanisms. In some parts of the country, fruits, nuts, and vegetables (12.7 percent of total farm production) are controlled by market orders whereas the same crop might not be controlled in another part. The California grapefruit crop, for example, is under a federal market order, but the Arizona grapefruit crop is not (see Anderson, 1982). The dairy industry (10.8 percent of sales) is also controlled via market orders, but these orders are supplemented by a complex subsidy system and federal government purchases of surplus products to support milk prices. All market order commodities are generally associated with large producer cooperatives that administer the marketing order (e.g., Sunkist, Sunsweet, Blue Diamond, Land O'Lakes).

Fourth, the **nonregulated portion of agriculture** includes livestock and its related functions such as the production of fodder. Such industries as beef cattle (23.7 percent of farm sales), hogs (6.6 percent), and poultry and eggs (9.0 percent) are subjected to little economic regulation by the federal government although there are some minor import quotas.

This brief discussion of the agriculture industry illustrates that the degree of federal economic regulation varies considerably from one farm sector to another. The reasons for this variation in the stringency of regulation will be discussed in the sections on regulatory politics.

Advocacy Coalitions

Agriculture learned early that influencing government was essential to its well-being. Numerous political organizations exist and can be divided into two groups—the general farm organizations and the commodity organizations. **General farm organizations** try to represent all farmers and speak for the entire agricultural sector. Five general farm organizations have attained some degree of political influence.

AMERICAN FARM BUREAU FEDERATION

The largest general farm organization with over 3.9 million members is the **American Farm Bureau Federation** (Browning 1992b, 452). The Farm Bureau was created through the efforts of the **USDA's Cooperative Extension Service**. Each county extension agent created a local farm bureau of progressive farmers to assist him or her in spreading the word about research and education. The Extension Service encouraged farmers through the local bureaus to adopt new agricultural techniques. These local farm bureaus were eventually joined to create state organizations, and in 1920 a national organization was formed (Tweeten, 1979a: 74). The Farm Bureau remains a federation with control by state units. The Farm Bureau is the most conservative of the general farm organizations, supporting free-market approaches to agriculture and allying itself with the Republican party. The organization's membership is dominated by Southern cotton farmers and Midwestern corn and hog producers (Anderson, Brady, and Bullock, 1977: 364).

NATIONAL FARMERS UNION

The **National Farmers Union (NFU)** is a more liberal farm organization that supports active government intervention on behalf of agriculture. It has strong ties to the Democratic party and often forms coalitions with organized labor (Anderson, Brady, and Bullock, 1977: 365). The NFU's base of support is among Midwestern wheat farmers, and it has about 250,000 members (Browning 1992b, 452). The NFU was greatly assisted in organizing by the Farm Security Administration during the depression (see Baldwin, 1968).

THE GRANGE

The Grange is the oldest general farm organization and can claim some credit for numerous reforms in the nineteenth century, including the Sherman Antitrust Act and the Interstate Commerce Act. In recent times, the Grange (with 300,000+ members; Tweeten, 1979a: 64) has not been aggressive politically and is not considered a major forces in agriculture policy. The Grange is composed of fruit, vegetable, dairy, and poultry farmers (Anderson, Brady, and Bullock, 1977: 365).

NATIONAL FARMERS ORGANIZATION

The **National Farmers Organization (NFO)** began as a protest movement by marginal farmers in the Midwest. It sponsored strikes and holding actions in the 1950s and 1960s in efforts to raise the prices paid to farmers for their products. The NFO has since developed into a traditional farm lobby organization with approximately 200,000 members.

AMERICAN AGRICULTURE MOVEMENT

The **American Agriculture Movement (AAM)** is the most recent general farm organization to grow out of a protest movement. Started in Colorado in 1977, the AAM sponsored farmer strikes and used tractorcades to dramatize the plight of farmers squeezed by low prices and high costs. Because AAM generally lacks a strong organizational structure, its permanence on the scene as a general farm organization is open to question (see Browne 1988).

COMMODITY ORGANIZATIONS

The general farm organizations are supplemented and surpassed by **commodity organizations** that represent farmers' interests in regard to a single commodity. Commodity organizations are necessary because different farm sectors often disagree on agriculture policy goals, thus preventing the general farm organizations from advocating any position. For example, grain farmers advocate high price supports for grains whereas livestock producers who feed grain to their animals favor lower price supports. Similarly, grain farmers who are heavily dependent on exports favor free trade whereas livestock producers and sugar producers favor import limitations. Because agricultural policy issues are decided on a commodity level, commodity organizations have gained influence at the expense of general farm organizations.

Almost every commodity is represented by a commodity organization. Among the more successful commodity organizations is the National Milk Producers Federation (NMPF). The NMPF is composed of dairy farmers and the giant cooperatives that market milk. It plays a major role in determining price support policies for dairy products (see Guth, 1980); and the giant coops such as American Milk Producers, Inc., Mid-America Dairymen, and Dairymen, Inc., are major contributors to political campaigns. The NMPF is not encumbered by the interests of nondairy farmers when pressing its policy goals. Among the other commodity organizations are the American National Cattlemen's Association, the National Wheat Growers Association, the National Turkey Federation, the National Cotton Council, the American Sugar Cane League, and the National Wool Growers Association. In 1981 and 1982 agricultural political action committees (mostly representing commodity groups) made $3.9 million in contributions to political candidates, about 5 percent of all political action committee or PAC contributions (Hagstrom, 1984: 422).

AGRIBUSINESS INTERESTS

Agribusiness interests represent themselves and work thorough trade associations on agricultural policy issues (see Browne 1988, 109-29). Agribusiness interests include traditional agricultural firms such as Cargill (a grain exporter), IBP (a beef packer), and Archer-Daniels-Midland (a grain processor). Less traditional agricultural interests such as food processors (e.g., Mars, Coca-Cola) are also active in agricultural policy issues.

Although agricultural interests are diverse enough to fight among themselves, they also have frequent opposition from the **ex/al groups** who are concerned with the externalities and alternatives in agricultural policy (Hadwiger 1982). Ex/al interests include environmental groups, conservation groups, alternative agriculture groups (e.g., The Agribusiness Accountability Project), and hunger groups (see Browne 1988, 130-49).

THE REGULATORY AGENCIES

Economic regulation of agriculture is conducted within the U.S. Department of Agriculture (USDA). Created in 1862, USDA has grown to 123,000 employees with an annual budget of $54 billion for fiscal year 1991. Employees of the Department of Agriculture generally do not think of themselves as regulators; rather, they perceive their role as assisting the farmer to receive fair prices and incomes. Recruited from the same state **land-grant colleges** of agriculture that produce the nation's farmers and agribusiness executives, USDA employees are technocrats with specific skills related to agriculture (see Talbot and Hadwiger, 1968: 240 ff; Hadwiger 1992, 284). Consistent with the assistance rather than the regulatory view, the department is decentralized with well over 90 percent of its employees located outside the Washington, D.C., area. Every county in the United States, including the totally urban ones, has at least one USDA office. Decision making in USDA is also decentralized, with the power located in the individual bureaus and the field units.

Tools to Regulate the Price of Agricultural Goods

The Department of Agriculture uses five specific tools to regulate the price of agricultural goods.

THE LOAN

First, the most commonly used tool to regulate prices is the **loan**. Numerous crops can be used as collateral for loans from the Department of Agriculture. Rather than sell his or her wheat, a farmer may choose to use it as collateral for a loan. Such action makes sense if the price of wheat is less than the loan rate and prospects for an increase in price are promising. Agricultural loans are **nonrecourse loans** so that the farmer may default on the loan with no penalty, and the government then keeps the crop. If prices rise, the farmer normally redeems the wheat and sells it; if not, he or she defaults on the loan. The loan rate becomes a **price floor** for a commodity because no farmer would sell a commodity for less than the government would loan.

TARGET PRICES

Second, **target prices** and **deficiency payments** are used to regulate prices and increase farm income. Crops such as wheat, corn, and cotton have target prices. With a hypothetical target price of say $2.30 a bushel for corn, for example, the system works as follows: The farmer sells his crop for whatever the market will bring. If the crop is sold for $2.10, the government pays the farmer $.20 a bushel so that the farmer receives the target price in income. Crops sold at prices higher than the target price receive no deficiency payments.

LIMIT PRODUCTION

Third, for some crops the USDA has authority to limit production through restricting the number of acres planted or the amount of the crop that can be sold. Use of **mandatory quotas** or **allotments** is not common. Tobacco is regulated in this manner as are some fruits, nuts, and vegetables under marketing orders that limit production (see later).

SET-ASIDE PROGRAM

Fourth, in times of great over-production, the department can use set-aside programs. Essentially a **set-aside program** pays farmers not to grow crops on a portion of their land. In 1984 the department established a program for the first time to pay dairy farmers if they decreased milk production (Wines, 1983h). Set-asides are often used in combination with loans and target prices because only those farmers who participate in set-asides are eligible for loans and deficiency payments. Although such links create incentives to participate in set-aside programs, set-asides are voluntary. The effectiveness of the set-aside programs as voluntary programs that rely on incentives (discussed later) may indicate how incentives programs would work in environmental regulation or workplace safety regulation.

IMPORT CONTROLS

Fifth, **import controls** are used to support the price of domestic production by limiting competition from foreign producers. Domestic sugar prices are kept high in this manner by limiting total imports via a series of national quota systems. Dairy products and, to a lesser extent, beef are also affected by import quotas.

USING REGULATORY TOOLS IN COMBINATION

Regulatory policies often combine a variety of these tools simultaneously. Dairy products, for example, are regulated by target prices, set asides (in the 1984 production year), and import quotas. Each commodity is regulated in slightly unique ways by an administrative unit that is in either the Agricultural Stabilization and Conservation Service or the Agricultural Marketing Service.

Agricultural Stabilization and Conservation Service

The **Agricultural Stabilization and Conservation Service (ASCS)** is the department's main price support regulator. It operates programs for wheat, corn, cotton, soybeans, peanuts, rice, tobacco, milk, wool, mohair, barley, oats, sugar beets, sugar cane, sorghum, rye, and honey. The specific mechanisms for supporting prices for these commodities are set by law; but normally loans, target prices, and set-asides are involved. ASCS programs are administered in the field. The secretary of agriculture appoints a committee to oversee each state program, and each county program is handled via an elected farmer committee supported by ASCS staff. The ASCS operates in conjunction with the Commodity Credit Corporation, a government corporation authorized to make loans and accept grain as collateral.

Agricultural Marketing Service

The **Agricultural Marketing Service (AMS)** is a multifunctional agency with control over agricultural marketing orders. A **marketing order** is a government-sponsored agreement among producers of a commodity that might specify quality controls, rate of flow to market, allocation of products to processors, or allocation of quotas to producers. Any group of growers can petition the secretary of agriculture to establish a marketing order. After hearings, such an order is adopted if passed by a two-thirds vote of producers.

Although marketing orders vary in content, they are essentially a government authorization for establishing a cartel to control the marketing of a commodity. In 1981, James Anderson (1982: 99) identified 47 marketing orders for 32 different fruits, nuts, or vegetables. An additional 56 milk marketing orders cover most of the major population areas except for California (MacAvoy, 1977: 7).

Resources

The major resource of both the Agricultural Marketing Service and the Agricultural Stabilization and Conservation Service is technical expertise. The entire Department of Agriculture prides itself on the technocratic orientation of its employees. Reflecting this orientation plus a common background is a high level of cohesion. Leadership is known for cultivating political support with Congress and the interest groups.

Both salience and legislative authority also affect agriculture regulators. Agricultural regulation reflects the interests of the agricultural sector most strongly during times when few outsiders are concerned with agricultural issues. Then policy decisions are generally made within the agricultural subsystems. Unfortunately for agricultural interests, agriculture and related issues have become more salient for large numbers of Americans. The high rise in food prices from 1973 to 1975 motivated many urban members of Congress to intervene in agriculture policy. The interrelationship between agriculture and foreign trade and foreign policy as well as recent escalations in the price of subsidy programs (USDA's budget often exceeds $50 billion) has meant that significant agricultural decisions are made outside the agriculture subsystems (see Youngberg, 1976; Barton, 1976; Peters, 1978).

Legislative authority consists of goal specificity, coverage of the policy, sanctions available, and procedures. The legislative authority of agencies regulating agriculture is distinctive in that it tends to be specific; the 1981 Omnibus Farm Bill ran over 182 pages. Congress sometimes sets the exact price support levels for some crops (and later regrets it, see the 1981 farm bill below), a specificity rarely found in other regulatory legislation. The coverage of agricultural regulation is also limited. Agricultural policy has always reflected an element of **volunteerism**. If farmers wish to forego the benefits of regulation (e.g., price supports), they need not comply with any of the restrictions (e.g., set-asides). Although some exceptions to this generalization exist in tobacco production and marketing orders, these affect only a small portion of agriculture's output. Correspondingly, the sanctions permitted to the Department of Agriculture are limited to the denial of participation in USDA programs. Finally, USDA procedures stress participation by farmers in local level decisions, thus turning the programs into a version of self-regulation.

Subsystems

Agriculture is not a single subsystem but rather many subsystems. Each major commodity has a specialized unit within the AMS or the ASCS to handle that commodity. Congressional subcommittees are also organized around commodity lines. The major battles with other advocacy coalitions do not occur within the subsystems but rather in the macropolitical system. The subsystems make a conscious effort to form a single agricultural coalition (usually at the House and Senate Agriculture Committees) before pressing issues in the larger political system (Browne 1988; Jones 1961).

Although the ASCS and AMS programs are central to the operation of the Department of Agriculture, USDA has many additional programs. These programs are often the source of coalitional allies for the regulatory programs. The largest program in the department is the **food stamp program**, which, in past years when agricultural prices were high, constituted more than one-half of the department's budget. Also included in the department are agriculture research and education programs, soil conservation programs, general loan programs via the Farmers Home Administration, and the Forest Service. Some units in USDA such as the Agricultural Research Service undercut the stability of the regulatory system by increasing productivity and, thus, driving down food prices (Rausser 1992).

THE ENVIRONMENT OF AGRICULTURE

This examination of the environment of agriculture includes an overview of both the economic environment and the technological environment.

Economic Environment

Agriculture has many characteristics of a competitive market; no single producer or buyer is large enough to influence the price of agricultural goods (at least in the long run), the grain of one farmer is easily substituted for the grain of another, and information is readily available about the supply and demand for commodities. The number of farms is large; over 2.1 million farms exist in the United States. Similar numbers are found within commodities; one million farms produce beef; 200,000 farms produce dairy products (Forste and Frick, 1979: 121). Even though some sectors of agriculture are more concentrated than others (e.g., feedlots, poultry producers), every sector has thousands of producers. Although agricultural economists note the concentration of agriculture today compared to agriculture in the past, when compared to other industries, agriculture is not concentrated at all.

Entry to agriculture, however, is moderately difficult, with a large capital investment necessary to become a farmer. A modest 400-acre corn farm in Illinois, for example, required a capital investment of $1.78 million in 1980 (Tweeten, 1981: 124). The ease of entry into agriculture characteristic of America's past during the Homestead Act no longer exists.

Profits in agriculture are attractive. From 1970 to 1978, Schertz (1979: 39) found that agriculture earned an annual return of 4.69 percent plus a capital gain of 11.59 percent for a total return of 16.28 percent. Few industries can match this return on investment. The 1970s were exceptionally good times for agriculture. Annual returns on investment for 1981-91 were 3.61 percent and capital gains were slightly negative; in real terms agriculture suffered a capital loss of about $200 billion during this time period. As a result, farms are often plagued by a problem of low cash flow (Gardner, 1981a: 11) and volatile profits.

Technological Environment

At one time in our nation's history, the technology of agriculture was fairly simple, and farmers were generally self-sufficient. In the twentieth century, however, this is no longer the case. The specialization of farmers to produce a single cash crop (**monoculture**) has turned agriculture into a complex industry. The farmer must make decisions on pesticides, fertilizers, plant, and animal hybrids, and tillage. Special tax provisions for agriculture as well as futures markets make the financial side of agriculture equally complex.

Agricultural technology is highly unstable. The Department of Agriculture and numerous state agricultural colleges spend millions of dollars a year developing new technologies. Major breakthroughs in mechanization, plant and animal productivity, and other areas have tripled the productivity of agriculture in the last 100 years (Ruttan 1982). The result has been major changes in the input mix of agriculture. Tweeten (1979b) found that agriculture inputs in 1940 were 17 percent land, 54 percent labor, and 29 percent capital; in 1976 these inputs were 22 percent land, 16 percent labor, and 66 percent capital.

Agricultural commodities have many substitutes for each other. Soybeans can be substituted for beef in our diets. One type of fruit can be substituted for another. Cattle can be fed corn, soybeans, or wheat (if the price is low enough) or be allowed to graze. Within limits farmers can shift production from one commodity to another.

THE POLITICS OF REGULATING AGRICULTURE

This examination of the politics of regulating agriculture includes sections on (1) preregulatory politics, (2) modern agricultural regulation, (3) the New Deal, (4) party conflict within the subsystem, 1948-1973, (5) opening the subsystems, and (6) does anyone have a farm policy?

Preregulatory Policies

Before 1933, government policy toward agriculture was **promotional** rather than regulatory. Government encouraged individuals to become farmers by selling federal land cheaply or by giving it away. Under the Homestead Act of 1862, individuals who resided on 160 acres of land for five years were given title to that land. From 1868 to 1879 some 70 million acres were **homesteaded**; from 1898 to 1917 another 100 million acres were homesteaded. All totaled, the U.S. government either gave away or sold 500 million acres of land to individuals (Tweeten, 1979a: 99). The result of the cheap land policies was an over-investment in agriculture, a problem not readily apparent in the nineteenth century because farmers were more self-sufficient. Over-investment in farming, however, becomes a major problem when farmers rely on cash crops as their sole source of livelihood.

After the Civil War, the federal government followed a policy of supporting research and education for agriculture. The Morrill Act established land-grant colleges, and research conducted at these schools was disseminated by the Cooperative Extension Service. Social investment in research and education exacerbated the over-investment in agriculture by increasing the productivity of individual farmers. Total output increased and prices fell.

Government policy also encouraged over-investment in farming by providing subsidized credit to farmers. Federal land banks and the USDA, and state government credit programs permitted farmers to borrow money at less than market rates. Consequently, more investment than optimal was made in farming resulting in over-production and low prices (Heady, 1983: 26).

By the turn of the century the economic structure of agriculture was set. An **institutionalized technological revolution** (via research at land grant colleges) aggravated the over-investment in agriculture resulting in chronic over-production.

Over-production is joined by three other sources of chronic economic hardship in agriculture. First, the supply of agricultural goods is a function of weather, soil conditions, and numerous other factors outside the control of individual farmers. In years with poor crops, therefore, those farmers with good crops will prosper. Second, the demand for food is fairly inelastic. If the supply of food increases and prices drop, consumers usually do not increase their food consumption more than marginally. As a result, small increases in oversupply result in major drops in prices. Similarly, small shortages result in large price increases. Third, entry and exit from farm production are delayed. Exit from farming has no impact on supply and demand until the next crop year; similarly, entry has a delayed effect on supply. These economic conditions resulted in periodic recessions in agriculture, a situation made more harsh by the government's hard money policies in the late nineteenth century.

Chronic economic hardship in agriculture is coupled with a long tradition of political action to correct such hardships. Numerous political movements from Shays' Rebellion to the Patrons of Husbandry to the Granger movement to the Greenback party to the Populist party had roots in agrarian discontent (see Taylor, 1953). Political action was sanctioned by the Jeffersonian ideal that small farmers were somehow more deserving and more noble than their urban cohorts (for a discussion, see Talbot and Hadwiger, 1968; Browne et al. 1992). Economic problems were to be addressed with political solutions.

Modern Agricultural Regulation

The first efforts to regulate farm prices and income came in the 1920s.[1] The preceding decade was a good one for agriculture, with strong demand and high prices. Following the end of World War I, however, demand and prices dropped. Rather than run candidates for Congress as agrarian movements in the past had, the American Farm Bureau organized members of both political parties who represented agricultural districts. The **Farm Bloc**, as the political organization in Congress came to be known, stressed both self-help and exports as the solution to the farm problem.

Self-help centered on the use of cooperatives to purchase raw materials and to sell farm products. In 1922 the Capper-Volstead Act exempted agricultural coops from

---

[1] The following historical sections on agriculture draw heavily from Anderson, Brady, and Bullock (1977) and from Tweeten (1979a).

antitrust laws. Such coops were to be regulated by the secretary of agriculture rather than the FTC, thus ensuring that, as combinations in restraint of trade, they would not be bothered by the government. Although the immediate impact of coops is minimal, in the long run they play a significant role in those commodities regulated by marketing orders.

Increased exports were the goal of the Farm Bureau's McNary-Haugen bills. The McNary-Haugen bills would have established a government corporation to purchase sufficient agricultural products to raise the price of farm goods to parity; **parity** is the price of farm goods that would be necessary to give farmers the same purchasing power as they had in the period 1910-1914. The government corporation would then dump any agricultural products not needed for domestic consumption on the world market at whatever price they would bring. Farmers would be paid a price for their production that represented a blend of domestic and international prices; these prices would be protected by **import controls**.

The McNary-Haugen bill was introduced in 1924 and actually passed both houses of Congress in 1927 and again in 1928. In both cases, President Coolidge vetoed the bill over concerns of cost and constitutionality. President Hoover's approach to declining farm incomes was the Federal Farm Board, authorized by the Agricultural Marketing Act of 1929; the Federal Farm Board had authority for $500 million in loans to cooperatives. By 1932 the board was an admitted failure, providing too little assistance too late; farm prices dropped 56 percent from 1929 to 1932 (Paarlberg, 1980: 20).

The New Deal

Franklin Roosevelt's solution to the depression problems of agriculture was similar to his initial solution for most industries—establishment of **government-sponsored cartels** to raise prices. The Agricultural Adjustment Act (AAA) of 1933 encouraged farmers to join together in marketing and price agreements. In addition, processors of agricultural goods were taxed, and those taxes were used to pay farmers who voluntarily reduced their acreage in production. To assist cash-flow problems, nonrecourse loans were permitted, using crops as collateral. The initial AAA program covered cotton, wheat, rice, corn, hogs, tobacco, and milk; in addition, sugar and peanuts were subjected to acreage controls. The commodities covered reflected, in part, Democratic party strongholds in the South and parts of the Midwest. The AAA programs plus some bad weather were successful in raising the price of some agricultural products by 1936 (Tweeten, 1979a: 459).

The Supreme Court, however, brought an end to the first New Deal in Agriculture. In *United States v. Butler* (1936), the Court held that the first AAA was unconstitutional because agriculture was a state matter and because the act taxed processors for a **special interest** rather than a **general interest** (Anderson, Brady, and Bullock, 1977: 378). Congress immediately finessed the Supreme Court decision via the Soil Conservation and Domestic Allotment Act of 1936. Under this law, farmers were paid to take **"soil depleting"** crops out of production; soil depleting crops were defined by Congress as those in oversupply (e.g., corn, wheat, and such).

The Supreme Court's decision did not affect the marketing order provisions of the AAA (although Congress repassed them anyway in 1937). Under these provisions, some industries such as the dairy industry organized cartels. Milk marketing orders, for example, set the price and production amount of fluid milk (milk used for drinking) with all excess production assigned to manufacturing (processing into cheese, butter, and such). **Surplus manufactured products** were then sold to the government to maintain prices above a specified level. Producers were paid a blend of the price of fluid and manufacturing milk (MacAvoy, 1977; Guth, 1980).

In 1938, with the Supreme Court taking a more tolerant view of the New Deal, a second Agricultural Adjustment Act was passed. The second AAA is the base legislation for agricultural regulation with subsequent acts passed as amendments to it. The AAA authorized **nonrecourse loans** to support crops at 52 to 75 percent of parity and provided for payments to set aside acreage. In addition, the act provided for a variety of programs to dispose of any surplus the government might acquire, including a commodity distribution program, the school lunch and school milk programs, subsidized exports, and even a forerunner of the food stamp program.

Early experience with the second AAA revealed that government agricultural programs were working at cross-purposes. The regulatory programs were designed to increase income by decreasing the supply of agricultural goods whereas the research and education programs were designed to increase productivity and thus supply. As a result, in 1938, although farmers reduced acreage under the AAA, total output increased.

Before the second AAA had time to affect agricultural production, the war in Europe fundamentally changed agricultural goals from restraining production to encouraging production. During the war and for two years afterward, prices were set at 90 percent of parity with few controls on production. Only such crops as tobacco faced production limitations after the war. When the wartime legislation expired in 1948, prices were to drop back to from 52 to 75 percent of parity.

Party Conflict Within the Subsystem, 1948-1973

The wartime legislation was intended to prevent a sharp postwar drop in farm prices similar to that after World War 1. Such a drop did not materialize because postwar reconstruction in Europe contributed to a strong demand for agricultural products. The 1948 expiration date of the war programs, however, permitted the government time to reexamine farm policy; several studies were commissioned (Cochrane and Ryan, 1976: 24), and a variety of different viewpoints were suggested.

Essentially, the issue was one of high versus low price supports with Democrats favoring the former and Republicans and the Farm Bureau favoring the latter. The year 1948 saw a compromise bill passed that extended the high price supports for two years to be followed by variable price supports established by the secretary of agriculture. After Truman's surprise victory over Dewey, however, the president reevaluated this position (Cochrane and Ryan, 1976: 29). Secretary of Agriculture Brannan proposed his famous **Brannan plan** designed to treat the farm problem as an income problem rather than a price problem. Under the Brannan plan, farmers would sell their goods at whatever price the market offered, and the government would then subsidize farm income with direct payments to farmers. All farm organizations except for the National Farmers Union opposed the Brannan plan, and it was defeated in Congress. Conflict over agricultural policy, however, was rendered moot by the Korean War, which greatly stimulated demand and increased farm prices.

The 1950s and 1960s saw an extension of the postwar farm politics with the parties taking similar positions. Under Secretary of Agriculture Ezra Taft Benson, the Republican party advocated a greater reliance on the market and low price supports whereas the Democratic party favored high supports. In general, prices in the 1950s were kept high, and the government owned large surpluses of various commodities.

In an effort to control the growing surpluses, President Kennedy advocated **supply management**—government efforts to impose real regulation and limit the supply of agricultural goods. The cornerstone of this policy was **mandatory production controls**. Unlike previous policies that permitted farmers to avoid regulation by foregoing subsidies, the Kennedy proposal would apply to all farmers. Congress, however, was unwilling to grant Kennedy all he wanted; instead, it authorized mandatory controls for the 1964 wheat crop if a referendum of wheat producers accepted such controls. The mandatory controls proposal was actively opposed by the American Farm Bureau, which campaigned against it during the referendum. The 1963 referendum rejected mandatory controls. President Johnson then sent agricultural policy back into the subsystem by inviting the various interest groups to write a Wheat-Cotton Bill (Hadwiger and Talbot 1965). From 1964 onward, agricultural programs were considered in a group to facilitate the formation of an advocacy coalition to pass the bills.

Opening the Agriculture Subsystems

By 1973 changes in the political system destroyed the careful efforts to resolve agricultural disputes within the confines of the agricultural subsystems. Four major changes occurred.

THE NUMBER OF FARMS DECLINED

First, as the nation continued to urbanize and as farms consolidated, the proportion of the population engaged in agriculture fell to less than 4 percent (and declined further to 2.1 percent by 1991). The farm sector became less and less important to the nation's politics.

REAPPORTIONMENT OF CONGRESS

Second, the decline in voters was exacerbated by **reapportionment**. Before the Supreme Court's decision in 1962 (*Baker* v. *Carr*) requiring apportionment on the basis of population, rural areas were greatly overrepresented in Congress. The number of congressional districts with over 20 percent of the population in farming fell from 154 in 1965 to 12 in 1973 (Anderson, Brady, and Bullock, 1977). To pass farm legislation, therefore, the agricultural coalition needed urban votes (Barton, 1976).

AGRICULTURE BECAME SALIENT

Third, food and agricultural policy became a salient political issue. In 1972, faced with two crop failures in a row, the Soviet Union decided to purchase grain rather than slaughter herds as they had in the past. The unprecedented Soviet entry into the market coupled with poor worldwide harvests resulted in demand that greatly exceeded supply.

In response, food prices jumped 20 percent in 1973, 12 percent in 1974 and 7 percent in 1975. Shortages developed, and consumers protested and boycotted some agricultural products.

PRESIDENTS BECAME INVOLVED IN AGRICULTURE POLICY

Fourth, agricultural policy became important enough for presidents to be involved (Youngberg, 1976: 59). Food exports became crucial to the nation's balance of payments situation, and food aid was a significant part of foreign policy. Both exports and aid dictated increased rather than limited production. With the explosion in the cost of government entitlement programs, agricultural programs that limited production were an attractive place to cut the size of government. Earl Butz, secretary of agriculture under Nixon and Ford, was a hard-core free-market advocate favoring unregulated production and sales.

Agriculture Policy in the 1970s and 1980s

The battle over the 1973 farm bill marked a turning point in the passage of agricultural legislation. Never again would the passage of a farm bill be an easy task with participation restricted to the agricultural subsystem only. The agricultural coalition was forced to vote for raising the **minimum wage** (a policy not favored in agriculture) in exchange for urban votes needed to pass the farm bill (Barton, 1976). In addition, rural interests had to grant concessions; even the bill was entitled the Agriculture and Consumer Protection Act of 1973. Two noteworthy changes in the 1973 act were **target prices** and **payment limitations**. Major grains were placed in a target price system whereby farmers received a check for the difference between the sale price of their crop and the target price.[2] Target prices, as in the Brannan plan, supported farm income but allowed consumers to benefit from a lower market price. In addition, the total amount of subsidies that each farmer could receive was limited to $20,000 (raised in later legislation to $50,000 with several loopholes).

The mid-1970s saw a brief **free-market era** in American agriculture. In general, prices were above targets so that few subsidies were paid except for milk, tobacco, and peanuts. The Department of Agriculture eliminated set-asides and encouraged all-out production. Unfortunately, American agriculture responded so well that by 1977 large surpluses were again being produced. Policy again changed to reimpose regulation. One permanent legacy of the mid-1970s, however, was agriculture's increased reliance on exports. One-third of all agricultural production was exported, some $40 billion in 1980 (six times the amount exported in 1970). Some crops became especially export-dependent; the nation exported 65 percent of its wheat, 65 percent of its cotton, 45 percent of its soybeans, 45 percent of its rice, 40 percent of its tobacco, and 30 percent of its feed grains (Penn, 1981: 18).

The 1977 farm bill (titled the **Food and Agriculture Act**) again faced the problem of surpluses but in a changed environment. Depressed agricultural prices and presidential

---

[2]Loan programs were retained with loan rates set below target prices.

pressures to limit the budget created conflicting pressures on Congress (see Peters, 1978). The farm bill was able to pass only because it contained provisions for the food stamp program. Under the leadership of New York City Representative Fred Richmond, rural legislators voted for increases in food stamps in exchange for urban votes for price supports. Several votes to delete such crops as peanuts from the program came close to passage. Despite the tenuous coalition and two weeks of floor debate in the House, the 1977 bill was essentially an incremental extension of the 1973 act.

The 1981 **Farm Bill** faced an even less promising environment than previous ones. With the 1980 election, the Republican party took control of the Senate. Republican control of the Senate coupled with the urban domination of the House provided a difficult environment for agriculture. In addition, President Reagan viewed agriculture as a promising area to target budget cuts and proposed that target prices be eliminated and that the secretary of agriculture have discretion in setting loan levels for all crops. Creating even greater difficulties was the Reagan proposal to cap all agricultural spending at $11 billion for four years and the separation of the food stamp program from the farm bill (Hagstrom, 1984: 424). The cap made agricultural groups compete for a fixed pie rather than logrolling to expand the pie, and eliminating food stamps hurt the urban-rural food coalition.

A stalemate developed between the Senate, supporting Reagan's position of lower price supports, and the House, favoring greater expenditures. Many urban legislators viewed the farm bill as a way to strike back at conservative Senator Jesse Helms for his advocacy of school prayer and human life legislation. Senator Helms represented North Carolina, a major tobacco producer, and was a strong supporter of tobacco subsidies. A compromise bill worked out between the administration, the Senate, and some members of the House proved so controversial that some of the House members on the conference committee refused to sign the conference report. The final bill passed the House by a slim two-vote margin.

Despite the difficult nature of passage, the 1981 bill was only a modest extension of the 1977 and 1973 policies. The changes were few. Most price support levels for crops were increased slightly, the dairy subsidies were reduced modestly, and some restrictions in the peanut program were eased. The 1981 conflict illustrated that portions of the farm coalition had become definite liabilities, especially when forming coalitions with urban legislators. The expensive programs for peanuts, cotton, and tobacco were alienating urban legislators and endangering the urban-rural coalition.

Two additional changes in agricultural regulation occurred between 1981 and 1985 (when 1981 bill expired). First, as a way to remove one of the irritants to successful coalitions, the tobacco subsidy program was removed from the budget in 1982 and funded by a tax on processors. Tobacco remained a heavily regulated crop, however, with strict production controls. By 1984 tobacco was in serious trouble; because tobacco price supports were kept high, imports took over 30 percent of the U.S. market. Second, the Reagan administration announced its payment in kind program (PIK) in 1983, whereby farmers would be paid in surplus farm products rather than cash. The program was an economic disaster; farm incomes dropped and government payments totaled 73% of net farm income. Neither action fundamentally changed the regulation of agriculture.

The 1981 farm bill and other agriculture experiences of the early 1980s illustrate the hazards of writing **detailed regulatory legislation** with minimal bureaucratic discretion. The 1981 farm bill assumed a continued demand for farm products and continued inflation. As a result, target prices were set to increase automatically every year. The wheat target price, for example, was set at $4.05 for 1982, $4.30 for 1983, $4.45 for 1984, and $4.60 for 1985. Because target prices are guaranteed, these prices encouraged farmers to increase production.

The worldwide recession, on the other hand, caused a slump in the demand for grains. This slump was exacerbated by the strong showing of the U.S. dollar in foreign markets, which increased the price of agricultural goods to foreign purchasers. Total farm exports dropped from $43.8 billion in 1981 to $26.3 billion in 1986. Net farm income dropped from a record $27.4 billion in 1979 to $14.2 billion in 1983 (ERS 1993, 16).

Encouraged by high target rices, farmers produced a record crop in 1981 and a large crop in 1982. Direct government support payments soared from $1.3 billion in 1980 to $16.7 billion in 1987. Government ownership of commodities skyrocketed; in 1983 the Commodity Credit Corporation owned 1.5 billion bushels of wheat, enough for two years of U.S. consumption. In an effort to reduce these inventories, the Reagan administration implemented the **payment in kind (PIK) program**. Farmers who had already set aside 20 percent of the land were eligible to set aside 10 to 30 percent more; rather than cash payments, these farmers would be paid in surplus government grains. Unlike normal set-asides, when 60 to 70 percent of farmers participate, the PIK program attracted over 80 percent of farmers, and nearly 20 percent of all cropland (82 million acres) was set aside. PIK's popularity could be traced to provisions guaranteeing 95 percent of wheat yields and 80 percent of other crop yields. With few marginal costs, potential profits were high.

Despite PIK payments valued at $9.7 billion in 1983, the price of other support payments ballooned to $9.3 billion for a total cost of $19.0 billion. In less than ten years, U.S. agriculture went from nearly a free market to being heavily subsidized with large surpluses. The blame can be laid at the feet of inflexible regulatory policies that encouraged production as demand fell.

1985 and 1990: Does Anyone Have a Farm Policy?

The 1985 **farm bill** was debated and passed during a major economic crisis in American agriculture. Exports had dropped dramatically as the result of the expensive dollar, farm incomes had declined precipitously, and the farm credit system was approaching bankruptcy (and was bailed out by the government in 1988). Such hard times generated the usual active farm protest groups (see Browne 1988). Interest groups were able to use the increased salience (several movies about hard times on the farm were released in this time period) including testimony by agricultural "experts" Sissy Spacek and Jessica Lange. Legislators representing agricultural areas faced strong interest group pressure on one side and a general reluctance to continue large farm programs on the part of urban legislators and the administration. The agriculture coalition won out by reducing program costs (by enacting lower loan, target price rates and providing greater flexibility in setting such rates), providing some benefits to environmentalists (a 34 million acre conservation reserve, Rausser 1992, 137), and by painting the Reagan administration as anti-farm. Such partisan efforts paid off the following year when Democrats regained control of the Senate in part by defeating three farm state Republican Senators.

For the 1990 **farm bill** renewal, the economic situation in agriculture had improved significantly yet had not returned to the good times of the mid-1970s. Mindful of the political costs paid by the Reagan administration, President Bush declined to submit a farm bill and left the process to Congress. Congress essentially enacted a continuation of existing policies with the addition of some environmental controls (wetlands set asides and pesticide record keeping) to gain nonagricultural support for the bill.

One minor market-oriented policy that was adopted was to permit farmers to change a portion of their plantings without forfeiting future subsidies (Rausser 1992, 143). The **Flex Program**, as it is called, designates 15 percent of a farmer's base acreage as flex acreage. These acres receive no subsidies and a farmer can grow any crops (with a few exceptions) in response to market demands. An additional 10 percent of base acreage is **optional flex land** and a farmer may also forgo subsidies on this land and grow alternative crops. In 1992 approximately one-half of flex land was used to plant different crops or left idle; only 7 percent of optional flex land was so used (GAO, 1993: 5). Neither the 1985 nor 1990 bills addressed any basic policy issues in agricultural regulation but rather incrementally extended programs with some modest reductions in costs.

WHO BENEFITS FROM AGRICULTURAL REGULATION?

Agricultural regulation is intended to benefit farmers; consumer benefits are considered secondary by agricultural regulators.[3] Despite the intent, not all agricultural producers benefit equally from regulation. Hog and egg producers, for example, are not regulated. The beneficiaries of the regulatory process are those sectors that are regulated —dairy products; wheat; feed grains; cotton; tobacco; sugar; and fruits, nuts, and vegetables. Other sectors of agriculture such as beef, pork, and chicken producers actually lose from regulation because regulation increases the price of the grains they use to feed their stock.

Some in Agriculture Benefit More than Others

Among those commodity producers that are supported by regulation, some producers benefit more than others. Despite the often heard rhetoric about farm policies designed to protect the family farm, the benefits of regulation have gone to the large farmer. In 1971, Schultze (1971: 16) found that the largest 20 percent of farmers received from 46.8 to 83.1 percent of the subsidies (depending on the specific crop). Thirty percent of direct farm payments went to 1 percent of the farmers (Anthan, 1980). In many cases. the distribution of farm subsidies was less equal than the distribution of farm income. In other words, economic regulation has benefitted the richer farmers; it has not assisted the poorer

---

[3]Consumers might indirectly benefit from farm programs. If such programs ensure an adequate supply of farm commodities from year to year, consumers might benefit in the long run. Whether such benefits are worth the extra costs is an empirical question.

farmers. A 1980 study by the Department of Agriculture (Lin, Calvin, and Johnson, 1980) came to a similar conclusion (see also Browne et al. 1992, 45). Recent historical research summarized by Kirkendall (1980) suggests that from the New Deal onward the intent of agricultural policy has been to benefit large farmers at the expense of small farmers. Such intent was predictable given the links of the USDA to progressive Farm Bureau members and the local autonomy of the programs (see Baldwin, 1968). Intended or not, the prime beneficiary of regulation has been the large farmer.

The reasons why some farmers such as corn producers benefit from agricultural regulation and others such as livestock producers do not is a function of politics pure and simple (for an alternative view see Gardner 1987). In the postwar years, the Agriculture Committees of the House and the Senate have been dominated by Southerners. Southern control of the key political posts plus the activities of the American Farm Bureau explain why Southern crops such as cotton, tobacco, and peanuts are heavily regulated in the interests of the producers. Other major beneficiaries such as the dairy industry can also be explained in terms of political activities. Milk is a highly organized industry with giant cooperatives handling the distribution of milk. These coops including such giants as American Milk Producers, Inc., MidAmerica Dairymen, and Dairymen, Inc., have devoted considerable resources to political influence ($1.7 million in 1982 PAC contributions alone). The infamous milk fund scandal of 1971 illustrates the coops' use of campaign contributions to influence congressional policy on milk price supports. Because price supports are funneled through the coops to the individual farmers, individual dairy farmers are unlikely to protest coop actions. The end result is higher prices and massive surpluses; at the end of 1983 the U.S. government owned 1.1 billion pounds of cheese, 578 million pounds of butter, and 1.71 billion pounds of powdered milk. Only major efforts of distribution and price support cuts plus a $2.0 billion government program to buy and slaughter dairy cattle (Bovard 1989, 78) were able to reduce these inventories by 1991.

The other major beneficiary of agricultural regulation has been wheat farmers. As Johnson (1981: 144) noted, the ratio of the support price of wheat to corn increased from 1.19 in 1964 to 1.62 for the 1979 crop year (and since stabilized at 1.45). Wheat farmers, generally represented by the National Farmers Union with its ties to the Democratic party, have been challenged less by urban Democrats than peanut, cotton, or tobacco programs. In sum, then, the beneficiaries of agricultural regulation reflect the political resources of each sector.

How Do Consumers Fare?

How do consumers fare in this process? The impact of agricultural regulation on consumers is fairly complex. Consumers gain in that they benefit from assured supplies, but they pay for assured supplies in terms of higher costs for agricultural products, 5 to 6 percent higher than in an unregulated market (Gardner, 1981b: 58; see also Rausser 1992, 141). Benefits to consumers vary a great deal in terms of specific commodities. Federal dairy programs, for example, penalize those individuals who drink fresh milk and at the same time benefit those persons who consume cheese and butter (Gardner, 1981a: 53). The only clear thing about consumer benefits is that agricultural regulatory policy is not designed to benefit consumers directly, and it does not consistently benefit consumers.

Argument: Agricultural Regulatory Programs Result in a Net Loss to Society

Overall, Gardner (1981a: 72) argues that agriculture regulatory programs result in a net loss to society. Gardner estimated farmers benefitted by $6.4 billion in 1978 (see also Rausser 1992, 141). These benefits were offset by $5.85 billion in increased costs to consumers and $1.44 billion in direct costs to the taxpayers. In 1978, a year with relatively low support costs, agriculture regulation resulted in a net loss of $1.5 billion to society. During the 1980s with direct annual costs exceeding $50 billion, the net loss to society must have been substantially greater.

Reform of Agricultural Regulation

Reforming the system of agricultural regulation requires a closer look at the economic reasons for regulation. Prices in agriculture are set by supply and demand. Supply is uncertain owing to forces beyond the control of the farmer, and demand is inelastic. This results in large fluctuations in farm income. The essential problem is that the market adjusts to changes in supply and demand faster than the industry can adjust. To withdraw from production or to enter production, a farmer must wait a year for such a decision to result in changes in supply. Prices, on the other hand, react immediately. The economic problem is that the market reacts too fast for individual producers to make rational decisions.

An effective government policy would attempt to deal with the great fluctuations in price without distorting long-run changes in price. This would permit individual farmers to withdraw gradually from the market without the trauma of bankruptcy sales. To stabilize the fluctuations in farm income, governmental policy needs to be flexible so that supports can be triggered in years with low farm prices and withdrawn in years of high farm prices. Establishing rigid price supports for four years in advance with built-in increases merely encourages over-production. Supports based on a moving average of farm prices over a five-year period and set at a reasonably low level would permit farmers to make rational long-run decisions about farming. Such supports could also be related to current surpluses with support levels lowered as surpluses expand.

SUMMARY

The administration of agricultural regulation is significantly different from other regulatory administration. Most differences are reflected in the legislative authorization that guides the program operations. First, agricultural legislation is more specific; the range of price supports and the various types of price supports are often set by law. Second, the agencies, as a result, exercise less discretion; their task is to encourage farmers to participate in such programs and administer the day-today details. Third, regulation relies almost totally on voluntary compliance by farmers. Restrictions on production except for a few crops are voluntary; participation is encouraged by subsidies, but in any normal year some 30 to 40 percent of farmers do not participate. Fourth, prices are supported by government payments rather than by raising the price to consumers. Target prices are direct government payments whereas such price supports as airline rates (prior to 1978) were reflected by higher consumer prices. Fifth, the regulation is for the benefit of farmers; little pretense of regulation in the interests of consumers is presented.

Given these differences, agriculture is a unique regulatory area. This uniqueness cannot, however, be attributed to differences in the economic or technical environment of agriculture. Agriculture's economic and technical environment resembles that of a perfectly competitive industry with a large number of producers and reasonably good sources of information (see Table 6.1). Some differences do exist, however. Production is uncertain, being in part a function of uncontrollable variables such as soil, weather, and other inputs. Demand is also uncertain, with high inelasticity of demand. Although barriers to entry exist in the form of large capital investments necessary for agriculture, these barriers to entry are not excessive.

The unique regulation of agriculture can be attributed to the political environment of the industry. Agriculture is populated by well-organized interest groups with a long history of using political means to solve the economic problems of agriculture. Agriculture groups do not need to be told how the political system works and are not hesitant about using it. This political efficacy is assisted by the Jeffersonian ideal of a nation of small farmers; farmers are somehow seen as more deserving than other interests (see Browne et al., 1992). The dominant focus of agricultural politics is Congress, which controls the process by writing detailed legislation every four years or so.

The regulatory bureaucracy in such a situation becomes a technocratic administrative arm. Although agriculture bureaus have a reputation for expertise and cohesion, they also share Congress' policy goals so that they do not become independent political operatives. Congress and the interest groups have close ties to the bureaucracy.

In recent years, the agricultural political system has been opened up to the participation of others. Agricultural affairs have been deemed too important to be left in the hands of the agricultural subsystems. The use of food as a weapon in foreign policy and the high cost of subsidy programs have attracted the interest of the president (until President Bush). President Clinton has yet to be called on to formulate an overall agricultural policy since the basic legislation was extended in 1990. The importance of food programs to urban consumers has provided a means of influence for nonrural legislators. The recent farm bills have reflected urban-rural coalitions, and farm interests have had to compromise their goals in the interests of passing legislation. Macropolitical trends are operating against the agricultural community; yet agriculture has been able to protect its policy benefits.

Table 6.1   A Summary of Agriculture Regulation

Economics

Ease of Entry	Hard
Number of Firms	2.1 million
Profits	Variable

Technology

Complexity	Moderate
Stability	Low
Substitutes	High

Subsystem

Bureaucratic control	Moderate
Industry coalition	Strong
Nonindustry coalition	Strong
Bureaucratic Resources:	
Expertise	High
Cohesion	High
Leadership	Moderate
Legislative authority:	
Goals	Specific
Coverage	Universal
Sanctions	Poor
Procedures	Fair

Involvement of Macropolitical Actors

Congress	Strong
President	Occasional
Courts	Weak

Chapter 7
Environmental Protection Regulation

Evan J. Ringquist[1]

Environmental protection exploded on to the national agenda in the late 1960s. Like most regulatory policies, environmental regulation is profoundly affected by crises or focusing events external to the regulatory environment itself. Following a series of such focusing events, from the publication of *Silent Spring* in 1962 to the outbreak of drinking water contamination in Milwaukee in 1993, federal responsibilities in environmental protection have grown to include the regulation of air and water pollution, solid wastes, hazardous wastes, noise and radiation pollution, pesticides, and most toxic chemicals traded in interstate commerce.

A variety of policy tools are used in environmental regulation. In many cases, traditional **command and control regulations** are used (e.g. equipment and design standards in air pollution control). In other instances, environmental regulation relies upon **market incentives** (e.g., tradable discharge permits), licensing and use restrictions (e.g., pesticides and some toxic chemicals), fiscal inducements (e.g., municipal waste water treatment grants), or providing information to the public (e.g., the Toxics Release Inventory). The tool selected depends upon the pollutant that is targeted and the period in which the regulatory statute was adopted.

This chapter has five parts. First is an overview of the policy environment and the policy subsystem in environmental regulation. Second is a discussion of four eras of advocacy coalition competition and policy development in pollution control. Third is an examination of the specifics of environmental regulation in water pollution control, air pollution control, hazardous waste management, and pesticides. Fourth is an evaluation of the outcomes of these regulations. Fifth is a discussion of future obstacles and opportunities in environmental regulation.

---

[1]Evan J. Ringquist is an assistant professor of Political Science at Florida State University. He received his PhD from the University of Wisconsin-Madison and previously taught at Texas Tech University. He is the author of *Environmental Policy at the State Level*, considered the seminal work on the role states play in environmental policy. His goals in life are to share a cheeseburger with Jimmy Buffett and a large mouth bass with Babe Winkelman.

THE ENVIRONMENT

All industries are affected by environmental regulation, though the most significant effects are felt by manufacturing facilities and local governments. Because environmental regulation covers the entire economy, many of the economic and technical variables discussed in other chapters can only be applied to decisions affecting individual industries rather than to the entire policy area (e.g., industries with few firms, high barriers to entry, and low profits will resist regulation more than other industries). The explanatory power of technical factors such as complexity, stability, and substitutes is similarly affected. Industries are less likely to be regulated closely if they have complex and stable technologies with few available substitutes. These caveats, however, do not mean that environmental variables are unimportant in environmental regulation.

Technological Uncertainty

Technological factors are critical in environmental regulation, though these factors usually deal with the technology of pollution control rather than the production technology of the regulated industry. Most early environmental regulation called for **pollution reduction goals** that were at or beyond the state of the art in pollution control technology. Supporters of these regulations claimed that they would force technological progress in these areas. Others, however, criticized such regulations as "policy beyond capability", and claimed that they were unnecessarily costiy, economically disruptive, and set up the government for policy failure and citizen disillusionment (Jones, 1975). While hindsight demonstrates that there was some truth to each position, disagreements regarding the technological feasibility of regulatory goals help structure the debate over environmental regulation to this day.

More recent environmental regulations place the majority of the burden of technological development on government. Market-like tools that rely upon the buying and selling of pollution permits require industries to develop new pollution control technologies to remain competitive. These tools also require that the regulator be able to monitor pollutant emissions immediately and continuously. The **monitoring responsibilities** of the regulator provide the stiffer test for technological innovation, since few examples of this technology are even at the demonstration phase and because nearly every incentive based regulatory scheme depends on the availability of this technology.

Complexity and Salience

Environmental regulation is a highly complex policy area. The knowledge necessary to model airborne pollutant plumes or determine the mutagenetic effects of a pesticide is not easily accessible to the average citizen. This complexity is made manifest in the thousands of hydrogeologists, atmospheric chemists, oncologists, engineers, and other professionals hired by environmental regulatory agencies. The complexity of environmental regulation is matched by its salience. Far from following the surge and decline of the "**issue-attention cycle**" (Downs, 1972), public support for environmental protection has remained strong for twenty-five years (Dunlap, 1989).

According to Gormley (1986a), the complexity and salience of a particular area of regulation not only determines the likely policy participants, but the environment in which policy debates take place as well. Where regulatory issues are both salient and complex, there is simultaneous pressure for accountability and expertise in the policy environment. High salience attracts journalists (looking for a story rife with conflict), interest groups (looking for public exposure) and elected officials (attracted by potential electoral rewards). On the other hand, high levels of complexity pose significant barriers to entry for substantive policy input from these participants. Critical decisions in areas of high complexity are made by upper level bureaucrats whose professional values attract them to difficult problems, and who have the technical expertise necessary to craft solutions to these problems. Decision making in environmental regulation closely resembles just such a policy environment.

THE SUBSYSTEM

This examination of the subsystem of environmental protection regulation includes an overview of the agency, other federal actors, state governments, and advocacy coalitions.

The Agency

Responsibility for most federal environmental regulation is vested in the **Environmental Protection Agency (EPA)**, an independent agency that reports directly to the president. The EPA administers regulations under more than two dozen statutes. The EPA is also the nation's largest regulatory agency. In 1992, the EPA had 18,000 employees (two-thirds of which were in the agency's ten regional offices) and a budget of $6.5 billion. Of this amount, $2.1 billion went to constructing municipal waste water treatment facilities, and $1.6 billion went to clean up abandoned hazardous waste dumps. This left only about $2.8 billion for all of the agency's other tasks (Rosenbaum, 1994).

AGENCY STRUCTURE

The EPA is unique structurally; it is the only regulatory agency (as opposed to a commission) that is not located in an executive branch department. The agency's structure also reflects its origin and its enabling legislation. Unlike many other regulatory agencies, the EPA was created not with the passage of an organic act, but through a reorganization plan proposed by President Richard Nixon. EPA received its air pollution control staff from the Department of Health, Education, and Welfare (HEW); its water pollution control staff from HEW and the Department of the Interior; its pesticide staff from the Department of Agriculture: all in all, the new agency received responsibilities and personnel from more than a dozen different agencies and bureaus (Marcus, 1980).

EPA's architects contemplated competing organizational structures for the new agency. The most prominent plan, offered by White House consultant Alain Enthoven, would have organized the agency into **functional units** (e.g., abatement, monitoring, enforcement, research, etc.) in order to facilitate coordinated environmental management.

The competing plan, supported by key members of the Ash council on government reorganization, maintained the structural division of program responsibilities as they were inherited from other agencies (e.g., an office of air pollution, water pollution, pesticides, etc.). Jealous of their autonomy, EPA's program managers supported the second alternative, as did the first EPA Administrator, William Ruckleshaus. While Ruckleshaus believed that this structure would allow the new agency to "hit the ground running," he expected the agency to reorganize along functional lines in the near future.

The functional reorganization of EPA never arrived. Fast on the heels of the new agency's creation, Congress passed separate pieces of legislation regulating air pollution, water pollution, and pesticides that reinforced the division of EPA into **media-specific offices**. To this day, EPA is organized along media-specific lines with Offices of Air and Radiation; Water; Solid Waste and Emergency Response; and Prevention, Pesticides, and Toxic Substances. In addition to these program offices, the agency has Offices of Policy, Planning, and Evaluation; Enforcement; General Counsel; Administration and Resource Management; and Research and Development organized along functional lines. EPA's media specific organizational structure and the reinforcing media specific legislation enacted by Congress create a situation where integrated environmental regulation is extremely difficult.

AGENCY RESOURCES

In response to regulatory complexity, EPA has developed a reputation for expertise. By recruiting employees who value environmental protection and reinforcing these values through a continuing socialization process, EPA has also developed a high level of cohesion and a strong sense of mission among personnel with widely different professional backgrounds. The legislative authority of the Environmental Protection Agency is somewhat unique. The enabling legislation is detailed: the **Clean Air Act (CAA)**, **Clean Water Act** (CWA), and **Resource Conservation and Recovery Act** (RCRA), particularly in their later amendments, contain provisions normally left to agency discretion. Regulatory goals are highly specific, as are the deadlines for meeting the goals. The EPA's coverage is universal, and its sanctions rate as moderate-to-strong among regulatory agencies (not so strong as the controls of the Food and Drug Administration and not so weak as the Equal Employment Opportunity Commission). Early environmental legislation left the EPA with significant discretion with regard to certain administrative procedures, but recent legislation has significantly reduced agency discretion in these areas.

Other Federal Actors

Other federal actors include the president, Congress, and the courts.

THE PRESIDENT

Presidents since Richard Nixon have taken a strong interest in environmental regulation. The salience of environmental regulation makes the area politically irresistible, as does the economic impact of these regulations. Presidents attempt to influence the regulatory environment through administrative appointments, executive orders, budgetary requests, legislative initiatives, and moral suasion. More often than not, however, presidents intervene in environmental regulation to advance specific environmental and economic policy goals rather than to articulate a broad vision for environmental protection (Shanley, 1992).

CONGRESS

Congress has always prided itself on the leadership its members display in environmental regulation. While the EPA must serve two masters (Congress and the White House), historically the agency has been much more comfortable serving the former than the latter (Marcus, 1980). Congressional support for environmental regulation, however, comes at the price of high levels of oversight. Environmental statutes are often crafted by different Congressional committees, which means that different program offices within EPA must be responsive to the priorities and values of these different committees. All told, the activities of the EPA fall under the jurisdiction of nine standing committees in the House, eleven in the Senate, and over 100 separate subcommittees. In fact, the agency is subject to so much oversight that the General Accounting Office (GAO), the investigative arm of Congress, maintains a permanent branch office at EPA headquarters (Rosenbaum, 1994).

THE COURTS

Over the past quarter-century, a majority of EPA decisions have been challenged in court (Wenner, 1994). In these instances, the courts are called on to determine what the law is and how it should be enforced: this makes the courts a critical player in environmental regulation. This enhanced role for the courts was made possible by a series of Supreme Court decisions during the late 1960s and early 1970s that liberalized **standing requirements** and increased environmental interest groups' access to the courts. Other decisions reducing the courts' deference to agency expertise made it easier for environmentalists to win these cases (Stewart, 1975). In fact, many of the environmental movement's most significant victories were won in the courts, not in Congress or at the EPA (Melnick, 1983). As the makeup of the federal bench changed over time, the role of the courts has changed as well (see below). The EPA can still expect to be sued roughly 100 times per year, however, solidifying the role of the courts in environmental regulation (Rosenbaum, 1994).

State Governments

While the federal government took the lead in environmental protection with the CAA of 1970, most pieces of federal environmental legislation contain **partial preemption provisions** whereby the states are expected to assume **primacy** for environmental regulation. Under partial preemption, states submit plans to the EPA demonstrating that they have the technical, administrative, and fiscal capacity to run their own pollution control programs. If the EPA is satisfied with the state plan, it turns over regulatory authority to the state with the understanding that the EPA can rescind this authority if the state does not live up to the requirements of the statute.

State governments play significant roles in five areas of environmental regulation:

First, states can set their own **goals** and **standards** for environmental protection, and while some states (e.g. Colorado) are prohibited by statute from adopting standards more stringent than those required by EPA, many states go beyond federal minimum requirements in this area.

Second, states **design** and **implement** their own programs. The overwhelming majority of states have accepted primacy for most pieces of environmental legislation. In addition, several states have adopted their own versions of federal regulations that do not have primacy provisions (e.g., state "superfunds"), while other states have developed programs that go far beyond federal regulations in acid rain prevention (New York and Wisconsin), toxic chemicals (California), pesticides (Iowa), and creating an "environmental bill of rights" (Minnesota and New Jersey) (Hall and Kerr, 1991; Ringquist, 1993).

Third, states do the majority of **monitoring and enforcement** of environmental regulations. In 1990, for example, state governments had monitoring responsibility for 45,000 sources of water pollution, while the EPA had responsibility for only 15,000. State air pollution control officials undertook 28,000 inspections during this same year, while federal officials completed only 2800 inspections (Lowry, 1992).

Fourth, states fund environmental regulatory programs, to varying degrees. In the early 1980s, states provided from 19 percent (Rhode Island) to 76 percent (California) of the cost of running pollution control programs, and state contributions have increased since that time (Davis and Lester, 1989).

Fifth, states play a small research and development role in environmental regulation.

Advocacy Coalitions

The advocacy coalition environment in pollution control regulation is generally bipolar. At one end we find the **"environmental quality"** advocacy coalition, made up of actors who's belief system revolve around a core that values environmental purity. At the other end we find the **"economic rationality"** advocacy coalition, who's participants belief systems reflect a core that values unfettered private enterprise. The traditional picture of advocacy coalition competition in this area has pitted grassroots public interest environmental groups against big polluting industries. While this sketch may have been true twenty-five years ago, it is less true today. The advocacy coalitions in environmental regulation have changed significantly over this period.

THE ENVIRONMENTAL QUALITY ADVOCACY COALITION

Though environmental groups still make up the largest block of players in the environmental quality advocacy coalition (the seven largest groups had 7.7 million members in 1990), they can no longer be seen as a unified force. The environmental movement has matured and diversified to include large, multi-issue groups (Sierra Club); smaller, more narrowly focused **"purist"** groups (Friends of the Earth); nonpartisan research and policy development centers (Resources for the Future); law and science groups (Environmental Defense Fund); **"radical"** deep ecology groups (Earth First!); and increasingly active independent state and local groups (Clean Water Action) (Bosso, 1994). While these groups may share certain core values, they display a dazzling variety of policy positions and political tactics.

Other actors have joined the environmental quality advocacy coalition over the last twenty years. The coalition lost strong advocates in Congress (John Blatnik, D-MN and Edmund Muskie, D-ME) and the White House (Jimmy Carter), but gained others (Henry Waxman, D-CA and Timothy Wirth, D-CO; Al Gore, D-TN). Certain industrial groups, such as the insurance, waste disposal, and pollution control equipment industries, have also adopted a more pro-environmental stance. As evidence mounted regarding stratospheric ozone depletion, global warming, and the immunological and reproductive effects of certain toxic pollutants, large sections of the scientific community also joined the environmental quality camp. Finally, significant numbers of social scientists and civil rights activists have allied themselves with the coalition as it has become more receptive to the concerns of economic efficiency and potential racial and class biases in environmental regulation.

THE ECONOMIC RATIONALITY ADVOCACY COALITION

Much as environmental groups are still major players in the environmental quality advocacy coalition, industrial groups continue to dominate the economic rationality coalition. While the players may have remained the same, the names and the tactics have not. During the early 1970s, industry relied heavily upon umbrella groups and trade association to press their policy positions. As this strategy proved generally ineffective, industry moved toward reliance upon lobbying by individual corporations. The late 1980s and early 1990s saw another shift, where industrial coalitions are setting up **nonprofit corporations** to lobby for regulatory change. These organizations benefit from a broad base, deep pockets, and names that invoke thoughts of civic-mindedness (e.g., the National Wetlands Coalition includes the real estate, petroleum, and natural gas industries, while the National Endangered Species Act Reform Coalition was organized by electric utility and agribusiness firms) (Carney, 1992).

One of the most interesting changes in the economic rationality advocacy coalition has been the remarkable increase in industry supported **conservative policy think tanks** (e.g., the Heritage Foundation, Manhattan Institute, Reason Foundation). These groups were nonentities twenty years ago, but with the increasing importance of analysis in policy debates, they have come to play a significant role in environmental regulation (Sabatier and Jenkins-Smith, 1993). Finally, as environmental protection has become a more partisan issue (Calvert, 1989), the economic advocacy coalition has picked up supporters in Congress and the White House.

The final addition to the economic advocacy coalition is the wide array of groups that make up the **"wise use"** movement. The 250 or so groups that march under the "wise use" banner run the gamut from true populist organizations made up of ranchers and four wheel drive enthusiasts, to public relations fronts for the timber, fossil fuel, and mining industries. What the groups share is a **grassroots lobbying style**, a sense that environmental regulation has gone too far, and an emphasis on the protection of private property rights. In 1991, 125 of these groups formed the Alliance for America as a counterpoint to grassroots environmental groups (Bosso, 1994).

FREE AGENTS

Along with the core members of the two competing advocacy coalitions are a variety of interested parties, or **"free agents,"** that may ally themselves with one of the two advocacy coalitions, depending upon the policy under consideration. Three groups exist. First, state and local governments have historically been allies of the environmental quality coalition, pressing the federal government for greater resources and going beyond federal requirements in several areas. With the recent rise of costly unfunded mandates in environmental regulation, however, states and localities are increasingly lining up with the opponents of environmental regulation. Second, several other federal agencies are routinely involved in environmental regulation (e.g., the departments of Agriculture, Defense, Energy, and Interior), and these agencies have allied themselves with both advocacy coalitions. By one estimate, these agencies will soon spend more for environmental protection than does the EPA (EPA Administrator, 1991). Third, since environmental regulations typically impose costs on manufacturing industries, labor unions have historically opposed environmental regulation. In an increasing number of instances, however, unions have allied with the supporters of environmental protection to protect jobs (e.g., coal miners and construction workers) or improve workplace safety (e.g., farm workers).

FOUR ERAS IN THE ENVIRONMENT OF POLLUTION CONTROL REGULATION

The four eras in the environment of pollution control regulation include (1) the era of nondecisionmaking, (2) federal control and environmental quality advocacy coalition dominance, (3) deregulation, devolution, and defunding, and (4) into the 1990s: policy learning and advocacy coalition compromise.

The Era of Nondecisionmaking

Environmental quality deteriorated rapidly in the United States after World War Two. The country experienced periodic episodes of severe air pollution and massive fish kills in lakes and rivers. These episodes caught the attention of a few observers, but none played the role of a focusing event around which advocacy coalitions could crystalize. Information regarding the economic costs and benefits of environmental pollution and the technical mechanisms of environmental damage and pollution control was nonexistent. With the exception of a few pieces of federal legislation that attempted to assess the scope of the problem and provide technical assistance to the states, environmental regulation remained the responsibility of state and local governments. By and large, environmental regulation was in a **pre-problem stage** (Crenson, 1971; Davies and Davies, 1975).

Federal Control and Environmental Quality Advocacy Coalition Dominance

Beginning in the late 1960s, a series of focusing events radically changed the environment surrounding pollution control regulation. In 1967 the oil tanker Torrey Canyon broke up off the coast of England, contaminating 250 miles of English and French beaches. In 1969, a Union Oil Company well off the coast of Santa Barbara blew out, and

20,000 gallons of crude oil a day washed up on California beaches. Ohio's Cuyahoga River became so polluted that it caught fire. Lake Erie had become little more than a sewage holding pond inhabited by green algae and carp. Finally, in April 1970, Earth Day raised the environmental consciousness of citizens across the country. Additional information that heightened the salience of environmental protection was provided by two reports from the Nader organization, *Vanishing Air* and *Water Wasteland*, that were highly critical of federal air and water pollution control programs (Esposito, 1970; Zwick and Benstock, 1971).

By 1970, public opinion polls showed that environmental protection was the most frequently cited public problem (Anderson, Brady, and Bullock, 1977). While we were still generally ignorant regarding the economic costs and technological complexity of environmental regulation, it was clear to the public that something had to be done. Politicians saw environmental protection as an opportunity to improve their public stature, and Congress fired the first shot in the war for the hearts and minds of environmentalists by passing the National Environmental Policy Act (see below). Over the next seven years, Congress would enact a dozen and a half pieces of new or significantly revised environmental protection legislation.

In February of 1970, President Nixon sent a special message to Congress seeking federal standards for industrial and municipal sources of pollution (Davies and Davies, 1975). Nixon's actions were viewed as a direct challenge to Edmund Muskie, a leader in the fight for stronger environmental regulation in the Senate, and the front-runner for the Democratic presidential nomination in 1972. As part of Nixon's initiative to take leadership in this area away from Muskie, the president submitted **reorganization plan number 3** to Congress (Davies and Davies, 1975). The plan proposed consolidating all pollution control efforts in the new Environmental Protection Agency. Established in December 1970, EPA had as its first administrator William Ruckelshaus. As an attorney, Ruckelshaus stressed court action to enforce the law. In the agency's first few years, some 185 law suits were filed against ITT, U.S. Steel, the City of Atlanta, and others. The announced agency policy was "to single out violators with the greatest visibility in order to get the message across" (Rosenbaum, 1973:124).

Deregulation, Devolution, and Defunding

The relative strength of the competing advocacy coalitions and the direction of environmental regulation changed beginning in the late 1970s. The impetus for this change was threefold. First, the seeds of change were planted as early as the **OPEC oil embargo** of 1973-74 which shifted public attention from environmental quality to energy supply concerns. Second, the embargo itself touched off a worldwide recession that brought high inflation, high unemployment, and declining labor productivity to the United States. The 1979 oil embargo exacerbated each of these factors. Third, several years of experience with the environmental policies enacted in the early 1970s had exposed the limits of **technology-forcing regulation**. Industry was faced with required water pollution control equipment that did not work, smokestack scrubbers that consumed five percent of the electrical output of power plants while producing thousands of tons of toxic sludge, and unreliable catalytic converters that reduced the fuel efficiency of automobiles.

Industrial members of the economic rationality advocacy coalition had regrouped during the mid-1970s, and were joined by several new conservative policy think tanks. Industry and think tank analysts painted regulation in general and environmental regulation in particular as the cause of much of the economic hardship of the decade (MacAvoy, 1979; Weidenbaum, 1981). In addition, they seized upon the shortcomings of technology forcing regulation and missed legislative deadlines as evidence that environmental regulation was misguided. In short, the coalition argued this new evidence proved that environmental regulation was technologically infeasible and economically ruinous.

Changes in the broader political environment also hastened change in environmental regulation. Opinion polls showed a dip in public support for environmental protection in the late 1970s (Dunlap and Scarce, 1991). These same polls showed that the electorate was becoming more conservative. The electoral consequences of the economic and ideological changes of the late 1970s were that the Republican party took control of the Senate for the first time in a generation, a coalition of Republicans and conservative Democrats established a working majority in the House of Representatives, and Ronald Reagan was elected president on an anti-regulation platform. To carry out his policy agenda in environmental policy, Ronald Reagan set out on a three-pronged strategy of deregulation, devolution, and defunding.

DEREGULATION IN THE 1980S

In pursuing deregulation, Reagan first began by cutting EPA's budget (a process begun by his predecessor, Jimmy Carter) and personnel. From 1979 to 1983, pollution control and compliance spending at EPA was cut by 60 percent. Between 1978 and 1983, EPA's research and development budget was cut by 75 percent, and the overall agency budget was reduced by 56 percent (Ringquist, 1993). By 1983, Reagan reduced the number of full time employees at the agency by 2,762 (Gottron, 1982).

President Reagan's second tactic in deregulation was appointing Anne Gorsuch Burford as EPA administrator, the first non-environmentalist to head the agency. Gorsuch-Burford supported the president's budgetary requests, personnel practices, and antipathy for environmental regulation. Along these lines, Gorsuch-Burford initially abolished the agency's enforcement office and reallocated the duties to other units, later recreating it as a separate but smaller unit. Enforcement efforts were reorganized four times in a ten month period in 1981 and 1982. In addition to constant restructuring, Gorsuch-Burford stressed voluntary compliance with pollution laws; a radical departure from the Ruckleshaus tactic of filing suit against the most visible polluters.

The president's third tactic in deregulation was **Executive Order 12291**, which required federal agencies to submit proposed regulations to the Office of Management and Budget (OMB) for benefit-cost analysis. Reagan was the first president to use **benefit-cost assessments** as the *sole* criterion for approving regulations. The EPA was singled out for particularly close attention in the implementation of executive order 12291; over half of the agency's proposed regulations were rejected or sent back to the agency for revisions, and agency rules were delayed an average of 64 days by the review process (Smith, 1984). On the surface, it seems reasonable to issue regulations only if their benefits exceed their costs. The technique of benefit-cost analysis, however, has notorious difficulty assessing the benefits and costs of environmental regulation and relies upon a series of highly unrealistic assumptions (Kelman, 1981c; Meier, 1984). In addition, the technique was manipulated for admittedly political ends within Reagan's OMB in an effort to scuttle environmental regulations, regardless of their benefits (Smith, 1984).

President Reagan's most enduring deregulatory legacy is found in the judiciary. Both Presidents Reagan and Bush consciously appointed judges to the federal bench who were hostile to regulation. By 1992, these Reagan/Bush appointees held nearly two-thirds of all federal judgeships, and a majority of seats on the Supreme Court. Predictably, the Supreme Court is now agreeing to hear more environmental cases, and the success rate of the environmental quality advocacy coalition in these cases is declining (Stewart, 1992; Wenner, 1994). The Washington, D.C. Circuit Court of Appeals, the site of many of the environmental quality coalition's victories in the early 1970s, is now much less receptive to these groups (Kovacic, 1991). Finally, environmental groups are finding it more difficult to launch court challenges in the first place because of a series of court decisions (led by Supreme Court Justices William Rehnquist and Antonin Scalia) that have imposed stricter requirements for standing on these groups (Schneider, 1992; Stanfield, 1988; Wenner, 1994).

DEVOLUTION IN ENVIRONMENTAL REGULATION

The second prong of President Reagan's approach to environmental regulation was **devolving policy authority** to state governments. In delegating and passing authority, the administration served the dual goals of reducing the reach of the federal government and returning policy responsibility to a level of government historically less supportive of environmental protection. Through the 1970s, the EPA had been reluctant to grant primacy for environmental regulations to state governments. But from 1981 to 1984, the delegation of environmental programs to the states accelerated rapidly. With new federal programs, new policy responsibilities, and a decrease in voluntary compliance resulting from the changed political climate, work loads in state environmental agencies doubled between 1980 and 1984 (Stanfield, 1984).

DEFUNDING ENVIRONMENTAL REGULATION

As the federal government devolved more responsibility to the states it simultaneously slashed federal contributions to these programs in an effort to shrink domestic expenditures. This **defunding** occurred across all policy areas as the overall value of federal aid to the states dropped 39 percent from 1980 to 1987 (ACIR, 1991). Reductions in federal support for environmental programs went even further. In 1979, **federal grants** to the states made up 43 percent of the EPA's budget. By 1988, these grants amounted to only 31 percent of a much smaller budget. Over this same period, federal support for state air pollution control programs fell by 54 percent and support for state water pollution control programs declined by 68 percent (CBO, 1988).

EFFECTS ON THE ENVIRONMENTAL PROTECTION AGENCY

The reaction of the Environmental Protection Agency to Reagan's deregulatory initiatives was threefold. First, agency activity levels dropped dramatically. Monitoring activity in the air program dropped 41 percent after the FY82 budget cuts and the appointment of Gorsuch-Burford, while abatement actions declined 69 percent (Wood, 1988). Enforcement actions experienced similar declines in other program areas (Wood and Waterman, 1993), while civil and criminal referrals to the Department of Justice fell from 252 in 1980 to 78 in 1981 (Davies, 1984). Second, morale dropped precipitously. For example, the turnover rate at EPA soared to 2.7 percent per month (Gottron, 1982). The agency's third reaction was to fight back. Internal documents were leaked to friendly members of Congress and the press to counter Burford's actions (Davies, 1984).

Responding to these leaks, between October 1981 and July 1982 Congress called EPA officials to testify before Congress some 70 times. During these hearings a number of senior staff resigned over policy conflicts with Burford (see *National Journal*, May 1, 1982). Congressional investigations also uncovered numerous improprieties in the hazardous waste program at EPA. After refusing to release documents relating to the hazardous waste investigation (citing **executive privilege**), Gorsuch-Burford was held in contempt of Congress. Other improprieties in the superfund program were traced to assistant administrator Rita Lavelle, and Lavelle and four of her assistants were fired on February 7, 1983. (Lavelle was later convicted of lying to a congressional committee.) By March 1983, Burford was seen as a major liability to the reelection of Ronald Reagan, and White House staff members pressured Burford into resigning. The housecleaning did not stop with Burford; in the next several months 20 top EPA officials were dismissed (Vig and Kraft, 1984).

President Reagan recouped some of his losses in the Burford affair by reappointing William Ruckelshaus to head the agency. Within months, Ruckelshaus was credited with operating an open management process and restoring morale to the agency (Mosher, 1983b). The Burford affair illustrates the power of the federal bureaucracy when the bureaucracy has political allies in Congress. Agency leadership that fails to consider the cohesion and values of career bureaucrats in an agency is leadership that is taking a major risk. Such action is especially risky if it is in opposition to the policy values held by key members of Congress.

EFFECTS ON THE STATES

The states reacted to the tactics of devolution and defunding in ways wholly unexpected by the Reagan administration. Between 1970 (when Congress shifted responsibility for environmental regulation to the federal government) and the early 1980s, state governments had undergone a remarkable transformation (Van Horn, 1992). By increasing the stability of their financial resources, the capacity of their legislatures, and the professionalism of their administrative agencies, most states were well equipped to shoulder additional responsibilities in pollution control. Impatient with the slow progress of environmental regulation at the federal level, many states became hotbeds of regulatory innovation (Lowry, 1992; Ringquist, 1993). Many states also replaced a significant portion of lost federal grants with their own sources of revenue (Lester, 1990). In short, by the end of the 1980s states had filled in many of the gaps in environmental regulation created by devolution and defunding.

Into the 1990s: Policy Learning and Advocacy Coalition Compromise

Reminiscent of a decade earlier, seeds of change in the regulatory environment were planted at the height of what appeared to be a fundamental change in the nation's political character. A number of focusing events turned public attention back toward the need for environmental regulation. Not the least of these focusing events was the Reagan assault on environmental regulation itself: budget cuts and the antics of presidential appointees helped to rekindle support for environmental protection in Congress, and flooded the memberships rolls and coffers of environmental groups across the nation. The 1986 accident at the Chernobyl nuclear power plant in Ukraine; the 1987 accident at the Union Carbide chemical plant in Bhopal, India; the 1989 grounding of the Exxon Valdez in Prince William sound; growing evidence of global warming and stratospheric ozone depletion in the late 1980s: these and other events helped push public support for environmental regulation to an all-time high by 1990 (Dunlap and Scarce, 1991).

Changes in the economic and technological aspects of the regulatory environment also helped to create conditions conducive to increased environmental regulation. First, research had demonstrated that the negative economic effects of environmental regulation had been significantly overstated, and in some cases simply did not exist (CBO, 1985). Second, a long period of economic expansion made citizens more willing to accept whatever economic costs might be associated with increased regulation. Third, many of the technical problems with pollution control equipment had been solved by the 1980s, and there was mounting evidence that this equipment had both reduced pollution emissions and improved environmental quality (CEQ, 1989).

More experience with pollution control regulations, more experience with each other, and the increased availability of economic and technical information provided bridges for cooperation between the environmental and economic advocacy coalitions that simply could not have existed earlier. For example, a number of environmental groups began listening to what economists had been saying for years; that traditional command and control regulations were a less efficient way of protecting environmental quality than were economic incentive approaches. Consequently, the Environmental Defense Fund and Resources for the Future became strong proponents of emission fees and tradable discharge permits (Kriz, 1992b). On the other hand, industry began to realize that in many instances pollution represents productive inefficiency, and that by reducing pollution a facility could lower costs and increase profits. These alterations in the positions of advocacy coalitions in response to experience and evidence are excellent examples of how **policy learning** takes place within subsystems (Sabatier and Jenkins-Smith, 1993).

This spirit of compromise was reflected in the political arena as well. When George Bush ran for president in 1988, one of the critical issues he chose to distinguish himself from his predecessor was environmental protection. Bush promised, in fact, to be "the environmental president." The new president followed up on this promise by appointing William Reilly, president of the Conservation Foundation and respected environmentalist, as EPA administrator. Bush also began to restore the EPA's budget, though by 1992 the agency's constant dollar budget was still barely half as large as it had been in 1978 (Ringquist, 1993). In the policy sphere, Bush oversaw the United States' participation in the international phase out of **chlorofluorocarbons** and helped craft the first reauthorization of the CAA in thirteen years (see below).

Cracks in the uneasy alliance of advocacy coalitions in environmental regulation began to appear in 1990, soon after President Bush signed the Clean Air Act Amendments. First, Bush proposed redefining **wetlands** in such a way that half of all remaining wetlands would have lost federal protection; a clear violation of his "no net loss of wetlands" campaign pledge (Huth, 1992). Next, a presidential commission compromised the Endangered Species Act by allowing clearcutting in the habitat of the northern spotted owl. Following in close succession were actions that allowed polluters to exceed emission limits for toxic pollutants without public notice or comment; the proposed elimination of public hearings and court challenges to oil, coal, gas, mineral, and timber sales and leases on public lands; and the weakening of several elements of the 1990 CAA. Many of these proposals emerged from the president's **Council on Competitiveness**, chaired by Vice President Dan Quayle. The commission, holding most of its meetings in closed session, solicited information from industry on where compliance costs were excessive and where regulations could be rolled back. Critics charged that this was the strongest assault on environmental regulations since the early years of the Reagan administration (Battaile, 1992; Waxman, 1992).

The replacements for Bush and Quayle, President Bill Clinton and Vice-President Al Gore, emphasized compromise and the positive relationship between environmental protection and economic growth during the campaign. Clinton has kept this promise of support for environmental protection by signing the global warming and biodiversity treaties crafted in 1992 at the United Nations' "earth summit" in Rio, and by appointing environmental advocates Carol Browner as EPA chief and Bruce Babbitt as secretary of Interior. In practice, each has maintained an approach that emphasizes compromise, whether the issue has been increasing grazing fees on public lands (Babbitt), assessing responsibility for improving water quality in the Everglades (Browner), or determining harvest rates for old growth forests in the Pacific Northwest (Clinton) (Hamilton, 1994; John, 1994). On the other hand, Clinton slightly reduced EPA's budget for FY94.

THE NATIONAL ENVIRONMENTAL POLICY ACT

Among the major threats to the environment in the 1960s was the federal government. The government operated hydroelectric plants, ran coal fired power plants, built thousands of miles of highways, managed millions of acres of public lands, sponsored research on pesticides, and so on. The **National Environmental Policy Act (NEPA)**, signed into law on January 1, 1970, established environmental protection as a goal of the federal government and created the **Council on Environmental Quality** to serve as the environmental equivalent of the Council of Economic Advisors. The act also required that all federal agencies prepare an **environmental impact statement** for major actions (Andrews, 1976; Ruff, 1981).

The provision for an *environmental impact statement* attempted to do three things. First, it established a procedure so that federal agencies would at least consider the environmental ramifications of their actions. Second, it permitted federal agencies to comment on the environmental impact of another agency's actions. Third, it permitted citizen access to the environmental impact statement. The third element proved to be the most influential even though it was added to the legislation as an afterthought. Citizens immediately took advantage of the opportunity to participate in environmental impact statements for major federal construction projects. In NEPA's first five years, some 400 court cases were filed to force agencies to comply with NEPA provisions.

Although the National Environmental Policy Act was initially important, its impact diminished over time. NEPA is essentially an act that changes agency procedures; it does not necessarily change their substantive actions. By altering agency procedures, however, the federal government's natural resources agencies gave greater consideration to environmental factors than they did before NEPA (Caldwell, 1982). By 1980 over 12,000 environmental impact statements were issued (Vig and Kraft, 1984). Environmental impact statements became an effective short-term tactic for environmentalists, allowing them to delay federal construction projects (Andrews, 1976). Some agencies, such as the Army Corps of Engineers, were profoundly affected by the act. The Corps changed from an agency little concerned with the environment to one that began to stress less environmentally damaging ways to control flooding (Mazmanian and Nienaber, 1979).

REGULATING WATER QUALITY

This examination on regulating water quality includes an overview of (1) the early efforts at water pollution control and the **Federal Water Pollution Control Act** (FWPCA) of 1972, (2) the Clean Water Act, (3) amending the FWPCA, (4) Criticisms of the FWPCA, (5) the Water Quality Act, and (6) reauthorizing the Clean Water Act.

Early Efforts at Water Pollution Control

The first piece of legislation reflecting an interest in water quality as an environmental and health issue was the **Water Pollution Control Act** of 1948. Like most pieces of early environmental legislation, this statute recognized water pollution as a potential problem and provided limited federal funds for studying the situation. The **Water Pollution Control Act** of 1956 sought to strengthen efforts at improving water quality through a grant program in which the federal government paid fifty-five percent of the construction costs of municipal waste water treatment facilities. The act also marked the beginning of the federal government's regulatory effort in water pollution control. If water pollution problems occurred, the Public Health Service (PHS) could call a conference to discuss the problem and pursue a solution in court, but only after the states had asked the PHS to intervene. The 1965 **Water Quality Act** was the first federal law to mandate state action to protect and improve water quality. The act now *required* states to set **quantitative water quality standards** for interstate waters within their borders and to develop **implementation plans** to meet these standards. If the state failed to develop standards, the federal government was authorized to promulgate them.

Implementing and enforcing these standards was left up to the states, but the **Federal Water Pollution Control Administration** was established to oversee the program.

In retrospect, these early efforts had limited success. Most states ignored federal admonitions to devise and enforce a system of water pollution permits because they feared that industry would leave the state rather than comply, and because they viewed the federal entry into water pollution control as an intrusion into state affairs. From 1956 to 1971, a total of 53 water pollution conferences were held; only four of these conferences progressed to the hearing stage, and only one resulted in a court suit (Lieber, 1983). In response, the federal government stepped in to take over primary responsibility in water pollution control.

The Federal Water Pollution Control Act of 1972—The Clean Water Act

Present surface water quality regulations are firmly rooted in the watershed **Federal Water Pollution Control Act (FWPCA)**, typically referred to as the **Clean Water Act (CWA)** of 1972. The Clean Water Act (CWA) received strong bipartisan support in Congress, and though President Nixon vetoed the legislation because of its $24 billion price tag, Congress easily overrode the veto (Davies and Davies, 1975). The CWA may be the most ambitious piece of environmental legislation ever passed at the federal level. In its zeal to satisfy the rising tide of environmentalism, Congress passed a law intended to attain the very ambitious goal of **zero pollutant discharge** in to the nation's waters by 1985. As an interim standard, the act set a goal of all waters being **fishable and swimmable** by 1983. To reach these ambitious goals, industrial sources of pollution were to install the **best practicable pollution control technology (BPT)** by 1977 and the **best available pollution control technology (BAT)** by 1983, while municipal treatment plants were required to install BPT by 1983 that achieved a secondary level of sewage treatment (e.g., removed 80 to 90 percent of organic wastes from sewage).

The FWPCA and the CAA amendments (see below) differed dramatically from normal regulatory legislation. Normal regulatory legislation sets vague standards such as "the public interest" and delegates most authority for meeting these standards to the regulatory agency. The approach embodied in the environmental regulation of the early 1970s was to set specific standards (e.g., BPT) with rigid deadlines for meeting these standards. The intent was to prevent the legislation from being subverted in the administrative process (Marcus, 1980).

IMPLEMENTING THE CLEAN WATER ACT

Under the FWPCA, states are responsible for establishing and implementing plans to meet national water quality goals. The act provides two major tools states may use to carry out this responsibility; **the municipal waste water treatment grant program (MWTGP)**, and the **National Pollutant Discharge Elimination System**. Prior to 1972, few states had taken advantage of the **federal waste water treatment grant program**, and most municipalities dumped untreated sewage directly into lakes, rivers, and oceans. Under the FWPCA, municipalities were now required to treat their sewage, but the federal government contributed seventy-five percent of the cost of constructing municipal waste water treatment plants. By paying cities to upgrade and expand their sewage treatment facilities, the MWTGP program subsidized municipal growth at the same time it sought to improve water quality.

Under the **National Pollutant Discharge Elimination System (NPDES)**, state and federal regulators provide **permits** to all facilities that discharge wastes into public waterways. The permits, which must be renewed on the average of every five years, also impose a strict set of reporting requirements on each facility. Periodically (though infrequently), state and/or federal regulators inspect both the facility and its reporting records for compliance and accuracy. The partial preemption provision of the FWPCA allows the states to accept responsibility for implementing their own NPDES programs, and thirty-eight states had done so by 1993 (Ringquist, 1993).

The FWPCA provided two methods by which NPDES permits could be given. The first method, and the method originally envisioned as standard operating procedure by many federal regulators, relies upon water quality standards like those called for in the 1965 Water Quality Act. When using water quality standards, the safe carrying capacity of a waterway is established for a number of pollutants. Permits are then issued to industrial and municipal dischargers so that the total amount of pollutants entering the waterway does not exceed its safe carrying capacity. The water quality based permitting system is ecologically sound, but it is extremely difficult to implement. Pollutant carrying capacities vary across seasons and years, and determining these capacities requires complicated water quality models and an extensive system of water quality monitors. This makes it very difficult to divide up the pollutant carrying capacity of a body of water among a large number of polluters.

Water quality standards were quickly abandoned in favor of **technology based standards** for issuing permits. Under the technology based approach, the EPA places uniform pollution control equipment requirements on all polluters in a particular industry or all polluters using a particular manufacturing process. While the technology based permitting approach avoided the difficulties inherent in water quality based permitting, it still left EPA in the position of determining best practicable treatment technologies for hundreds of different industrial classifications. After a long delay, EPA finally established 642 **industrial subcategories**, each with its own separate treatment guidelines (Ruff, 1981). The real advantage of technology based permits comes in monitoring and enforcement: rather than testing the waste water at each facility, inspectors simply make sure that the facility has the required pollution control equipment in proper working order.

Amending the FWPCA

The FWPCA was amended in 1977 while the environment surrounding pollution control regulation was in flux. Industries lobbied for relaxation of the 1972 standards, arguing that they were impossible to meet and that the 1985 "zero discharge" goal could never be met. Congress responded to these pressures. Sources that acted in **"good faith"** to meet the 1977 policy of BPT but failed to do so were given until 1979 to meet the standard. The 1983 BAT standard was weakened to best conventional pollution control technology (BCT), effective for 1984. Although the **"zero discharge"** goal remained in the legislation, the 1977 amendments placed its attainment far in to the future (Marcus,

1980). Later amendments in 1981 extended the BAT deadline for municipal treatment plants to 1988 and reduced to 55 percent the federal share of constructing these plants.

Criticisms of the FWPCA and Its Amendments

Experience with federally directed water quality regulation identified a number of shortcomings of the FWPCA and its amendments:

First of all, nearly all federal regulation under the CWA focused on **point sources of water pollution** (i.e., pollution from industrial facilities and municipal sewage plants), but by the late 1980s **nonpoint sources of water pollution** (e.g., pollution from farmland, mines, construction sites, and urban runoff) accounted for nearly two-thirds of the pollutants reaching American waterways (Rosenbaum, 1991).

Second, though the FWPCA required EPA and the states to regulate toxic water pollutants, controlling these pollutants was generally ignored during the 1970s and 1980s. For instance, the 1972 statute required EPA to set toxic pollutant effluent standards for fifty industrial categories, but by the late 1980s, the agency had developed regulations for fewer than half of these (Schneider, 1992).

Third, several policy observers had become concerned about the cost of the federal municipal waste water treatment grant program. This program quickly grew to become the largest expenditure in the EPA budget, funneling over $45 billion in grants to municipalities from 1972 to 1988 (EPA, 1989).

Fourth, most indicators suggested that progress toward improving water quality was very slow (see below).

The Water Quality Act of 1987

The **Water Quality Act** of 1987, passed nearly unanimously over the veto of President Reagan, sought to address the shortcomings of previous water quality legislation, increase the use of water quality based permits, and return more responsibility for water pollution control to the states. The act addresses nonpoint water pollution by directing the states to assess the seriousness of nonpoint source pollution and to minimize the impact of these pollutants on the environment. Under the WQA, states are required to prepare a nonpoint pollution assessment identifying major sources of nonpoint pollution. States and localities are then directed to devise implementation plans incorporating "**best management practices**" (BMPs) that will control these nonpoint pollution sources (EPA 1990; Hansen et al., 1988). The states are assisted in nonpoint pollution control efforts by an EPA nonpoint source pollution task force and the Departments of Agriculture, Commerce, and the U.S. Geological Survey.

Prior to the mid-1980s, surface water regulation emphasized the traditional pollutants of bacteria, nutrients, sediments, and oxygen demanding wastes. The 1987 WQA, however, focuses more attention on **trace toxic elements** in water such as pesticides and heavy metals. **Toxic pollutants** are the most significant remaining problem in industrial and municipal effluent (EPA, 1990). The WQA requires states to develop lists of waters impaired by toxic pollution, and then develop individual impact control strategies (e.g., new NPDES permits) for each of the point sources contributing to this toxic pollution (EPA, 1990). States were supposed to have these toxic discharge control programs in place by 1990, and though only 35 had done so by 1991 (Schneider, 1991), all states are expected to have completed toxic discharge control programs by 1994.

The 1987 WQA also seeks to control toxic water pollution by requiring municipalities to adopt aggressive **industrial pretreatment programs**. In pretreatment, industries that produce toxic pollutants are required to treat their effluent to remove these toxins before releasing the remainder of their waste stream in to municipal sewage systems. An increasing number of industries are discharging their wastes into municipal sewer systems, and most municipal treatment facilities are not equipped to handle toxic substances. At best, the substances pass through the facility unaffected, and at worst they can damage the facility itself, rendering the treatment of other wastes difficult or impossible. An estimated 35 percent of all toxic chemicals reaching the nation's waters do so by passing through municipal treatment systems (EPA, 1988).

Finally, the 1987 WQA changed how the construction of municipal waste water treatment plants is funded. The municipal waste water treatment grant program was replaced by a series of one-time grants to the states for municipal waste water treatment. States use these grants to set up **revolving loan funds**, and municipalities that want to build or upgrade waste water treatment facilities receive loans out of these funds. The loan fund greatly reduces federal support for municipal waste water treatment, but most municipalities presently have secondary level treatment plants or better, and the loan fund allows the states to follow their own funding priorities when constructing waste water treatment plants. Thirteen states had fully operational revolving loan funds by 1990 (EPA, 1990). In a final municipal treatment note, the EPA issued a set of rules in 1994 regulating the toxic pollutant content and disposal of the seven million metric tons of sludge produced annually at municipal waste water treatment plants.

Reauthorizing the Clean Water Act

The **Clean Water Act** will not be revised until the 1995-96 Congressional session. The debate over reauthorizing the CWA is an excellent example of the new era of political competition in environmental regulation, as members of each advocacy coalition have aggregated into large nonprofit lobbying organizations. The **Clean Water Working Group**, for instance, contains the American Farm Bureau Federation, the National Agricultural Chemical Association, and over thirty other agribusiness concerns. The **Water Quality Task Force** is made up of the National Association of Manufacturers and over 150 affiliated organizations. Even members of the environmental quality advocacy coalition have adopted this tactic: the **Clean Water Network** is made up of the National Resources Defense Council and 450 fellow travelers including labor unions, fishermen, and surfers (Carney, 1994).

Elements of the revised CWA are beginning to take shape. Some, such as increasing EPA's authority to limit the use of toxic chemicals that eventually find their way into surface water, will strengthen the role of the federal government. Most changes, however, will strengthen the role of state and local governments in water pollution control. Proposals from the White House and Congressional committees will allow states more options in developing best management practices to control nonpoint sources of pollution, roll back the deadlines for municipal compliance with stormwater runoff regulations, and make municipal stormwater facilities eligible for federal construction grants. Finally, the act will likely encourage the development of watershed management plans that allow states and localities to determine methods for protecting wetlands and water quality, and increase state and local authority for collecting permit fees to pay for implementing these plans (Catalina, 1994).

AIR QUALITY REGULATION

This examination of air quality regulation includes (1) early air pollution control efforts, (2) the Clean Air Act of 1970, (3) the Clean Air Act Amendments of 1977, (4) criticisms of the 1970 and 1977 Clean Air Acts, and (5) the Clean Air Act Amendments of 1990.

Early Air Pollution Control Efforts

As far back as the 1880s, Chicago and Cincinnati had laws regulating smoke emissions, and in 1952 Oregon became the first state to pass comprehensive statewide air pollution legislation and establish a state air pollution control agency (EPA, 1988). As air pollution problems emerged in Los Angeles and other urban areas, the federal government responded with the 1955 **Air Pollution Control Act** and the **Air Quality Act** of 1960. Both acts authorized research into the sources of air pollution. Little happened in this area, however, until President Kennedy called for federal action against air pollution. The Congressional response was the 1963 Clean Air Act and amendments to the Air Quality Act in 1967. These acts sought to induce states to set voluntary air pollution standards and to develop plans for attaining these standards. The acts also empowered the new National Air Pollution Control Administration to create a set of **Air Quality Control Regions** across the country, study the effects of air pollution, provide grants and training assistance to the states for air pollution control, and hold air pollution control conferences if requested to do so by a state.

The federal enabling legislation of the 1960s was intended to induce states to step up their own efforts in air pollution control, but these inducements fell far short of their intended effects. For example, though the **Clean Air Act** empowered the federal government to intervene in interstate air pollution problems, this intervention could only come at the request of the states. From 1965 to 1970, only eleven air pollution abatement actions were taken under the Clean Air Act (Smith, 1992). A few states (and some localities) began to successfully grapple with air pollution control problems near the end of the decade (see Jones, 1975), but for the most part states tended to ignore the suggestions and incentives for controlling air pollution provided by early federal legislation.

The Clean Air Act of 1970

Electoral considerations played a part in how the federal government responded to increased pressure for action in air quality regulation. President Nixon and Democratic presidential contender Senator Muskie proposed increasingly strong clean air programs in

Congress. Congress eventually embodied most of the Muskie proposals in the Clean Air Act Amendments of 1970, which were passed by huge bipartisan majorities. The Clean Air Act is recognized as the flagship piece of federal environmental policy. Never before had Congress established specific goals that were nonincremental changes from current policy, that required the cooperation of all 50 states, and that were to be accomplished in a short time period.

NATIONAL AMBIENT AIR QUALITY STANDARDS

The Clean Air Act gave the EPA 120 days to issue **National Ambient Air Quality Standards (NAAQS)** for the criteria pollutants of nitrogen dioxide, sulfur dioxide, total suspended particulates, carbon monoxide, hydrocarbons, and photochemical oxidants (the oxidant standard was later changed to a standard for ozone, and a lead standard was added in 1978). There are actually two standards for each pollutant: a **primary standard** designed to protect human health "with an adequate margin of safety", and **secondary standards** designed to protect property, crops, and the environment. The CAA also empowered the EPA to study the effects of toxic air pollutants (e.g., benzene, vinyl chloride, heavy metals, etc.) and set standards for these pollutants as necessary. States are ultimately responsible for meeting national ambient air quality standards through **State Implementation Plans (SIPs)** that include a combination of existing source performance standards, new source performance standards, monitoring and enforcement programs, and innovative state programs (see below).

Although Congress was fairly specific about EPA actions, the agency's discretion in setting the standards was virtually unlimited because the scientific study of pollutants was just beginning. Congress explicitly recognized that this scientific uncertainty might pose problems, and thus directed the EPA to reconsider these standards every five years. Despite the limitations of knowledge, EPA responded to Congress's mandate with six NAAQS in 1971. The scientific problems involving NAAQS were illustrated in 1979, when the EPA revised the ozone standard. Little research had been done, and that which had did not present consistent findings concerning the effects of ozone. The revision effort was controversial, with environmentalists pressing to retain the current standard (.08 parts per million, or ppm) and industry advocating a substantially weaker standard (.25 ppm). Eventually, EPA selected a standard of .12 ppm that left everyone dissatisfied (Landy et al., 1990).

STATIONARY SOURCES EMISSION STANDARDS

The Clean Air Act required state pollution control agencies to set emission standards for **existing stationary sources of pollution** (e.g., smelters, coal fired power plants, factories). The CAA also required the EPA to set uniform emission standards for new stationary sources of pollution. Like existing source performance standards, **new source performance standards (NSPS)** are established on an industry-by-industry basis. The NSPS are more stringent, however, in that they require these sources to install the best available control technology. Once consequence of this policy is that older and dirtier plants have been kept in operation longer than they would have been without the policy

(Crandall, 1983). Rather than improving air quality, stringent NSPS may have retarded progress toward improved air quality in the short run.

REGULATING AUTOMOBILE EMISSIONS

The Clean Air Act established specific **goals and rigid timetables** for **automobile emissions**. Emissions of carbon monoxide and hydrocarbons had to be reduced by 90 percent by 1975, and nitrogen oxides had to be reduced by 90 percent by 1976. Immediately, the auto industry claimed that the standards were technologically infeasible (though foreign manufacturers were able to meet these standards with little difficulty, see White, 1981), and pressed the EPA for a one year delay. When Ruckleshaus refused the delay, the companies sued (*International Harvester* v. *Ruckleshaus*, 1973); and the courts remanded the case to the EPA stating that its refusal must be justified by the facts in the situation (Ruff, 1981). In the meantime, the OPEC oil embargo had radically changed the political environment surrounding pollution control, and Ruckleshaus granted the one year extension. The Ruckleshaus decision was probably influenced by Chrysler's failure to meet the standards. Rather than shut Chrysler down, Ruckleshaus capitulated.

The auto industry, having accomplished all it could through the administrative branch, turned its attention to Congress. During the early 1970s, Detroit was facing stiff foreign competition and new fuel economy, emissions, and safety regulations, so the industry's motivations for regulatory relief were clear. The automakers were fairly new at lobbying Congress, however, and were not successful until they convinced the United Auto Workers (UAW) to take the lead. The automakers threatened to close down assembly lines and throw thousands out of work rather than produce cars that would result in $10,000 fines. The automaker-UAW coalition was successful in using the political environment of the mid-1970s to weaken the Clean Air Act. In the Energy Supply and Environmental Coordination Act of 1974, emission standards were delayed for all automobile pollutants.

The Clean Air Act Amendments of 1977

The Clean Air Act was reauthorized in 1977. As the reauthorization deadline approached, it was clear that many of the goals of the CAA of 1970 would not be met, and several of the 1977 amendments either relaxed the stringency of air quality regulations or rolled back the dates for attaining clean air goals. For example, the 1977 CAA delayed State Implementation Plan approval deadlines from 1977 to 1982, and delayed the deadline for meeting NAAQ standards from 1979 to 1987. Schedules for attaining automobile emission reductions for hydrocarbons and carbon monoxide were extended into the 1980s, and automobile nitrogen oxide emission standards were relaxed from a 90 percent to a 75 percent reduction. In addition to relaxing existing pollution control regulations, the 1977 amendments extended regulation into new areas.

REGIONAL COAL CONFLICT

A number of **coal-fired utilities** met the emission reduction requirements of the 1970 CAA without installing pollution control equipment. This was possible because many stationary sources of pollution could meet the emission standards simply by switching from more polluting high sulfur coal to less polluting low sulfur coal. This strategy did not sit well with either high sulfur coal interests or environmental groups. In response, a coalition of Eastern mine owners, United Mine Workers, and environmentalists proposed that all coal be **"scrubbed"** regardless of its initial sulfur content; otherwise, the coalition argued, low sulfur Western coal would have an unfair competitive advantage. Congress responded to this pressure by requiring all new coal fired power plants to adopt the best **technological system of continuous emission reductions** (e.g., smokestack scrubbers) (Ackerman and Hassler, 1981).

PREVENTING DETERIORATION

The 1970 Clean Air Act required strong pollution controls only in areas that were not currently meeting NAAQ standards. Environmental groups feared that this would induce polluting industries to locate in areas with clean air and lead to the pollution of areas with exceptionally clean air across the country. To prevent this, the Sierra Club sued the EPA, and in 1972 the Supreme Court ruled that State Implementation Plans must include provisions to prevent the degradation of air quality in those areas that currently exceeded federal air quality standards (*Sierra Club* v. *Ruckleshaus*, 1972). The EPA responded by developing **prevention of significant deterioration (PSD)** regulations in 1974, and Congress formalized EPA's guidelines as a set of legislative PSD requirements in the 1977 CAA. Under PSD, all **air quality control regions (AQCRs)** attaining NAAQ standards were designated Class I, Class II, or Class III. Almost all AQCRs were originally designated **Class II**, which allows some degradation of air quality. States can reclassify Class II areas (with EPA approval) to either **Class I** (for pristine areas around national parks or wilderness preserves) or **Class III** (where air quality is allowed to degrade to NAAQS levels).

IMPLICATIONS FOR THE STATES

Both the altered new source performance standards and prevention of significant deterioration requirements affected the states. Many Southern and Western states saw these regulations as attempts by the high sulfur coal producing and industrialized states of the East to hamstring industrial development in the relatively clean spaces of the West (Ackerman and Hassler, 1981; Crandall, 1983). The 1977 CAA also formally recognized the interstate nature of air pollution problems and required states to provide **"adequate assurance"** that stationary sources of pollution within one state's borders would not prevent the attainment of NAAQS in neighboring states (Freedman, 1987). This prohibition has not been supported in practice. During the 1980s, Wisconsin sued Illinois, and states in the Northeast sued states in the Midwest over cross boundary air pollution, but in each case the courts refused to take substantive action (Lowry, 1992).

Criticisms of the 1970 and 1977 Clean Air Acts

The Clean Air Acts of 1970 and 1977 were criticized from a number of perspectives. Environmentalists felt that several of the pollution control provisions in the acts were not strong enough. As evidence of these weaknesses, environmental groups pointed to automobile emission standards that had either remained the same or been relaxed since 1970, a lack of progress in reducing urban air pollution, the absence of pollution controls aimed at acid rain and toxic air pollutants, and feeble enforcement efforts. Many economists argued that uniform emission reduction standards and the "command and control" provisions characteristic of environmental regulation in general were inefficient and often ineffective. Most economic policy analysts suggested an increased use of economic incentives and market-based pollution control mechanisms to overcome these problems of inefficiency and ineffectiveness. Overall, the 1977 CAA has been criticized for increasing electricity prices, increasing dependence upon imported oil, increasing sulfur dioxide emissions, and placing southern and western states at a disadvantage in industrial development and coal production (Navarro, 1981).

Disagreements over how a new CAA should address these criticisms and shifts in the power of the competing advocacy coalitions led to intense political debates throughout the 1980s. President Reagan briefly attempted to weaken the act when it came up for reauthorization in 1982, but this effort was quickly abandoned when it became clear that public and congressional support for the act was strong enough to thwart this executive initiative. While congressional support for the Clean Air Act was strong, powerful figures such as Senator Robert Byrd from West Virginia and Representative John Dingell from Michigan prevented Congress from strengthening either the acid rain or automobile emission provisions of the act. Furthermore, even if Congress could have developed a new Clean Air Act acceptable to a majority of members, there was not enough support to override a certain presidential veto. Thus, the provisions of the 1977 act were kept in place during the 1980s through a series of congressional continuing resolutions.

The Clean Air Act Amendments of 1990

The deadlock over clean air policy was broken in 1990 when Congress and the Bush administration were able to agree on reauthorization of the Clean Air Act. The 1990 CAA amendments significantly strengthened the act, and it is clear that the architects of the law listened carefully to critics of the earlier legislation.

REQUIREMENTS OF THE 1990 AMENDMENTS

The requirements of the 1990 amendments have three thrusts:

First, the amendments seek to address **urban air problems**. The amendments require that all new automobiles sold after 1993 reduce their emissions of nitrogen oxides by 60 percent and hydrocarbons by 35 percent (from 1990 levels). The act also doubles the required lifespan of **automobile pollution control equipment** (to 100,000 miles) and requires the use of **reformulated automotive fuels** in those cities with the worst smog problems. These requirements will be tightened again in 2003 unless the EPA deems that they are unfeasible or unnecessary. In addition, the 1990 CAA gave all states (not just California) the option of exceeding federal automobile emission requirements. So far, California, eleven northeastern states and Washington, DC have decided to exceed federal mobile source emission standards. Finally, all **ozone nonattainment areas** have been placed on strict attainment schedules ranging from 1993 (for cities with small ozone problems) to 2010 (for cities with severe ozone problems).

Second, the 1990 CAA attempts to control **toxic air pollutants**. Beginning in 1993, all sources that emit significant amounts of toxic pollutants must obtain a permit from the

EPA. If toxic polluters exceed the emissions allowed by their permits, they are subject to civil fines and criminal prosecution by the EPA or empowered state agencies. Environmental agencies are not the only toxic pollutant watchdogs under the 1990 CAA. The act contains a provision modeled on the Clean Water Act that allows any citizen (or environmental group) to sue an industry for excessive toxic air pollutant emissions. The goal of this air pollution permit program is a seventy-five percent reduction in the emission of over 180 toxic chemicals.

Third, the 1990 amendments address the acid rain problem by requiring a fifty percent reduction in sulfur dioxide emissions and significant **reductions in nitrogen dioxide emissions** by 1995. These goals will be met in large part by using **marketable emission permits** that allow utilities to buy and sell the right to emit sulfur and nitrogen dioxides. Initially, 110 of the nation's dirtiest utilities will be able to trade these permits, and by the year 2000 nearly all coal fired utilities will be allowed to trade in the emission permit market. Over time, the number of permits (and thus the level of allowable pollution) will be reduced, though the EPA does have the authority to issue more permits if necessary (Cushman, 1991).

PROBLEMS OF IMPLEMENTATION

Implementation of the 1990 CAA has been uneven, and most progress has been driven by pressure from the states. The first sale of emission permits under the 1990 CAA took place in May of 1992. The Tennessee Valley Authority (ironically, a federally owned utility) purchased the rights to ten thousand tons of sulfur dioxide emissions from Wisconsin Power and Light for between $2.5 and $3 million (Wald, 1992a). The second sale of emission permits took place barely a week later, this time between Wisconsin Power and Light and the Dusquene Power Company in Pittsburgh. Interestingly, it was the stricter air pollution control regulations in Wisconsin that turned Wisconsin Power and Light's extra emission reductions into a valuable asset that the utility could sell. These initial sales notwithstanding, the volume of trading in air pollution futures on the Chicago Mercantile Exchange has thus far proved to be a bit of a disappointment.

The remainder of the implementation experiences under the 1990 CAA are not so positive. The complexity of the new law itself has made implementation difficult: where the CAA of 1970 took up only 50 pages, the 1990 version was over 800 pages long. In addition, Congress required the EPA to manage the nearly impossible task of writing 55 new regulations in two years. Overall, Congress placed over 100 separate deadlines into the act (Rosenbaum, 1994). Carrying out the provisions of the law was made even more difficult by President Bush's election year moratorium on all new federal regulations and by the objections of Vice President Dan Quayle's Council on Competitiveness.

Legislative complexity and executive obstacles caused the EPA to miss deadlines for issuing toxic pollution permit guidelines, new car pollution equipment requirements, automobile inspection and maintenance requirements, and standards for reformulated automotive fuels (Wald, 1992b). The regulations that were promulgated close to the deadlines made it easier for industries to exceed toxic air pollution emission limits and exempted a number of utilities from having to participate in the marketable emission permit program (Cushman, 1991). Several states have become impatient with what they perceive as federal efforts to delay or weaken new clean air regulations. By late 1992, states were faced with the prospect of being fined for noncompliance with regulations that EPA had yet to produce (Cushman, 1993; Rosenbaum, 1994). In response, nine states sued the EPA failing to carry out the provisions of the 1990 CAA (Wald, 1992b). Pressure from environmental groups, states, and the courts prompted EPA to begin issuing new CAA regulations in late 1992, and the pace of regulatory promulgation has accelerated under the Clinton administration.

REGULATING HAZARDOUS WASTES

Environmental regulation distinguishes between **contemporary hazardous wastes** and **pre-existing hazardous wastes**. Hazardous waste regulation is also unique in that the focusing events leading to the adoption of the enabling legislation occurred during what was otherwise a difficult period for environmental protection.

The Resource Conservation and Recovery Act

The storage, treatment, and disposal of contemporary hazardous wastes are regulated under the **Resource Conservation and Recovery Act** of 1976 (RCRA). The RCRA was actually a set of amendments to the **Solid Waste Disposal Act** of 1965, and the hazardous waste sections of the act were included almost as an afterthought (Davis, 1993). RCRA required the EPA to identify and classify hazardous wastes, develop a cradle-to-grave **tracking system** for these wastes, and regulate those facilities that would store, treat, or dispose of these wastes. RCRA also contains the familiar partial preemption provisions that allow states to administer their own hazardous waste programs.

Under RCRA, **hazardous wastes** are defined as any waste testing positive for toxicity, corrosivity, ignitability, or reactivity. In addition to chemicals meeting these criteria, over 500 substances have been listed by the EPA as hazardous in their own right. Responding to pressure from the regulated industries, Congress exempted from hazardous waste classification certain types of waste that would fail these tests (e.g., oil and gas drilling sludges). Our best estimate is that between 255 and 277 million metric tons of hazardous wastes are produced annually in the U.S., though only two percent of producers are responsible for roughly 95 percent of this waste (McCarthy and Reisch, 1987).

The EPA or the authorized state agency tracks hazardous wastes by means of a **manifest system**. Any person engaged in the production and storage, transport, treatment, or disposal of hazardous wastes must file a manifest which identifies the source of the waste, the type and amount of the waste, and the final destination of the waste. Individual state manifests were replaced in the mid-1980s by a standard federal manifest form. The manifest system was intended to create a hazardous waste management data base, and to minimize the illegal disposal or "**midnight dumping**" of hazardous wastes. The manifest system affects only a small portion of hazardous wastes, since no more than 10 percent of all hazardous wastes produced are transported and disposed of off site (Dower, 1990).

In designing performance standards for facilities that would store, treat, or dispose of hazardous wastes (e.g., STD facilities), EPA was again venturing into the frontiers of scientific knowledge. For example, no one at the agency really knew how to design a safe and effective **hazardous waste incinerator**. Soon after the passage of RCRA, however, the discovery of Love Canal made the consequences of poorly designed hazardous waste disposal facilities front-page headlines (see below). Love Canal brought increased advocacy coalition and Congressional pressure to bear on EPA in developing hazardous waste facility performance standards. Increased salience also highlighted the technical difficulties faced by EPA, and these factors combined to delay the creation of performance standards.

Regulations for storage and treatment facilities were issued in January 1981, regulations for incinerators were issued in June 1982, and regulations for hazardous waste landfills were finally issued in January 1983, nearly seven years after RCRA became law (Lieber, 1983). With regulations in place, EPA could now begin case-by-case evaluations of the 14,000 existing STD facilities for the purpose of issuing permits to these facilities. The costs of complying with RCRA regulations eventually forced over two-thirds of these facilities out of business, creating a shortage of approved capacity for the treatment and disposal of hazardous wastes (Davis, 1993).

Amending Resource Conservation and Recovery Act

RCRA was reauthorized as the **Hazardous and Solid Waste Amendments** (HSWA) of 1984. According to hazardous waste policy scholar Roger Dower, HSWA "can only be described as among the most detailed and restricting environmental requirements ever legislated" (Dower, 1990:165). In HSWA, Congress extended RCRA regulations to **small quantity generators** (e.g., those facilities that generated between 100 and 1000 kilograms of hazardous waste per month), even though these generators produced less than five percent of all hazardous wastes. Congress also banned untreated hazardous wastes from landfills unless it was proven that this disposal technique posed no risk.

More than any other piece of environmental regulation, HSWA is a product of the conflict between Congress and the president over the direction of environmental policy. Dissatisfied with EPA's slow progress in promulgating regulations and issuing permits, Congress required the agency to develop treatment and disposal standards for one-third of all high volume wastes by 1988, for all high volume hazardous wastes by 1990, and for all remaining hazardous wastes by 1991 (Dower, 1990). Congress was also extremely distrustful of the regulatory direction of EPA under President Reagan, and consequently legislators took on the role of regulators. Congress placed within HSWA standards for everything from the permeability of landfill liners to allowable pollutant concentrations in hazardous waste incinerator stack gasses. If the EPA did not develop approved treatment and disposal standards by the deadlines, "**hammer clauses**" within HSWA meant that these congressionally designed standards would take effect (Rosenbaum, 1989). The EPA met most of the regulatory guidelines within HSWA, and by 1993 there were over 500 commercial STD facilities and nearly 3700 on-site STD facilities across the country with RCRA permits (EPA, 1993).

The Comprehensive Environmental Response, Compensation, and Liability Act

Love Canal, located in Niagara Falls, New York, was an uncompleted canal used as a toxic chemical dump by the Hooker Chemical and Plastics Company. In 1953, Hooker covered the dump site and deeded the land to the Niagara Falls Board of Education. Eventually, an elementary school and a playground were built on the site, and several hundred homes were built around the site. After heavy rains in 1976, chemicals leaked from the site into area basements; eventually, the canal itself overflowed and toxic waste entered the environment. The Love Canal was declared a **disaster area** by the federal government, and evacuation of the area began (Brown, 1981).

The Love Canal incident immediately raised the salience of hazardous waste regulation, and revealed a weakness in the 1976 RCRA; it applied to current waste sites only and did not affect abandoned waste sites such as Love Canal. Because the Love Canal problems were not noticed until 23 years after the site had been closed, some process was needed to find hazardous waste sites and clean them up.

The congressional response to Love Canal was the **Comprehensive Environmental Response, Liability, and Compensation Act (CERCLA)** of 1980, better known as "**superfund**." Unlike other environmental legislation that developed over decades, CERCLA was created whole-cloth, by a lame duck Democratic Congress before a transition to a new Republican president. Designed to clean up hazardous wastes sites, the bill was initially opposed by the Chemical Manufacturers Association because the law provided for a system of compensating those injured by exposure to hazardous wastes. To save the legislation, the **injury provisions** were deleted (Mosher, 1983a). While CERCLA contains no partial preemption provision, several states have created their own versions of CERCLA.

CERCLA contains numerous provisions. First, the law requires EPA to assess all abandoned toxic waste sites across the country. The EPA has identified over 30,000 such sites, but the General Accounting Office estimates that between 130,000 and 425,000 possible hazardous waste sites exist (GAO, 1987). Each site is evaluated according to its level of toxicity and the potential for human and environmental exposure to hazardous wastes, and the most dangerous sites are placed on the **National Priorities List (NPL)**. Second, the EPA attempts to get responsible parties to clean up the abandoned site in compliance with guidelines established by the agency. If responsible parties refuse to undertake clean up or cannot be found, the agency itself can begin cleanup.

CERCLA imposes a condition of strict, joint, and several liability based on the "**polluter pays**" principle. **Strict liability** means that parties can be held responsible for cleanup costs even if they complied with all applicable regulations when they disposed of their wastes. **Joint liability** means that several parties may be help responsible for clean up costs. **Several liability** means that a single responsible party may be held liable for all site clean up costs, regardless of how much waste that party actually disposed of at the site. The assumption behind **joint and several liability** is that responsible parties will search out and sue other responsible parties in order to recoup the costs of cleanup. The joint and several liability provision can lead to abuse, however, as when a pizzeria in New York was sued for clean up costs on the assumption that it may have disposed of empty insecticide cans that eventually ended up in a superfund site (Landy and Hague, 1992).

CERCLA provides two funding mechanisms for cleanups undertaken by the EPA. First, the agency is supposed to recover cleanup costs by suing or settling with responsible parties. Second, the law created a $1.6 billion fund (the "superfund) financed by a feedstock tax on the petroleum and chemical industries (86 percent) and general revenues (14 percent) that the agency could draw upon to cover cleanup costs. In practice, the agency has succeeded in recovering few costs from responsible parties (Dower, 1990).

Amending Superfund

The cleanup of abandoned hazardous waste sites progressed slowly, and soon it became clear that the problem was larger and more expensive than was envisioned in 1980. One respected estimate pegged the total cost of cleaning up the most dangerous hazardous waste sites in the country at $68 billion (GAO, 1987). The **Superfund Amendments and Reauthorization Act (SARA)** of 1986 extended and replenished the superfund to the tune of $8.5 billion. Most of the fund was still bankrolled by the feedstock tax and general revenues, but SARA also included a general business environmental tax amounting to 0.12 percent of all corporate earnings above $2 million.

In reauthorizing CERCLA, Congress added prohibitions on companies filing for **bankruptcy** to avoid liability under superfund. The legislature also directed the EPA to increase the use of out-of-court settlements in an effort to entice responsible parties to share cleanup costs. In response, the number of settlements under CERCLA increased from 13 in 1981 to 565 in 1988 (Dower, 1990). Congress added a nonregulatory element to hazardous waste policy with the **Emergency Planning and Community Right To Know Act (EPCRA)**; Title III of SARA. EPCRA required industry to inform communities about potentially dangerous chemicals and processes used in day-to-day operations. Industry was also required to report yearly emissions toxic chemicals in the Toxics Release Inventory. All of these data were made available to the public so that communities could plan for toxic emergencies and so consumers and communities could make informed decisions in their selection of products and corporate neighbors.

Overhauling Superfund

Legislative authorization for CERCLA expired in October 1994, and authority for the feedstock tax that finances the superfund expires one year later. Many in Congress oppose extending authorization for the tax unless CERCLA undergoes a major overhaul. Almost no one is satisfied with the performance of CERCLA, with reasons for dissatisfaction ranging from the slow progress of cleanup to the fact that over one-third of all expenditures under the program (e.g, several billion dollars) have gone to legal fees, not to cleanup (Kriz, 1994a; Landy and Hague, 1992; Mazmanian and Morrell, 1992).

The reauthorization debate thus far has made for some odd bedfellows. Hazardous waste generators and many municipalities are advocating relaxed cleanup standards for superfund sites; generators want to reduce their liability costs, while municipalities want to unlock scores of potential industrial development sites presently off-limits because of toxic contamination. Insurers would also like relief from potentially huge liability claims under the law, and advocate a tax on insurance companies to pay for cleanup costs. Environmental groups and the waste management industry support the strict liability provisions and cleanup standards in the present law, while civil rights groups want more cleanup resources targeted in poor and minority communities that contain disproportionate concentrations of toxic waste sites (Commission for Racial Justice, 1987).

President Clinton set up an interagency panel to recommend changes to CERCLA, but even the agency representatives disagree on how to best address the shortcomings of the law. One item that the panel did agree on was to eliminate liability for pre-1980 hazardous wastes that were disposed of in compliance with pre-1980 regulations. Vice-president Gore, however, rejected this recommendation and threw his support behind a proposal from a coalition of industrial generators, environmental groups, civil rights advocates, and academics that would let an Administrative Law Judge allocate liability for pre-1980 hazardous wastes (Kriz, 1994b). The most likely scenario has Congress limiting liability for pre-1980 hazardous wastes, changing the funding mechanism for superfund, and allowing tiered cleanup standards depending upon the proposed use for the former superfund site.

REGULATING PESTICIDES

The EPA is responsible for regulating pesticides, but pesticide regulation is far different from other types of environmental regulation. In the first place, where traditional environmental regulations regulate the **externalities** from the production of consumer products (e.g., air and water pollutants), pesticide legislation regulates the products themselves. Secondly, unlike the CAA, CWA, and RCRA, pesticide statutes require EPA to **weigh the benefits** of these products with the risks posed by their use before issuing regulations.

Pesticides have grown into a huge industry in the United States, with production at over a billion pounds and sales of over $5 billion annually by the late 1980s (Kriz, 1988). EPA's authority to regulate pesticides comes from the **Federal Insecticide, Fungicide, and Rodenticide Act (FIFRA)** of 1947. The purpose of the 1947 act was to protect farmers from ineffective or excessively dangerous pesticides. In the political climate of the early 1970s, however, FIFRA was reauthorized and amended in 1972 to emphasize environmental protection. The EPA regulates pesticides much as the Food and Drug Administration regulates drugs. In order for any pesticide to be sold, it must be registered by the EPA. The FIFRA amendments of 1972 required the EPA to produce by 1974 registration standards that ensured pesticides were safe, environmentally benign, and effective.

Implementing FIFRA

Evaluating and registering new pesticides is a manageable task, given that the EPA receives from 15 to 25 requests for new pesticide registrations each year. In addition to registering new pesticides, however, FIFRA required the EPA to evaluate and register the roughly 50,000 existing pesticides on the market, and to complete this task by October of 1976. According to Christopher Bosso, the reaction among EPA careerists to these requirements was "disbelief." (Bosso, 1987). In an effort to target resources, the agency adopted the **"Rebuttable Presumption Against Registration" (RPAR)**. Under RPAR, EPA petitioned industry for information on those pesticides that it had reason to believe posed **unreasonable risks** (identified through complaints) or that were **supported by inadequate data**. If the agency was satisfied with the quantity and quality of this additional information, the pesticide was presumed safe without formal toxicity testing. The agency also conserves resources by relying upon independent private laboratories to assess the safety and effectiveness of pesticides. This magnified the difficulties surrounding pesticide regulation when in the late 1970s, the country's largest private chemical testing firm (Industrial Biotest) was discovered to have falsified data and tests on over 200 EPA registered pesticides (Bosso, 1987).

After evaluating all relevant data, the EPA can place **restrictions** on the production, use or distribution of a pesticide, or refuse to register it. Once these restrictions are in place, the EPA trains commercial pesticide applicators. Pesticides in agriculture and industry can be applied only by trained applicators, though homeowners face no such restrictions. The EPA can also cancel a pesticide's registration and remove it from the market (e.g., ban the pesticide: see Dorfman, 1982). EPA banned DDT in 1972, and has since banned over 30 other pesticides. Under the FIFRA amendments of 1972, for every pesticide EPA banned, the agency had to compensate the manufacturer for product costs and sales revenue lost as a result of the ban. These costs are not inconsequential: in FY89, EPA's budget for pesticide testing and registration was $45 million, while its budget for indemnification (e.g., compensation) was $53 million (Kriz, 1988).

Criticisms of FIFRA

Within EPA, the original **Office of Pesticide Policy** was criticized for a lack of expertise and a pro-pesticide orientation that clashed with the agency's overall support of environmental values. This criticism has its roots in the fact that the original pesticide office was staffed by the **"dregs"** from the Department of Agriculture and the Food and Drug Administration who's primary clientele prior to 1970 were farmers and pesticide manufacturers. A more concrete set of criticisms is targeted at the slow pace of progress in pesticide registration. By the mid-1980s, the EPA had assessed the environmental and health effects of only six of the more than 600 active ingredients used in the manufacture of pesticides. Moreover, the agency had not even begun testing the majority of the 40,000 pre-1972 pesticides still on the market (Kriz, 1988).

We can find four reasons for EPA's slow pace of pesticide evaluation:

First, there is tremendous pressure to keep pesticides in use and little organized pressure to withdraw pesticides. Maney and Hadwiger (1980:210) estimated that pesticides increase the profit from farming by approximately $20 per acre; the economic incentive to continue use, therefore, is strong.

Second, the analysis of pesticides is exceedingly complex. No data on the impact of most pesticides on human beings exists before the pesticides are used, and information on harmful effects often takes years to gather (Dorfman, 1982:19).

Third, the pesticide program is constantly distracted from any long-term regulatory efforts by a series of crises. Media attention on the "pesticide of the month" followed by congressional hearings requires the agency to drop long-run programs and respond to immediate pressures.

Fourth, the pesticide program at EPA suffers from a chronic shortage of resources.

Amending Pesticide Regulation

Congress, with the prodding of both advocacy coalitions in environmental regulation, has been trying to overhaul FIFRA for the past two decades. As of yet, only a few minor changes have been made in pesticide regulation. Amendments to FIFRA in 1978 relaxed **data reporting requirements** on industry, and required the EPA to compensate manufacturers when information that the manufacturers classified as **trade secrets** was required in the pesticide registration process. During the Reagan administration, pesticide regulations were relaxed administratively when the EPA abandoned the **genotoxic theory of toxicity** (which assumes that pesticides cause cancer by mutating cell DNA) and adopted the **epigenetic theory of pesticide toxicity** (e.g., that these chemicals do not alter the genetic makeup of cells). In theory, genotoxic chemicals are more dangerous (Wines, 1983c).

In 1986, members of the National Agricultural Chemical Association and large environmental groups met to forge a compromise proposal for a comprehensive reform of FIFRA. The bill seemed headed for passage when it was derailed at the last instant by grassroots environmental groups and farmers who were uncomfortable being excluded from the negotiating process. By the late 1980s, congressional agricultural committees were in danger of losing jurisdiction over FIFRA because of their inability to craft a reform proposal. To avoid this possibility, the committees decided to reform the legislation piece by piece, rather than attempt a comprehensive overhaul as had been done with SARA in 1986 and the WQA in 1987.

The resulting reforms, enacted in 1988, eliminate the indemnification provisions of FIFRA. Now if the EPA bans a pesticide, compensation is made to a limited number of applicators (e.g., farmers) rather than to the chemical manufacturer. Second, the 1988 amendments require the EPA to review all active pesticide ingredients and make registration decisions on the more then 19,000 existing pesticides on the market by 1997 (Kriz, 1988). Though EPA was allowed to charge higher registration fees to pay for the **accelerated review process**, by the end of 1992 the agency had completed reviews of only 2 pesticide ingredients. Pressure for comprehensive reform of FIFRA is again building in response to a National Academy of Sciences report that found children are much more susceptible to pesticides than previously thought, and in response to a 1991 Supreme Court decision that allows localities to enact stricter pesticide limits than required by the EPA (Kriz, 1992a).

EVALUATING ENVIRONMENTAL REGULATIONS

This section evaluating environmental regulations includes sections on (1) evaluating enforcement, (2) the economic effects of environmental regulation, and (3) regulatory effects on environmental quality.

Evaluating Enforcement

We can distinguish between two types of compliance monitoring in environmental regulation. First, under **initial compliance monitoring**, the EPA or the appropriate state agency inspects a facility to determine if it has installed the required pollution control equipment. Second, in **continuous compliance monitoring**, the agency inspects facilities to determine if the pollution control equipment is functioning properly and the quality of the facilities' waste stream. In general, EPA has only made a half hearted effort at continuous compliance monitoring, and this has encouraged widespread violation of environmental regulation (Russell, 1990). For example, between 1978 and 1983, the General Accounting Office estimated that 82 percent of NPDES permittees were in violation of their permits at least once during any 18 month period. Thirty-one percent of these facilities were significant violators (e.g, they exceeded allowable discharge levels by more than 50 percent for multiple months). While significant noncompliance rates dropped to around ten percent by 1988 (EPA, 1990), certain industries (e.g., steel) have been in violation of a majority of environmental regulations for decades (Meier, 1985).

EPA relies upon **industry self-monitoring** to assess compliance with environmental regulations under the CAA, CWA, and RCRA, but audits to assess the accuracy of these self-monitoring efforts are fairly uncommon. In the early 1980s, major polluting facilities were audited between one and three times per year, while smaller facilities were audited about once every year (Russell, 1983). The frequency of audits had changed little by the early 1990s (Russell, 1990). Moreover, those audits that were undertaken were not designed to catch violators. The majority of audits are announced ahead of time, and inspectors rarely test pollution control equipment or test effluent during these audits (Magat and Viscusi, 1990; Russell, 1990).

EPA's lax enforcement style continues after a violator has been identified. Under EPA's distinction between violations and **"significant violations,"** only significant violators are subject to EPA sanctions, and even this process involves bargaining between EPA and the facility (Downing and Kimball, 1982). EPA's policy for significant violations is to set civil fines at a level that equals the economic benefits the facility received from noncompliance, plus a penalty. In practice, EPA's civil fines are small (Russell, 1990); on average, as little as 0.1 percent of a facility's compliance costs (Crandall, 1983). EPA does little better in using its authority for criminal prosecution. Between 1982 and 1989, the agency referred 258 cases to the Justice department for prosecution. Of these, only 125 were prosecuted, and 72 percent of these resulted in convictions. The average sentence for being convicted of an **environmental crime** during this period was six months (Russell, 1990).

Critics of EPA's monitoring and enforcement record suggest three changes. First, devote more resources to continuous compliance monitoring of a facility's waste stream, particularly through the use of remote sensing equipment. Second, target resources by linking the frequency of inspection to a facility's historic violation rate. Third, stringently enforce the civil and criminal penalty provisions of environmental statutes. These reforms are especially critical as EPA continues to rely upon self-monitoring, and as the agency relies increasingly upon market incentives in pollution control.

The Economic Effects of Environmental Regulation

This examination of the economic effects of environmental regulation includes an overview of both the costs and benefits of regulation and the second order economic consequences.

COSTS AND BENEFITS OF REGULATION

EPA's budget of $6.5 billion accounts for less than one-half of one percent of the total federal budget, but federal expenditures make up only a small portion of the total cost of environmental regulation. The EPA estimates the total costs of environmental regulation at just under $130 billion for 1995. Of this figure, over $100 billion is paid by private industry (EPA Administrator, 1991). More important than the cost of regulation, however, is a comparison of regulatory costs and benefits.

Given the shortcomings of benefit-cost analysis in environmental protection, we have to be careful in interpreting these figures. Several analyses have pegged the annual cost of pre-1990 air quality regulations at between $8.6 billion and $16.8 billion, while the probable benefits of these regulations ranged from $4.6 billion to $51.2 billion (Crandall, 1983; Freeman, 1982; and Gottron, 1982). One evaluation of air quality regulations similar to those adopted in the 1990 CAA concluded that the benefits of these regulations exceed their costs (Kamieneicki and Ferrall, 1991), though another reaches just the opposite conclusion (Krupnick and Portney, 1991). Benefit-cost assessments of water quality regulations estimate the costs of these regulations at between $23.2 billion and $30.8 billion annually and the benefits of these regulations at $5.7 billion to $27.7 billion (Freeman, 1990). Overall, then, the benefits of air quality regulation appear to outweigh the costs, and the benefits of water quality regulations are nearly equal to their costs. Only in hazardous waste regulation is there a consensus that regulatory costs far outweigh regulatory benefits (Dower, 1990).

SECOND ORDER ECONOMIC CONSEQUENCES

Environmental regulations may also have important **second order economic consequences** for inflation and unemployment rates, productivity, and international industrial competitiveness. In reviewing the literature on this topic, the Congressional Budget Office (1985) estimated that by the mid-1980s inflation was roughly 0.13 percent higher than it might have been in the absence of environmental regulation, but this inflationary effect was diminishing (though the 1990 CAA temporarily reversed this trend). **Productivity rates** were depressed slightly by environmental regulations during the 1980s, but in the long run many economists expect these regulations to have a positive effect on productivity by channeling investment to more efficient firms (CBO, 1985). Portney, (1981) estimated that environmental regulation would actually have positive short term and long term effects on employment. Finally, early environmental regulations did not place the United States at a competitive disadvantage with respect to Japan, West Germany, or Canada (CBO, 1985). A more recent analysis found that the U.S. spent a higher percentage of its gross domestic product for environmental protection than did Great Britain or France, but spent the same or less than Japan and Germany (EPA Administrator, 1991).

Regulatory Effects on Environmental Quality

Evaluating the environmental effects of pollution control regulations is more difficult than it appears. In fact, the EPA estimated that in 1991, only three of the agency's 23 major programs had monitoring adequate to identify program success or failure (EPA, 1991). The data that are available paint a generally positive portrait of the effectiveness of environmental regulation.

AIR QUALITY

From 1970 to 1991, emissions of all six criteria pollutants declined from three percent (nitrogen oxides) to 95 percent (lead). Similarly, from 1974 to 1991, atmospheric concentrations of all criteria pollutants decreased between 24 percent (nitrogen dioxide and carbon monoxide) and 94 percent (lead) (EPA, 1992), and the average acidity of rainfall declined significantly during the 1980s (CEQ, 1993). Air quality has also improved dramatically in the most polluted urban areas. The California Air Resources Board reported that between 1982 and 1991, the California basin experienced a 50 percent drop in the number of hours that air pollutant concentrations reached hazardous levels (NWF, 1993). New York City went all of 1992 without violating the NAAQS for carbon monoxide, the first time this had happened in twenty years (NWF, 1994).

While air quality has improved since 1970, there has been some disagreement as to whether regulation caused these improvements. Broder (N.D.), Crandall (1983), and MacAvoy (1979, 1987) all conclude that regulation has been ineffective, and trace improvements in air quality to changes in industrial production and fossil fuel use. Crandall goes so far as to argue that federal regulation has been counter productive, since air quality appeared to improve more rapidly prior to 1970. Each of these studies has serious flaws, however, (e.g., Crandall reaches his conclusion by simply "eyeballing" some data even he recognizes are questionable) and their conclusions have been largely discounted. For example, White (1982) found that CAA requirements significantly reduced nitrogen oxide emissions from new cars, while Ringquist (1993) demonstrated that states with stronger regulatory programs experience greater reductions in pollutant emissions and greater improvements in air quality.

WATER QUALITY

The EPA does not have a system of monitors to measure changes in water quality over time. In order to evaluate the effectiveness of water quality regulation, we have to rely upon data from state water pollution control officials and the U.S. Geological

Survey's National Stream Quality Accounting Network (NASQUAN). Evaluations of state officials show that between 1972 and 1982, water quality generally improved across the country (ASIWPCA, 1984). Moreover, while in 1974 only one-third of the nation's waters met a fishable-swimmable use designation, by 1993 this figure had increased to two-thirds (Wayland, 1993). Finally, in evaluating data from over 400 NASQUAN stations, Lettenmaier, et al., (1991) discovered improvements in water quality associated with increased dissolved oxygen levels and decreased concentrations of fecal bacteria, dissolved solids, and phosphorus. These researchers also found that water quality had degraded at a number of monitoring stations because of increased concentrations of nitrogen, chlorides, and heavy metals.

As with air quality, there is some debate as to whether environmental regulations are the cause of these changes in water quality. When we look at specific pollutants or local waterways, water quality regulations have proven remarkably effective. Magat and Viscusi (1990), for instance, found that these regulations significantly reduced pollution discharges from the pulp and paper industry. Similarly, upgrading municipal waste water treatment plants significantly improves water quality immediately downstream from those plants (GAO, 1986). On the other hand, researchers have been unable to demonstrate a causal connection between regulation and nationwide changes in water quality (Gianessi and Peskin, 1981; Ringquist, 1993; Vaughn and Russell, 1982). While regulations targeting point sources of pollution do improve water quality locally, most of the improvements from these efforts are overcome downstream by increased nonpoint water pollution.

HAZARDOUS WASTES

Evaluating the environmental effects of hazardous waste regulation, particularly the Resource Conservation and Recovery Act, is nearly impossible. Unlike for air and water pollution, there are no good indicators of environmental quality with regard to hazardous wastes. In fact, we do not even have good data on the amount of hazardous wastes produced, nor on how the majority of these wastes are disposed of (Dower, 1990). Evaluating CERCLA is a bit easier, if only because superfund records allow us to count cleaned hazardous waste sites. Since 1980, over $13 billion has been spent on superfund, and the EPA has assessed over 11,000 hazardous waste sites, placed 1660 of these sites on the National Priorities List, and completed cleanups at 217 sites. Each completed **cleanup** takes an average of 11 years and costs over ten million dollars (Dower, 1990; Kriz, 1994b). While some progress has been made, the pace of cleanup under superfund has been excruciatingly slow, and one study estimated that a third of all program money has been spent on legal fees instead of **site remediation** (Kriz, 1994b). The most comprehensive evaluation of the program, in fact, dubbed it a "superfailure" (Mazmanian and Morrell, 1992).

Evaluating Title III of SARA (the Emergency Planning and Community Right To Know Act), presents a much brighter picture of the effectiveness of hazardous waste regulations. Title III required most industries to track their emissions of toxic chemicals and report these emissions in the **Toxic Release Inventory (TRI) report**. SARA carries no sanctions for industrial toxic chemical emissions. Like Environmental Impact Statements under NEPA, the TRI simply creates a public record of the potential for environmental damage from certain activities. The first TRI in 1987 found that industry had released nearly 5.2 billion pounds of toxic chemicals into the air, land, and water. By all accounts, even industry was surprised by this figure, and many corporations vowed to reduce their emissions of these chemicals. The 1992 TRI showed that releases of toxic chemicals to the environment had fallen to 3.16 billion pounds, a decrease of nearly 40 percent. Transfers of toxic chemicals for off site disposal also declined by over 40 percent (EPA, 1994).

NEW OBSTACLES TO ENVIRONMENTAL REGULATION

Environmental regulation, like most regulation, has always faced opposition. Within the past few years, however, the opponents of environmental regulation have adopted a new set of tactics with the potential to radically alter the terms of the debate in environmental protection. Discussion below covers the four most prominent of these tactics; the "private interests" argument, and the "unholy trinity" of property rights, unfunded mandates, and risk assessment. Future environmental regulations will have to either debunk these charges or accept them and alter the substance of regulations accordingly.

Private Interests in Environmental Regulation

Members of the environmental quality advocacy coalition have traditionally held an ethical trump card in that they are motivated by selfless "**public interest**" concerns, while their industrial opponents are motivated by **private greed**. In fact, spending public resources to benefit the nonregulated general public instead of the regulated industries is what separates environmental regulation from occupational regulation or instances of regulatory capture (see Chapter 1). Increasingly, however, critics of environmental regulation are attempting to recast this **public benefit-private benefit** debate by highlighting examples where environmental regulations have conferred significant material benefits on a few while providing little environmental benefit to the general public (Greve and Smith, 1992; Yandle, 1989).

One of the earliest examples of using environmental regulations to confer **private benefits** is the **scrubbing requirement** of the 1977 Clean Air Act amendments. Recall that this requirement did little to improve air quality, but did safeguard the jobs of high-sulfur coal miners and the profits of Eastern mine owners (Ackerman and Hassler, 1981). Landy and Hague (1992) claim that retaining the strict liability provisions of CERCLA will not improve environmental quality, but will line the pockets of attorneys and waste management companies and advance the "leftist" political agenda of environmental groups. In a similar vein, Greve (1992) argues that the citizen suit provisions of the CWA and the new CAA allow environmental groups to collect huge out of court settlements from facilities that violate their discharge permits, but that these cases rarely improve the quality of the facilities' waste streams.

The most recent example of this phenomenon is EPA's June, 1994 decision to require the use of ethanol in reformulated gasoline in an effort to reduce urban ozone levels

(Strong, 1994; see also Adler, 1992). Under most conditions, ethanol burns cleaner than traditional gasolines. Gasoline laced with ethanol costs more, however, and under certain circumstances (e.g., hot summer temperatures) gasoline laced with ethanol evaporates more quickly, sending more VOCs into the atmosphere and possibly worsening the ozone problem. While the debate between ethanol and competing methanol producers was cast as a contest between small farmers and big oil companies (the methanol based ethers used in reformulated gasoline come from petroleum products), in reality over 80 percent of the ethanol produced in the United States comes from the Archer Daniels Midland company, which stands to reap billions of dollars in additional ethanol sales thanks to the EPA decision.

Property Rights

The past five years have witnessed an avalanche of cases where federal and state governments have been sued if environmental regulations in any way reduce the value of **private property**. The basis for these suits is found in the **"takings clause"** of the fifth amendment, which states "...nor shall private property be taken for public use without **just compensation**" (historically, this clause has been used to compensate owners when their land has been taken for highways, canals, and other public necessities). In a 1887 decision, the Supreme Court held that an owner's use of private property could not be "injurious to the community." A 1987 decision reaffirmed that when the federal government acts to prohibit a **nuisance-like activity** (e.g., regulates the use of private property in order to avoid public harm), there is no taking (Moore, 1992).

This interpretation of the law was challenged beginning in the mid-1980s. In an influential book published in 1985, University of Chicago law professor Richard Epstein argued that 100 years of common law was in fact wrong, and that the government must pay property owners whenever environmental regulations limit the value of their property (Epstein, 1985). Takings claims against the federal government are heard by the Court of Claims, and Chief Judge Loren Smith (a Reagan appointee) took Epstein's writings to heart. Traditionally a legal backwater, under Smith's direction the Court of Claims has become a haven for defenders of property rights (Moore, 1992). In 1991, for example, the Court required the federal government to pay $226 million in claims and hundreds of millions of dollars in interest on those claims. Currently, the backlog of takings cases before the Court of Claims opens the federal government to more than $1 billion in potential property judgments.

In some instances, decisions of the Claims Court appear to go too far. For example, in order to protect an aquifer already showing signs of contamination, the Army Corps of Engineers refused to grant a permit to a Florida company wanting to quarry limestone on 98 acres of a 1560 acre holding. The company had already realized substantial profits from mining the remainder of the holding, and the land was still valued at nearly $4,000 per acre even without mining rights. In *Florida Rock Industries* v. *U.S.* (1990), however, the Court awarded the company $1 million in compensation for the taking of all use of the property. In its ruling, the Court explicitly stated that the burden placed on the private property owner outweighed any public benefit from protecting the aquifer (Wenner, 1994).

The Supreme Court has moved closer to supporting the takings perspective of the Court of Claims. In the 1987 decision discussed above, four justices dissented, arguing that the federal government should reevaluate its land use regulations to determine if they really focus on nuisance damages (Moore, 1992). In 1992, the Supreme Court decided the most significant takings case in a century, *Lucas* v. *South Carolina Coastal Council*. In the Lucas case, the plaintiff had purchased two lots on a barrier island off the coast of South Carolina. In order to prevent erosion and protect coastal habitats, the state prevented Lucas from developing the lots. In its decision, the Supreme Court overturned the finding of the South Carolina supreme court in deciding that Lucas was a victim of taking due to the "total destruction of the value of his property" (Funk, 1993). Perhaps more chilling for environmentalists than the decision itself was fact that President Bush's attorney general for the environment and natural resources urged the Supreme Court to abolish all nuisance exemptions and require compensation in all cases of the taking of private property (Moore, 1992). The Court extended the protection of private property rights and requirements for compensation to state and local governments in *Dolan v. Tigard* (1994).

Supporters of environmental regulation are highly critical of the actions of the Court of Claims and the Supreme Court's *Lucas* and *Dolan* decisions. First, they decry the abandonment of 100 years of common law, and suggest that the Supreme Courts recent direction is propelled more by Justice Antonin Scalia's political agenda than by solid judicial reasoning (Sullivan, 1993). Second, the courts have been criticized for ignoring the long tradition in property law distinguishing **development rights** from property rights. In this tradition, restricting development is not the same as taking property, and land has value outside of its development potential (Blumm, 1993). Third, environmentalist argue that actions under laws from the Clean Water Act to the Endangered Species Act will come to a standstill under the new interpretation of "takings" claims. Still, a number of bills have been introduced in Congress that would require the federal government to compensate any person or company when environmental regulations reduce the value of the owner's property.

Unfunded Mandates

State and local governments feel that they have been beset by huge costs from recent **unfunded federal mandates** in environmental regulation. Federal requirements for implementing best management practices for nonpoint source water pollution control, water quality testing under the **Safe Drinking Water Act**, and treatment requirements for urban stormwater runoff could potentially cost state and local governments hundreds of billions of dollars (Claiborne, 1994). Columbus, Ohio, for instance, has estimated that complying with federal environmental regulations will cost the city nearly $1 billion during the 1990s. California has threatened to return authority for its Safe Drinking Water Program to the EPA because it is too costly and requires excessive testing standards for little environmental benefit (Hayes, 1993).

The opposition of state and local governments to environmental regulation is an example of the shift in the composition of advocacy coalitions discussed above. Traditionally, state and local governments have been supportive of environmental protection, with state governments often going beyond federal requirements in many areas.

This support evaporated, however, when federal regulatory mandates began to set state and local spending priorities. In the words of Michael Evers, general counsel to the Senate Environment and Public Works Committee, "there's a different climate on the Hill. Today, your primary adversary on many of these issues isn't the National Association of Manufacturers—it's the National Governor's Association" (Kriz, 1994c:1097).

Members of the environmental quality advocacy coalition are deeply skeptical of "unfunded mandate" complaints, seeing these complaints as stalking horses used by those who want to weaken environmental regulation. These groups feel that many states and localities inflate the costs of federal mandates for political gain and to insulate themselves from taxpayer criticism at home. In addition, these groups contend that since drinking water and urban runoff are municipal problems, it is not unrealistic to expect municipal governments to pay for addressing them. Nevertheless, over a dozen bills have been introduced in Congress to try and relieve some of the financial pressure placed on state and local governments by federal mandates. The most far reaching bill, sponsored by Senator Dirk Kempthorne (R-ID) would require the federal government to pay for all public costs of complying with federal laws and regulations (Claiborne, 1994).

Risk Based Regulation

FIFRA, the **Toxic Substances Control Act (TSCA)**, and other pieces of legislation require the EPA to balance the benefits of regulations with the risks posed by the regulated substances. In addition, from the 1970s to the 1980s, regulatory priorities at the EPA moved from reducing **bulk pollutants** to reducing exposure to less obvious **trace pollutants** having the potential to threaten human health (Landy et al., 1990). The EPA has turned to risk analysis and risk based regulation in a effort to better target its resources, and as a methodology for carrying out the requirements of FIFRA and TSCA (Andrews, 1994).

Risk based regulation rests on the twin foundations of risk assessment and risk management. **Risk assessment** brings together biologists, chemists, epidemiologists and other professionals to evaluate the toxic effects of a particular chemical (usually the cancer risk, less often noncancer health or ecosystem risks). Risk assessment asks the question, how risky is this situation or substance? (Patton, 1993). **Risk management** takes into account the technical feasibility and cost of reducing risks and the economic and social consequences of attempting risk reduction (e.g., increased unemployment, loss of choice in the marketplace, etc.). Risk management asks the question, what shall we do about the risk? (Cleland-Hamnett, 1993; Patton, 1993).

In 1984, EPA chief Ruckleshaus endorsed the use of risk assessment and risk management in EPA decisionmaking. Risk assessment was welcomed as a managerial tool that could help EPA set regulatory priorities, and as a political tool that could help the agency shift the terms of the debate over environmental regulation from economic benefit/cost analysis to scientific decisionmaking where the EPA had a **comparative advantage** (Andrews, 1994). Internal reports in 1987 and 1990 were critical of EPA's regulatory priorities from the perspective of risk assessment. For example, the reports found that while experts rated indoor air pollution, radon exposure, and stratospheric ozone depletion as high risk factors, most agency resources were targeted at the relatively low risk problems of point source water pollution and abandoned hazardous waste dumps (EPA, 1987; EPA and SAB, 1990). In response to these reports, William Reilly in 1991 directed all EPA regional offices to use comparative risk assessment to justify their annual budget requests. The EPA has also created the Integrated Risk Information System (IRIS) data base containing toxicity data for over 500 different chemicals. Finally, the agency provides technical and financial assistance for **pilot projects** at the state level that emphasize risk based regulation.

Environmental groups are less critical of risk based regulation than they are of the property rights crusade or complaints about unfunded federal mandates. Still, most members of the environmental quality advocacy coalition have reservations about relying upon risk analysis and risk management to make regulatory decisions. Three concerns exist:

First, risk assessment faces enormous **data limitations**. Only very sketchy data are available for assessing the risks posed by most substances, and these data generally focus on cancer risks as opposed to other health risks or ecosystem risks. This allows for the exercise of large amounts of discretion in determining risk levels and establishing regulatory priorities. In fact, one study showed that while a majority of the social scientists and attorneys at EPA were supportive of using risk analysis to make regulatory decisions, over two-thirds of the biomedical and environmental scientists opposed this strategy because of these data limitations (Rycroft, et al., 1988).

Second, reliance upon highly technical risk assessment models can effectively exclude many stakeholders from participating in regulatory policy making. Decisions may be made by savvy technical experts without the input of citizens who's estimates of risk might be affected by irrational fears. In fact, the EPA has been criticized for failing to reeducate citizens regarding environmental risks (Landy, et al., 1990).

Third, quantitative risk assessment was designed to evaluate the risks from specific chemicals. The environmental challenges of the 1990s, however, do not fit this mold. Most of the new environmental problems we face have **multiple causes** (e.g., nonpoint source water pollution), **cross environmental media** (e.g., acid rain), or **cross international boundaries** (e.g., global warming). Quantitative risk assessment is not very useful here. In response, the EPA has moved toward using comparative risk assessment, a methodology that uses both quantitative and qualitative assessments of risk to produce an expert ranking of possible environmental risks. Both the 1987 and 1990 EPA studies used comparative risk assessment to recommend regulatory priorities.

Despite the reservations of environmentalists, Senator Daniel Patrick Moynihan (D-NY) is proposing an Environmental Risk Reduction Act that would require EPA to seek independent advice in **ranking environmental risks** and **setting regulatory priorities** (Hayes, 1993). A separate bill to elevate the EPA to cabinet level status was derailed by a proposed amendment that would have required the agency to undertake risk assessment and cost-effectiveness studies of all new regulations. Supporters of EPA claimed that the risk assessment requirement would have proved so burdensome that the agency would have been effectively shut down (Cohen, 1994).

Even if the EPA did use comparative risk assessment to establish regulatory priorities, this would affect regulatory decision making only at the margin. Legislative mandates force EPA to spend 90 percent of its water budget on point sources of pollution (as opposed to more serious nonpoint sources), 80 percent of its ground water budget on cleaning up contaminated aquifers (though preventing aquifer contamination is a much more effective strategy), and allow the agency to spend only two percent of its total budget on the high risk problems of ozone depletion, global warming, and species diversity (Hayes, 1993; Rosenbaum, 1994).

NEW TOOLS IN ENVIRONMENTAL REGULATION

Efforts at environmental protection have revolved around traditional **command and control regulations** where the EPA tells a facility which pollution control technology it must use and then penalizes the facility if it refuses to comply with the requirements. While command and control regulations have produced noticeable reductions in pollution (see above), they are not without their shortcomings. Four weaknesses exist:

First, command and control regulations do not adapt well to changes in technology. The pace of development in pollution control technology can outstrip regulatory requirements, but because of the terms of a facility's permit it has no incentive to adopt the new technology.

Second, command and control regulations force all facilities within an industry to reduce pollution by the same amount. Some facilities may find it less expensive to reduce pollution than do others, however, making the uniform reduction requirements economically inefficient.

Third, command and control regulations are traditionally organized around a single pollutant or a single media, while many pollutants travel across media. In some instances, single media pollution regulations have actually exacerbated pollution problems elsewhere. For example, smokestack scrubbers and waste water treatment plants both produce millions of tons of toxic sludge that have typically been dumped in the ocean or deposited in landfills.

Fourth, rulemaking in environmental regulation is a time consuming process, particularly when most of these rules are held up by court challenges (Alm, 1992).

A number of regulatory innovations are presently being used in an effort to circumvent the shortcomings of the command and control approach. The most common of these innovations is the use of market incentives in pollution control, but **integrated environmental management** and various "**nonregulatory**" approaches to environmental protection are also gaining in popularity. By some accounts, these alternatives to command and control regulations represent the next frontier in environmental protection (Freeman, 1994; John, 1994).

Economic Incentives in Pollution Control

There are literally dozens of suggested market mechanisms in environmental protection; from effluent fees, to tradeable discharge permits, to subsidies for pollution reduction (Downing, 1984). All of the market-like techniques share two characteristics. First, they provide polluters with an incentive to reduce pollution instead of a disincentive *not* to reduce pollution (e.g., they use a carrot instead of a stick). Second, these techniques allow all facilities (in theory) to reduce pollution to a level where the marginal cost of reduction is equal to its marginal benefit, producing an efficient level of pollution reduction in each firm.

Incentive mechanisms in pollution control are not new. In the late 1970s, the EPA instituted a number of market-like approaches to air pollution control. For example, the EPA's **"bubble"** program focuses on facilities with multiple sources of pollution. Rather than set standards for each source, the EPA places an imaginary "bubble" and a single pollution limit over the entire facility and lets the facility decide how do best allocate pollution controls among the sources (Liroff, 1986). Under a separate **offset program**, industrial facilities that want to build or expand in a nonattainment area must pay for pollution reductions at another facility in the area that will more then offset increases in pollution from the new facility. By 1992, polluting sources had made use of 50 bubbles (some of them covering entire communities) and over 2500 offsets (Morgenstern, 1992).

The use of economic incentives in pollution control took off in the 1990s, particularly transferable discharge permits. Under a **transferrable discharge permit** scheme, facilities that can reduce pollution at relatively low cost do so, and sell the excess pollution reduction credits to facilities who find it more expensive to reduce pollution. The 1990 CAA amendments created a system of marketable discharge permits in order to reduce emissions of sulfur dioxide and nitrogen oxides 50 percent (see above). The amendments also created a market for toxic air pollutant emissions, and now facilities can make trades involving multiple toxic air pollutants. Finally, under the 1990 CAA the **tradeable discharge permit** scheme for reducing chlorofluorocarbons (initiated in 1988) was expanded internationally (Morgenstern, 1992).

In a related decision, the EPA has created a **mobile-stationary source trading program**. Patterned after a 1990 Unocal experiment in California, utilities are now allowed to purchase old, polluting automobiles, destroy them, and count the emissions that would have otherwise come from the vehicles as a pollution reduction credit. This is cost effective for the utilities, since it is often cheaper to purchase old cars than to install additional pollution control equipment. The program also improves air quality, since approximately 86 percent of carbon dioxide and hydrocarbons from mobile sources come from pre-1980 automobiles (*EPA Journal*, 1992). The size and duration of the pollution reduction credit depends upon the make and age of the car.

Market-like pollution controls are now being suggested for areas other than air pollution. For example, some analysts are proposing **pesticide application permit auctions** to encourage farmers to use pesticides more effectively and efficiently, thereby reducing total pesticide use (Freeman, 1994). Others have suggested a simple pesticide user fee to encourage conservation in pesticide use (Williams, 1992).

The most exciting experiment along these lines might be the **point-nonpoint source pollutant trading program** now in place in North Carolina. Eighty percent of the nutrient pollution in the Tar and Pamlico rivers in North Carolina comes from agriculture. The EPA has helped the state devise a **watershed management plan** for this region, and the state, the Environmental Defense Fund, and a dozen waste water treatment plants have agreed to install a pollutant trading program in the watershed; a sort of **"water bubble"**

(Letson, 1992). First, the state placed a limit on total nutrient pollution in the watershed (425,000 kilograms in 1994). For every kilogram of nutrient pollution above this limit, a facility pays a tax of $56 (this money goes to pay for pollution control improvements on farms, ranches, and mines in the watershed). The treatment plants can chose to reduce their pollution by installing additional pollution control equipment, or by paying for best management practice controls on farms and ranches in the watershed. Participants in the program expect to meet 80 percent of the required pollutant reductions through these trades (*ENR*, 1992).

After years of protest, many (but not all) environmental groups now support the use of economic incentives in pollution control. Present experiments with market incentives in environmental protection, however, still leave four important questions unanswered.

First, while environmentalists are becoming more comfortable using economic analysis to select the most efficient method of reaching environmental goals (e.g., **cost effectiveness analysis**), they remain uncomfortable using economic analysis to select the goals in the first place (e.g., **benefit-cost analysis**).

Second, the competing advocacy coalitions often differ on just where to set levels for these economic incentives. For example, the EPA believed a carbon dioxide tax of $6.51 per ton would be an effective tool to combat global warming, but the Department of Energy pegged the effective tax rate at $140 per ton (Kriz, 1992b).

Third, many groups are uncomfortable with the potential **distributional consequences** of these tools. For example, older facilities in inner cities often find it more costly to reduce pollution. These same facilities would thus be most likely to purchase pollution reduction credits instead of reducing pollution, exacerbating a situation in which poor and minority neighborhoods are exposed to disproportionately high levels of pollution (Asch and Seneca, 1978; Bullard, 1990; McCaull, 1976).

Fourth, any scheme of pollution trades requires accurate and constant monitoring of actual levels of pollution being released into the environment. The EPA does not presently have such a monitoring system, nor do the states. California is experimenting with **continuous stationary source pollutant monitors** that are linked to that state's central computing system, and Wisconsin is testing remote sensing equipment to monitor automobile exhaust, but these technologies are still in the developmental stage. In this sense, market incentives in pollution control are truly technology forcing regulations.

Integrated Environmental Management

While command and control regulations have reduced emissions of some pollutants (e.g., atmospheric sulfur dioxide), in many cases these "**reductions**" have simply displaced the pollutant into a different medium (Dryzek, 1987). In addition, many of the new environmental problems we face have significant cross-media components (e.g., acidified streams and toxic contamination of the Great Lakes both stem from air pollution). To be truly effective, environmental regulations must begin to recognize Barry Commoner's **first law of ecology**: "everything is connected to everything else" (Commoner, 1972). Regulators have tried to incorporate this perspective through various forms of integrated environmental management.

The first efforts at **integrated environmental management** approached the problem from a **geographic perspective**, attempting to track and control pollution across several political jurisdictions through complex ecosystem models. In the early 1980s, the EPA funded pilot programs in integrated environmental management in Kanawha Valley, West Virginia; Baltimore, Maryland; Philadelphia, Pennsylvania; and Santa Clara Valley, California. From the beginning, the programs suffered from a lack of resources. In FY87, EPA's Geographic Branch had only 12 people and a budget of $1.3 million. Each demonstration project ran into serious problems with ecosystem modeling, data management, and cross jurisdictional political cooperation. Most also lacked an evaluative mechanism, and the projects were shut down in the late 1980s (Cohen and Weiskopf, 1990). A number of states also attempted to reorganize their environmental bureaucracies to emphasize integrated environmental management. Here too, agencies found it difficult to overcome the cost, data, and political obstacles to integrated environmental management. Most of these state programs reverted to using integrated environmental planning to streamline the regulatory process, rather than as a tool for truly integrated environmental decisionmaking (Rabe, 1986).

The next effort at integrated environmental management was organized around particular industries instead of geographic regions, and focused on the environmental permitting process. Most facilities require permits under several environmental statutes, but there is little or no coordination to determine where it might be most effective to reduce pollution. Regulators rarely check to see if the requirements of one permit increase the volume of waste elsewhere. As early as 1981, EPA attempted **industry wide, cross-media permit integration**, but abandoned the effort in 1985 as unproductive (Cohen and Weiskopf, 1990). Once again, the states took over the leadership role in integrated environmental management, and unlike experiences in the early 1980s, many Great Lakes states appear to be having some success in using integrated permitting within particular industries (Rabe and Zimmerman, 1994).

Federal interest in integrated permitting was rekindled during the 1990s. Successful state experiences might be one reason for this renewed interest. A second reason might be the EPA's experience with environmental permitting at the Amoco oil refinery in Yorktown, Pennsylvania. The agency was going to require the refinery to install costly pollution control equipment on its refinery stacks in order to reduce the emission of ozone generating VOCs. A plant-wide analysis, however, showed a much greater reduction in VOCs could be achieved at much lower cost by controlling emissions at the refinery's riverside loading docks; a source not regulated under the CAA. In response to this and other evidence, Congressional debate over reauthorization of the CWA includes a provision for integrated environmental permitting. In addition, EPA chief Carol Browner has pledged to take a "**holistic**" approach to environmental protection that emphasizes integrated environmental management. Along these lines, the heads of EPA, DOE, USDA, and the Department of the Interior now hold monthly meetings to discuss integration in policy goals and effects (Ember, 1993).

Nonregulatory Tools in Environmental Protection

This examination of the nonregulatory tools in environmental protection includes sections on (1) regulatory negotiation, (2) pollution prevention, and (3) environmental dispute resolution.

REGULATORY NEGOTIATION

The most "regulatory" of the **nonregulatory tools** in environmental protection is the **negotiated rulemaking process** now being used at EPA. In traditional rulemaking, the only formal opportunity regulated parties or other stakeholders have to participate in the process is through the notice and comment procedure after the proposed rule has already been drafted. In negotiated rulemaking, representatives from the regulatory agency sit down with representatives from the affected groups and negotiate a proposed rule. The negotiation process is supposed to produce regulations that are easier to comply with, easier to enforce, and less likely to be challenged in court.

Negotiated rulemaking (part of a larger process known as regulatory negotiation, or **"reg-neg"**) had its debut at EPA in 1982 (Lassila, 1992). Under the political climate of the time, negotiated rulemaking was seen as little more than letting the regulated industries write their own rules. Over time, however, members of the environmental quality advocacy coalition grudgingly recognized some of the benefits of negotiated rulemaking. EPA's present **"workgroup"** approach to adopting major new rules typically includes over fifty agency staff members plus representatives of major stakeholder groups (Rosenbaum, 1994). Negotiated rulemaking was codified as standard operating procedure in all regulatory agencies by the Negotiated Rulemaking Act of 1990.

Some observers even advocate a negotiated approach to compliance and enforcement in regulation, in effect transforming the regulatory inspector from a police officer into a **consultant** (Bardach and Kagan, 1982). While the opportunities for abuse are obvious, in certain instances this approach may work. Burby and Paterson (1992) evaluated compliance with nonpoint source water pollution prevention performance standards at dozens of construction sites in North Carolina. Some of these sites were overseen by state inspectors who took a traditional adversarial approach to compliance, while others were overseen by local inspectors who took a more cooperative approach. Local inspectors completed nearly four times as many inspections per site, and these sites complied with the performance standards at nearly twice the rate of sites overseen by state inspectors.

POLLUTION PREVENTION

The EPA is trying to forge **cooperative relationships** with industry in an effort to prevent pollution before it is produced. This effort was launched in 1989 with the creation of EPA's **Office of Pollution Prevention**, and was strengthened when Congress enacted the Pollution Prevention Act of 1990. EPA's first major pollution prevention initiative was the **33/50 program** whereby the agency hopes to help industries reduce emissions of 17 toxic chemicals 33 percent by 1992 and 50 percent by 1995. Over 800 companies are currently participating in the program, and the agency offers workshops and industry-specific technical assistance to all program participants. The second pollution prevention initiative is the **Green Lights program** in which EPA works with companies and state and local governments to install energy efficient lighting systems. Participants in the Green Lights programs agree to survey their lighting needs and install energy efficient lighting systems within five years. In return, the EPA connects participants with utilities who provide them with technical and financial assistance for lighting retrofits. Participants also get to promote their participation in the program on their products and in their advertising (Andrews, 1992).

The EPA is also attempting to take pollution prevention to state governments and federal research labs. For example, an EPA scientist was assigned to help incorporate environmentally friendly design principles into the new Denver international airport. Now completed, the airport uses power plant fly-ash in the runway cement, daylighting and low flow water fixtures in the terminal, natural gas fleet vehicles, and recycles its deicing fluids (McGraw, 1992). Finally, Congress is considering a proposal to redirect some of the Department of Energy's nuclear weapons labs to produce "**green technologies**" for industry that incorporate pollution prevention principles (Browning, 1992a).

ENVIRONMENTAL DISPUTE RESOLUTION

Environmental dispute resolution (EDR) is an approach to environmental regulation that emphasizes cooperation and consensus building. In traditional EDR, a neutral mediator brings together the various interests involved in a dispute and they attempt to fashion a compromise upon which all participants can agree (Amy, 1990). EDR is most often used in land use or development disputes, but has been advocated as an approach that is well suited to disagreements over environmental regulations as well (Crowfoot and Wondolleck, 1990). Initial efforts at using EDR as an alternative to litigation were undertaken in the mid-1970s at the University of Washington's Office of Environmental Mediation. By 1990, environmental mediation centers had sprung up in 15 states, and the EPA was considering expanding its use of EDR outside of the negotiated rulemaking process (Amy, 1990).

CONCLUSION

Who benefits from environmental protection? At first glance, environmental regulation appears to be an issue that seeks to redistribute benefits from polluters to the general public. On closer examination, however, the relationship might not be so simple. A few environmental regulations clearly confer private benefits. Moreover, as long as pollution controls are uniformly imposed on all plants within an industry and the industry can effectively compete with imports, pollution controls are probably translated into higher prices. Because the general public pays these prices, environmental regulation both benefits and costs the same group of people in the abstract. The general support for such policies illustrates that benefits are perceived to exceed the costs.

If we leave the macro level, pollution regulation has some redistributive effects within and between industries. One distributional impact is that pollution control imposes greater costs on dirtier industries, thus raising their prices and reducing demand. Such sanctions are economically rational, because pollution regulation does nothing more than reimpose externalities on the firms producing them. A second distributional impact is on smaller firms. Pashigian (1983) found that pollution control imposed a greater cost on small firms than it did on large firms. To some extent, pollution control has economies of scale. If such a bias is deemed significant, subsidies for pollution control could be granted to small business. On the other hand, the liberal tax provisions for investments in pollution control probably make such incentives unnecessary (see Downing, 1984).

In sum, then, environmental protection places restrictions on the regulated for the benefit of the nonregulated. This policy orientation reflects some of the variables discussed in Chapter 2, such as high issue salience, a well-organized nonindustry advocacy coalition, and a bureaucracy equipped with ample resources. Table 7.1 provides a summary of these and other variables involved in environmental regulation. At times, short-term political forces can alter the direction of policy somewhat, but such occurrences are fluctuations from the overall trend.

The politics of pollution regulation is influenced greatly by the issue's salience. Since environmental protection burst on the scene in the 1960s, it has consistently remained important to most Americans. Public opinion polls generally show strong support for environmental protection and significant support for stronger action. Such a level of salience explains the heavy participation in environmental policy by political elites.

Salience and congressional activism go hand in hand. While Congress perceives regulation in general as a legislative responsibility, no regulatory area is as close to Congress as environmental protection. As a counterweight to Congress stands the president. Environmental policy is too important for even presidents not to take an active role. Although presidents have exerted significant influence via appointments and budget controls, in general, presidential impact has been less than that of Congress. The courts have also played a role in environmental policy by forcing administrative action or providing an alternative forum for disputes (Melnick, 1983). Changes in the composition of the judiciary, however, mean that the courts are a much less hospitable place for environmental groups than was true in the 1970s.

Within the subsystem, three actors with ample resources operate. Because environmental regulation is complex, the Environmental Protection Agency plays a major role. EPA's major resource in building a power base, however, has been the cohesion of its employees. EPA employees, even though they are recruited from numerous professions, have developed a commitment to the organization and to environmental protection. With allies in Congress, they were able to resist the initiatives of Anne Burford in the 1980s. This cohesion, coupled with unusual expertise for a regulatory agency and generally positive leadership, has made the agency a factor that must be considered in environmental protection. Legislative authority assists the EPA in its battles. Goals are specific, coverage is universal, and sanctions are good even though they are not used frequently. In such circumstances, regulation favoring the regulated is not likely.

Within the subsystem, EPA faces competing advocacy coalitions. The economic rationality advocacy coalition is well organized and well funded. In opposition, environmental groups have used the salience of environmental protection to build a fairly strong competing advocacy coalition. Although the environmental quality coalition cannot match the industry groups in terms of size and resources, in practice it does not have to do so. Because environmental groups advocate policies with a fair amount of diffuse

Table 7.1   A Summary of Environmental Regulation

Economics	
Ease of entry	Varies
Number of firms	Vary
Profits	Variable
Technology	
Complexity	Varies
Stability	Varies
Substitutes	Varies
Subsystem	
Bureaucratic control	Moderate
Industry coalition	Strong
Nonindustry coalition	Moderate
Bureaucratic resources:	
Expertise	Strong
Cohesion	Strong
Leadership	Strong
Legislative authority:	
Goals	Specific
Coverage	Universal
Sanctions	Good
Procedures	Good
Involvement of Macropolitical Actors	
Congress	Strong
President	Strong
Courts	Moderate

public support, they need fewer resources to accomplish their ends than does industry.

If recent developments are a sign of new trends, the future of environmental regulation will be very different from its past. First, the targets of regulation are changing from **large, remote industrial facilities** to **smaller, more tangible actors** such as dry cleaners and farmers. Second, concerns such as global warming and stratospheric ozone depletion are beginning to shape U.S. environmental regulatory decisions, adding an international dimension to the politics of pollution control. Third, no longer content to be excluded from environmental decisionmaking, civil rights groups are calling attention to the disproportionate levels of pollution suffered by many working class and minority communities. The entry of these groups into the policy subsystem lends a more populist flavor to policy debates in environmental protection. Fourth, the emergence of property rights claims, unfunded mandates, and risk analysis present important new challenges for advocates of environmental protection. Fifth, developments in regulatory negotiation, pollution prevention, and environmental dispute resolution suggest that the future of environmental regulation may evolve to be less adversarial. Taken together, these changes have the potential to reshape the politics of environmental regulation.

Chapter 8
Workplace Safety and Health Regulation

Lael Keiser[1]

Occupational safety and health regulation is probably the best known and most controversial federal regulatory enterprise. The Occupational Safety and Health Administration (OSHA), the principal federal agency involved, has been condemned for imposing large costs on business for little safety gain. Shortly after it was created, OSHA became the favorite whipping boy of politicians running for office. Despite the controversy, occupational safety and health regulation is a fairly traditional form of regulation. OSHA, through the rulemaking process, establishes standards for safety (e.g., specifications regarding the strength of ladders) and health (e.g., workers shall be exposed to no more than x parts per million of a chemical). OSHA then inspects workplaces for compliance with these standards and levies fines for failure to comply. The basic form of regulation is similar to that of the Environmental Protection Agency.

THE SUBSYSTEM

This examination of the subsystem of workplace safety and health regulation includes an overview of (1) the agencies involved, (2) advocacy coalitions, (3) the environment, and (4) occupational safety before the Occupational Health and Safety Administration.

The Agencies

The regulation of occupational safety and health at the federal level is handled through a three agency system. The most visible agency, **Occupational Safety and Health Administration (OSHA)**, is located in the Department of Labor and is headed by an assistant secretary of labor, who reports directly to the secretary of labor. OSHA issues health and safety standards, inspects firms for compliance, and fines firms for

---

[1]Lael Keiser is a PhD candidate in political science at the University of Wisconsin-Milwaukee. An honors graduate of Lawrence University, she previously worked as a staff member for Senator Paul Simon of Illinois. Her research focuses on the role of bureaucracy in public policy with special emphasis on social service bureaucracies.

Dutch 801 Roman

violations. The agency is decentralized with most activities conducted by 94 field offices. In fiscal year 1993, OSHA had 2,300 employees and a budget of $288,300 million. OSHA shares some safety regulation tasks with other federal regulatory agencies such as the Nuclear Regulatory Commission and the Mine Safety and Health Administration which have jurisdiction over specific industries.

OSHA is not a research agency. The research that forms the basis for regulation is done in the **National Institute of Occupational Safety and Health (NIOSH)**, a small agency in the Department of Health and Human Services. In addition, if businesses wish to contest OSHA decisions, they can appeal to the **Occupational Safety and Health Review Commission (OSHRC)**. OSHRC is an independent agency that adjudicates contested OSHA fines, provisions of corrective action orders, and the adequacy of inspections.

Workplace safety and health is another area of regulation that is greatly influenced by **federalism**. State governments that meet certain criteria (see below) can opt to enforce federal workplace safety and health laws with state agencies. States that qualify are not subject to enforcement by OSHA. State workplace safety regulators tend to be independent of federal control and likely to pursue policies different from those of the federal government.

Because OSHA is the major action agency at the federal level, it will be the focus of our discussion. OSHA has generally not developed the resources to become a powerful political actor. Because NIOSH is the prime research agency, OSHA does not have a reputation for expertise. By cultivating the **professional values** of industrial hygienists and safety engineers, however, it has become somewhat cohesive. Limiting the use of cohesion and other resources has been OSHA's lack of good leadership; even when leadership has not been hostile to regulation, it can normally be characterized as poor to average.

Two other political resources are worthy of note—**salience** and **legislative authority** (see Chapter 2). Occupational safety and health is a salient issue. To be sure, it does not have the salience of environmental protection, but it maintains its salience at a consistent level year after year. The reason for this persistent salience is that occupational safety and health is a labor-management issue with two highly organized advocacy coalitions taking opposite positions on most issues (see Sabatier 1988).

High salience means that political actors have been motivated to intervene in the regulatory subsystem with great frequency. Such intervention is often highly partisan because labor and management have links to different political parties. Congress has continually been involved in the administration of occupational safety and health policy since its inception. Policy implementation at times has been so controversial that since 1978 presidents have addressed OSHA issues and established elaborate review procedures for OSHA initiatives.

Salience in worker safety and health is such that advocacy coalitions rarely accept defeat without exhausting all avenues of influence. Interest groups that fail to convince OSHA of their position usually then sue the agency to have the regulation set aside. Virtually every OSHA health rule ever issued was involved in a **court battle**. After the court rules (generally in favor of OSHA), the losing party usually presses Congress or the president to intervene in the process and change the outcome. High salience determines that there are no quick, final decisions.

OSHA's legislative authority differs little from that of other regulatory agencies. The legislative goals are vague, encouraging OSHA to protect the health and safety of workers so far as is possible. Little specific guidance is given in the 30-page **Occupational Safety and Heath Act** (note the brevity compared to 200-page laws for regulating agriculture and the equally detailed Clean Air Act). Initially, OSHA covered most businesses involved in **interstate commerce**. In 1977, however, Congress exempted small farms, and in 1981 with a targeting policy the agency **exempted** a large number of firms from inspections (see below). OSHA has the capability to impose financial sanctions on businesses and seek injunctions to compel compliance. The size of the fines actually imposed are small, thus reducing their impact.

Advocacy Coalitions

OSHA's policy sphere contains two well-organized advocacy coalitions. Overall **business viewpoints** are represented via the Business Roundtable, the National Association of Manufacturers, or the National Federation of Independent Business. **Individual industries** are almost always represented by trade associations such as the Chemical Manufacturers Association. In addition, individual companies often represent themselves. In general, industry groups are large campaign contributors, especially after the election laws were rewritten to permit corporations to establish political action committees. Industry groups often have the support of academic economists who study safety and health issues. The industry coalition has many of the advantages Rourke (1984) details for effective interest group articulation, including resources, prestige, status, and knowledge about the system. Industry groups generally press for no regulation or weak regulation of occupational safety and health.

Industry is opposed in its anti-OSHA lobbying by an advocacy coalition headed by **organized labor**. One labor spokesperson characterized the Occupational Safety and Health Act as "the single most important piece of labor legislation since the National Labor Relations Act of 1935" (Quoted in Pettus 1982: 611). Because the National Labor Relations Act is often referred to as the Magna Charta of organized labor, the high priority of workplace safety and health is evident. Although the AFL-CIO often presses for stronger regulation, the key union is the Oil, Chemical, and Atomic Workers Union because they have developed the scientific expertise on safety issues that is used to counter the arguments of industry (Viscusi 1983: 564). Union can often count on various safety and health professionals as allies. Since 1987 a major safety advocate has been the National Safe Workplace Institute. The coalition has been weakened in recent years as union membership has dropped; membership in the oil and chemical workers union for example, dropped in the 1980s from 145,000 to 100,000 (Victor 1990a: 1942).

The Environment

The reach of OSHA is **economy-wide**. All industries are subject to OSHA's general regulations, and some industries such as lumbering are subjected to specific regulations. Because the reach of OSHA is so broad, the normal economic and technological environmental variables considered in other chapters have less relevance for explaining the general direction of OSHA regulation. Such economic factors as the number of firms, the ease of entry, and industry profits vary from industry to industry as do such technological variables as complexity, stability, and substitutes. When a rule applies specifically to a **single industry**, these variables are important. For example, the OSHA effort to limit cotton dust exposure (see below) was strongly resisted by the textile industry because the industry's economic status was fairly dismal. The textile industry suffered from low profits and strong competition from imports; resistance to health standards that would require large investments was predictable.

One technological factor that is important, however, is that of availability. Occupational safety and health regulations are subject to the same problems that environmental regulations face—often standards are set that cannot be met with the current technology. Under such circumstances, the rulemaking process becomes a highly technical debate over the scientific feasibility of meeting the standards.

Occupational Safety Before the Occupational Safety and Health Administration

Workplace dangers were not suddenly discovered in 1970 when OSHA was created. Injuries, deaths, and illnesses related to specific occupations had been documented for years. The **National Safety Council** estimated that, in 1970, 14,000 persons were killed in work-related accidents and 2.2 million persons were physically disabled; in addition, some 5.7 million accidents resulted in 1.7 million lost workdays annually (Kelman 1980: 236). Although these figures showed large decreases from the 1920s (Shaffer 1977: 198), from 1966 to 1970 injury rates increased rapidly (Smith 1976: 8).

Data on workplace safety were based on estimates taken from business and hospital records; many criticized these estimates as far too low (see Ashford 1976: 3). Compared to statistics on occupational disease, however, **accident data** were fairly reliable. Ashford (1976: 93), a highly respected expert in this field, estimated that 100,000 persons died from occupationally-related diseases and that 400,000 new cases of **occupationally-related illnesses** occurred annually.

Before 1970 the regulation of worker health and safety was left to the states.[2] In fact, most states had adopted a law regulating workplace safety by 1900 following the lead of Massachusetts (Kelman 1980: 238). Two different methods of compensating injured workers were tried. The first option was to treat an occupational injury as a **tort** and use the legal system to determine damages. A worker injured on the job could sue his or her employer. The effectiveness of lawsuits was limited by court interpretation. To collect damages from an employer, an employee usually had to prove (1) that the employer was negligent, (2) that the employee was not negligent (had not contributed to the danger), and (3) that no fellow workers were at fault (see Buchholz 1982: 304). Consequently the legal system rarely compensated injured workers.

---

[2]There were a few notable exceptions to this policy. Coal mine safety and working conditions for longshoremen were federal concerns. In addition, federal contractors had to have safety plans. For an excellent analysis of coal mine safety, see Lewis-Beck and Alford (1980).

The second option for the states was the enactment of workers' compensation laws. **Workers' compensation laws** are essentially no-fault insurance laws; employers are required to carry insurance or pay directly to compensate workers injured on the job. The system is administered by quasi-judicial state agencies usually called Workmen's Compensation Courts.

Workers' compensation law had a shaky start. Many laws were declared unconstitutional before the courts accepted this form of regulation. By 1948 every state had adopted some form of workers' compensation law (Shaffer 1977: 197), and 85 percent of all workers were covered (Nichols and Zeckhauser 1981: 213). Under the workers' compensation system, large firms have an incentive to improve safety on the job because their insurance premiums are based on their **accident records**; small firms' insurance rates are based on **industry-wide averages**, so they have little incentive to incur additional costs to improve safety.

Although workers' compensation programs varied from state to state, in general, they had five weaknesses as a method of protecting workers from unsafe conditions:

First, the **benefits** paid by the system were fairly low; in 1940 state systems paid an average of 66 percent of before-accident wages for a total disability; by 1970 this had fallen to 50 percent in some states (L. White 1983: 117).[3]

Second, the system was slow, often taking several years to provide benefits; in fact, businesses had an incentive to slow down the process because benefits did not have to be paid (and thus be reflected in insurance rates) until final disposition.

Third, the system was **compensatory** but not **preventative**. The system provided only weak incentives for businesses to improve the safety of their plants and, as a result, appeared to have no impact on the incidence of industrial accidents (Shaffer 1977: 197).

Fourth, workers' compensation generally ignored **occupational diseases**. Unlike an injury that could be traced to an on-the-job accident, an occupational disease might be attributable to only one of the worker's employers (if the disease had a long latency period) or even to off-the-job exposure. One indicator of the workers' compensation system's inability to handle occupational diseases is that 13 percent of the Social Security System's disability funds are devoted to individuals with disabilities resulting from occupational diseases (L. White 1983: 118).

Fifth, the workers' compensation system was inefficient. On the average, only 65 percent of insurance premiums were paid out in worker claims; in some states the figures were as low as 50 percent (L. White 1983: 113). Because premiums are invested and draw interest until needed, benefits as a percentage of earnings were even lower.

---

[3]A disabled person will generally need less income to maintain the same standard of living as a person working, in theory. Because the disabled person does not have work-related expenses, benefits were set at a percentage of pre-disability wages. The exact percentage necessary to restore full purchasing power is open to question.

ESTABLISHING FEDERAL REGULATION

This examination of establishing federal regulation includes an overview of the (1) politics of creation, (2) the Occupational Safety and Health Act, and (3) rulemaking procedures.

The Politics of Creation

Despite the weaknesses of the workers' compensation system and the large number of individuals killed and injured on the job, the 1960s saw no great push for federal regulation. Unlike other areas of social regulation, no political entrepreneur seized on occupational safety as an issue. Even the Nader organization came to occupational safety late; the Nader exposé of workplace dangers was not published, for example, until three years after OSHA legislation was passed (Page and O'Brien 1973). Instead, occupational safety and health reached the political agenda via a series of idiosyncratic events (see Kelman 1980).

A speech writer for President Lyndon Johnson, Robert Hardesty, had a brother who worked in the Bureau of Occupational Safety and Health, a research unit in the Department of Health, Education, and Welfare. As the result of his brother's urging, Hardesty occasionally slipped references to occupational safety and health in some of Johnson's speeches (Kelman 1980: 239). At the same time Assistant Secretary of Labor Esther Peterson became concerned with health conditions in mining and raised the issue with the secretary of labor.

In late 1967, Secretary of Labor Willard Wirtz was looking for new legislative proposals to suggest to the president. After the interest expressed in the issue by Peterson, Department of Labor executives discovered the references to occupational safety and health in the president's speeches (Kelman 1980: 239). A proposal on occupational safety and health, therefore, appeared to be one that would gain the president's approval. The White House accepted the proposal and included it in the president's **legislative program** even though the Department of Labor did little to lobby for its inclusion (Kelman 1980: 239). Occupational safety and health, therefore, was not placed on the agenda via such normal mechanisms as interest group pressure, political entrepreneurship, or external crisis. Rather, Kelman (1980: 240) attributed its placement on the agenda to bureaucrats looking to push good causes as well as some highly idiosyncratic events.

With an administration proposal, Congress scheduled hearings in 1968. During the hearings, the controversial nature of workplace safety was established. Labor organizations testified in favor of strict regulation of the workplace to enhance safety. The National Association of Manufacturers and other business organizations argued that the record on occupational safety was not so bad and that most accidents were the fault of workers not business. Business generally opposed any federal efforts. Neither house passed legislation in 1968.

In 1969 three events created an environment conducive to passage of occupational safety and health legislation (see Kelman 1980: 241). First, a late 1968 mine disaster in

Farmington, West Virginia, killed 78 miners, thus increasing the issue's salience. Second, the AFL-CIO made the issue a legislative priority. Third and perhaps most important, Richard Nixon presented his own legislation as part of his strategy to woo the blue-collar workers in the silent majority.

President Nixon's bill, however, was significantly different from the one proposed by the Johnson administration. Nixon proposed that safety regulation rely primarily on **voluntary industry compliance**; in addition, Nixon's proposal did not authorize rulemaking but would have relied on case-by-case corrections. **Fines** were permitted only if the firm engaged in willful violations of the law (Kelman 1980: 255). Nixon's law would have been administered by a new independent agency, the National Occupational Safety and Health Board.

The nearly unanimous votes by which the Occupational Safety and Health Act passed both houses of Congress masked the highly partisan legislative struggle. The legislation was reported out of committee in the House despite a Republican boycott of committee meetings. Floor amendments to change the legislation resulted in a series of party-line votes. In general, the Democrats won most of the floor fights, but in one concession to conservatives, the law permitted states to enforce the federal law (see L. White 1983: 136). In December 1970, President Nixon signed the Occupational Safety and Health Act into law.

The Occupational Safety and Health Act

The goal of the **Occupational Safety and Health Act (OSH Act)** is "to assure so far as possible every working man and woman in the nation safe and healthy work conditions." The act made two significant changes in occupational safety and health regulation policy. First, the policy was **nationalized**, with the federal government established as the dominant regulator in place of the states. To be sure, states could continue to operate programs if they were "**at least as effective**" as the federal program; but to operate a state program, the state had to provide one-half of the funds. Approximately one-half the states operate their own programs. Second, the emphasis changed from compensation of the injured and ill to **prevention** of injury and illness. The workers' compensation system remained in place for compensating injuries.

The details of how injuries and illnesses would be prevented were left to the **bureaucracy** (F. J. Thompson 1982: 203). The task facing the bureaucracy was enormous. The legislation covered all firms in interstate commerce, at the time some 4.1 million establishments with 57 million employees. Only federal, state, and local governments were **exempted** (Smith 1976: 7). Although the regulatory agency was faced with a task as impossible as that facing the Environmental Protection Agency, it had one advantage; the act did not require completely safe and healthy workplaces by a specified time.

The act created two new bureaucracies and changed the name of a third. The basic operation of the act was entrusted to the Occupational Safety and Health Administration (OSHA). OSHA was given the **power** to issue rules and enforce the rules it issued. OSHA was delegated **quasi-legislative** (adopting rules), **quasi-executive** (conducting inspections), and **quasi-judicial** functions (determining whether an employer was in violation of the rules and if so, the amount of the fine for violations). The agency's **rulemaking**

power was broader than that of most other regulatory agencies. In addition to the authority to adopt rules under rulemaking procedures similar to the **Administrative Procedures Act (APA)**, OSHA could also adopt temporary emergency rules without following APA procedures if a "**grave danger**" existed. In addition, OSHA was given the authority to promulgate any "**consensus**" industry standards as rules in the first 28 months of the agency's life.

OSHA's location in the **Department of Labor** is significant. The Department of Labor employs individuals with sympathies for organized labor (see Seidman and Gilmour 1986). In Democratic administrations, the political appointees as well as the career bureaucrats see organized labor as their clientele. Within such an organizational environment, OSHA could be expected to give greater attention to labor union concerns than to those of private industry. Republican administrations are usually more favorable to private industry.

The second agency created by the 1970 act was the **Occupational Safety and Health Review Commission (OSHRC)**. OSHRC is an appeals commission established to adjudicate contested OSHA decisions. OSHRC has always operated independently from OSHA; it has used different criteria for enforcing the law and usually reduces OSHA fines. OSHRC once went so far as to hold that businesses need not comply with safety regulations if compliance would be **unduly costly** (compared to the OSHA view that costs should not be considered, see Harter 1977: 36).

The Occupational Safety and Health Act also changed the name of the Bureau of Occupational Safety and Health to the **National Institute of Occupational Safety and Health (NIOSH)**. The act left the agency in the Department of Health, Education, and Welfare (now Health and Human Services). NIOSH continued with its research on occupational safety and health issues and was given the authority to suggest new regulations to OSHA.

Of these agencies, OSHA was clearly the most important. The tone for the agency was established with the initial recruitment of personnel. Individuals hired to work for OSHA were generally safety and health professionals such as safety engineers and industrial hygienists (Kelman 1980: 250). According to Kelman (1980: 250), the professions shared commonly held values that indicated the future direction of regulation. Both professions are concerned with **preventing** accidents and health hazards; the question of cost is not usually asked. OSHA, therefore, was populated by employees whose professional values consisted of "**doing good**" (Kelman 1980; F.J. Thompson 1982).

Unlike other agencies such as the Federal Aviation Administration or the Environmental Protection Agency, where agency leadership played a strong role in creating an organizational ideology, in OSHA the ideology grew out of professional norms. This ideology was reflected in the agency's regulations. The ideology had a preference for **engineering standards**, that is, specifying a standard and also specifying how that standard should be met. Included as part of engineering standards was the belief that **personal protective gear** would not solve any problems. When faced with controlling exposure to an **occupational hazard** (e.g., cotton dust), OSHA regulators, therefore, would require the air in the workplace to be cleaned rather than require individual workers to wear respirators (Kelman 1980: 252).

In addition, OSHA employees distrusted the goodwill of employers. Almost four of five OSHA inspectors responded in a survey that many employers would ignore standards (Kelman 1980: 255). One illustration of the strength of professional values in determining regulatory outcomes in this area is Kelman's finding that occupational safety and health policies are similar in Sweden and the United States despite the vastly different degrees of influence of business and labor. The similarity, he argues, can be attributed to the values of health and safety professionals (see Kelman 1981b).

Rulemaking Procedures

The general **rulemaking procedure** for OSHA is similar to that for other regulatory agencies, and it is illustrated in Figure 8.1. The rulemaking procedure is complex in part because there are so many interested parties that participate. Normally the process begins with NIOSH conducting a literature review of the hazards involved in exposure to substances or dangerous conditions and proposing that OSHA author a regulation in the area. OSHA, however, need not respond to NIOSH initiatives. OSHA may also undertake the rulemaking process on its own initiative or in response to an individual petition.

At this point OSHA begins the normal rulemaking process: **notice of a rulemaking procedure** is published in the *Federal Register*, and **public hearings** are held. OSHA hearings are often long and controversial because both labor and management groups (as well as public health people) can be expected to present evidence and dispute the evidence of others. OSHA is also required to do some **cost analysis** on its proposed regulations. As a nonindependent agency, OSHA was required to file **inflationary impact statements** under President Ford, was challenged by the economic analysis of the Council on Wage and Price Stability under Carter, and must clear its regulations with the Office of Management and Budget under Reagan, Bush and Clinton. Despite the pressures for **cost-benefit analysis**, until the 1980s OSHA had successfully *avoided* doing such analysis before issuing rules. The final rule must then be published in the *Federal Register* before it takes effect.

OSHA also has the authority to issue **temporary rules** when an emergency exists and when going through the full rulemaking process would delay correction of the problem. Under such circumstances, OSHA can issue a temporary emergency rule, but must then begin normal rulemaking procedures to issue a permanent rule. In addition, OSHA had authority to bypass normal rulemaking procedures in the first 28 months (see the following section).

Experience has shown that the OSHA rulemaking process is cumbersome and slow. By an optimistic count, OSHA issued no more than 40 rules in its first two decades using this procedure. Many of these rules deal with minor matters, however; the number of major health-oriented rules was less than a dozen.

IMPLEMENTING THE LAW

The examination on implementing the law includes an overview of (1) the inspection process, (2) implementing safety regulations, and (3) the shift to health regulation.

Figure 8.1   Overview of the OSHA Rulemaking Process

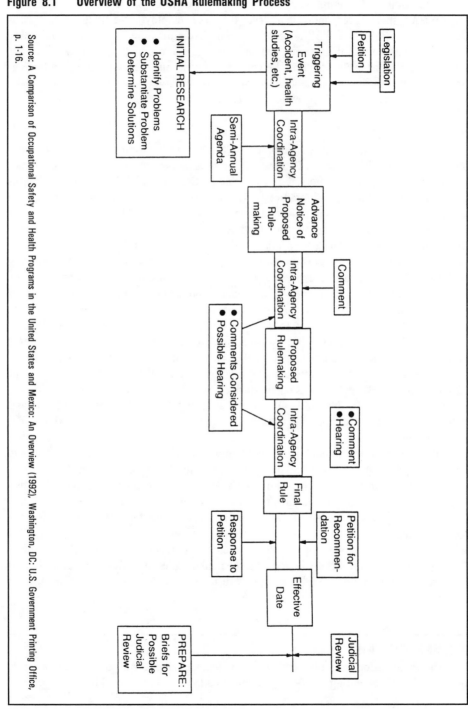

Source: A Comparison of Occupational Safety and Health Programs in the United States and Mexico: An Overview (1992), Washington, DC: U.S. Government Printing Office, p. 1-16.

The Inspection Process

OSHA regulations are enforced by **on-site inspections** conducted by OSHA personnel. A firm might be selected for inspection for four reasons:

First, OSHA engages in targeted inspections. Because OSHA does not have the personnel to inspect the millions of U.S. workplaces, it sets priorities for inspections. In general, targeted inspections focus on more **hazardous occupations** such as lumbering, meatpacking, longshoring, and so on.

Second, OSHA conducts inspections as part of accident investigations.

Third, inspections are scheduled if the agency receives **complaints** about unsafe work conditions. Initially, a large portion of OSHA inspections resulted from worker complaints. Experience showed, however, that compliance-inspired inspections found few safety violations. Such a record suggests that workers probably used the OSHA process to harass employers.

Fourth, OSHA conducts follow-up inspections to determine if previous violations have been corrected (see Buchholz 1982: 311).

An OSHA inspector can find five different types of violations:

First, **other-than-serious violations** are those that have no direct relationship to job safety; the remedy is to give notice of such a violation but not to issue citations or levy fines.

Second, **nonserious violations** are those with a direct relationship to safety but unlikely to cause death or serious injury. Such violations are subject to a penalty of up to $1,000 at OSHA's discretion.

Third, **serious violations** are those that might probably lead to death or serious harm; serious violations are subject to a mandatory penalty of up to $7,000 fine.

Fourth, **willful violations** occur if an employer is aware of a hazardous condition and makes no reasonable effort to eliminate it. Penalties of, at a minimum $5,000, to a maximum of $70,000, may be proposed for willful violations. If a willful violation results in the death of an employee, OSHA can fine an individual employer $250,000 and fine a corporation $500,000. If an employer fails to correct the practice or condition that caused a violation in the past, they are subject to repeat violations which can be as high as $70,000.

Fifth, since 1986, OSHA has followed a policy of imposing **"egregious" penalties**.

Companies can be fined for several instances of the same violation. If a company is cited for unsafe equipment, for example, OSHA can cite the company for each piece of that equipment or each worker affected by the equipment. In fiscal year 1991, OSHA used this citation policy 14 times with an average penalty per inspection of $1,905,753 (United States Department of Labor 1993: 11). Egregious penalties can only be imposed if the employer is found in violation of the law with actual knowledge of the violation and if the employer has made no reasonable effort to eliminate the problem. In addition, violations must be associated with conditions that cause worker fatalities, and persistently high rates of injuries or illness.

When citing companies under egregious penalties, OSHA encourages the negotiation of **Corporate-Wide Settlement Agreements**. These agreements specify steps that the employer must take to remove the dangerous condition and a date for completion of this task. Since 1986, OSHA has reached settlements with companies in over ninety percent of the cases involving penalties for egregious violations (United States Department of Labor 1993: 12).

The OSHA inspector does not levy **fines** on employers. After completion of the inspection, the inspector presents his or her findings to the **OSHA area director**, who determines the fine. Any employer who wishes to appeal either the size of the fines or the citation can file an appeal with the Occupational Safety and Health Review Commission.

Many employers with egregious penalties have **appealed** the citations to the Occupational Safety and Health Review Commission and have had the fines reduced and the policy declared a violation of Administrative Procedures Act (Sapper and Yohay 1993). Other administrative law judges have, however, found in favor of egregious penalties (Tyson 1992: 21). According to the Assistant Secretary of labor, OSHA will be expanding the use of egregious penalties during the Clinton administration (quoted in *Occupational Hazards* 1994 56:11-12).

In addition to monetary sanctions, OSHA can also impose **non-monetary sanctions** on companies that violate the OSH act. OSHA inspectors can find that a situation presents an **imminent danger** to employees; under such circumstances, the employer is required to correct the situation immediately. OSHA can seek **court injunctions** to correct imminent dangers. OSHA can also refer cases to the United States Department of Justice for possible **criminal prosecution**.

Implementing Safety Regulations

Safety regulation rather than health regulation was the first priority of the early OSHA. This priority reflected the interests of the advocacy coalition supporting the legislation, and the actions of OSHA in this area created a controversy that engulfed the agency. Many of OSHA's political problems can be attributed to a single major mistake made by the agency in 1971.

The Occupational Safety and Health Act permitted OSHA to adopt any **consensus national safety and health standards** within two years and 120 days without going through the normal rulemaking procedure. Rather than carefully examining the consensus standards before adopting them, OSHA after only five months issued some 4,400 standards. In part the issuance of these standards reflected the agency's desire to take dramatic actions even though it had a small budget and few trained staff (see Shaffer 1977: 203; F.J. Thompson 1982: 203).

The adopted standards came from two sources. First, 45 percent of the standards came from two **private standards-setting organizations**, the American National Standards Institute and the National Fire Prevention Association. These standards were generally recommendations to business on accepted procedures in industry such as the number and location of fire extinguishers, construction of ladders, guarding of equipment, and the like. Second, the remaining standards were **federal government safety standards** for those firms with federal contracts in excess of $10,000; these standards were issued under the Walsh-Healy Act. The 4,400 standards covered 250 pages in the *Federal Register* and referred to numerous other documents that contained thousands of pages. The total volume of rules in practice, therefore, was overwhelming.

A careful review of the consensus standards would have revealed that wholesale adoption was a serious mistake. The standards were dated, were highly technical, and had serious gaps. The **dated aspect** of the standards was the most amusing. One regulation prohibited the use of ice in drinking water for employees; this standard survived from the days when ice was cut from the top of polluted lakes. The highly technical nature of the standards also created some problems. The standard for ladders was difficult to read without a degree in industrial engineering; 140 standards for ladders were included covering such topics as the types of wood that could be used and the thickness of each of the parts. Despite the volume and the technical detail, the consensus standards had some serious gaps. Almost all the standards dealt with workplace safety, with little attention paid to worker health (Harter 1977: 35).

In an effort to establish a reputation as a stringent regulator, OSHA gave its inspectors **little discretion** in citing violations. A combination of silly rules and rigid enforcement was bound to generate controversy. Story after story surfaced about OSHA's citing business for broken toilet seats, failure to hang fire extinguishers an exact distance from the floor, and other violations that only remotely related to safety (see Nichols and Zeckhauser 1981). In the process, OSHA's reputation was irreparably damaged.

As OSHA discovered its error of acting in haste, it also discovered that issuing rules was easier than repealing rules. To withdraw a rule, OSHA had to go through the **elaborate rulemaking process** established by the Occupational Safety and Health Act even though the rules were issued without using this procedure. A few rules were corrected via this process in the early years of the agency, but little overall progress was made.

Under President Carter, Dr. Eula Bingham, a respected professor of occupational health, was appointed to head the agency. In December 1977, Bingham purposed to eliminate 1,100 **consensus-standards rules** (F.J. Thompson 1982: 205). During the rulemaking hearings, OSHA discovered that even ineffective rules gather supporters; organized labor strongly opposed the withdrawal process. The repeal hearings drew over 200 witnesses and filled three volumes. In October 1978, OSHA repealed 928 of the initial consensus standards and rewrote several others. The **fire prevention standards**, for example, were reduced from 400 pages (including those incorporated by reference) to 10 pages.

Although the Bingham-sponsored process corrected many problems with OSHA regulations, the agency received little credit. Critics continued to cite the old regulations as examples of abuse (see Nichols and Zeckhauser 1981); both business and congressional critics intensified efforts to restrict OSHA. OSHA became in **myth** something far greater and more disruptive than it was in practice; the agency represented the symbol of **overregulation** to many businesses and the symbol of protection from occupational hazards to many unions. Neither view was especially accurate.

The record shows that OSHA can learn from its mistakes, however. An examination of early enforcement data showed that OSHA generally deserved its nit-picking image; from 1973 to 1976 over 98 percent of all OSHA citations were for nonserious violations.

Only two percent of the citations were for serious, willful, and repeat violations. After 1977, however, the OSHA record improved. Although the agency issued fewer citations, more citations were for serious hazards. The number of citations for serious, willful, and repeat violations increased from 9,420 in 1976 to 31,245 in 1979 (Pettus 1982: 600). This trend has continued; in 1991 OSHA cited companies 101,407 serious, willful and repeat violations (United States Department of Labor 1993: Appendix C-1). The data show a clear reorientation of OSHA's priorities in safety inspection.

The Shift to Health Regulation

This discussion of the shift to health regulation includes (1) stress on safety, (2) early health efforts, (3) changes in priorities, and (4) a comprehensive policy.

STRESS ON SAFETY

In its early years, OSHA focused primarily on safety regulation to prevent accidents and on-the-job deaths. The initial consensus standards were almost exclusively **safety standards**. With few health standards on the books when the agency emphasized enforcement, it meant safety enforcement. From 1972 to 1979 the proportion of the agency's budget devoted to the development of health standards ranged between three and seven percent (F.J. Thompson 1982: 209).

The early concentration on safety rather than health reflected the priorities of the individuals who supported the **Occupational Safety and Health Act** and OSHA's implementation of it. Other than such problems as black lung, organized labor showed little concern for health issues. Occupational health, however, is a far more important concern. Approximately 136,000 persons contract occupationally-related diseases every year (Wilson 1988: 2430). There are seven to ten times more deaths from occupational diseases than from industrial accidents.

EARLY HEALTH EFFORTS

Because OSHA's initial consensus standards contained few health-related rules and because the rulemaking process was fairly cumbersome, progress on health regulation was slow. In 1972 OSHA issued its first **health regulation**, on exposure to asbestos. The year 1974 saw two rules, one governing several carcinogens and one governing vinyl chloride (see Doniger 1978). A rule for coke was issued in 1976; and in 1978 six rules were issued covering arsenic, benzene, cotton dust, lead, acrylonitrile, and DBCP. From 1978 to 1984 no additional new health rules were issued even though NIOSH had identified 2,000 suspected carcinogens.

Rulemaking in the health area was gradual for two reasons other than the inherent slowness of the process. First, the scientific base needed to write rules was weak. OSHA rulemaking, similar to that of the EPA, is based on the theory that a **dose-response curve** exists that shows a relationship between exposure to a substance and subsequent development of a disease. Often the regulations established a **threshold** below which exposure to a substance is considered safe. Establishing threshold and dose-response curves are difficult. Scientists are not permitted to experiment on human beings (with some exceptions), and **ecological studies** (i.e, non-experimental field research) do not control for all the other causes of disease. As a result, information on **toxicity** is generalized from animal studies and such generalizations are limited by differences between animals and human beings in both response and toxicity.

More recent research demonstrates the complexity of the underlying science of **chemical exposure**. Scientists have often assumed a **linear relationship** between exposure and disease. That is, if exposure to 100 ppm produces cancer in 50 percent of the subjects, then exposure to 50 ppm will produce cancer in 25 percent of subjects, etc. Research, however, has revealed at least two nonlinear dose response curves. For vinyl chloride very small doses are toxic but stronger doses have no greater effect because the body has a limited capacity to absorb vinyl chloride. For formaldehyde, exposure has little impact until a threshold of about 10ppm,; after that threshold risks skyrocket (Gladwell 1990: 39). If different chemicals each have different types of dose-response curves, the scientific problems of estimating safe exposure levels increases exponentially.

The second reason that rulemaking in heath was gradual was that rulemaking hearings were turned into an **adversarial process** by the coalitions representing business and labor. Business organizations generally pushed for weak standards or no standards, stressing the costs of compliance. Unions, on the other hand, argued that exposure standards should be set as low as possible. Both sides documented their position with scientific and economic data. OSHA generally followed a policy of trying to please both groups; the rule usually established a fairly stringent standard but allowed business a period to time to phase in compliance. The end result frequently pleased neither group; often both business and labor challenged the rule in court for different reasons.

CHANGES IN PRIORITIES

In the late 70s, OSHA administrator Eula Bingham announced that OSHA would change its policies to focus on health issues (Harter 1977: 39). Bingham's new priorities were reflected in both inspections and rulemaking. She increased the number of inspections focusing on health from 8 percent in 1976 to 19 percent in 1979 (Pettus 1982: 601). The number of **citations** for serious, willful, and repeat health violations in the same time period quadrupled. In the rulemaking area, Bingham initiated or hurried several rulemaking procedures. As noted earlier, in 1978 six major health-related rules were issued, more than had been issued in OSHA's entire previous history.

The change in priorities, although welcomed by most observers of OSHA, was not without difficulties. Business and labor were no more in agreement on health standards than they were on safety standards. Both parties sought court intervention in the process; the success of one suit involving benzene (see later) called into question the entire decision-making process used by OSHA. Until this issue was resolved in 1981, new health rules were held up. The government handled many health issues on a **case-by-case basis**. This approach, however, was characterized by delay. The conflict over the cotton dust standard started, for example, in 1974 and lasted until 1981 when the Supreme Court ruled to support OSHA's standard (see American Textile Manufacturers v. Donavan 1981).

The **cotton dust issue** was not completely settled, however, with the Supreme Court decision. Industries still had four years from the time of the decision to comply. In addition, compliance with the standard can be determined only with inspection, an activity that was de-emphasized after 1981.

A COMPREHENSIVE HEALTH POLICY

Not only is the case-by-case approach to regulating health hazards slow; too many carcinogenic substances exist to regulate them effectively in this manner. If NIOSH's estimate of over 2,000 **workplace carcinogens** is correct, at the rate of 11 rules in the first decade of OSHA, total coverage would take centuries.

In 1980 to provide a more comprehensive approach, OSHA announced its **cancer policy**. The agency, based on scientific research, would classify suspected carcinogens into two groups. If conclusive evidence exists that a substance causes cancer, that substance would be placed in **category I**. Conclusive evidence consists of either one study linking the substance to cancer in human beings or one study revealing cancer in mammals if the mammalian study meets certain research design criteria. For any substance placed in category I, one of two actions will be taken. If a substitute for the substance exists, the use of the suspected substance will be **banned**. If no substitutes exist, exposure to the substance must be reduced to the lowest feasible level.

Category II includes all those substances for which tests show a suggestion of carcinogenicity. Substances in category II are subject to less strict standards to be determined on a case-by-case basis. In 1980, OSHA announced a list of 207 substances that would be evaluated for inclusion in category I or category II (AEI 1981: 30).

Before the cancer policy could be implemented, it was delayed by the benzene decision; and then the 1980 election changed presidents and, therefore, OSHA administrators. With an agency leadership more concerned about the burdens that regulation places on industry, a policy change in cancer policy was announced in 1981. The clause requiring that category I carcinogens be reduced to the lowest feasible level was deleted. Such a deletion implied that **cost factors** would be considered in setting individual standards for category I substances.

In 1988 OSHA announced a proposed rule that would set exposure standards for 428 **chemicals** (compared to the 24 chemicals subject to standards at that time). The OSHA proposal was consistent with a strategy advocated by Mendeloff (1979); he argued that workers would be better off if many chemicals were subject to modest regulation rather than a few chemicals with stringent regulations. The OSHA proposal received strong support from business and was criticized by labor groups as well as safety advocate Nicholas Ashford (Mattingly 1988). That the standards were moderate was beyond question. For 200 of the substances, NIOSH had already recommended exposure standards. In only 15 cases were the OSHA standards as stringent as the NIOSH recommendations. In the last days of the Reagan administration, OSHA promulgated standards for 370 of the chemicals under consideration.[4]

---

[4]The timing of the OSHA chemical exposure rule suggests that politics played a role. The proposed regulation was published during the campaign at a time when George Bush trailed in the polls. The effort might have been seen as a way to get weak standards established and force the next administration to go through a long involved process to strengthen individual standards.

In 1992, however, a federal appellate court struck down the **generic standard** for permissible exposure limits arguing that it was too vague (*AFL-CIO v. OSHA* 1992). The court ordered that the standards revert to those in use prior to the acceptance of the generic standards. Those chemicals that were not included in the original standards would go unregulated. The Clinton administration decided not to appeal this decision and to let Congress rewrite the standards in its reform of the OSH Act. Permissible exposure limits will be central in the reform debate.

During the 1990s, other health issues became salient besides chemical exposure limits such as exposure to hepatitis and the HIV virus in the workplace. During the Bush and Clinton administrations, OSHA promulgated standards regulating the handling of these blood borne pathogens.

In addition, OSHA has become concerned with impact of **indoor air quality** on workers' health. Currently, OSHA is creating standards that would regulate ventilation systems and smoking at work. The smoking standard should prove to be highly contentious and salient, and threatens to divide unions in their traditional support of OSHA standards.

THE POLITICS OF OCCUPATIONAL SAFETY AND HEALTH ADMINISTRATION

Because the actions of OSHA are salient, political actors frequently intervene in the regulatory process to influence decisions. As both labor and business have strong ties to the political parties, when either one loses a regulatory battle, appeals to political officials are almost **automatic**. The actions of OSHA have been the subject of influence efforts by interest groups, Congress, the president, and the courts.

Congress

Congress has served as a focal point for criticism of OSHA. When OSHA adopted rules or conducted inspections, it imposed costs on business. The heads of small and large businesses are often active in politics at the local level and are heavy **contributors** to election campaigns. As a general rule, such persons have access to members of Congress when they wish to complain about a regulatory agency.

Congress has been responsive to these complaints, both by providing a forum for criticism via hearings and by occasionally taking action. In 1977, Congress added a rider to the OSHA appropriations bill, **exempting** farms employing fewer than ten persons from OSHA regulations. The rider has been continued in subsequent years.

Numerous other proposals to limit OSHA's powers have also been considered. In the first six years of the agency, one hundred bills a year were introduced that would have restricted OSHA (Shaffer 1977: 192). Generally, the bills proposed exemptions for small business or a legislative veto for OSHA rules. Although none of these bills passed, they did suggest to OSHA that policies needed to be changed. In a 1979 effort to respond to these demands, OSHA exempted **small businesses with good safety records** from some recordkeeping requirements. OSHA estimated that 1.5 million businesses with 5 million employees were exempted by this policy.

After 1981 when OSHA became a less aggressive regulator, congressional attempts to restrict OSHA declined. In their place were hearings held by supporters of organized labor. Such hearings were used to encourage OSHA to be more aggressive in regulating workplace safety.

After twenty years of minor changes in OSHA law, Congress began to work on revising the Occupational safety and Health Act of 1970 in the 1990s. In 1992, the House Education and Labor Committee wrote an overhaul of the act, but was unable to win the support of Republicans in the full House. With the new Republican Congress, advocates remain hopeful that OSHA will be reformed.

Presidents

Presidents have been involved in OSHA policy only in a general sense. Every president since Gerald Ford has attempted to create a review system that would subject OSHA decisions to outside analysis. President Ford required **inflationary impact analysis**. President Carter required economic analysis of **costs** through his Regulatory Analysis Review Group and the Council on Wage and Price Stability. President Reagan and President Bush required **cost-benefit analysis** by the Office of Management and Budget. In addition, incumbent presidents found OSHA useful during elections campaigns; both Nixon in 1972 and Ford in 1976 denounced OSHA's "unjustified harassment of citizens" (Singer 1976: 973).

In terms of actual personal involvement in the OSHA process, however, the record is less clear. Kelman (1980: 254) could find no evidence of direct presidential involvement in OSHA decision making prior to 1978.[5] In 1978 the Council of Economic Advisors Chairman Charles Schultze attempted to persuade Jimmy Carter to intervene on the cotton dust regulation. After lobbying by organized labor and the Department of Labor political appointees, however, Carter supported the OSHA rule (Kelman 1980: 262).

The **Office of Management and Budget (OMB)** currently reviews OSHA rules. In 1984 OMB forced OSHA to modify its proposed ethylene oxide rule to eliminate a short-term exposure limit (Corrigan 1986: 1054).[6] One study found OMB was twice as likely to change or challenge an OSHA rule as a rule from other regulatory agencies (Victor 1989a: 2891).

The president's major impact on OSHA policies has been through the appointment process. Carter's appointment of Eula Bingham resulted in a reorientation of agency priorities from regulating safety to regulating health hazards. President Reagan's appointment of Thorne Auchter dramatically improved the relationship between OSHA and business. Kelman (1980: 262) recognized the president's ability to influence OSHA when he stated, "The most dramatic step a president could take to make OSHA responsive

---

[5]Intervention by other executive branch personnel, however, did occur. In 1977 the Department of Labor's Office of Policy, Evaluation, and Research blocked a noise exposure rule. The office argued that only rules with more benefits than costs could be approved.

[6]This rule is not an example of OSHA initiative. OSHA was required to issue the rule as the result of a federal court case.

to his political views would be to appoint a head of the agency (say, an economist) who is strongly committed to changing agency decisions on regulation." Neither President Bush nor President Clinton have made appointments that have drastically altered OSHA.

President Clinton will have an increased opportunity to affect OSHA, however, by participating in the reform efforts. Because the Clinton administration has come out in support of the Comprehensive Occupational Safety and Health Reform Act, it seems likely that Congress will alter the OSH Act sometime during the Clinton presidency.

The Courts

To a degree rivaled only in environmental protection, losers in administrative battles on occupational safety and health seek court intervention. Fourteen of the first eighteen major OSHA health regulations were challenged in court—often by both business and labor (Shapiro and McGarity 1989: 1269). Although all the major health regulations, except the benzene regulation were subsequently upheld by the courts, the actions of the court system have resulted in changed policies and procedures.

The Supreme Court served notice early that it would be involved. In 1974 an emergency rule regulating the exposure of agricultural workers to pesticides was disallowed because OSHA failed to demonstrate an emergency existed (*Wall Street Journal*, August 20, 1974: 1). In *Atlas Roofing Company v. OSHRC* (1977), the method of assessing fines by OSHA was challenged as a violation of the constitutional requirement of **trial by jury**. The Supreme Court held that this constitutional provision did not apply to administrative fines. In Marshall v. Barlow's the Supreme Court held that OSHA inspectors could not inspect a plant without a **warrant**. Although this decision initially appeared devastating (because the law prohibited notice of inspections), in practice its impact was minor. Warrants were required only if businesses refused to admit inspectors, and only 1.5 percent of employers did so after the ruling (Job Safety 1978: 13). In addition, warrants were easy to obtain because OSHA did not have to prove probable cause but only had to state that the inspection was part of its systematic inspection process.

More disrupting for the agency was the Supreme Court's decision on benzene (*Industrial Union Department v. American Petroleum Institute*). Medical studies showed that exposure to benzene in concentrations greater than 100 parts per million (ppm) was linked to leukemia. Although few valid data exist on lower levels of exposure, in 1978 OSHA reduced its benzene standard from 10 parts per million to 1 part per million. A federal Court of Appeals set aside the benzene regulation in 1978, holding that OSHA could not legally regulate benzene exposure without determining whether "the benefits expected from the standard bear a **reasonable relationship** to the costs imposed." The court's decision implied that OSHA regulations must yield benefits in excess of costs. The decision had a chilling effect on rulemaking activity. A moratorium was placed on new heath rules in 1978, reflecting the uncertainty about their validity.

When the Supreme Court reviewed the benzene case, it failed to clarify the issue. The Supreme Court accepted the Circuit Court's decision but rejected its reasoning. Four of the five majority judges held that the rule was invalid because OSHA did not demonstrate that a 1 ppm standard was more beneficial than a 10 ppm standard. Only one justice unambiguously supported cost-benefit analysis.[7] The issue of cost-benefit analysis was resolved one year later in *American Textile Manufacturers v. Donavan* (1981), when the Court held that cost-benefit analysis for health standards was *not* required by the Occupational Safety and Health Act. In combination, the benzene case and the cotton dust cases established that OSHA must justify its regulations in terms of benefits but need not use cost-benefit analysis; the decisions do not prevent OSHA from using cost-benefit analysis if it so desires.

More recently, the Supreme Court has stepped in to resolve controversy over **overlapping** state and federal regulatory programs. In 1992, the Court ruled that OSH Act preempted state licensing statutes concerning the handling of blood borne pathogens (*Gade v. National Solid Wastes Management Association*).

The OSHA situation clearly shows the advantage of **delay** in appealing to the courts. As the legal process unfolds, implementation of a regulation is delayed. Industry gains by delay alone because it gives the industry more time to conduct business without the additional costs imposed by the regulation. The cotton dust standard is a good example. Issued in 1978, it was delayed by the court suit until 1981; with a four-year phase-in period, the regulation did not become effective until 1985. Even without winning court cases, benefits can be gained.

Courts, however, send mixed signals to OSHA. As the result of suits by unions, OSHA is frequently ordered to issue rules immediately; the rules are often then delayed by a court review resulting from a business suit. As excellent example is the 1971 OSHA rule that required employers to provide drinking water, toilets and hand washing facilities to all workers; the rule exempted farm workers. In 1972 a Latino farm workers' organization petitioned OSHA to extend the rule to farm workers. OSHA did not; the organization sued, and in 1975 a federal court ordered OSHA to extend the rule. In 1977 the federal Court of Appeals reversed the case but asked OSHA for a **timetable** for issuing the rule. When OSHA failed to submit a timetable, the district court again ordered a rule to be issued. The Appeals Court in 1979 again reversed and required a time table. In 1982 OSHA agreed to submit a rule by 1985. In 1985 OSHA sought a two year delay to encourage states to act in this area. In 1987 the Court of Appeals required OSHA to issue a rule in 30 days; OSHA finally did. Sixteen years of court battles with different courts providing mixed signals eventually produced a farm workers toilet rule (see Shapiro and McGarity 1989: 55).

Although federal courts sometimes expand safety and health protection; they also sometimes restrict OSHA. In 1993, for example, a federal appeals court ruled that OSHA could not hold a structural engineer of a construction site responsible for safety violations (*Reich v. Simpson, Gumpertz and Heger, Inc*).

Many federal appellate court decisions over standards have repercussions for OSHA policy making. In 1991, for example, a federal appeals court objected to OSHA's failure to conduct an **industry-by-industry** assessment of the **lockout-tagout standard** (*International Union, UAW v. OSHA* 1991). The standard mandated procedures involving

---

[7]A revised benzene rule was not issued by OSHA until 1987.

the service and maintenance of machines and required that machinery be unplugged before it was cleaned or repaired. The court argued that the language in the OSH act requires a cost-benefit analysis of safety standards (the Supreme Court had already ruled that cost-benefit analysis was precluded for health standards). This case threatens OSHA's ability to make standards that cover many different industries (Locke 1991). In 1992 the courts further impeded OSHA's movement toward generic and broad standards. The court struck down OSHA's generic standard for permissible exposure limits because OSHA failed to show that the new standards lessened health risks or that they were economically or technologically feasible (*AFL-CIO v. OSHA* 1992).

Political Leadership

OSHA leadership has played a key role in the politics affecting the agency. The first OSHA administrator, George Guenther, recognized the political value of OSHA during the 1972 campaign. Guenther drafted a memo to the undersecretary of labor, stating that OSHA would issue no controversial rules during the campaign and suggesting that OSHA was a good sales point for fund raising (*National Journal* December 7, 1974: 1837). Guenther's lack of management caution in promulgating the early consensus standards was one reason why OSHA became a point for potential **fundraising**.

Guenther was not the only politically involved person to head OSHA. Morton Corn, the first OSHA head with professional qualifications, eventually resigned over the lack of political support for the agency. Both Eula Bingham and Thorne Auchter, although they disagreed as to who OSHA's constituency is, were more receptive to what they saw as the political constituency of OSHA. By using this political support, both Bingham and Auchter were able to redirect OSHA policies. More recent OSHA heads have had less impact on the organization. Robert Rowland served only one year and had little impact on the agency. John Pendergast (1986-89) and Gerald Scannell (1989-92) were health and safety professionals with good reputations but did not have the impact that either Bingham or Auchter did. It is too early to accurately assess the impact of President Clinton's appointee, John Dear. Because the political leadership of OSHA during the Reagan presidency had the most impact on OSHA, Reagan's initiatives will be briefly discussed.

THE REAGAN INITIATIVES

One of Ronald Reagan's issues in his quest for the presidency was the **overregulation** of American business. His transition teams were highly critical of the Carter administration's regulatory fervor and had several suggestions about limiting regulation. In general, Reagan appointed regulatory critics to head the regulatory agencies. OSHA was no exception; Thorne Auchter was named assistant secretary of labor for occupational safety and health.

In 1980 Auchter coordinated Florida political events for Reagan. His experience with OSHA was as an executive with his family-owned construction firm; one of his areas of responsibility was safety and health. Auchter's firm had been cited by OSHA 48 times for safety violations and fined $1,200. In the early 1970s he had also served on the committee that wrote a Florida state OSHA implementation plan.

Auchter's tenure affected both agency rulemaking and enforcement. First in **rulemaking**, OSHA did not engage in any major innovations. Some rules were issued; a few rules were strengthened; some were weakened; but the agency did not develop a reputation for aggressive rulemaking. Second, **enforcement** activities of OSHA were dramatically altered; Auchter wanted to eliminate OSHA's police officer image. Each of these efforts merits further discussion.

Rulemaking

As noted before, the rulemaking process is fairly complex. Reducing the amount of regulation via withdrawing rules is a slow process that, given the inevitable court challenges, would provide few immediate benefits. Auchter's rulemaking policy, therefore, was not a wholesale elimination but rather an unhurried look at minor rules.

Initially, the Auchter OSHA appeared to favor weaker standards than the Bingham agency. In 1981, OSHA changed its cancer policy; **category I** carcinogens (those that were confirmed causes of cancer) would not automatically have to be reduced to the lowest feasible level (Kosters 1982). Levels would be established on a **case-by-case basis**. Nothing happened on this policy until 1988 when OSHA proposed its comprehensive chemical exposure rule (see above). Also in 1982, OSHA withdrew the **walk-around rule** that required firms to pay for the time of union representatives who accompanied OSHA inspectors during walk-around inspections. In July 1982 the agency restricted **workers' access** to medical and safety records. In March 1983, OSHA issued its rule on worker exposure to noise, a rule held over from the Carter administration. Essentially, the noise rule reduced the amount of testing and the number of warning signs required in order to lower the costs imposed on business.

Although these actions were praised by business and condemned by labor, the record of the Auchter OSHA was not so clear-cut. In 1981 the lead exposure level was reduced by 75 percent (Kosters 1982). Auchter also took an active role in pressing OMB to release an OSHA regulation on the labeling of hazardous substances (Wines 1983i: 2012). In 1983 a newly revised asbestos rule surprised many people when it established a stricter exposure standard (Wines 1983i: 2008). In April of 1983 OSHA announced it would reissue the benzene rule with a lower exposure limit than the one currently on the books.

Auchter's mixed record on rulemaking was attributed to two factors. First, Auchter was conceded to be a good manager and a fairly good political infighter. One White House official attributed Auchter's occasional willingness to press for stronger rules to his management background; "[H]e was a construction executive in a family-owned firm. In that sort of situation, when you're the boss, you're the boss" (cited in Wines 1983i: 2012). Second, others attributed Auchter's actions to congressional criticism and the example of Anne Burford. The asbestos rule was issued shortly after a critical congressional hearing. Congressman David Obey has been especially critical of OSHA; he condemned the agency for failing to issue emergency regulations on EDB and ethylene oxide even though both substances met the criteria for emergency regulations and the courts had ordered OSHA to issue an ethylene oxide regulation (Wines 1983i: 2011).

Enforcement

Thorne Auchter's greatest impact was in enforcement, particularly in three areas.

First, OSHA changed its **priority system** policies for determining which firms to inspect. OSHA exempted all industries with a **lost workday rate** due to injuries below the national average. Individual firms in high-risk industries were also exempted if they had a low lost workday rate. This policy exempted some three-fourths of the businesses in the United States from OSHA inspection (Wines 1983i: 2009; Viscusi 1982: 34). The remaining fourth accounts for nearly 75 percent of all worker injuries.

The priority system was widely criticized. By using average workdays lost for an entire industry, an unsafe firm within a safe industry would avoid inspection. In addition, injury data collected by industry is highly suspect; many injuries are not reported, or injured workers are required to report to work even though no work is assigned (L. White 1983). A GAO (1988: 3) report reviewed three studies and found **underreporting** of injuries in 75%, 23% and 50% of the firms studied. Injury data calculations are also based on total employment, so that firms with large white-collar employment often can have unsafe manufacturing plants and still report low injury rates. Perhaps most important, using injuries as the criterion for inspections downplays those industries with health problems because injury rates reflect safety problems only. Economist W. Kip Viscusi (1983: 23) argued that the injury rate criterion was misguided; a frequent critic of OSHA, Viscusi argued that inspections should be targeted on the basis of the risks involved and the degree of hazard. Injury rates do not reflect either of these phenomena.

Second, the emphasis was changed to rely on **voluntary industry cooperation** (Wines 1983i: 2009). An increase in consulting visits reflected this policy. **Consulting visits** are designed to advise firms on how to comply with the law; citations are not issued during such a visit. The number of consulting visits increased from 22,000 in 1980 to 28,000 in 1982. OSHA regional directors were instructed to make inspections less confrontational and were told that they would be evaluated negatively if the number of contested violations was large. Contested violations dropped from 22 percent in Bingham's last year to 5 percent in 1982. Clearly, inspections were less confrontational than in previous years (according to critics, this indicated less vigorous regulation).

Third, the level of **enforcement** was reduced. In two years the number of OSHA inspectors dropped 26 percent from 1,328 to 981 (Wines 1983i). In 1982 (compared to 1980, the last year of the Carter administration), the number of citations for violations dropped 22 percent, citations for serious violations dropped 47 percent, citations for willful violations dropped 90 percent, and citations for repeat offenses dropped 64 percent. Total fines levied dropped 69 percent to $5.8 million (Wines 1983i: 2013). In health areas, the record was even less active. Regarding testing for compliance with the asbestos standard, the number of tests dropped from 8,606 to 2,636. Citations in the area dropped by 60 percent and fines by 76 percent.

Similar to some other regulatory areas, then, occupational safety and health saw significant efforts to deregulate. The deregulation, however, did not eliminate regulations; to the extent that OSHA regulations have been pruned, that process occurred under Bingham. Deregulation for the Auchter OSHA was a deregulation of enforcement, a reduction in the amount of enforcement activity, and a reliance on voluntary compliance.

Although OSHA's enforcement policy was widely criticized, Auchter argued that the policy had a major impact on worker safety. As evidence, he cited a decline in workdays lost due to injury; the figure dropped from 5.9 days per 100 workers in 1979 to 4.7 in 1983 (Glen and Shearer 1984: 9). These raw figures, however, also reflect the decline in injuries normally associated with economic recession (see Viscusi 1983). The data presented in Table 8.1 on work days lost confirm the lack of impact of the Auchter strategy. Lost workdays increased as the economy improved.

Table 8.1   Workdays Lost Due to Injury or Illness per 100 Workers

Year	Rate
1981	8.3
1982	7.7
1983	7.6
1984	8.0
1985	7.9
1986	7.9
1987	8.3
1988	8.6
1989	8.2
1990	8.3

Source: National Safety Council, *Accident Facts*.

OSHA After Auchter

While periodically articles are printed contending that OSHA is making a comeback (see Corrigan 1986; Victor 1989a; Smith 1991), workplace safety was not a priority of the Reagan and Bush administration. Neither administration was quick to fill OSHA **vacancies** when they occurred. The strategy was to nominate individuals with health and safety credentials from business organizations (Pendergast from 3M and Scannell from Johnson and Johnson). These individuals had good public relations skills and in comparison to Thorne Auchter appeared to be OSHA advocates. In 1990 Secretary of Labor Elizabeth Dole was able to get a modest increase in the OSHA enforcement budget (Victor 1989a: 2890).

Like Reagan and Bush, OSHA does not seem to be a **top priority** of President Clinton. Clinton did not appoint a leader of OSHA until well into his presidency. Clinton's appointee, John Dear, did not assume the leadership of OSHA until April of

1993, one and a half years after Clinton assumed office. Unlike Bush and Reagan, however, Clinton has closer ties to organized labor and is expected to support labor's position on OSHA. Despite this, Clinton passed over union candidates to head OSHA in favor of John Dear, former head of Washington State's Labor and Industries Department. Neither labor nor industry opposed Dear's confirmation (Hanson 1993: 52). Although it may be too early to tell, Dear seems moderate in his approach and is known for his ability to compromise between labor and industry positions (Hartley 1994: 4).

One reason for the perception of a revitalized OSHA has been the OSHA policy of stressing **high fines**. Fines were almost nonexistent in the Auchter years; in 1985 only $23,000 in fines were proposed by OSHA. Bolstered by OSHA's interpretation that a violation could be counted for each worker exposed to a hazardous condition, OSHA levied some major, highly publicized fines after serious industrial accidents. Union Carbide was fined $1.4 million in 1985, Chrysler paid a $294,000 fine in 1987; Phillips Petroleum was fined $5.6 million in 1990 after a refinery explosion; and USX Corporation was fined $7.3 million in 1989. While such penalties are newsworthy, these are proposed fines. OSHA has collected only about one-third of these large fines (Victor 1989a: 2891) and even at full amount, they are a trivial portion of the corporation's assets.

EVALUATING OSHA POLICY

OSHA's activities have frequently been denounced as both costly and ineffective by critics. Given organized labor's support for the agency, this view is hardly unanimous. In the two decades since the creation of OSHA, several scholars have examined the effectiveness of OSHA regulations. These studies can be divided into studies of enforcement and studies of impact.

Enforcement

Even before the Reagan administration, the enforcement of OSHA standards was considered weak. The criticism of the enforcement efforts included these: (1) Few firms are ever inspected, (2) firms that are inspected are cited for minor violations only, (3) inspectors do not find major health problems, and (4) the size of the fines is trivial. Although OSHA has improved in the areas of violations, fines and health problems, OSHA still faces criticism that it is ineffective.

FEW INSPECTIONS

With at most 1,050 federal inspectors (OSHA's peak) supplemented by a similar number of state inspectors, many firms will avoid inspection. According to Robert Stewart Smith (1976: 62), "Only 1.3 percent of all covered plants were inspected in fiscal year 1973, implying the typical establishment will see an OSHA inspector once every seventy-seven years, about as often as we see Halley's Comet." Similarly, an AFL-CIO report estimated that a company can be expected to be inspected once every eighty-four years (Geisel 1992: 2). OSHA recognized that the agency would not be given sufficient resources to inspect all workplaces, so it established a system of inspection priorities from the beginning. In the 1970s, OSHA targeted the longshoring, roofing and sheet metal, meat packing, lumbering, and miscellaneous transportation equipment industries for closer inspection because the accident rates in these industries were high (Smith 1976: 67). Within these industries, larger firms were inspected before smaller firms (Pettus 1982: 599). In the 1980s and 1990s, OSHA has focused on the **construction industry**. Fifty three percent of all federal inspections occur in that industry. In addition, OSHA currently targets inspections towards the **petrochemical industry** and industries with **high ergonomics hazards** such as meat packing (United States Department of Labor 1993: 80). Despite the targeting, resources are inadequate. In fiscal year 1993, only 3.9 percent of all inspections are follow up inspections (phone interview with the Occupational Safety and Health Administration).

TRIVIAL VIOLATIONS

Early criticism of OSHA focused on the prevalence of trivial violations. In the early days of OSHA, inspectors were given little discretion and were required to cite every violation. From 1973 to 1976, for example, the number of serious, willful, or repeat violations never exceeded 3 percent of total citations in any one year. The focus on minor matters gave rise to the view that OSHA was citing industries for "Mickey Mouse" violations such as broken toilet seats. By the 1990s, however, OSHA had improved this situation. In 1991, 67.1 percent of all violations were serious (United States Department of Labor 1993: 81).

SAFETY EMPHASIS

Inspectors were initially drawn from the ranks of safety engineers and, as a result, were better trained to detect safety violations than health violations. Smith (1976: 33) estimated that the agency spent four to five times more on safety regulation than on health regulation; in 1974 the agency inspected 100 percent of the targeted industries for safety violations but only 5 percent for health violations.

Again, this emphasis changed in 1977 with the arrival of Eula Bingham. The proportion of inspections devoted to health increased from 8 percent in 1976 to 15 percent in 1977 and 19 percent in 1979 (Viscusi 1983: 18). This change in emphasis, however, did not continue. In 1992 health inspections were still only 21 percent of all inspections (Department of Labor 1993: 20). Although some progress has been made, safety inspections still dwarf health inspections.

MINOR PENALTIES

Although OSHA's record on penalties has been terrible, legislation raising the allowed penalty amount and OSHA's policy of imposing egregious penalties has improved OSHA's ability to penalize violators. In the agency's first three years the average fine for a serious violation was only $600 (Harter 1977: 37). By 1991, however, the **average initial penalty per serious and repeat violation** rose to $4,458 (United States Department of Labor 1993: 84). In addition, under the new egregious penalty policy, OSHA can fine companies unprecedented amounts. In 1991 OSHA fined companies cited with egregious penalties an average of $1,905,753 per inspection (United States Department of Labor 1993: 11).

One company shut down its doors in protest to an egregious penalty. OSHA fined the Dayton Tire Company $7.4 million for violating the lockout/tagout standard which resulted in the death of one worker and injuries to several others. In response to the fine, the Dayton company shut its doors until it obtained a restraining order from a federal district court blocking the fine. The case is still pending in court.

Although some companies receive large fines under the egregious penalty policy, most companies are fined for one violation. Only fourteen violations were egregious in 1992 (United States Department of Labor 1993: 11). The majority of fines are, therefore, fairly minor. Such fines can hardly be an incentive to business to correct problems and can be trivial to a large corporation. The trivial nature of these fines to a large corporation, however, is not totally OSHA's fault. The size of fines per violation is limited by law, and OSHRC often reduces the fines.

In combination, all these factors indicate that OSHA enforcement can be characterized as weak. The combination of low risks of inspections and low fines are not adverse enough to encourage businesses to change behavior.

Not all companies have, however, the same chance of getting **investigated**. A relationship exists between enforcement of the OSH Act and unionized companies. Weil (1992) finds that OSHA investigates and cites **unionized companies** more than non unionized companies in the construction industry. Inspections are longer and penalties are higher in union companies than in their non union counterparts (see also Fairris 1992; Scherer et al. 1993a).

Impact

Given the weak enforcement level of the Occupational Safety and Health Act, the impact of OSHA on occupational safety and health cannot be great. Although several scholars have attempted to estimate OSHA's impact, any efforts to evaluate the program comprehensively are limited by three **data problems**. First, good data on the impact of health regulations do not exist because occupational diseases have long **latency periods**. It may be decades before the impact of health regulations is reflected in occupational death rates; in addition, death rates are a poor indicator of occupational health impact because several other factors also affect the rates. Nichols and Zeckhauser (1981: 216) note that the impact of health regulations may never be resolved. Second, **plant-by-plant data** are not available (Viscusi 1983: 85); as a result, industry-wide data that lump safe plants together with dangerous plants must be used. Third, in 1971 the Bureau of Labor Statistics changed the definitions of workplace injuries and accidents; data before 1970, therefore, are **not comparable** to data after 1971. Unfortunately, the change in definition occurred at the same time as the creation of OSHA, thus confounding any evaluation with measurement error.

Two widely cited early studies of OSHA showed little impact of occupational safety regulation. Mendeloff (1979) compared pre- and post-OSHA injury rates and found no difference between them. Viscusi (1982) found no relationship between the number of inspections, the size of penalties levied, and the injury rate for 61 industries. Both of these studies have serious data flaws. Mendeloff is essentially comparing data under two different definitions, and Viscusi has eliminated any firm-specific as opposed to industry-specific impacts of OSHA and does not recognize that firms might be inspected because they have high injury rates. In a simpler study, Nichols and Zeckhauser (1981) examined post-OSHA data only; they found that from 1972 to 1978 injuries declined by 13.8 percent but that workdays lost rose by 24.2 percent. Because both injuries and workdays are affected by numerous other variables, such as the state of the economy and the experience of the workers, simple comparisons such as these have little value.

A few other studies have attempted to disaggregate accident data, and these studies showed positive, but modest impacts. By examining the types of accidents most likely to be affected by OSHA regulations such as accidents involving people caught in machinery, Mendeloff (1979: 117) found a 30 percent reduction. This translates into an overall reduction of from 2 to 3 percent in all accidents. Smith (1979) found a 16 percent reduction in injury rates in plants than had been inspected in 1973 and a 5 percent reduction for those inspected in 1974. The impact was greater in smaller plants. Even though these studies found small, but positive results, they have many of the same data problems that plague the other studies.

More recent studies have found modest but statistically significant impacts for OSHA. Viscusi (1986) found that a 10 percent increase in OSHA enforcement was associated with a 2 percent decline in workplace injuries; in a similar study Scholz and Gray (1990) found a similar increase in enforcement was associated with a 1.5 percent decline in injuries. Gray and Jones (1991) examining twelve years of data suggested that an OSHA inspection reduced the level of citations by about fifty percent in the next inspection. Furthermore, using panel data from 1979 to 1986, Scholz and Grey (1990) find that inspections imposing penalties induce a 22% decline in injuries in the inspected plant during the following few years. **Panel data** allows researchers to examine changes in injury rates in particular companies over time. This alleviates the difficulties inherent in comparing unlike companies. The sample that was used in this study, however, is biased toward large companies and their findings may not be accurate for smaller inspected companies. In addition, their findings do not reveal any impact of OSHA on companies that are not inspected. Other recent studies have examined the impact of changes in OSHA's policies. Ruser and Smith (1990) could find no impact of OSHA's greater emphasis on accurate plant accident records.

At a theoretical level with **perfect enforcement**, the amount of reduction in accidents and injuries that occupational safety and health regulation could reduce is open to question. The National Safety Council (cited in Nichols and Zeckhauser 1981: 115) found that 19 percent of industrial accidents were the result of human causes, 18 percent were the result of environmental causes (such as unsafe working conditions), and 63 percent were the result of both human and environmental causes. They estimated that perhaps only 25 percent of all industrial accidents were preventable. Bailey (1980: 7), in fact, argues that little more can be done to eliminate on-the-job accidents.

Both the potential impact of OSHA and the actual impact of OSHA are still empirical questions. The data problems in the area are so severe that we may never know if regulation improves safety. In occupational health, both the nature of occupational diseases and limitations of data have prevented any studies to date. To conclude that OSHA has been ineffective or effective would be premature.

CURRENT POLITICAL ISSUES

Similar to many other areas of regulation, new issues in occupational safety and health develop faster than old issues are resolved. Seven current issues in addition to those discussed earlier are shaping the debate over occupational safety and health regulation. These issues are the effectiveness of state-run programs, the impact on small businesses, the use of higher wages to compensate workers for risky jobs, the workers' right to know about chemical hazards, repetitive motion injuries, the overall benefits and costs of OSHA, and the pending legislation to reform the OSH act. Each will be discussed in turn.

State-Run Programs Have Incentives to Limit Occupational Safety and Health Regulation

Under the Occupational Safety and Health Act, states may opt to administer the law if the state program is **"at least as effective"** as the federal program. States wanting to operate their own programs must have plans for doing so approved by OSHA; OSHA then provides **funding** equivalent to 50 percent of the operating costs of the state program. Although the exact number of states operating mini-OSHAs varies somewhat, approximately half the states chose to operate their own programs.

A potential problem with state-operated programs is that states have incentives to engage in **limited regulation** of occupational safety and health. Such regulations impose costs on business and in extreme cases might eliminate the marginal revenues necessary to operate the firm. Because states want to attract and keep industry, Rowland and Marz (1982) argue that a process they call **Gresham's law of regulation** will occur. States with lax regulation will attract industry from states with stringent regulation; as a result, states will compete to have lax regulation and attract business. Because the federal government has an incentive to regulate one state differently from the others, the Gresham's law analogy implies that federal regulation will be more stringent than state regulation.

In an analysis comparing 22 state OSHA programs with the federal program operated in 28 states, Marvel (1982: 21) found that the federal program held more inspections, found more violations, issued more citations, and levied greater penalties. The differences were major; in 1978 the penalties were 10 times larger in federally regulated states. These statistically significant findings held even when the industrialization of the state was controlled. The Marvel study was done at a time when the federal OSHA was an aggressive agency; its generalizability to a period with a quiescent federal OSHA is open to question.

Thompson and Scicchitano (1987: 103), in a study covering both the Carter and the Reagan years, found that the federal OSHA focused more on health inspections than the state-run programs. State programs, however, conducted more total inspections. During fiscal 1990 state-run OSHA programs conducted 93,162 total inspections while OSHA conducted only 54,557 (Victor 1990c: 441). Focusing on just inspections, however, presents a misleading picture since state-run programs levy far fewer fines than does OSHA (Waldman 1989: 44).

Scholz and Wei (1986: 1263) in a systematic assessment of state and federal OSHA programs, found that state-run programs were more responsive to political forces and the safety environment. In some states that means an aggressive program; in others, a token program. Illinois, for example, brought criminal charges against corporation executives after a chemical worker died in that state (*National Journal* 1989: 373). California's program had the reputation of being much more stringent than the federal OSHA and was even able to survive an effort by the governor in 1987 to turn enforcement responsibility back to the federal government (Victor 1990c: 443). Weak programs also exist such as the one in North Carolina during the early 1990s (see below).

The pattern of state-run programs during the Reagan administration demonstrated how the federal system can act as a check on national government efforts. When the federal government reduced its enforcement and issued fewer serious violations in 1982 and after, state-run programs continued enforcement at the same level (Scholz and Wei, 1986: 1263). As the emphasis on health issues declined in the early 1980s at the federal level, state-run programs began to increase their effort in this area (Thompson and Scicchitano 1987: 103). This pattern continued even though federal budget cuts meant that OSHA did not fully fund the 50% obligation for state-run programs (Victor 1990c: 441).

As another indicator that state regulation is more accommodating to industry than federal regulation, Marvel (1982: 26) found that more federal citations are contested than are state citations. In addition, in states where a larger proportion of the state population is employed in **manufacturing** (i.e., the businesses regulated by OSHA), states generally conduct fewer inspections. The federal government, on the other hand, conducts more inspections in states where manufacturing is a larger part of the economy.

Such behavior on the part of states has some impact. Marvel (1983) showed that states operating their own programs were able to attract **new investment**. These states had faster industrial growth rates than those states with federal programs; they also had slightly higher industrial accident rates. Such differences could increase; under Thorne Auchter, OSHA removed federal inspectors completely from the 21 states that operated their own occupational safety and health programs, thus eliminating any federal oversight of state administration (Wines 1983i: 2009).

A 1991 fire in a North Carolina chicken processing plant that killed 25 workers and injured 50 others intensified the debate surrounding oversight of state occupational safety and health programs and concerns over the adequacy of such programs. North Carolina's program was considered so weak that OSHA began proceedings to revoke the state's authority to run the program (Victor 1992: 1123). Despite OSHA's responsibility for overseeing state programs, this was the first time a revocation had been considered. Legislative action in the North Carolina state legislature to toughen its state program appeased OSHA before it took action.

In response to the fire, Congress also requested a General Accounting Office (GAO) investigation into federal oversight of state programs. GAO's primary concern with OSHA's oversight was the standards it used to evaluate state programs. According to the GAO, OSHA has little information or standards with which to judge whether a program has achieved desired outcomes or results (GAO 1994). The GAO faulted OSHA for measuring **state program compliance** relative to OSHA's own performance. To determine compliance, OSHA assesses whether states conduct similar activities as those conducted by OSHA. The GAO argues that this asks states to meet a "moving performance target." The GAO recommended that OSHA emphasize measures of program outcome and evaluations of the effectiveness of specific programs features instead of assessing state programs on their similarity to federal activities. OSHA has taken steps to comply with the recommendations of the GAO. While moving toward some absolute criteria of assessing state programs. OSHA believes, however, that some activity measurement is necessary and proper for oversight purposes and that the OSH act requires such measurement (GAO 1994: 68).

Impact on Small Business

Small business has been especially critical of OSHA; legislation to grant small firms relief has been introduced in nearly every congressional session since 1970. Small business claims that OSHA regulations are especially burdensome to plants with limited capital. One reason for this apparent bias, however, may well be the safety record of larger business. Larger firms are generally unionized and as a result have been pressed by their unions to improve on-the-job safety. Larger firms also see a direct correlation between injury rates and workers compensation insurance costs. Consequently, large firms are safer places to work than are small firms (Butler 1983: 73; Marsh 1994: 1). In addition, the fixed costs of safety or health investment can be spread over more output in a large business than in a small one. OSHA regulations, therefore, may appear more burdensome to small business because large businesses have already made some safety investments and because the relative investment is larger for a small firm (see Bartel and Thomas 1985; Viscusi 1985).

Although systematic data on impact is limited, a study by Pettus (1982: 601) showed that OSHA imposed larger costs on large businesses than on small ones. Establishments with ten or fewer employees had 37 percent of the inspections in 1976 but only 29 percent in 1979. In 1979 less than 0.8 percent of small businesses were inspected by OSHA. Of the far more costly health inspections, more than seven times as many large businesses were inspected as small businesses (reflecting the agency's priority system that inspects larger firms first). In no year did more than 1,330 of the nation's 2.2 million small businesses receive a health inspection visit from OSHA. More recently, Scherer et al. (1993b) find that OSHA reaches settlements and reduces penalties by a larger amount for large manufactory firms than it does for small manufactory firms. OSHA inspects, however, more large businesses than small ones. Although an inspected small business may feel persecuted by OSHA, overall small business has had little contact with OSHA.

Risk-Based Wages

Some economists argue that government safety regulation duplicates a process that is handled by the **free market**. Recognizing that some hazardous occupations such as stunt performers are paid fairly well for taking risks, these economists propose that hazardous jobs in general have to pay more to attract workers. The solution to workplace hazards, therefore, is to **provide information** concerning the hazards associated with various occupations and let individual workers make the tradeoff between higher wages and safety. In theory, employers will make safety improvements if the marginal costs of safety measures are less than the marginal costs of risk-based wages.

The topic of **risk-based wages** has received some empirical analysis. Bailey (1980: 36) noted that workers in hazardous jobs were paid less than workers in safe jobs, but that this was a function of the low-skill levels of workers in hazardous jobs. To control for such variables as skills, age, education, and union membership, elaborate multiple regression models are used to estimate the additional wages paid for high-risk occupations. Using such techniques, Smith (1976: 30) found that wages were 1.5 percent higher in occupations where the risk of on-the-job death was doubled. Leigh (1981: 776) in two separate estimates, found wage premiums of 2.2 percent and 0.8 percent for a doubling of risk (see also Leigh 1984). Leigh found no impact for occupational disease. Occupational disease impacts are difficult to find because mortality rates for various occupations are affected by numerous variables other than exposure to health hazards; one of the occupations with a high mortality rate, for example, is short-order cooks, not one of the more hazardous occupations. Leigh and Gill (1991) have correctly noted that all these studies estimated risk based wages for male workers. Their study of risk and female workers found that females in unionized plants received wages 9.2 percent higher (for the increase in one additional death per 100,000) but that females in nonunionized plants received wages 2.7 percent lower. Unions, Leigh and Gill suggest, play an important role in informing workers about the job-related risks.

Other studies have attempted to measure risk premiums in other ways; Viscusi (1983: 44) compared wages of persons who perceived that their job was dangerous with those who did not and found that the former were paid $925 more per year. Although this amount is small at the individual level (45 cents per hour), when aggregated, it totals $2 million per industrial death or about $69 billion nation wide.

These findings on risk-based premiums are statistically significant but substantively trivial. If we take the Smith estimate, a worker earning $15,000 per year in an occupation with a mean death rate of 24 per 100,000 workers would earn $225 more a year than a person working in an occupation with 12 deaths per 100,000 (about the national average). This **risk-based premium** translates to approximately 11 cents an hour, hardly an incentive to increase risk to life. Smith (1976: 31) argues that differentials need not be large because the incentive operates for the marginal worker only. This assumes that a worker can rationally assess risk probabilities of 0.00012 versus 0.00024, however; and studies show that most individuals have difficulty making decisions based on low probability events (see Nichols and Zeckhauser 1981: 207). As Viscusi (1983: 107) notes, "a typical worker in a hazardous occupation does not receive enough additional remuneration to be obvious to the casual observer."

These studies show that a worker in a hazardous occupation would be far better off **unionizing** the plant than seeking direct compensation for on-the-job hazards. Viscusi (1983: 55) found that the presence of a union in a plant doubled the rise in salary associated with risk (see Leigh and Gill 1991 on unions and women). In fact, unions per se have a far greater impact on wages than any risk premium; Leigh (1981: 776) found that unions had from 10 times to 300 times greater impact on wages than did job hazard premiums.

One reason for skepticism concerning the use of risk-based wages to compensate for safety dangers (other than the trivial amount of the increase) is that these studies have **methodological problems** so severe that the findings may not be valid. In general, these studies use survey data that cut across a variety of industries. Because industry-specific factors are difficult to control, a more valid study would focus on a single industry to determine if unsafe plants pay higher wages than safe plants. In addition, the entire concept of controlling for age, education, unionization, and other factors may be inappropriate. These studies tell the worker in a hazardous job that he or she is paid more than other persons with similar skills in similar plants; they do not tell the workers that he or she is actually paid less than workers in safer plants (such plants tend to be unionized, have more experience workers, have better educated workers, and so on). In an artificial statistical sense, therefore, a worker in an unsafe plant is paid better, but in terms of money in the pay envelope that worker is paid less.

Finally, whether or not labor would respond to such small incentives to undertake risky jobs is open to question. In a theoretical world, incentives would create a response because moves between jobs are assumed to be costless. In the **real world**, changing jobs is never cost free; a move might reduce seniority and its wage incentives; and if relocation is required, additional costs must be incurred. In addition, in a small town with a textile mill, the choice might not be between working in a safe plant and an unsafe plant but between working in an unsafe plant and not working at all.

The Workers' Right to Know About Chemical Hazards

The National Institute of Occupational Safety and Health (NIOSH) estimates that one million workers are exposed to hazardous substances throughout their workday, and 20 million workers are exposed at sometime during the workday (Matlack 1987: 832). In 1975 OSHA began a rulemaking process to require that all hazardous substances they handle and related safety precautions. Some 40 states and local governments placed pressure on OSHA to issue the rule by passing their own laws requiring notification. In 1986 OSHA finally issued its **hazard communication rule**, but applied the rule only to manufacturing plants. Since a wide variety of service industries also handle hazardous substances, the rule was perceived as incomplete (Matlack 1987: 833). In 1987 OSHA extended the rule to all plants when it was ordered to do so by the federal Court of Appeals. Having a rule and having a successful rule are two different things, however. The General Accounting Office (1991a: 4) issued a highly critical assessment of OSHA's hazardous communication standard; GAO found that 52 percent of all employers were not in compliance with the regulation four years after the regulation was issued.

Repetitive Motion Injuries

With organized labor as the major agitator for greater OSHA enforcement, OSHA was late in responding to hazards in white collar employment. Some 26 states and localities considered legislation on **video display terminals** and Suffolk, New York has adopted legislation (Matlack 1988: 3070, 3072). Video display terminals raised among other issues the injuries caused by repetitive motion. According to the 1992 Bureau of Labor Statistics Annual survey of Occupational Injuries and Illnesses, the number of repetitive trauma disorders increased from 37,000 in 1985 to 184,000 in 1990. When OSHA became involved in this area, its focus was in manufacturing not office employment. In 1988 OSHA levied a $4.3 million fine against meatpacker John Morrell & Co. for willfully mishandling repetitive motion injuries. A citation against U.S. West was dropped when it agreed to change equipment and introduce training to prevent future injuries. OSHA also negotiated the establishment of programs to combat repetitive motion injuries with Chrysler Corporation and at Sara Lee meat processing plants (Victor 1989a: 2890). OSHA gives citations for mishandling repetitive motion injuries under its general duty clause. This clause maintains that employers have a general duty to provide a place of employment free from recognized hazards, *regardless* of whether the hazards are regulated by specific standards. Debate exists as to whether the OSH Act supports OSHA's use of the clause to prosecute alleged ergonomics violations (Kolesar 1992). Because of the high incident rate of repetitive motion injuries, OSHA has made ergonomics a high priority. OSHA is in the process of creating standards to prevent cumulative trauma disorders. These standards are due for release. OSHA has encountered difficulty, however, in establishing the exact scientific relationship between certain activities and various **cumulative trauma disorders** (Reynolds 1993).

Costs and Benefits of OSHA

Whether or not OSHA generates greater benefits than costs has been an issue just as it has in environmental regulation and consumer protection. Although OSHA itself did little cost-benefit analysis, its regulations have not been free from such efforts. OSHA is located in the Department of Labor. Because it is not an independent agency, its actions are subject to review at the presidential level and are governed by the numerous executive orders issued concerning regulation. Currently, OSHA regulations must be cleared through the Office of Management and Budget, an organization that performs some limited cost-benefit analysis.

Cost-benefit analysis in regard to OSHA has been controversial and difficult to do because most of the benefits of OSHA policies are incommensurable. That is, the benefits of OSHA, injuries prevented and lives saved, are benefits that cannot be purchased in the market; none of the attempts to place a **value on human life** or human health have been satisfactory (see M.S. Thompson 1980). To circumvent this problem, Thorne Auchter advocated **cost-effectiveness analysis** whereby different standards are contrasted in terms of the dollar cost required to save an individual life.

Even the cost side of OSHA is subject to dispute. The best cost data belong to industry, but industry has an incentive to overestimate OSHA compliance costs. For example when OSHA reduced the exposure standard for vinyl chloride in 1974 from 500 ppm to 1 ppm, industry estimated that the standard would shut down the polyvinyl chloride industry and severely damage the plastics industry. The loss to gross national product was estimated at between $65 and $90 billion with 1.7 to 2.2 million jobs lost. The actual total costs were $250 million (a price increase of about 6 percent), and few jobs were lost (Greer 1983: 451).

With questionable cost estimates and no accepted technique to estimate benefits, **cost-benefit ratios** for OSHA regulations have varied greatly. Mendeloff (1979: 188) found that the 1972 asbestos standard produced 72 different cost-benefit ratios, some with more benefits than costs and others with more costs than benefits.

Estimates of the total costs imposed by OSHA have not been large. Mendeloff (1979) found that the total annual costs that OSHA imposed on industry ranged between $0.5 billion and $2.5 billion. According to Pettus (1982: 612), "In the first decade, inspection costs and costs of compliance with OSHA regulations, even in health, apparently have not been heavy, despite the body of rhetoric to the contrary." Good cost-benefit analysis might prevent some of the more extreme claims made about OSHA regulations; unfortunately, quality studies are limited by both biased cost estimates and the inability to measure benefits.

The Comprehensive Occupational Safety and Health Act

Legislation to reform the 1970 Occupational Safety and Health Act has been in Congress since 1991. Without the support of the Bush administration, however, reform legislation died. The Clinton administration has, however, come out in support of the reform. Because of this, advocates are hopeful that the OSH act will be reformed during the Clinton presidency.

If passed, the bill would subject employers to tougher **criminal penalties** for certain health and safety violation; require employers to establish **labor-management safety and health committees** and **written safety and health programs**; extend the protection of the OSH act to all state and local government workers; eliminate OSHA's use of cost-benefit analysis when deciding whether to issue safety standards; force OSHA to investigate all serious incidents involving the hospitalization of workers and fatalities and force OSHA to inspect worksites in response to all complaints of violations, including anonymous ones. The proposed act would also affect OSHA's **standard setting process**. OSHA would be required to respond to requests for new safety or health rules within ninety days; if a standard is found warranted, OSHA would be required to issue a proposed rule within 12 months. In addition, the bill would return the permissible exposure limits for many chemicals to the 1989 standard (see above) and require that OSHA update its permissible exposure limits every three years based on recommendations from the National Institute for Occupational Safety and Health.

The reform bill, the **Comprehensive Occupational Safety and Health Reform Act**, has sparked major controversy among industry, labor, Congress and the administration. Industry claims that the reform is too costly, will increase paperwork, will shut down business and decrease companies ability to compete in a global economy. Labor leaders argue, on the other hand, that the current OSH act does not adequately protect the health and safety and workers. Most of the provisions in the act are supported by labor and opposed by industry. Industry claims that the bills have been written by the AFL-CIO and that the administration's support of the bill is an effort to appease labor for Clinton's support of the NAFTA agreement (Victor 1994: 837).

Although the reform act has sparked major debate, it does not dramatically increase the resources of the Occupational Safety and Health Administration. Many OSHA advocates believe that the reform will not have a substantial impact on the safety and health of workers unless it increases the agency's resources. Both the federal government and state governments combined spend only about $380 million to promote workplace safety and health; this contrasts with the $1.1 billion that various federal agencies spend to protect fish and wildlife (Geisel 1992: 36).

Much debate has focused on the expansion of criminal sanctions and the creation of joint management-labor safety and health committees. Each of these issues will be briefly discussed.

CRIMINAL SANCTIONS

The reform bill expands **criminal liability** for violations of the OSH Act. Directors, officers, or agents of an employer could be held criminally liable for violations. In addition, the penalty or fine may not be paid out of the assets of the employer on behalf of the individual. The bill would elevate criminal offenses from misdemeanors to felonies and create a new felony offense for **willful violations** of standards that result in "**serious bodily injury.**" Industry strongly opposes the increase in criminal sanctions. Opponents of the bill fear that it will lead to increased resistance to inspections, increase litigation, and lead to a delay in the abatement of hazards. Concern also exists over the difficulty in defining serious bodily injury.

Proponents of the provision argue, however, that these fears are unfounded. The Assistant Secretary of Labor contends that only about 600 out of 101,000 OSHA inspections in fiscal year 1993 resulted in findings of willful violations involving serious bodily injury (Victor 1994: 838). Expanding criminal sanctions will not affect the majority of business. In addition, proponents argue that current penalties for willfully neglecting the safety and life of workers do not fit the seriousness of the crime. Assistant Secretary Dear stated, "You don't have to meet with many survivors of serious injuries (and families) of workers killed on the job to get a sense that they really don't understand why it's a bigger penalty to harass a wild burro under federal law than it is to willfully neglect safety and health and kill or seriously injure a worker" (quoted in Victor 1994: 838).

SAFETY AND HEALTH COMMITTEES

The proposed act would require companies having more than eleven employees to set up **health and safety committees** composed of equal numbers of employee and employer representatives. The committees would have broad powers to review the company's safety and health program, conduct inspections and propose corrections. The administration supports the creation of safety and health committees. The administration hopes that the committees will serve as whistle blowers to OSHA and help the agency improve its targeting of **unsafe industries**. Industry opposes the committees claiming that they would create an adversarial environment, allow unions to mount organizing campaigns in non-union companies and impose rigidity to the process (Victor 1994: 836).

Although labor originally supported this provision, concern developed that these committees violate the National Labor Relations Act by creating company unions that have the power to negotiate worker's issues. Although the amendment establishing safety and health committees was originally supported by the House Education and Labor

Committee, it was soon dropped after labor voiced its concerns. This shift in position by the chairmen of the committee, William Ford, increased the partisan bickering over the bill and weakened its chances of gaining bipartisan support (Victor 1994: 837).

CONCLUSION

Who benefits from occupational safety and health regulation? If an effective program of regulation existed in the United States, workers would benefit greatly, and industry would absorb some of the costs. The impact on industry would not be all negative, however, for effective regulation would reduce workers' compensation insurance premiums and possibly even avoid situations like that of the Manville Corporation, where suits for asbestos exposure exceeded the net worth of the company. Because the current policy is far from effective (limited by minor penalties and a lack of funding), an assessment of who benefits is more difficult. The safest conclusion is that workers benefit a small amount (workers in nonunion plants who lack bargaining power over safety issues benefit least) and industry bears a small cost.

The reasons why occupational safety and health regulation benefits labor rather than industry can be directly tied to two variables, the environment of the agency and the values of the agency employees (see Table 8.2). Located in the Department of Labor, OSHA is in an environment that supports policies favorable to organized labor. Although this support is greatest in Democratic administrations, it remains in Republican administrations. If the agency were located in the Department of Commerce, OSHA would probably be a far different regulator. In addition, agency employees have incorporated the values of the safety engineering and industrial hygienist professions. Their orientation is to protect workers even if protection requires that industry spend large amounts of money to do so.

Even though OSHA may be predisposed to favor labor, it lacks the resources to impose its policies on the regulatory subsystem. OSHA has failed to develop a high level of expertise (see Shapiro and McGarity 1989: 7); it lacks sufficient resources for its assigned duties and has few effective sanctions. Although recent agency leadership has been fair, generally an absence of strong leadership has hurt the agency.

The actions of OSHA are highly salient; for any proposal, highly organized advocacy coalitions will both support and oppose it. Consequently, OSHA cannot dominate politics even within the subsystem. OSHA politics has become institutionalized as labor-management politics. As a result of the high salience, outside political elites have frequently intervened in the regulatory subsystem. Presidents have designed systems to monitor OSHA rules. President Carter and President Reagan both appointed individuals who fundamentally changed OSHA policies. Congress, in turn, has stressed continual oversight; hearings before 1980 were forums to criticize agency actions; some hearings after 1981 were used to criticize the enforcement policies of Thorne Auchter and his successors. Hearings under the Clinton administration have focused on the debate surrounding the overhaul of the OSH Act. Finally, courts are as active in this area as they are in any regulatory area other than those where courts serve as the decision maker (e.g., antitrust). Agency decisions will be subjected to court scrutiny via appeals from the coalition that loses in front of the agency.

Table 8.2   A Summary of Worker Safety and Health Policy

Economics	
Ease of entry	Varies
Number of firms	Varies
Profits	Vary
Technology	
Complexity	Varies
Stability	Varies
Substitutes	Vary
Subsystem	
Bureaucracy	Weak
Industry coalition	Strong
Nonindustry coalition	Strong
Bureaucratic resources:	
Expertise	Moderate
Cohesion	Low
Leadership	Moderate
Legislative authority:	
Goals	Vague
Coverage	Almost Universal
Sanctions	Poor
Procedures	Fair
Involvement of macropolitical actors	
Congress	Strong
President	Strong
Courts	Moderate

Although the salience of occupational safety and health is generally high, the salience will vary with variations in the economy. Both for the entire economy and for individual industries, salience will increase as the economy slows down. A sluggish economy means that firms will have fewer discretionary funds and will likely resist any regulatory attempts to impose greater costs. When the economy is robust, however, safety and health costs are easier to absorb.

Chapter 9
Regulating Drugs

Alexander Grant[1] and Sharon Olmstead [2,3]

This chapter provides readers with a basic understanding of the Food and Drug Administration (FDA), the regulatory framework for ensuring safe and effective drug products, and the influence of consumers in building that framework. It traces the historical development of laws passed during the 20th century designed to protect consumers and make public participation an integral part of the decision-making process at the FDA.

The issues that arose in drug regulation during the past ten years, those that are currently under consideration, and the issues projected as future policy decisions confronting the agency will serve to illustrate the role consumers have in the development of public health policy at the FDA. The chapter focuses primarily on the drug regulation efforts of the Food and Drug Administration.

REGULATORY SUBSYSTEM

Among the many federal regulatory agencies, none touch the day-to-day lives of citizens as directly as does the Food and Drug Administration (FDA). Twenty-five cents of every consumer dollar is spent annually on the FDA regulated products.

[1]Alexander Grant has been the Associate Commissioner for Consumer Affairs at the Food and Drug Administration since 1979. He serves as principal advisor to the Commissioner on consumer affairs policy and emerging issues. Mr. Grant joined the Food and Drug Administration in 1972, as Director of Consumer Affairs, Office of Professional and Consumer Programs. He has received numerous awards including the 1991 Meritorious Executive Rank Award, the Public Health Service Superior Service Award, the 1993 Philip Hart Award, and the 1994 Esther Peterson Award for consumer excellence.

[2]Sharon Olmstead joined the Office of Consumer Affairs of the Food and Drug Administration in 1994, as a Consumer Affairs Specialist working on drug regulation and women's health issues. Ms. Olmstead began at the Food and Drug Administration in 1991, in the Division of Metabolism and Endocrine Drug Products, Center for Drug Evaluation and Research. She has a bachelor's degree in biology from Old Dominion University and is completing a master's degree in health education at the University of Maryland.

[3]Special acknowledgement is given to Marcia Trenter and Karen Garthright for their technical assistance on this chapter.

The mission of the FDA is to ensure that: (1) foods are safe, wholesome, and sanitary; human and veterinary drugs, biological products, and medical devices are safe and effective; cosmetics are safe; and electronic products that emit radiation are safe; (2) regulated products are honestly, accurately, and informatively represented; and (3) these products are in compliance with the law and FDA regulations; noncompliance is identified and corrected; and any unsafe or unlawful products are removed from the market. In addition, the FDA is also responsible for regulating such products as vaccines, serums, and blood, including blood banks; the sanitation of the food, water, and sanitary facilities on interstate vessels, trains, planes, and buses; and color televisions, cellular phones, and microwaves.

Located in the Department of Health and Human Services, the Food and Drug Administration is one of eight agencies within the **U.S. Public Health Service**. The FDA, however, is the only regulatory agency within the Public Health Service. The Center for Drug Evaluation and Research, located in the Office of Operations at the FDA, is responsible for ensuring that all human drugs manufactured for interstate sale, are safe and effective with truthful and informative product labeling (see Figures 9.1 and 9.2).

The FDA's proposed budget for **fiscal year (FY)** 1995 is $988 million, an increase from FY 1994 of $54 million. The agency has also requested an increase in full-time employee positions from 9,370 in FY 1994 to 9,693 in FY 1995. The increase in funding resources, if approved, will be allocated to the centers that regulate drugs, biologics, and medical devices. The agency has reduced its reliance on appropriated funds, those approved by Congress and supplied by taxpayer dollars, through legislation that allows the FDA to collect **user fees** from the various industries it regulates. Therefore, the $988 million requested includes $343 million in user fee collections. The funds requested for appropriation by Congress total $645 million, down from $873 million appropriated in FY 1994. In comparison to the drug industry's billions spent in drug development and drug marketing, the FDA's budget is a mere drop in the bucket.

The FDA functions autonomously under specific laws, regulations, and budgetary constraints. The agency, however, does not function in a vacuum. The influences on FDA policies and procedures are illustrated in Figure 9.3 depicting the external influences on the FDA. The degree to which each external influence affects the FDA varies.

The executive branch, for example, exerts its political ideology to shape the policies of all federal agencies. Under the Bush administration, the president's **Council on Competitiveness** was established as a vehicle for private industry to voice its concerns about government regulation. The free enterprise philosophy of the Republican party was apparent in the recommendations of the Council on Competitiveness that the FDA eliminate the requirement for phase 1 clinical data (e.g., safety/toxicity testing) for new drugs; increase the number of foreign studies used to support new drug applications in the U.S.; and use outside consultants to review early clinical data for new drugs—all in an attempt to accelerate the drug approval process, thereby shortening the time it takes to get a new drug to market. The Bush administration also flexed its pro-life position by imposing an import ban on the abortifacient **RU-486**, effectively preventing the importation of this drug for personal use.

Figure 9.1   Organization Chart for Public Health Service

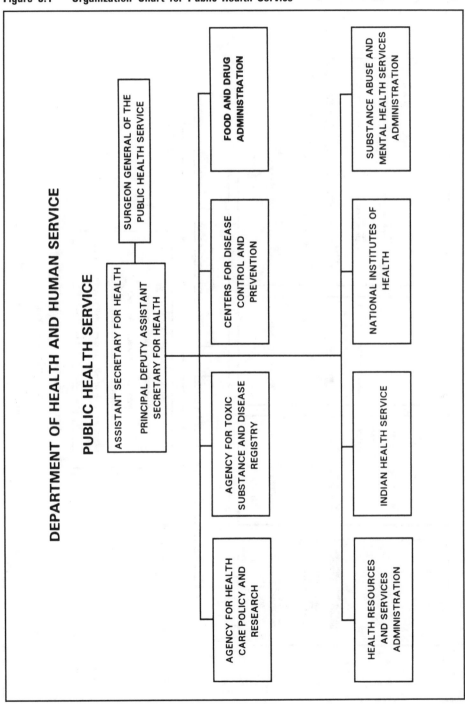

Figure 9.2   Organization Chart for FDA

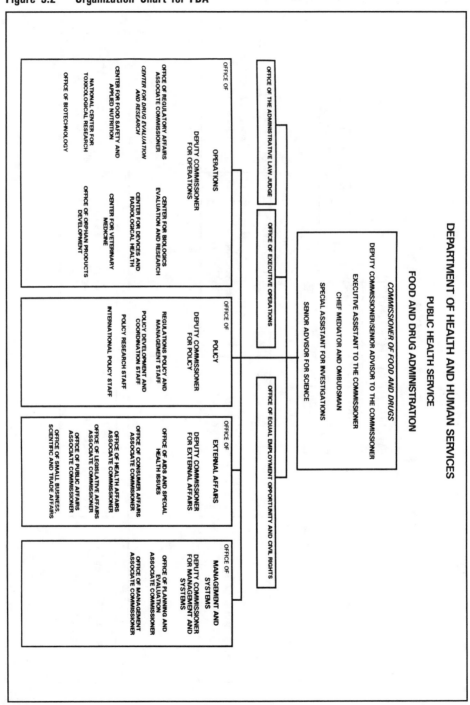

Figure 9.3   External Influences on FDA

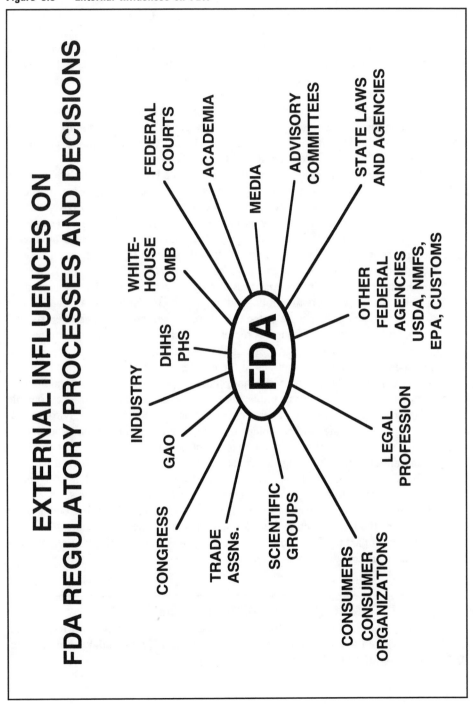

With the change in administration following the 1992 elections, the political ideologies also changed. On January 22, 1993, President Clinton, in one of his first official acts, issued a memorandum directing Health and Human Services Secretary Donna Shalala to assess initiatives to promote the testing and licensing of RU-486 for nonsurgical abortions in the United States. In May 1994, it was announced that the U.S. patent rights to RU-486 would be donated to a not-for-profit corporation to further expedite testing and licensing of this drug in the U.S. The executive influence from the president does not usually impact the day-to-day functioning of the agency. Although the commissioner of the FDA is a politically appointed position by the president, the position must answer to the Secretary of the Department of Health and Human Services, another politically appointed position which answers directly to the president.

The **legislative** influences impact the FDA through the laws established by **Congress** and the interpretation of those laws by the **courts**. The influence felt by congressional actions vary. For example, the Senate approves the appropriations for the FDA's budget. Therefore, this particular influence very intimately affects the FDA's ability to carry out its mission. The agency also answers to the Congress during congressional hearings on the topics of most congressional interest, which are usually brought to their attention through their constituencies. FDA policies and practices are greatly influenced by Congress, however, the laws that are drafted and passed by Congress are usually influenced by constituencies made up of both public and private sector individuals. Congress is theoretically a vehicle for the people of the U.S. to voice their concerns and interests, and therefore, those laws passed by Congress represent the ultimate in **public participation**. The public can also influence FDA policies through direct dialogue with the agency. These methods will be further examined in the chapter.

The FDA also works jointly with many other federal agencies on a number of different issues and products. For example, the Federal Trade Commission is responsible for regulating the advertising for over-the-counter drug products; the Environmental Protection Agency regulates the pesticides that are acceptable for use on products for consumption, the Department of Agriculture is responsible for the regulation of meat and poultry; and all habit-forming drugs approved by the FDA must be registered with the Drug Enforcement Agency. In recent years, the joint efforts of FDA and other agencies have resulted in new efforts to protect the consumer from harmful products.

Before these and the many other external influences can be fully understood, a basic understanding of the laws affecting the FDA should be examined. The context in which these influences impact the FDA will be reflected in the evolution of the food and drug laws and public participation policies.

HISTORY: THE EVOLUTION OF THE FOOD, DRUG & COSMETIC ACT

This examination of the evolution of the Food, Drug & Cosmetic Act includes an overview of (1) the **Pure Food and Drug Act of 1906**, and (2) the **Federal Food, Drug, & Cosmetic Act of 1938**.

Pure Food and Drug Act of 1906

During the early stages of the consumer movement, prior to 1906, the regulation of food and drug products was the responsibility of individual states. Variations from state to state in these laws resulted in an inability of states to enforce their regulations. Products deemed legal in one state were considered **adulterated** in a neighboring state, and a lack of consistency in labeling requirements made it impossible for consumers to truly know the contents of the products they purchased (Janssen, 1981).

In 1883, Dr. Harvey Wiley, a professor from Purdue University, left academia to become the Chief Chemist of the Division of Chemistry in the U.S. Department of Agriculture. Dr. Wiley and his colleagues began developing scientific methodology to test foods and determine their actual content. Dr. Wiley helped establish that many of the product labels were written without regard for the contents or made unsubstantiated health claims (Janssen, 1981). Twelve young male employees of the Department of Agriculture volunteered to test the safety of food additives such as borax, sulfites, and saccharin. They ate meals laced with these substances and were then tested for adverse effects. The volunteers became known as Dr. Wiley's **Poison Squad** (see Figure 9.4).

His experiments on food additives, however, brought him public attention. Dr. Wiley led a campaign to expose the misleading information provided by many food and drug manufacturers and to bring the regulation of food and drug products under the authority of the federal government (Janssen, 1981).

The National Consumers League (NCL), a vital participant in the early fight for a federal law governing food and drug products, was created in 1899 by women who worked with labor and women's organizations to address consumer issues such as child labor, minimum wages, and adulterated foods and drugs. NCL was not alone in their efforts. Other organizations like the American Medical Association and the American Pharmaceutical Association, and the well-known author Upton Sinclair, who exposed filthy conditions in meat packing plants, joined in the fight to raise consumer awareness of the need for a federal food and drug law. Several popular magazines, including *Good Housekeeping*, *Ladies Home Journal* and *Colliers Weekly*, undertook a new role of helping to raise awareness about this socially-relevant issue. By 1903, Dr. Wiley was working with his consumer partners in pressing for the passage of a federal law addressing public safety. He credited these partners with turning the tide of opinion in favor of the Pure Food and Drug Act which was passed in 1906 (Janssen, 1981).

The Pure Food and Drug Act of 1906 gave the federal government the authority to prevent the shipment of "adulterated" or "misbranded" foods and drugs across state lines. This law defined the terms "**adulteration**" and "**misbranded**"; however, the burden of proof was placed with the government to prove that a drug promoter intended to mislead the consumer. A drug promoter could simply claim that it was not his intent to mislead the consumer and the case would be dismissed—effectively limiting the FDA's authority to prevent unsafe drugs from entering the market (Janssen, 1981). The law mandated that certain **dangerous drugs** (e.g., heroin, cocaine, morphine) and alcohol be labeled and their amounts stated. It established the **U.S. Pharmacopeia and National Formulary** as the official compendia for drug standards. The law, however, did little to control the use of dangerous and fraudulent drugs and devices. While weaknesses in the law had been discussed and debated for years, it took catastrophic incidents to propel further action.

Figure 9.4   Poison Squad

THE "POISON SQUAD," AN INTERESTING AND UNIQUE ORGANIZATION OF
TWELVE VOLUNTEERS

Source: FDA Historical Office

Federal Food, Drug, & Cosmetic Act of 1938

In the early 1930's, **dinitrophenol**, widely used for weight reduction, resulted in deaths and hundreds of cases of blindness, agranulocytosis (a potentially fatal blood disorder), and other serious adverse reactions. In 1937, more than 100 people in 15 states, most of them children, died as a result of taking a liquid form of the drug sulfanilamide. This new liquid formulation, **Elixir Sulfanilamide**, contained diethylene glycol (a chemical cousin of antifreeze) and was marketed without **toxicity testing**. New drugs were not yet required to be proven safe prior to marketing.

These tragedies prompted Congress to pass the Federal Food, Drug, and Cosmetic (FD&C) Act of 1938, considerably expanding consumer protection by requiring safety testing of new drugs prior to approval for marketing. This law required drug manufacturers to submit a **new drug application (NDA)** with safety data to the FDA for review and approval prior to marketing the product (Janssen, 1981). The law also mandated that drug labeling include adequate directions for use. This law provided consumers with an assurance that approved drug products were safe for use.

In the late 1950s and early 1960s, Senator Estes Kefauver, troubled by the large profits and markups of pharmaceutical manufacturers, held a series of congressional hearings. As these hearings on the economic aspects of the industry progressed, defects in the safety and efficacy of drugs were revealed. Additionally, the hearings showed drug advertisements were frequently misleading, and numerous drugs existed that had no clear advantages over other drugs (Quirk, 1980; Nadel, 1971).

In 1961, Senator Kefauver introduced a bill to amend the Federal Food, Drug, and Cosmetic Act. The bill required that drugs be proven both safe and effective before marketing. (Quirk, 1980; Janssen, 1981). Once again, a catastrophic event influenced legislative action. At the same time this legislation was being debated in Congress, an application for approval of **thalidomide**, a sedative-hypnotic, was pending at the FDA. This drug was used extensively in Europe before it was determined that the product was a **teratogen** (a drug or substance causing birth defects in the fetus). Thousands of malformed babies were born as a result of their mothers taking the drug during pregnancy. Fortunately, a new medical officer at the FDA named Dr. Francis Kelsey did not act on the application because of a lack of data to support its safety.

Just prior to passage of the Kefauver amendments, the FDA issued new regulations for drug testing because thalidomide had been very widely distributed in the U.S. under the guise of investigational use. Congress used this incident to pass the 1962 amendments. In addition to requiring drug manufacturers to provide substantial evidence to support the drug's effectiveness and safety, the sixty-day review period previously required under the 1938 law was also eliminated, providing the FDA the opportunity to review the application fully and make marketing approvals based on substantive reviews (Janssen, 1981; Quirk, 1980; Nadel, 1971). The law gave the FDA enhanced authority to inspect manufacturer's production and quality control records. Jurisdiction over prescription drug advertising was transferred from the Federal Trade Commission to the FDA. Now under the FDA, prescription drug advertising began receiving more attention and scientific reviews of material content.

AGENDA SETTING: PUBLIC PARTICIPATION

The historical review of the legislation passed to regulate the investigation, manufacturing, and marketing of drug products illustrates the role consumers took in establishing federal laws to protection the public from unsafe, ineffective, and misleading products. Public participation in the actual process of drug development and approval was enhanced by further legislation and the specific actions of several administrations targeting consumer participation in the governmental decision-making process.

There is a strategic and critical need to include public participation in the decision-making process. The issues related to drug regulation are complex, controversial, and confounding. **Consumer input** is necessary for the government to have balanced decision making. The challenge is how to implement the public participation in a meaningful way.

Administrative Practices and Procedure Act

The authorities given to the FDA to review and approve new drug products under the FD&C Act promote public participation. The FDA relies heavily on public input through testimony at **advisory committee meetings** and **public hearings**, **written comments**, and **citizen petitions** from consumer organizations, industry, health care professionals, and the scientific research community. The importance of public participation in the government's decision-making process was legally recognized in 1946, when Congress passed the **Administrative Practices and Procedures Act**.

During the 1950s, consumer activity moved away from drug regulation and focused primarily on food related issues. The laws established to this point seemed adequate to protect the consumers from dangerous drug products. In December 1952, the FDA hired sixteen consumer consultants in the field, because the FDA believed that **informed consumers** would require less protection. The consultants served as liaisons between the agency and the public on a wide variety of consumer problems (Swann, 1992). The federal government also began to recognize the benefits of an informed consumer.

In 1962, President John F. Kennedy established the Consumers' Bill of Rights, providing consumers with the rights to choice, information, safety, and the right to be heard. President Kennedy believed the right to be informed and the right to be heard would provide the foundation for two-way dialogue between consumers and government. The Consumer Advisory Council was founded to implement the goals of this bill. The **Freedom of Information (FOI) Act**, passed in 1966, provided the public with another mechanism to access the federal government. The FOI Act provided access to government information, which improved the public participation process by allowing consumers to gather information on government decisions and actions.

The Development of Consumer Affairs Activities at the FDA

Spurred on by President Kennedy's Consumer Bill of Rights of 1962, the FDA created three consumer-related branches in its new **Bureau of Education and Voluntary Compliance: A Consumer Information Branch**, which developed educational materials for consumers and answered queries to headquarters; the Consumer Consultant Branch, which planned programs for consumer education through the consultants, and the Consumer Survey Branch, which evaluated consumer interests and attitudes. In the mid-1960s, the consumer education program began focusing on three target audiences: the elderly, primary and secondary school teachers, and labor forces of all economic brackets. Consumer Specialists now were expected to devote about half of their time to conferences or workshops for these audiences (Swann, 1992).

By the late 1960s, the nature of the resource materials used to educate consumers began to change. Consumer Specialists employed Spanish language press releases, radio and television scripts, and pamphlets; they carried out mass distribution of reprints from *FDA Papers* and its successor, the *FDA Consumer*; and they used one-page fact sheets to apprise consumers of particular issues. By the end of the decade there were 20 Consumer Specialists and 10 part-time Consumer Consultants. By 1972, this doubled. The FDA currently has 43 Public Affairs Specialists and Technicians in the field educating consumers on FDA issues and encouraging their input on agency policy (Swann, 1992).

United States Office of Consumer Affairs

President Nixon answered the consumer movement by establishing the **U.S. Office of Consumer Affairs (USOCA)** in 1971. The director of this office was charged with advising and representing the president on matters of consumer interest, identifying and coordinating federal consumer protection activities, and improving the effectiveness of governmental consumer programs. During that same year, the Administrative Conference of the U.S. established the criteria for public participation in administrative hearings.

Federal Advisory Committee Act

In 1972, Congress established the **Federal Advisory Committee Act**. This law provided an opportunity for the general public to participate in the policy process by serving on advisory committees and panels to federal regulatory agencies. The agency needed to balance the input from industry with solid information from the public. The FDA, therefore, used this opportunity to foster an open-door policy for consumers. Several changes were implemented to inform the public of proposed policies as well as improve consumer participation through public testimony and written comments. The FDA extended the minimum time for public comment on proposed the FDA regulations and policy statements from 30 to 60 days. The extension was designed to provide consumers, whose resources were limited, with more time to research the issues under consideration and more effectively participate in the process. A preamble in lay language was also required for all *Federal Register* proposals clearly explaining the background and reasons for the action to be taken. In addition, a summary of the comments received during the public comment period, including the FDA's response, must accompany the publication of any final rule. With the establishment of the Federal Advisory Committee Act, the FDA began appointing consumer representatives to the advisory committees established to advise the FDA.

The FDA recognized in the early 1970s that consumers should be provided with an opportunity to dialogue directly with the agency. In 1979, the **Office of Consumer Affairs** was established within the Office of the Commissioner. This office serves to inform and educate consumers about the FDA's policies and programs and how they impact on public health; facilitates dialogue between consumers and the agency; and ensures consumer input into agency decision making.

Esther Peterson, the consumer advisor to President Jimmy Carter, recognized the importance of the consumer affairs offices within the government and the need to raise the stature of these offices to report directly to the agency head. When Ms. Peterson began considering a prototype to implement this change she looked to the Office of Consumer Affairs (OCA) at the FDA. President Carter issued an **Executive Order 12160** in 1979, modeled after OCA. The order outlined the five elements required in federal consumer programs: (1) the establishment of professional a consumer affairs staff, (2) public participation in the development of all agency rules, policies, and programs, (3) the development of informational materials for consumers, (4) education and training for staff on federal consumer policies, and (5) the development of avenues for consumer complaints. The **Consumer Affairs Council**, established under the executive order, was chaired by Esther Peterson with membership from all cabinet level federal agencies. It was through her leadership and coordination that the implementation of effective consumer programs was ensured.

By the late 1980s, consumers were members of 35 FDA advisory committees. In addition to consumer representation on advisory committees, consumers and patients can access the agency when pending drug applications or current health issues are discussed before an advisory panel through public testimony or written comment. The agency has continued to improve consumer participation at the FDA. During the 1990's, OCA recognized the special needs of women and patients with life-threatening illnesses, such as AIDS and cancer, through the implementation of programs targeting these populations. The agency has narrowed its focus on these issues by establishing the Office of Women's Health and the Office of AIDS and Special Health Issues to provide specialized attention to the public health concerns of women and patients with life-threatening diseases.

DRUG DEVELOPMENT

In order to fully understand the impact consumers have on drug development and the policies governing that process, the reader must also understand the actual drug development process. That is, what is involved in the process to make a new drug available to the public.

The regulatory procedures established for new drug development under the current law require extensive clinical testing of a product and a thorough review of the data and approval by scientific experts at the FDA before a drug product can be introduced into the market. The data submitted to the FDA must support the drug's safety and effectiveness in the prescribed patient population.

Clinical data to support the approval of a new drug is usually collected from clinical trials carried out by researchers in several phases under an **investigational new drug (IND) application** submitted to the FDA. The initial human trials are conducted in a **phase 1** study to establish the pharmacological and metabolic actions of the drug and any adverse reactions or side-effects in 10 to 50 subjects. If favorable results are obtained from a phase 1 trial, the sponsor can move on to **phase 2**. This phase evaluates the drug's activity and safety in patients with the intended disease, usually including 50 to 200 subjects. **Phase 3** trials are conducted to confirm the safety and efficacy data collected in phase 1 and 2 with two adequate and well-controlled trials that enroll 200 to 1000 or more subjects. Following the completion of clinical trials, the manufacturer of the drug will submit all the relevant clinical data to the FDA in a **new drug application (NDA)**. The data in the NDA is reviewed by a team usually consisting of a medical officer, a chemist, a pharmacologist, a statistician, and a biopharmaceutics reviewer. When a review is near completion, the agency often solicits input from an advisory committee and the public regarding the approvability of the drug product. If the data submitted to FDA supports the safety and efficacy claims made by the manufacturer, the drug will be approved for marketing (see Figure 9.5).

In the years following the 1962 amendments, the FDA has been repeatedly criticized for the length of time required to bring new drugs to the market. The phrase **"drug lag"** was coined during the post-1962 era to describe the relationship between regulatory

Figure 9.5 Drug Development and Approval Process

THE DRUG DEVELOPMENT AND APPROVAL PROCESS

It takes 12 years on average for an experimental drug to travel from lab to medicine chest.
Only five in 5,000 compounds that enter preclinical testing make it to human testing.
One of these five tested in people is approved.

	Preclinical Testing		Clinical Trials: Phase I	Clinical Trials: Phase II	Clinical Trials: Phase III		FDA		Phase IV
Years	**3.5**	FILE IND AT FDA	**1**	**2**	**3**	FILE NDA AT FDA	**2.5**	**12 Total**	
Test Popula-tion	Laboratory and animal studies		20 to 80 healthy volun-teers	100 to 300 patient volunteers	1,000 to 3,000 patient volunteers		Review process/ approval		Additional post-marketing testing required by FDA
Purpose	Assess safety and biological activity		Deter-mine safety and dosage	Evaluate effectiveness, look for side effects.	Verify effectiveness, monitor adverse reactions from long-term use.				
Success Rate	5,000 compounds evaluated		5 enter trials				1 approved		

Source: Wierenga and Eaton (1993)

stringencies and decreased access to new drug products (McFadyen, 1981). The criticism about the FDA's drug lag led to significant policy changes in the 1980s and 1990s. As described below, potential beneficiaries of successful new drugs (consumers) again actively worked with the FDA to effect changes in this process.

POLICY DECISIONS: IMPACT ON DRUG REGULATION

Advocacy coalitions interested in drug regulation include consumer and patient groups, health professionals, scientists, and the pharmaceutical industry. The focus on regulation and the desired policy changes varies for each group. AIDS patients and the fight for earlier access to experimental drugs is a good example, although the initial policies to allow early access began with those drugs used to treat cancer. The policy changes implemented during the 1980s and 1990s have benefitted not only AIDS patients, but also those individuals suffering from other life-threatening and serious illnesses such as cancer, Alzheimer's disease, advanced multiple sclerosis, and advanced congestive heart failure.

AZT and Other Therapies

Three factors impacted on changes in the approval of AIDS therapies: (1) patients with the disease usually died, (2) the health care community could not provide a treatment, and (3) patients were organized and politically active (Vogel, 1992). **AIDS patients** demanded access to **experimental drugs** before the normal FDA testing phases were completed. The demands of AIDS patients highlighted the willingness of individuals with life-threatening diseases to accept increased risks associated with medical treatments for potential benefits gained.

AIDS groups, impatient with the drug lag, implemented an entirely new strategy to force the agency to focus on the drug approval process. Their tactics included a large demonstration at FDA headquarters in which AIDS patients blocked the entrances to the building in a successful effort to shut down the FDA. In a meeting with AIDS activists, planned by the FDA to be conciliatory, the then Commissioner Frank Young was pelted by tomatoes (see Figure 9.6).

The FDA's Office of Consumer Affairs played a pivotal and lead role in establishing lines of communications with the AIDS community through a series of meetings with activists. During this same period (1987), the agency finalized a major initiative to provide **expanded access** to promising experimental drugs for seriously ill patients before approval. This procedure provides patients with life-threatening diseases such as cancer, Alzheimer's disease, advanced parkinson's disease, advanced congestive heart failure, and AIDS, with access to investigational drugs under a specific treatment protocol before the drug has been approved.

In 1988, the FDA proposed a process to **expedite** the development and approval of drugs intended to treat life-threatening and severely debilitating illnesses. The FDA met with members of the AIDS community, consumer groups, health professionals, industry, and members of the scientific community involved in AIDS research to develop the new

Figure 9.6   A Growing Number of AIDS Activists Change Their Mind

FIGHTING FOR THEIR LIVES

Frustrated by a lack of anti-AIDS drugs, about 1,000 activists demonstrated in front of the FDA's headquarters in Rockville, Md., this month. They hoped to persuade the FDA to let them take experimental medication before it has been proved effective.

Source: *Time*, October 31, 1988

①If there was a single, unifying battle cry among protesters, it was the charge that the Federal Government's delays in approving experimental treatments were responsible for killing thousands of desperately ill AIDS patients.

Source: FDA/Office of Consumer Affairs

②A growing number of AIDS activists change their mind.

■Medicine
Let's Not Be Too Hasty

Activists who once clamored for speedier approval of AIDS drugs now favor a more deliberate approach

Source: *Time,* September 19, 1994

③Doctors and patients start to complain that the speeded-up approval process didn't provide them with enough information to make an intelligent decision about which drug to use.

procedures. The most fundamental change in the procedures was that the FDA assisted the manufacturers in designing the phase 2 clinical trials with the goal that phase 3 clinical trials may not be necessary for approval (53 FR 41516). This new process became known as **"subpart E"**, named after the section of the code of federal regulations defining this process.

If approval is granted, the FDA may seek an agreement from the sponsor to conduct certain postmarketing or **phase 4** clinical trials. Such a study may evaluate different dosages or administration regimens, longer periods of drug exposure, and the effectiveness of the drug in different patient populations. A phase 4 study can provide additional data on the risks, benefits, and optimal use of the drug (53 FR 41516). The agency piloted this program with zidovudine (AZT). AZT, the first AIDS drug using the expedited process, was approved in 107 days, reducing the normal approval time by almost 18 months (53 FR 41516).

In 1990, FDA, with significant input from the AIDS community, including patient advocates, health professionals, the research community and the pharmaceutical industry, developed the **parallel track protocol policy**. This policy is limited to only those drugs developed for treating AIDS and HIV-related illnesses. Parallel track protocols differed from the treatment protocol established in 1987 because they could begin treating patients at the same time the controlled clinical trials designed to establish efficacy were accruing patients. The treatment protocols were typically begun at the end of the clinical investigations or after the accrual for the controlled clinical trials was complete.

In 1992, the FDA developed an **accelerated approval process** for new drug therapies to treat serious or life-threatening illnesses. The approval may be based on surrogate or disease-indicator endpoints rather than survival endpoints. In addition, drug sponsors are required to conduct postmarketing studies to establish the drug's clinical benefit on survival (57 FR 13234). Overall, the drug approval process has been significantly speeded up in recent years. The FDA approved 85 new drugs and biological products in 1994 with a median approval time of only 19 months.

CURRENT ISSUE: THE MOVEMENT TO SWITCH PRESCRIPTION DRUGS TO OTC STATUS

The FDA is faced with many challenging issues. It is through these issues that FDA policy is molded. Because there are so many drug issues currently pending at the FDA, we will focus only on one issue, the movement to switch prescription drugs to over-the-counter status. This multi-faceted issue will illustrate the different issues the FDA is facing within this area of drug regulation.

Today's consumer has more choices in **over-the-counter (OTC) medications** than consumers 20 years ago, due to changes initiated by FDA and the drug industry. In 1972, the FDA began a comprehensive **safety and effectiveness review** of all active ingredients in OTC drug products. Most marketed products had never been reviewed for safety and efficacy prior to this point. This review was the result of the 1962 amendment requiring **effectiveness data** before market approval would be granted. This undertaking involved over 700 active ingredients used in more than 300,000 different drug products. The agency, with the help of 17 advisory committees, began reviewing active ingredients by **drug class** (e.g., antihistamines, antifungals, and anti-cough medicines). It was during this review process that the initial prescription to OTC switches were made. Antihistamines are an example in which the advisory committee recommended increasing the dosage available in OTC to prescription dose. Drug manufacturers could legally begin to marketing the prescription dose recommended by the panel (Segal, 1991).

Prior to 1951, distinctions between prescription and OTC drug products did not exist (except for narcotic-containing products). In 1951, the Durham-Humphrey amendment to the FD&C Act defined the difference between a **prescription drug** and **OTC drug** and provided a statutory requirement that drugs which are unsafe for use except under a physician's supervision must be dispensed only by prescription. Nonprescription drugs or OTCs were considered safe for consumer use with adequate directions and warnings on the label (Segal, 1991).

The initial prescription drug candidates approved for OTC status were not met with the same enthusiasm as seen in today's market. Consumer organizations were concerned about the safety issues of adequate directions for OTC use to prevent misuse, labeling of warnings and side effects, and possibly interactions with other drug products.

The Process of Switching to OTC Status

Prescription drugs on the market can also be switched to OTC status by other mechanisms: an NDA or a supplemental NDA submitted by the drug manufacturer or a citizen's petition by an interested party requesting the FDA to amend the OTC monograph for the particular active ingredients. Dr. Michael Weintraub, Director, Office of OTC Drug Evaluation, spoke about the FDA's philosophy regarding the switch of prescription drugs to OTC status. He stated that, "The agency treats each application or switch as a unique event. Each application will be presented to the Nonprescription Drug Advisory Committee supplemented with members of the specialty committee" (Interview, 1994).

Rogaine and Tagamet

Recent examples in which the **Nonprescription Drug Advisory Committee** recommended against OTC availability of a product include such drugs as Rogaine and Tagamet. Rogaine (minoxidil 2% topical solution), used to treat baldness in men and women, was not switched to OTC status at this time based on the limited effectiveness of the product and concern for the safety of patients who may misdiagnose the reason for their hair loss or misuse the product. Tagamet (cimetidine), currently available under prescription for the treatment of ulcers, was approved in 1983. The manufacturer subsequently requested OTC status for the treatment of episodic heartburn using a lower dose than the prescription product. The panel recommended against approval of OTC status at this time based on the potential interactions with other prescription drugs. OTC drug products cannot carry the same level of toxicity as prescription drugs, and the product should be effective in most users. If either of these criteria is not met, the drug would need physician supervision to ensure that appropriate patients received the drug.

Acyclovir

Another recent candidate for OTC switch was **Acyclovir**. Burroughs Wellcome submitted a supplemental NDA to switch acyclovir to over-the-counter status for the treatment and suppression of recurrent genital herpes (a sexually-transmitted disease). Acyclovir has been marketed since 1985, under prescription as Zovirax for the treatment of first episode and recurrent genital herpes. In 1985, the FDA also approved the oral formulation of acyclovir for the treatment of herpes zoster and chicken pox, and for the suppression of recurrent genital herpes.

The application was presented at a public hearing before an FDA panel in May 1994. The Nonprescription Drugs Advisory Committee and the Antiviral Drugs Advisory Committee were also present to hear the public comments. The agency conducted an extensive outreach to the public announcing this meeting, and calling for public comment. If approved for OTC use, acyclovir would be the first systemic antiviral product on the market without a prescription, hence without physician consultation. The agency was interested in receiving public comment on the following issues: (1) the implications of unrestricted availability of acyclovir for the transmission and asymptomatic shedding of herpes simplex virus; (2) the incidence and clinical significance of acyclovir-resistant herpes simplex; (3) the ability of patients to self-diagnose genital herpes (i.e., without consultation of a physician); (4) the potential for misuse for unapproved OTC indications such as chickenpox, shingles, and other viral illnesses; (5) the potential for adverse effects on the fetus; and (6) general issues of safety and the incidence of adverse drug events during widespread, unrestricted use. These questions were posed to the general public including consumers, health care professionals, scientists, and other federal agencies.

The committee heard seven hours of public testimony from patient advocacy groups, individual patients, and medical associations, as well as the Centers for Disease Control and Prevention (CDC). The public hearing on this issue illustrates the commitment made by the FDA to seek out public comment during the decision-making process, particularly on a potentially controversial issue. Although the FDA is only charged with the regulation of specific products for safety and efficacy, the agency heard comments regarding the social implications surrounding the unrestricted use of a drug for a sexually-transmitted disease; the economic impact of such a switch on **cost reimbursement** from insurance companies; and the therapeutic benefits reported but not yet proven to decrease the transmission of HIV. Many groups voiced their concern regarding the elimination of patient counseling provided by the physician. The American Social Health Association (ASHA), however, presented data from a 1991 study published in the Journal of Sexually Transmitted Diseases, in which 60% of the patients with herpes simplex virus surveyed reported that poor or insufficient counseling and information was provided by their health care provider.   The most divisive topic discussed during the hearing was viral resistances. The CDC cautioned the FDA to defer approval of the OTC switch until a review of the evidence indicates that the public health benefit outweighs any negative effects, specifically viral resistance. The National Women's Health Network (NWHN), a leading advocacy group for women's health, and an avid proponent of patient self-diagnosis and treatment, opposed the switch for the single reason of resistance. They stated that the FDA must address the potential development of acyclovir-resistant strains of genital herpes before NWHN will consider supporting this switch.

The administrative hearing closed with a summary discussion by the advisory committee members and a commitment to meet again for final recommendations to the FDA on the approvability of this application. Although approval of acyclovir as an OTC drug product remains unresolved, the agency has begun to address the issue of resistance in both humans and animals as recommended during the acyclovir hearing and during a joint session of the Veterinary Medicine Advisory Committee and the Anti-Infective Drugs Advisory Committee in May 1994.

Oral Contraceptives

An example in which the public has independently begun providing input to the FDA on a possible candidate for OTC switch is oral contraceptives or birth control pills. During the past decade, the movement to switch the pill from prescription to OTC status has gained momentum in the women's health community. To date, the FDA has not publicly addressed this issue. In June 1993, the Henry J. Kaiser Family Foundation, a private foundation devoted exclusively to health issues, held a two-day forum to discuss the "pros" and "cons" of the availability of oral contraceptives without a prescription. Issues addressed included safety, effectiveness, barriers to use, economic impact of a switch, and the international experience (Samuels, 1993).

The National Women's Health Network (NWHN) has taken a position in opposition to the proposed switch. Cindy Pearson, Program Director, stated, "The NWHN believes with adequate information women can self-screen for the contraindication and be alert to potential adverse reactions." The safety issue concerns long term use at an earlier age and a possible link with breast cancer. The NWHN believes that these questions need to be addressed before the pill should be available without a prescription. Another concern involves the effectiveness of the pill once counseling is eliminated from the prescription process. In foreign countries, the pill is available OTC; however, the social marketing system present in those European countries provides counseling at the time of oral contraceptive purchase. Family planning clinics in the United States continue, even with counseling, to field questions about oral contraceptive use and antibiotics, discontinuation of the pill because of spotting episodes, or discontinuation because of amenorrhea (lack of a menstrual period). Ms. Pearson voiced NWHN's concern that "without counseling, women will use the pill in ways that will result in decreased effectiveness" (Interview, 1994)

At the Kaiser Forum, Carol Scheman, the FDA's former Deputy Commissioner for External Affairs, presented the policy issues that will face the FDA if the pill is considered a candidate for OTC status. The FDA must consider scientific criteria for any product switch. Nevertheless, the FDA cannot ignore the impact an OTC switch may have on public health, such as third party reimbursements, access to health care, and misconceptions regarding sexually-transmitted diseases (Scheman, 1993).

FUTURE POLICY DIRECTIONS

There are at least three areas of future concern of the Food and Drug Administration: (1) the AIDS epidemic, (2) the effectiveness of OTC labeling, and (3) the ways that various subpopulations respond to medications.

The AIDS Epidemic

It would be difficult to project the future policies of FDA without further consideration of the AIDS epidemic and its continued impact on public health. As the number of individuals infected with HIV approaches one million, AIDS and HIV-related illnesses will remain a priority in public health policies. As the access to new therapies improves, we have seen a strengthening of the advocacy groups representing AIDS patients. Whether through the modest improvements in medical therapies that are helping to extend the lives of those individuals infected with disease or through greater diversity of representation in these advocacy groups, the tide may be turning regarding **risk acceptance** in this community. During a recent public hearing of the Anti-Infective Drugs Advisory Committee, an AIDS advocate expressed concerns regarding surrogate endpoints as evidence for the safety and efficacy of a new drug called stavudine. His concerns focused on the safety of stavudine and the possible unknown risks that might prevail through the accelerated drug approval process.

Effectiveness of Over-The-Counter Labeling

Freedom of choice, driven by the health promotion and disease prevention movement, will continue to affect the drug area. Cindy Pearson, National Women's Health Network, summarizes consumer concerns about access by stating, "The right to choose is meaningless without the right to know" (interview, 1994). In the OTC drug arena, the FDA Office of OTC Drug Evaluation is nearing completion of its safety and efficacy review of all active ingredients in OTC drug products, a process that has taken nearly 20 years and resulted in the removal of thousands of products containing ineffective ingredients. The agency has turned its attention to the effectiveness of **OTC labeling** to convey adequate information to consumers. Current law requires that OTC labels state the intended uses and results of the product; adequate directions for use; and warnings against unsafe use, side effects, and adverse reactions. The monograph establishes the substantive content of the labeling for each active ingredient. The positioning of such information has been left to the discretion to the manufacturer. Generally, the majority of information found on an OTC drug product is puffery or information to embellish the appeal of such a product. For example, "smooth taste" or "4 out of 5 doctors prefer," are acceptable statements provided that the information is truthful and not misleading.

During a recent joint hearing of the Nonprescription Drug Advisory Committee and the Arthritis Drugs Advisory Committee in September 1994, the FDA presented a preliminary proposal to redesign the format for OTC drug labeling, including directions for use, warnings of adverse reactions, and drug interactions. Dr. Weintraub, Director, Office of OTC Drug Evaluation, indicated that the agency recognizes that "Consumers want to take charge of their health. Therefore, they are reading the labels more carefully to better understand appropriate medication use." The proposed changes will address print size, legibility, terminology, and standardized text and format of mandatory information. The agency has likened these proposed changes in format to the new nutritional food labeling introduced in 1994. A **standard format** would provide consumers with the ability to locate specific information about a product at the same location on any OTC drug label. The agency recognizes the importance of consumer and industry input during this process, particularly in the methodology development needed to test the success of such changes. The presentation at the public hearing was the first of many steps towards addressing the changing needs of the consumer.

Subpopulation Response to Medications

Another area in which interest has been growing to develop or improve public health policy involves differences in the way various **subpopulations** respond to medications and how physicians can effectively and safely interpret these differences. In a recent article, the FDA identified factors, such as ethnicity, gender, age, body size, and fat content, that can influence an individual's response to a drug (Merkatz, 1993). The FDA has taken several major steps to encourage development of data to ensure that the safety and efficacy of drugs are adequately studied in the full range of patients who will receive therapy (58 FR 39406). The agency will look to the industry to begin collecting data that will improve the efficacy of drug therapies by calculating dose based on physiologic criteria rather than extrapolating dosage based on results obtained from white, middle-class males. In September 1994, several chapters of the AIDS advocacy group ACT-UP were joined by women's organizations in a demonstration at FDA headquarters. The protesters held a mock trial in which the FDA was placed on trial for failure to require the inclusion of women in clinical trials. This issue will continue to mold the FDA's policy in the future and provides another example of consumers utilizing tactics to bring attention to public health issues that they feel have not been adequately addressed by the government.

SUMMARY

A summary of regulation at the Food and Drug Administration is shown in Table 9.1. As the nation prepares to enter the 21st century, the FDA is met with many challenges. The agency must continue to protect the public health while at the same time provide for greater freedom of choice as demanded by consumers. The FDA has evolved into a federal agency in which public participation in policy development has become paramount. The regulations governing the development of new drug therapies, particularly those designed to treat serious and life-threatening diseases, have undergone dramatic changes to allow earlier access. Access to prescription drugs as over-the-counter drug products has also increased. Consumers have seen their **self-help movement** influence FDA and its position to provide consumers with greater access to drug therapies. As the consumer organizations continue to coordinate their efforts and gain strength to meet the issues of the next century, the FDA will work to ensure that public participation in the decision making process is met.

Table 9.1   A Summary of Food and Drug Administration Regulation

Economics

Ease of entry	Moderate
Number of firms	2 million
Profits	High

Technology

Complexity	Moderate
Stability	Varies
Substitutes	High

Subsystem

Bureau control	Weak
Industry coalition	Moderate
Nonindustry coalition	Moderate
Bureaucratic resources:	
Expertise	High
Cohesion	Low
Leadership	Moderate
Legislative authority:	
Goals	General
Coverage	All
Sanctions	Moderate
Procedures	Moderate

Impact of macropolitical actors

Congress	Strong
President	Strong
Courts	Moderate

Chapter 10
Food Safety Regulation

Mary L. Carsky[1]

From the time of the first federal food legislation in the first decade of this century, food safety regulation centers on providing a safe and wholesome food supply. The first statutes, passed in 1906, defined those products that were considered foods and contained provisions on the adulteration and misbranding of food products. Since that time, there has been a tremendous change in the types of food products available. Today's complex national and international systems for agricultural production, processing/manufacturing, merchandising, and packaging require a broader range of controls. Herbicide and pesticide residues, irradiation, E. coli bacteria, toxicity of additives and supplements, and sanitary conditions of processing facilities are some of the safety issues addressed by current regulatory actions. Legislative action to ensure wholesomeness of the food supply in the present environment includes consideration of foods' ability to offset chronic illnesses, provide nutritional value, and disclose information that will enable consumers to make rational choices.

THE SUBSYSTEM

This examination of the subsystem of food safety regulation includes an overview of the agencies involved and the associated advocacy coalitions.

The Agencies

Responsibility for regulating the food supply and monitoring food safety rests primarily in the hands of two federal agencies. The **United States Department of Agriculture (USDA)** specifically the **Food Safety and Inspection Service (FSIS)** is

---

[1]Mary L. Carsky, associate professor of marketing at The University of Hartford, Barney School of Business and Public Administration, completed her PhD in consumer studies at Virginia Tech. She has published several articles on grocery shopping behavior and consumer use of information in the supermarket. She has conducted a study of food labeling preferences and presented testimony on behalf of the New England Food and Drug Officials at the Food and Drug Administration hearings in Atlanta in December 1989.

responsible for enforcing regulations on meat and poultry, and the **Food and Drug Administration (FDA)** in Health and Human Services is responsible for all other food products. Responsibility for monitoring pesticides is shared between the **Environmental Protection Agency (EPA)** and the Food and Drug Administration. Others are either shared with or allocated to individual states.

Early in the century abuses in the meat packing industry and the adulteration of processed foods prompted passage of the **Pure Food and Drugs Act** and the **Federal Meat Inspection Act** in 1906. These two laws gave the Agriculture Department broad jurisdiction over food in interstate commerce. Over the years, laws and programs have been created in response to problems in specific food sectors and responsibility for enforcement has been spread about in a piecemeal fashion leading to regulatory fragmentation, gaps, inconsistencies and even conflicts across jurisdictions as well as substantive issues on enforcement, and statutes which conflict with one another (Hardy, 1990).

Through early legislation, Congress gave the USDA responsibility for monitoring food processing to prevent the adulteration of foods. Amendments to the Pure Food and Drugs Act in 1930 (McNary-Mapes Amendment) and in 1938 gave new powers to the Department of Agriculture to set legally enforceable standards, affirmative labeling requirements, and better enforcement of sanitary conditions in food processing. These government mandates were assigned to the Food and Drug Administration within USDA. In 1940 the FDA was transferred out of the Department of Agriculture to the Department of Health and Human Services (HHS). As food regulation evolved toward more sophisticated surveillance, **pesticide control provisions** of the FDA were transferred to the Environmental Protection Agency (Hardy, 1990).

Over the years, significant food safety mandates have been assigned by Congress to nine federal agencies lodged in four different Cabinet Departments and two independent agencies. While FDA is charged with enforcement of legislative mandates, a second agency in HHS, the **Public Health Service** monitors **foodborne illness**. The Environmental Protection Agency (EPA) monitors pesticide residues. Four separate agencies within USDA regulate different segments of the food industry: (1) **Agricultural Marketing Service monitors egg production**; (2) **Animal and Plant Health Inspection Services monitors live food animals**; (3) **the Federal Grain Inspection Service oversees grain and oilseed crops,** and (4) **Food Safety and Inspection Service enforces statutes on food processing**. The **National Marine Fisheries Service in the Department of Commerce**[2] **and the Bureau of Alcohol, Tobacco and Firearms, within the Department of the Treasury**, are responsible for their respective products.

State and local governments participate in the regulation of food safety. Combined state monies are equal to the total level of federal resource allocations (Hardy, 1990: 230). More than 380 state agencies carry responsibilities similar to the FDA. State programs are lodged in **Departments of Agriculture, Health, Consumer Protection, and in Offices**

---

[2]The Department of Commerce Seafood Inspection is voluntary and affects approximately ten percent of the seafood sold in the United States. In 1993 an Office of Seafoods was created within the FDA.

of Attorneys General (Porter and Earl, 1992). Arrangements between federal and state regulators differ by product category. For example, **meat inspection** is almost completely federalized; USDA develops the rules, and only states deemed to be "equivalent" are delegated authority to inspect meat in interstate commerce.[3] By contrast, **milk inspection** is conducted by all states under guidelines established jointly with the FDA; the FDA audits the performance of state inspection. The EPA pesticide program follows another model; the EPA contracts with states for nearly all enforcement with minimal auditing. State and local ordinances often differ from the federal law either because the state feels the federal law in inadequate (e.g., Maine has banned the use of BST growth hormone in cattle) or because the federal law does not meet the specific needs of the state or locality. For example, Minnesota and Wisconsin have regulations for labeling wild rice (Porter and Earl, 1992: 125).

Advocacy Coalitions

Historically, food processors have supported national food legislation in order to obtain uniformity in regulatory requirements and to build credibility for the food supply (Porter and Earl, 1992). **Food producers and sellers** are a diverse group comprised of farmers, processors, distributors, retailers, and food service providers. These are represented by a number of trade associations which routinely lobby Congress on legislation which will affect their industries. Recently, for example, a coalition of 11 trade associations including the Council of Farm Cooperatives, the American Meat Institute, the National Food Processors Association, the National-American Wholesale Grocers' Association and the International Food Service Association voiced opposition to safe handling labels on the basis that the scope of labeling was too broad (Panetta Criticizes..., 1993).[4]

The **Association of Food and Drug Officials (AFDO)**, a coalition of food and drug officials at the federal, state and local levels, was established in 1887. AFDO's purpose is "to promote and foster such regulation as would tend to protect public health and prevent deception...also to promote uniformity in legislation and rulings..." (Jones, 1912). While AFDO has worked for uniformity, the organization prefers "uniformity through cooperation..." rather than federal preemption of food safety standards. Recently AFDO studied the need for the petition process for states to petition FDA for an exemption from the Nutrition Labeling and Education Act. AFDO's position is that because state and local needs differ, the law must provide for exemptions to federal uniformity policies (Porter and Earl, 1992). Since its beginning, AFDO has developed model state laws and regulations and worked to harmonize different state programs.

The consumer interest in food safety has been represented by The Center for Science in the Public Interest. The Center, which is an advocacy group under the Nader umbrella, serves as a watchdog over the food industry. The Safe Food Coalition (SFC) organized

---

[3]Game meat and fowl are inspected by state inspectors.

[4]The trade associations supported labeling for ground meat and poultry products "that are not presently labeled with handling and cooking instructions." (Panetta Criticizes...1993: 23).

in 1986 following the passage of the Processed Products Inspection Improvement Act (PPII) which eliminated continuous inspection of processed meat and poultry. In 1993 the coalition rallied around the prevention of food borne illness and called for the implementation of a science-based set of regulatory principles known as **Hazard Analysis Critical Control Points (HACCP)**. The coalition includes interest from public health, citizen groups, labor organizations, and retired persons. Representatives include members of the Consumer Federation of America, National Consumers League, Consumers Union, Public Voice and the former Assistant Secretary of Agriculture, Carol Tucker Foreman (Reinventing Meat..., 1993).

THE ENVIRONMENT

This section on the environment of food safety regulation includes an overview of the economics and the technology.

Economics

The processed food and beverage industry (SIC 20) is the nation's largest manufacturing sector. Approximately 380,000 firms process, wholesale and retail the nation's food supply. In 1993 the value of food and beverage industry shipments reached an estimated $404 billion. (Food and Beverages..., 1993).

Although the food distribution system is the country's largest marketing system, its present growth rate is below the rest of the economy. In 1980, the food sector employed 11.5 percent of U.S. workers and contributed 11 percent of the value added to the gross domestic product (GDP). A decade later in 1990 the food industry employed 9.5 percent of workers and its contribution to GDP fell to 9.5 percent (Gallo, 1990).

The slowed growth rate in the food industry can be attributed to several factors. Changing consumer demographics, increased automation and productivity, and economic conditions have had an effect. In 1993, the U.S. population grew by less than one percent and food expenditures, as a proportion of disposable income, declined to 11.4 percent. Dollar expenditures for food increased by three percent over the previous year to $647 billion. However, as the number of single person households increases, the population ages, and as more women enter the work force, more meals are being consumed away from home. Expenditures for food-away-from home accounted for 32.6 percent of food and beverage purchases in 1993 (Food and Beverages..., 1993).

The food market is internationalizing. U.S. firms' ownership of foreign food processing firms and direct investment in foreign food processing, wholesaling, and retailing firms more than doubled during the 1980's (Gallo, 1990). U.S. exports of food reached $22.5 billion in 1992. Exports of higher value-added foods such as frozen fruits and vegetables, ice cream, bakery, and breakfast cereal are increasing to meet the demands of a rising middle class in developing and emerging countries. Between 1989 and 1993, exports of higher value foods increased 16 percent annually (Food and Beverages..., 1993).

The food distribution system is highly diverse with size ranging from the local baker to the giant conglomerates (e.g., Phillip Morris Company, PepsiCo, RJR Nabisco). During the 1980's industry concentration increased, in part, because of the number of mergers and leveraged buyouts. Food processing experienced 2,500 of these transactions while wholesaling, retailing, and food service combined had over 1,600 mergers and buyouts. In spite of the increased concentration, the top 50 processing firms control only 48 percent of the market, the top 20 retailing firms control 36.5 percent and the top 50 food service[5] firms control just 22.3 percent.

Although the industry has become more concentrated, competition has intensified at all levels. This competition is reflected in an increasing number of new product introductions, consumer advertising expenditures, and retail promotions. Limited shelf space coupled with the high number of new introductions has led food retailers to command **slotting allowances**.[6] Manufacturers might pay $2 million in slotting fees to introduce a new product to the national market (Gallo, 1990).

Food firms are the largest advertisers spending more than $12 billion annually in direct advertising. In 1990, eating and drinking places and food stores each spent about $1.7 billion. Mass media expenditure for food processors was $6.3 billion and the redeemed value of manufacturer's coupons was estimated at over $2 billion (Gallo, 1990). In 1990, media advertising expenditures accounted for 30 percent of promotional dollars; nearly 45 percent was allocated to trade promotions to the retail industry and the remaining 25 percent went to consumer promotions (Donnelley, 1991).

Profits vary greatly from firm to firm within each segment of the industry. Mergers and leveraged buyouts in the 1980's increased debt, but also increased productivity and cost stability; modest growth contributed to increasing profits over the industry (Industry Surveys, 1993). Profit margins for the food industry as a whole were approximately 12.5 percent in 1992. This represents a steady increase since 1977 at which time the industry average profit margin was 9.1 percent (Food, Beverages..., 1993).

Technology: Complexity, Stability, Substitutes

Food processing technology is a large-batch and continuous-processing technology but it is not complex. New processing techniques such as irradiation, advances in plant biotechnology, and rapid method microbial testing combined with science-based inspection procedures are, however, increasing the complexity of food production. Also, growing evidence of the connection between food and health has led consumers to call for more information about the nutrients in foods they consume. And, recent outbreaks in food poisoning have accelerated changes shifting the burden of inspection and analysis away from the regulators to the food processing industry.

New and informative food labels may be more difficult for foreign food and beverage processors not accustomed to such extensive product analysis and disclosure requirements, particularly those required under the provisions of the **Nutritional Labeling and Education Act** (NLEA). The North American Free Trade Agreement will provide the

---

[5]Industry concentration figures (1987) are the most recent available (Gallo, 1994).

[6]**Slotting allowances** are fees paid to the retailer for shelf space allocation to new products. In addition to slotting allowances, some retailers are charging **"failure fees"** to recoup costs of removing failed new products from their distribution system (Gallo, 1990).

impetus for uniformity and harmonization of inspection procedures and standards as the agreement begins mutual tariff reductions between the United States and Mexico. Some view the new NLEA requirements as a barrier to trade that could be challenged by GATT and NAFTA (Food and Beverages..., 1993).

The structure of food retailing is changing. In 1992, non-traditional grocery sales outlets—hypermarkets, wholesale clubs, deep discounters, and food mass merchandisers accounted for seven percent of sales and approximately one percent of competing units. By 1997, non-traditional outlets are expected to account for 11 percent of sales and 1.5 percent of competing units. Non-traditional high volume retailers operate on low margins, but substantial profits are achieved through volume sales (Food and Beverages..., 1993).

AGENDA SETTING: A SAFE AND HEALTHFUL FOOD SUPPLY

The earliest government actions for consumer protection were centered on food safety. The federal food laws passed in 1906 (Pure Food and Drug Act and Meat Inspection Act) continue to be the basis for food regulation in the United States. The Pure Food and Drug Act, amended in 1930 and again in 1938 to become the Federal Food, Drug, and Cosmetic Act has remained virtually unchanged with the FDA serving as the lead federal agency. Within USDA, the Food Safety and Inspection Service (FSIS) administers a comprehensive system of inspection laws.

Over time, innovations in product formulations, processing, packaging, and distribution have vastly increased the number of food products which must be regulated. Since 1990 more than 10,000 new products have been introduced annually, and in 1991 there were 230,000 packaged food products on grocery store shelves (AER, 1994; Gallo, 1990; Food and Beverages..., 1993). Products are becoming technically more complex as new ingredients, additives, and processing techniques are introduced. Revolutions in food packaging and marketing are posing new challenges to food safety assurance (Hardy, 1990: 228).

Despite the years of growth and change in the food supply, the statutory structure for ensuring food safety has not changed. Since 1938 piecemeal amendments have been made to food safety laws, creating a patchwork of regulations involving numerous federal agencies. Inspection methods have not kept pace with the changes. FSIS still relies heavily on visual inspection while current technology allows scientists to measure micronutrients and very low levels of contaminants in foods—levels which formerly escaped detection. These changes point to a need to reexamine of established levels of **acceptable risk** as well a search for new control and inspection methods.

Recent public scares about food contamination such as the Alar pesticide residue and Chilean grape scare in 1989, and the more recent E. coli outbreaks associated with tainted hamburger have brought food safety to the forefront. Increasingly aware of the linkage between diet and health, consumers want, not only to be protected from hazards, but also they desire a food supply that will promote health and longevity. They want **"chemical free"** foods which are friendly to the environment and, finally, they want complete and accurate information on the foods they consume.

THE LAW AND AGENCY PROCEDURES

The **Food and Drug Administration** (FDA) and the **Food Safety and Inspection Service** (FSIS) are charged with primary responsibility for monitoring the safety and wholesomeness of the food supply. The regulatory approaches of the FDA and USDA differ significantly. The USDA's Food Safety and Inspection Service carries out mandatory and continuous inspection of all meat and poultry slaughtering and processing facilities. FSIS currently employs 9,411 full-time inspectors and 1,269 veterinary medical officers who monitor 6,675 firms.[7] By contrast, the FDA Center for Food Safety and Applied Nutrition (CFSAN) is responsible for monitoring all foods except meat, poultry, eggs, and liquor in interstate commerce. The FDA employs approximately 1,000 who monitor the more than 46,000 companies handling food (Schwade, 1994; Hardy, 1990; McWilliams, 1994).

FSIS AND FOOD SAFETY

Inspections procedures of the FDA and FSIS differ as mandated by law. The intensity of surveillance in the meat and poultry sector is unmatched anywhere else in the food system for reasons that have more to do with history than with science. In 1906 when the Federal Meat Inspection Act was passed, the major public health concerns were animal disease and filth. Scientific tools were limited and inspection depended largely on the keen senses of the inspectors. The system has evolved, but inspection is still predominantly visual. Animals are inspected before they are slaughtered and again during processing. Inspectors stand at carcass production lines and look for signs of disease including tumors, filth, and bruises (*Food Chemical News*, 1993-1994). This type of inspection cannot detect chemical or microbial contamination, the latter of which is the primary human health hazard present in the food supply.[8]

The heavy reliance on visual inspection of carcasses and lack of microbial testing by FSIS has received heavy criticism. According to a recent General Accounting Office report, continuing to use "inflexible statutory requirements and labor-intensive inspection procedures that are of limited value in detecting microbial pathogens, FSIS is not able to target its resources on the principle health risk associated with meat and poultry—microbial contamination" (FSIS Should..., 1994:41). Many large processing plants voluntarily conduct microbial testing, but such programs are too costly for smaller facilities and FSIS is unable to provide assistance or guidance to small processors. The

---

[7]According to Joe McWilliams, of the FSIS personnel office the number of inspectors increased by 160 following the well publicized E. coli outbreak in Washington state in January 1994.

[8]USDA announced stricter inspection standards for poultry in July 1994. In August the agency announced that a new rapid test had been developed to detect **"high levels"** of invisible bacteria on meat and poultry. The usefulness of the test is questionable. It cannot identify specific bacteria such as salmonella or E. coli 0157:H7, the contaminant in the "Jack-in-the-Box" hamburgers in January 1994, nor can it detect low levels of bacteria (Sugarman, 1994a).

agency has also been criticized for not building upon the information developed by plants through microbial tests to be able to provide assistance. FSIS has not collected, analyzed, or disseminated microbial testing information developed by the processors in which its inspections required periodical review of the plants' testing programs (FSIS Should..., 1994).

Since passage of the Wholesome Meat Act of 1967 and the Wholesome Poultry Products Act of 1968, products for sale in both interstate and intrastate commerce are subject to federal regulation.[9] Any state able to demonstrate that its inspection of meat plants was **equivalent** to the USDA was delegated the authority to make such inspections and received 50 percent of the cost through a contract agreement with USDA. As state budgets were cut, many states realized that they could opt out of this program, saving their 50 percent costs and USDA would be required to do the inspections (White Paper..., 1994). The state of Connecticut, for example, withdrew from the program in 1976 and saved $300,000 (Heslin, 1994).

FSIS not only inspects facilities, but its approval is required on the design of a meat processing facility, including such items as the placing of equipment and processing flows. Both materials of construction and individual pieces of equipment must be approved. Any ingredients added in processing and all product labels must be approved by the agency. The USDA has the authority to gain access to plant records, detain foods suspected of violations, shut down a piece of equipment, or shut down an entire plant with a court order (Hardy, 1990).

Following an outbreak of E. coli contamination, in January 1994,[10] USDA developed mandatory **Safe Handling Labels** to be placed on raw meat and poultry products. The final rule was published in the *Federal Register* on March 28, 1994. The Safe Handling Instructions include five statements and accompanying pictographs.[11] Products intended for further processing by an inspected establishment as well as some cooked products such as sausages are exempt from the label requirement. (Safe Handling Labels..., 1994).

FDA AND FOOD SAFETY

The FDA has two broad areas of authority in food safety: (1) inspection of food products and food processing/handling facilities, and (2) the approval of new foods, food additives, and pesticides. The FDA inspectors are authorized to cover every link in the food chain including farms, warehouses, ports of entry, processing plants, transportation

---

[9]Prior to the 1967 legislation, only meat products to be sold interstate were subject to FSIS inspection.

[10]This E. coli 0157:H7 outbreak was traced to the consumption of undercooked hamburgers served at selected Jack-in-the-Box restaurants. The outbreak affected more than 500 people in Washington, Idaho, California and Nevada and resulted in four deaths.

[11]"Safe Handling Instructions—This product was prepared from inspected and passed meat and/or poultry. Some food products may contain bacteria that could cause illness if the product is mishandled or cooked improperly. For you protection, follow these safe handling instructions. Keep refrigerated or frozen. Thaw in refrigerator or microwave. Keep raw meat and poultry separate from other foods. Wash working surfaces (including cutting boards), utensils, and hands after touching raw meat or poultry. Cook thoroughly. Keep hot foods hot. Refrigerate leftovers immediately or discard."

vehicles, restaurants, and supermarkets. The frequency of FDA inspections varies widely across food sectors. High-risk sectors, such as certain imported foods and facilities with a history of violations, receive the most attention. In FY'93 the FDA's Center for Food Safety and Applied Nutrition issued 291 warning letters, ordered 663 recalls and 47 seizures, and obtained seven injunctions and two prosecutions (FDA Internal..., 1994).

Food Product Inspection

Food Products are inspected for contamination or adulteration which would render products unsafe for the general public. Food is **adulterated** if it is produced in an unsanitary plant, contains ingredients or additives harmful to human consumption, or contains decomposed, putrid, or filthy portions (Porter and Earl, 1992). The amount of adulteration or contamination permitted varies according to the source and type of contamination. Some foods contain contaminants that cannot be avoided. Freshwater fish, for example, often contains high levels of polychlorinated biphenls (PCBs), and peanut butter contains alphatoxins; both are hazardous to human health. Such contamination is regulated by **threshold levels** which are generally measured in terms of acceptable number of parts per million (ppm). **Unintended ingredients** such as pesticide residues, rodent hairs, and package residues are also regulated by threshold levels.

Food products adulteration can present a health/safety hazard, a reduction in wholesomeness, or both. The Pure Food and Drug Act of 1906 addressed health/safety adulteration. The Federal Food, Drug and Cosmetic Act of 1938 addressed **wholesomeness** of the food supply by giving the agency powers to engage in economic regulation, to set legally enforceable food standards, and to establish affirmative labeling requirements (Hardy, 1990: 229). Consequently, the FDA examines food products' adulteration from both wholesomeness and safety perspectives. A recent example was the Chilean grape scare of 1989 in which the imported grapes were contaminated with cyanide. By contrast, several cases involving adulteration of juices diluted with sugar water or less expensive juices represent reductions in wholesomeness and **economic fraud**. Yet, another condition of economic fraud occurs when a manufacturer **misbrands** food. In this later instance, the food is not adulterated, but the consumer is deceived. In 1993 the FDA seized 2,400 cases of Procter & Gamble's Citrus Hill orange juice for using **"fresh"** on the label when the product was, in fact, produced from concentrate (Colford, 1993).

The fish and shellfish industry represents a high risk sector. Seafood is known to carry pathogens and to contain natural toxins, parasites, and chemical contaminants such as nickel cadmium, chromium, and lead (FDA Issues..., 1993). Oversight of the seafood industry historically has been weak. The FDA reportedly inspected less than one percent of domestic and about three percent of imported fish. The voluntary inspection of the National Marine Fisheries covers less than 10 percent of domestic consumption (Hardy 1990). Consumption of seafood has been on the rise and public perception of its safety has been declining (Survey: Variance..., 1994). In 1991 the FDA established the Office of Seafood (OSF) with a 60 percent increase in funding for seafood inspection (Foulke, 1993). OSF is the first federal office to establish guidelines for **Hazard Analysis Critical**

Control Points (HACCP), a science-based safety assurance methodology for monitoring product safety.

Inspection of Food Processing and Handling Facilities

Inspections of food processing and handling facilities are not continuous and ongoing as those of FSIS.[12] The FDA also lacks the legal powers to gain access to plant records, detain foods suspected of violations (except at ports of entry), withdraw inspection, and close facilities.[13] For plant or facilities violations, **warning letter** is commonly sent to a firm "alleging deviations from **Good Manufacturing Practice** regulations in the...(type of facility)." Violative products can be detained by an embargo available through cooperating state agencies or court **injunctions**. In 1992 the Justice Department brought more than 30 injunctions on behalf of the FDA (Justice Department..., 1993).

In 1992 the FDA devoted 255 staff years to inspecting 53,000 food stores (FDA, FSIS Merger..., 1993). The agency's jurisdiction extends to 48,000 facilities which process and handle foods. The FDA also contracts a share of inspections to state inspectors. In 1972 the FDA was given $5.4 million to contract with states for inspection services in the area of basic food sanitation (White Paper..., 1994). The number of inspections contracted to the states varies from year to year and from state to state—depending somewhat on the states' resources available to complete the inspections. Over the past few years, budgetary constraints have led to a decrease in the number of state inspectors. For example, since 1986 the number of state inspectors in the food division of the Connecticut Department of Consumer Protection has dropped from 38 to 15 and in the past year Arizona has lost 14 inspectors (McGuire, 1994; Heslin, 1994).

Food Additives

Food additives are substances added to food in processing to delay spoilage, improve nutritional value, enhance taste, reduce cost, or enhance other characteristics. The **Food Additives Amendment** (also known as the **Delaney Clause**) of 1958 requires that only those additives that do not cause cancer in man or animal be generally recognized as safe for human consumption. The amendment requires that manufacturers prove the safety of new food additives prior to placing them in food products for human consumption. The 600 additives in common use prior to January 1, 1958, which had not been found to cause cancer were therefore **"generally recognized as safe"** and comprised the **GRAS list**. Food products which contained an additive found to cause cancer in either man or animal were removed from the market. Unlike other areas of food regulation where small traces of foreign matter or minute contamination is permissible, food additives found to be carcinogenic face an **absolute zero standard**.

---

[12]Resources of the FDA have not kept pace with increasing responsibilities. Current resources have dropped to a level where the agency can only inspect food processing facilities on average about once every eight years (GAO: FDA..., 1994).

[13]Many states have power to seize food, detain equipment, and close facilities. FDA sometimes relies on cooperating state agencies to take action (Hardy,1990: 240).

At the time the Delaney Amendment was passed, consumers' consumption of processed foods was increasing, and the zero cancer risk standard was a reasonable approach to regulation. Since 1958, however, the ability to detect minute amounts of a chemical in food has far outpaced the ability to assess the effects of tiny residues on humans. Recently developed chromatographic separation techniques make it possible to detect parts per trillion of almost any chemical. With the current level of technology, few substances on the GRAS list would meet the standard (Hardy, 1990).

The **zero cancer risk** of Delaney is particularly controversial on the issue of pesticide residues. A 1970 amendment to the **Federal Fungicide, Insectitide, Pesticide, and Rodenticide Act (FIPRA)** transferred the pesticide program to the Environmental Protection Agency (EPA). The EPA has been granted the authority to set threshold levels for pesticide residues, but the EPA is also required to uphold Delaney. A pesticide residue can be allowed on a fresh fruit or vegetable if that pesticide has a tolerance set by the EPA under Sec. 408 of the Federal Food, Drug & Cosmetic Act or if the EPA has granted an exemption from the tolerance. By contrast, if a residue is present on a raw commodity which is further processed, the Delaney clause takes precedence and the zero tolerance standard is enforced. As a result of further amendments to FIPRA (1972, 1978, 1988), few new pesticides were registered during the 1980's because of the Delaney clause, and as a result older, less safe, but GRAS approved pesticides have continued in use (Winter, 1993). In October 1994, the EPA announced that it was starting the process (because the EPA lost a court decision) to take action to review and possibly eliminate over 30 pesticides.

Food additives which are toxic or found to be allergens are not subject to the Delaney amendment. These are not banned from the market but treated either through warning labels or through allowable threshold levels. For example, in 1986 the FDA adopted a regulation limiting the use of sulfiting agents. The regulation specifies that sulfites must be declared on the label if they are present above a given level (Porter and Earl, 1992).[14]

WHOLESOMENESS OF THE FOOD SUPPLY

In addition to monitoring food safety, the FDA and USDA are charged with responsibility for overseeing the wholesomeness of the food supply. The **Federal Food, Drug, and Cosmetic Act** (FFD&C) of 1938 gave FDA the authority to define **"standards of identity"** for common foods, that is to specify the ingredients for such foods as mayonnaise, ketchup, jelly, and fruit juices. FFD&C also specified that every processed, packaged food contain the name of the food, its net weight, and the name and address of the manufacturer or distributor. In addition, a list of ingredients was required for those foods not having standards of identity (FDCA; P.L. 75-717). In 1973 FDA and USDA issued regulations requiring nutritional labeling on foods containing one or more added nutrients or whose label or advertising included claims about the food's nutritional

---

[14]In 1984 the FDA required that sodium content be added to the list of optional nutrients on the nutrition label (Kurtzweil, 1993).

properties or its usefulness in the daily diet. Thus, nutritional labeling was voluntary but prescribed a standard format (FDA, 1973).

NUTRITION EDUCATION AND INFORMATION

In 1946, USDA identified seven basic food groups on which its dietary guidelines were based; in the 1950's this was reduced to the "Basic Four." Regulations for nutritional labeling established in 1973, were based on these guidelines. The primary focus during at the time was on "getting enough nutrients." As more has been learned about human nutrient requirements, the dietary guidelines have changed. Since 1977, the focus of dietary guidelines has been directed toward avoiding excess intakes of food components linked to chronic diseases (Welsh, Davis, and Shaw, 1992).

Consumers have become more interested in nutrition through the years. They are generally aware of the link between diet and health and are increasingly concerned about food additives and pesticides. Many are searching for pure and natural products which they believe to be free of the hazards of chemicals introduced into foods. They are looking to reduce fat, cholesterol, and sodium intake while demanding the good taste which these nutrients contribute (Fuller, 1993). In the 1980's food processors began to emphasize nutritional benefits and utilize health claims to promote their products.

Consumer interest, marketing strategies, and mounting evidence linking food and health led to efforts to reform food labeling policy. By the late 1980's, the dietary guidelines had changed substantially. New guidelines then called for a diet that is sufficient in nutrients without excesses.[15] Improved food label information was viewed as a way to assist consumers in making food choices that would be more healthful. In 1989 the FDA published an **Advance Notice of Proposed Rulemaking** and, with FSIS, held hearings to find out what consumers, food manufacturers, and health professionals wanted on the food label (FDA, 1989).

In November 1990, the **Nutrition Labeling and Education Act (NLEA)** became law. This legislation has been referred to as one of the government's most aggressive initiatives to help people eat better (Sugarman, 1994b). The NLEA requires mandatory nutritional labeling on nearly all processed foods regulated by the FDA and authorizes appropriate health claims on the labels of such products.[16] **Flavorings** and **color additives** must be identified by name, such as FD&C Yellow No 6 (Kurtzwell, 1993). In 1991 the FSIS joined the FDA in announcing proposals to implement many of the law's provisions.

---

[15]The USDA and DHHS 1990 Guidelines are: (1) eat a variety of foods, (2) maintain a healthy weight, (3) choose a diet low in fat, saturated fat, and cholesterol, (4) choose a diet with plenty of fruits and vegetables (5) use sugars only in moderation, (6) use salt and sodium only in moderation, and (7) if you drink alcoholic beverages, do so in moderation (Saltos, 1993).

[16]Exemptions include plain coffee and tea, flavorings, and spices which contain virtually no nutrients and foods prepared on site, such as bakery, restaurants food, bulk food that is not resold, and foods produced by small businesses. A **small business** is defined as one with food sales of less than $50,000 a year or total sales of $500,000. FSIS defines a small business as one that employs 500 or fewer people and produces no more than a certain amount of poundage (Kurtzweil, 1993).

The mandatory labeling requirements of FSIS and FDA are similar.[17] The regulations take up 961 pages in the *Federal Register* of January 6, 1993 including 900 pages for the FDA's 27 final regulations and three proposals, and 61 pages for the FSIS's one final regulation and one proposal (Mermelstein, 1993).

NLEA Calls for Information and Education About Nutrition

The NLEA calls for activities to educate consumers about nutrition and using information on the food labels. It also requires nutritional label information to be conveyed so that consumers can understand the food's relative significance in the context of a total daily diet. Thus, it was necessary to educate the public on the components of a **healthful diet** (dietary guidelines), and then to develop a common language to link diet to the nutritional label.

The Human Nutrition Information Service of USDA developed the **Food Guide Pyramid**, a graphic illustration of the dietary guidelines. The graphic organizes foods into five groups and conveys three essential elements of a healthy diet: the proportion of food to choose from each major food group; the moderate or restrictive use of fats, oils, and sugars; and the variety of foods to be consumed. The American Heart Association, the American Dietetic Association, the Center for Science in the Public Interest, and other professional groups concerned with health and nutrition have applauded the graphic Pyramid, particularly for its clear representation on the proportion of foods comprising a healthful diet (Food Guide Pyramid..., 1992).[18]

In developing the Pyramid, research was conducted to establish nutritional goals, set serving sizes, develop **nutrient profiles** (nutrients one would expect from an average serving), and determine the number of servings for a healthful diet. The goals for some foods were based on the **Recommended Daily Allowances (U.S. RDAs)** and on the Dietary Guidelines for Americans. Because not all foods had such reference values, new classifications and new terminology were developed. The U.S. RDAs were replaced by **Recommended Daily Intake (RDI)**. The **Recommended Daily Value (RDV)** designates levels of nutrients for which no set of standards previously existed (e.g., fat, cholesterol). The RDI and RDV combine to form the Daily Value. The new term, **Daily Value (DV)** serves as the common language linking the dietary guidelines to the nutritional label.

The New Food Label

The nutrition panel on the new food label includes a revised list of nutrients (selected for their relationship to current health concerns), uniform serving sizes across all product lines, and the nutrients must be listed in terms of the "% Daily Value" based on 2,000 and 2,500 calorie diets. Acceptable nutrient claims such as "lite" and "lean" are clearly defined by the FDA. A complete list of ingredients must appear on all processed food packages.

---

[17]One exception to the similarity is that FDA permits seven specified health claims and FSIS does not (Nutritional Labeling, 1993).

[18]A major criticism of the "Basic Four" was that it communicated a message that the diet should comprise equal amounts of the four food groups.

The standards of identity for foods such as peanut butter or jelly no longer exist.[19] Also, FDA-certified color additives and flavor enhancers must be identified by name (Kurtzweil, 1993). To encourage a healthier diet, standards have been developed for voluntary labeling of raw fruits, vegetables, and fish (Focus on Food Labeling, 1993).

IMPACT OF POLICY DECISIONS

Food policy decisions affect the daily lives of all citizens. To the extent that food laws are amended in response to changing environmental factors, policy decisions are generally beneficial, but their implementation is costly. The FDA estimates that new nutritional labels are expected to cost its regulated processors $1.4-$2.3 billion and cost government $163 million over the next 20 years.[20] Nutritional labeling on meat and poultry products are projected to cost the industry between $218-$272 billion over the same period. The potential benefits of decreased rates chronic diseases such as high blood pressure, osteoporosis, and allergic reactions to food will well exceed the costs (Mermelstein, 1993).

The American Meat Institute estimates that labeling for Safe Handling Instructions will cost the entire meat and poultry sector $135 million annually in addition to one-time, up-front costs of $50-$100 million. The annual cost of foodborne illness in the U.S. ranges from $5.2 to $6.1 billion, with $3.9 to $4.3 billion attributable to meat and poultry products. If the labels are 10 percent effective, the reduction in cases of food borne illness has been estimated to result in savings of $4.1 and $9.2 billion against costs of $757.4 to $876.4 million (Safe Handling Instructions, 1993).

Implementation of **Hazard Analysis Critical Control Point** (HACCP) procedures for monitoring food processing will require fewer state and federal resources, and will put much more of the burden of safety assurance on industry. Implementation and maintenance of these systems will be costly and difficult. Processes for identifying and correcting hazards, identifying critical control points, and monitoring procedures need to be developed. These will require new equipment for monitoring and recordkeeping along with more highly trained personnel (Hardy, 1990; USDA FDA HACCP..., 1993).

CURRENT ISSUES

Growing awareness of the link between diet and health, outbreaks of foodborne illness, new technologies, and internationalization of the marketplace are shaping food

---

[19]The former standards of identity required that foods, which did not follow the standard recipe, be labeled **"imitation."** Thus, a jelly which did not contain 45% sugar could not legally be called a "jelly," but rather it had to be called a "spread" or an "imitation jelly."

[20]This may be a conservative estimate. Others have indicated that the cost will more likely be closer to $7.0 billion. Firms must analyze their recipes, redesign labels and packaging, and dispose of obsolete packaging materials. Laboratory analysis can cost up to $2,000 per product. One firm doing an analysis estimated it will cost about $1,800 to relabel a saltine cracker package (Knight-Ridder, 1994).

policy. Controversy surrounds such issues as irradiation of meat and poultry, food additives and pesticides, vitamins and supplements, and genetically engineered foods. In addition to substantive issues, alternatives to the present regulatory structure, as it has existed, are being examined.

Cohesive Food Policy

Conflicting regulations and overlapping authority of nine regulatory agencies[21] at the federal level have made it nearly impossible to develop a cohesive food policy. Alternative proposals to combine all food safety enforcement under one agency are currently under consideration. A single agency would be better able to develop policies and procedures to be universally applied across the system and to more easily harmonize with those of other countries.

Diet and Disease

Awareness of the possible effect of diet in reducing the risk of disease has led to an increase in consumer interest in supplements and herbal treatments. A recent FDA report invokes both food additive and drug law provisions for herbal treatments. **Health claims for supplements** that are identical to those granted for foods under NLEA are currently permitted. Supplements are required to contain a **nutrition facts panel**, similar to that on conventional foods. There is considerable evidence that health claims made for some supplements are not substantiated, and that some herbal treatments have been found to be unsafe (Supplement Industry..., 1993; FDA, 1993; Farley, 1993). Legislation is pending in Congress to exempt health claims on nutritional supplements from FDA regulations, and the Food and Drug Administration is firmly against any such exemption.

Foodborne Illnesses

Recent outbreaks of **foodborne illness** have brought attention to the inadequacy of USDA's visual inspection policies. Science-based HACCP principles, which focus the identification of potential hazards and their points of control during processing, are amenable to standardization. Canada expects HACCP to be fully implemented in its food processing facilities this year. FDA and USDA are working on efforts to shift toward HACCP processes during this decade. The World Food Organization has endorsed HACCP processes as being amenable to the development of equivalency for food inspection and certification in international trade (HACCP, ISO 9000..., 1993).

---

[21]The nine agencies include: (1) FDA and (2) Public Health Service in HHS; the (3) Agricultural Marketing Service, (4) Animal and Plant Health Inspection Service, and (5) Federal Grain Inspection Service and FSIS in the Department of Agriculture; (6) National Oceanic and Atmospheric Administration and (7) the National Marine Fisheries Service in the Department of Commerce; (8) Bureau of Alcohol, Tobacco and Firearms in the Department of Treasury; and (9) the U.S. Environmental Protection Agency (Hardy, 1990:231).

Irradiation

Irradiation is recognized as having both safety and economic benefits. Contamination of meat and poultry and resulting foodborne illness could be significantly reduced by irradiation (Oliver, 1993). Both FDA and USDA have approved its use for meat and poultry, and a recent World Health Organization study reaffirmed its safety (Need for..., 1993). Food scientists posit that irradiation is an alternative to the use of fumigants; it can reduce post-harvest food losses, ensure hygienic quality, and facilitate wider trade (Pszcozola, 1993). Some groups question irradiation and suggest that it can have serious side effects (Water & Food..., 1993), although evidence remains lacking.

Food Additives and Pesticides

Policies on food additives and pesticides are also being reevaluated. The technical ability to detect the presence of substances in "parts per trillion," has led to a reconsideration of the "zero risk" requirement imposed by the Delaney Amendment. Proposals to the Congress have suggested that a **"negligible risk"** standard replace the absolute "zero tolerance," particularly for pesticide residues. The "zero cancer risk," unique to this country, poses a potential barrier to the distribution of food products throughout North America (Miller, 1993).

Biotechnology

Gene splicing technology has the potential to create crops with resistance to disease and pests, and having tolerance to various environmental factors, thus reducing reliance on pesticides. Biotechnology is capable of producing foods with health benefits and longer shelf lives (Olempska-Beer, Kuznesof, DiNovi, and Smith 1993; Sudduth, 1993). A bioengineered tomato was approved by the FDA in 1994 and a banana awaits approval. Current FDA policy does not require labeling of genetically altered foods so long as they do not contain allergens that would normally not be present. Recently, Bovine seratropin (rBST) for cattle to increase milk production has been approved by USDA without a labeling requirement. Uncertainty about the safety of this technology has led several states to preempt the federal regulation and require labeling on diary products from cattle treated with rBST (BST Labeling..., 1994).

International Acceptance of Food Products

The acceptability of technological advancements, the standards for ingredients and labeling, and tolerances as well as assessments of risk are currently being considered for acceptability by the international marketplace. In 1992 the value of U.S. food processing exports was $22.7 billion; exports exceeded imports by $0.7 billion (AER, 1994). The **General Agreement on Trade and Tariffs** (GATT), which is to be replaced the World Trade Organization (WTO), and the **North American Free Trade Agreement** (NAFTA) call for a gradual reduction in tariffs allowing free exchange across North American borders. Policies and regulations need to be harmonized with the international community and ISO 9000 standards will have to be met for our products to be marketable in the European Union and beyond.

FUTURE POLICY DIRECTIONS

Future food policy will be molded by international food standards and developing technologies as well as by food growers and processors along with consumers and public interest groups. New food legislation must provide for regulations that integrate all components of the food system and deal with all aspects of safety including labels and standards. Policy decisions must consider the adequacy of enforcement and must be in harmony with the international food market (Miller, 1993).

The development of new food technologies will depend on maintaining the balance between protecting consumers' health and fostering product developments. New substances which lower the risk of disease do not currently fit well into the existing categories for food and food ingredients. Also, a new regulatory framework may need to be developed to adequately assess novel ingredients, functional foods, and new packaging technologies which will raise food safety issues not heretofore considered (Food Safety..., 1994).

Novel ingredients are macro ingredients used as a substitute for or to replace majority dietary components such as fats and sugars. Safety and nutrition concerns will center on identifying long term effects of novel ingredients. Some scientists are concerned that the consumption of novel macro ingredients could cause adverse nutritional effects. Because current law does not permit weighing potential benefits against risk when reviewing food additives, it would be difficult to conduct human tests.

Foods formulated with additional vitamins and nutrients are often claimed to have health benefits; this will remain controversial. There also are concerns about the safety of increasing the consumption of certain naturally occurring food chemicals that could prove to be toxic to humans. These new products, termed **neutraceuticals** or **functional foods**, blur the distinction between food and drugs. The level of scientific substantiation that these foods will be required to demonstrate has yet to be determined.

New packaging technologies raise new questions about safety. For example, new **"modified atmosphere refrigerated packaging"** retards the growth of microorganisms that cause evidence of food spoilage, but does not necessarily eliminate organisms that can survive in a refrigerated environment. **Recyclable packages** raise the question of whether trace amounts of chemicals and other substances could remain in the recycled material after it is made into food-use packaging. In addition, limitations in FDA authority could impair the agency's ability to regulate food packaging technologies (GAO recommends..., 1993).

Food products produced by new technologies will be imported into the United States. The ability of current regulatory agencies to regulate such imported foods is uncertain. Unless these foods are so labeled, it may be difficult to distinguish them from traditional products. Internationally accepted standards and certifications will need to be developed for foods developed by new technologies and, as for all other food products, standards will need to be harmonized across international borders.

SUMMARY

A summary of food regulation is shown in Table 10.1. Food safety regulation has undergone dramatic changes within the past few years, and continuing change can be expected into the next century. Regulatory change will be fueled by countervailing interests on the supply side and the demand side. On the **supply side**, food growers and processors will be requesting approvals for products developed by new technologies (e.g., irradiation, bioengineering). Suppliers will also be clamoring for harmonization of standards to facilitate international trade. On the **demand side**, single-issue constituency groups will exert pressure on the FDA and FSIS for stricter guidelines and increased oversight of the industry. Current calls for labeling of food "treated with radiation" and dairy products produced from rBST treated cattle are merely a foreshadowing of what is to come. Special interest groups are likely to seek labeling of pesticides, fumigants, waxes, antibiotics, and other substances used in food production. In addition, people with food sensitivities may call for easy identification of foods that are milk-free, gluten-free, and monosodium glutamate-free.

The food industry is multi-tiered with numerous firms at each level of the distribution chain, from the farmer to the processor to the retailers. At almost every level, there is some niche within the industry that has few barriers to entry. Occupational licensing is virtually absent; frequently no educational preparation is required. For example, farm produced fruits and vegetables, jams and jellies, and baked goods are routinely sold at local farmers' markets without oversight. Food served in home day care facilities and small group homes for the elderly is not routinely monitored by state health inspectors, unless a problem with foodborne illness occurs. Such additional needs can be placed against the current difficulty of overseeing the more than 380,000 reporting firms that process, wholesale, and retail food.

Within the subsystems, the FDA and USDA exercise control over the food industry. Both agencies have developed expertise and leadership. Over the past decade their policies have become more cohesive. Dietary guidelines and food labeling, for example, have been built upon the combined expertise of the agencies. Because of the salience of the food industry, the agencies have attracted consumer protection advocates. Those advocates with strong leadership skills are often able to tip the balance of regulatory activity in favor of the consumer. State agencies cooperate with the FDA and USDA by enforcing policies and conducting inspections. The benefit to consumers from the state agency activities varies.

Agency control is counterbalanced by industry and nonindustry coalitions. Food and agriculture coalitions are well organized, well financed, and have traditionally exerted strong influence over regulatory activities. This is particularly true within USDA. Consumer advocates point to such actions as the recent USDA approval of rBST growth hormone to increase milk production and to the FDA's approval of the bioengineered tomato. Both were approved without a labeling requirement to inform consumers these foods were modified.

Although nonindustry coalitions are generally viewed as weak, underfunded, and single-issue oriented, they appear to be gaining momentum, and the consumer's voice is being heard. At the state level, for example, Vermont has responded to consumer concerns

Table 10.1   A Summary of Consumer Protection

Economics	
Ease of entry	Easy
Number of firms	380,000
Profits	Vary
Technology	
Complexity	Moderate
Stability	Low
Substitutes	High
Subsystem	
Bureau control	Strong
Industry coalition	Strong
Nonindustry coalition	Weak
Bureaucratic Resources:	
Expertise	Moderate
Cohesion	High
Leadership	Moderate
Legislative authority:	
Goals	General
Coverage	All
Sanctions	Good
Procedures	Fair
Impact of macropolitical actors	
Congress	Weak
President	Weak
Courts	Weak

by requiring labeling of milk from cows treated with rBST. The Clinton administration has called for stricter food safety and inspection standards, and serious consideration is being given to combining all food regulatory activities under one agency, an agency outside of USDA.

The macropolitical actors exert a weak influence on the direction of food regulation. The legislative authority over the food industry is guided by the goal of providing a safe and wholesome food supply that is affordable to the consumer and profitable to the producer. Congress has given broad powers to FDA and to USDA to oversee the operation of virtually all sectors of the food industry. The trend since the Reagan administration has been toward national uniformity in food safety legislation, with states cooperating in carrying out the legislative mandates. Over the past few years, however, states are once again beginning to legislate on issues that are unique to their jurisdictions.

The generally nonpolitical environment of consumer protection is becoming more important in forging the direction of food industry regulation. Both technology and economics are expected to become more important in the future. Foods produced with the aid of new technologies will reshape definitional standards. Technological advances in testing and detection will change modes of food inspection. With the implementation of HACCP methods the burden of inspection will be shifted from the regulatory agency to the food processor. This shift is at least partially attributable to the decline in government resources for inspection. Those who reap the profits from the food industry will be expected to bear a higher proportion of the costs for ensuring the safety of the food supply. Furthermore, as the nonpolitical environment becomes more dominant, the adversarial relationship between the regulatory agencies and the industry will become more cooperative. Industry and regulatory agencies will be required to work together to ensure a safe and wholesome food supply.

Chapter 11
Consumer Product Safety Regulation

Mary Ellen R. Fise[1]

The Consumer Product Safety Commission (CPSC) is one of the most important consumer agencies in terms of having the ability to affect American citizens, through the products they use, each and every day of their lives. Young or old, rich or poor, all consumers use many of the products within CPSC's jurisdiction prodigiously throughout their lives. One of the youngest consumer agencies (it just celebrated its 20th anniversary), it is still struggling to establish an identity—both with the many industries it regulates and with the American public as a whole. Like many "Twenty-something" year-olds, the CPSC has achieved some accomplishments for which it can be proud, but still has a long span of challenges ahead.

THE SUBSYSTEM

This examination of the subsystem of consumer product safety regulation includes an overview of the Consumer Product Safety Commission and its program areas.

The Agency

The **Consumer Product Safety Commission (CPSC)** is an independent regulatory agency charged with protecting consumers from hazards associated with an estimated 15,000 different consumer products. These include items used in and around the house, school, or in recreation, but exclude those regulated by other federal agencies, such as

---

[1]Mary Ellen R. Fise is Product Safety Director of Consumer Federation of America. In this position she represents consumers before Congress and the regulatory agencies on a variety of consumer health and safety issues. In 1992, she served on the Clinton administration transition team on the Consumer Product Safety Commission. Fise has also worked for the National Consumers League, the public interest law firm of Swankin & Turner, and the Maryland Public Interest Research Group. She has a bachelor of science degree in consumer economics from the University of Maryland and a law degree from the University of Baltimore. She is the co-author of *The Childwise Catalog* (Harper Collins, 3rd edition, 1993), a consumer guide for parents.

food, drugs, cars, and boats.[2] In other words, most of the products consumers use or are exposed to on a daily basis—whether they are their toasters, carpeting, clothing, lawn mowers, or children's toys, for example—are CPSC's responsibility. Injuries and deaths associated with products used in the home are staggering. In 1993, for example, there were an estimated 18.9 million injuries, 6.6 million disabling injuries, and 22,500 deaths that occurred unintentionally in the home (National Safety Council, Accidents Facts, 1994 Edition, 98). Many of these incidents are related to products used in the home and result in billions of dollars of health care costs and property damage.

Congress established the CPSC in 1972 in order "to protect the public against unreasonable risks of injury associated with consumer products" (15 U.S.C. 2051). In addition to this purpose, the agency's enabling legislation, the **Consumer Product Safety Act**, also includes the following purposes: to assist consumers in evaluating the comparative safety of consumer products; to develop uniform safety standards for consumer products and to minimize conflicting state and local regulations; and to promote research and investigation into the causes and prevention of product-related deaths, illnesses, and injuries" (15 U.S.C. 2051(b)).

The agency administers six acts (see below). CPSC has the authority to **set mandatory standards**, **ban products**, **order recalls** of unsafe products, or **institute labeling requirements**. The agency also provides information to the public about hazardous products. CPSC learns about product-related injuries and deaths through a variety of sources, including the National Electronic Injury Surveillance System, consumer complaints, in-depth investigations by CPSC staff, and other data bases and sources.

Leadership of the agency is vested in a chairman and commissioners. The Consumer Product Safety Act provides for presidential appointment of five commissioners, with one commissioner designated by the president as chairman; the commissioners elect a vice chairman. In order to foster independence, no more than three commissioners can be affiliated with the same political party. At this writing, there were only three commissioners serving; there are two vacancies, leaving the agency at its statutory minimum needed to take action.

CPSC is headquartered in Bethesda, MD, suburb of Washington, D.C. The agency has three regional offices—New York, Chicago and San Francisco.

Within the agency, there are the Offices of the Secretary, Congressional Relations, General Counsel, Inspector General, Equal Employment, Budget, Planning and Evaluation, Information and Public Affairs, Hazard Identification and Reduction, and Compliance and Enforcement. Key professional staff directing these offices include: an Executive Director, General Counsel, seven Associate Executive Directors, the Director of the Office of Program Management and Budget, and the Director of the Office of Information and Public Affairs.

---

[2]See for example, Chapter 9 on Regulating Drugs, Chapter 10 on Food Safety Regulation, Chapter 12 on Automobile Safety Regulation, and Chapter 7 on Environmental Protection. In addition to foods and drugs, the Food and Drug Administration also has jurisdiction over cosmetics and medical devices. Other agencies that affect consumer product safety include the Federal Aviation Administration (airplanes), the U.S. Coast Guard (boats), and the Bureau of Alcohol, Tobacco and Firearms (firearms).

Program Areas

The agency has three key program areas: (1) Hazard Identification and Reduction, (2) Compliance and Enforcement, and (3) Information and Public Affairs.

The **Office of Hazard Identification and Reduction** has two separate programs. **Hazard Identification and Analysis** is responsible for the collection and analysis of consumer injury and death data. These data are analyzed to determine whether more investigation is needed and preliminarily whether hazard reduction strategies would be appropriate. **Hazard Assessment and Reduction** takes the data developed by the Identification and Analysis program and develops solutions (such as a standard, ban or labeling requirement) to address the hazards. Alternatively, the CPSC may pursue a **non-regulatory solution**, such as providing information about the hazard to the public.

Both the Hazard Identification and Analysis and Hazard Assessment and Reduction programs rely upon the Directorates for Epidemiology, Economic Analysis, Engineering Sciences, and Health Sciences for relevant technical, environmental, economic, and social impacts of projects and proposed solutions.

The **Compliance and Enforcement** staff supervises compliance and administrative enforcement activity under all administered acts, and reviews proposed standards and rules with respect to their enforceability. This office is also responsible for identifying and acting on safety hazards in consumer products already in distribution, promoting industry compliance with existing rules, and conducting litigation before an administrative law judge. It also directs the enforcement efforts of the field offices, monitors corrective action plans, and enforces statutory provisions requiring firms to identify and report product defects which could present possible safety hazards.

The **Information and Public Affairs** program is responsible for the development, implementation, and evaluation of a comprehensive national information and public affairs program designed to promote product safety. The office manages the CPSC toll-free Hotline which accepts consumer complaint information and gives out information on product recalls and other safety issues. Implementation of the commission's media program nationwide and serving as the agency's spokesperson are also functions of this office.

THE HISTORY OF THE CONSUMER PRODUCT SAFETY COMMISSION

CPSC has had a checkered history in its first 20 years of existence. Because the regulation of consumer product hazards is often complex, the agency has had to struggle to develop technical expertise. That struggle has been complicated by the fact that the agency often has to rely on industry for information. Simultaneously it has experienced a turnover of chairmen and/or commissioners, severe budget and staff cuts, and congressional amendment of its procedures for promulgation of safety rules. These roadblocks were not those envisioned by the panel that recommended the formation of the agency.

President Lyndon Johnson appointed a **National Commission on Product Safety** in 1968 to investigate the problems of product safety. In its June 1970 report, this commission documented numerous dangers involving consumer products. It found that 20 million persons were injured each year in using consumer products, 10,000 persons were permanently disabled, and 30,000 were killed. The annual monetary cost of these accidents was estimated to be $5.5 billion (Pittle, 1976: 131). The National Commission on Product Safety argued that **industry self-regulation** was "chronically inadequate" and that certification programs by independent laboratories were weakened because they depended on industry for operating funds (Bureau of National Affairs, 1973: 23). The chairperson of the National Commission on Product Safety testified before Congress that an effective administrative agency could prevent as many as 4 million accidents and 6,000 deaths a year.

Alternative Proposals for a Product Safety Agency

Immediately after the report of the National Commission on Product Safety, bills to create a Consumer Product Safety Commission were introduced in both houses of Congress. In 1971, President Nixon tried to head off strong legislation by proposing educational programs in the Department of Health, Education, and Welfare (HEW) rather than a new regulatory agency (Bureau of National Affairs, 1973: 27). Nixon's proposal was ignored by Congress.

General Hazards Targeted Instead of Specific

The major issue in 1971 was not whether to create a product safety regulator but what kind to create. The Nixon administration and business leaders favored regulation by existing departments (characterized by the National Commission on Product Safety as limited). Senator Magnuson and consumer advocates favored a new independent commission. Under Magnuson's leadership, the Senate Commerce Committee reported a strong bill that included not only consumer products but also transferred regulation of food, drugs, cosmetics, and meats to the new CPSC (Bureau of National Affairs, 1973: 29). In conference with the House, the jurisdiction of food, drugs, cosmetics, and meats was left in their original agencies. The bill's quick passage can be attributed to the noncontroversial nature of consumer protection in 1971. Serious opposition to consumer protection had not yet formed.

Rulemaking Was Different at the CPSC

Passage of the Consumer Product Safety Act (CPSA) marked a change in the congressional approach to hazardous products. Prior efforts (fabrics, refrigerators, and so forth) were targeted at specific hazards. The 1972 act took a general position against hazardous products and vested authority to move against such hazards in a regulatory agency (see Pittle, 1976: 131).

As originally enacted the CPSA rulemaking followed an innovative process called the **offeror system**. CPSC did not issue rules by itself; rather, it advertised the area of rulemaking and received proposals (from **offerors**) to write the rule. One or more offerors were selected; and they were required to have participation by consumers, small business, and retailers in the process. The finished rule was then submitted to CPSC, which could either accept or reject it (Bardach and Kagen, 1982: 181). The congressional intent was to maximize participation in the rulemaking process.

In its early years, the agency was criticized for its slow response to consumer problems. In its first four years, CPSC issued only three rules, covering swimming pool slides, matchbook covers, and architectural glass. CPSC's failure to issue more standards and the slow nature of its actions were not entirely its own fault. The cumbersome offeror system with its emphasis on maximum participation slowed down the rulemaking process greatly. In addition, by failing to set priorities, CPSC spread its resources too thin and attempted to address too many issues.

Early Problems at the CPSC

Numerous studies criticized the ineffectiveness of CPSC circa 1977. In 1976 the General Accounting Office criticized the agency for inefficiency, poor management, and poor enforcement. In 1977 the GAO revealed that the offeror process for rulemaking was taking approximately 2½ times longer than the 330 days permitted by law. A 1976 House Commerce Oversight and Investigations Subcommittee report found that the agency failed to set priorities and that participation efforts resulted in long delays in enforcement. A Civil Service Commission (now Office of Personnel Management) survey of CPSC employees discovered that only 43 percent of the agency's personnel felt the agency was doing a good job. Even an internal management task force found that the commission was failing short of reaching its legislative mandate (Lammers, 1983: 86).

CPSC's performance from 1972 to 1977 resulted in a loss of congressional support and only lukewarm consumer support. Contrasting with this support was strong opposition from the business community. Even President Carter, a strong advocate of consumer protection, considered abolishing the agency in 1977 and assigning its functions to the Food and Drug Administration and the Environmental Protection Agency (Lammers, 1983: 86). As the result of some vigorous internal lobbying, particularly by Esther Peterson, Carter's Special Assistant for Consumer Affairs, the administration changed its mind and supported reauthorization of the CPSC.

Early Reauthorizations Resulted in Improvements

After subjecting CPSC to a series of critical hearings, Congress grudgingly reauthorized the agency. Congress made several changes in the authorizing legislation. The CPSC chairman would serve at the pleasure of the president, the offeror process was modified, and the commission was encouraged to use voluntary industry standards. Implicit in the reauthorization was the threat that the agency might be abolished when its authorization expired in 1981.

The administration of CPSC improved after the 1978 reauthorization. Carter-appointed Chairman Susan King emphasized voluntary industry standards. Of the 75 standards adopted between 1978 and 1981, only five were mandatory; the rest were developed voluntarily by the industries (Lammers, 1983: 90). Even the agency's abysmal record in court improved. Prior to 1978 the agency lost almost every major court case it argued; after 1978 (until 1981) it won 17 of 21 cases (Lammers, 1983: 87).

CPSC's record on safety recalls also showed some results. Relying on toll-free hotlines, hospital injury room monitoring systems, and manufacturers for information about product hazards, it recalled millions of consumer products. The actual recalls, however, were of limited success because locating owners of consumer products is difficult. As a result, less than 50 percent of recalled products (up from 20 percent prior to 1977) were actually retrieved (Tobin, 1982: 295). CPSC estimated that these recalls prevented a million accidents between October 1977 and September 1980, approximately 1 percent of the total.

Reauthorization Through the Difficult 1980s

CPSC's performance under Susan King in all likelihood saved the agency. Following the 1980 election, President Reagan proposed that the commission be abolished. Had the agency's record in 1981 been similar to its record in 1978, the agency might not have survived reauthorization.

Despite improvements, CPSC faced a formidable array of enemies in its 1981 reauthorization. In addition to Ronald Reagan, the CPSC reauthorization was opposed by OMB Director David Stockman and Senate Oversight Chairman Robert Kasten. The eventual reauthorization placed numerous constraints on CPSC. CPSC rules were subjected to **one-house veto**, the offeror process was abolished, and rulemaking procedures were drastically altered. See discussion below on the CPSA.

The congressional restrictions placed on the CPSC were minor compared to the Reagan administration actions. CPSC was subjected to massive budget and personnel cuts as part of the Reagan budget process. In 1982 the budget was reduced by 30 percent with a 27 percent reduction in agency staff. The agency continued to engage in setting priorities for consumer protection, but administered the priorities with reduced numbers of personnel. This budget and staff drain continued throughout most of the 1980s (see discussion below on budget and staff). Conservative appointments of chairmen and commissioners contributed to a growing malaise at the agency and a serious staff morale problem. Promulgation of regulations plummeted to an all-time low (see Fise, The CPSC: Guiding or Hiding from Product Safety?, 1987).

COALITIONS IN PRODUCT SAFETY

This examination of coalitions in product safety includes coalitions of advocates for product safety as well as business coalitions.

Coalitions of Advocates for Product Safety

During the agency's first two decades of operation, several public interest consumer organizations emerged as advocates of product safety issues. These groups have filed petitions with the agency seeking standards or bans of dangerous consumer products. They have conducted surveys examining the availability of dangerous consumer products. On Capital Hill, they have lobbied Congress for statutory changes in CPSC laws, affecting the structure of the commission and the procedures by which it operates, and have sought enactment of product specific legislation when the agency itself has refused to take action (see discussion below, for example, on the Child Safety Protection Act). These groups have also supported increased appropriations for CPSC. Finally, these groups have challenged in court the agency's action or inaction, arguing, for example, that CPSC acted in an **"arbitrary and capricious manner"** in failing to promulgate a rule. The following groups are among those that have been most active on CPSC issues.

CONSUMER FEDERATION OF AMERICA

The **Consumer Federation of America** (CFA) has been a long standing supporter of a strong CPSC and was a frequent critic of the agency in the 1980s and early 1990s. The CFA is a non-profit association of some 240 pro-consumer groups. It files petitions seeking agency action on issues such as formaldehyde, methylene chloride, toy choking hazards, crib toys, bicycle helmets, baby walkers, bunk beds, and waterbeds. The group also lobbies Congress with respect to CPSC authorization and appropriations and has challenged agency action in federal court.

CONSUMERS UNION

Consumers Union (CU), the publisher of *Consumer Reports* magazine, has also been an ardent CPSC critic along with the CFA and has been active on CPSC issues before the agency and Congress. CU is effective in using testing data gathered for *Consumer Reports* magazine articles in advocating its positions before CPSC.

U.S. PUBLIC INTEREST RESEARCH GROUP

The **U.S. Public Interest Research Group** (U.S. PIRG), the national association of state Public Interest Research Groups, conducts local surveys on product safety issues, such as toys and playgrounds, to expose unsafe products. Along with other groups, U.S. PIRG lobbies Congress and CPSC on a host of CPSC-related issues and has challenged CPSC in court.

PUBLIC CITIZEN LITIGATION GROUP AND PUBLIC CITIZEN CONGRESS WATCH

Two Public Citizen organizations, **Public Citizen Litigation Group and Public Citizen Congress Watch**, are also active on CPSC matters. Congress Watch lobbies with other groups on CPSC reauthorization and appropriation. Public Citizen Litigation Group has acted as attorney of record for several consumer group clients in challenging CPSC action and has also participated in agency rulemakings.

NATIONAL SAFE KIDS CAMPAIGN

The **National SAFE KIDS Campaign**, the coordinating body for hundreds of state and local SAFE KIDS chapters, are dedicated to protecting children from unintentional injury. SAFE KIDS has focused on bicycle helmets, tap water scalds, smoke detectors, baby walkers, as well as many other issues affecting childhood injury. In addition to these issues, it lobbies on CPSC issues before Congress and the CPSC.

INSTITUTE FOR INJURY REDUCTION

The **Institute for Injury Reduction** is a membership organization of individuals, many of whom are trial attorneys, committed to measures to reduce consumer injury. The Institute conducts surveys, issues reports, and advocates before the CPSC.

AMERICAN ACADEMY OF PEDIATRICS

In addition to these consumer groups, two other types of organizations have advocated the need for safer consumer products. The medical community, and in particular, the **American Academy of Pediatrics (AAP)**, has been involved in a number of issues affecting children's safety. AAP joined with many of the consumer groups listed above in decrying the agency's failure to ban all-terrain vehicles for children and joined with consumer groups in petitioning the agency for a ban of dangerous baby walkers.

ATTORNEY GENERAL'S OFFICE OF THE STATE OF NEW YORK

The other entity that has been a force in affecting policy at the Consumer Product Safety Commission has been the **Attorney General's Office of the state of New York** (especially during Robert Abrams tenure as NY Attorney General). The NY Attorney General's office joined with Consumer Federation of America in filing petitions on toy choking hazards, crib toys, and waterbeds. It also joined with the CFA in challenging the CPSC failure to regulate the chemical methylene chloride. In addition, it has filed, with other state Attorney General's (AG) offices, amicus briefs on the all-terrain vehicle issue and has worked with other AG offices to forge an agreement with carpet manufacturers to inform the public about chemical emissions from new carpet.

Business Coalitions

Because CPSC authority is economy-wide, the regulated industry encompasses almost the entire manufacturing sector. The relevant business coalition varies, therefore, from issue to issue. A flammable fabrics rule will see action by textile manufacturers, a toy safety rule by toy makers, and lawn mower rule by lawn-mower manufacturers. On a more general level, the Chamber of Commerce and the National Association of Manufacturers have opposed what they see as regulatory excess on the part of CPSC and have been involved in discussions and debates before Congress regarding amendments to the CPSC's statutes.

THE ENVIRONMENT

This examination of the environment of product safety regulation includes an overview of budget and staffing levels as well as agenda setting.

Budget and Staffing Levels

The CPSC has had a troubled budget and staffing history. It began its operation in fiscal year 1974 (its first full year) with a budget of $34.7 million and a staff of 786. Its budget rose to a high of $43.9 million in 1979 and its staff reached a high of 978 employees in 1980. During the Reagan and Bush administrations, the CPSC budget received great slashes followed by some very modest increases, with the greatest cut coming in 1982 when its budget was reduced from $42.1 million (1981) to $32.1 (1982) Between 1980 and 1984, the number of staff positions was cut from 978 to 595.

In the past seven years, CPSC has managed to obtain $1-3 million dollar increases but has lost an additional 40 employees. See Table 11.1 below. The agency's 1995 appropriation marks the first time in the agency's history that the number of staff has fallen below 500—to 487 employees. The consumer and health community believe the agency's budget and staffing levels are inadequate and have provided Congressional testimony and correspondence on this matter on numerous occasions. For example, a letter to Congressional appropriations committee members in 1993 from 28 consumer and health groups called upon Congress to begin increasing the agency's budget over the next few years with an eventual goal of $55 million (letter to Chairman Barbara Mikulski, Senate Subcommittee on VA, HUD and Independent Agencies, May 19, 1993).

Despite the small increases in their budget, the CPSC has not been able to keep pace with the demand for resources that its broad consumer product jurisdiction requires. Without the necessary funds the agency must often discontinue projects or restructure them over several years. Their testing laboratories lack proper equipment and their computer capabilities have been limited. Enforcement staff is hampered in its negotiations for recalls because it does not have enough resources to conduct investigations in a manner that will foster successful court challenges. The new Clinton-appointed CPSC Chairman, Ann Brown, has vowed to do "more with less" and agency insiders believe this will be her greatest challenge in coming years.

Agenda Setting

Over the years, the agenda of CPSC has been determined primarily from three sources:

First, the agency's own in-house data gathered from a variety sources indicates **trends** in consumer product hazards. These data include those collected by the agency from death certificates, hospital injury reports, and consumer complaints (see above under Hazard Identification and Reduction). The agency's compliance staff also becomes aware of hazard trends through its own investigations or as the result of manufacturer reports of substantial product hazards required to be reported by law (see Compliance and Enforcement above).

Second, the agency also has instituted regulations for the establishment of **priorities** for commission action (see 16 C.F.R. section 1009.8). Priorities are decided by majority vote of the commission. Votes on all requests for appropriations, an annual operating plan,

Table 11.1   Consumer Product Safety Commission Resources

Year	Budget Authority	FTEs[†]
1974	34,776,000	786
1975	36,954,000	890
1976	39,564,000	890
1977	39,759,000	914
1978	40,461,000	900
1979	43,940,000	881
1980	41,350,000	978
1981	42,140,000	891
1982	32,164,000	649
1983	34,038,000	636
1984	35,250,000	595
1985	36,500,000	587
1986	34,452,000	568
1987	34,600,000	527
1988	32,696,000	519
1989	34,171,000	529
1990	35,147,000	529
1991	37,109,000	511
1992	40,200,000	515
1993	42,100,000	515
1994	42,286,000	502
1995	42,509,000[‡]	487

[†]This column represents the staffing ceiling established for the agency in each year. The term **FTE** or **full-time equivalent** has been used since 1980. One FTE is equal to 2080 hours per year. From 1974-1979 the figures in this column represent positions (or people).

[‡]In addition to this, the 1993 appropriation included $6.3 million in relocation funding to pay for the agency's move to new offices.

and any revisions reflect these priorities. The CPSC also designates specific priority issues each year. The public is invited to submit comments or to appear at an annual hearing on priorities. The commission examines the following eight criteria in establishing specific priorities: (1) frequency and severity of injuries; (2) causality of injuries; (3) chronic illness and future injuries; (4) cost and benefit of CPSC action; (5) unforeseen nature of the risk; (6) vulnerability of the population at risk; (7) probability of exposure to hazard; and (8) additional criteria.

Third, the agency agenda is also affected by **petitions** filed by outside parties. While the specific petition provision of the Consumer Product Safety Act (CPSA) was repealed in 1981 (formerly section 10 of the CPSA), the right to petition the agency still exists by virtue of the right of petition found in the Administrative Procedures Act (5 U.S.C. section 553(e)). Generally, several petitions are filed each year seeking promulgation of a standard or ban of a consumer product in order to address a product hazard. (See discussion above regarding consumer organizations for examples).

THE LAW AND PROCEDURES
The CPSC is charged with carrying out six statutes.

Consumer Product Safety Act (15U.S.C. 2051)
The Consumer Product Safety Act (CPSA) was signed into law on October 27, 1972. This broad statute sets out the agency's jurisdiction, its powers (bans, mandatory standards, recalls), as well as the commission structure and organization. It contains onerous **information disclosure provisions** restricting, for example, the release of information that identifies a manufacturer's name. The CPSC must rely on voluntary consumer product safety standards, rather than promulgate a mandatory standard, whenever compliance with the voluntary standard would eliminate or adequately reduce the risk of injury and it is likely there will be substantial compliance with the voluntary standard. Although not technically a part of the Consumer Product Safety Act, the law now contains amendments addressing some product-specific laws; these include a mandatory standard on automatic garage door openers and lawn mowers as well as bans of lawn darts and butyl and isopropyl nitrites.

Section 6(b) of the Consumer Product Safety Act requires that before CPSC can release any information that identifies a manufacturer, it must first send the information to the manufacturer and allow the manufacturer to comment on the information or dispute its release. This requirement has two effects: (1) the release of product safety information to the public is delayed, and (2) the agency must use some of its already scarce resources to complete this notification process. The CPSC staff reports that release of information is delayed for many months and sometimes years. The agency estimates that processing 6(b) requests costs the CPSC approximately $454,000 per year. It takes the staff four times as long to fill these requests as all other Freedom of Information requests. The CPSC is the only federal health and safety agency required to go through this procedure.

Federal Hazardous Substances Act (15 U.S.C. 1261)
The Federal Hazardous Substances Act (FHSA) was passed in 1960. Its original intent was to require **precautionary labeling** of hazardous household chemical products. The Act specifically defines **hazardous substances** as those that are: toxic, corrosive, irritants, strong sensitizers, flammable, combustible, or those that generate pressure through decomposition, heat or other means. The warning or caution labels seen on household cleaners, paints, and other substances used in the home, are required by this law. Through

amendments to this law, the Act's jurisdiction expanded to include toys and other products intended for children that present an electrical, mechanical or thermal hazard. The CPSC has regulated toys, cribs, rattles, pacifiers, walkers and other products for children using their FHSA authority.

Poison Prevention Packaging Act (15 U.S.C. 1471)

The Poison Prevention Packaging Act (PPPA) was signed into law in 1970 to address the risk to children from ingestion of hazardous household substances. The Act establishes **child-resistant packaging standards** for certain household products. Any product subject to the standards must be contained in **child-resistant packaging**, unless the manufacturer also packages the substance in a package that is not child resistant and the package that is not child resistant contains a conspicuous label stating: "This package for households without young children."

Flammable Fabrics Act (15 U.S.C. 1191)

The Flammable Fabrics Act, enacted in 1953, was in response to fires involving children who were wearing highly flammable clothing. The purpose of the act is to protect the public through the adoption of federal standards of flammability covering all textiles used for wearing apparel and interior furnishing. The law prohibits the manufacture, sale, or importation of any fabric, article of wearing apparel, or interior furnishing that fails to meet standards promulgated under the Act. This law has been extremely effective in reducing children deaths associated with children's sleepwear—from 60 per year (during the early 1970s) to less than 5 per year (early 1990s).

Refrigerator Safety Act (15 U.S.C. 1211)

The Refrigerator Safety Act was enacted in 1956. This law requires all household refrigerators manufactured after October 1958 to have safety devices enabling them to be opened from the inside in order to prevent entrapment and suffocation inside the refrigerator. The value of the Act is evidenced by the continuation of deaths in products manufactured before the safety device requirement went into effect. Between 1980 and 1988, for example, 59 children died when they became trapped in **old-style latch-type** refrigerators and freezers. (Childwise Catalog: 342)

Fire Safe Cigarette Act (15 U.S.C. 2054)

The Fire Safe Cigarette Act, passed in 1990, addresses cigarette-ignited fires and directs CPSC, along with the National Institute for Standards and Technology's Center for Fire Research, to: (1) develop a standard test method to determine cigarette ignition propensity; (2) compile performance data for cigarettes; and (3) conduct studies to develop valid predictive capability regarding cigarette ignition. In addition, CPSC was charged with implementing a study to collect baseline and followup data about the characteristics of cigarettes, products ignited, smokers involved in fires, and costs of cigarette-ignited fires. This Act essentially represents followup legislation to the Cigarette Safety Act of 1984, which required studies that found that the value of a cigarette with less of a likelihood to ignite furniture and mattresses would prevent property damage and personal injury. Both Acts seek to address the fact that cigarette-ignited fires are the leading cause of fire deaths in the United States.

IMPACT OF POLICY DECISIONS

The CPSC argues that its actions have saved lives and money. From 1977 to 1989, deaths associated with consumer products decreased by 13 percent; from 25,000 per year to 21,600 per year. From 1979 to 1991, injuries associated with consumer products have decreased by 14 percent. Commission actions are estimated to save society about $2.5 billion each year (see, CPSC Long Range Planning Committee, Second Paper: Implementing the Mission of the Consumer Product Safety Commission, January 6, 1992: 22-23). In 1992, the agency estimated that since 1973, it had issued: 50 mandatory standards or special packaging requirements; 40 product bans; and 60 requirements for product labels. Additionally, in 1990-1991, CPSC recalled 59 million product units and stop importation of 405 shipments of violative products (23-24).

RECENT AND CURRENT ISSUES

Responding to an outcry from consumer organizations that the agency had failed to take action to protect children, Congress in 1993-1994 passed specific legislation (described below) directing CPSC to work on toy and bike helmet safety. Also, in 1994 with the appointment of Ann Brown as chairman of the agency, the CPSC came roaring back to life and instituted several new rulemakings and other safety initiatives. A few of these are described below.

Toys

In 1987, in response to a petition by a consumer group and a state attorney general, CPSC began examining toys that pose a choking hazard to young children. A rulemaking was begun, but later terminated by the commission. Countering the termination of this rulemaking, Congress, in 1994, enacted the **Child Safety Protection Act**. This legislation specifically addressed toys and bicycle helmets (see below). The law requires toys intended for children ages three through five and that contain small parts to bear a prominent warning of the choking hazard these small parts pose to young children. The labels are also required on packages of marbles, small balls, and balloons. Also, balls that are intended for children under age three must be at least 1.75 inches in diameter so as not to pose a choking hazard (59 Fed.Reg.33932 and 59 Fed.Reg. 33925).

Bicycle Helmets

The Child Safety Protection Act (see above) also requires that CPSC develop a uniform federal standard for bike helmets. The standard must address, among other things, the risk of bike helmets' rolling offing off during falls and the need for special protection of childrens' heads. While this standard is being developed all manufacturers must comply with one of three **voluntary standards** (American National Standards Institute, Snell, or American Society for Testing and Materials) or any other standard the CPSC deems appropriate. Between 1984 and 1988 2,985 bicyclists in the United States died from head injuries that required hospital emergency room treatment. It is estimated that 85% of all head injuries suffered by bicyclists could be prevented by using bicycle helmets. (Congressional Record, November 20, 1993, S 16889) (59 Fed. Reg. 41719).

Five-Gallon Buckets

Infants, 8-14 months of age, are at risk of falling into and drowning in five-gallon buckets. The increased popularity of these buckets, which come filled with paint, drywall compound, or other substances, or can be bought empty, has been accompanied by a rise in deaths. The agency estimates that 40 children per year drown in such buckets. The CPSC voted in 1994 to publish an Advance Notice of Proposed Rulemaking and will examine regulatory options, including labeling and a performance standard for buckets (59 Fed. Reg. 35058, July 8, 1994).

Upholstered Furniture

Fires involving upholstered furniture cause more deaths than any product under the CPSC's jurisdiction, claiming an average of 1,000 victims each year and resulting in over 2,000 injuries, and destroying $300 million of property annually. In 1994, CPSC published an Advance Notice of Proposed Rulemaking to address fires occurring when small open flames ignited upholstered furniture. These fires were estimated in 1991 to result in approximately 150 deaths, 580 injuries, and $66 million in property losses (59 Fed. Reg. 307 35).

Walkers

In 1994, CPSC also began a rulemaking to examine injuries and deaths associated with baby walkers. The commission specifically targeted this rulemaking because of the 18,500 injuries that occur each year from baby walkers' falling down stairs. This issue was raised with CPSC in a petition filed by consumer groups and pediatricians (59 Fed. Reg. 39306).

Drawstrings on Children's Clothing

Alarmed about children who were strangling and dying when drawstrings on the hoods and necks of their clothing caught on playground equipment and other surfaces, CPSC worked with children's clothing manufacturers and retailers to voluntarily modify or eliminate strings from children's clothes. There were at least 12 deaths and 27 near-strangulations between 1985 and 1994. Nearly 30 manufacturers and retailers joined the voluntary program (CPSC Press Release No. 94-103, July 7, 1994 and Update, August 19, 1994).

Window Blind Cords

Between 1981 and 1994, 140 children died when they strangled on window blind and drapery cords. Typically the young victims, most under the age of two, were playing with cords hanging beside their crib or near the floor. CPSC warned parents of the danger and is working with window covering manufacturers and retailers to provide consumers with free tassels for the cords which will allow the noose-like feature of window blind cords to be eliminated (CPSC Consumer Product Safety Alert, July 1993, and information from Office of Information and Public Affairs, September 1994).

Window Falls

To respond to the 70 deaths each year resulting from falls out of windows and the 42,000 emergency room treated injuries associated with falls and windows occurring annually, CPSC convened a roundtable in July 1994 to begin to examine risk reduction strategies. Manufacturers, retailers, physicians, consumer advocates and others participated (CPSC Window Falls Roundtable, Hazard Sketch, July 27, 1994).

Flammable Chiffon Skirts

In August, 1994, CPSC announced a stop sale and recall of a popular style of rayon/cotton blend skirt, which is dangerously flammable. The skirts, which fail the **Flammable Fabrics Act** and burn faster than newspaper, are long, full and two layered, with a sheer chiffon layer of fabric over a gauze lining. When the agency first announced the recall, it had received no reports of injuries associated with the skirts. However, within a week of the recall announcement, CPSC received several reports of past incidents of the skirts catching on fire and burn injuries. This recall is a good illustration of the importance of media coverage in obtaining greater information from consumers about adverse product experience (CPSC Press Release No. 94-117 and 94-119, August, 1994).

FUTURE POLICY DIRECTIONS

Given the breadth and magnitude of the CPSC's jurisdiction, it seems clear that CPSC will remain an important consumer agency. In 1994, the American public began to get a taste of what a strong and vocal Consumer Product Safety Commission was all about under the new leadership of Chairman Ann Brown. Because of Brown's ability to capture headlines and media interest, and therefore the public's attention, it may be difficult for CPSC ever to return to its old ways. Members of Congress with oversight and appropriations authority may hold future chairmen up to the "Brown standard," at least in terms of public education about product hazards (if not the initiation of regulatory measures). While conservatives may relish returning to the quieter, slower, moribund days of CPSC, consumer advocates now recognize that what they pushed for during the Reagan/Bush 80s is, in fact, possible. They will be loathe to let the CPSC, Congress, or the American public forget what the CPSC is capable of doing (as it has in Chairman Brown's era) if an attempt to diminish the agency's activity or power is resurrected.

With its arsenal of regulatory powers, CPSC has the ability to significantly affect consumer deaths and injuries associated with consumer products for many years to come. In 1988, Vice President Al Gore, then chairman of the Senate Consumer Subcommittee, concluded that CPSC is a vital consumer agency when he stated:

> Products of all sorts touch the lives of Americans more directly and more often than we can imagine, and it is essential that we act to revitalize the CPSC and stop this erosion of public confidence in the Federal Government's product safety activities. The CPSC is too important an agency to permit it to wither and die (Congressional Record, October 21, 1988, S17179).

SUMMARY

Table 11.2 provides a summary of Consumer Product Safety regulation. The Consumer Product Safety Commission (CPSC) has struggled through its early years to establish itself as a consistent and tough regulator of consumer products. Now in the beginning of its third decade, it biggest challenge is carrying out its responsibilities with a meager budget and reduced staffing level.

With some 15,000 different products within its jurisdiction, CPSC is significantly challenged to keep track of the many firms it regulates and oversees. In some cases the products are simple and straight forward, requiring minimal technical expertise to understand the operation of the products and their possible hazards. In other cases, the products are highly sophisticated and complex, requiring CPSC staff to be up-to-date on the latest manufacturing developments and inventions. Likewise, depending upon the product, the profits recognized from sales of products within CPSC's jurisdiction varies. The effect on profits of CPSC action (such as a recall) is similarly dependent upon the type of product and possible associated hazards.

Consumers have clearly benefitted in the areas where CPSC has taken action. Whether it be reducing clothing fire deaths, strangulations in baby cribs, or decreasing children's access to hazardous substances, the agency, through its use of standards and bans, has changed the way certain products are made.

The CPSC has been most effective in addressing risks to young children and it continues today to emphasize the issues that affect the very young. It has a much less successful record in reducing long term chronic hazards associated with consumer products (e.g., toxic exposures). In part, this probably reflects our society's willingness to be more accepting of risks that it can not perceive as well.

Leadership of the Consumer Product Safety Commission has varied and, not surprisingly, the chairmen have often reflected the political leanings of the president that appointed them. The reduction of the number of commissioners—from five commissioners (as prescribed in the Consumer Product Safety Act) to three—may have had some effect on the resulting decisions. Establishing a consensus among five persons, each of whom bring his or her own concerns to the bargaining table, is a different process than establishing a quorum of two—where a commissioner simply has to convince one other colleague to vote with her/him. While the reduction in the number of commissioners has

Table 11.2   A Summary of Consumer Product Safety Regulation

Economics	
Ease of entry	Easy
Number of firms	Over 1 million
Profits	Vary
Technology	
Complexity	Moderate
Stability	Varies
Substitutes	High
Subsystem	
Bureau control	Moderate
Industry coalition	Moderate
Nonindustry coalition (consumer)	Strong
Bureaucratic resources:	
Expertise	Moderate
Cohesion	Moderate
Leadership	Strong
Legislative authority:	
Goals	General
Coverage	Broad
Sanctions	Good
Procedures	Cumbersome
Impact of macropolitical actors	
Congress	Strong
President	Strong
Courts	Moderate

diminished commissioner-associated costs for the agency, it has caused other problems. During times when there is a vacancy, the CPSC is left with two persons and may not be able to conduct business at all.[3]

---

[3]Congress amended the agency's law allowing two persons to constitute a quorum for conducting business for a six-month period. The Commission has consisted of just two persons twice in recent history (November 1993-March 1994) and (October 1994-present).

There is substantial interest in the consumer advocacy community in the actions (or inactions) of this agency. Cross-professional coalitions between consumer advocates, state government officials and the public health community have increased the strength of the public interest representation before the CPSC. During times of increased activity by the agency (whether it be more recalls or more rulemakings) the business community has also become energized. Similarly, when individual states attempt to regulate consumer products, the business interests affected has sometimes sought federal action by CPSC (or Congress) to preempt state law.

As new consumer products are developed, the CPSC is constantly challenged to keep abreast of these products and any potential hazards that may be associated with their use. Because there is no pre-market approval of consumer products (within CPSC's jurisdiction) this often means that the agency must respond after the fact, or in other words, after a consumer has been injured or died. With thousands of consumer products under its authority and new technologies and designs developing rapidly, the CPSC's challenge to keep up is monumental. Despite all of CPSC's hard work and best intentions, when it comes to product safety, **"caveat emptor"** is still an appropriate slogan for today's consuming public.

Chapter 12
Automobile Safety Regulation

Judith Lee Stone[1]

Today's younger generations have grown up expecting much from private and public providers of automobile safety. It seems logical this would be the case, until a look at the history of auto safety and its various stages of development reminds us that it was not quite three decades ago that federal statutes protecting auto consumers from the manufacture of unsafe cars and auto supplies were adopted, followed shortly by other laws governing fraudulent behavior, consumer information, and other safeguards for cars, drivers and highway environments. Nothing short of a revolution occurred in the 1960s when these laws were passed.

In the **current era**, regulation can be a four-letter word in some camps, but much of auto safety regulation has become almost mainstream in the mind of the general public, in that consumers both expect and demand safety in their automobiles. Few car dealerships would sell many cars without collapsible steering columns or padded dashboards, but it was not very long ago that these standard features were unheard of. Soon, air bags and antilock brakes will join the list of safety features to be expected, and will no longer be touted as "advancements." Another illustration of the high expectations for safety is the surprise on the faces of mothers and fathers buying minivans, sport utility vehicles, and compact pickup trucks, for family use, when they discover that these vehicles usually fall behind regular passenger cars in meeting a required vehicle safety standard schedule. Despite the fact they are the fastest growing segment of new car market, they are not yet required to meet federal motor vehicle safety standards at the same pace.

---

[1]Judith Lee Stone is president of Advocates for Highway and Auto Safety, a coalition of consumer, safety, public health, law enforcement and insurance organizations working for improved public policies for safer highways. She has lived in Washington, D.C. for 27 years, and has worked in both the House and Senate, for the federal government, and for non-profit advocacy groups. All but 10 of those years have been devoted to the highway safety field. Stone is one of the last people left in the United States who believes good government is not only possible, but necessary. She received a degree in sociology, with a minor in journalism, from Northwestern University, and came to Washington the year before Richard Nixon was elected president. Unlike Garman, she, her husband, step-daughter, and golden retriever rarely eat together, much less by candlelight, in their Capitol Hill home and are looking to be inspired by such unusual behavior.

The story of automobile safety regulation, still underway, is a uniquely American government/private sector success story. Its pieces are not easily understood or explained, and like a lot of phenomena, generate a thousand points of view.

THE SUBSYSTEM

This examination of the subsystem of automobile safety regulation includes an overview of the agencies and the constituencies involved.

The Agencies

The **National Highway Traffic Safety Administration (NHTSA)**, one of ten agencies within the **U.S. Department of Transportation (U.S. DOT)**, regulates the automobile manufacturing industry in three major areas: (1) **safety**, (2) **damageability**, and (3) **fuel economy**. NHTSA has far-reaching authority to set minimum safety standards that must be met by every manufacturer selling cars and certain related products such as tires, child safety seats and motorcycle helmets in the United States. The agency also administers a $125 million grant program for the states to conduct various traffic safety programs, such as anti-drunk driving, safety belt use, speed control, motorcycle safety, and emergency medical services programs. This program is funded by the Highway Trust Fund (fueled by the gas tax).

NHTSA's enforcement office is responsible for auto safety defect recalls, and the rulemaking office also regulates the manufacture of heavy trucks, including braking, **conspicuity** (how well the truck can be seen on the road, particularly at night), and other vehicle issues, although the **Federal Highway Administration** (FHWA), another DOT agency, is responsible for trucking operations on the highways, as well as roadway environment safety.

Damageability in motor vehicles is primarily addressed in manufacturing design. The insurance industry and consumer organizations encourage auto manufacturers, and urge the government to encourage auto manufacturers, to produce vehicles able to withstand impacts without incurring extraordinary repair costs. The major statute governing damageability issues is the Motor Vehicle Information and Cost Savings Act, adopted in 1972, and amended several times thereafter. Despite statutory authority and strong committee report language directing the agency to act on that authority, damageability takes a back seat to safety at NHTSA. Indeed, support for these consumer information programs is weak within the agency. One good example is bumper strength. The auto industry is reluctant to design strong bumpers, erroneously claiming it would be necessary to make a heavier bumper, resulting in less fuel economy. Both the agency and manufacturers say consumers do not really care about bumper strength, although insurance polls continually show the opposite. After a strong bumper standard was rescinded in the early years of the Reagan Administration, NHTSA has avoided the issue whenever it can, paying little attention and giving no support to insurance and consumer arguments and crash test data pointing to many hundreds, even thousands of dollars in repair costs due to weak bumpers. NHTSA and supporters of the auto industry on Capitol Hill say bumper strength should be debated and resolved among the insurance and auto industries. Frustrated consumer groups have gone to state legislatures to pass laws in California, Hawaii and New York requiring bumper strength to be displayed on a sticker so that buyers will know before the purchase whether the bumper will survive a fender bender without breaking the bank.

The **fuel economy research program** resides at NHTSA, with certain **corporate average fuel economy (CAFE)** levels set by law that must be met by manufacturers. The government was aggressive in establishing CAFE goals in the 1970s, but retreated hastily throughout the 1980s and 1990s under pressure from auto manufacturers. Legislative and media CAFE battles involving environmental and safety activists on one side, and the manufacturers on the other, take place regularly, including throughout the Clinton-Gore campaign for the presidency in 1992. Very little has occurred, voluntarily or legislatively, to improve fuel economy in the vehicle fleet since the beginning of the CAFE standards in the 1970s. It is easier and less costly for the carmakers to brag about achievable fuel economy levels far into the future, indeed into the next millennium, than to put cars in the dealerships that are more fuel efficient today.[2]

NHTSA's budget in FY1994 (October 1, 1993-September 30, 1994) was a total of $298 million, with approximately $10 million specifically set aside for rulemaking activities. It makes sense to subtract the state highway safety grant program from the total ($125 million) as none of those funds are spent for regulatory programs. The NHTSA budget is difficult to analyze because monies for operations and research are lumped together, making it impossible to separate out precisely how much administrative funding is devoted solely to regulatory activities. But there is a specific budget for rulemaking research and a few special **"line items"** inserted in the budget during the appropriations process in Congress. The number of employees is 667, but that number includes employees in ten regional offices who are not at all involved in rulemaking activities or administration. Dr. Ricardo Martinez is head of NHTSA.

This is a relatively small agency, given the size of the industry it regulates and problems it is in business to address, but it has a highly visible, targeted, controversial and at the same time popular mission: to reduce death and injury due to motor vehicle crashes.

Since its creation in the late 1960s, NHTSA's list of accomplishments has been extraordinary. Despite growing numbers of motorists and vehicle miles travelled every year, the annual death toll has decreased to 40,115 fatalities in 1993, down from the peak of 54,589 in 1972 and 53,543 fatalities in 1969 just after passage of the two major safety acts (see "The Law and Procedures"). The death rate per 100 million vehicle miles traveled declined from 5.0 to 1.8 (Insurance Institute, 1994).

As the nation struggles to understand violence and the use of firearms, another major injury prevention issue in our society, many look to the auto safety movement as a model.[3]

---

[2]At a technology fair sponsored by the U.S. Department of Transportation in October 1994, automakers displayed a prototype vehicle that would provide three times the current fuel economy, at some undetermined time in the future, but likely not until the middle of the next century.

[3]See speech, U.S. Surgeon General M. Joycelyn Elders, Lifesavers National Conference on Highway Safety Priorities, March 1994.

A large number of factors contribute to this success story, and the climate within which the many changes occur to bring about the successes shifts with political changes in administrations and leadership capabilities. Particularly in recent years, other government agencies outside U.S. DOT have influenced NHTSA's overall mission and program, as the motor vehicle crash problem became more popularly defined in public discourse as a public health issue. Those agencies are primarily within the U.S. Department of Health and Human Services (HHS). Because regulatory activities addressing the motor vehicle crash problem are defined as public health solutions, they are often less vulnerable to attack by anti-government regulation forces, who find it easier to criticize economic regulation.

Constituencies

In a nation of 258 million people, 194 million cars and other motor vehicles, and 172 million licensed drivers, NHTSA has undoubtedly among the broadest and most diverse constituencies of any government agency. The largest regulated industry is the auto industry, but the trucking and tire industries must also meet certain regulatory criteria promulgated by the agency. Although not strictly regulated by NHTSA, the insurance industry has enormous stakes in rulemaking outcomes and other agency programs, including its legislatively-mandated damageability activities. The state grant program has generated numerous constituencies attempting to change driver behavior, including law enforcement, medical and emergency response personnel, state government officials, victim's groups and others. Finally, Congress itself, the nation's governors, and local elected officials are major constituents of NHTSA.

ADVOCACY COALITIONS

The auto industry is represented by the **American Automobile Manufacturers Association (AAMA)**, representing only General Motors, Ford and Chrysler (since 1993), and the **Association of International Automobile Manufacturers (AIMA)**. In addition, each individual company is usually represented before the agency and on Capitol Hill by Washington office staff or hired counsel, or by a public relations or law firm on a particular matter.

Generally, the auto industry favors moderate or **no regulation**. It prefers change to take place through marketplace forces, especially in the 1990s political environment. An environment that assumes, in many camps and usually erroneously, that most major vehicle safety regulations are already in place, with only minor "tinkering" necessary.

Numerous pro-auto safety regulation groups continue to push for additional, tough auto safety rules, and work often in large coalitions organized around specific issues, such as air bags, head injury, side impact, and rollover protection. These informal coalitions consist increasingly of public health and victim's groups, such as the National Head Injury Foundation, Mothers Against Drunk Driving, and the American College of Emergency Physicians. Traditional consumer groups join forces with insurance, law enforcement, and civic organizations to focus attention and advocate additional government action to improve auto safety. These coalitions have often succeeded in altering regulatory outcomes, telling their stories and making their points effectively in the popular media.

Many of these advocacy groups also support strong measures to be taken by the government, in both the driver behavior and roadway environment programs. Aggressive grass roots campaigns, specializing in individual, local contacts with members of Congress, on behalf of stronger regulation, have been effective (see National Journal, June 11, 1994).

CHANGING APPROACH TO AUTO SAFETY REGULATION

This is a change from the early days of highway and auto safety, when most organizations favored a more singular approach to problem solving. Stark divisions in philosophy among diverse groups were common throughout the 1960s, 1970s and 1980s, with Ralph Nader and other consumer leaders believing primarily in vehicle safety solutions as the most effective approach, and more traditional safety organizations vesting enormous energy in educational attempts, usually unsuccessful, to change driver behavior. In the 1990s, there is more "cross-fertilization" in philosophies about where the solutions lie, with a deeper understanding and sophistication about the need to take aggressive action in all areas.

One other major change is the expansion of types of advocacy coalitions involved in auto safety issues. As the public demands more safety built into automobiles, not only because they know it can be done but because the car represents a significant investment from the family budget, there is a growing recognition among constituencies in a wide variety of interest groups of the impact of auto safety, or lack of it. Also, as costs to society of motor vehicle crashes are more carefully and realistically documented by the federal government agencies, such as the Centers for Disease Control and Prevention and respected academic institutions, the convincing case can be made by advocacy coalitions that it is highly cost-effective to build safety into the vehicle in the first place. **Prevention** is "in" and manufacturers accept, indeed promote, the fact that "**safety sells**."

THE ENVIRONMENT

This examination of the environment of automobile safety regulation includes an overview of the economics, the technology, and the sociology of the subject.

Economics

The auto industry (manufacturers, suppliers, sales and service) represents the largest industrial sector of our nation's economy. Over 4 million U.S. jobs are directly associated with the $600 billion-a-year industry. (The number of jobs totals 13 million if you include highway construction, truck drivers, petroleum works and transit). The 1992 Democratic presidential campaign recognized the importance such an industrial base plays when it spawned the now-famous slogan, "It's the economy, stupid."

Auto safety regulation is controversial because it is often portrayed by the industry as burdensome, although the positive contributions made by regulatory changes are widely recognized and enjoy broad public support (NHTSA, 1979).

As safety advances are incorporated into vehicles both through regulatory requirements and voluntary industry efforts, it is apparent that safety does sell. Consumers perceive auto safety regulation as **public health and safety regulation**, rather than economic regulation, and for this type of measure there is significant public support.

In the early 1990s, the national debate about the need to reform the national health care system began in earnest at the same time air bags, anti-lock brakes and other auto safety devices had become household words. This follows a 25-year battle between the auto industry on one side, and the insurance industry and consumer and safety groups on the other. The cost of motor vehicle injury to the society, and to the individual family, had been well-documented in numerous landmark national and state studies, beginning in the mid-1980s (see Rice & MacKenzie, 1989). Proponents for stronger auto safety regulation are well-armed with facts and statistical justifications for taking action and for tying the issue to health care. No longer is the issue strictly economic feasibility (for the industry) versus public safety. Now the arguments involve those same issues, but factor in extraordinary multi-billion dollar costs to society in the equation. The cost of one serious head injury over the lifetime of one individual is often many millions of dollars. (see testimony, Sabatini, 1992). This has changed dramatically the debate around the viability of any highway or auto safety countermeasure, including the effect of regulation on the economic health of the industry.

Competition to sell safer automobiles was enhanced, in part, when the domestic auto industry—instigated by Chrysler's decision in 1989 to make driver-side air bags standard equipment on every car—became more aggressive in **marketing safety features**. Legislation in 1991 mandated installation of both driver and passenger side air bags in all cars and **multi-purpose passenger vehicles (MPVs)** by the end of the 1990s, and several other rulemaking proceedings (see Intermodal Surface Transportation Efficiency Act, P.L. 100-17, 1991).

At the same time, foreign manufacturers were expelled from the industry's largest trade association, the Motor Vehicle Manufacturers Association (MVMA), which was re-named the American Automobile Manufacturers Association (AAMA) and includes only the three domestic companies (GM, Ford and Chrysler). There appeared at this time to be a shift in emphasis within the domestic auto industry toward more marketing of safety in the interest of gaining a **competitive edge** over foreign auto manufacturers, particularly the Japanese. Early voluntary installation of air bags in more lines of domestically-produced cars is an example of this change in strategy, as well as making anti-lock brakes widely available. Making these safety features standard in all lines allowed the domestic manufacturers to make claims that their vehicles, even small cars, were safer than similarly-sized foreign autos. In the late 1980s and early 1990s, safety not only became marketable, but internationally competitive.

Technology

Automobile technology borrows much from the aerospace industry and the science of space exploration. The **Motor Vehicle Safety Act** of 1966 (see chapter section "Agenda Setting: The Law and Procedures") created a **"technology-forcing approach"** (see Graham, 1988) in the environment that had the practical effect of guiding the auto industry toward existing technologies to implement auto safety regulations. Many of those technologies, including air bag sensing and inflator devices, had already been developed by the aerospace industry, as had crushable foam and other occupant protection systems. Therefore, the technologies usually were in place, framing the debate more around questions of costs and economic feasibility for the industry.

MOVING TOWARD A LEVEL PLAYING FIELD

Government requirements for less pollution, better gas mileage and safer vehicles resonate in an environment where the technology of automaking is complicated and extraordinarily competitive, making the regulator's task difficult. Although it is hard to find many in the industry willing to publicly admit it, auto safety regulation has had a very positive effect on the economic health of the automobile industry, as standardization creates a "**level playing field**" for the overall industry, producing certainty in the field with **performance** (rather than design) **standards** that can be met however the industry chooses. Investments by the industry in research and production are more stable, with a more certain payoff in a clearly-defined period of time.

There is nothing to stop any company from exceeding government requirements for safety, and some have taken advantage of the very positive environment for safety by marketing extensive **voluntarily-installed technological advances**. (See Toyota Previa minivan advertisement stating they meet and exceed government safety standards before they were required to.)

Much sophisticated research has been produced since the mid-1980s on the cost of injury to society. Despite this fact, research funding for **biomechanics**, the science of injury control, has been dramatically reduced in recent years. Because the setting of most important motor vehicle safety standards relies upon such biomechanics research, NHTSA's role in coordinating and moderating the debate around each issue has been diminished as a result. The negative effect of this paucity of research dollars for a public health problem that kills 40,000 people a year, seriously injures hundreds of thousands a year, and costs the society over $137 billion annually, is dramatic. Rules governing enhanced side impact, rollover, pedestrian protection, and roof crush have not been promulgated, in part, because research is inadequate. Whole blocks of time measured in years have been lost due to a lack of resources.

INTELLIGENT VEHICLE HIGHWAY SYSTEMS

One controversial issue in the early to mid-1990s has been the hundreds of millions of dollars siphoned off highway and auto safety research coffers into those of the **Intelligent Vehicle Highway Systems (IVHS)** program. (Nearly $200 million was budgeted in FY 1994 for IVHS research, development and deployment; this compares to $10 million for all auto safety rulemaking and $5 million for biomechanics research.) The word "**safety**" is prominent in literature and discussions advocating expansion of this relatively new program, but little specificity is offered. IVHS is administered and fostered primarily in the Federal Highway Administration, although NHTSA's research program devotes a relatively large percentage of its dollars to IVHS.

IVHS is formally defined as "the use of advanced computer, electronics and communication technologies that could increase the effectiveness of the entire surface transportation system." The program has four operational goals: (1) to improve safety, (2) to reduce congestion and improve accessibility, (3) to improve energy efficiency and environmental quality, and (4) to enhance economic productivity.

The three institutional goals of Intelligent Vehicle Highway System are: (1) to develop the U.S. IVHS industry, (2) to revitalize the transportation profession, and (3) to serve as a model for technology development and deployment.

Just how much safety is advanced in and by IVHS is yet to be determined, and there is much skepticism in the safety advocacy community that safety sounds good and plays well on Capitol Hill, but is little more than lip service. Virtually none of the early projects, now in research and development, have a safety focus.

Whatever **up-front costs** are associated with incorporating safety technology in motor vehicles are reduced as the systems are made **standard**, rather than optional or on only some models. Such costs incurred by the industry are balanced and compared in the debate with costs of motor vehicle crashes to society and families.

Sociology

Auto safety has been shaped over a period of thirty years by two powerful movements: **consumers** and **victims**. Vehicle safety regulatory issues were closely associated with Ralph Nader (see next section "Agenda Setting: The Law and Procedures"), who deserves most credit for the system we have today, and with victim's issues with **Mothers Against Drunk Driving (MADD)**. MADD formed in the early 1980s, and in ten short years grew into the most successful grassroots victims' organization in the history of the nation.

Federal and state government programs promoted alcohol safety on the highways since the inception of the **State and Community Highway Safety Grant** (Section 402 of the 1966 Highway Safety Act), and laid a solid foundation of research and problem identification. But MADD and all the forces that have come into play[4] around its emergence and the development of other victim's organizations have played the key role in changing the national definition of **acceptable driving behavior** in a very short time, which has led to the reduction of the number of **alcohol-related motor vehicle fatalities** from 25,165 in 1982, to 17,461 in 1993; that amounts to a drop of almost one-third over the last 12 years. Never before has there been such a dramatic reduction in traffic fatalities, over just a decade, accompanied by significant societal attitude and behavioral change. No longer is it in vogue to joke about drinking and driving, as it used be on late night talk shows and in the movies.

---

[4]Buoyed by channeled grief and victims' stories, highway safety and public health activists advocated successfully for tougher anti-drunk driving laws in every state in the nation, beginning in 1981 and 1982. Community support began to grow for stronger law enforcement and judicial actions to combat drunk driving. The federal government passed supporting legislation in 1984, including a mandatory uniform national drinking age of 21. Changes in the laws and heightened enforcement are directly commensurate with the formation and growth of Mothers Against Drunk Driving (MADD).

The drunk driving movement's success has affected the entire field of highway and auto safety by teaching society that the victim's story has a force behind it strong enough to actually shift societal behavior, over time. Although alcohol and drunk driving represent a big percentage of the motor vehicle crash problem, **"single-issue groups"** like MADD recognize the impact of their support for solutions to other problems, such as low safety belt use rates, excessive speed, and inadequate vehicle safety measures. MADD's eventual involvement in issues other than drunk driving has increased the effectiveness of the auto safety lobby, especially through emphasis on telling the victim's story, and convincing decisionmakers that stronger measures of all sorts might have prevented the tragedy from happening in the first place.

It is tempting to assume that the anti-drunk driving movement and increases in safety belt use (from 15% in the early 1980s, to 66% in 1993) are nearly singularly responsible for the relatively low fatality rate in the early 1990s (1.8 fatalities per 100 million vehicle miles traveled in 1993, compared to a rate of 2.6 a decade earlier). These impressive statistics undoubtedly signify major changes in driving behavior, but they occurred precisely at the time air bags were coming into the vehicle fleet in large numbers and passenger car side impact protection improved. Also, the population aged, putting greater numbers of more experienced drivers on the roads. The point is that it has never been wise to analyze and evaluate the motor vehicle crash problem from a "magic bullet" perspective. Safer vehicles, improved driver behavior and better roadway environments all contribute to the outcome. More importantly, they do not exist in isolation from one another as crucial disciplines that interact with each other to create one overall system with the ultimate goal of reducing death and injury.[5]

Congress recognized this interaction when the highway safety and motor vehicle safety statutes were adopted simultaneously in 1966, and again in 1991 with passage of the **Intermodal Surface Transportation Efficiency Act** (ISTEA). That omnibus legislation included major changes, overseen by public works committees in the House and Senate, in the roadway construction and highway safety programs, as well as an authorization bill for the motor vehicle regulatory program at NHTSA. Inclusion of the NHTSA motor vehicle authorization bill in the **Intermodal Surface Transportation Efficiency Act** (ISTEA) was opposed by the auto industry, led by Rep. John Dingell (D-MI), chair of the powerful House Energy and Commerce Committee, who fought against its provisions requiring agency action on air bags, head injury, child booster seat, and rollover protection. With adoption of ISTEA, all three major areas of

---

[5]Science and good data tell us there are certain undertakings in auto safety that have a **high payoff**: passive, or automatic protection built into the vehicle, that does not require action on the part of the occupant, is certainly one of these. For example, when air bags are standard equipment on both the driver and front seat passenger side of all vehicles (by the end of the 1990s) it is expected that as many as 9,000 lives a year will be saved. Coupled with manual safety belt use, which is not automatic but highly effective when used, even more death and injury can be avoided. Another extremely high payoff program was the 55 mph speed limit in 1974, when there was an immediate annual savings of several thousand lives attributable almost totally to the lowering of the national maximum speed limit.

consideration—highways, drivers and the automobile—were wrapped together in one program for the 1990s.

The decade of the 1990s may be looked upon as the time in highway and auto safety when the principles embodied in the major safety acts adopted in 1966 truly came together to fully work on behalf of the motoring public, who now know that it is possible to create a healthier and safer environment by demanding prevention at all levels—in the car, behind the wheel, and in the roadway system. Media interest in the various stories involving victims, regulation of the auto industry, community activism, and conflict between the industry and consumers, remains at a surprisingly high level.

AGENDA SETTING: THE LAW AND PROCEDURES

This examination overviewing the legal and procedural aspects of agenda setting in automobile safety regulation includes a review of the legislation passed during the 1960s and 1970s, the administration of the National Highway Traffic Safety Administration, and the decade of the 1980s.

The 1960s and 1970s: Legislation

Most of us associate the topic of automobile safety regulation and reform with Ralph Nader, as well we should. But before Nader's *Unsafe At Any Speed* was published in the mid-1960s, others wrote and held congressional hearings on safety problems with American autos. Congressman Kenneth Roberts held hearings on auto safety from 1956 to 1964; the muckraking book *The Insolent Chariots* by John Keats publicized safety deficiencies, and minor legislation was passed during this period requiring the General Services Administration to set safety standards for automobiles purchased by the federal government (Nadel, 1971:32). Automobile manufacturers generally opposed these early efforts, arguing that driver error was the major cause of accidents, a factor that could not be controlled by federal regulation.

The real push for change came in the early 1960s. With the introduction of high-powered muscle cars, traffic fatalities increased from the 1950s level of approximately 38,000 a year to more than 50,000 by 1965 (see Meier and Morgan, 1982: 161). Perceiving an issue that would generate public support and favorable publicity, Senator Abraham Ribicoff scheduled hearings on automobile safety (Nadel, 1971: 139).

Two factors generated a great deal of media attention for the Ribicoff hearings. The first was the presence on the committee of Robert Kennedy, a visible senator of that time. Kennedy pressed General Motors personnel into admitting that the company spent only $1.5 million on safety research the previous year despite profits of $1.7 billion. The second factor was the testimony of an obscure lawyer named Ralph Nader who had recently published a book called *Unsafe at Any Speed*. Nader argued that automobiles, the GM Corvair in particular, had designed-in safety defects. These safety defects became important during the **"second collision"** in an accident (the driver impacting the inside of the car).

Strong safety regulation was actually helped by a political blunder by GM. The company hired private detectives to investigate Nader. When news of the investigation was revealed, followed by GM's lame excuse that it wanted to know if Nader was behind the rash of Corvair suits filed against the company, sales of *Unsafe at Any Speed* skyrocketed. Hearings were reconvened, and automobile executives weakly submitted to embarrassing questions (Nadel, 1971: 141). Momentum built for legislation to regulate automobile safety, and Nader's subsequent successful lawsuit against GM provided the seed money for his public interest groups.

The **National Traffic and Motor Vehicle Safety Act of 1966** empowered the National Highway Safety Bureau in the Department of Commerce (now the NHTSA in the Department of Transportation) to establish **"reasonable, practicable, and appropriate"** safety standards for automobiles and to create a **systematic and open system of reporting safety defects**.

Over the next eight years, Congress passed a variety of other traffic safety laws. The Highway Safety Act of 1966 provided grants for states to operate highway safety programs resulting in such innovations as raised center-line bumps, breakaway sign posts, and sand-filled barrier cushions (see Menzel and Feller, 1977). That same act established grants, to be apportioned to and administered by representatives of the states' governors, addressing alcohol safety, occupant protection, speed, emergency medical services, and other driver behavior issues. The **National Traffic and Motor Vehicle Safety Act** was amended in 1969 to cover tires and in 1974 to require that all recalled vehicles be repaired free by the manufacturer. In 1974, NHTSA was given joint administration over the National Maximum Speed Limit (then 55 mph) with the Federal Highway Administration (FHWA).

NHTSA Administration

The NHTSA approach to vehicle regulatory administration is two-pronged: (1) regulations that apply to all new cars sold, and (2) recalls of vehicles when safety defects are discovered. By 1982 NHTSA had issued more than 50 safety regulations for vehicles. Among the requirements of the agency's regulations are dual braking systems, windshield wipers, lap and shoulder safety belts, child restraint systems, head rests, and collapsible steering columns (Greer, 1983: 436).

On the safety defect front, NHTSA conducts its own field tests and also provides a hotline for consumer complaints about automobile safety. NHTSA has legislative authority for **fining** automobile companies that fail to conform to safety regulations, but it generally relies on **voluntary recalls**. A **recall** may be requested if a defect is safety-related and creates an unreasonable risk of accident or death (Tobin 1982: 282). From 1966 to 1993, NHTSA presided over the recall of 177 million vehicles sold in the United States.

Although the recalls are termed voluntary, they are hardly that. The automobile companies and NHTSA have frequently been at loggerheads over recalls. Auto companies generally dispute claims of safety defects and then reluctantly agree to a recall after the evidence accumulates. NHTSA determines recalls on a case-by-case basis; such a process usually results in bargaining with the companies about the content, scope or wording of the recall (Tobin, 1982: 283). For recalls to work effectively, owners must be notified and vehicles must be repaired at no cost to the motorist. Studies estimate that only 60 to 70 percent of recalled vehicles are repaired.

The conflict between NHTSA and the auto companies is also evident in the rulemaking process. The auto companies consistently testify before Congress that safety regulations greatly increase the price of automobiles, usually for marginal safety gains. They have a strong ally in Rep. John Dingell (D-MI). In the late 1980s and early 1990s, their cry has been "we're doing this anyway, so why go to the expense and trouble of setting a standard when it is not needed?" Despite the fact auto companies have increased their safety activities by marketing air bags, anti-lock brakes, and other safety applications, it is still the case that government regulation of the industry plays a crucial role in **"pushing the envelope"** of safety technology, creating an important arena where investment and outcome are more stable and certain, and future safety advances are more readily incorporated into vehicle lines. This is especially true as different types of vehicles come into the market that lag behind the regulatory compliance schedule for regular passenger cars: minivans, light trucks and sport utility vehicles. These vehicles are increasingly purchased by families as the **principal passenger car** (over one-third of new cars purchased in the United States in the early 1990s were these types of vehicles), and they fall in a separate category—**multipurpose vehicles (MPVs)**—that have only recently been required to meet the same set of safety standards as traditional passenger cars. Some manufacturers take advantage of the popularity of both these vehicles and safety by incorporating enhanced safety features before the deadline imposed by the government, and then aggressively marketing this fact.

The 1980s: Dry Times for Regulation

When Ronald Reagan won the 1980 presidential election, a new 12-year era began during which very few major vehicle regulations were promulgated by NHTSA. Indeed, the effort to deregulate the auto industry was launched early in the decade when political appointees rescinded the **5-mph bumper standard** (which had been in effect for only a few short months) and the much-debated **"passive restraints"** (air bag) rule. The administration was promptly sued by insurance companies and consumer groups, whose opposition was sustained by the Supreme Court which held that the U.S. DOT (NHTSA) could not withdraw a rule without going through the same process that was necessary to issue a rule (*Motor Vehicle Manufacturers Association v. State Farm Mutual Automobile Insurance Company*). As a result, the withdrawal of the rule was not permitted; NHTSA was told it could withdraw the rule only if evidence supported withdrawal. NHTSA interpreted this decision to mean that they must study the issue further. In 1984 a new air bag rule was issued, with a pro-safety transportation secretary, Elizabeth Dole, at the helm. This new rule would not become effective if enough states to total two-thirds of the nation's population passed laws requiring safety belts by 1987. Thus ensued a well-funded effort by the auto industry to pass safety belt laws that qualified under the terms of the rule in as many of the 50 states as needed. Many laws were passed, surpassing two-thirds of the population within a few years, although most of the state laws did not meet the requirements spelled out in the rule and would not be counted toward the necessary percentage. Auto manufacturers were uncertain about the outcome of the safety belt issue, and began preparing for the eventual installation of air bags. In 1989, Lee Iaccoca, CEO of Chrysler Corporation, announced that it "was possible to teach an old dog new tricks" and reversed his years-old position against air bags by making them standard equipment for drivers of all new Chrysler models. This signalled victory for pro-air bag forces, and other manufacturers soon followed.

The practical effect of this passive restraint rule, therefore, was to gain both safety belt use laws in most states and standard equipment air bags on the driver side. Only in hindsight was it possible to analyze the outcome; most parties in the debate were too suspicious of each other to be objective about the substance at the time. Putting ulterior motives aside, most evaluations give the Dole rule high marks for gaining both air bags and greatly increased safety belt use.

Despite the fact the Reagan administration finally gave us air bags, albeit on the rebound, other **vehicle crashworthiness areas**, such as side impact, rollover, roof crush, and pedestrian safety were virtually forgotten during the decade of the 1980s, especially for multipurpose vehicles (vans and light trucks). Research continued, but not until legislation was passed in 1991 requiring NHTSA to address these rulemakings (with varying degrees of aggressiveness) did the rulemaking schedules pick up speed. (see ISTEA). This law also required air bags be made standard equipment on both driver and passenger sides, in cars and MPVs, on a phased-in schedule by **dates certain** at the end of the decade of the 1990s. Most auto manufacturers plan to meet the requirement ahead of schedule, if air bag suppliers can meet the increased demand. The result of this amazing turnaround is that automobiles sold in America today have the finest occupant protection systems in the world, and thousands of lives have been saved in a very short period of time.

IMPACT OF POLICY DECISIONS

The impact of NHTSA on its environment has been controversial, yet highly beneficial. In earlier years, auto companies contended that NHTSA rules greatly increased costs with few compensating safety benefits. To support their arguments, they cited conservative economic studies (see Peltzman, 1975) that argued these safety regulations imposed more costs than benefits.

What makes policymakers skeptical of these arguments, however, is the common sense perception that automobile safety has improved. The traffic fatality rate ceased its rapid increase after 1965 and began a slow, steady descent. Alcohol-related fatalities began decreasing when the victims movement blossomed, spurred by MADD, and safety belt laws were adopted by most states throughout the 1980s, further decreasing the annual death toll. By the time manufacturers were installing standard-equipment air bags in the late 1980s and early 1990s, progress in reducing deaths and injuries due to motor vehicle crashes was being measured by leaps and bounds—in 1993, just over 40,000 were killed on the nation's highways, a full 10,000 less than a decade before.

This success story can be told many different ways, but there is no doubt that safer vehicles have been a large factor in the enormous reduction. President Clinton's secretary of Health and Human Services, Donna Shalala, credits auto safety successes for the longer lives we are all now living as a nation. Because safety regulations have occurred simultaneously with improvements in highways and laws governing driver behavior, it is difficult to discern their precise impact. For instance, NHTSA estimates air bags are saving approximately 500 lives per year, but safety researchers in the private sector believe the number is significantly higher. It is clear, however, that building safety into the vehicle in the first place provides **prevention** in a way no drunk driving, safety belt, or traffic control law can ever do.

The imposition of costs on the automobile industry is one aspect of safety regulation that cannot be ignored. From an economic standpoint, however, safety regulation simply incorporates the cost of safety into the vehicle price; safety is paid for up front rather than after the fact through injuries. Safety regulation has raised the **cost** of automobiles, but to argue that safety regulation is the cause of the problems faced by the automobile industry is difficult to maintain. Economist Michael Levine (1982:118) has argued that safety requirements actually help the American automobile manufacturer compete with foreign imports. Recent ads extolling the safety features of American automobiles show that Detroit is now recognizing this fact.

Other impacts of NHTSA's policy decisions include:

- the creation of a "**level playing field**" for auto manufacturers and those seeking to influence them; issues are debated through agency regulatory procedures; known agendas result in targeted, clearly directed investments by the industry.

- the creation of a "**safety marketplace**," where manufacturers compete rigorously for dominance in the safety field; combined with reasonable regulation, safety marketing flourishes and companies profit from safety.

- the importance of **consumer information** in such a competitive environment increases, as does the need for more advanced testing procedures to push the industry toward higher levels of crashworthiness and crash avoidance.

CURRENT ISSUES

In the mid-1990s, there are several issues on the table of automobile safety regulation:

Reevaluate Current Generation of Federal Motor Vehicle Safety Standards

The current generation of federal motor vehicle safety standards needs to be evaluated, as a body of work, to address the changing types of vehicles in the market. More than one-third of new passenger vehicles purchased in the United States today are in the multipurpose vehicle category—either vans or light trucks—many are bought as family vehicles. Occupant protection standards set in the 1970s require a 30 mph crash test into a fixed barrier; many believe this requirement should be raised to 35 or 40 mph, and the test should be changed to an **offset crash**, rather than **fixed barrier** (see IIHS Special Report, July 1994). The **New Car Assessment Program (NCAP)**, a crash test program that provides consumer information about the crashworthiness of vehicles in crash tests at 35 mph is being studied in 1994 to determine if the threshold should be raised to 40 mph and consumer information about the results should be simplified.

What is "Appropriate" Regulation?

How much automobile regulation is moderate, appropriate regulation? As the first generation of motor vehicle safety standards nears a close, it becomes more difficult for regulators and politicians to define the degree to which automobiles should be regulated, even to force technology in a positive direction. This is especially true when political decisions must be made in a pro-business environment, because few businesses will say much of anything positive, publicly, about regulation, even if they believe it is helpful. It is easier, therefore, for regulators to spend more time getting drunk drivers off the road and increasing safety belt use rates—important activities—far easier to define as achievable goals, and very popular and visible with the public.

A good example of this dilemma is the Clinton administration's decision to drop research and rulemaking on vehicle rollover stability protection, and substitute **consumer information labeling** about rollover propensity. Although nearly 10,000 people are killed annually due to rollover crashes, many of which happen in the more unstable and very popular sport utility vehicles, NHTSA announced their decision to drop rulemaking because they believed such action could lead to elimination of a class of vehicle, among other reasons. Automakers were reported to be "secretly delighted" because it had been assumed there would be a rollover rule promulgated, as design changes were "inevitable" for such a huge portion of the fatality universe. It was assumed by many in the safety advocacy community that the administration wished to go easy on the auto industry, perhaps even at the behest of the White House, who had made no secret about its support of the domestic auto industry. Consumer information labelling, as a concept, is more popular with that community, and DOT apparently believed consumers would be satisfied with information, and no safety standard. This calculation could not have been more wrong. Many groups protested the decision and petitioned the agency for reconsideration.

NHTSA Still Lacks Aggressiveness

Nearly two years into the Clinton administration, many believe the regulatory program under a Democratic administration sympathetic to business and high-tech advancement is barely more aggressive than previous Republican regimes. No NHTSA Administrator was in place a full year and a half into the Clinton administration. It is clear that the White House would not choose someone with a pro-regulation stance for this consumer regulatory agency.

Funds for Proven Auto Safety Efforts Continue to be Diverted

The Intelligent Vehicle Highway Systems program receives enormous levels of funding from the Highway Trust Fund and the general fund (approximately $120 million proposed for Fiscal Year 1995), at the same time biomechanics and other highway safety research struggles to maintain very low levels of funding ($5 million budget request for biomechanics in FY93.)

FUTURE POLICY DIRECTIONS

Auto safety regulation appears to be headed in several directions:

Expanding the New Car Assessment Program

The **New Car Assessment Program** (NCAP), a crash test program that provides consumer information and rates new cars on crashworthiness will likely be expanded and improved to include more cars, higher crash test speeds, and different crash test modes. Data from the NCAP program provides the basis for the successful, privately published *Car Book* (Gillis, 1994) from which consumers learn about safety attributes of new cars. Vehicles in the NCAP are crashed at 35 mph, above the 30 mph requirement for federal motor vehicle safety standards. This has had the effect of pushing the industry to compete and exceed government standards.

Developing a "New Generation" of Automobile Safety Standards

A new push for the "next generation" of auto safety standards will develop, particularly to accommodate new types of vehicles already on the road (multi-purpose vehicles) and new safety technologies. Making small cars safer will be the greatest challenge, seconded only by appropriating adequate government funds.

Defining Auto and Highway Safety as Public Health Remedies

Further definition of auto and highway safety as major public health remedies will occur, using **societal cost** studies to advocate additional funding and legislative action.

Improving Coordination Among Government Agencies

Coordination among government agencies both within U.S. DOT and across cabinet departments will increase to address the motor vehicle crash problem (see Transportation Research Board, Safety Management Systems workshop, July 1994). Federal and state government agencies concerned with and responsible for particular disciplines and programs will attempt to communicate better in the interest of cost-saving and increased efficiency in the delivery of safety in the roadway environment, among drivers and passengers and in the vehicle itself.

SUMMARY

Table 12.1 provides a summary of automobile safety regulation. It includes descriptions about economics, technology, subsystem, and the impact of macropolitical actors.

Auto safety regulation has had a dramatic, positive effect in keeping fatalities and injuries down, considering the potential size of the problem. The bank of regulations promulgated in the 1960s and 1970s have produced a general standard and demand for safety unmatched in the world. However, the national vehicle fleet is changing, and will continue to change into the 21st century, forcing an overall review of current standards and creation of a new generation of safety rules.

Table 12.1   A Summary of Automobile Safety Protection

Economics

Ease of entry	Moderate to difficult
Number of jobs	4 million
Profits	Vary

Technology

Complexity	High
Stability	Moderate
Substitutes	Moderate

Subsystem

Bureaucracy control	Moderate
Industry coalition	Strong
Nonindustry coalition	Moderate to strong
Bureaucratic resources:	
Expertise	Strong
Cohesion	Weak
Leadership	Weak to moderate
Legislative authority:	
Goals	General and specific
Coverage	All
Sanctions	Good
Procedures	Fair

Impact of Macropolitical Actors

Congress	Moderate
President	Strong
Courts	Strong

Auto manufacturers have finally decided that safety sells, so there is not as much argument with NHTSA that safety standards are necessary; it is the level and degree of standard that is debatable for them. In some cases, such as the rollover stability standard abandoned by the Clinton administration in 1994, auto industry and government officials make the case that consumer information, other safety measures (such as safety belt use and better door locks) and market forces produce adequate safety.

Although Congress clearly directed NHTSA to move forward aggressively in various auto safety areas (air bags, head injury, side impact, rollover) in ISTEA in 1991, budgets for NHTSA's supporting research and rulemaking activities are meager, and not nearly enough to do the job. Congressional support for program expansion in most agencies is dwindling due to deficit control and **anti-government rhetoric**, although most credit the lion's share of weak budgets for NHTSA rulemaking activities to auto industry advocacy and to the chairmanship of the House Appropriations Transportation Subcommittee in the early 1990s. The subcommittee was chaired by Rep. Bob Carr (D-MI), who forcefully represented his home state and the auto industry throughout his tenure, until he left the House of Representatives to run for the Senate in 1994.

Like other industries, the auto and its supply industries favor **international harmonization of safety standards** to facilitate international trade. Because American safety standards are usually of a high quality, advocates fear harmonization could weaken existing standards.

It is expected that auto safety advocates and other public health constituencies will continue to push for higher standards that will provide additional crashworthiness for emerging vehicle fleets, into the next century.

Better definition of and support for meaningful and specific safety in the Intelligent Vehicle Highway Safety program is a must for the advocacy community, particularly because so many resources are diverted from traditional research and demonstration programs to this new, very future-oriented technology program.

The auto industry is complex, and constitutes an enormous percentage of the economy. The need and demand for safety technologies offer numerous opportunities to inventors and other entrepreneurs to enter the market, although the major manufacturers, both domestic and foreign, exercise primary control over the final product.

In the subsystems, NHTSA is the official agency regulating the auto, and its influence within the industry has shifted considerably in the nearly 30 years of its existence. Although small in number, NHTSA's regulatory staff are highly knowledgeable and professional people who see the need for government oversight of this mega-industry. Information about technological and other advances are often shared, to each other's benefit, between government and industry, and comments to the various rulemaking dockets are carefully reviewed. But a combination of political and economic forces have taken their toll on the NHTSA research and rulemaking staffs, limiting their ability to play as major a role in advancing auto safety as they did in the earlier days.

Advocacy groups continue to push for more resources for the agency, and for continued congressional and executive branch leadership on behalf of auto safety, and new, non-traditional constituencies are paying more attention to the regulatory issues. The emergence of injury control as a public health epidemic and a full program within the Centers for Disease Control (motor vehicles are fully a third of the national injury picture) has helped define the motor vehicle crash problem more widely and dramatically. For example, for the first time in the history of a major NHTSA rulemaking, the National SAFE KIDS Campaign and the National Head Injury Foundation joined Advocates for Highway and Auto Safety and the Insurance Institute for Highway Safety in signing the 1994 petition to reconsider NHTSA's rollover stability decision.

Media campaigns objecting to questionable industry advertising, especially for unlimited speeds in the new "muscle" cars, have been effective from time to time. Examples include a successful effort by several safety groups to coerce Nissan to pull an advertisement first shown in a prime time Superbowl advertising slot showing its newest sports car outrunning a supersonic jet. Ford Motor Company voluntarily stopped showing an ad depicting a young soccer team in the back of a pickup truck (although the truck was not moving, the implication was they had just arrived at the field) when they were telephoned about it after a safety advocate saw it during a weekend show. Nonindustry coalitions do hold sway over industry activities in this way, although NHTSA itself has no official authority to limit the content of auto industry advertising. (The Federal Trade Commission governs advertising practices, and thus far has been reluctant to enter this debate.) Only one company has actual guidelines governing responsible advertising as regards safety.

Auto industry trade associations and coalitions are well funded, with large staffs and influential leaders. The domestic trade association, American Automobile Manufacturers Association, hired Andrew Card, former secretary of transportation in the Bush administration, as its president just as the Clinton administration took office. Card, as did his members, worked closely with the new administration on the **North American Free Trade Agreement** (NAFTA), and had lead responsibility lobbying for employer mandates in health care reform for Clinton. Clearly, this close relationship with the Democratic White House has been beneficial to the domestic auto industry.

The insurance industry continues to influence the regulatory program, both through litigation (air bags and bumpers) and by supporting other groups advocating legislation for auto safety measures. NHTSA has no formal regulatory authority over the insurance industry, except to require insurance data on automobile theft.

Nonindustry coalitions are often single-issue in focus, or limited in the areas they wish to influence. Involvement of more groups in regulatory issues, however, is expanding, due to special efforts by aggressive advocacy groups to include them and to an existing and growing bank of data documenting high benefits of vehicle safety standards. Influence by nonindustry coalitions and organizations is often exerted in the media, as a counterforce to extensive auto industry resources and lobbying activities. The more diverse the coalition supporting the issue, and the more personal the individual story highlighting the need for action, the more interested the media seems to be.

The impact of macropolitical actors on auto safety regulation is varied. Congress' control over and direction to NHTSA is moderately strong, although it has diminished some in recent years. Fewer members of Congress demonstrate leadership in auto regulatory oversight, although those that remain committed take strong stands in favor of reasonable and forceful regulatory activity. Statutory guidance is clear and direct, although NHTSA's response to its mandates ebbs and flows with changes in leadership in the administrator's office, in the secretary's office, and at the White House.

The role of the president and other executive branch officials has always had a high impact on the outcome of auto safety regulation, as has that of the courts. A landmark ruling from the Supreme Court forced the Reagan administration to reissue the standard that gives us air bags, and as an additional bonus, state safety belt use laws. The auto industry, and particularly domestic manufacturers, is recognized by both Republican and Democratic administrations as a powerful force in our fluctuating economy. As long as the recovery, growth, and success of this huge industry remains primary to a healthy economy, arguments for regulation that will create "undue burdens" on the industry will likely fall on unsympathetic ears.

The challenge for **pro-regulatory** forces for the rest of the decade and for 2000 and beyond is to continually educate newly elected and appointed officials about the short and long term cost benefits of auto safety regulation, and to organize the American public around the issues. The public now demands and expects reasonable safety to be built into new cars, and expects their government to help make this happen.

Chapter 13
Depository Institutions Regulation

Jing J. Xiao[1]

In the 1980s, one of the most salient issues was deregulation of the banking industry. Failures of a huge number of banks and thrifts greatly influenced the national economy and consumer well being. For example, consumers have nearly $300 billion above the insurance limit at **Federal Deposit Insurance Corporation (FDIC)-insured institutions**. Because a 1991 law limits the FDIC's options for handling bank failures, **uninsured depositors** (including some who thought their deposits were insured) lost money in nearly half of all the bank failures in 1992, compared to less than 15 percent of the bank failures in previous years (FDIC, 1993: 5).[2] How to effectively and efficiently regulate the troubled banking industry will remain a critically important issue in the 1990s.

Even though many kinds of financial institutions offer products and services that were traditionally provided by banks, **depository institutions** in this chapter refers to commercial banks, savings associations, savings banks, and credit unions. These depository institutions make loans and offer banking services to businesses and individuals that are regulated by a complicated subsystem, involving several federal agencies and many state agencies.

---

[1]Jing J. Xiao is assistant professor of consumer economics at University of Rhode Island. Mr. Xiao received his PhD in consumer economics from Oregon State University in 1991. He is the winner of the 1992 Dissertation Award of American Council on Consumer Interests. Xiao is the author of *Modern Family Economics* (Shanghai People Press, 1993), and the co-author or contributor of several other books. His current research interests include family saving and investing behavior and the impact of financial deregulation on consumer well-being.

[2]In response to a Freedom of Information Act request (Garman, 1994a), the Federal Deposit Insurance Corporation reports that of twelve insured banks that failed through the first eleven months of 1994, eight institutions had deposits that were not covered over the insured amount of $100,000. In those institutions, there were "619 depositors who had insured deposits of $14,211,827." In recent years, the FDIC has recovered approximately 82 percent of uninsured deposits and returned those amounts to those with uninsured deposits within a couple of years. Therefore, one can conclude that the 619 underinsured depositors at the eight banking institutions might eventually recover an estimated $11,653,698; this would amount to an aggregate loss of $2,558,129 for those depositors, or an average uninsured loss of $41,326.80 per underinsured depositor.

This chapter will first introduce agencies that have direct responsibilities to regulate depository institutions. Then follows a description of advocacy coalitions, including the regulated depository institutions and their lobbying groups; and the nonregulated, the consumer organizations concerned about the banking regulation. Environmental elements, such as macropolitical actors, economic factors, and technologies, affecting the agenda setting of banking regulation are also discussed. Three major events of the past decade, the deregulation of the banking industry, the savings and loans bailout, and the truth in savings legislation are then addressed in turn, emphasizing the processes of agenda setting and impact on consumer well being. Following is a discussion of current issues including fair lending, regulatory consolidation, interstate banking, and mutual funds sales. The last section concludes the chapter by providing an overall assessment of the banking regulation and predictions of future trends in this field.

THE SUBSYSTEM

This examination of the depository institutions regulation subsystem includes an overview of the key federal regulatory agencies, their resources, advocacy coalitions, and the regulatory environment.

The Regulatory Agencies

The United States maintains a **dual banking system**. A bank or any other type of depository institution can be chartered by either the federal government or any one of the state governments. Banks can switch from national to state charters and vice versa. Because of this dual banking system, **two sets of regulatory agencies** exist at federal and state levels. The major federal agencies regulating banking activities are the **Office of the Comptroller of the Currency (OCC)**, the **Federal Reserve System (FRS)**, the **Federal Deposit Insurance Corporation (FDIC)**, the **Resolution Trust Corporation (RTC)**, the **Office of Thrift Supervision (OTS)**, and the **National Credit Union Administration (NCUA)**. All states have their own **banking departments**. The choice of **charter** (state or federal) determines whether a bank's primary regulator will be a state or a federal agency. Most federal regulation of state-chartered banks is **optional**. For example, state-chartered banks may join the FDIC and/or the Federal Reserve. Thus, virtually all state-chartered banks are jointly regulated by federal and state authorities. These banks are subject to at least two separate government examinations and to the administrative rules and regulations of more than one agency (Friedman, 1989: 199).

OFFICE OF THE COMPTROLLER OF THE CURRENCY

The Office of the Comptroller of the Currency, an agency in the **Department of the Treasury**, was created for the purpose of establishing and regulating a national banking system. The **National Currency Act** of 1863 provided for the chartering and supervising functions in this connection. The income of the OCC is derived principally from assessments paid by national banks and interest on investments in U.S. Government obligations.

This agency charters new banking institutions that desire chartering as national banks. Supervision of existing national banks is aided by the required submission of periodic reports and detailed on-site examinations. In addition, the Comptroller considers applications for mergers in which the resulting bank will be a national bank and applications from banks to establish branches. The Comptroller of the Currency also promulgates rules and regulations for the guidance of national banks and bank directors. The Office of the Comptroller had a 1992 budget of $305 million and 3,508 personnel (U.S. Government, 1994: A919-920).

THE FEDERAL RESERVE SYSTEM

The Federal Reserve System, or the "**Fed**" as it is popularly known, administers the national banking system. It is one of the most powerful and independent agencies in the federal government. The system is governed by the Board of Governors of the Federal Reserve System. Members of the board are appointed for 14-year terms and can only be removed via impeachment.

The Federal Reserve System operates under the provisions of the **Federal Reserve Act** of 1913, as mended, and other acts of Congress. The Board of Governors determines general monetary, credit, and operating policies for the system as a whole and formulates the rules and regulations necessary to carry out the purposes of the Federal Reserve Act. The Fed regulates, examines, and approves mergers for those state banks that are also members of the Federal Reserve System. It also administers the reserves that all member banks must maintain with the Fed and it regulates the activities of bank holding companies. The Fed has substantial monetary powers that have made the agency the major player in national economic policy.

The Fed levies upon the Federal Reserve banks, in proportion to their capital and surplus, an assessment sufficient to pay its estimated expenses. No government appropriation is required to support operations of the Board of Governors of the Federal Reserve System. The Board's 1991 operating expenses were $115 million with a staff of 1,520 (U.S. Government, 1994: A1267-1268).

FEDERAL DEPOSIT INSURANCE CORPORATION

The Federal Deposit Insurance Corporation (FDIC) created by the **Banking Act of 1933** to provide protection for bank depositors and to foster sound banking practices, is a government corporation that insures bank deposits up to $100,000 for each account. Any state bank may opt to insure its deposits with the FDIC, and insurance is compulsory for national banks. With insurance comes regulation. The FDIC regulates all state banks that receive FDIC insurance but are not members of the Federal Reserve System. Its regulation covers the same economic soundness, consumer protection, and merger laws that the Fed and the Comptroller provide for other banks.

Because of the banking crisis in the mid-1980s, the FDIC's regulatory responsibility was expanded by the **Federal Institutions Reform, Recovery and Enforcement Act (FIRREA)** of 1989. This law established several new agencies to take over functions formerly provided by the **Federal Home Loan Bank Board** (FHLBB) that was dissolved by the same law. These agencies are the **Office of Thrift Supervision** (OTS), the **Resolution Trust Corporation** (RTC), the **Savings Association Insurance Fund** (SAIF), and the **FSLIC Resolution Fund** (FRF). SAIF and FRF, along with the original regulating body, now renamed as Bank Insurance Fund (BIF), are administered by the FDIC. RTC and OTS will be introduced separately in the following two sections.

The **Bank Insurance Fund (BIF)**, a public enterprise revolving fund, derives its income principally from insurance assessments paid by insured banks. The fund represents the accumulated net income of the BIF and is reserved for the protection of depositors in insured banks and for payment of administrative and insurance expenses. In 1992, the operating budget was $343 million[3] with 11,799 employees (U.S. Government, 1994: A1067-1068).

The **Savings Association Insurance Fund (SAIF)** insures depository institutions formerly insured by the **Federal Savings and Loan Insurance Corporation** (FSLIC)[4]. Starting in 1993, SAIF receives assessments paid by its members. Beginning in 1994, SAIF is appointed conservator or receiver of failed thrifts. Its 1992 operational budget was $102 million with a staff of 652 (U.S. Government, 1994: A1069-1070).

The **FSLIC Resolution Fund (FRF)** is the successor to FSLIC assets and liabilities from resolved cases. FRF will terminate upon the disposition of all its assets, and any net proceeds would be paid to the Treasury. FRF's 1992 operational obligation was $39 million and had 1,498 employees. Its budget is expected to decrease over years. In 1994, its operational budget is estimated to be $20 million with a staff of 1,185 (U.S. Government, 1994: A1070-1071).

RESOLUTION TRUST CORPORATION

The FIRREA of 1989 established the **Resolution Trust Corporation (RTC)** to dispose of insolvent thrift institutions. RTC has an **Oversight Board** to provide general policy direction and to review its performance. Its seven members including the Secretary of the Treasury as Chairperson, the Chairman of the Fed, the Chairman of the FDIC, the Director of the OTS, the RTC Chief Executive Officer, and two members appointed by the president with the advice and consent of the Senate.

Sources of funds for the RTC include income and sale proceeds from assets acquired during the course of resolving thrift cases, the sale of capital certificates to the Resolution Funding Corporation (a privately capitalized financing entity also established by FIRREA), and funds appropriated prior to 1993. Under present law, the Oversight Board may direct that the unused funds be transferred to the SAIF for SAIF losses, if needed. RTC is planned to be terminated on December 31, 1996. Upon its termination, all assets and liabilities of the RTC will be transferred to the FRF, managed by the FDIC. RTC's 1994 budget and personnel are estimated as $1.24 billion and 5,752, respectively (U.S. Government, 1994: A1138-1140).

---

[3]The operating budgets reported here exclude undistributed items, such as undistributed resolution outlays.

[4]FSLIC was a subsidiary of the Federal Home Loan Bank Board (FHLBB) that offered deposit insurance to savings and loan associations before 1989.

OFFICE OF THRIFT SUPERVISION

The **Office of Thrift Supervision (OTS)**, located in the Treasury Department, was also created by the **Financial Institutions Reform, Recovery, and Enforcement Act (FIRREA)** of 1989. The Office assumed the regulatory functions of the Federal Home Loan Bank Board dissolved by the same act.

The Office charters, regulates, and examines federal thrifts, all of which are insured by the **Savings Association Insurance Fund** (SAIF). In addition, the Office cooperates in the examinations and supervision of state-chartered thrifts insured by SAIF. The Office sets capital standards for federal and state thrifts and reviews applications of state-chartered thrifts for conversion to federal thrifts. It also reviews applications for establishment of branch offices. Income of the office is derived principally from assessments on thrifts, examination fees and interest on investments in U.S. Government obligations. This agency has a 1992 budget of $253 million and 2,527 personnel (U.S. Government, 1994: A920-921).

THE NATIONAL CREDIT UNION ADMINISTRATION

The **National Credit Union Administration** (NCUA) was established in 1970. Before 1970, from 1934 to 1969, authority for regulating credit unions was shifted among several different agencies. NCUA is governed by a three-person board appointed by the president and confirmed by the Senate.

NCUA's activities include chartering new federal credit unions, supervising established federal credit unions, making periodic examinations of their financial condition and operating practices, and providing administrative services. The operating fund is reimbursed for the insurance fund's share of the agency's administrative expenses by the insurance fund. The reimbursement percentage, which is reviewed and adjusted periodically, is currently at 50 percent. The regulatory functions of NCUA were budgeted for $82 million with a staff of 996 in 1992 (U.S. Government, 1994: A1105-1106).

STATE BANKING COMMISSIONS

All states charter commercial banks, and some states charter savings banks, savings and loan associations, and credit unions as well. A **state charter** is granted upon investigation of the applicant's background and a finding that the bank meets the state's capital requirements. States examine the institutions they charter, rule on their acquisitions and branching applications, and issue advisory opinions on acquisition applications received from bank holding companies. States also examine most of the U.S. branches and agencies of foreign banks (Friedman, 1989: 199).

In general, states have a reputation for lax regulation of banks (Spellman, 1982: 23). Many differences between federal and state regulation have been documented, including definitions of what constitutes a loan or capital, restrictions on underwriting securities or purchasing stock, and restriction on mergers, foreign affiliates, and branches (Stone, 1979: 25).

OTHER REGULATORY AGENCIES

A variety of other regulators operate in the financial institutions area. The antitrust division of the **Justice Department** is responsible for enforcing antitrust laws in connection with bank mergers and bank holding company acquisitions. **Finance companies** are regulated in terms of consumer protection by the Federal Trade Commission and by the state regulation. **Investment companies and money market mutual funds** are governed by the rules of the Securities and Exchange Commission. Some aspects of **private pension funds** are regulated by federal laws. Insurance companies are regulated by state agencies. These other regulators occasionally play a role in the subsystems of federal financial institutions.

Agency Resources

Because financial regulation is fairly complex, the various federal regulators have all developed a reputation for expertise. Each has the cohesion to operate in secrecy; sometimes financial institutions are closed, for example, before any outsiders know the institution is being examined. Leadership is less positive. Although many regulatory heads have effectively managed these agencies, few have become known for innovative leadership outside the regulatory subsystem.

Banking became highly salient in the mid-1980s because of a huge number of **bank failures**. Between 1945 and 1982, an average of less than ten banks failed every year and the total number of problem banks on the FDIC's **watch list** stood at only 200 out of an industry total of over 14,000 institutions. But from 1982 to 1987, more than 600 banks failed. And in 1988 more than 1,500 banks, with total deposits of almost $250 billion, were on the FDIC's list of **problem banks** (Friedman, 1989: 203-204). The recent banking crisis resulted in serious political concerns that caused the passage of several important banking laws. These laws required reorganizing of the subsystem of banking regulation (see later on).

Financial regulators have a generous grant of **legislative authority**. First, legislative **goals** are more specific than the vague "public interest" standards of transportation regulation but less specific than the detailed goals of agricultural policy. This grants the regulatory agencies a good deal of discretion. Second, each agency **covers** only a portion of the industry, thus fragmenting power; but within the specified portion, coverage is almost universal. All financial regulators have generally unrestricted rulemaking powers. Third, the agencies have a wide variety of sanctions. Institutions that violate regulations may be required to write off loans, individuals may be forced out of a relationship with an institution, and institutions may be closely by the regulators. The discretion is unlimited. Fourth, agency procedures place no specific limitations on the activities of the agencies.

The federal government's **major goal** in regulating banks is to protect banks, their depositors, and the communities in which they operate from bank failures. Banks must **operate prudently** and have **sufficient liquidity** (or access to it) to prevent a loss of public confidence in the safety and soundness of the banking system. Another regulatory goal is to **promote competition in banking**. The federal government also seeks to use regulation to protect bank owners from management fraud and excessive risk taking and to assure them a reasonable rate of return on capital invested. A final goal of federal regulation is to protect consumers of bank credit and bank services from **discrimination, deception, and abuse of their rights** (Friedman, 1989: 193).

Compliance examinations are generally conducted by bank examiners who are specifically trained to review consumer protection laws and regulatory compliance. All federal bank regulatory agencies operate under a **common set of guidelines** to ensure uniform enforcement of consumer regulations. The regulatory agencies generally agree on overall examination procedures, while there are some differences in the emphases of financial ratios, methods used for off-site monitoring, information storage and release policies, and so forth (Gordon, 1992: 2). Special instructional manuals are used for each regulation, and an examination checklist is followed. Each consumer law and regulation is covered by a special report complete with procedures for detecting and correcting violations (Friedman, 1989: 221).

The decision to impose specific enforcement actions generally depends on the **composite capital adequacy, asset quality, management, earnings, and liquidity (CAMEL) rating** the institution receives during its periodic examinations. If the CAMEL rating is poor, a bank or thrift will probably be subject to formal or informal enforcement cation. **Informal enforcement actions** include a board resolution or commitment letter and a **memorandum of understanding (MOU)**, a document drafted by the regulators and agreed to by the institution. The **formal enforcement action**, which is more common, is the **cease and desist order (C&D)**. C&D can both prohibit some actions and mandate others. The most serious and direct threat to bank management and directors is a **civil money penalty (CMP)**. CMPs are generally imposed for violations of laws or regulations or for violations of orders or written commitments such as C&D or MOUs (Rockett, 1994: 60-62).

Advocacy Coalitions

Major depository intermediaries that are most concerned about banking regulations are commercial banks and thrifts. **Thrifts** refer to savings associations, savings banks, and credit unions, since the early effort of these financial intermediaries was to encourage thrift among workers. In addition, a number of nonprofit organizations play active roles in advancing consumer's interests in the area of banking regulation.

COMMERCIAL BANKS

Commercial banks are the full-service institutions that people normally identify as banks. Ranging in size from the California-based Bank of America to the local bank in a rural community, approximately 12,000 banks have assets in excess of $2.9 trillion (FDIC, 1991; Federal Reserve System, 1994: 85). In a subdivided financial world (e.g., pre-1970), commercial banks serviced the day-to-day needs of depositors (usually checking accounts and large savings accounts) and loaned money on short-term notes to business. Commercial banks are usually formed as **stock companies**, an economic characteristic that distinguishes them from thrift institutions.

Commercial banks, as can be imagined, are a powerful political force in the United States. They have the prestige, resources, and dispersion that Rourke (1984) deems necessary for influence. Some 280 **political action committees** are bank related (Keller, 1982: 191). The banking industry is not monolithic, as the **large money center banks** (e.g., Chase Manhattan, Citibank, Marine Midland) often have goals that differ from those of small rural banks. Large banks often represent themselves, but the **American Bankers Association (ABA)** has advocated the interests of big banks in deregulation efforts and many other issues. Smaller banks are more likely to belong to the Independent Bankers Association of America and identify with its concerns about competition from larger banks. Regulatory issues of current concern to commercial banks include **Community Reinvestment Act** reform, regulatory agency consolidation, and interstate banking (Smith, 1994: 16).

SAVINGS ASSOCIATIONS AND SAVINGS BANKS

Savings associations, normally called **savings and loans (S&Ls)**, were designed as a specialized financial institution to provide funds for purchasing houses. A savings association in the pre-1970s era attracted long-term savings from the small saver and loaned this money to individuals to purchase homes under long-term mortgages. Savings banks like savings associations originally developed because commercial banks were not interested in offering savings accounts to individuals (Mayer, 1974: 190). Based on a **mutual** system of organization (that is, they have no stockholders; depositors technically purchase an interest in the bank), **savings banks** are state chartered and located mostly in the Northeast. They were designed to encourage saving (especially among the working class) and invested initially in government bonds and later in home mortgages (Spellman, 1982: 20). In the United States, about 2,500 savings associations and savings banks have assets over $1 trillion (Kidwell, Peterson, and Blackwell, 1993: 524; Federal Reserve Board, 1994: 93).

Even though savings associations vary greatly in terms of size and the role they play in long-term finance, they have generally spoken with a unified voice in lobbying efforts. The **Savings and Community Bankers of America**, which created by the merger of the United States League of Savings Institutions and National Council of Community Bankers in 1992, now represents the nation's savings associations and savings banks (Daniels and Schwartz, 1993: 58).

Savings banks have developed less political clout than other depository institutions for both resource reasons and motivational reasons. In terms of resources, savings banks, because they are regionally concentrated, do not have access to a great number of legislators. In addition, savings banks did not suffer a great trauma from the economic depression of the 1930s and, as a result, had no motivation to seek government help. In fact, they often turned down offers of **government assistance** (e.g., deposit insurance) to avoid regulation. Savings banks were organized as the National Association of Mutual Savings Banks until 1982. At that time they merged with a small savings and loan association to form the National Council of Savings Institutions.

CREDIT UNIONS

Credit unions are depository institutions that serve a defined group of persons based on a common bond of employment, association, or residence. Normally affiliated with an employer, credit unions accept deposits (they refer to deposits as the **purchase of shares** in the credit union) and make installment loans to members. Credit unions seek to provide cheap funds for member loans while at the same time earning higher interest for member deposits. They have the potential to do this because the common bond (knowing the member) reduces the risk of bad loans and because operating overhead is reduced to a minimum (often with volunteer labor). Credit unions are generally small; about 12,700 credit unions have assets of $280.7 billion (NCUA, 1992:6; Federal Reserve System, 1994: 93).

Credit unions are represented by the **Credit Union National Association (CUNA).** Although greatly dispersed throughout the country, credit unions have some organizational liabilities. By providing services in a somewhat closed market, credit unions can escape the financial pressures that squeeze other institutions. If demand for loans dries up or interest rates are too low, credit unions often deposit their funds in commercial banks. Current concerns of NCUA are court cases on credit union's liberal membership recruitment, regulatory consolidation, and Truth in Savings compliances ("NCUA's Hot Topics", 1994: 20-21).

CONSUMER INTEREST ORGANIZATIONS

Among major consumer interest organizations involved in the legislative process of banking regulation are the Consumer Federation of America and Consumers Union. **Consumer Federation of America** is an organization representing over 240 national and state consumer groups. One of its members, **Consumers Union**, the publisher of the influential *Consumer Reports* magazine with an estimated five million circulation, is also active in promoting consumers' interests in the banking legislation.

Both groups voiced consumer concerns in front of congressional hearings on banking deregulation (Brobeck, 1991). Some current concerns of these groups include defending against the banks' attempts to roll back regulations, encouraging the administration to appoint tough new regulators to provide effective implementation of such laws as the Community Reinvestment Act and other fair lending laws, restructuring the banking regulatory agencies, and encouraging the legislation on bank mutual fund sales (CFA News, 4/1993: 2; 4/1994: 2).

Regulatory Environment

This examination of the depository institutions regulatory environment includes an overview of the macropolitical actors, economic factors, and technology.

MACROPOLITICAL ACTORS

Congress, presidents, and courts are three macropolitical actors that have avenues to intervene on regulatory policy issues. In the 1980s and early 1990s, Congress passed several important laws first **deregulating**, then **reregulating** the financial institutions. House and Senate Banking Committees, under the leadership of the chairmen in different periods, Senator Jake Garn (1981-1986, R-UT), Senator William Proxmire (1986-1988, D-WS), Senator Donald W. Riegle (1989-, D-MI), Representative Fernand J. St. Germain (1980-1988, D-RI), Henry B. Gonzalez (1989-, D-TX), who played active and prominent roles in pushing passages of these laws. Also, the informal personal contacts by member of Congress with those in the regulatory agencies has the potential to influence the policies of those agencies. The macropolitical influence was exemplified when the Senate conferees were willing to give up other conditions to keep Danny Wall's job, the then-Chairman of the **Federal Home Loan Bank Board**, when negotiating a major re-regulation law in 1989; this occurred in part because Wall was a former chief banking aid of Senator Garn (Day, 1993: 117).

Presidents have provided some of the leadership in major legislative efforts, especially during the banking crisis of 1980s. Then-President Bush released his plan to solve the savings and loan crisis, which brought the passage of a major re-regulation law in 1989. President Clinton's proposal of regulatory consolidation later played a leading role in the legislatively mandated reform of the U.S. banking regulatory system.

Court rulings also have influenced the subsystem that regulates the banking industry. In 1979 the D.C. Circuit Court of Appeals consolidated three cases regarding the automatic transfer of funds by banks, share drafts by credit unions, and remote service units by savings associations, and speeded the pace of deregulation of the depository institutions (Conte, 1979: 1364).

ECONOMIC FACTORS

Economic factors that influence the banking industry are ease of entry, number of firms, and profitability. Entry varies among the different types of depository institutions. Credit unions are without a doubt the easiest institution to open whereas commercial banks appear to be the most difficult. Under the 1927 **McFadden Act**, **interstate banking** was restricted. However, many states now permit interstate banking in some way, typically through bank holding companies. As a result, entries to local markets by out-of-state bank holding companies are common in many states.

Through the 1980s banking crisis, the number of banks and thrifts decreased. In the early 1980s there were over 14,000 commercial banks, 4,600 savings associations (savings associations and savings banks), 460 savings banks, and 23,000 credit unions. One decade later, the number of commercial banks, savings institutions, and credit unions decreased to 12,000, 2,500, and 12,700, respectively. The number of banks is predicted to continue decreasing. It is estimated that in 2010, there will be about 5,500 independent banking organizations. At the same time, the proportion of domestic banking assets accounted for by the largest 50 and 100 banking organizations will rise sharply to 70% and 87%, respectively, compared with 52% and 65% in 1989 (Hannan and Rhoades, 1992).

The **profitability** of depository institutions varies by the type of institution and the time frame being considered. In 1991 the average return on assets for the year was .56 percent, up from an average of .49 percent in each of the previous two years. More than 89% of commercial banks were profitable in 1991, the highest proportion since 1982 (FDIC, 1991: 10). High profits at commercial banks were seen again in 1994. The picture of savings institutions is not as good as that of commercial banks. All savings associations and savings banks lost money in the late 1980s and early 1990s (Kidwell, Peterson, and Blackwell, 1993: 523). The situation of credit unions is the best in recent years. The average return on assets increased to 1.3% in 1992 from .8% in the previous year (NCUA, 1993).

TECHNOLOGY

Technology used in banking can be categorized as relatively simple and substitutable. At a rudimentary level, the process of taking deposits and making loans does not differ significantly from that of the moneylenders of the middle ages. The technologies of commercial banking, savings associations, savings banks, credit unions, and other financial intermediaries are easily substituted for one another. However, new developments in technology in the 1980s provided banks and thrifts more opportunities as well as competitors that demand regulatory responses.

In the 1980s, banks and thrifts became computerized and **electronic funds transfer (EFT)** became common among depository institutions. With computers and electronic network technology, banks and thrifts were able to achieve faster transactions and a tightly linked network of financial institutions helped transform the market for money from a local market to a national and international market.

The popularity of **automated teller machines (ATMs)** helped banks and thrifts to circumvent laws against **branch banking**. ATMs are technically not branches because they do not offer the full services of a bank such as loans. With nationwide systems of ATMs honoring the cards of all members, a form of interstate banking was established.

Technologies such as computers, electronic funds transfer, automated teller machines, and electronic data interchange (EDI) now used by banks and thrifts are also utilized by nonbanks, such as VISA, American Express, AT&T, Merrill Lynch, and General Electric. Nonbanks do not offer all the services of a depository institution, such as accepting deposits. **Nonbanks** offer credit cards, home banking, automated teller machines, and nonbank lending and deposit products which provide payments system functionality such as money-market mutual funds and cash management accounts with checking and payment-card features. Because consumers want information along with monetary transfers and nonbanks are providing it, the traditional payment system used by banks has been challenged (Furash, 1994).

DEREGULATION OF FINANCIAL INSTITUTIONS

In the early 1980s, the U.S. government deregulated depository institutions. The deregulation was accomplished by two important banking laws: the **Depository Institutions Deregulation and Monetary Control Act** (DIDMCA) of 1980 and the **Garn-St. Germain Depository Institutions Act** of 1982.

Background

Before the 1980s, the depository institutions were strictly regulated under two laws created five decades earlier. Through the **McFadden Act** of 1927, the federal government severely limited interstate banking. As a response to the collapse of the banking industry during the Great Depression, the **Glass-Steagall Act**, a portion of Federal Banking Act of 1933, created the Federal Deposit Insurance Corporation (FDIC) and restricted the products and prices of banking institutions. Commercial banks could no longer underwrite securities or act as securities brokers. The **Banking Act of 1935** required the Federal

Reserve to impose ceilings on savings interest rates and to prohibit interest payments on checking accounts; this was known as **Regulation Q**. The general intent of all the depression-era legislation was to ensure financial soundness of banks by limiting risks, including the risks of competition (Spellman, 1982: 27). Moreover, the legislation **"firewall"** against catastrophes was created between the banking and securities industries in the United States.

Because of the banking acts of the 1930s, the depository institutions had clearly defined roles in the financial system. Commercial banks were to service the daily needs of depositors and make short-term loans to local businesses. Savings associations and savings banks were to service the long-term needs of savers and loan money for mortgages. Credit unions were to service long-term saving needs and make low-risk personal loans.

However, the environment of depository institutions had changed so much by the 1970s that it fundamentally changed the financial industry and led to industry-requested legislative responses. The situation could be summarized as two environment factors and three financial innovations.

TECHNOLOGICAL CHANGE

One environmental factor was technological change. Computerization of financial industries and the linking of financial institutions via networks eliminated any physical barriers to the transfer of funds over long distances. Also, funds could be electronically moved from savings into other investments. Both environmental factors created possibilities for banks to conduct interstate banking, or nonbank activities, which were actually prohibited by the banking laws.

HIGH INTEREST RATES

The second environmental factor was the high interest rates caused by policies of the Federal Reserve in late 1970s that emphasized monetary policy management by tightening the aggregate supply of money. The resulting high interest rates caused large depositors to withdraw their funds from depository institutions and put them into other investments such as the newly created **money market mutual funds** that paid greater returns. In addition, passbook savings and demand deposits became attractive sources of funds for the competitors of depository institutions, such as investment and insurance companies, since the spread between the interest rates paid to borrow funds and market lending rates were greatly increased.

CHANGE INDUCED INNOVATIONS

The changing environment also stimulated innovations. Three innovations emerged in the 1970s: (1) the creation of money market mutual funds, (2) new methods of permitting interest on demand deposits, and (3) the dissolution of geographic barriers.

THE CREATION OF MONEY MARKET MUTUAL FUNDS The invention of **money market mutual funds** was initially a response from investment companies because the **Securities and Exchange Commission** deregulated brokerage commissions and a prolonged slump in the stock market occurred during the mid-1970s. Investment companies wanted to become strong competitors. As a result, money market mutual funds soon became serious competitors to banks and thrifts. Money market mutual funds provided small investors indirect access to financial instruments normally restricted to the large investors. They even provided checking services and cash advances via special checks and credit cards, and consumers could borrow money while still receiving market interest rates on funds invested (Frank, 1981: 39).

The situation caused a gross disintermediation. **Disintermediation** refers to the shift of funds that were previously routed through the intermediation market (financial intermediaries) to the direct credit market. The **gross disintermediation**, coined in the early 1970s, describes the outflow of funds from one financial intermediary subject to deposit rate ceilings to another financial intermediary not subject to deposit rate ceilings (Kidwell, Peterson, & Blackwell, 1993: 34). The Federal Reserve then attempted to restrict money market mutual funds by imposing a 15 percent reserve requirement on them in 1980, but the Fed soon eliminated the requirement because it lacked proper legal authority.

NEW METHODS OF PERMITTING INTEREST ON DEMAND DEPOSITS Although depository institutions were not allowed to pay interest on checking accounts (technically called **demand deposits**), banks and thrifts invented several ways to circumvent the regulation in the 1970s. The regulatory subsystem actually encouraged these activities. A special savings account that allowed checking-writing privileges, named a **negotiated order of withdrawal (NOW)**, was invented by a savings bank in Massachusetts, and legalized because of a 1972 court decision. In 1975 and 1978, Congress authorized banks in New England and New York to offer NOW accounts. The National Credit Union Administration in 1974 permitted credit unions to offer "**share drafts**" that were, in effect, checks drawn against credit union accounts, and thus equivalent to NOW accounts. In the same year, savings associations were authorized by the Federal Home Loan Bank Board to set up **remote service units** in commercial locations. Such units allowed depositors to withdraw cash from ATM machines, thus enabling savings accounts to perform the equivalent function as checking accounts (which savings associations technically could not offer). In 1975 the Federal Reserve approved **telephone transfers** for commercial banks that allowed a depositor to shift money by phone from a savings account to a checking account, perhaps in time to cover checks written. In 1978 the Federal Reserve went further and permitted **automatic funds transfers** from savings accounts to cover checks written in a checking account.

THE DISSOLUTION OF GEOGRAPHIC BARRIERS Geographic and industry barriers set by the McFadden and Glass-Steagall Acts were challenged by two additional factors in late 1970s. One factor was the **grandfathered bank holding companies**. A holding company could establish a subsidiary to engage in nonbank activities while continuing to operate banks through other subsidiaries. In addition, a holding company could purchase banks in more than one state and thus "branch" across state lines. While this loophole was closed by the **Bank Holding Company Act** of 1956 regarding multibank holding companies, and by the amendment of 1970 regarding single-bank holding companies, some of the activities were exempted via a grandfather clause. In addition, a number of financial institutions used their dispersed geographic locations as a basis to move into banking functions while avoiding the restrictions of banking laws.

GROWING COMPETITION

During the 1970s, depository institutions attempted to invade the turf of the other depository institutions while protecting their own. They had successfully persuaded their regulators to ease up on some restrictions. However, such relaxations were challenged in court by the other financial institutions. A number of cases were consolidated by the D.C. Circuit Court of Appeals in ABA v. Connell (1979), and the circuit court gave the Congress until December 31, 1979, to authorized the services in question (Conte, 1979: 1364).

Agenda Setting

Under the leadership of Fernand St. Germain, the chair of the Subcommittee on Financial Institutions of the House Banking Committee, the House acted first. St. Germain's bill simply repealed the prohibition against paying interest on checking accounts and allowed all depository institutions to offer them; this bill quickly passed the full House on September 11, 1979.

On the Senate side, Senator William Proxmire, chair of the Senate Banking Committee, had his own bill. It would phase out limits on interest payments over a ten-year period, permit NOW accounts, and reduce the minimum deposit for a money market certificate to $1,000. After four days of debate and adding amendments, the Senate bill passed on November 1, 1979.

The conference immediately deadlocked since the House opposed issues other than interests on checking accounts. With the December 31 deadline approaching, a temporary compromise was proposed. The law, PL 96-161, which passed quickly by both houses, authorized the three accounts challenged by ABA v. Connell for three months, until March 31, 1980, thus giving the committee more time to act. The 90-day delay gave sufficient time to hold hearings on some of the disputed points. On March 5, 1980, the conference reached a compromise, and agreed to a bill incorporating federal reserve membership conditions, which was introduced by the House, with Senate provisions. The most important law deregulating depository institutions, the **Depository Institutions Deregulation and Monetary Control Act (DIDMCA)** was finally passed.

The trend of deregulation continued even though the DIDMCA passed. Three factors in early 1980s combined to demand new legislation: (1) the continued outflow of funds to money market mutual funds, (2) changes in the supply and demand for money, and (3) the 1980 congressional election. Money market mutual funds, which did not exist for everyday investors five years earlier, had attracted a total of $180 billion at their peak during the early 1980s. The large outflow of money from depository institutions to money market mutual funds motivated commercial banks to seek deregulation so they could compete for these funds. Another factor was the **worldwide economic recession** during which interest rates dropped dramatically. This created a two-edged sword for the thrifts because housing sales dropped, and there was little demand for mortgages. The third factor was the regulatory subsystem. President Reagan appointed supporters of deregulation to the key financial regulatory positions. In addition, Senator Jake Garn, the new chair of the Senate Banking Committee, became a strong advocate of fundamental changes to deregulate depository institutions.

In a major shift of position, the representatives of some 15 financial industry groups met in early 1982 to resolve their differences and push for new legislation (Wines, 1982: 1500). A Senate bill represented the results of this meeting that would grant broader powers to thrift institutions in exchange for authorization of banks to engage in property and casualty insurance. The House under St. Germain's leadership was considering a bill with provisions for federal aid to thrifts but no new powers for either institution.

The Senate banking Committee, in response to pressure from the insurance and securities industries, reported out the revised bill without any new powers for banks. Representatives of commercial banks denounced the measure as a "saving and loan sweetheart bill" and withdrew their support. Despite the differences between this bill and St. Germain's, a conference committee compromise passed both houses and was signed into law on October 15, 1982. To gain support from banking interests, authority to offer market interest rate accounts was immediately granted to depository institutions (Puckett, 1983: 88).

The Laws and Procedures

The Depository Institutions Deregulation and Monetary Control Act (DIDMCA) of 1980 made the most significant changes in U.S. banking regulations, the powers of the Federal Reserve, and the Federal Reserve's control of monetary policy since the 1930s. The Federal Reserve gained powers to impose reserve requirements on deposits held by all commercial banks, savings banks, savings associations, and credit unions, to establish discount rate policy that could apply to every depository institution in the country, to price and provide payments services directly to all depository institutions, and to shape the growth of the nation's evolving electronic payments networks.

DIDMCA profoundly altered the competitive relationship between banks and thrift institutions, strengthened the ability of consumers to obtain higher interest rates on **time deposits**, and gave depository institutions across the country the power to offer new types of interest-earning transaction accounts (such as NOW accounts). It allowed thrifts to make consumer loans and issue credit cards, phased out deposit rate ceilings by April 1, 1986, and allowed NOW accounts at all depository institutions.

Many DIDMCA provisions were self-implementing or implemented by the private sector, except for Regulation Q. The law transferred the control over interest rates to a **Depository Institutions Deregulation Committee (DIDC)**, composed of the heads of the Federal Reserve, the FDIC, FHLBB, and NCUA, the secretary of the Treasury, and the Comptroller of the Currency. DIDC was instructed to phase out all interest rate controls in six years. In June 1981, DIDC adopted a plan to phase out Regulation Q by deregulating those deposits with the longest maturity on August 1, 1982, and then, the short-term deposits on August 1, 1985. The savings associations were displeased with the "rapid" pace of the plan and they counterattacked. They convinced DIDC to withdraw an increase to 6 percent on the interest cap on passbook savings and challenged DIDC's other actions in court; and they were successful in delaying the implementation of the DIDMCA. During this period, in March 1982 the National Credit

Union Administration withdrew from the DIDC deregulation process and immediately removed all interest rate controls for credit unions.

The **Garn-St. Germain Act** of 1982 substantially extended the powers of banks and thrifts and the activities of bank regulatory agencies beyond those established by the DIDMCA. It enabled banks to offer **money market deposit accounts** (which were government insured) to compete with existing money market mutual funds. It provided for additional assistance to the struggling thrift industry, such as allowing merger-related assistance from the FDIC to prevent savings banks and savings and loan associations from failing, providing for emergency acquisition allowances to banks seeking to buy a failing thrift institution, authorizing thrift institutions to issue net worth certificates to maintain their capital bases, and expanding their lending and investing powers. It also increased the lending powers of commercial banks. It further exempted the first $2 million in transaction accounts and other reservable liabilities of every depository in the nation from reserve requirements, which released most of the nation's 20,000 credit unions from reserve requirements (Friedman, 1989: 210-211).

Two months after the Garn-St. Germain Act, DIDC authorized both **money market demand accounts** (checking accounts that paid rates competitive with money market mutual funds) and **super-NOW accounts** effective in January of 1983. In June of that year with an October effective date, DIDC corrected an absurdity in the regulations that deregulated short-term funds but kept an interest rate cap on some longer-term deposits. For all intents and purposes, the economic side of depository institutions was finally deregulated in terms of interest rates in 1983.

The Impact of Deregulation

Deregulation of depository institutions in the early 1980s brought both good and bad news for consumers. The good news was that banking consumers began to receive substantial interest payments on certain checking accounts and increased interest rates on savings accounts. In 1989, for example, commercial banks paid several billion dollars in interest on the more than $70 billion in NOW and Super-NOW accounts (Federal Reserve System, 1989: A19). The bad news for consumers included increased bank fees and closing of bank branches. Between 1980 and 1983 the levels of bank service charges and fees rose at a rate two to four times the increases in the general price level (Canner and Kurtz, 1985: 609). Between 1978 and 1982, the service charges collected by commercial banks on deposit accounts more than doubled—from $4.9 billion to $10.8 billion (Hertzber, 1984). At the same time, banking institutions sought to control costs by closing old branches and slowing the opening of new ones. Between 1979 and 1983, the number of branch closings increased while the number of openings declined (Dennis, 1984).

The deregulation-related changes were of little benefit to most low-income households and harmed many others (Brobeck, 1991: 171-177). For the poor and near poor, fees paid to banking institutions rose more rapidly than for the most affluent. The low-income households also began to lose some access to bank branches. Moreover, the least affluent Americans were dropping out of the banking system. A study found that in the New York City between 1977 and 1984, the city lost 65% of its bank branches while the suburbs gained 8%. Among the poorest communities in the New York City, 16 neighborhoods were without a branch, and 8 had only one by 1984 (Spix, 1986). Some evidence showed that the growing availability of electronic funds transfer, particularly automated teller machines (ATM) seemed not to benefit the poor appreciably. The negative effects of financial deregulation on the low-income consumers were reflected as well by their very negative attitudes toward the deregulation.

SAVINGS AND LOAN (S&L) BAILOUT

In the mid-1980s, financial institutions "crashed and burned" with increasing frequency. By the end of 1987, over 500 mortgage-oriented savings associations were **insolvent**, and even worse, the then-insurer of these savings associations, the **Federal Savings and Loan Insurance Corporation** (FSLIC) was insolvent too. To deal with this and other troublesome issues, the **Competitive Equality Banking Act**, which passed in 1987, not only recapitalized the FSLIC, but also provided safeguards for the FSLIC's insurance premium base. FSLIC-insured savings associations were forbidden from switching to FDIC insurance for one year, and institutions switching insurers were to be assessed a costly "**exit fee**" designed to discourage switching. But the situation did not get better. During 1988, approximately 450 financial institutions **failed** (equally divided between thrift institutions and banks). The rapidly growing numbers of institutions that failed or became insolvent endangered the national economy, and pushed the then-President Bush to assign a high priority to restructuring the U.S. deposit insurance system in general and the thrift institutions in particular. The president's initiative, after long debate by Congress, resulted in the passage of the **Financial Institutions Reform, Recovery, and Enforcement Act** (FIRREA) of 1989.

Agenda Setting

President Bush announced his plan to resolve the crisis in the savings and loan industry and to place federal deposit insurance on a sound basis on February 6, 1989. Two months later, the Senate approved its version of the savings and loan rescue and reform bill that was very close in spirit to the administration's plan. Another two months later, the House adopted its version of the bill, including on-budget financing, tougher capital standards, and an affordable housing program (Barth 1991: 142). There were three major differences between the two bills. The House bill banned thrift investments in junk bonds, and the senate version permitted such investments if limited to 11 percent of a thrift's portfolio. The House bill required that Wall, the then-Chairman of the Federal Home Loan Bank Board, be reappointed by the president and reconfirmed by the Senate, and the Senate bill allowed Wall automatically to remain as the nation's chief thrift regulator of a newly proposed agency. In addition, the House bill contained one provision that likely would elicit a veto threat from President Bush: it put the entire cost of the bailout **on-the-budget** but exempted it from the **Gramm-Rudman budget limits** (targeted limits for overall government spending). The White House wanted to keep S&L spending largely off the budget (Day 1993: 326). These differences turned out to be major debating issues at the congressional conferences. Finally, the Senate conferees gave up everything to win Wall the job of heading the agency that would regulate thrifts, and the House conferees, having won every major point of substance, reluctantly agreed to keep Wall in. On a sunny morning, August 9, 1989, President Bush signed the bailout bill into law (Day, 1993: 336).

The FIRREA Law: Beginning the $500+ Billion Bailout

The FIRREA made major changes in the financing of deposit insurance and the structure of financial institution regulation. It also provided for the "bailout" of insolvent thrift institutions (Kidwell, Peterson, and Blackwell, 1993: 502-506).

The FIRREA transferred chartering and some other regulatory powers for the savings associations from the Federal Home Loan Bank Board (FHLBB) to a newly created **Office of Thrift Supervision**, which is located in the **Treasury Department** and under the direct control of the administration. The powers of the FHLBB were stripped away because it had been subject to extensive influence by the savings associations and had not adequately protected its deposit insurance fund. Another new federal insurance institution, the **Savings Association Insurance Fund (SAIF)**, as a subsidiary of the FDIC, assumed responsibilities for insuring thrift deposits. The FDIC continued to supervise the Federal Deposit Insurance fund for banks, now called the **Bank Insurance Fund (BIF)**. The SAIF was under the control of the FDIC because bank failures were not as serious as thrift failures and it was assumed that the FDIC's examination and insurance standards were much sounder than those of the insolvent Federal Savings and Loan Insurance Corporation (FSLIC). The law required both banks and thrifts pay higher insurance premiums for their federal deposit insurance. It also tightened up capital requirements for thrifts.

To address the issue of how previous problems encountered by the thrifts deposit insurance fund were to be resolved, the FIRREA provided for the sale of at least $50 billion in government backed bonds. The proceeds of the bond sales were to go to a new institution called the **Resolution Funding Corporation (RFC)**, which was also to obtain funding from SAIF and the Federal Home Loan Banks. The funds were to be transferred to the Resolution Trust Corporation (RTC), which was to assume the responsibility for all problem institutions **shut down, merged,** or **assisted** by the FSLIC. The RTC was to use the $50 billion obtained from the sale of the bonds plus the funding provided directly or indirectly by thrift institutions to pay for losses on assets acquired from failing thrifts.

The FIRREA toughened the penalties for managers and directors of dishonest savings institutions, established higher standards for appraisals, and provided for more vigorous enforcement of regulations and laws related to the operation of all federally-chartered or insured financial institutions. The FIRREA also let banks buy healthy thrifts.

The Impact of the Law

To "bailout" the troubled banks and thrifts, the actual cost to the taxpayer will range from a minimum of $130 billion (the cost of newly authorized government backed debt) to about $300 billion (a figure that also included the cost of interest on that debt as well as an allowance for future possible losses) (Kidwell, Peterson, and Blackwell, 1993: 505). There are other estimations of the cost up to $500+ billion under different assumptions, which amounts to about $5,000 for each and every adult taxpayer (Garman, 1993: 677; White 1991: 197).

To reduce both the potential for systemic problems in the banking system and bank regulatory agencies' incentives to follow a **too-big-to-fail policy**, the Congress passed the **Federal Deposit Insurance Corporation Improvement Act** in 1991. The law strictly controls regulators' abilities to protect or extend the lives of large banks while keeping other policy tools for dealing with **systemic risk**. To avoid a repeat of the savings and loan situation, the law granted heavy controls both to the government and outside third parties. The law requires banks to meet new capitalization standards, follow stringent outside audit rules, and establish stricter internal controls. Bankers dislike the law and have asked for reform, since they believe that they cannot increase lending without some relief from regulations ("Reforming FDICA ...", 1993).

TRUTH IN SAVINGS

More than twenty years ago, a family economics professor deposited $500 in twin savings accounts—same rate, same date of deposit and activity, same New York City bank—but received a different amount of interest on each account a year later. The posted balances were $548.20 and $543.22. How were the interest payments figured? That question led him to find the facts that banks used different daily rates for the same quoted annual rate, and there was no regulation on the accuracy of quoted rates (Morse, 1992a). As a serious scholar and passionate consumer advocate, Professor Richard L. D. Morse at Kansas State University started his twenty-plus years lobby for the passage of the **Truth in Savings Act**.

Agenda Setting

Truth in Savings bills have been introduced in Congress since 1971. It took twenty years of almost continuous legislative battles, until 1991, to pass the Truth in Savings Act in Congress. The ideas of Truth in Savings originated even earlier (Morse, 1987; 1992b: 83-85).

The roots for **Truth in Savings** were planted in 1961 and exposed in the 1963 report of the **Consumer Advisory Council** to then-President Kennedy. The idea of Truth in Savings was first expressed by Senator William Proxmire and Treasury Under Secretary Joe Barr in a colloquy over whether an 18% Annual Percentage Rate (APR) truthfully represented a 1.5% monthly percentage rate. Advised by Professor Morse, a graduate student, Jackie Pinson, researched the ways bankers were paying interest on savings. The findings were published in an article entitled "Maybe We Need 'Truth in Savings,' Too" in the February 1971 issue of *Changing Times*. A legislative aide to Senator Vance Hartke telephoned after reading the article and asked whether Morse had any plans for legislation. With the help of Morse, Senator Hartke and Representative Bill Roy introduced bills on Truth in Savings in Senate and House, respectively, in 1971. Another similar bill was introduced by Representative Henry Gonzalez (Morse, 1992b: 83). Truth in Savings bills required disclosure of three rates: (1) the **periodic percentage rate (PPR)**, (2) the **annual percentage rate (APR)**, and (3) the **annual percentage yield (APY)**. The bills were referred to their respective committees, but no hearings were held. The bills died (Morse, 1987).

In the 93rd and 94th Congress, Truth in Savings bills were reintroduced, but neither the House nor Senate passed any bill until the 99th Congress. Representative Lehman reintroduced his bill in the 99th Congress and again in the 100th Congress. It was amended and passed by the House of Representatives. Senator Christopher Dodd introduced a similar bill, which was amended into the **Financial Modernization Act** of 1988, and passed by the Senate. No legislation ensued for lack of a conference report reconciling differences between the House-

and Senate-passed bills. The same situation was happening when Representative Lehman's bill was passed by the House and Senator Dodd's bill was incorporated in the **Money Laundering Act** and passed by the Senate. During this period, Dr. Morse testified and exhibited his research findings in many hearings held by several congressional subcommittees (Morse, 1992b: 84-85).

In the 102nd Congress, Representative Lehman reintroduced Truth in Savings. Representative Gonzalez included Truth in Savings in a comprehensive banking reform bill. Representative Esteban Torres introduced a different Truth in Savings Act. And Representative Jim Slattery introduced a separate bill with many consumer-friendly provisions. It included three recommendations which Dr. Morse had initiated: (1) that for the purpose of computing interest, **"annual"** would mean 365 days; (2) that the balance on which interest is computed would be the **daily balance**; and (3) that depository institutions would provide depositors with a statement of account activity sufficiently informative for the depositor to **verify computations**. The House Consumer and Monetary Affairs Committee considered both bills and amended most of the Slattery additions into the Torres bill, recommending it to the full House for passage. It passed (Morse, 1992b: 85).

The conference committee considered both the House and Senate bills in its consideration of the banking bill, the Federal Deposit Insurance Corporation Improvement Act of 1991. Truth in Savings was included in consideration of the act, and Senate conferees yielded to the House version. The Torres bill was accepted and recommended for passage. As a result, the Truth in Savings Act became law with the signing by the president on December 19, 1991 (Morse, 1992b). The Federal Reserve Board issued proposed regulations in April 1992, and final regulations, known as **Regulation DD**, in September 1992. The mandatory compliance date for Truth in Savings Act was June 21, 1993.

The Truth in Savings Law

The Regulation DD contains three principal provisions: (1) a requirement for depository institutions to provide consumers with information about the **terms of deposit accounts** before an account is opened, (2) regulation of the content of deposit account advertising, and (3) **mandated methods of calculating** the deposit account balance upon which interest is calculated. It required depository institutions to use clearly defined terms, such as **annual**, **APY (annual percentage yield)**, and **APR (annual percentage rate)**. Annual will mean 365 days. Confusion as to whether a year is 365, 360, 366, 372, and so on that were used by banks before have been eliminated. APY expresses the amount of interest that would be expected from a $100 deposit in 365 days. APR expresses the annualized rate paid each period. For example, if an institution compounds quarterly, its APR will be 4 times its quarterly rate. If it compounds monthly, its APR will be 12 times the monthly, and 365 times the daily rate if it compounds daily. The law asks banks to pay on the full amount of principal in the account for each day, in which banks have to drop unfair and complex methods which had been so difficult to explain to consumers, such as Low Balance, LIFO (last-in, first-out), FIFO (first-in, last-out), and Investible Balance. Banks must provide full disclosure of fees, charges, and penalties and how these are computed. Any time limitations imposed also have to be fully disclosed.

The Truth in Savings law gives banks freedom to compound and credit interest as institutions wish, simplifies training of bank service personnel with standardized terminology, and provides an opportunity to involve consumers in their getting a better understanding of how interest works. Moreover, this law can give depositors a sound basis for their confidence in the savings system. The law is considered both consumer, and banker, friendly (Morse, 1992b: 99).

Evaluation of Truth in Savings

Even though the Truth in Savings Act is viewed as a victory of consumers in banking regulation, many critics argue that further legislation is still needed. For example, the Annual Percentage Yields (APY) are not directly comparable with those quoted for Treasury bonds, money market mutual funds, or yields on other investments. Consumers need information of this kind when they make saving and investment decisions when selecting different types of financial instruments. The law only defined several key terms, but did not require the disclosure of "**Centsible Interest**," a term coined by Dr. Morse. Centsible Interest is based on daily compounding of daily balances and expressed in cents per $100 (Morse, 1992b: 85). This is "unit price" in banking accounts and would help consumers more easily compare interest rates when choosing different account categories.

When the Fed wrote the regulation to implement the Truth in Savings law, they permitted depository institutions to use one or two alternative methods of determining the balance, thereby making it impossible for consumers to take pencil and pad to verify the bank's calculations.

CURRENT ISSUES IN DEPOSITORY INSTITUTIONS REGULATION

This examination of current issues in depository institutions regulation includes an overview of fair lending, interstate banking, regulatory consolidation, and mutual funds sales.

Fair Lending

Lending discrimination is prohibited by four federal laws, the Fair Housing Act, the Equal Credit Opportunity Act, Community Reinvestment Act, and Home Mortgage Disclosure Act. However, subtle **discrimination** still exists. This issue has been raised because of the results of several recent studies and investigations.

A preliminary analysis of 1990 **Home Mortgage Disclosure Act (HMDA)** data indicated that significant differences in loan denial rates among racial and ethnic groups. As a result, the Fed authorized the Federal Reserve Bank of Boston to conduct a detailed study that might answer some of the questions rased in the preliminary review of the HMDA data. In 1993, a study from the Federal Reserve Bank of Boston found that differences in borrower credit and loan characteristics explain about two-thirds of the racial disparity in mortgage lending in the Boston area. African-Americans and Hispanics applying for mortgages in the Boston area were about 60% more likely to be denied credit than whites after controlling for differences in credit worthiness. The HMDA data for 1992 revealed that 36% of black applicants for mortgage loans were turned down, while only 16% of white applicants had their loan applications denied

(Lindsey, 1994). In June 1993, *The Washington Post* published the results of a 6-month investigation of the mortgage lending practices of Washington, DC-based banks and thrifts. The series indicated that mortgage loans were made in white neighborhoods at twice the rate they were in black areas with equivalent income levels.

Regulatory agencies responded to this issue promptly, and sometimes concertedly. In May 1993, the federal bank regulatory agencies issued a letter to the chief executive officers of all depository institutions to address concerns that minority consumers and small business owners were experiencing discrimination by lenders.

President Bill Clinton announced in July 1993 a **Community Reinvestment Act (CRA)** reform initiative to increase lending in underserved communities and streamline, clarify and make the CRA regulatory process more objective. The old CRA had been criticized as "a little more than a piece of paper bearing empty threats" (Risen, 1994: 16). As a result, the four federal bank and thrift regulators proposed to replace 12 subjective factors then used to assess an institution's CRA performance with three **"tests"** using objective, performance-based standards in these areas: (1) a lending test, (2) a service test, and (3) an investment test ("Regulators Seek ...", 1994: 10). The four bank regulatory agencies also announced several initiatives to implement President Clinton's program to improve the availability of credit to businesses and individuals. The Federal Reserve Board modified amendments to **Regulation B**, which prohibits lending discrimination, in early December 1993. As an early signal of the Clinton initiative, the Shawmut National Corporation's application to acquire a New Hampshire savings bank was rejected by the Fed based on concerns about the bank's compliance with the fair lending laws.

Ten federal agencies issued a **joint discrimination policy** in March 1994, which represented the first effort to define both **discrimination** and **acceptable remedies** to in a manner affecting most private lenders. The Justice Department also opened fire on fair-lending issues. It recently settled three lending discrimination cases (Cocheo, 1994).

Some remaining major issues are to eliminate unnecessary paperwork for lenders and impose tougher penalties on banks and savings associations that have poor marks under the Community Reinvestment Act. Bankers are lobbying for including credit unions under CRA-like requirements to create a "level playing field." Consumer advocates have challenged the elimination of the current twelve CRA assessment factors that are beneficial for consumers. Finally, two weaknesses of the CRA reform proposal are the provision offering exemptions from full-scale CRA examinations to institutions with $250 million or less in assets under certain circumstances and the provision emphasizing one-shot quickie investments. (CFA News, 2-3/1994: 3).

Interstate Banking

In August and September 1994, House and Senate, respectively passed bills to permit banks to operate branches across state lines. Both bills would remove the few remaining barriers to interstate banking, preempting states' rights to continue to restrict such activities. President Clinton indicated that he would sign the bill (Glater, 1994), and he did.

As a result interstate banking is increasingly becoming a reality in the United States. All states except Hawaii now permit their banks to be acquired by bank holding companies headquartered in some other states. A few states allow banks to branch across state lines, and the new federal law will permit interstate branch banking except in states that specifically exempt themselves. The number of multi-state bank holding companies has risen to 178 as of June 30, 1993, and the share of domestic commercial banking assets held by out-of-state organizations has increased to 21.3% until the end of 1992 (Savage, 1993).

Empirical evidence explains the reasons why many states allow entry of banking for out-of-state banks and documents the consequences of relaxing interstate banking laws. States with regional banking difficulties have motives to adopt relatively unrestrictive interstate banking laws (Gunther, 1992a). States with low bank capital levels are more likely to permit national interstate banking without reciprocity (Gunther, 1992b). Out-of-state and out-of-region banks, excluding money center banks, have profited most from these law changes and money center banks have been least positively affected by the law changes which implies that the opening of interstate banking opportunities to other than money center banks is to "level the playing field" (Goldberg, Hanweck, and Sugrue, 1992). The relaxation of statewide branching laws has led to an increase in the number of new branches but not to an increase in the number of new banks, possibly reflecting a substitution toward branch entry (Amel and Liang, 1992). The effects of the New England regional interstate banking compact, formed in 1982-1984, upon competition were examined over the period 1983-1988 (LeClair, 1991). The results suggest that the interstate banking has benefitted those states involved in terms of competition indicators. In addition, the fear that interstate competition would lead to excessive concentration in the banking industry appears unfounded. Interstate banking results in an increase in profitability that benefits only the small and medium-sized banks, while the increase in systematic risk applies only to medium-sized and large banks (Beng, 1991).

The Fed supports the interstate banking and its representatives believe that interstate banking and branching and broader insurance authority would provide wider household and business choices at better prices, increase competitive efficiency, eliminate unnecessary costs, encourage the reduction of risk through geographic and product diversification, and pave the way for the development of a truly nationwide banking system with geographically diversified lending and funding sources. The proponents of interstate banking observe that consumers in multi-state areas would gain more convenient access to their accounts and related services.

Consumer groups have traditionally opposed interstate bank branching on the grounds that it would lead to dangerous concentration and to reduced lending and fewer banking services in many communities, particularly poor communities. It is possible that interstate banking threatens the tie between a bank and its local community and consumers (CFA News, 4/1994: 2).

Regulatory Consolidation

In 1993 bills were introduced in both the House and Senate to overhaul the nation's fragmented and duplicative system of regulating banks and thrifts. The administration unveiled its own proposal, which was similar to the two bills, in November that year. The plan was designed to merge the supervisory functions of the Federal Reserve, the Federal Deposit Insurance Corporation, the Office of the Comptroller of the Currency, and the Office of Thrift Supervision into a single **Federal Banking Commission**. The FDIC would continue to provide deposit insurance, and the Federal Reserve would continue to conduct monetary policy, but the two agencies would largely lose their supervisory roles. The intent of this proposed reconstruction of banking regulation system is to realign the bank regulators along the lines of their core functions: deposit insurance, central banking, and safety-and-soundness regulation. It is estimated that the reconstruction would save some $150-$200 million a year.

Issues surround the regulatory consolidation are mainly three: (1) role of the Federal Reserve System, (2) necessity of the consolidation, and (3) inclusion of credit unions. The Fed opposes the proposal of regulatory consolidation and has offered its own reform plan (Greenspan, 1994). Experts from the Federal Reserve System argue that the Fed historically has served as a crisis manager. If the agency had no power to supervise banks, its role of crisis manager would be seriously handicapped. The role described by the proposals would undermine the Fed's ability to carry out its mission as the U.S. central bank.

Argument against the idea of the regulatory consolidation points to the necessity of competition among regulatory agencies. Whether or not to include credit unions in the process of the regulatory consolidation is another controversial issue debated by the representatives from banks and credit unions. All current proposals do not include NCUA into the proposed National Banking Commission. Bankers, however, point out that credit unions should be subject to all banking regulations. Representatives of credit unions argue that credit unions are subject to virtually all regulations banks are, with the exception of Community Reinvestment Act, but that they have their own guidelines for practicing fair lending.

Mutual Funds Sales

This issue was initially raised by a study conducted by North American Securities Administrators Association and American Association of Retired Persons. The October 1993 survey indicated that more than 80% of bank customers are unaware that annuities and mutual funds sold by banks are not insured by the Federal Deposit Insurance Corporation. Another survey conducted seven months earlier by the *Money* magazine showed that only around 10% of bank representatives can correctly answer questions regarding the FDIC insurance coverage, which implies the great potential of bank representatives misleading bank customers (Kobliner, 1993). Also, bad investment advice and outright lies about safety in bank's mutual fund sales were found in an investigation conducted by *Consumer Reports* magazine ("Should You ...", 1994).

In response, the FDIC launched a series of efforts to bolster the bank and consumer awareness of the issue. The FDIC provided an addendum banks could reprint and provide along with the "Your Insured Deposit" pamphlet. The agency also started to publish a consumer newsletter that dealt with deposit insurance issues and operate a consumer hot line that used a combination of pre-recorded advice selected by push-button phone menus and live operators to provide advise about FDIC insurance coverage and other issues.

To respond the criticism by consumer advocates and general consumer dissatisfaction on this issue, the American Bankers Association and five other national banking trade associations prepared a set of guidelines titled **"Retail Investment Sales: Guidelines for Banks."** These guidelines go much further than simply addressing the fact that mutual funds are not insured. They serve as an action plan for banks that want to make certain that all aspects of their effort to expand into retail investment sales are correct and above board and that they treat consumers fairly ("Sales Guidelines ...", 1994: 51).

Consumer advocates have urged congressional action on this issue. They demand that three key measures be contained in legislation: (1) stressing the separation of an insured institution's name and logo from an uninsured product, (2) separating the location of insured activity within a bank from the location of the marketing of uninsured products, and (3) separating bank employees who handle insured funds from those who peddle uninsured products (CFA News, 4/1994: 2).

CONCLUSION

Depository institution regulation generally has benefited both the regulated and nonregulated, since the major goals of the regulation are safety and soundness of the banking industry, which is essential for a healthy economy. However, the practices of banking regulation in the 1980s have brought mixed consequences for both depository institutions and banking consumers. Deregulation of the banking industry in the early 1980s provided banks and thrifts more freedom to offer interest on savings and checking accounts and to expand business into nonbanking areas. This helped banks and thrifts to compete with other financial intermediaries, but it is one of major reasons for the failure of a huge number of banks and thrifts. Consumers enjoyed higher interest on checking accounts, higher interest on savings accounts, and numerous other new financial products offered by banks and thrifts. But taxpaying consumers (then, now and tomorrow) also must pay the $500+ billion bailout costs through increased taxes to pay for the S&L crisis and failures. Consumers also continue to pay higher service fees to financial institutions while having fewer bank branches available. The negative impact of deregulation on the poor has been even more onerous.

Table 13-1 provides an assessment of factors associated with the subsystem of depository institution regulation. The subsystem of regulating depository institutions is unique, compared to other sectors of the society, because of the dual banking system and culturally historic reasons. Several federal agencies and dozens of state agencies currently regulate some aspects of all depository institutions. The expertise and cohesion of these agencies are strong, but the leadership is moderate. Goals of these regulatory agencies are specific and sanctions and procedures are adequate in achieving those goals. The thrift and banking crisis of the 1980s has brought banking issues into national attention, and the continuing salience of these concerns highlights the importance of depository institution regulation. The regulatory agencies as an important part of the subsystem were changed because of the FIRREA of 1989, and it is likely to change again during the legislative battles of 1990s.

The regulated in banking regulation are strong. Depository institutions today—numbering only three-quarters of the total a decade ago—are financially stronger than they were in the 1980s and they are better able to compete with other types of financial institutions. Historically, banks and thrifts have asked for and gained many favors from the regulatory agencies. When presented with proposals for a uniform banking regulation body, the viewpoints of depository institutions varied. Consumer organizations play an important role in advancing the interests of consumers in the legislative and regulatory efforts as well as in law enforcement in the banking industry. Other financial institutions that are intermediaries and

Table 13.1   A Summary of Depository Institutions Regulation

Economics	
Firms	Many
Entry	Easy
Profits	High
Technology	
Complexity	Low
Stability	Low
Substitutes	High
Subsystem	
Bureaucratic control	Strong
Industry coalition	Strong
Nonindustry coalition	Strong
Bureaucratic resources:	
Expertise	Strong
Cohesion	Strong
Leadership	Moderate
Legislative authority:	
Goals	Specific
Sanctions	Good
Procedures	Good
Involvement of Macropolitical Actors	
Legislature	Strong
President	Moderate
Courts	Weak

those which offer banking, insurance, and investment products but are not regulated by the depository institution subsystem will voice their desires as the debate continues around regulatory consolidation. As has been said in the past, all any one group wants is an unlevel playing field. What would benefit society the most is a more level playing field for all types of financial institutions that offer banking and related nonbanking products and services.

Congress always has important functions in defining regulatory agencies of the subsystem. The banking committee members, especially the chairmen, historically and currently, play critical roles in setting the regulatory agenda and in proposing important legislation. Presidents generally have not been very concerned with banking regulation until a national crisis happens. During such crises, presidents often assume a leadership role to reconstruct the banking industry in an effort to regain consumer confidence in the government and the economy. The role of courts in depository institution regulation has been passive but decisive on critical issues.

Profitability and technology innovation are major reasons that attract nonbanks to invade the banking industry while at the same time depository institutions try to expand into nonbanking areas. The interwoven aspects of banking and nonbanking activities has blurred the boundaries of these industries and it challenges the current regulatory configuration. Future regulation of depository institutions is likely to cover some nonbanks.

The regulatory system may very well be changed during the next Congress, since the current structure, which reflects a series of historical accidents since the 1930s, does not effectively and efficiently regulate the evolving U.S. banking industry. The future regulatory structure might be a combination of several versions proposed by the president, Congress, and the Federal Reserve Board. In designing the future regulatory system, balance will be sought between maintaining the soundness and safety of banks and thrifts and creating a level playing field for banks, thrifts, and other nonbank institutions that offer similar products and services. New technologies, such as information highway resources, will be used in regulating banks and thrifts to increase efficiency and reduce regulatory burdens to some degree. Because of the complexity of banking products and the providers themselves allowed by current and expected future laws, it is likely that consumers will continue to be confused when purchasing and using financial products for purposes of saving, insuring, and investing. To protect the interests of consumers, the regulatory agencies will demand that banks and thrifts provide better information to consumers themselves. This information will aid the understanding of numerous innovative financial products and services, deposit and investment insurance coverages, interest rates, and other financial terms. The information will be provided through various mechanisms, including computer and other advanced technologies, in more understandable, clear, and straightforward ways than currently used.

Chapter 14
Credit Regulation

Gong-Soog Hong[1] and Ramona K. Z. Heck[2]

Early credit legislation and regulation as described in this chapter have been hailed as some of the major achievements of today's modern consumer movement (Garman, 1994: 31-57). Recent developments in the area of credit regulation are best viewed as refinements of the earlier baseline legislation. Past the flurry of legislation in the 1960s and 1970s, more recent times have brought maturity to this area of regulation. As alluded to in the previous chapter on depository institution regulation, the deregulation and reregulation of the banking and thrift industries along with the appearance and growth of nontraditional **"bank-like"** institutions have resulted in the offering of a variety of financial services including an array of credit sources and arrangements (Kidwell, Peterson, & Blackwell, 1993: 645-677). The current areas of credit growth are credit card instruments, and much recent regulation has been aimed at this major market area.

This chapter describes the major agencies involved in the regulation of all **major credit markets**. Next, advocacy coalitions are delineated including among others a description of credit bureaus. Then, the chapter focuses on the history, current status and dimensions, and the general credit environment including credit cards, traditional closed-

[1]Gong-Soog Hong is assistant professor in the Department of Consumer Sciences and Retailing, Purdue University. She holds a PhD from Cornell University and an MS degree from Utah State University. She teaches consumer and family economics courses for undergraduate and graduate students. Her current research interests include aging and financial well-being, health care, employee benefits, and family-owned businesses. She is a reviewer for the *Journal of Family and Economics Issues and Home Economics, Family and Consumer Sciences Journal*, and *Research on Aging*. Her work has been published in the *Home Economics Research Journal, Journal of Family and Economic Issues, Journal of Home Economics*, and various conference proceedings.

[2]Ramona K. Z. Heck is associate professor in the Department of Consumer Economics and Housing, Cornell University. She holds the designation of J. Thomas Clark Professor of Entrepreneurship and Personal Enterprise at Cornell University. Her current research interests include family-owned business, home-based employment, and working families and employers' benefits. She is Editor of the *Journal of Family and Economic Issues*, on the editorial boards of the *Family Business Review* and *Journal of Consumer Affairs*, and is a member of the Overseas Advising Board for the *Journal of Consumer Studies and Home Economics*. Her work has been published in the *Family Business Review, Journal of Consumer Affairs, Journal of Family and Economic Issues, Journal of Consumer Studies and Home Economics, Journal of Home Economics, The Service Industries Journal*, and *Science*.

end contracts for consumer credit, and residential mortgages, This section is followed by a detailed description of the major federal consumer credit and mortgage legislation in three areas: consumer information, consumer protection, and fair and efficient allocation. Finally, current issues and future policy directions are explored.

THE SUBSYSTEM

This examination of the subsystem in credit regulation includes an overview of the agencies involved, advocacy coalitions, and the environment.

The Agencies

Different federal agencies are responsible for the enforcement of credit laws depending on the particular creditors involved. The **Office of Comptroller of the Currency (OCC)**, which was established by the National Currency Act of 1863, has **chartering and supervisory power** over nationally chartered banks that constitute about 30 percent of the nation's banks. The **Federal Reserve System**, established in 1913, supervises state member banks that comprise about seven percent of all banks. Thus, the Board of Governors of the Federal Reserve System, known as the "**Fed**," is accountable for enforcement of the credit laws when state-chartered banks that are members of the Federal Reserve System violate the law. The **Federal Deposit Insurance Corporation (FDIC)** is responsible for regulating state-chartered banks that are insured by the FDIC, but are not members of the Federal Reserve System. As an independent federal agency established in 1933, the FDIC supervises primarily state nonmember banks that make up 61 percent of the nation's banks.

The **National Credit Union Administration (NCUA)** is in charge of enforcing the law when a federally chartered credit union is involved. When a **state-chartered** credit union is involved, the laws of individual states prevail. Laws at that level typically include the **Uniform Commercial Code** (UCC), small loan regulations, usury laws, little FTC act, **Uniform Deceptive Trade Practices Act**, **Consumer Fraud Act**, and **Uniform Consumer Sales Practices Act** (Garman, 1994: 316-317). Administratively, states regulate credit through the state Attorney General's Office, State Banking Department, State Corporation Commissions, and Office of Consumer Affairs (OCA). The Federal Trade Commission (FTC) has jurisdiction over mortgage banks, consumer finance companies, and retailers including auto dealers, department stores, car rental companies, and gasoline companies to ensure that consumers are not deceived, misled, or mistreated in the credit market. The **Division of Credit Practices** in the Federal Trade Commission (FTC) is in charge of enforcement of advertising regulations; state attorneys general and state Offices of Consumer Affairs also oversee credit advertising.

The **Office of Thrift Supervision (OTS)**, established by the 1989 **Federal Institutions Reform, Recovery and Enforcement Act (FIRREA)** to replace the Federal Home Loan Bank Board (FHLBB), regulates thrift institutions. The **Federal Savings and Loan Insurance Corporation (FSLIC)** is responsible for the state savings and loan associations insured by the FSLIC only. The **state banking commissions** supervise all of the uninsured banks that are not regulated by any of the federal agencies (Lash, 1987: 26-31; Kidwell, Peterson, & Blackwell, 1993: 536-537; Kapoor, Dlabay, & Hughes, 1994: 174; Money Management Institute, 1988; Wolf, 1989: 164-167). These agencies have a number of means to enforce credit laws, such as issuing cease and desist orders, levying fines, removing bank officials, revoking charters, or terminating deposit insurance.

Besides the agencies mentioned above, the Department of Housing and Urban Development (HUD), Department of Justice, Office of the Comptroller of the Currency (OCC), Federal Trade Commission, and Commission on Civil Rights enforce federal laws in **real estate lending practices** to ensure efficiency and fairness in the mortgage market.

In addition, the federal government has created and continues to support and regulate three main agencies to facilitate the operations of the **secondary mortgage market** and simultaneously offer liquidity and geographic flow of funds to the primary mortgage market: (1) Federal National Mortgage Association (FNMA-Fannie Mae), (2) Government National Mortgage Association (GNMA- Ginnie Mae), and (3) Federal Home Loan Mortgage Corporation (FHLMC-Freddie Mac) (Brueggeman & Fisher, 1993: 715-756; Kidwell, Peterson, & Blackwell, 1993: 256-259). These agencies offer investment securities to garner moneys to purchase mortgages from the primary market lenders.

Advocacy Coalitions

The Federal Reserve System and the Office of Comptroller of the Currency promote **consumer welfare** in the credit market. They have Offices of Consumer Affairs at all of their regional offices and handle consumer complaints. There also are state agencies that enforce the state laws. All states have Banking Commissions, Credit Commissions, Savings and Loan Commissions, and Consumer Credit Commissions. They deal with consumer credit issues including state usury laws. Consumers are also protected by the state Office of Consumer Affairs (OCA) that is most often positioned under the Office of the Attorney General. The National Association of Attorneys General (NAAG) is the primary coordinating mechanism for state enforcement authorities by providing a forum for the chief legal officers from 50 states and five jurisdictions (Garman, 1994: 50).

Consumer organizations often work with other groups to accomplish their objectives. The Consumer Federation of America (CFA) is a Washington, D.C. based coalition of over 240 national, state, and local organizations. The coalition has over 50 million members of consumers, farmers, cooperatives, laborers, and others. The Consumer Union (CU) is a consumer product-testing organization that publishes *Consumer Reports* magazine and is involved in consumer advocacy. The U.S. Public Interest Research Group (PIRG) is a group of professionals who are interested in consumer issues and conduct research on consumer issues. There are other organizations such as National Consumers' League (NCL), Public Citizen, and National Credit Union Association. On any particular consumer credit issue, the consumer groups may work with state and federal governments, businesses, academic institutions, and civil rights groups to achieve goals.

Credit bureaus across the U.S. maintain credit record information on over 80 million consumers. More than 2,000 local credit bureaus are connected to major firms such as TRW Credit Data, Equifax, and Trans Union. Credit bureaus are the middle man; they collect information from merchants and institutions that grant credit, store it and sell it to legitimate third parties. As a part of the credit application review, creditors buy credit reports from the credit bureau. Generally, however, credit bureaus do not assign credit ratings (Garman, 1994: 556; Kapoor, Dlabay, & Hughes, 1994: 159; Wolf, 1989: 116). American Financial Services Association, Bankcard Holder of America, and National Foundation for Consumer Credit, Inc. are national nonprofit organizations that are dedicated to educating consumers in the wise use of credit.

The Environment

This examination of the environment of credit regulation includes sections on the development of credit markets, current credit industry, lending limits to consumers, and loan rate ceilings.

DEVELOPMENT OF CREDIT MARKETS

Credit has generally been available as long as there have been organized markets (**National Commission on Consumer Finance** [NCCF], 1972). The availability and use of credit can be dated back to Biblical times and earlier with guidelines denoting unfair **usury practices and rates** (Leviticus 25:35-37; Deuteronomy 23:19-20). Throughout the Middle Ages and colonial America, consumers and producers who were in need of cash borrowed against future income much in the same way modern consumers and producers do. However, early lending practices tended to involve mainly loans with low principals, **simple interest rates**, and short terms. Such loans were made with installment payback schedules. However, most consumer credit arrangements, including common short term mortgages, involved borrowing a specified sum and making *only* interest payments over the term of the loan until the entire principal became due at the end of the credit term or time period (Brueggeman & Fisher, 1993: 111-114).

Usury Laws During these earlier times, state usury laws also operated to set maximum interest rates that could be charged depending on the type of credit arrangements. Although usury laws sought to protect consumers against high interest rates, these state imposed interest rate ceilings usually resulted in limiting credit availability because the ceilings were set too low to make it profitable for lenders to lend money at such low rates.

Small Loan Laws At the turn of this century, the Uniform Small Loan Law allowed exceptions to state usury laws and, therefore, increased the availability of credit and the expansion of consumer credit markets (NCCF, 1972). As the U.S. economy matured and became more oriented toward consumer goods, over time consumer credit usage rose as well as the amount of consumer credit outstanding in the economy. Consumer incomes were rising and, in turn, increased consumers' ability to repay credit and their willingness to assume debt. Many households began accumulating assets including homes and accordingly these same households began accumulating debts to finance such asset ownership (NCCF, 1972).

Amortization The economic conditions during the Great Depression of the 1930s caused many individuals and families to default on their consumer credit loans and mortgage foreclosures were common. Post-Depression lending both for consumer credit loans and residential mortgage became synonymous with **amortization** which is a scheduling of repayments of both interest and principal over the entire term (e.g., time period) of the credit arrangement or contract (Brueggeman & Fisher, 1993: 114-119; Winger & Frasca, 1993: 201-204).

Amortization left the consumer with a more balanced repayment schedule but it complicated the calculation of **effective interest rates**. Under an amortized repayment schedule, the simple interest rate is no longer the effective interest rate because the principal is paid back along with the interest over the course of the loan thereby lowering the **effective borrowed amount** to about one-half the amount borrowed at the beginning of the loan. As a rough approximation, the effective interest rate of an amortized loan is about twice the simple interest rate.

Effective Interest Rates In the case of credit cards described next, the effective interest rate depends on how the account balance is defined before it is multiplied by the quoted monthly interest rate. The **Truth in Lending Act** of 1969 established standards for disclosures of effective interest rates in annual terms—**APR** or **annual percentage rate** (Winger & Frasca, 1993: 201-204). Thus, consumers could more easily compare credit costs amongst various lenders offering different credit rates and terms. The **Real Estate Settlement Procedures Act** of 1974 brought full disclosure and uniformity to mortgage lending practices (Brueggeman & Fisher, 1993: 231-239).

Growth of Consumer Credit As early as 1900, some hotels issued **credit cards** to regular patrons. By 1914, large department stores and gasoline companies also issued credit cards to the most highly valued customers. Credit cards were, however, first made broadly available in the U.S. by major department stores in the early 1950s. The cards were issued to customers for convenience in managing accounts. Customers were expected to pay the bill in full when they received the monthly bill. A penalty of one or one and a half percent was typically imposed if the full payment was not made within the billing period. Gradually, consumers were allowed to pay their bills either in full or by installment. Retailers such as Sears Roebuck and Company and Montgomery Ward Company were the leaders of this shift to a revolving or option accounts. These accounts were a useful means of financing major household appliances and other durables for consumers (Canner & Luckett, 1992; National Commission on Consumer Finance, 1972).

Commercial banks entered the consumer credit market as they recognized the potential profitability of providing open-end financing to consumers in early 1960s. To make bank cards more attractive to consumers who already had department store cards, the same grace period of twenty-five to thirty days was offered. The banks, however, imposed **service fees** on card-honoring merchants. By the mid to late 1960s, credit cards were used broadly by individual consumers. The majority of consumers were convenience users who paid the balance in full and avoided finance charges. For many years, bank credit card operations were marginally profitable. The profit, however, increased as efficiency in credit card operation improved. More bank credit cards were issued to consumers and widely used by the mid 1970s. Bank cards have grown rapidly at an average annual rate of 28.7 percent since 1967 and shared 38.4 percent of credit card markets in 1977 (Garcia, 1980). When profits were reduced in the late 1970s and early 1980s due to a declining economy with high inflation, **annual fees** on credit cards were imposed to supplement interest income. More restrictive lending practices were also adopted by banks and the growth of credit use was curbed temporarily.

Usury Rate Ceilings   The 1978 Supreme Court decision, *Marquette National Bank v. First of Omaha Service Corporation*, decreed that nationally charted banks must provide credit at the **rate ceilings** of the state in which they are located. Many states have **usury laws** that sets the legal interest-rate maximums that can be charged by credit lenders. In states with usury laws, consumers may pay lower interest rates than those in other states (Garman, 1993: 223). Many national banks that operate nationwide by bank holding companies moved to the states that raised or removed the rate ceilings on credit cards. These developments helped the banks to restore their profits in the credit operation (Canner & Luckett, 1992).

CURRENT CREDIT INDUSTRY

In 1993 the growth of consumer credit outstanding in the economy and mortgage credit was more rapid than in recent years (Board of Governors of the Federal Reserve System, 1994b). As of 1992, consumers held about $741 billion in consumer debt and $4 trillion in mortgage debt outstanding (Board of Governors of the Federal Reserve System, 1994a). **Revolving credit** (e.g., open-ended credit arrangement like credit cards) now represents the largest amount of outstanding consumer debt, nearly 36 percent of all consumer credit outstanding.

Commercial banks are the leading lender in both these consumer credit and mortgage credit markets. Finance companies rank second in the amount of outstanding consumer credit held and credit unions are third in the consumer credit market. Savings institutions and savings and loan associations were the second largest mortgage lender and life insurance companies were third in the market. Consumer credit rates in 1992 averaged about 9 percent for new 4-year car loans, about 14 percent for 2-year personal loans, and nearly 13 percent for 10-year mobile home loans (Board of Governors of the Federal Reserve System, 1994a).

Almost 6,000 commercial banks and other depository institutions issue general-purpose credit cards with a VISA or Master Card brand label. About 12,000 depository institutions act as agents for issuers and distribute cards to consumers. Major retailers such as Sears and J.C. Penney also continue to provide **store-specific credit cards**. Small retailers provide store-identified credit cards to their customers but their credit card operations are usually managed by other institutions. As many types of institutions are competing in the credit market, consumers are offered a variety of credit services (Canner & Luckett, 1992).

LENDING LIMITS TO CONSUMERS

Loans to individual consumers comprise about 18 percent of total bank lending. The **National Bank Act** prohibits national banks from lending more than 10 percent of their unimpaired capital and surplus to any one customer. For example, if the bank has a capital-to-asset ratio of 5 percent, then a maximum of 0.5 percent of its total assets can be loaned to a single borrower. This rule assures diversification within the bank's loan portfolio and limits risk. **Insider lending** is also limited. The Federal Reserve **Regulation O** sets the aggregate lending limit for loans to any one insider (e.g., directors, executive officers, and principal shareholders who own more than 10 percent of the voting stock) and specifies other restrictions regarding loans to bank officers. However, the lending limits do not apply to the sales of federal funds and investments in the securities of the federal government and federal agencies (Lash, 1987: 56-58). The OCC regulates national banks' real estate lending that comprises about one-fourth of their total lending. The banks are allowed to invest 100 percent of either total capital and surplus or 70 percent of time and savings deposits in home mortgage loans (Lash, 1987: 64-65).

LOAN RATE CEILINGS

Financial institutions and finance companies are restricted on the rates that they can charge on consumer loans. **Loan rate ceilings** vary widely from state to state. Currently, 14 states specify ceilings above 18 percent per year and 16 states do not specify ceilings at all (Canner & Luckett, 1992). Ceilings are intended to protect consumers from paying high rates for credit. They pose no problems as long as the ceiling exceeds the interest rate in a competitive market. When the rate ceilings become binding, they may cause some problems. Studies done in Arkansas and in the Washington, D.C area, where rate ceilings are low, indicate that the market adjusted to the rate ceilings by charging higher prices on the goods sold on credit to compensate for losses incurred on their credit operations. Thus, consumers paid higher prices under the restrictive rate ceilings (Kidwell, Peterson, & Blackwell, 1993: 710; Peterson & Falls, 1981). Sullivan (1980: 20) also concluded that commercial banks operating under restrictive loan rate ceilings charged higher service charges on demand deposit and checking accounts than those operating in less restrictive markets.

Companies that specialize in small loans, such as Household Finance Corporation and Beneficial Finance Corporation, are regulated by **small-loan laws**. The maximum amount of loan and interest rate that can be charged are limited (e.g., 48 percent on loans less than $500 and 36 percent on loans from $500 to $2,000). Limits on these rates vary state by state. In general, the rates for small loans are higher because small loan companies make high-risk loans that have higher default rates (Garman, 1991: 243).

COSTS OF CREDIT REGULATION

Costs associated with consumer credit regulation include direct and indirect compliance costs incurred by imposing consumer credit regulations. **Direct compliance costs** comprise the costs of developing, implementing, and operating loan applications plus costs associated with processing, granting, and collecting procedures. Conforming to the laws requires using legal resources, developing new forms, training personnel, developing and updating computer procedures, and compiling and keeping records. Collection costs may also rise when geographic restrictions are imposed on loan allocations (e.g., Community Reinvestment Act).

Indirect cost is represented by the lost efficiency that will reduce profits of financial institutions. It occurs when fewer products are produced or a lower quality of products are produced as a result of regulation. For example, when lender compliance with the **Equal Credit Opportunity Act (ECOA)**, which prohibits obtaining certain information about the credit applicant, reduced the percentage of good loans accepted by up to two percent and increased the acceptance of bad loans by two and a half percent. Thus, the indirect cost here is a decrease in the profit predicted to be from two to 16 percent (Shinkel, 1976: 174-179). To increase profits, creditors may restrict cheap credit to the best credit risks among their consumer loan applicants and charge less qualified applicants higher rates. This amounts to charging **variable rates** for lending. Therefore, consumers will either have to pay more to obtain credit in a regulated environment or will be forced not to use credit because they can no longer obtain it (Heggstad, 1981; Peterson, 1980).

Another cost of usury laws is the reduced supply of credit in states that have such laws. Credit lending rates that are set at below-market levels limit credit supply and a key result is that consumers may have difficulty obtaining credit. Those who are hurt most tend to be young or low-income consumers who are either entering the marketplace without having a well-established credit record or are perceived as a high-risk group. In general, higher rates are charged on loans with the greatest credit risk, the longest maturities, and the highest administrative cost. Such loans are usually demanded by either young or low-income consumers. This group of consumers is likely to be denied credit by creditors.

Usury laws also tend to fuel inflation by raising consumer demand. When interest rates are less than the inflation rate, consumers tend to buy now and pay later. Increased demand causes an increase in prices (Hanna, 1994: 559-560; Lash, 1987: 57-58; Pace, 1980).

Providing reasons for **credit rejection** also raises the cost of credit operations because the process of credit application is formal and needs to be completed fully. In the short-run, financial institutions and taxpayers bear the costs of consumer credit regulation and enforcement. But in the long-run, the costs of regulation are passed on to consumers in one way or another.

FEDERAL CONSUMER AND MORTGAGE CREDIT LEGISLATION

There are three types of credit regulation: (1) to inform consumers about interest rates and finance charges on credit; (2) to protect consumers from potential abuse by imposing loan rate ceilings, to restrict debt collection procedures, and to establish procedures for billing errors; and (3) to help ensure an effective and fair credit allocation by prohibiting lenders from discriminating against consumers based on borrowers' socio-demographic characteristics.

Credit Laws That Provide Consumer Information

Legislation that promotes consumer education includes the Truth in Lending Act, the Consumer Leasing Act, the Real Estate Settlement Procedures Act, the Home Mortgage Disclosure Act, and the Fair Credit and Charge Card Disclosure Act.

TRUTH IN LENDING

The **Truth in Lending Act (TILA)** of 1969, also known as **Title 1** of the Consumer Protection Act, is designed to improve consumer awareness of interest rates. The law requires that lenders disclose uniform and meaningful information regarding the full cost of credit, such as the **finance charge** and **annual percentage rate (APR)** of interest in plain language on credit purchase agreements and loan applications. The **total finance charge in dollars** includes all interest and fees that must be paid to receive the loan. The **APR** is the rate of interest paid over the loan period. Both the total finance charge and the APR must be shown before consumers sign the contract. Credit customers are entitled to request an itemization of the amount financed if the creditor does not automatically provide it. The act is intended to assist consumers to engage in more informed comparison shopping in the credit market. All consumer credit transactions under $25,000 are covered by the Truth in Lending Act. Mortgages used to buy a personal residence are covered, regardless of the loan amount. The Act applies to an institution or business that offers credit such as banks, credit unions, savings and loans, retailers, and retail businesses.

As a part of Truth in Lending Act, the **Federal Garnishment Act** of 1970 limits the portion of an employee's wages that can be garnished. The law requires that the maximum portion of aggregate disposable earnings of an individual for any workweek may not exceed 25 percent of his/her disposable earnings for that week or an amount by which disposable earnings for that week exceed 30 times the federal minimum hourly wage, whichever is less. The act prohibits employers from firing an employee because of a wage garnishment.

CONSUMER LEASING ACT

The **Consumer Leasing Act** (CLA) of 1976 requires disclosure of information that may help consumers compare the cost and terms of one lease with another and with the cost and terms of their contracts. The personal property leased by an individual for a period of more than four months for personal, family, or household use is covered. Also covered are long-term rentals of cars, furniture, appliances, and other personal property. The Act limits any extra payments including license, registration, or maintenance fees and regulates lease advertising.

REAL ESTATE SETTLEMENT PROCEDURES ACT

The **Real Estate Settlement Procedures Act (RESPA)** of 1974 is administered under **Regulation X** of the Department of Housing and Urban Development (HUD). The Act is designed to inform buyers and sellers of the settlement costs, to eliminate kickbacks or referral fees, to limit the amounts of money home buyers are required to place in an escrow account, and to improve the record keeping of land title information. Lenders are required to provide the mortgage loan borrowers with an information booklet explaining the settlement process, a good faith estimate of the settlement cost, and a uniform settlement statement that discloses all fees and charges at closing within three days of the application.

In 1983, RESPA was amended to cover **controlled business arrangements** and the law now requires a disclosure of whether a lender has an ownership stake in the referred settlement service company. In 1992, HUD amended RESPA to cover **first-lien refinancing** of federally related mortgage loans. This includes almost all first-lien and residential loans, both conventional and government. Currently, RESPA covers all refinancing and temporary loans issued with commitments by the lender to provide permanent financing with or without conditions. For **home equity lines of credit**, lenders can substitute disclosures required by the Truth in Lending Act for RESPA disclosures (Chamness, 1994)

HOME MORTGAGE DISCLOSURE ACT

The **Home Mortgage Disclosure Act (HMDA)** of 1975 is implemented under Federal Reserve **Regulation C**. It requires federally regulated lending institutions, including independent mortgage companies, in metropolitan areas to report where they make their mortgage and home improvement loans by census tract or zip code. Information about the type of loan, location of the property, race or national origin, gender, and annual income of the applicants and borrowers is required to be disclosed. Lenders also disclose loans originated or purchased during a year, the loans they sold, classified by the type of secondary market purchaser, and may indicate the reasons or denial of other applications. The purpose of the law is to provide information to help regulators (e.g., Federal Reserve System) and the public see whether housing needs of a community are served by financial institutions. In other words, the lending practices of an institution are checked to see whether it is involved in the practice of **redlining** (refusing to make loans in undesirable neighborhoods).

FAIR CREDIT AND CHARGE CARD DISCLOSURE ACT

The **Fair Credit and Charge Card Disclosure Act** of 1988 requires that credit card issuers reveal the details of pricing prior to signing up for consumer credits. Required to be disclosed are the method used to calculate the annual percentage rate (APR), if the rate is variable, the method used to calculate the monthly balances, all fees associated with the credit card, and grace periods. Consumers can use the information provided with the application form to make the best decision on their credit card choice.

Credit Laws That Provide Consumer Protection

Legislation that provides specific consumer protection include the Fair Credit Reporting Act, the Fair Credit Billing Act, the Fair Debt Collection Practices Act, the Electronic Funds Transfer Act, and the Home Equity Loan Consumer Protection Act.

FAIR CREDIT REPORTING ACT

The **Fair Credit Reporting Act (FCRA)** of 1971 ensures that a consumer's credit file contains accurate and up-to-date information. The Act especially protects consumers from the circulation of inaccurate, incomplete, or obsolete credit information. It allows consumers to examine the accuracy of their files, and it defines the steps consumers can take to correct or remove inaccurate, out-dated, or biased information from their files. If credit is denied because of unfavorable information in a consumer's credit file, the name and address of the credit reporting agency must be disclosed to the consumer. Consumers can—at no charge—then request to review their file. The agency must disclose the contents of the file and the sources of the information. The agency must also inform consumers what organizations or individuals have requested the credit file in the past 6 months. If incorrect or incomplete information is found during the review process, consumers can request an investigation. Any information that cannot be substantiated by the credit bureau must be removed from the consumer's credit file. If the consumer disagrees with the data in file, the **consumer's comments** can be added to the file. All **adverse information** must be deleted after 7 years, with the exception of bankruptcy. Bankruptcy information can be retained for 10 years. The law also **limits the liability** of unauthorized use of credit cards, including telephone credit cards. If consumers notify the credit-card company within two days of a lost or stolen card, they are not legally responsible for any charges. After two days, consumers are liable for only $50 for any false charges.

The consumer reporting industry controls 450 million credit files on individual consumers and processes almost 2 billion pieces of data per month. A survey conducted by Consumers Union indicated that over 48 percent of the credit reports reviewed contained inaccurate information. Between 1990 and 1993, the Federal Trade Commission received more complaints regarding the credit reporting industry than any other industry. About 20 percent of the complaints filed with the FTC concern errors in consumer credit reporting source (Committee on Banking, Housing, and Urban Affairs, 1993a: 1-3).

In 1993 Congress reviewed bills that seek a balance between the needs of consumers and businesses, and various issues were discussed. The **Consumer Reporting Reform Act** of 1994, passed by both the House and the Senate but held up by the threat of a Republican filibuster, requires creditors and credit bureaus to furnish accurate credit information and to investigate and update disputed data within 30 days of a complaint. The House bill also requires that when one unit of a company makes an adverse credit, employment, or other decision based on information about an individual that was obtained from an affiliate, the denying unit must tell the consumer where it acquired the data. The Senate bill applies only to credit and insurance denials. The bill also requires that the credit bureau provide free credit reports to unemployed consumers, those who are on welfare, and victims of credit-reporting fraud. All others should be charged no more than $3. (Committee on Banking, Housing, and Urban Affairs, 1993a: 3-31). President Clinton indicated that he will sign such a bill into law when, as expected, it again passes Congress during the 1995-96 session.

FAIR CREDIT BILLING ACT

The **Fair Credit Billing Act (FCBA)** of 1975 sets up a procedure for the prompt correction of errors on a credit account and prevents damage to one's credit rating while settling a dispute. The FCBA generally applies to "**open-end**" credit accounts that include credit cards, revolving charge accounts, and overdraft checking. When a mistake is found in a bill, a written billing error notice must be forwarded to the creditor within 60 days after the first bill containing the error was mailed. The billing error must be acknowledged by the creditor in writing within 30 days after it is received, unless the problem is resolved within that period. The problem should be resolved within 90 days after the acknowledgment. The FCBA limits the amount of time that certain information can be kept in a credit file and establishes procedures for consumers and creditors to follow when billing errors occur on periodic statements of credit accounts. Consumers who have made a credit card purchase of a defective product or service for over $50 can generally withhold payment until the problem has been resolved. Creditors who fail to comply with the rules in correcting billing errors forfeit the amount owed on the item in question, up to a total of $50. It also requires creditors to promptly credit customers' accounts and to return overpayments if requested. The FCRA permits merchants to give cash discounts of up to 5 percent to customers who pay by cash instead of using credit.

FAIR DEBT COLLECTION PRACTICES ACT

The **Fair Debt Collection Practices Act (FDCPA)** of 1978 is designed to eliminate abusive, oppressive, and deceptive debt collection practices. It specifies the collection procedures that prohibit unfair, abusive, and deceptive practices by debt collectors. Borrowers are entitled to a written notice from the debt collector and instructions on what to do if they do not owe the money. Borrowers have 30 days from receipt of the written notice to respond to the debt collector and to deny the debt. The FDCPA sets the procedures for debt collectors to follow when contacting the credit user and restricts the contact made by debt collectors with a third party involved. It further defines that the collection process should not interfere with the consumer's life at home or at work. Consumers also have the right to tell the debt collector not to call and the collector must respect the request. When the law is violated, consumers have the right to sue a collector in a state or federal court within one year.

ELECTRONIC FUNDS TRANSFER ACT

The **Electronic Funds Transfer Act (EFTA)** of 1978 provides consumer protection in electronic banking. The act covers automatic teller machines (ATMs), point-of-sale terminals, telephone transfers, and computer transactions. In case of unauthorized use, the consumer's liability is limited to $50 if the financial institution is notified within two business days after the card has been lost or stolen. If not reported within the time frame permitted, the consumer may be liable for up to $500. If an unauthorized transfer on the statement is not reported within 90 days, the consumers' liability is unlimited. A number of states have additional laws to protect consumers in electronic transactions.

HOME EQUITY LOAN CONSUMER PROTECTION ACT

The **Home Equity Loan Consumer Protection Act (HELCPA)** of 1988 is designed to reduce abuses in the home-equity loan market. The Act requires lenders to disclose terms, rates, and other conditions, such as miscellaneous charges or fees for the home equity line of credit with the application. If the disclosed terms change, the consumer can refuse to accept the change and is entitled to a refund of fees paid for the application. It also prohibits lenders from changing the terms of a loan after the contract has been signed and calling in loans before maturity.

Credit Laws that Provide for the Fair and Efficient Allocation of Credit

Legislation aimed at providing fair and efficient allocation of credit includes the Fair Housing Act, the Equal Credit Opportunities Act, and the Community Reinvestment Act.

FAIR HOUSING ACT

The **Fair Housing Act (FHA)**, known as Title 8 of the 1968 **Civil Rights Act**, prohibits discrimination in mortgage lending on the basis of race, gender, religion, handicap, familial status, or national origin when selling, renting, or financing housing and also in the advertising of housing. The law is designed to prohibit unfair practices in the housing market. It is enforced by the Department of Housing and Urban Development, the Justice Department, and the Comptroller of the Currency.

EQUAL CREDIT OPPORTUNITY ACT

The **Equal Credit Opportunity Act (ECOA)** of 1975, known as Title VII of the Federal Consumer Credit Protection Act, prohibits lenders from discriminating against borrowers on the basis of their age, race, sex, marital status, national origin, color, religion, or receipt of public assistance. The Act does not guarantee consumers will receive credit, but it requires that creditworthiness be judged uniformly. Creditors are not allowed to make an inquiry about the sex or marital status of credit customers. The Act requires that the same criteria be applied to both males and females. Married women do not have to disclose their husband's income or their childbearing plan when applying for credit. Women also can apply for credit in their own name regardless of their marital status.

The ECOA establishes disclosure requirements for lenders. A consumer must be notified of a credit decision within 30 days of submitting a completed credit application. If the lender's rejection letter does not state the reason for rejection, consumers can request it in writing. Consumers can also review the data in their file at the credit reporting agency—for free—when the data files are the basis of the rejection. Consumers can sue the creditor for actual damages plus punitive damages of up to $10,000 if they can prove that the creditor discriminated against them.

COMMUNITY REINVESTMENT ACT

The **Community Reinvestment Act (CRA)** of 1977, implemented by the Federal Reserve **Regulation BB**, encourages federally insured commercial banks and savings associations to help meet the credit needs of their communities, especially low- and moderate-income neighborhoods, in a manner consistent with safe and sound banking practices. The CRA requires mortgage loan records to be identified and compiled by geographic region. The key to compliance is to treat all potential borrowers equally. Each depository institution must adopt a **Community Reinvestment Act statement** for its delineated community. The files of public comments on the institution's credit policies and the recent **Community Reinvestment Act** (CRA) must be kept for review. The institution's records of meeting those credit needs are reviewed annually by preparing a written evaluation of the institutions along with the assignment of a concluding rating supported with facts. The Fed, FDIC, and NCUA conduct such reviews.

Historically, the Community Reinvestment Act, however, has been an empty threat to banks since government regulators almost never enforced it. In 1993, President Clinton requested changes in CRA implementation to: (1) reduce excessive paperwork, (2) include consumers, small businesses, and community development lending, and (3) increase the objectivity of the evaluation system. The Clinton administration also proposed to strengthen the CRA by establishing stringent numerical standards for a bank's lending, investment, and service practices in poor areas. Under the proposed and later revised regulations, lenders are expected to meet the needs of their entire service areas through a combination of consumer, residential, small business, and community development lending. The lenders would be judged by how much money they lent to the poorest inner-city areas relative to their market share for lending in the area (Risen, 1994; Sniderman, 1994). Action is expected on these CRA-related proposals during the 1995-96 Congress.

CURRENT ISSUES

As the consumer credit industry has grown and consumer credit use increased, the number of problems associated with consumer credit have escalated. The major current consumer credit concerns are briefly summarized as follows.

Heavy Use of Consumer Credit

The consumer credit industry has grown dramatically since the 1970s. Over $700 billion in consumer installment credit is now outstanding. In 1993 American consumers charged more than $350 billion on their bank credit cards and paid $36 billion in credit card interest. The average balance carried by a typical consumer recently was $2,733; that person also paid about $460 in interest (Layer, 1994). There are five reasons for the growth of the **credit industry**: (1) easy accessibility, (2) low minimum payments, (3) convenience, (4) demographic changes, and (5) aggressive marketing.

The number of credit cards outstanding has nearly doubled since 1980 with over one billion cards today. Approximately 70 percent of all US households have at least one card up from 50 percent in 1970. About three-quarters of card-holding households have more than two credit cards with the average number of credit cards held by all card-holding households approaching nine (Canner & Luckett, 1992).

The required **minimum payment** decreased from 5 percent in the mid-1980s to only 2 or 3 percent today. It is, therefore, easier for consumers to take on a large amount of debt. Such small minimum repayment requirements can easily extend what formerly was about a three-year payback time period to ten years or more. Consumers pay high interest payments to banks and other credit card companies which raises the ultimate cost of their purchases substantially.

Acceptance of credit cards has grown vastly. Credit cards are accepted for any purchase including groceries, telephone services, IRS payments; they also allow cash advances at a cost. The high divorce rate has affected credit card borrowing, too. When the divorced and separated no longer share their housing and durables, they individually use more credit for new purchases. Marketing strategies used by the credit industry also affect consumer acceptance and willingness to pay interest as they are offered extremely low minimum payment terms, flexible payment choices, and interest-free periods (Canner & Luckett, 1992; Luckett & August, 1985; The Boston Company Economic Advisors, Inc., 1992). Consumers who have a good credit record are especially targeted with offers of a preapproved line of credit and services such as a rebate on purchases, travel discounts, rental car insurance, travel accident insurance, and extended warranties on purchases. As a result of this unnecessary credit-card soliciting many consumers accept a second or third VISA card. Consequently the use of credit cards increases (Garman, 1994: 551).

Haynes (1989) has suggested that a credit variable or factor needs to be added to demand analyses on a standard basis. Researchers have begun to study the effects of credit use on food expenditures (Kirby & Capps, 1994) and suggest that further study is needed to examine its effect on other household expenditures. Other research has explored the theoretical implications of households using open-end credit to manage financial risk as an alternative to insurance (Eisenhauer, 1994). Still other researchers have examined credit card ownership and usage among traditional groups such as the elderly who are not usually associated with this type of credit (Mathur & Moschis, 1994).

Consumer Privacy at Risk

Credit reporting agencies collect information concerning credit histories and the financial status of 90 percent of all Americans. The original purpose of the agencies was to maintain and provide consumer credit information for businesses and consumers. However, they expanded their business by selling the consumer credit information to their customers, such as retailers, insurance companies, lenders, businesses that sell mailing lists, prospective employers, and government agencies. Consumers have lost control over how their personal information is circulated and consumer privacy is threatened (Committee on Banking, Housing, and Urban Affairs, 1993a: 1-3; Wallace, 1992; Westin, 1992). Personal information from auto loan applications, courthouses, mail-in coupons, and changes in residence are combined with consumers' credit files. This type of information is readily available for marketers at a price. Based on the consumer information provided, certain groups of consumers are targeted depending on the products involved. Almost all consumers are affected by these marketing efforts and their privacy is endangered. Consumers can contact the Direct Marketing Association (DMA) and request their names be purged from further solicitations (Garman, 1994: 558).

Interest Rates That Are Too High

Interest rates on credit cards have fluctuated within a narrow range and have been higher than those on other types of credit. From the end of 1981 through the beginning of 1991, the average credit card interest rate varied very little and averaged more than 18 percent (Board of Governors of the Federal Reserve System, 1994c). The stable credit card rates suggest that the credit market is not competitive. Banks argue that delinquencies, bankruptcies, and the operating costs have forced costs upwards. However, competition has grown for the banks as new firms have entered the market and challenged established credit card issuers by aggressively pricing their credit card products.

Congressional efforts have also been made periodically to set a national ceiling for credit card rates. After the attempt made by the Congress in 1991, the credit market became competitive by offering lower interest rates to consumers. The average credit card interest rate in 1993 was 16.30 percent. The publicity about the high rates of interest on credit cards and difficulty encountered by card issuers in acquiring new customers may have contributed to the growing interest rate competition in a relatively mature credit market.

The **two-cycle average daily balance method** to calculate the balance of a credit account doubles the effective interest rate by eliminating the grace period on new purchases. It does so by eliminating the grace period received for the previous month each time the credit account carries a balance. As a result, consumers are charged a doubled interest. This misleading practice allows creditors to overcharge consumers legally (Garman, 1994; 557).

Consumer information and consumer behavior in selecting their credit card choice(s) are important factors in reducing credit card rates. Consumers should be educated on how to select and use credit. Many consumers do not bother to search for the best credit choice. Some consumers do not even know how much they pay for interest charges. Efforts should be made by consumer educators to raise the knowledge of credit users. However, consumer advocates argue that credit card usage can not be reduced by consumer power alone; government involvement is essential. Active involvement of both government regulators and consumers can affect creditors' practices.

Equal Opportunity Is Not So Equal

A persistent racial discrimination problem in lending practices was revealed in the 1992 Home Mortgage Disclosure Data. The denial rate for conventional home purchase loans was much higher for African-Americans (36 percent) and Hispanic-Americans (27 percent) than for whites (16 percent) with similar credit circumstances (Committee on Banking, Housing, and Urban Affairs, 1993c: 68). Banking regulators and the industry acknowledged that mortgage lending discrimination is a serious problem that must be corrected. A new fair lending law enforcement agreement between HUD and the Justice Department was announced in a Senate Hearing in November of 1993. A concerted effort on the part of the Justice Department, HUD, federal financial institutions, and the regulatory agencies was made to strengthen enforcement of fair lending and CRA, to eliminate racial **discrimination** in lending practices (Committee on Banking, Housing, and Urban Affairs, 1993b: 56-62; 1993c: 54-58).

The CRA reform proposed by the Clinton administration in 1993 emphasized the banking community's efforts to assess community credit needs, product development activities, and advertising practices relevant to disadvantaged segments of its service area. The proposed new rules are intended to radically alter the scope of coverage, compliance criteria, and enforcement methods. Regulators appear to loath imposing strict numerical quotas on lenders. A more objective lender-evaluation process will serve minority and low- to moderate-income consumers with their fair share of loan activity (Sniderman, 1994).

As the number of non-married women increases, enforcement of the Equal Credit Opportunity Act also needs to be strengthened to protect non-married women from discrimination in the credit market. Unfair treatment of these women will affect not only their well-being but also that of the children living with them.

Consumers Lack Credit Information

A recent study by Princeton Survey Research Associates (1994) indicated that many consumers had **poor knowledge** of the grace period, fees, and charges associated with credit use and were confused about fixed and variable interest rates. Consumers may be even more confused since the current Truth in Lending Law does not require creditors to inform consumers when the interest rates on variable-rate credit cards are changed. Holders of variable-rate credit cards are forced to pay higher interest payments without being informed.

Credit insurance (e.g., credit life, credit disability insurance, and job loss) is not well understood by consumers although it is widely marketed by the creditors. Most of these insurance policies are overpriced yet they are sold to more than half of consumers with installment loans. Over 70 percent of credit insurance premiums are commissions for salespeople. It is clear that many consumers do not fully understand why they purchase the insurance. Critics argue that much of the success of the credit insurance industry is due to both consumers' ignorance and aggressive practices by lenders.

Credit life insurance is probably the worst consumer rip-off because purchasers rarely get value for money. The average payout ratio is 40 percent or less. In other words, only 40 percent of premium dollars was paid to the insurance policy holders. Lack of competition and weak regulation by state insurance commissioners have contributed to the financial waste by consumers.

Credit card or debit card registration services are another consumer rip-off. Credit card and other companies that sell a credit card registration service register the consumer's card numbers and arrange, for a fee, for the cancellation and replacement of any lost or stolen credit cards. This is a totally unnecessary service because if consumers can pull together all their credit card numbers for a card registration service, they also can do the last step—notify the credit card issuers themselves (within two days to avoid legal liability) in the event of theft or loss. Consumers must know the value of the services prior to their purchase.

"Ratio-less" Credit Scoring Is Here

The factors or variables used to predict default and delinquency in credit contracts may need to be reexamined in light of heavier debt loads and expanded use of credit as a substitute for insurance, as suggested by Eisenhauer (1994). Traditionally, prediction has been achieved by using a **credit-scoring approach**. This involves modeling default behavior using a statistical methodology known as discriminant analysis to determine levels or thresholds of characteristics associated with a particular behavior, such as default. Leonard and Banks (1994) have reexamined this approach in an attempt to simplify the credit decisionmaking process and make it more effective.

In the area of mortgage lending, some lenders are considering operating under new rules or the so-called **"cashflow underwriting"** instead of conventional debt ratios which evaluate applicants based on specific financial characteristics (Cocheo, 1994). This approach is formally known as the **Alternative qualifying process (AQP)**. AQP considers how well applicants manage current financial situations and does not require the traditional lending ratios such as the total debt-to-income ratio used by the lending industry.

SUMMARY OF CREDIT REGULATION POLICY DIRECTIONS

Credit regulation has been maturing as the credit markets have become more complex and the demand for consumer credit has increased. Table 14.1 summarizes all elements of credit regulation. The status of the credit regulation system is presented separately for both consumer credit and mortgage lending since the regulatory agencies, creditors, and consumer demands differ between these two types of credit.

The federal government enforces credit laws to ensure that credit is allocated in the most socially desirable manner and to service consumers in the credit market. However, the current regulatory structure has been criticized as being irrational and ineffective with considerable

Table 14.1   Summary of Credit Regulation

	Consumer Credit	Mortgage Lending
Economics		
Easy of entry	Easy	Moderate
Number of firms	26,700+	13,200+
Profits	High	Moderate
Technology		
Complexity	Moderate	Moderate
Stability	High	High
Substitutes	Moderate	Moderate
Subsystem		
Bureau control	Moderate	Strong
Industry coalition	Strong	Strong
Nonindustry coalition	Weak	Moderate
Bureaucratic resources:		
Expertise	Moderate	High
Expertise	Moderate	High
Cohesion	Moderate	High
Leadership	Weak	High
Legislative authority:		
Goals	General	General
Coverage	All	All
Sanctions	Fair	Good
Procedures	Good	Good
Impact of Macropolitical Actors		
Congress	Moderate	Moderate
President	Weak	Weak
Courts	Weak	Weak

overlap among the different agencies. Cooperative efforts among the regulatory agencies is required to ensure fair and efficient credit allocation in the economic marketplace. Consumers need more protection than ever because the credit market continues to become more sophisticated using advanced marketing skills, new uses for data, and leading-edge technology. There are also a number of obsolete regulations in part because of the consistent lag behind technological innovations in the credit market. As database technology advances rapidly in the credit market, it is imperative that credit regulators revise some of the existing regulations (e.g., Regulation E) or devise new ones (e.g., Consumer Credit Reform Act) to protect consumers in a changing credit market.

The legislative attempt to set a national credit rate ceiling in 1991 motivated competitive development in the credit market. The credit market has since become more intensely focused on rates. Since the beginning of 1992, all the nation's largest issuers have reduced their rates by 2 to 4 percentage points for selected low-risk groups of cardholders. Consumers now face a wide range of interest rates in their credit choices.

Credit card lenders are offering "quantity discounts" to selected consumers by charging lower rates on higher balances. Even though rates may be lower, lenders profit by gaining customer accounts with larger unpaid balances. The increasingly competitive credit card market is using a number of similar marketing strategies. As a result, the market for consumer credit increasingly will be **segmented** by the rate structures developed by creditors that are based on the profitability of each structure. As a result, consumers will increasingly face choices between variable-rate and fixed-rate credit card plans, and more consumers will shift credit balances from one card account to another account. It is not clear how these changes would affect consumers in the future credit market, especially those from low- and middle-income groups. Meanwhile, consumers will continue to communicate their problems and concerns in credit use with consumer organizations and government agencies.

Credit availability in general and especially for specific groups such as minorities and women continues to be a problematic area. Stronger enforcement of antidiscrimination laws and regulations by government may be one solution; establishing preferential lending programs may be another. Given the known effect of interest rate ceilings in limiting availability of credit, possible policy conflicts will become evident if a national interest rate ceiling on credit cards is again proposed. The examination of credit scoring systems and the innovative use of **"ratio-less"** underwriting for mortgages may address some of the traditional barriers for some potential borrowers in the lending world. Further educational efforts may also assist consumers in knowing how best to use their credit alternatives.

Chapter 15
Housing Regulation

Carol B. Meeks[1]

The private market for housing differs from markets for other goods and services because housing is in a relatively fixed location, is durable, and provides services not only from the unit itself but also from the quality of the neighborhood environment and the larger community. The **housing delivery system** involves a complex set of interrelationships between the private market activity of producers, sellers and buyers, and government policymakers and regulators. Although housing markets are local, there is multi-level regulation of housing. Governments regulate all phases of housing production and distribution. There are regulations on the structure and location of housing, component manufacturing, and the construction and distribution process as well as financing and sales transactions. Rental housing transactions are also regulated. The number of housing regulations has escalated in recent years due to concerns with perceived damage caused by past developments as well as increased concerns with health and safety, energy conservation, environmental preservation, and needs of special groups.

The majority of housing regulations are enacted at the local level under the **police powers** delegated to the government. Police power is the state's inherent right to regulate an individual's conduct or property to protect the health, safety and welfare of the community. However more states are moving toward regional and statewide housing regulations, particularly on land and environmental questions as well as building codes, rather than local regulation.

---

[1]Carol B. Meeks received her PhD from The Ohio State University. She is currently professor and head in the Department of Housing and Consumer Economics at The University of Georgia. Meeks has worked for the Senate Committee on Banking, Housing and Urban Affairs; the Economic Research Service at the United States Department of Agriculture; Cornell University; and the University of Massachusetts. She is the author of a textbook *Housing*, as well as numerous articles. Meeks has served on the board of directors of the National Institute of Building Sciences, American Council on Consumer Interests, and American Association of Housing Educators. She is chair of the Manufactured Home Construction and Safety Standards Consensus Committee. She has been a consultant to numerous organizations, including the Department of Housing and Urban Development, National Association of Home Builders, Manufactured Housing Institute, Massachusetts Institute of Technology, Yale University, and National Institute for Consumer Research (Oslo, Norway).

THE SUBSYSTEM

This examination of the subsystem in housing regulation includes an overview of advocacy coalitions and the environment.

Advocacy Coalitions

The largest lobbying group related to housing is the **National Association of Home Builders (NAHB)** with 155,000 members, and 824 local groups. They are concerned with current developments in all phases of homebuilding. The **Industrialized Housing Manufacturers' Association** has 82 members who focus on manufacturing of modular housing in the eastern United States. Manufactured housing has a separate organization with 171 members known as the **Manufactured Housing Institute**.

Real estate interests are represented by the **National Association of Realtors**, which has 805,000 members along with 50 state and 1,848 local groups. There focus is more directly related to regulations impacting housing transaction and financing.

The **Housing Assistance Council** represents needs of low income households, particularly rural households. The **National Coalition for Homeless** advocates for the homeless through training, newsletters, and technical assistance. The **American Association of Retired Persons (AARP)** has been an active advocate for improved housing for older individuals. They have had extensive impact on manufactured housing regulation.

Environment

The home building industry is characterized by a large number of relatively small firms operating in limited geographic areas (NAHB, 1992). Builders of less than 25 homes accounted for 77 percent of starts in 1991 while builders of over 100 homes accounted for only 8 percent of production. Entry into and exit from production is easy with limited capital and technological costs.

On the other hand, modular and manufactured home production is more capital intensive. **Modular housing** is factory produced according to state laws and regulations whereas **manufactured housing** is produced according to federal standards. Thus what distinguishes the two types of housing is the regulatory authority under which they are constructed rather than the method of construction. There were approximately 100 manufacturers of HUD-Code[2] homes active in 1993, operating a total of 230 plants nationwide or 40 percent fewer than a decade ago (NCSBCS, 1993). Production is highest in the Southeast with the leading producer states being Georgia, North Carolina, and Alabama.

HOUSING CONSTRUCTION REGULATION

At the federal level, the majority of housing activities are centered in the **Department of Housing and Urban Development (HUD)** although the **Farmers Home Administration**

---

[2]HUD is the Department of Housing and Urban Development.

(FmHA) programs are located in U.S. Department of Agriculture. Regulations pertinent to housing are also developed by the Environmental Protection Agency (EPA), Department of Energy (DOE), Federal Emergency Management Agency (FEMA), as well as private organizations. The National Institute for Standards and Technology (NIST) also provides much of the research and technological work for regulations.

Traditional Housing Regulation

Traditional housing regulation is for the protection of health, welfare, and safety of the occupants. Building codes and standards exemplify this type of regulation. **Building codes** are local laws that specify the standards that builders must meet in construction or rehabilitation. **Housing codes** govern the maintenance and occupancy of buildings. There are nearly 10,000 jurisdictions with building codes in the United States today (Colwell & Yavas, 1992).

Under **Federal Housing Administration (FHA) mortgage insurance programs**, housing units had to meet the **FHA/HUD Minimum Property Standards for Housing**. This has been a major stimulus to improving the quality of housing. Today, HUD field offices will review local codes which may be acceptable; the **Council of American Building Officials (CABO)** performs similar functions. FHA also has requirements for site design, wells, and energy conservation.

Often local communities adopt one of three regional model codes promulgated by: (1) the Building Officials and Code Administrators International (BOCA), which produces the **National Model Code**, (2) the Southern Building Code Congress International (SBCCI), which authors the **Standard Model Code**, or (3) the International Conference of Building Officials (ICBO) which publishes the **Uniform Model Code**.

The Council of American Building Officials (CABO) coordinates efforts to standardize the families of codes created by the three organizations. CABO sponsors two additional codes which are accepted nationwide: the **Model Energy Code** and the **One-and Two-Family Dwelling Code**. Both are referenced in the three regional codes which have now adopted similar formats.

The use of different years of the model codes and the local modifications of them have lead to great diversity across jurisdictions in building codes, despite the fact that most local jurisdictions reference one of the model codes. A **single national residential building code** would eliminate these differences and allow for economies of scale. A single national code is currently under discussion and it is just a matter of time until a national code becomes a reality. The organizational structure that it will take and the timing are the major questions delaying final action.

Manufactured Housing Regulation

The only type of housing currently regulated at the national level is manufactured housing. The **National Manufactured Housing Construction and Safety Standards (NMHCSS) Act** of 1974 established federal standards (1) for design and construction of manufactured homes to protect the safety and health of the owners or occupants, (2) to reduce the number of personal injuries and deaths and the amount of insurance costs and property damage resulting from manufactured home accidents, and (3) to improve quality and durability. Affordability must be balanced against these goals. Implemented in 1976, the federal standards preempt all state and local laws. MHCSS consolidated under one department of government regulations that existed in 45 of the 50 states.

Responsibility for regulation of manufactured housing resides in the Department of Housing and Urban Development (HUD). As HUD's contractor, the **National Conference of States on Building Codes and Standards (NCSBCS)** monitors HUD's **third-party inspection system** of manufacturer compliance with the MHCSS. In addition, all builders of HUD-Code homes are required to submit monthly production reports to NCSBCS.

There are several avenues for changes and input into the federal regulations. There is a **National Manufactured Home Advisory Council** under the direction of HUD which provides advice to the Secretary on manufactured housing standards issues. There are also two consensus committees that make annual suggestions to HUD for changes in the standards.

A **National Commission on Manufactured Housing** was created by Congress as part of the **Cranston-Gonzalez National Affordable Housing Act** of 1990. The purpose of the commission is "to develop recommendations for modernizing the National Manufactured Housing Construction and Safety Standards Act of 1974." The commission is composed of 16 members appointed by Congress and a member appointed by the Secretary of HUD. Commissioners represent state and local elected officials, the manufactured housing industry, consumer organizations, building code officials, and homeowners. The commission is to assess the effectiveness so the Act and development recommendations for legislative and regulatory revisions to the present law.

Current federal law requires that manufactured housing have a **permanent chassis** attached because it was expected that the housing unit would be moved. This expectation no longer holds true for the majority of manufactured housing units. Some of the issues the commission is required to consider are: (1) whether a permanent chassis is needed and the effect of the removal of the permanent chassis on affordability and durability, (2) whether the current system of inspections and enforcement is adequate and whether the financing source should be changed, (3) development of a system for reviewing and updating the standards annually, (4) impact of financing manufactured housing on the actuarial soundness of the federal mortgage insurance program and secondary market programs, and (5) compliance with state requirements for implied or expressed warranties. The final commission report was scheduled for release last year.

Modular Construction Regulation

The modular building industry is primarily under state regulation, except that there is a move toward the establishment of an **interstate coordinating compact for industrialized buildings**. The **Industrialized Building Commission (IBC)** is a government agency created by legislative action in three charter states: Minnesota, New Jersey, and Rhode Island. The purpose of the IBC is to jointly administer the industrialized and modular building regulations of the participating states. The long term goal of the IBC is to involve all 50 states and the U.S. territories in its compact so there will be a single national (although non-federal) process for acceptance and approval of industrialized production. The compact does not authorize the participating states to exercise any powers they could not exercise in its absence nor do the states delegate any sovereign powers to the IBC.

On July 9, 1993, the IBC adopted rules, regulations and administrative procedures. As of February 1, 1994, it is mandatory that housing meeting the requirements for the IBC's member states bear an **IBC certification label** which signifies that the building bearing it is in full compliance with the construction standards and requirements of the states and that the construction was overseen by qualified evaluation and inspection personnel. The IBC controls the shipment of factory-built houses from 33 states into the three charter states.

ACCESSIBILITY TO HOUSING

Access to housing is important to individuals. Regulations related to accessibility are primarily focused on **discrimination**. However, fundamental **economic accessibility** may have an impact on a greater number of individuals and families.

The **Fair Housing Act** prohibits discrimination in housing based on race, color, religion, sex, national origin, handicap, or familial status (includes individuals or families with children under 18 years of age and pregnant women). It is against the law to deny housing; refuse to rent, sell or negotiate; or to offer different terms and conditions for any of the listed reasons. **Discriminatory advertising** is prohibited as well as denying that housing is available when it is. It is illegal to adopt and enforce discriminatory zoning and land use ordinances.

Housing for older people, however, is not required to serve families with children. To be exempt under the law, such housing must be intended for residents 62 years or older, have at least 80 percent of the units occupied by at least one person 55 years of age or older, and provide significant services and facilities for older persons.

The Americans with Disabilities Act makes it illegal to design and construct most multifamily dwellings of four or more units, ready for first occupancy after March 13, 1991 unless they are accessible to people with disabilities.

Economic accessibility is not determined primarily by regulation, although **rent control laws** would provide one type of price control. Rent control was first used in the United States during World War I and was revived again in World War II (Willis, 1960; Drellick & Emery, 1939). Congress extended rent control through 1954 with a series of legislative acts. The tenant movement of the 1960s increased interest in rent control. The Nixon administration froze rents for 90 days in 1971 and restricted annual rent increases for 13 months afterwards (Achtenberg, 1973).

Rent control is generally used when a large share of the population cannot obtain reasonable quality housing at affordable rents (Meeks, 1980). The effectiveness of rent control depends on how inflated rents are and the methods used to determine rent increases. Rent control is often unfair to both tenants and landlords. It favors long-term residents over new ones and those who have high mobility. Rent control encourages black marketing and may favor those who can afford the entrance fee. Landlords of rent-controlled apartments may have to meet more regulatory requirements and may earn lower profits than those with uncontrolled units. Moorhouse (1972) found that rent control lowers the optional level of maintenance during an inflationary period. Rent control is only a short-term solution to housing shortages. In the long run, it will leads to decreased investment in rental property, causes poor maintenance and abandonment, and creates a black market for rent controlled housing (Meeks, 1980).

Economic accessibility is provided primarily through government programs sponsored by the Department of Housing and Urban Development and the Farmers Home Administration. These programs are aimed at low- to moderate-income households. Congress has defined **moderate income households** as those whose incomes are between 80 and 120 percent of median income for the area; **low-income households** are those with incomes between 50 and 80 percent of a median area income; **very low income households** are those with incomes less than 50 percent of median area income. **Median area income** is determined annually by the Department of Housing and Urban Development. Programs may provide **noncash assistance**, such as land for home sites or technical help, mortgage insurance or loan guarantees, interest subsidies for builders or consumers, subsidies for capital development costs, or direct cash payments to occupant families, public agencies, private organizations, or property owners. In addition, tax credits are allowed for mortgage interest payments and property taxes. At times tax credits have been allowed for energy conservation and other selected programs.

SAFETY ISSUES IN HOUSING

Because of the lack of attention to benefit/cost analysis in residential building construction regulation, state health and safety regulations are primarily based on the notion that higher standards are always better regardless of cost. Four safety issues dominating the national scene are: (1) fire protection, (2) lead-based paint cleanup, (3) stair safety, and (4) natural hazards such as seismic or wind safety.

Fire Protection

Fire safety regulations are promulgated by the **National Fire Protection Association (NFPA)**, which has provided this service to the nation for a century. According to Hall and Cote (1991), every hostile fire requires an initial heat source, an initial fuel source, and something to bring them together. Usually it is a human being who commits an immediate act or omission. At times the delayed effect of an error in design or installation is a causative factor. **Prevention** can be directed to any of these three factors. Changes in **product design** may result from regulation, compliance with voluntary codes or standards, a voluntary industry-wide effort, and in response to consumer demand. Some product design proposals have high costs relative to the problem they address and may involve the loss of other significant features desirable to builders and consumers.

Smoking materials are the number one cause of fire deaths, accounting for three of every ten deaths (Hall and Cote, 1991), and most begin with the ignition of upholstered furniture, mattresses, or bedding. Heating equipment malfunction is the leading cause of home fire incidents while cooking equipment is the leading cause of home fire injuries. Unattended cooking is the principal behavioral factor. The **National Electrical Code**

promulgated by the NFPA has widespread use and enforcement. This has contributed to the small role played by electrical systems in fire safety.

Because fire prevention will never be 100 percent successful, **fire protection strategies** are developed. Strategies include engineered redundancy and in-depth defense. Hall and Cote (1991) note that no one system should be considered disposable and no one system should be considered a panacea. They note that smoke detectors cut the risk of death by one-half. They further report that the presence of automatic sprinklers will cut the chances of dying in a fire by one-third to one-half and property loss per fire by one-half. The **National Association of Home Builders** (NAHB) position on residential fire sprinklers is that they should be optional and cost-effective. Mandatory sprinklers would add another layer of regulation and decrease affordability of residential housing. The NAHB Research Center is working with the U.S. Fire Administration to demonstrate low-cost, low-flow residential fire sprinklers in a national program. NFPA has developed a Life Safety Code which subjects properties to its requirements.

Lead-Based Paint Cleanup

Lead poisoning has been identified as a major health hazard for young children for many years (Rabin, 1989). Heavily leaded paint was used in homes built before 1978 and paint is the major source of poisoning. Thus national and regional attention has been focused on this issue.

Within HUD there is an Office of Lead-Based Paint Abatement and Poisoning Prevention which provides direction to HUD's lead-based paint activities. Programs are directed toward state and local governments that have filed a **Comprehensive Housing Affordability Strategy**. Programs help build the capacity to inspect for lead-based paint hazards, develop cost-effective methods for the reduction of lead-based paint hazards in housing for low- and moderate-income families, and provide information dissemination.

In 1992 the Federal National Mortgage Corporation Foundation made a special grant to create the National Center for Lead-Safe Housing, a collaboration between the Enterprise Foundation and the Alliance to End Childhood Lead Poisoning (FannieMae, 1993). The Center develops, tests and promotes the nationwide adoption of cost-effective strategies for preventing lead poisoning. It is to recommend model legislation and regulations for use by states and cities to reduce led paint hazards and develop ways to finance lead hazard reduction. It works with the insurance industry to find ways to provide liability insurance for property owners and contractors to meet established standards.

Stair Safety

The appropriate size of stair treads and risers continues to be a major national building issue. Pauls (1993) noted that the cost of stair-related injuries exceeds ten billion dollars each year in the United States. It has been suggested that a change in stair and riser tread would reduce stair accidents. Although several studies on stairway incidents exist (Templer, 1975; Carson, Archea and Carson, 1978; Archea, Collins and Stahl, 1979; Templer, Archea, and Cohen, 1985), all have major flaws. There is no research base that would suggest an optimal stair tread or riser size, although housing experts believe that there must be one. Most of the previous studies cited used small nonrandom samples, were in a public building, or did not control for relevant factors. Pauls (1993) supports a 7" riser and an 11" tread as the appropriate geometry for stairs in dwellings. The National Association of Home Builders reports that such a change would increase costs of construction by $6 billion in year one and $5 billion annually beyond with a $5,000 additional cost per new home (NAHB, 1993). Changes in design plans are one factor in the cost. For smaller housing units, an increase in square footage may be needed to accommodate the longer stairways. The model code organizations continue to discuss the most appropriate stair geometry.

Natural Hazards

In four of the past five years, natural disasters have caused at least four times the amount of damage budgeted by the federal government in its emergency fund (Healey, 1994). These disasters have included earthquakes, hurricanes, and floods. Probably the most coordinated federal regulatory effort is related to seismic safety. The **Building Seismic Safety Council (BSSC)** which receives substantial funding from FEMA has given strong leadership to developing national regulations. It is a public-private cooperative effort based primarily on volunteers who are experts in their respective areas. The seismic regulatory provisions developed by BSSC have been adopted by all the model codes.

Hurricane Andrew, with its winds of 140 miles and higher, brought massive devastation to South Florida as well as national attention to the need for higher wind safety standards (Interagency Hazard Mitigation Team Report, 1992). The costliest disaster in United States history, Hurricane Andrew destroyed or inflicted major damage on 75,000 single family homes, manufactured homes, and apartments. Approximately 160,000 people were left homeless. Insurance costs and costs of clean up were astronomical. Although Florida legislation required that structures in the coastal building zone be designed for a 100-year storm event, many homes were damaged due in part to the unusual strength of Andrew. There have been some policy suggestions that building in coastal areas be limited or outlawed.

Not only has the United States recently been beset by hurricane damage, large sections of the Midwest received extensive flood damage. FHA will not insure new housing units built in **flood plains**. If a prospective owner plans to build housing in an area that has been designated as a flood plain he must obtain a letter of exemption stating the given parcel of land is not actually in the flood plain. For instance, a given parcel of land may be higher than the surrounding land but included in the original geographic designation as part of a flood plain. Owners of existing housing units may purchase federal flood insurance and mortgage holders will require that they do so at the time of purchase.

Looking toward the future, there is discussion of a **Multi-Hazards Council** which would examine regulations in terms of the interactive impact on the array of natural hazards. For insurance purposes, communities would probably be graded on their risk level, code requirements, and enforcement efforts just like communities are graded today on the fire protection provided.

ENVIRONMENTAL ISSUES IN HOUSING

Three environmental issues are highlighted here: (1) energy conservation to promote natural resource conservation, (2) indoor air quality, and (3) wetlands. These three environmental issues have a major impact on construction and sale of housing and land.

Energy Conservation

Within housing, **energy conservation** at the national level has focused on the building structure itself and the equipment within that structure. Although there have been attempts to establish federal residential structural requirements for energy conservation, these have not been successful. The Model Energy Code developed by CABO has been adopted by all of the model code organizations. Further work is under way to have the **American Society of Heating, Refrigeration and Air Conditioning Engineers (ASHRAE)** publish a consensus energy standard to be known as "**90.2.**" This would then replace the Model Energy code and as a consensus standard would be more acceptable to communities.

The design of home appliances are determined not only by market forces but also by government regulation. Early regulation of appliances were centered around safety. The first federal legislation to impact appliance design was the **Child Entrapment Act** of 1957, passed to prevent children from becoming trapped in abandoned refrigerators. Doors were required to be able to be opened by an internal force of 15 pounds. The **Radiation Control for Health and Safety Act** of 1967 regulated color televisions which emitted x-rays and microwave ovens which emitted microwaves. The Consumer Product Safety Commission, established in 1973, has influenced safety requirements for household appliances in such areas as immersion protection on portable hair dryers, tipping requirements for electric space heaters, thermal cut-off devices for coffeemakers, and electrical grounding requirements for refrigerators.

Home appliances are one of relatively few energy-using products subject to federal regulations. The **Energy Policy Conservation Act** of 1975 called for voluntary appliance **energy efficiency standards** and established the now familiar **Energy Guide** appliance labeling program. Amendments to the Act in 1978 authorized the Department of Energy to set energy efficiency standards for major home appliances on a phased-in time schedule. Since 1975, appliance energy efficiency has steadily improved. Today's appliances use 30 to 60 percent less energy than models built in 1972 (see Figure 15.1). Changes in the law in 1987 established that appliance standards require the maximum improvement that is technologically feasible and economically justified.

The Clean Air Act amendments and the International Montreal Protocols signed by the U.S. in 1987 require the phaseout of **chlorofluorocarbon compounds (CFCs)** which deplete atmospheric ozone and contribute to global warming. Today's appliance are being redesigned to use new types of chemicals, **HCFC's**, that are less harmful to the ozone layer. The appliance industry goal is to completely eliminate the use of these ozone-depleting chemicals by 1996, in advance of the date required by the Clean Air Act (Weizeorick, 1993).

Figure 15.1   Major Home Appliance Energy Use Reductions

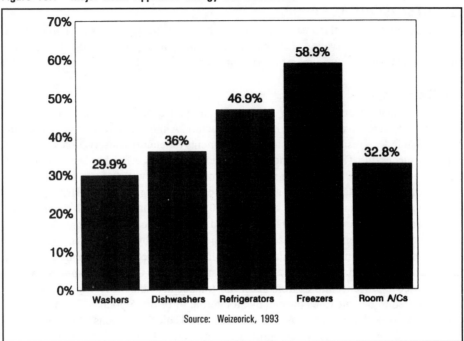

Source: Weizeorick, 1993

On March 4, 1994, the Department of Energy issued a Notice of Proposed Rulemaking and Public Hearing that will effectively eliminate the use of **electric resistance water heaters**. DOE suggests that a heat pump water heater will be more energy efficient over the lifetime of use. Future directions in appliance regulation will be concerned with such items as water consumption in clothes washers, recycling and conservation of appliances themselves, and the possible dangers of electromagnetic fields (Weizeorick, 1993).

Indoor Air Quality

Concern with **indoor air pollution** began in the early eighties as the impact of tighter homes for greater energy efficiency became more dominant (USGAO, 1980). Since more time is spent indoors than out, indoor air pollution may pose a more serious health problem than outside environmental pollution. Harmful pollutants found indoors include: radon, carbon monoxide, formaldehyde, nitrogen dioxide, and other biological agents. Smoking also contributes to indoor air contamination.

Federal agencies have been reluctant to invest resources to study indoor air problems because they lack clear responsibility for addressing the issues. Federal actions have, therefore, been piecemeal. Most of the attention of federal agencies has been directed toward requirements of the Clean Air Act and the amendments to it (USGAO, 1994). Concern with indoor air quality is the basis for ventilation standards developed by the model code organizations.

Radon which is blamed for between 7,000 and 30,000 lung cancer deaths annually is a colorless, odorless, and tasteless radioactive gas present to some degree in rocks and soils (Henderson, 1994). Laquatra and Chi in a study of housing in central and western New York State reported that up to 66 percent of rental units had excessive radon levels. This number was in contrast to 41 percent of owner-occupied homes costing less than $40,000 and 36 percent of homes worth more than $40,000 (Henderson, 1994). The Federal National Mortgage Association will no longer purchase loans on rental properties for which assessments of environmental risks have not been made.

The Environmental Protection Agency is also concerned with radon in homes. They have developed a program to educate consumers on the health hazards and to assist builders in mitigating radon levels. The EPA does not have mandatory regulations regarding radon in homes. EPA has prepared a **Model Standards and Techniques for Control of Radon in New Residential Buildings** which is suitable for adoption in building codes. It contains a prescriptive approach to assist builders in implementation and calls for the installation of passive systems in high radon potential areas and urges, but does not require radon testing for new homes. CABO has adopted the model for use in its **One- and Two-Family Dwelling Code**. Some states are considering regulations that would require homes to be **certified free from radon** at the time of sale. In communities with high radon levels, testing kits are usually readily available to consumers so that they can determine the level of contamination.

Wetlands

Wetland policy has important implications for housing development. Property owners are required to obtain individual **permits** under **Section 404** of the **Clean Water Act** for construction on sites deemed to be wetlands. Albrecht and Good (1994) found that the federal permit program is not working They reported that it took the average applicant 373 days to get through the individual permit process, and during the process 63 percent of the individual applications in 1992 were withdrawn. Of the 410 applications received that year, one-fourth impacted less than 1/4 acre of wetland; just under half impacted less than one acre. Thus there is a processing cost as well as a high time cost to housing development with minimum environmental benefits.

There are several bills in Congress to amend the Clean Water Act and to revise the wetlands program. A proposal by a group of House Public Works and Transportation committee members would reform federal wetlands regulation by providing a clear definition of wetland for purposes of federal regulatory protection under the Clean Water Act. The proposal also would classify wetlands into three categories and provide regulatory protection based on function and value; transfer all wetland permit authority to one agency and establish an administrative appeals program; institute a wetland mapping program; and establish a compensation plan for landowners whose property value is significantly diminished due to the existence of a jurisdictional wetland. While the National Association of Home Builders is supportive of this proposal, many environmental groups are opposed to sections of the proposal and will attempt to kill any bill that might weaken current legislation. Two organizations playing roles in this issue are the Environmental Protection Agency and the Army Corps of Engineers.

CONCLUSION

Because of the complex nature of the regulatory environment for housing, only key issues have been examined. It is the complexity of housing which increases the need for regulation so that the consumer can expect high quality service from the housing unit selected without needing to understand the technical processes which created the product. Thus, housing regulation is not likely to decline in the foreseeable future. Quality and safety of newly constructed units will continue to rise but along with this will come increased costs. The key variables in housing regulation are outlined in Table 15.1.

The creation of housing is primarily by many small builders. Entry to the market is easy. Although many of the components of housing are highly sophisticated, the majority of the units are traditional **stick-built units**. Production of modular and manufactured units require greater capital investment and higher-level management skills.

At some point, there will be a single national building code which will help reduce variance in structural requirements between local jurisdictions. The weak link in such a system is that enforcement will continue to be local and, therefore, variable.

The fragmentary nature of housing regulation will remain, in part, because of the wide array of housing activities that must be regulated. This will continue to hurt both producers and consumers.

Because of their individual interests, the advocacy groups for housing are often aligned on different sides of an issue. The groups representing producers and suppliers have different positions than those representing low-income or elderly individuals. There is no group that represents the housing concerns of all families and households.

Table 15.1   A Summary of Housing Regulation

Economics	
Firms	Many
Entry	Easy
Profits	Vary
Technology	
Complexity	Low/high
Stability	Cyclical
Substitutes	High
Subsystem	
Bureaucratic control	Variable
Industry coalition	Strong
Nonindustry coalition	Somewhat weak but growing
Bureaucratic resources:	
Expertise	Low to high
Cohesion	Low
Leadership	Low
Legislative authority:	
Goals	Specific/general
Coverage	Varies by community
Sanctions	Poor
Procedures	Poor
Involvement of Macropolitical Actors	
Legislature	Moderate
Governor	Weak
Courts	Moderate

Chapter 16
Telecommunications Regulation

Samuel A. Simon[1]

In the broad spectrum of telecommunications, this chapter focuses on eight separate areas of regulation: the subsystem, advocacy coalitions, the environment, agenda settings, the law and agency procedures, the impact of policy decisions, current issues, and future policy directions. This chapter examines the key organizations within the telecommunications industry and it analyzes the conflicts those organizations face during times of change in the areas of regulation and technological development. Only by monitoring vigilantly legislative and regulatory actions of this industry can one keep informed of the changes and conflicts that threaten the economic viability of corporations in particular and consumers in general.

THE SUBSYSTEM

This examination of the subsystem in telecommunications regulation includes an overview of the agencies involved at both the federal and state levels of government.

The Agencies

There are four entities that assess, develop, and implement telecommunications regulations, two on the federal level and two on the state or local level: (1) the Federal Communications Commission (FCC or Commission), (2) the National Telecommunications and Information

[1]Samuel A. Simon is President, Issue Dynamics, Inc., a Washington, D.C. based consumer affairs consulting firm. Mr. Simon received his J.D. from the University of Texas School of Law in 1970, cum laude, and his Bachelor of Arts from the University of Texas at El Paso, in 1967. He is the author of two books, *Reverse the Charges, How to Save Money on Your Phone Bill*, (Pantheon, 1984); and *After Divestiture, What the AT&T Settlement Means for Business and Residential Service*, (Knowledge Industries, 1985). Mr. Simon wishes to thank Edward S. Hammerman, J.D., for his assistance in researching and writing this chapter.

Administration (NTIA), (3) the state regulatory commissions, often called the Public Service Commission (PSC) or Public Utilities Commission (PUC) in each state, and (4) local consumer protection offices or cable regulation offices.

The **Federal Communications Commission (FCC)** regulates interstate and foreign communications by cable, radio, satellite, television, and wire. The FCC is responsible for the orderly development and operation of broadcast services and the provision of rapid, efficient, nationwide, and worldwide telephone and telegraph services at reasonable rates. The FCC's responsibilities also include the use of communications for promoting safety of life and property and for strengthening the national defense.[2]

The Federal Communications Commission is composed of five members, appointed by the president with the advice and consent of the Senate. The president designates one of the members as the Chairman.[3] In appointing commissioners and bureau chiefs within the current administration, at times key political contacts weighed more heavily than pure competency.

The **National Telecommunications and Information Administration (NTIA)** was established in 1978 by combining the Office of Telecommunications Policy in the Executive Office of the President and the Department of Commerce's Office of Telecommunications to form a new agency reporting to the Secretary of Commerce.[4] NTIA's principal duties and functions include serving as advisor to the president on telecommunications and information policy. NTIA develops and presents U.S. plans and policies at international communications conferences and coordinates U.S. Government positions in consultation with the Federal Communications Commission, the U.S. Department of State, and other federal agencies. NTIA also prescribes policies for managing use of the radio spectrum.[5] NTIA provides **grants** to extend delivery of public telecommunications services to as many citizens of the United States as possible. It also strives to increase ownership and management of telecommunications businesses and properties by women and minorities, and to strengthen capabilities of existing public television and radio stations providing telecommunications services. Most recently, NTIA has focused its efforts on creating a national information infrastructure, known as the **"information superhighway."**

Nearly every state has a **state regulatory commission** responsible for regulating rates and service of **public utilities** (gas, electricity, and telephone). This is often called a **Public Service Commission (PSC)** or **Public Utilities Commission (PUC)**. These agencies are often established by provisions in state constitutions, though increasingly state laws establish the legal requirements for regulation. As cable television service has spread

---

[2]The Federal Communications Commission was created by the Communications Act of 1934, 47 U.S.C. §§ 35, 151 (1988), and was assigned additional regulatory jurisdiction under the provisions of the Communications Satellite Act of 1962, 47 U.S.C. §§ 701-744 (1988).

[3]In 1994, after two vacancies from the Bush administration were filled, the Commission regained a full board. The Commission is led by Chairman Reed Hundt (Democrat), and Commissioners James Quello (Democrat), Andrew Barrett (Republican), Susan Ness (Democrat), and Rachelle Chong (Republican).

[4]Reorganization Plan No. 1 of 1977 (5 U.S.C. app.) and Executive Order No. 12046 of March 27, 1978 (3 CFR, 1978 Comp., 158).

[5]In accordance with Executive Order No. 12046, issued under section 305 of the Communications Act of 1934, as amended 47 U.S.C. § 305 (1988).

its coaxial cables across the nation, local governments[6] have undertaken the role of regulator as they have issued **franchises** (permits) to these companies to offer cable and in some cases telephone service. This local regulation is typically performed by **local consumer protection offices** or **cable regulation offices**.

ADVOCACY COALITIONS

This examination of the advocacy coalitions in telecommunications regulation includes an overview of the industry coalitions, the public coalitions, and the public interest and consumer coalitions. Various groups represent myriad interests in the telecommunications industry. Where specific interests were once represented by the efforts of major lobbyists for the monopolistic dominant carriers of telephone service, now the emergence of new technologies creates multi-faceted issues needing new advocates.

Advocacy coalitions address increasingly complex and diverse legal issues, such as cable television subscription rates, local exchange competition for wired telephone service, and competition for wireless telecommunications services. Due to the convergence of the new generation of wireless telephone and data services, both advocacy coalitions and the FCC hope to raise industry aspirations of providing substantially new and increased competition for cellular telephone companies, which will lead to lower costs as well as newer and improved services for consumers.

Industry Coalitions in Telecommunications

Increasingly different parts of the telecommunications industry are organizing themselves for regulatory and legislative advocacy. As Congress continues to undertake in 1995 the first major overhaul of the nation's communications laws since 1934, these coalitions are crucial in pursuing the primary objective of industry—to promote policies favorable to existing and planned business structures. Although the communications industry is subject to regulation on federal and state levels, it is best if the industry's advocates view federal and state regulatory policies as **opportunities for**, rather than **obstacles to**, economic success.

Industry coalitions can change based on the particular issues debated. The following are important coalitions:

---

[6]In 1984, Congress enacted legislation that prohibited local governments from regulating the rates of cable companies, the Cable Communications Policy Act, 98 Stat. 2779 (1984) (codified at 47 U.S.C. §§ 521-559 [1988]). In 1992, Congress passed a new law to regulate rates and empower cities and states to have a greater role in regulating service. See, note 11, infra. Some states, such as Connecticut, regulate cable on a statewide basis, though most states allow municipalities to regulate cable.

LOCAL TELEPHONE COMPANIES

All local telephone companies have generally the same objective. The Regional Bell Operating Companies[7] have worked together advocating rules that enable them to compete in **new lines of business**, such as information services and video dialtone, while limiting the ability of other industries, such as cable companies, to enter their businesses right away.

CABLE COMPANIES

Cable programmers (e.g., CNN, USA) and cable system operators (e.g., TCI, Time-Warner) working through the National Cable Television Association (NCTA), their trade group, have lobbied on the federal and state levels for over a decade to gain rules favorable to their positions. Initially, these groups butted heads against **over-the-air broadcasters** that saw cable as a direct threat to their audiences and financial status. More recently, cable companies have sought to keep telephone companies from using their **coaxial cable networks** to offer cable-like services. As technology changes, it is increasingly possible for cable and telephone companies to enter each other's businesses and markets. The issue is generally what the **rules of entry** will be in the future and who will provide what service. Imagine watching "The Late Show with David Letterman" over your telephone line and talking to a relative attending college over the student's dormitory's coaxial cable.

NEWSPAPERS AND PUBLISHERS

The publishing industry has long fought the entry of cable, broadcast, and telephone companies into services that could be attractive to local advertisers. The **Newspaper Association of America** (previously, the American Newspaper Publishers Association) seeks to protect newspapers from increased competition from any source. They oppose permitting telephone and cable companies to **"publish"** information and they try to limit the authority and business opportunities of these other potential market entrants.

LONG DISTANCE COMPANIES

With the break-up of the Bell System in 1982, long distance telephone service has grown enormously. The key players are AT&T,[8] MCI, and Sprint. There are a number of smaller long distance providers, including those companies that buy minutes of long distance services **"wholesale"** from the three big companies, and **"re-sell"** this time to the

---

[7]The Regional Bell Operating Companies are NYNEX (northeastern states: Maine, Massachusetts, New Hampshire, Rhode Island, Vermont), Bell Atlantic (mid-atlantic states: Delaware, District of Columbia, Maryland, New Jersey, Pennsylvania, Virginia, West Virginia), BellSouth (southern states: Alabama, Florida, Georgia, Kentucky, Louisiana, Mississippi, North Carolina, South Carolina, Tennessee), Southwestern Bell (southwestern states: Arkansas, Kansas, Missouri, Oklahoma, Texas), Ameritech (mid-western states: Illinois, Indiana, Michigan, Ohio, Wisconsin), US West (northern and mountain states: Arizona, Colorado, Idaho, Iowa, Minnesota, Montana, Nebraska, New Mexico, North Dakota, Oregon, South Dakota, Utah, Washington, Wyoming), and Pacific Telesis. (western states: California, Nevada).

[8]AT&T is the new name of what used to be American Telephone and Telegraph Company. The name was changed legally in 1994.

public. These companies have united to compete and offer long distance service. In the very near future, Congress may allow local exchange companies to provide long distance service, not only in their regional service areas, but across the country and around the world.

COMPUTER INDUSTRY

The computer and software companies are new entrants into the telecommunication debates. Sensing a large financial interest in these issues, the computer industry formed the **High Performance Computer Consortium (HPCC)** to advocate greater federal commitment to developing the **national telecommunications infrastructure**. They have become important advocates for the "information superhighway" that the Clinton administration promotes.

Public Coalitions in Telecommunications

Telecommunications regulation is balanced among federal, state, and local authorities. Control over the public airwaves has always been the responsibility of the FCC and the federal government, but authority over the regulation of telephone and cable service has been less certain. Even today, the division of authority over the regulation of telephone service results in considerable tension between state and federal authorities. States seek to control as much as possible in the telephone and cable industries, while the federal regulators seek to expand their authority to create a **single national policy** for the entire telecommunications industry.

The major advocacy coalitions involved in these debates include the following:

STATE COALITIONS

The **National Association of Regulatory Utility Commissioners (NARUC)**, which is the association of the state regulatory commissions, is the leading advocate for strong state authority over telephone and cable regulation. Similarly, the **National Conference of State Legislatures (NCSL)** represents the interest of state legislatures in Washington, D.C. NCSL advocates strong state authority over telephone and cable regulation. The **National Governor's Association (NGA)**, is also a strong advocate for state authority.

CITY COALITIONS

The **National Association of Cities**, the **National Conference of Mayors**, and the **National Association of Counties** form an important coalition advocating strong local authority in the telecommunication arena. Increasingly, competition arises not only between state and federal authority, but also between state and local authority. As telephone companies seek to offer cable services, and cable companies seek to offer telephone services, the local and state authorities challenge each other over authority to regulate and to tax these entities. Neither level of government wants to lose possible sources of revenue.

Public Interest and Consumer Coalitions in Telecommunications

As telecommunications issues have peaked in importance during the last few years, so too have the number and types of public interest and consumer coalitions. Historically, advocacy coalitions in telecommunications divided themselves along the **lines of technology**. In broadcasting, there existed coalitions concerned with improving the quality of television, with some focusing on children's television (Action for Children's Television, now superseded by the Center for Media Education), others focusing on television violence, and still others concerned generally about listeners' and viewers' rights (National Citizens Committee for Broadcasting).

Today, as the technological lines blur, so do the interests of the various coalitions. New coalitions emerge while others refocus their **agendas**. Agendas differ sharply among some of the coalitions, from those that focus solely on the interests of lowering subscription rates, to other coalitions that point to the need for more and improved service to consumers. The following are the major public interest and consumer advocacy coalitions with their key agendas indicated:

CONSUMER ADVOCACY COALITIONS

Traditional consumer groups are becoming more involved in telecommunications. Their agendas typically represent the interest of the consumer in **lowering service rates**. These groups often participate in legal actions, such as **rate proceedings**, on the federal and state level. Prominent among proponents for legislative change is the **National Association of State Utility Consumer Advocates (NASUCA)**, which is the association of the official state agencies responsible for representing consumer interests in utility cases (usually rate cases) at the state level. NASUCA also has a Washington, D.C. office, and it often lobbies at the FCC and participates in congressional hearings. Also important in this area is the **Consumer Federation of America (CFA)**. CFA, an alliance of 240 state, local, and national consumer and labor organizations, often advocates for lowering rates for consumers at the FCC and in selected state proceedings. Both CFA and NASUCA juxtapose themselves to policies that may result in increased cost to consumers, even when that raised cost would increase investment in infrastructure and expand new services to residential consumers.

TECHNOLOGY COALITIONS

Two new, pro-technology coalitions have emerged to support the growing importance of information technologies. The first coalition, the **Electronic Frontier Foundation (EFF)**, was founded by the former head of Lotus Development Corporation ("the spreadsheet company"), Mitch Kapor. EFF, working closely with some industry segments, particularly computer and software companies, advocates for a more rapid deployment of **advanced digital technology** in the telephone network. Their goal is to create the modern equivalent of a "plain, old 'data'" (POD) network, similar to that of the voice telephone system used today (called POTS for "plain old telephone service").

The second coalition, the **Alliance for Public Technology (APT)**, advocates for the deployment of a national telecommunications infrastructure to the home, assuring greater **access to technology** by consumers. As the public interest coalition of other public groups, APT seeks to foster greater access to the benefits of technology by consumers, even if it means that consumers must pay somewhat higher service rates. Both of these groups occasionally find themselves in opposition to the more traditional "consumer" groups, such as CFA and NASUCA, whose goals tend to focus primarily on lowering subscription rates.

ACCESS COALITIONS

The **Media Access Project**, one of the oldest advocacy groups in Washington, D.C., is one of the key advocates for access to telecommunications, broadcast, cable, and now multi-media services by alternate, **non-commercial voices**. These advocates want to assure that media owners do not maintain a monopoly over the ideas and programming that is heard by the American public. In the cable arena, the **Association for a Democratic Media** (formerly, National Association of Cable Programmers) argue for increased cable access channels. Public television stations lobby through their Washington, D.C. advocates to maintain access to **allocated broadcasting frequencies** (radio and television), to secure legal rights to be carried on cable systems (**must-carry rules**), and to gain access to the new **technology platforms**.

Other access coalitions seeking greater access to new telecommunications technologies, as **producers of programming and content**, include libraries, local governments, and non-profit organizations. A subset of access coalitions is **minority advocates** who seek greater diversity in ownership of the media, including new media. They advocate for set-asides, tax certificates, and preference in allocations of frequencies and licenses.

PUBLIC EDUCATION COALITIONS

Public education remains an important part of promoting consumer interests. A key number of consumer advocates work primarily to assure consumers have access to information to assure that they can be effective purchasers. An effective example, the **TeleConsumer Hotline**, is a collaborative effort of the Consumer Federation of America and the **Telecommunications Research and Action Center (TRAC)**, financed by the telecommunications industry. The Hotline provides consumer assistance on selecting long distance telephone carriers and how to make decisions on buying local equipment. TRAC produces information on rates of the major long distance carriers.

RURAL COALITIONS

In telecommunications, geographic deployment of technology is extremely important. Rural interests seek to assure that their rates and services are as affordable and robust as those for the more urban areas of the country. The **urban-rural conflict** has been a historic battle in telephony, with much of public policy focused on assuring that **rate subsidies** are available to rural consumers. Here, the rural telephone industry often works together with government agencies to support rural telephony and rural consumers.

THE ENVIRONMENT

This examination of the environment in telecommunications regulation includes an overview of the economics of the industry and the convergence in technology.

The Economics of Telecommunications

Telecommunications is one of the most lucrative industries in the United States. Ninety-eight percent of all households own television sets. Ninety-four percent of the households purchase telephone service and more than ninety percent is **passed by** (has the option to connect to) cable television (about sixty percent actually subscribe).

Television and radio, collectively the **"broadcast industry,"** like newspapers, are **advertiser supported**. Their economics and existence depend on delivering audiences to advertisers. This paradigm has lasted for nearly fifty years. Where the advertiser's product is the good or service shown during commercials, the **product** in broadcasting is the audience and the revenue generated is the **price** advertisers pay to reach these viewers. Thus, the larger the audience, the more revenue generated. Increasingly, as new forms of competition for readers and viewers develop, the economics of broadcasting are changing. Now national networks are losing market share to new cable networks (e.g., HBO, Showtime). As more consumers subscribe to cable services and as more cable operators provide new services, viewers are more apt to **"channel surf,"** and skim programming from channel to channel, making it more challenging for programmers and advertisers to grasp viewers' attention and expendable income.

The fees and charges associated with advertising and over-the-air television have never been regulated. Although extensive federal government regulations exist, many regulations were adopted to protect and to assure a **diversity of voices** in broadcasting and a variety of information services.[9] Over-the-air broadcasting typically is referred to as **"free TV,"** and it seeks continually to maintain its unique, but diminishing role in the marketplace.

Telephone and cable typically generate their revenue from monthly subscription rates for service. Similarly, the new on-line computer services share per-month subscription rates. Increasingly, these services are also beginning to rely on advertising and **"transactional"** revenues. That is, by prompting the sale of goods and services over their systems, the on-line services receive revenues or commissions on the sales produced by their advertising. Thus, cable shopping services, and on-line services such as Prodigy, now emerge which sell services over their own networks.

Telephone service was regulated traditionally as a monopoly, based on the type of regulation adopted for other common carriers, particularly railroads. Known as **"rate-of-return"** regulation, the profits and prices of the telephone companies were heavily regulated. Governed by the **Communications Act** of 1934, the goal of regulation was to

---

[9]These have included rules limiting the power of the three major television networks (ABC, CBS, and NBC), rules to assure local broadcasters covered important public issues, and rules to assure that political broadcasting was available to all candidates.

achieve **"universal service,"** assuring that all United States' citizens had access to affordable telephone service. Many early policies were designed to promote universal service. For example, the cost of installing telephone service was set low to encourage people to hook into the network, while at the same time increasing the cost of traditional telephone service. Similarly, regulators allowed long distance telephone service to subsidize the expense of local telephone service, also keeping local service costs low.

Today, new policies have evolved, promoting competition in telecommunications. With competition gaining prominence, totally new regulatory systems are becoming necessary. The **"cross-subsidies"** that were built into the system originally to keep local rates low are no longer viable. Traditional rate-of-return regulation is being abandoned as too costly and inefficient and is being replaced by **price-only regulation**.

The economics of cable television historically have involved primarily the cost of subscribing to the cable service. As cable television struggled to get off the ground in the 1970's, the industry sought to overcome the patchwork rules that existed throughout the country with virtually every major city having its own regulations. In 1984, Congress enacted laws (Cable Communications Policy Act, Pub. L. No. 98-549, 98 Stat. 2779 [1984]) that assured cable television service would not be regulated by localities and stripped away completely the authority of cities and states to adjust prices. With this new found freedom, cable rates increased dramatically, as did their offered services. Even though cable channels multiplied and subscriptions to the cable systems soared, rates also skyrocketed. In 1992, responding to consumer outrage, Congress adopted a new regulatory system, limiting the prices of cable system operators.[10] Rates have been cut nearly seventeen percent since the enactment of the 1992 **Cable Act** (Farhi, 1994: B1).

At the same time, cable operators and networks are discovering new sources of revenue. Evolving from a single subscription scheme, cable systems are becoming sophisticated marketeers of programming and services. Increasingly, rates for "premium channels" such as HBO and Showtime count for larger portions of revenues. Similarly, "pay-per-view" is an important new source of revenue, where cable systems charge for new shows on a per-show or a la carte basis.

Advertising is also making its way into cable systems. Many of the cable networks today are advertiser-supported, like over-the-air broadcast stations. Cable News Network, CNBC, and others sell advertising for their networks and offer advertising minutes for sale by the local cable operator, just as the traditional television networks offer "spots" to television stations to sell local advertising. Finally, home shopping channels pay local cable operators a commission on the sales made over the local cable operator's system.

The Convergence in Telecommunications Technology

The cable, broadcast, telephony, and computers industries are all merging because the technology used by them is converging. This **convergence** is keyed to digital technology,

---

[10]Cable Television Consumer Protection and Competition Act of 1992, Pub. L. No. 102-385, 106 Stat. 1460 (1992)(to be codified as amended at 47 U.S.C. §§ 521-555). In 1994, the Commission reduced cable service subscription rates by seventeen percent.

which is the ability to convert image and sound into a binary code of ones and zeros. Known as **"multi-media,"** the new technology means that in the near future the telephone, television, and computer all might offer competing services.

Technology evolves constantly in telecommunications. The competition to provide faster microprocessors, larger information storage capacities, and the ability to transmit simultaneously voice, video, and data through wires, fiber optic cables, or wireless communications creates a ferociously competitive business and an overburdened regulatory environment.

The introduction of **personal communications services (PCS)**, a broad term that covers pocket telephones, advanced paging, wireless fax machines, personal desk assistants, and computers that communicate over-the-air, illustrates how the diverse areas of telecommunications are now converging and competing for limited space over conduits and in the radio frequency spectrum.

Two new forms of licensed technology competing for limited space in the radio frequency spectrum are **direct broadcast satellite (DBS)** and **high definition television (HDTV)**, or **advanced television (ATV)** as it is known in regulatory circles. DBS is a new conduit created to compete directly with cable service providers by providing similar content to identical customers. The advantage of DBS is that any consumer in the continental United States is capable of receiving the satellite signals after purchasing an eighteen-inch in diameter satellite receiver antenna. DBS will be particularly popular in two areas: (1) with people living in remote or rural areas that are not passed by cable, and (2) with consumers who wish to purchase existing programming not offered by their local cable operator. A disadvantage to DBS is that it carries no local programming.

The future medium of television viewing, HDTV, lies a quantum leap away from your parents' old cathode ray tube. HDTV uses an extra-wide screen with more scan lines of horizontal resolution, which is a result of more information being transmitted to your television set than existing broadcast signals provide. HDTV will deliver images rivaling movie screens, coupled with CD-quality sound. Under the latest regulatory scheme, broadcasters will send programming in two formats: conventional signals and high definition. In order to provide the new formats of signals, DBS or HDTV, the radio frequency spectrum must be reallocated, allowing for the provision of these new services, which in turn spurs the regulatory behemoth to flex its overburdened muscles.

Although no industry is amenable to regulation, the burden the Federal Communications Commission shoulders to regulate telecommunications is necessary to provide these emerging technologies to American consumers who learn to use and enjoy these services in our evolving environment.

AGENDA SETTING

On September 15, 1993, the Clinton administration released the *National Information Infrastructure: Agenda for Action* (Agenda) which outlined general goals and principles for a **National Information Infrastructure (NII)** (Brown, 1994: xix). Since the release of the Agenda, President Clinton and Vice President Gore have emphasized the need for developing the NII as an information superhighway for all Americans (Brown, 1994: xix).

To implement the goal at the federal level, the administration formed the **Information Infrastructure Task Force (IITF)**. The IITF's **Telecommunications Policy Committee**, responsible for formulating consistent administration positions on key telecommunications issues, updates and revises governmental policies in order to make real the information superhighway (Brown, 1994: xix). In doing so, consumers, business, labor, and academia should have every opportunity to use the NII. And if the NII was not enough, the Organization for Economic Cooperation and Development formed a task force to create the **Global Information Infrastructure (GII)**, creating an information-rich, global village consisting of electronic huts through the use of earth-orbiting satellites and undersea, fiber-optic cables.

THE LAW AND AGENCY PROCEDURES

There has been a veritable explosion in legal issues concerning telecommunications regulation since the 1960s (Zuckman, 1988: xix). Practitioners and students of telecommunications regulation studying these issues are aware of and often frustrated by the fact that telecommunications technologies develop much more rapidly than their regulations. As a result, lawyers, businesspersons, and students frequently must grapple with important consumer protection questions based on the legal practices of by-gone days. Until recently, past law, although at times antiquated, adequately dealt with consumer protection of telecommunications regulation. However, with the emergence and convergence of new technologies, new issues involving consumer protection arise.

The Federal Communications Act

There is a general unease with the present federal Communications Act, with a strong sense that more problems loom ahead. As the technologies blur into each other, as local and state governments clash with the federal government, and as international competition, digitization, and other trends of our information age march forward, major adjustments to the Communications Act appear necessary (Firestone, 1992). In the particular area of common carrier telephone service, there is a blurring of lines between private and public carriers and the controversy concerns whether the Communications Act requires tariff filings even in fully competitive markets with statutory ownership limitations.

Before attempting to comprehend such complex common carrier conditions, one must travel back to the beginning of common carrier regulation to learn from where telecommunications regulation hales. The statutory scheme for telecommunications regulation originated as an adaptation of the Interstate Commerce Act of 1887, initially developed for railroads (24 Stat. 379, 1887). Congressional deliberations in 1934, giving rise to the Communications Act, barely changed the Interstate Commerce Act's scheme, which was the impetus of a major economic force requiring national regulation. Title II of the Communications Act initiated the federal regulatory scheme for telephone service as a logical extension of common carriers like the railroads. Central to this concept was that no common carrier has the right to **discriminate** between person or places, or to give preferences in any manner (Cullom, 1886: 39). From the Communications Act, rate provisions were born and consumers had access to non-discriminatory rates that even today are arguably just and reasonable.

Deregulation in Telecommunications

Perhaps nothing better illustrates the deregulatory thrust of the present Federal Communications Commission than its recent repudiations of one of the fundamental pillars of broadcast regulation—the **Fairness Doctrine** (Zuckman, 1988: 455). The Fairness Doctrine arose out of a series of FCC rulings which for over two decades were thought to have been codified by Congress in its 1959 Amendments to Section 315(a) of the Communications Act (Pub. L. No. 86-274, 1959). The 1959 amendments specifically relieved broadcasters' obligations "to operate in the public interest and to afford reasonable opportunity for the discussion of conflicting views on issues of public importance" (Pub. L. No. 86-274, 1959). Traditionally, this language acted as legislative shorthand which through law enacted a dual license obligation: first, to devote a reasonable amount of broadcast time to the discussion of controversial issues; and second, to do it fairly by affording reasonable opportunity for the presentation of opposing views[11] (Zuckman, 1988: 456). In a 1986 United States Court of Appeals decision (Telecommunications Research, 1987), the entire Fairness Doctrine was thrown into confusion when the court held that the Fairness Doctrine was not a codified, congressionally mandated statutory obligation, but was the FCC's creation and the FCC was free to apply the doctrine or to eliminate it. In 1987, the FCC repealed the Fairness Doctrine, reasoning that it chills speech and "contravenes the First Amendment and thereby disserves the public interest" (Syracuse Peace, 1987).

IMPACT OF TELECOMMUNICATIONS POLICY DECISIONS

Despite the wide array of positions held, a consensus on the impact of telecommunications policy decisions is considerable. One result characterizes telecommunications systems as providing sufficient competition at every level. This competition entails open entry and exit of firms, choices for consumers, and allows consumers to take advantage of a full array of new and existing telecommunications services from call waiting to video dialtone. Benefits participants have frequently identified positive impacts through the enactment of telecommunications policy, including the enhancement of education, health care delivery, diversity of information services, and economic efficiency (Entman, 1991).

CURRENT ISSUES

By opening up a large portion of the airwaves for new wireless telephone and data services through auctioning off portions of the radio frequency spectrum, the Federal

---

[11]See also *Red Lion Broadcasting v. Federal Communications Commission*, 395 U.S. 367 (1969); 47 C.F.R. § 73.1910.

Communication Commission has set the stage for fierce technological competition to serve American consumers[12]. Conventional market wisdom holds that wireless communications will be increasingly popular. The popularity of new technology acts as a double-edged sword. The first edge cuts out market participants who cannot compete or succeed in their new ventures. The second edge carves out niches for new services and competition, which in turn slashes prices for consumers.

Success in this new industry is hardly assured. New telecommunications systems cost billions of dollars to create. Consider the costs of designing, building, launching, and monitoring satellites in space or laying rubber-coated fiber optic cable across the floor of the Atlantic Ocean. Even with new digital technologies in use, new entrants still must compete against well established participants, such as cellular telephone service providers. The Federal Communications Commission has set a few guidelines on how the newly allocated frequencies can be used, but it can be assured that the FCC will endeavor to put all participants on a level playing field[13].

FUTURE POLICY DIRECTIONS IN TELECOMMUNICATIONS REGULATION

Under current leadership, the Federal Communications Commission, National Telecommunications and Information Administration, and the Clinton administration are focusing on a much more **economic approach** towards telecommunications regulation. One policy goal is to increase competition to such a level that the government can abstain from regulating these new services in truly competitive markets. The government is well on its way to achieving this goal by implementing the 1993 Budget Act which reshapes government organizations at the Federal Communications Commission by proposing new regulatory schemes by transforming today's common carrier and private radio services into commercial mobile radio and private mobile radio services (Pub. L. No. 103-66, 1993) and by establishing new international and wireless service bureaus. By promoting effective competition, current deregulation may lead to restraint.

SUMMARY

Having peered through the looking glass of telecommunications regulation, one must account for what was learned. In a nutshell, the eight separate areas of telecommunications regulation are divided into five distinct groups: economics, technology, the subsystem, bureaucratic resources, and the involvement of macropolitical actors. Table 16.1 provides a summary of telecommunications regulation.

---

[12]See comprehensive policy review of use and management of the radio frequency spectrum, *Notice of Inquiry and Request for Comments*, 54 Fed. Reg. 50,694 (1989).

[13]*In re* implementation of sections 3(n) and 332 of the Communications Act, regulatory treatment of mobile services, *Notice of Proposed Rule Making*, 8 FCC Rcd. 7988, 58 Fed. Reg. 53, 169 (1993).

Table 16.1   A Summary of Telecommunications Regulation

Economics	
Firms	Many
Entry	Easy/Difficult
Profits	Vary
Technology	
Complexity	High
Stability	Low/High
Substitutes	Low/High
Subsystem	
Bureaucratic control	High
Industry coalition	Strong
Nonindustry coalition	Strong
Bureaucratic resources:	
Expertise	High
Cohesion	Low
Leadership	High
Legislative authority:	
Goals	General
Coverage	All
Sanctions	Firm
Procedures	Thorough
Involvement of Macropolitical Actors	
Legislative	High
Federal agencies	High
Courts	High

Economics

Many firms participate on the telecommunications playing field. For some firms, such as software companies and minor computer hardware manufacturers, entry into the field is easy because initial start-up costs are relatively small. For larger firms attempting to enter larger, more competitive markets, such as the major telecommunications services like telephone and cable, financial burdens exist and entry is more expensive and difficult.

Profits vary among the players due to the **level of regulation** within their specific service area. Profits are high in unregulated service areas and profits are satisfactory based on **just-and-reasonable rates of return** in regulated service areas.

Technology

Technology is extremely complex in this area of regulation and it evolves constantly to higher levels of compatibility in an effort to become more user-friendly. Due to the incessant introduction of new conduits and faster microprocessors, stability is less certain for emerging technologies and much higher for those technologies that are more accepted and considered standard. Substitutes for technology are low for government-approved modes of transmission, but substitutes are much higher for components providing the transfer of information.

Subsystem

Within this regulatory scheme, bureaucratic control is high under the current administration. Control is justified by the goals of revamping the antiquated policies and rules behind today's telecommunications infrastructure. Although control is high, competition is keen, which will lead to less bureaucratic control as a result of governmental deregulation. Industry coalitions that promote deregulation and spur industry competition have strong voices. Their opinions are requested and respected within the subsystem. Nonindustry coalitions are respected too, due to the hard work and logical messages voiced by public advocates like the Alliance for Public Technology, who assures consumers' voices are heard in Congress, at NTIA, and at the FCC.

Bureaucratic Resources

Expertise and leadership are high because the experts and leaders are culled from the industry pool. Overall, cohesion is low, due to the myriad issues presented and conflicts created. Legislative authority is high in the regulated industries because Congress and the administrative agencies create the laws and regulations by which the industry participants must abide. Goals are general, broad, and vague, usually aiming to serve the "public interest." Bureaucratic coverage sweeps over all forms of interstate and foreign communications by cable, radio, satellite, television, and wire. Sanctions can be harsh, but only if they are enforced. Most violations go undisciplined until injured parties file complaints. Procedures are thorough, but painstakingly laborious giving rise and reason to the term, **"bureaucratic red tape."**

Involvement of Macropolitical Actors

Telecommunications regulation dances on the razor's edge of cutting technology. As a result, involvement by federal and state legislatures, federal agencies, and the courts remains high.

CONCLUSION

Protecting the interests of consumers in this advanced information age will enable U.S. citizens and businesses to compete in the global economy while generating good jobs and stimulating economic growth for the nation. In order for the future policy directions of telecommunications regulation to become a reality, every consumer—rich or poor, urban or rural—must have access to the benefits of the new telecommunications revolution (Gore, 1994: 1). The challenge for consumers is not developing new technology. The challenge is developing new policy that holds true to our basic principles. Consumers must advocate stronger positions of maintaining and gaining more access to telecommunications services. "Whether their words come from the quill pens that wrote and then signed the Declaration of Independence or from the laptop computers of the 1990's college student, better communications and consumer protection lead to greater market freedom and economic growth (Gore, 1994: 1).

Chapter 17
State and Local Consumer Protection

S. Lee Richardson[1]

State and local consumer protection has played an interesting role in the history of the United States. As recently as 30 years ago, consumer protection via government regulation largely did not exist. Today, strong consumer protection statutes and regulations exist in all states and virtually all communities. This chapter examines the subsystem of state and local consumer protection, overviews state and local consumer protection, and outlines the state legislative schemes to protect consumers before concluding with an epilogue.

THE SUBSYSTEM

The state and local regulatory system for consumer protection is influenced by some unique structural differences as well as particular interest groups. The chief executive of a state must share responsibility with one or more other elected state officers. Notable among these is the elected **attorney general**, the chief law enforcement official. Attorneys general have to answer to voters, not governors, and they are responsible for most consumer protection activities including enforcement and much consumer complaint handling. In some states, mediation and policymaking, to some degree, are in the executive branch. Moreover, the unique role of attorney general combines regulatory authority with executive authority of an elective office.

Consumer protection duties in the states are further complicated by the occurrence of specialized state agencies with authority over certain industries. **Regulated utilities** are monopoly franchises and generally fall under the regulatory authority of an appointed **public**

[1]S. Lee Richardson is a G. Maxwell Armor Eminent Scholar and professor of marketing at the University of Baltimore. He has been president of two state consumer advocacy organizations, the Louisiana Consumers' League and the Maryland Citizens Consumer Council. He served in the White House Office of Consumer Affairs under Presidents Carter and Nixon and was acting director in 1977-78. He is currently a board member of the Consumer Federation of America and has served twice as its elected president.

service commission or **public utilities commission**. Insurance and financial institutions are usually heavily regulated by executive branch appointees, typically through a **insurance commission**, a **banking commission**, and a **securities commission**, or some combination thereof. States may venture on a selective basis into regulation of many other industries and the apparatus to regulate them may be most anywhere in the executive branch. An example is a **department of weights and measures**. Also, much **licensing and occupational regulation** includes consumer protection provisions. And, **agricultural regulation** often contains health and product standards quality dimensions with consumer impact.

Consumer protection at the local government level often is a "hit or miss" situation. Some cities may have consumer protection agencies that administer various laws and have the traditional functions of licensing or weights and measures. As a rule, however, most cities and counties, except the largest ones, do not have a central consumer agency to handle consumer complaints, much less administer laws and provide for law enforcement.

Most law enforcement at the local level is through the offices of **district attorneys** or **state attorneys**. District and state attorneys are typically elected and are administratively separated from the mayor or county executive. The local agenda of law enforcement officials is much more concerned with criminal law—the everyday consumer civil litigation instances are of low priority.

Interest group influence on consumer protection legislation is diffuse and specialized by topic. **Consumer advocacy groups** at the state level exist in all states, although they typically have no paid staff and few resources, often operating out of homes and using post office boxes. Some consumer advocacy groups specialize in problems of the poor (e.g., high-interest credit terms, high fees to cash checks) or some other specific priority issues (e.g., utilities). Nonetheless, many are quite credible with legislative, executive, and press interests.

The state government is often influenced by local media that have found consumer information reporting, and even some consumer investigative reporting, popular with their audiences. In recent years, however, the newspapers have reduced their investigative reporting relative to that done on television. Much of this type of journalism concerns issues in consumer finance, investments, housing, automobiles, and food.

Media and other special interest groups influence state and local politics. Most media is local in nature, often covering a rather small geographic area. However, those media in state capitals and other big cities often have a major influence on the state regulatory systems.

There are some unique organizations and interest groups peculiar to state and local consumer protection. Most of the major state agencies and local governments in the nation are closely tied to various organizations that propose and draft **uniform laws and regulations**. In drafting consumer protection laws and regulations, state legislators and attorneys general have relied on such processes as well as guidelines from the **Federal Trade Commission (FTC)**. State and local consumer advocacy groups have ties to larger organizations, such as the **Consumer Federation of America (CFA)** and the **Public Interest Research Groups (U.S. PIRG)**. The larger groups sometimes are influential in state and local consumer protection. Government consumer protection agencies at the state and local level have ties through the **National Association of Consumer Agency Administrators (NACAA)**.

The state attorneys general are affiliated through the **National Association of Attorneys General (NAAG)**. Utility, insurance, securities, and banking regulators likewise have specific professional associations that propose regulations, although these have been historically denounced for their lack of genuine interest in consumer protection measures.

OVERVIEW OF STATE AND LOCAL CONSUMER PROTECTION

Although the states' earliest attempts at curbing deceptive trade practices date back to the early 1900s, the most significant state and local legislation came about as a result of the resurgent consumer movement of the 1960s. Although the focus of this chapter is consumer protection at the state level, first it is necessary to gain both a historical perspective of the political and economic environment from which it was born as well as an understanding of the federal legislation from which it evolved.

Historical Background of State and Local Consumer Protection

For most of the nineteenth century, the government assumed a paternalistic role in its relationship with private enterprise by providing a **favorable regulatory climate** conducive to business growth. The Industrial Revolution, coupled with the construction of an extensive railway system for transporting goods, marked a shift from small local operations and markets to a single national market. The rise and dominance of big business during the late nineteenth century, fostered by the government's laissez-faire approach to regulation of industry, led to the demise of many small manufacturing operations[2]. Large retailers, especially department stores and chains, developed quickly in rapidly growing large cities which further squeezed many smaller local merchants out of business.

Because it was more profitable to cooperate rather than compete, owners of large businesses often formed **mini-cartels**, known as **pools**, and collusively agreed to either limit production or charge identical prices. Meanwhile, consumer transactions became more and more impersonal as mass production by distant firms increasingly replaced local manufacturing and large retailing organizations replaced many smaller independent neighborhood stores. False and misleading claims by advertisers became prevalent and the doctrine of **caveat emptor** (let the buyer beware) displaced personal trust in consumer purchase transactions.

THE PROGRESSIVE ERA

The **progressive era** generally covered the time period beginning with the inauguration of Theodore Roosevelt in 1901 up to the beginning of World War I in 1917. Rooted particularly in the urban middle class, the primary objective of progressive era was effectuating social improvement by way of governmental intervention. Although the government's role in big business had begun a very gradual shift from being paternalistic

---

[2]For example, between 1800 and 1900, the number of farm tool manufacturers fell by two thirds; the number of leather goods manufacturers fell by three fourths.

and helpful toward a more regulatory stance, this process was greatly impeded by the power and influence of the industrial elite who had infiltrated many high political levels through either bribery[3] or appointment[4].

The public grew increasingly frustrated by the ability of greedy business owners to shape or deter legislation[5] and feared the control that big business had achieved over resources and markets. Theodore Roosevelt, however, who had succeeded McKinley as president in 1901, believed that big business was beneficial to the country "especially when regulated by 'big' government." The Roosevelt administration, with the support of the general public, began a period of reform that moved toward a more regulatory-oriented and heavier-handed government. This period of massive reform continued through the Wilson administration.

The progressive era spurred reform at both the federal and state levels. While state and local reform focused primarily on strengthening **participatory democracy**, federal efforts focused on **economic reform** and bringing unbridled big business into check. The authority of the **Interstate Commerce Commission** was strengthened, legislation prohibiting child labor was passed, and the **Federal Reserve System** was created. In effect, a number of regulatory agencies were established and delegated authority to enforce needed reform. For example, in response to deplorable conditions in the meatpacking industry, the Pure Food and Drug Act was passed in 1906, which ultimately led to the creation of the Food and Drug Administration (FDA) some years later. Also, with the passage of the Federal Trade Commission Act in 1914, the **Federal Trade Commission (FTC)** was established to regulate competitive trade practices.

The first rumblings of **consumerism** were at the state level and surfaced in 1911 when *Printer's Ink*, an advertising industry trade journal, proposed a model statute aimed at curbing deceptive advertising in newspapers and other publications. Approximately 40 states adopted all or part of the model statute and, although there were efforts at enforcement, the net effect on deterrence was minimal. The whole wave of domestic reform might have continued, but was derailed by a change in national priorities as America entered World War I in 1917.

THE FEDERAL TRADE COMMISSION, THE PRECURSOR TO STATE REGULATION

The Federal Trade Commission was established in 1914, not as a consumer protection agency, but to protect businesses from **"unfair methods of competition,"** such as deceptive trade practices. Because many people felt the monopolistic practices of big business posed a serious threat to the future of capitalism and American democracy by the elimination of smaller businesses, public opinion favored the FTC's creation.

---

[3]"When I want to buy up any politician, I always find the anti-monopolists the most purchasable. They don't come so high," said William H. Vanderbilt.

[4]Under the Constitution, senators originally were appointed by state legislatures. At the turn of the century, the U.S. Senate contained 25 industrial millionaires, thus earning it the nickname, the "Millionaires' Club." The 17th amendment to the Constitution, enacted in 1913, abolished the practice of appointment to Senate seat.

[5]Fundamental government structure underlies the progress, or lack of, specific reforms.

Congress amended the Federal Trade Commission Act in 1938 with the **Wheeler-Lea Act** which added two significant provisions. First, it granted the FTC broader authority to stop false advertising of food and drugs by allowing criminal penalties and permitting expedited preliminary **injunctions** against violators. Second, it prohibited "**unfair and deceptive acts and practices affecting commerce**." This provision, in effect, gave consumers the same protections afforded businesses by the 1914 FTC Act. The Wheeler-Lea amendment made no attempt to define "unfair and deceptive acts," thereby allowing the FTC to maintain the flexibility needed to circumvent new and evolving fraudulent schemes by wrong-doers.

However, the FTC had only been delegated authority to provide injunctive relief. From its inception, the FTC's role had been to prevent abuse, not to punish it. Thus, originally the FTC was not authorized to seek civil penalties or restitution for injured parties[6] The use of injunctions to halt unfair methods of competition between businesses was appropriate. For the individual consumer, however, an injunction was an unsuitable remedy.

PRIVATE ACTIONS AGAINST FRAUD

During these times, an injured consumer could, of course, pursue a private action against the violator under **common law fraud theory**. However, one of the many elements[7] that must be proven for a showing of fraud is that of **fraudulent intent** by the violator, which is extremely difficult to prove. In addition, the legal costs of pleading and litigating a case of fraud usually typically far exceeded the amount of restitution the aggrieved consumer could hope to recover. Therefore, the expense and uncertainty of litigation generally deterred the pursuit of meritorious claims by consumers as the economics of law, in practice, made common law fraud theory useless to most individual consumers.

Consumerism Comes of Age in the 1960s

This examination of consumerism coming of age includes developments in the American economy, state legal initiatives in consumer protection, the codification of the philosophy of the consumer movement, the growing momentum of the consumer movement, and the leadership of Ralph Nader.

DEVELOPMENTS IN THE AMERICAN ECONOMY

The end of World War II in 1945 began an era of unprecedented growth in the American economy. Post-war prosperity, new products, and easy credit led to a long-lasting "spending spree," and it marked the beginning of a more **consumer-oriented society**. Through the 1950s and early 1960s, increasingly persuasive advertising and

---

[6]Financially injured or wronged.

[7]The specific elements to prove fraud vary slightly from state to state. Generally, fraud can be shown when a false misrepresentation was known by its violator to be false and it was made intentionally by the violator with the aim that the misrepresentation was to be acted upon by the plaintiff. Further, it must be shown that the plaintiff relied on the misrepresentation, was induced by the violator to act upon it, and not knowing it to be false and through the exercise of reasonable care could not have ascertained it to be false.

technologically complex products had transformed the marketplace into an arena in which the uninformed consumer was clearly disadvantaged. Reliance on deceptive advertisements by manufacturers and retailers made victims of unsuspecting consumers.

STATE LEGAL INITIATIVES IN CONSUMER PROTECTION

A number of state governments recognized the inadequacy of the Federal Trade Commission Act as a deterrent to unfair trade practices and deceptive advertising. By the late 1950s, they began drafting their own piece-meal statutes aimed at protecting unwary consumers from fraud and deceit[8].

The **Uniform Commercial Code** (UCC) was drafted in the late 1950s and subsequently adopted by all states except Louisiana. Although intended for merchants, the UCC does not specifically preclude consumers from seeking redress under it. **Section 2** of the UCC contains a number of provisions that restrict the activities and conduct of parties in oral and written contracts which can be readily applied to consumer transactions. However, the UCC state laws provided consumers with only a slightly more effective means of resolution through the courts. For example, the UCC applies only to transactions for moveable goods exceeding the value of $500, which obviously eliminates its application to small consumer purchases. Moreover, as the name of this legislation implies, the UCC was intended to provide a uniform standard of conduct—mostly **contracts**—for merchants in commercial transactions with other merchants.

In sum, contract law remedies, whether under the UCC or common law contract theory, generally provide the prevailing party with **restitution only** (with no award of attorney's fees or court costs). Also, contract law does not include punitive damages to deter future violations. For consumers, therefore, the only advantage of contract law over common law fraud theory was that violations were easier to prove. Still, the potential cost of litigation was still a deterrent in most consumer cases.

THE PHILOSOPHY OF THE CONSUMER MOVEMENT IS CODIFIED

In President John F. Kennedy's 1962 message "On Protecting the Consumer Interest" he proclaimed the following four basic **rights of consumers**:

1. The **right to safety**, including the right to be protected against the marketing of goods which are hazardous to health or life;
2. The **right to be informed**, including the right to be protected against fraudulent, deceitful, or misleading information, advertising, labeling, and other such practices, and the right to be given the facts necessary to make informed choices;
3. The **right to choose** among a variety of products and services at competitive prices; and
4. The **right to be heard**, including the right of consumer interests to receive full and sympathetic consideration in the formulation of government policy.

---

[8]Among the first to draft fairly comprehensive consumer protection statutes were New York and Rhode Island, passing statutes in 1957.

In his conclusion, Kennedy pronounced a need for greater recognition of these rights in the marketplace as well as a need for new legislation and a strengthening of existing consumer protection programs. President Kennedy also established the **Consumer Advisory Council**, thereby incorporating consumer affairs into governmental policymaking. Although the laws pertaining to consumer protection rest squarely on the concept of deception instead of the four basic rights of consumers, Kennedy's message served to establish a national standard of responsibility toward consumers as well as to exemplify his administration's intended role in consumerism. This standard greatly affected consumer protection at the state and local levels as it quickly became the ideological underpinning of the consumer movement throughout the country.

THE GROWING MOMENTUM OF CONSUMERISM

Kennedy's message reverberated at all levels of government, and one result was increased federal-state cooperation. By the mid-1960s, the FTC was quite active in pursuing consumer protection and antitrust issues and had established cooperative relationships with state enforcement officials. Recognizing that its ability to effectively handle the volume of meritorious complaints was restrained by both its resources to police unfair and deceptive practices and its inability to seek damages or restitution for injured consumers, the Federal Trade Commission encouraged the states to pass their own legislation. Such legislative actions, therefore, empowered the states and localities to pursue local consumer matters.

In the atmosphere of the Kennedy message, numerous developments occurred in the mid-1960s (Richardson, 1976). The Consumer Federation of America became the premiere national advocacy group, and approximately 200 state and local advocacy groups formed. Federal laws were passed related to automobile safety, consumer loans, food packaging, and meat and poultry inspection. Thus, consumer protection became much more politically visible than just a few years before.

THE LEADERSHIP OF RALPH NADER

Ralph Nader was the most prominent and most vocal consumer advocate of the 1960s and 1970s. Nader is best known by many for his role in exposing the safety hazards of General Motors' Corvair automobile through the publication of his book, *Unsafe at Any Speed* in 1965. In the mid-1960s, Nader recruited groups of young associates—nicknamed by the press as "Nader's Raiders"—who investigated and exposed environmental threats by corporations as well as the inactivity of government agencies directly involved in consumer issues. In 1968, Nader blasted the Federal Trade Commission for its focus on trivial matters while ineffectively attacking the more significant issues (Cox, Fellmeth & Schulz, 1969), thereby prompting the agency to assume a more aggressive stance on consumer issues.

Various Nader groups successfully lobbied for radiation control, improved automobile safety, and better meat standards, among other things. In the 1970s, Ralph Nader was instrumental in influencing legislation that created the Environmental Protection Agency, the Occupational Safety and Health Administration, and the Consumer Product Safety

Commission. As with the Federal Trade Commission Act, reform at the federal level often encouraged and influenced legislation at the state and local levels.

STATE LEGISLATIVE SCHEMES TO PROTECT CONSUMERS

During the 1960s, it became increasingly evident that state legislation was needed. Several **model consumer protection laws** were proposed during the late 1960s and early 1970s. Given that these were only model statutes, state legislatures were free to adopt them in either their entirety, in some amended form, or not at all, depending on what, if any, provisions were deemed beneficial for a particular state. The following represents a brief description of each of the four model statutes that are in effect across the United States.

Uniform Deceptive Trade Practices Act

The **Uniform Deceptive Trade Practices Act (UDTPA)** was drafted in 1964 and revised in 1966. It was approved by the National Conference of Commissioners on Uniform State Laws. The UDTPA preceded the Federal Trade Commission's proposal that states draft their own consumer protection laws. It represented an attempt at circumventing inconsistency among the consumer protection laws that had begun developing in those states acting on their own initiative. The UDTPA provides a list of 11 prohibited trade practices[9] and contains a **catch-all provision** prohibiting "...conduct which similarly creates a likelihood of confusion or misunderstanding."[10] The UDTPA, in its model form, allows injured consumers to seek injunctive relief from future violations of the act, but does not provide for monetary damages or restitution. Note that states that used the UDTPA as the basis for their consumer protection laws did, in many cases, expand its legislative scope to provide for government enforcement and monetary damages.

Unfair Trade Practices and Consumer Protection Act

In 1967, the FTC, in conjunction with the Committee on Suggested State Legislation of the Council of State Governments, drafted the **Unfair Trade Practices and Consumer Protection Act (UTPCPA)**. The UTPCPA grants the authority of state attorneys general to **adopt regulations, issue subpoenas**, and **conduct hearings**. It also permits the attorney general to seek **injunctive relief** and **civil penalties** in some circumstances, and to seek forfeiture of a corporate franchise for violations of the act. The FTC drafted an amended version in 1971 that provides for **private causes of action** by consumers against violators of the act and permits the attorney general to seek **restitution** on behalf of injured consumers.

This model statute offered three alternatives for states to consider adopting:

---

[9]These include false or misleading price comparisons, bait and switch tactics, trademark and tradename infringement, disparagement, and misrepresentations of the standards, origins, or quality of goods.
[10]7A U.L.A. 305-09.

(1) The first alternative tracks the language of Section 5 of the FTC Act[11] prohibiting "unfair methods of competition and unfair or deceptive acts or practices in the conduct of any trade or commerce."

(2) The second alternative, intended for those states that had already enacted antitrust legislation[12], does not ban unfair trade practices, but declares unlawful, "...any false, misleading, or deceptive acts or practices in the conduct of any trade or commerce."

(3) The third alternative defines and prohibits 12 specific illegal practices related primarily to false advertising, and further declares unlawful, "...any act or practice which is unfair or deceptive to the consumer."

Uniform Consumer Sales Practices Act

The **Uniform Consumer Sales Practices Act (UCSPA)** was approved by the National Conference of Commissioners on Uniform State Laws in 1971. This statute was intended to provide merchants with predictable standards for their conduct and to bring about uniformity among state laws on consumer sales practices by making them consistent with **Federal Trade Commission** policy. This model statute prohibits both unconscionable and deceptive sales practices and provides a non-exclusive list of 11 deceptive sales practices (which are quite similar to the 11 prohibited trade practices delineated in the UDTPA), as well as factors a court would consider in evaluating a claim of **unconscionability**[13].

Little FTC Acts

By 1981, all states and the District of Columbia had adopted one of the three proposed statutes in either its model form or a hybrid version. These state laws, modelled after the Federal Trade Commission Act, were dubbed "Little FTC Acts," and provided enforcement at the state level, generally through the state attorney general's office. These acts embodied the substance of the FTC Act in that they adopted the FTC's mandates and interpretations and provided for restitution and other remedies appropriate to consumer needs. Although the Little FTC Acts vary somewhat from state to state, practices that are illegal in one state will likely be illegal in all others as well.

STATE AND LOCAL CONSUMER PROTECTION TODAY

Virtually all state consumer protection acts provide the aggrieved consumer with a **private cause of action**, a provision absent in the FTC Act that permits both individual consumers and government entities the ability to file lawsuits. The states' acts permit either the aggrieved consumer or the attorney general to seek restitution damages.

---

[11]15 U.S.C. § 45.

[12]To both enable enforcement at the state level and close loop-holes in the federal law, many states had begun enacting their own antitrust statutes.

[13]These include: (1) whether the transaction was excessively one-sided in favor of the seller, (2) whether the seller made misleading statements from which the buyer was like to rely, and (3) whether the price grossly exceeded the price at which similar goods or services are commonly sold.

Approximately 35 states' acts provide remedies that exceed actual damages, including double damages, treble damages, punitive damages, or minimum statutory damages. Also, approximately 40 states' acts permit a prevailing plaintiff to recover attorneys fees.

The Changing Role of the Federal Trade Commission

The inactivity and lethargy of the Federal Trade Commission caused it to be known as "the little old lady of Pennsylvania Avenue." Nader's 1968 investigative report initiated an another inquiry by the American Bar Association into the Federal Trade Commission's activities. Nader's accusations of inactivity and trivial pursuits were confirmed. Partly in response to the criticism, the enhanced awareness (or public disclosure) of the agency's weak and docile image, Congress amended the FTC Act in 1975 with the powerful Magnuson-Moss Warranty-FTC Improvement Act. Besides requiring manufacturers to disclose the warranty terms of consumer products, Magnusson-Moss provided the agency with the "muscle" to obtain civil penalties and assess significant fines for violations of the FTC Act (La Barbera, 1977).

But by the time the Federal Trade Commission's shortcomings were remedied with new leadership and by the Magnusson-Moss Act, a great number of states had already begun their own enforcement efforts under their Little FTC Acts. The consumer protection reputation of the FTC and the states improved significantly during the 1970s.

The 1980s Reagan years resulted in enormous cuts in the FTC budgets and serious attempts to gut the consumer protection missions of the agency. In 1983, the Reagan-appointed FTC Chair James Miller successfully replaced the strong **"tendency or capacity to deceive"** standard the Federal Trade Commission had long used in evaluating cases of misrepresentation with the more strict **"reasonable person standard."** This new interpretation, which was inconsistent with either case law or legislative intent, had the effect of crippling the agency's ability to effectively prosecute advertisers who unfairly and deceptively targeted the undereducated and the poor. Fortunately, although the states had, until that point, followed the FTC's case law interpretations in enforcing their Little FTC Acts, most states ignored the FTC's weak new standard for deception. Therefore, the Little FTC Acts of those states became more strict than the federal law in consumer deception and misrepresentation cases.

Variations and Recent Developments in Consumer Protection Law

Many states have continued to expand their laws with **"problem-specific"** consumer laws and regulations that address particular activities. Examples include laws aimed at automobile odometer tampering, pyramid investment schemes, time-share property sales, door-to-door solicitation cooling-off periods, new car lemon laws, warranty restrictions by manufacturers, and health club memberships.

Additionally, laws regulating banking, insurance, agricultural products, professions, health care, housing, and others often contain specific consumer protection provisions. Sometimes such state legislation is modelled after federal law, however, state laws often are stronger or more comprehensive in their provisions, enforcement, or penalties. There are some instances where states and the federal government divide jurisdiction over industries in a unique fashion (e.g., federal and state-chartered financial institutions regulations).

EPILOGUE ON STATE AND LOCAL CONSUMER PROTECTION

It is important to note that the Little FTC Acts are limited to enforcement only in consumer-merchant transactions. Consumers who buy goods or services from other consumers are exempt from protective coverage. However, such wronged consumers can seek relief under common law fraud theory. For consumer to consumer purchases, the doctrine of **caveat emptor** still prevails. Merchants who buy goods from other merchants are generally subject to the provisions of the Uniform Commercial Code which primarily governs commercial transactions. Unfortunately for small businesspersons, whose disputes often do not meet the $500 statutory minimum value for coverage under the UCC, the drafters of the Little FTC Acts exempted merchants from coverage.

Caveat emptor is not the philosophy underpinning consumer law, but it is a practical approach for consumers shopping in today's marketplace. A healthy skepticism is necessary for consumers. Trust is essential, and although it can be found it is not universal. The key is for consumers to become as informed as possible prior to purchasing decisions. Purchasing decisions should be based on, not just the product itself, but any and all follow-up service that may be needed.

Although the vast majority of businesses are honest and work to establish and maintain solid relationships with customers, there are dishonest retailers selling reputable goods and reputable retailers selling inferior goods. Mail-order consumer and tele-marketing transactions are especially troublesome. Consumers can generally save themselves a great deal of aggravation later by examining the consumer information resources they have at hand before they make purchases because no amount of legislation or regulation is a substitute for good judgment.

SUMMARY

State and local consumer protection, greatly expanded in the past thirty years, has been shaped by political, economic, and other social forces including the consumer movement. Its history is tied to federal law and regulation. And, since the 1960s states have tended to move somewhat in concert in expanding their individual consumer protection legal and regulatory systems. Table 17.1 overviews the regulatory aspects of state and local consumer protection.

State and local consumer protection centers primarily around legal concepts of unfairness and deception that, in spite of the Reagan attempt to weaken them, have been dramatically broadened in the past three decades. While states originally looked to the FTC in developing such law, they have made their own interpretations and modifications which are often far more comprehensive in their applications than the federal law from which they were modelled. While the FTC languished in the 1980s, states expanded consumer protection law and enforcement efforts.

But enforcement of consumer protection law at the state level is not ideal in all circumstances. When violations occur that are either nationwide or regional in nature, separate actions in each affected state results in the inefficient use of judicial resources

Table 17.1   A Summary of State and Local Consumer Protection

Economics	
Ease of entry	Moderate
Number of firms	400
Profits	NA
Technology	
Complexity	Moderate
Stability	High
Substitutes	Moderate
Subsystem	
Bureau control	Moderate
Industry coalition	Strong
Nonindustry coalition	Moderate
Bureaucratic resources:	
Expertise	Moderate
Cohesion	High
Leadership	Moderate
Legislative authority:	
Goals	General
Coverage	All
Sanctions	Good
Procedures	Fair
Impact of Macropolitical Actors	
Congress and state legislatures	Strong
President and governor	Moderate
Courts	Moderate

and fragmented enforcement efforts. An injunction in one state does not prevent the wrong-doer from continuing the same practices elsewhere. In such cases, when possible, enforcement at the federal level is preferred for its expediency. Using federal resources, ultimately, fewer consumers will be harmed. When state must lead in consumer protection cases, increased communication and cooperation among the states aimed at stopping violators quickly is needed.

Today consumerism is on a plateau of activity that has prevailed since the late 1970s when a significant piece of consumer protection legislation was defeated (the Agency for Consumer Advocacy). This has been followed by efforts to stymie federal agency regulation. This pattern was reflected in some states as well. A great number of consumer agencies in the states were cut back or eliminated during budget crises in the 1980s, but this occurred while consumer protection legislation and regulation grew and improved.

Attorneys general are usually quite active in consumer protection cases and they have been extremely critical of federal lapses. Where scams and frauds have appeared, states have been quick to respond. Scam operators using the mails, telephones, and faxes, however, often could be stopped more quickly with federal action. Preying upon senior citizens in particular, the nation is awash in solicitations from skilled direct marketers offering gold coins, oil and gas leases, penny stocks, foreign lottery tickets, telephone industry investments, pyramid company participations, and many other dubious investments that vary with popular opinion and preferences for quick ways to make fortunes. Based on a recent study of consumer complaints at the state level by the Consumer Federation of America and the National Association of Consumer Agency Administrators, the top five areas of consumer complaints are new/used car sales, home improvements, auto repairs, mail order, and telemarketing.

In the **past**, the companies that were scrutinized most carefully by state consumer protection authorities were mostly neglected industries with serious flaws in the marketing, pricing, and the products they offer. The lack of value for money in many insurance products has led to a number of improvements at the state government level. Utilities are generally well regulated and a number of states have forced price reductions or refunds for consumers. Widespread failures and mergers among financial institutions have made most state banking regulators more willing to act to protect depositors.

The **future** of consumer protection will likely be shaped by forces in the economy, government, and society at large. Specific predictions are difficult. While state and local consumer protection efforts have expanded rapidly in recent years, they lagged considerably behind the apparent need for them before consumerism became politically powerful. Whether consumer protection needs go begging, are met, or are overreached, depends largely on the ability of consumer advocates and state and local legislatures to respond in a timely manner to the dynamics of the marketplace and other social forces that create deficiencies in the American-style capitalistic marketplace.

Chapter 18
Contemporary Consumer Protection

James L. Brown[1]

The extraordinarily broad range of forums in which contemporary consumer protection policy is formulated is evolving in response to a number of societal trends. Political, economic, and technological developments are combining in complicated ways to focus an increasing proportion of substantive consumer protection activity in federal and state administrative rulemaking agencies. This rulemaking emphasis poses a number of structural challenges for consumer activities and for their legislative champions.

This chapter on contemporary consumer protection includes an overview of the subsystem, the current regulatory environment and its future directions, the politics of consumer protection, future policy directions, and an example of current consumer protection activities.

THE SUBSYSTEM

Consumer protection activity ultimately involves the creation, shaping, promotion, and balancing of various economic interests. These interests include those of consumers, in all their many manifestations, and those of commercial entities. These **commercial entities** are mainly businesses and professionals that provide (or would provide) goods or services to consumers.

For reasons described below, those that would "protect" consumers most typically have relied upon the various direct means, mechanisms and processes of government to that end. A number of current trends are discernable which affect the particular methods of government consumer protection frequently pursued. Given the remarkably expansive

[1]James L Brown is Director, Center for Consumer Affairs, University of Wisconsin-Milwaukee, where he also is an associate professor. Brown received his bachelor of arts degree from Princeton University; his law degree is from the University of Wisconsin Law School. He was a staff attorney with Milwaukee Legal Services concentrating in consumer law issues. Brown has served as president of the Wisconsin Consumers League. He serves on a number of corporate, civic, and community organization boards, including the Electronic Funds Transfer Association, TYME Corporation, the Consumer Financial Education Foundation, and the Consumer Federation of America.

reach of modern American governmental activity and the extent to which its mandates are sought in the name of protecting consumers, it is worthwhile preliminarily and briefly to survey the landscape of consumer protection.

Responsibilities for Consumer Protection

There literally is no one agency with exclusive responsibility for consumer protection activity, either on the federal or state level.[2] The other chapters in this volume demonstrate the breadth of and enumerate the agencies addressing the specific substantive topics susceptible to consumer protection activities. Accordingly, no attempt is made here to list all the agencies, bureaus, commissions, departments, task forces, etc. which address consumer protection activity in its totality. Rather, an overview is attempted, with pertinent examples. And, at the end of the chapter, an example is given, demonstrating a number of the forces at work, the players involved, and the complexity of their interrelationships.

All three branches of government—legislative, executive and judicial—are extensively involved in the process of determining, promoting or otherwise assessing, adjusting and adjudicating relative economic interests (e.g., **consumer protection**). Further, this activity is regularly (and often concurrently) occurring at different levels of government—federal, state, and local. Thus, assessment of the arena(s) in which most consumer protection activity occurs involves a matrix with cross-relationships, conflicts, or both, not only between different branches of government, but also between similar governmental units on different jurisdictional levels.[3]

Initiators of Consumer Protection Activities

Among the numerous initiators of consumer protection efforts are:

(1) **Executive branch officials**, such as Presidents, Governors, Mayors, Attorneys General, specific Agency or Department chiefs, mid-level bureaucrats, and officials at virtually each level in between;

(2) **Legislators**, including their mushrooming staff;

(3) **Consumer advocates** (hereinafter, "**consumerists**") from generalized national consumer organizations, such as Consumer Federation of America, Consumers Union, or the National Consumers League (or their counterpart organizations in the various states);

(4) **Topic-specific organizations** (e.g., Public Voice for Food and Health Policy, Center for Auto Safety, and other [often Nader-inspired] groups);

---

[2]Though there has existed a Special Assistant to the President for Consumer Affairs since the Johnson Administration, that office does not typically engage in the formation of specific legislative or regulatory proposals.

[3]As technological developments have been brought to bear and regulatory changes implemented to bring more unique, complex, and unfamiliar services and goods to consumers from more remote (and often non-traditional) purveyors of those particular services or goods, the interplay, and often the conflict, among various levels of government has become more complex and, often, contentious. One of the most contentious subjects in numerous recent federal consumer protection proposals involves the scope and degree of **federal preemption** of state strictures.

(5) **Broader interest groups** with particular topical consumer concerns (e.g., the American Association of Retired Persons, or many organized labor organizations);

(6) Numerous **individual businesses** with obvious financial and competitive interests at stake in the outcomes of regulatory activities;

(7) **Business trade associations**[4] (e.g., generalized interest groups, like the Business Roundtable, as well as, specific industry groups, such as the American Bankers Association, the American Medical Association, the American Automobile Manufacturers Association, etc.); and,

(8) **Standards setting organizations**, such as ANSI (The American National Standards Institute) or ASTM (The American Society for Testing and Materials).

Also important in the larger realm of consumer protection activity is the role of the **media**. Most typically, however, the media is primarily a means for advocates attempting to shape public opinion (and thus policy formation) to their own ends, as it is relatively rare for the media to initiate specific consumer protection efforts.

Federal and State Agencies Involved in Consumer Initiatives

The range of **federal executive branch agencies** involved in consumer protection activity is breathtaking, involving over 40 distinct entities. A list of the agencies so involved on a primary, secondary or tertiary level encompasses nearly every agency in the federal government.

PRIMARY CONSUMER PROTECTION AGENCIES

It may be helpful in appreciating the extent of consumer protection activity to categorize agencies and their activities. **Primary consumer protection agencies** are those agencies whose explicit principal responsibilities include the protection of consumers, such as the Federal Trade Commission[5], the Consumer Product Safety Commission[6], and the Food and Drug Administration[7]. Similarly, at the state level, virtually all state statutory

---

[4]Trade associations often quite naturally tend to include as many constituent members as possible, primarily to expand both their membership rosters and their financial bases, and thereby their political influence. In the context of many consumer markets which involve ever more discriminating targeting of increasingly narrow segments of consumers, the ability of these trade associations to formulate a unified **"industry position"** regarding specific consumer protection proposals is severely challenged. This, in turn, can have significant impact on the outcome of relevant consumer protection efforts by, for example, affecting occasional coalitions that some industry groups may establish with consumerists in opposition to other industry groups. For example, recent efforts to restrict the limited antitrust exemption applicable to certain segments of the insurance industry precipitated substantial withdrawals from and the restructuring of at least two major industry trade associations, as well as affecting in various complex ways a number of competing or alternative proposals addressing the subject matter involved.

[5]The Federal Trade Commission is charged with protecting consumers both through its consumer protection and its antitrust divisions.

[6]The Consumer Product Safety Commission has wide-ranging authority to establish standards involving the safety of a broad range of consumer products, and has significant powers both to preclude various products from coming to market and to compel the withdrawal of unsafe products from markets.

[7]The Food and Drug Administration is one of the oldest of federal agencies engaging in the protection of consumers, dealing with the safety of ingested products.

regimens grant generalized consumer protection responsibility and authority to a specific agency or agencies, such as the Department of Justice (the Office of the Attorney General) or the Department of Agriculture (reflecting the original focus of consumer protection activity on the purity and safety of foodstuffs).[8]

SECONDARY CONSUMER PROTECTION AGENCIES

Secondary consumer protection agencies are those agencies which, while they are assigned important consumer protection functions, also have other responsibilities which may (though they need not necessarily) supersede their consumer protection activities where conflict exists (e.g., the Federal Reserve Board). The "Fed", while it has numerous important specific consumer protection responsibilities[9], nonetheless has other explicit responsibilities—in this case, determination and stabilization of national monetary policy, and ensuring the safety and soundness of financial institutions—which are at least as (if not, more) important from the standpoint of public policy formation and implementation. On the state level, specific departments or commissions dealing with topics as diverse as insurance, professional regulation and licensing, securities, transportation, and utilities might fit in such a category.

TERTIARY CONSUMER PROTECTION AGENCIES

Yet another level of executive branch activity exists, performed by tertiary consumer protection agencies. This would include agencies whose activities affect consumers "perhaps significantly" but essentially only as an outgrowth of their other activities (e.g., the U. S. Postal Service, the Interior Department, or the Department of State).

Others Involved in Consumer Protection Activities

Intergovernmental task forces attempting to coordinate federal consumer protection policy have representatives from literally dozens of departments and agencies. Given the intricate involvement of government in so many different areas of economic activity, it is not surprising that consumers' interests are so broadly affected by governmental decisions, and thus, presumably potentially in need of protection.[10]

---

[8]Agencies such as these typically have jurisdiction over the so-called **UDAP statutes** (Unfair and Deceptive Acts and Practices). These are statutes of general applicability encompassing purveyors of goods and services broadly, as contrasted, for example, with credit strictures which would apply only to entities extending consumer credit.

[9]For example, the creation and interpretation of the various titles of the Consumer Credit Protection Act, encompassing such diverse subtopics as the Truth-in-Lending, Fair Credit Billing, Fair Credit Reporting, Equal Credit Opportunity, Electronic Funds Transfer, Truth-in-Savings, Delayed Funds Availability, and numerous other Acts.

[10]Among the statutory purposes of the federal Department of Commerce is the charge to "*foster, promote, and develop* the foreign and domestic commerce, the mining, manufacturing, shipping, and fishery industries, and the transportation facilities of the United States..." 15 USC 1512 (emphasis supplied) And, since virtually all economic transactions involve both a provider and a consumer, it hardly seems unusual or radical that a government statutorily charged with "fostering, promoting and developing" the interests of one party to such transactions should also be concerned with the well-being of the other party to those transactions (e.g., the consumer).

A further dichotomy is observed (which is the subject of extensive discussion later in this chapter) between on the one hand the legislative branches of government, and on the other, the administrative rulemaking agencies, which are, of course, housed within the executive branch. These agencies are typically assigned by statute the tasks of "fleshing out" the particulars of the enacted legislation in the form of **administrative rules** (which generally carry the full force of law) and interpretations thereof.

Legislative bodies recognize, implicitly and explicitly, their need for both the **substantive expertise** and the **political insulation** which these agencies provide. However, they often insist, for both substantive and political reasons, on retaining **oversight authority** over the **work product** of these agencies (e.g., their rules and interpretations). That is to say, they generally wish to be positioned relatively easily to review, and where desired, amend or block implementation of administrative rules.[11]

Judicial Outcomes of Consumer Protection Activities

On an entirely different level, significant consumer protection activity also occurs within the **judicial branches of government**. Litigation initiated by advocates of various economic positions can seek many outcomes, among them:

- **injunctions/temporary restraining orders**;
- **cease and desist orders**;
- **mandamus**[12] or other special orders; and/or
- **penalties**, individually, or collectively through such means as **class-action lawsuits**; these can involve either civil or criminal sanctions, or both.

Judicial consumer protection activity most typically is focused upon the **effectiveness** (or even the existence) of particular consumer protection mandates or directives, although occasionally it may involve the creation of specific consumer rights.[13] Where legislative or regulatory enactments actually establish what steps purveyors of goods or services must or must not take, judicial actions typically address the **adequacy** of those steps as against the **legislatively-created standard**.

Without meaningful sanctions, either governmentally created (and enforced publicly by prosecution or through private legal causes of action), or imposed through the economic actions of markets, purveyors would be largely free to ignore such strictures. In many instances, purveyors have been quite content to do so. Judicial activity is

---

[11]Thus, there generally exists a process—formalized or otherwise—by which legislative review of administrative regulations regularly occurs. To paraphrase Yogi Berra, when it comes to creating consumer protection norms (in the administrative rulemaking context), "It ain't over 'til it's over; and even then, it ain't over!"

[12]This refers to a judicial procedure wherein a court directs a specific governmental agency to perform various duties assigned to it by statute which the party initiating the judicial proceeding contends it has been refusing to do as required under the authorizing statute.

[13]For example, litigation to enforce existing anti-discrimination statutes may result in judicial orders creating **"set-aside"** programs targeting particular classes of consumers for benefits related to but distinct from the rights created by the statutes underlying the litigation itself. The right created is the avoidance of discrimination; the explicit benefit—not specifically provided for in the statutes themselves but occurring as a result of their judicial enforcement—would be, for example, homeowners' insurance programs targeted in inner cities.

undoubtedly important, even critical, in consumer protection. But, it is clearly distinct from the process by which the content and extent of the enacted mandates or standards are established. This is because judicial activity typically applies only to the parties actually involved in the litigation.[14]

THE CURRENT REGULATORY ENVIRONMENT AND ITS FUTURE DIRECTIONS

This overview of the current regulatory environment and its future directions includes an examination of seven factors: (1) an analysis of the consumerist preferences for mandates, (2) the scope of technological change, (3) the pace of technological change, (4) the "hate-love" relationship between the public and its government(s), (5) the business preferences for regulatory consideration, (6) demographics as an indicator of the Balkanization of consumer interests, and (7) the push for economic development efforts (jobs) conflicts with consumer interests.

The Consumerist Preference for Mandates

Organized consumer protection efforts—historically as well as in relatively contemporary times—have generally gravitated naturally toward **mandates**, most typically accomplished by **governmental means**.[15] That is to say, they have usually involved legislative, regulatory or (less commonly) adjudicated interjections into markets[16] founded upon the coercive power of societal legal norms. Consumerists, by both temperament and experience, have generally been predisposed more favorably toward this sort of legalistic, regulatory response to the perceived problems of consumers. Their legislative champions are by definition, and for obvious political reasons, similarly inclined.

IMBALANCE OF POWER IN THE MARKETPLACE

This predilection undoubtedly stems from both the actual and perceived imbalance in bargaining power between most purveyors and most consumers. Governmentally-founded intervention is perceived as the most direct and effective means of restoring some semblance of comparability in effective bargaining power as between the parties to a consumptive transaction. And, implicitly, restoring this balance—in its own way, an inherently economically traditional and "conservative" notion if ever there was

---

[14]As below, the universal applicability of most legislative/regulatory enactments to most if not all providers in a given market contributes substantially to the preference demonstrated by most consumerists for advocacy in these forums. **Judicially-based advocacy** is typically viewed as an important but ancillary component of an overall strategy for achieving consumer protection. This seems accurate notwithstanding the development of quite sophisticated consumer protection advocates whose primary function is the bringing (or the support) of litigation, such as the National Consumer Law Center.

[15]"[A]ctivists like Ralph Nader...tend[s] to restrict **consumerism** to efforts directed toward government intervention on behalf of consumers." Maynes, "Consumerism", Cornell Consumer Close-Ups, 1993-94:6, Ithaca, 1994.

[16]"Consumerism...responds to the failures and helps improve the functioning of the price mechanism that lies at the heart of a market economy." Maynes, ibid.

one—thereby "protects" consumers.

While consumer informational programs, picketing, or adverse publicity campaigns, for example, can be effective in individual cases involving specific sellers or even selected markets, coercing providers by legalistic means to alter their behavior is both more compelling and more likely to encompass most if not all providers in a given market. Less favored as a tactic is appealing through **market incentives** to relative **competitive positions** (e.g., economic) that might (and then, only someday) accrue in favor of or against individual providers in reforming specific practices objected to by consumerists.

Thus, specific governmental consumer protection efforts typically have taken the form of legislative enactments, administrative rulemaking exercises, or, less commonly though still importantly, through litigation. **Litigation** is generally clearly distinct from legislative and administrative agency advocacy in its goals, its processes, and its outcomes. And, while it can have a significant impact, it is often directly influential only on the parties to the litigation.

POLITICAL SALIENCE AND TECHNICAL COMPLEXITY AFFECT LEGISLATION AND RULEMAKING

As between legislation on the one hand and administrative rulemaking (hereinafter **"regulation"**) on the other, different circumstances have been identified which seem most typically to concentrate the focus of consumer protection activity in one or the other forum. Among the most important of these are the political salience and the technical complexity of the subject matter involved.[17]

However, there appears to be a noticeable shift occurring influencing this dichotomy. Our modern **"consuming society"** is very complex, with its proliferating and diverse products and services, aimed at ever more **transient consumers** whose tastes and preferences are rapidly evolving. These products and services are offered by ever more dispersed and unfamiliar or **nontraditional purveyors**. This complexity is leading to a seeming change in the preferred forum most usually resorted to by consumerists for consumer protection efforts. While very broad-brush consumer protection efforts via legislated means have continued (e.g., truth-in-savings, food labelling, etc.) an ever greater proportion of consumerist effort and ultimately consumer protection activities, have increasingly been focused within regulatory arenas.

This is not to suggest that consumer protection efforts in toto generally have become less common; on the contrary, there is evidence to suggest that, if anything, they may be increasing in frequency. Rather, the scope of legislated efforts, relatively speaking, has become more broad brush and less detailed. Legislators, seeing (perhaps, seeking?) ever more consumer protection "problems" in need of attention, nonetheless to a greater extent than ever, tend only to identify and broadly define generic "problems," against which consumers need protection.

By the same token, the detailed substantive terms of specific consumer protection strictures—derided by opponents as "micro-management"—have narrowed and deepened to ever more complex levels of sophistication. This has been accompanied by a shunting of a greater portion of the bulk of the substantive work of consumer protection *away* from

---

[17]See, for example, Meier, **Regulation: Politics, Bureaucracy and Economics**, 1985: 16 et seq.

the halls of the legislatures and *into* the maw of the administrative agencies. Put another way, legislators are inclined, more than ever, to enunciate "**broad rights**," and leave to administrative agencies the often tedious but crucial work of devising means for implementing those rights in a politically and economically feasible manner.[18]

This poses a number of significant challenges for the consumer protection community, which will be briefly discussed below. As such, any assessment of contemporary consumer protection must then begin with an examination of those various forces and influences occurring throughout society which affect the manner and processes in which the preferred forum for consumer protection efforts—legislation or regulation—is selected. A number of relatively distinct societal trends seem to be propelling this shift.

The Scope of Technological Change

Several, until relatively recently, fledgling industries have spawned a torrent of new consumer products and services. The applications, for example, of consumer electronics, computer-based data processing, expanded telecommunications capabilities, and biotechnology to name but a few, were virtually unheard of by most consumers only a short time ago. Many of their manifestations have appeared in forms with which consumers typically possess virtually no familiarity.

Developing these **technologies** to the point where they can be economically applied to consumer-size transactions (as contrasted with wholesale or commercial transactions) has hastened the development described below. The potential benefits to consumers of such heretofore unfamiliar products and services are undeniable in many instances.[19] Yet, the range and scope of potential problems for various categories of consumers are equally, if not more, expansive.

LEGISLATORS YIELD TO REGULATORS

Comparatively speaking, legislative bodies typically lack the expertise, the time and the inclination even to begin to address and comprehend the more advanced intricacies, the greater uncertainties, and the numerous and diverse implications for distinct groups of consumers of these new technological applications. Despite the political attractiveness of designing and enacting legislative responses to new "problems," most legislators seemingly (at least implicitly) recognize the structural difficulties they encounter in attempting to intelligently address emerging concerns in detail. The statutory process is less well equipped than are regulatory agencies both in terms of substantive expertise and in its procedural capacity to respond in a timely manner to evolving concerns.

---

[18]In part, this reflects the finite (often quite limited) ability of legislators to obtain within existing political contexts sufficient votes necessary to achieve enactment of various provisions. Support for broader legislative goals is often easier to come by than is support for more detailed, more specific requirements, which will typically evoke outcries—and thus, overt opposition—from those most specifically affected by the "costs" and "burdens" attendant to such mandates.

[19]For example, Automated Teller Machines, caller ID (identification) services, or cellular phones, to name but a few.

REGULATORY AGENCIES POSSESS EXPERTISE TO DEAL WITH TECHNOLOGICAL CHANGE

Specific regulatory agencies have, of course, always enjoyed at least the theoretical advantages of more refined, sophisticated, topical, and substantive expertise. Indeed, important specialized areas of regulation of extraordinary complexity and with enormous consumer protection implications have evolved over the years as a result, (e.g., public utility or insurance ratemaking, or food/drug testing). But, the sheer degree of complexity in the new range of consumer products and services makes the legislative/regulatory dichotomy more pronounced.

The Pace of Technological Change

While more evolved regulatory substantive expertise is not a particularly new or recent development, the relatively recent **acceleration in the rate of change** of offered products and services makes the importance of the relative advantages enjoyed by regulatory agencies more significant as a factor affecting the preferred forum for consumer protection activity. And, the rate at which new products and services are being developed and offered by an ever-expanding array of providers to ever more far flung markets is clearly accelerating.

Perhaps no subject matter area better demonstrates this increase in the pace of introduction of new products and services by ever more purveyors than **consumer financial services**. The application of evolving computer technological capabilities and telecommunications devices to consumer-size financial products on an increasingly cost-effective (and thus, enabling) basis has spawned a plethora of variable-rate savings, investment, and loan instruments previously unheard of by the typical consumer. These include sweep accounts; money market asset management accounts, with literally dozens of features; variable-rate credit/debit/asset accounts with ever more exotic features and enhancements, and ever more complex, pricing regimens; etc. **"Smart cards"** and **home banking** loom on the horizon, or in some instances, are already in operation. The financial community's ability to tailor products specifically to individual wants and needs gives consumers ever greater choices. And, in so doing, also presents heightened concerns for those consumers.[20]

Creating or changing a statute is generally a relatively time-consuming process. Administrative rulemaking or interpretive action, by contrast, can be, despite its often frustratingly protracted duration, comparatively speedy. The mushrooming pace, then, of the introduction or offering of new products and services, and thus, the more rapid

---

[20]Further, the capacity to provide such products and services over great distances without any face-to-face contact with consumers has helped drive enormous political pressures to relax or eliminate legal constraints which previously had limited (often very severely) the range of possible providers from which consumers could obtain these increasingly particularized products and services. Not only are geographical limitations falling, so too are barriers which had formerly segregated entire industries. **"Banking"** services are now available from both traditional "banks" and also from brokerage firms, thrifts and insurance companies. As these barriers have become ever more porous, many consumers now obtain ever more complex financial services from ever more distant and nontraditional sources. In short, consumers are now faced at a cascading rate, with more products and services, from more providers, often located at greater distances, and operating in the form of completely unfamiliar corporate entities.

development of associated consumer concerns, further enhances this relative advantage of regulatory consideration. The capacity of regulatory agencies to assess and respond more quickly to ever more rapidly emerging developments becomes relatively even more attractive to consumerist efforts as the pace of new product introductions accelerates.

The "Hate-Love" Relationship Between the Public and Its Government(s)

Jimmy Carter was elected President in 1976 in large part by successfully portraying himself as an "outsider" to Washington, and, by extension, to "government" generally. He thus distinguished (and presumably largely exempted) himself from the implicit corrupting influences and disingenuous practices broadly perceived as being inherent in the political establishment and its participants. Ronald Reagan perfected this appeal with the pithy: "Government is not the solution; it's the problem."[21] Incumbents oxymoronically seek to manage the neat trick of running for reelection as "outsiders." The abundance of jokes regarding public employment ("I'm from the government; I'm here to help you.") reflect the breadth of public disdain for governmental processes generally.

PEOPLE HATE GOVERNMENT BUT LOVE THE BENEFITS

This hostility has mushroomed notwithstanding the simultaneous seemingly nearly universal efforts to obtain governmental benefits or subsidies of one form or another on the part of individuals, groups, organizations, businesses, trade unions, other units of government, etc. Even as the aggregated public reviles the functioning of government, its multitudinous subgroupings seek favor and benefits ever more aggressively and competitively from it. The proliferation of legislative and regulatory lobbying efforts is seemingly at odds with a dedication to controlling or reducing, let alone eliminating, the scope of governmental involvement in ever more realms of societal activity.

PROPOSALS TO EXPAND GOVERNMENT MEET OPPOSITION

Recall that consumerists are predisposed to seek to further their goals through appeal to the creation of new or expanded governmental strictures or mandates (often accompanied by bureaucratic structures, with their attendant direct expense and attendant political vulnerability). Such efforts will intrinsically generate less public support (or conversely, more opposition) simply by virtue of the proposed expansion of the reach and involvement of government. These efforts will collide head-on with the growing public antipathy to governmental activities per se. Government is portrayed (and ridiculed) by those objecting to consumer protection efforts as the **"National Nanny."**

BROADLY-STATED CONSUMER PROTECTION CONCERNS MAY RECEIVE SUPPORT

On the other hand, identification of broadly-stated consumer protection concerns, if characterized in terms of consumer needs, does not, at least to the same degree, run afoul of the generic hostility to ever more extensive governmental involvement. By identifying

---

[21]Their previous experience as governors of large states somehow did not disqualify them as "outsiders" to government.

broad topics of concern—often directly in statutory enactments characterized, for example, as "findings"—legislators can obtain the political advantages of perceived diligence and sensitivity to consumer concerns and demands while avoiding the targeted criticisms aimed at those who would impose relatively specific remedies, with their attendant costs, both financial and philosophical.

For example, the Congress (and many states) have identified **access to credit** and **access to insurance** as broadly agreed upon needs for most consumers. Reasonable access to such services, has broadly accepted political appeal. Despite enunciating a right to have reasonable access to these services, legislators have proposed to leave to the regulatory agencies the involved and thorny questions. Attempting to devise mechanisms by which to measure the extent of these problems is difficult enough, let alone developing an apparatus to expand access to such services.

LEGISLATORS SHIFT THE BURDEN OF CONSUMER PROTECTION TO REGULATORS

The recognition of the public for identifying the problem is thus captured by the elected legislator, while the revulsion of the public against the specific burdens inherent in explicit mandates—which will surely be criticized by the affected industries as expensive—can simultaneously be neatly shifted onto the regulatory agencies. The popular parlance tellingly speaks not of legislative, but rather regulatory burdens. Perhaps the ultimate condemnation of one's mental thought processes today is to be guilty of **"bureaucratic thinking."**

The Business Preference for Regulatory Consideration

This resulting tendency of legislatures generally to identify broad issues of concern and consign to the regulatory agencies the responsibilities for identifying and implementing detailed consumer protection responses is often encouraged by the purveyors of goods and services themselves. The relationship between regulators and the regulated has long been a subject for academic review. Some have even viewed the regulators as having been effectively "captured" by the regulated.[22] To the extent this view may be even partially accurate, there would exist a logical, indeed, a structural preference among industries facing governmental consumer protection impulses to prefer that the bulk of the substantive determinations leading to legalistic strictures be made in those forums in which they feel best able to present, assert and achieve their preferences—the regulatory agency.

While most academics feel that the relationship between regulatory agencies and those regulated is much more complex than to allow so simple a notion as "capture" by the regulated industry, the forum of preference remains the same. Even if (as seems the case) a regulator is not in fact "captured," businesses have other reasons"and increasingly compelling ones"to prefer addressing consumer protection concerns in the regulatory milieu.

---

[22]Huntington's, (1952) study of the Interstate Commerce Commission was the first of several articles presenting this argument.

More evolved, technologically-based products and services almost by definition pose more complex problems for policymakers. For example, variable rate consumer loans have become feasible economically only with the application of computer-based technologies. It is only in recent times that these technologies have become **cost effective** when applied to the relatively small amounts involved in most consumer transactions. Essentially, the technologies enabling such loan instruments have allowed lenders to transfer interest rate risk (as contrasted with credit risk) previously borne by lenders to consumers. Since consumers thus face increased uncertainty (the flip side of the marketing appeal of "flexibility") over the entire term of such a loan, the possibilities for consumer misunderstanding or abuse or both are increased. The greater complexity of the loan creates more concerns at the time of the formation of the loan; the ongoing exposure to interest rate shifts creates concerns over the term of the loan. And, as a result, the "need" for consumer protection is greater.

It takes a much more detailed understanding of the nuances of such loan instruments, both at formation and during the term of the loan, in order to design and promulgate effective consumer protections. This more detailed understanding almost invariably will lead to a greater appreciation of the difficulties (and costs) posed for businesses by broad-brush prohibitions or mandates.

As a result—and regardless of whether or not an industry in fact might have "captured" its regulators—it will increasingly prefer regulation in administrative agencies to legislative controls, given the greater understanding of (or, at least, sensitivity to) its needs that more technically expert overseers can logically be expected to possess.

Similarly, as products become more complex, the expertise and technical competency necessary to assess those products and their implications will largely be possessed by those either within an industry or at least with significant experience with the involved industry. As a result, the industry itself—already a primary source of technical expertise regarding specialized industries—is likely to become even more overwhelmingly the source of regulatory agency personnel. This leads of course to a greater appreciation and sympathy for industry positions within the agency, which will in turn further strengthen the current industry preference for the regulatory forum in which to determine its fate.

Demographics as an Indication of the Balkanization of Consumer Interests

The decline in the frequency of consumer problems needing and realizing legislative relief is only relative, not total. Many consumer problems still do (and are likely to continue to) attract legislators' attention. The particular topics, problems, or subjects of these efforts, however, have been influenced by **demographic changes**. Those consumers most likely to be **voters** (e.g., the consumers to whom most legislators, regardless of political stripe, wish to appeal) are characterized by a strong correlation among age, income, and propensity to vote. This has resulted in the increased tendency of legislative consumer protection efforts to be focused on the needs of middle-class and upper-middle class consumers.

MIDDLE-CLASS AND UPPER MIDDLE-CLASS GAIN CONSUMER PROTECTIONS

For example, and notwithstanding the so-called "deregulation era" of the 1980s—the "Reagan Revolution" aimed at getting the government "off the back" of the people—in just five years[23] 49 out of 51 jurisdictions nationally enacted, usually by overwhelming, bipartisan majorities, at least one (and in many instances, several versions of a so-called) **Lemon Law**. These laws were intended to create, protect and effectuate the warranty rights of buyers of new motor vehicles. The new motor vehicles to which such laws attach are of course typically acquired by more affluent consumers. Poorer consumers typically don't buy new cars. As a result, both the legislative inclination to act, and the tendency to do so with uncharacteristic statutory specificity, are not surprising.

The class of consumers protected by such a law will be aggressively courted directly by legislators wishing either to protect them, to curry political favor with them, or both. In this context, the specifics (and the attendant costs) of oversight burdens are not seen as carrying the negative political baggage described above. Accordingly, legislators have incorporated often quite specific provisions directly into statutes aimed at this category of consumer (e.g., number of days out of service or number of repair attempts creating the presumption favoring a vehicle buy back by the warrantor).

Legislative consumer protection efforts have increasingly aimed at such relatively segmented and generally upscale markets as health spas, time share arrangements, investment scams and the like. Less affluent consumers, of course, are not exempt from being abused in these markets. However, the prevalence of legislative recognition of perceived inequities and the impulse as a result toward protective action in markets dominated by more affluent consumers is greater, and further, is likely to increase. By contrast, consumer issues which cut across economic class lines or which more closely address issues of greater impact to less affluent consumers, are likely to be more specifically addressed in administrative agencies, to the extent that they attract governmental attention and intervention at all.[24]

Further, the very dynamics of marketplace economics itself will work to compound this regulatory trend. Simply by virtue of their economic characteristics, more affluent consumers are generally relatively less disadvantaged by the actions of **unfettered markets**. Given their relative economic attractiveness to sellers, they will typically have more options among which to choose. These options will typically entail more **"value"** in the sense that competitive forces will tend to ameliorate abusive practices between greater numbers of would-be sellers. These consumers generally also have higher levels of education and economic sophistication, and are thus better able to avoid stumbling into consumer problems ab initio. In short, they are inherently less likely to be subject to objectionable consumer abuses in the first place. In street terms, richer consumers are less likely to get ripped off. Thus, it follows that, relatively speaking, their needs for consumer protection in any form from government will be less.

---

[23]Beginning in Fall, 1983, in Connecticut and California.

[24]For example, contemporaneous with the sweep of Lemon Laws across the nation in the mid 1980s, the Federal Trade Commission considered—and ultimately—rejected a Trade Regulation Rule addressing various consumer concerns regarding *used* cars.

LESS ECONOMICALLY SOPHISTICATED CONSUMERS ARE SUBJECT TO MORE ABUSES

On the other hand, less affluent, less educated, generally less economically sophisticated consumers, will likely be relatively more frequently subject to abusive practices, however defined. This follows, given: (1) their more perilous economic and educational statuses; (2) their relatively narrower margins to absorb the negative economic impacts of marketplace practices, thus lowering the effective standard for "abuse"; and (3) the sharper practices often following naturally in riskier or higher-priced/lower-value markets inhabited primarily by less affluent consumers.

Legislators will be more inclined to act directly to protect more affluent consumers. But, relatively speaking, these consumers will generally have fewer compelling consumer protection needs. Lower-income consumers, on the other hand, might be expected to have relatively greater needs, but to be of less political appeal to legislators. Taken together, these phenomena will further accelerate the tendency toward the concentration of consumer protection activities in regulatory and administrative as opposed to legislative forums.

The Push for Economic Development Efforts (Jobs) Conflicts With Consumer Interests

Consumerists have always engaged in a mix of activities which are at least in tension if not in outright conflict with one another.[25] They have sought markets in which **aggregate output is maximized**, on the theory that with more product available, more consumers can obtain such product at more advantageous prices. While many in the environmental movement are increasingly questioning this notion, most consumerists, at least implicitly, still generally seek the maximum quantitative availability of products and services of acceptable quality.

At the same time, consumerists have also sought to **reform or restructure markets** so as to **redistribute**, or make more widely available products and services to populations which unfettered markets would not reach—quantitatively, qualitatively, or both. This type of activity stems back at least to the seminal work, *The Poor Pay More*.[26] Efforts aimed at assuring **enhanced access** (either more affordable, or at all!) to basic banking services, or homeowners' insurance in urban central cities, for example, are classic examples of this type of activity.

The current ubiquitous efforts at virtually all levels of government to promote economic development—"jobs, jobs, jobs"—are entirely consistent with the first consumerist goal of output maximization. They are, however, often perceived as being in direct conflict with the latter goals of market access/product redistribution, whether they actually are or not.

Thus, for many of the same reasons which led legislators sensing the prevailing public distaste for government to prefer leaving to the regulatory agencies the specifics of consumer protection, similarly, legislators seeking to promote economic development (most legislators today) don't wish to be seen as imposing unnecessary burdens on

---

[25]See, for example, Brown (1986: 53).
[26]Caplovitz, (1963).

business in the form of specific consumer protections, and (arguably) thereby inhibiting job creation. They will predictably prefer to leave these tasks—to the extent they undertake them at all—to the administrative agencies.

THE POLITICS OF THE ECONOMICS OF CONSUMER PROTECTION

Related to the twin goals of economic development and job creation is the notion of assessing and balancing the competing costs and benefits of various proposed regulations. Having succeeded in defeating consumer protection efforts in too few instances largely on **equitable grounds**, many opponents have increasingly relied upon **economic arguments** to dilute, derail, or defeat such efforts. In some contexts, **economic impact analyses** are statutorily required to be considered prior to promulgation of new laws. Indeed, this tactical development is by no means limited to consumer protection measures.

This is certainly by no means necessarily inappropriate. Many consumer protection efforts are clearly intended to reshape unfettered marketplace functioning, and have as an inevitable consequence, redistributionist impacts. Thus, it is, as a matter of public policymaking, clearly appropriate to attempt to assess attendant costs—especially economic costs—to determine who bears them, and to determine if incurring such costs is well-founded when balanced against the supposed benefits to be realized. This seemingly follows as a matter of public policy formation in any society purporting to be democratic.

The danger, however, to consumer protection efforts is that such costs often fall (or are claimed to fall) disproportionately on specific, identifiable entities or groups. And, where those entities are politically organized to be able to affect governmental activities (and increasingly they are, since it is clearly in their economic interests to be so), they can often succeed in defeating such efforts. Specific regulatory **"burdens"** will often engender targeted, concentrated opposition. This contrasts with the frequently less focused, less intense support generated favoring more amorphous **"protections."**

This type of opposition is generally more successfully asserted in the regulatory forum. Since it often entails weighing economic costs incurred by certain parties on one side against equitable or even more ephemeral health and safety concerns on the other, this is a balancing which opponents would prefer to occur in the less publicly visible forum of administrative law. The emotional and political appeal of "protecting" consumers will naturally be more effective in the more emotional and political environment of a legislative body. The essentially political appeal of "ripped off" individuals is likely to be relatively less persuasive in administrative forums.

Further, the often mind-numbing complexity of the involved economic concepts and analyses doesn't usually lend itself well to legislative debate. Coupled with the generally greater substantive appreciation which more technically competent regulators are likely to have for the "burdens" of such costs, the likelihood of success in opposing redistributionist consumerist efforts there is usually likely to be greater.

FUTURE POLICY DIRECTIONS: IMPLICATIONS AND CHALLENGES FOR CONSUMER PROTECTORS

There are five implications and challenges for consumer protectors: (1) the need for technical and substantive expertise, (2) consumer protections proposals will face great frustrations, (3) the importance of ongoing relationships with regulatory personnel, (4) the need for different tactics to influence regulatory agency personnel, and (5) the expanding role of information provision as a means for consumer protection.

The Need for Technical and Substantive Expertise

Consumerists and their allies within both the legislative and regulatory arms of government will need to become more technically expert substantively. This evolution is already well under way. The sophistication of consumer organizations and the proficiency of their technical expertise have increased dramatically. They have also become ever more topically specialized.[27] Given the burgeoning complexity of consumer products and services, they will need to become even more so in the future.

This, however, poses a significant structural personnel problem for consumerists in an era when employability generally is becoming ever more linked to specialized, often technical expertise. As advocates become more knowledgeable and skilled, they become more attractive and salable as prospective industry employees. Skilled and expert consumerists—be they in advocacy organizations or within government—will find the opportunities to obtain significantly higher-paying employment in industry increasing. As these persons respond to these attractions, the difficulties in attracting and retaining replacements will only become greater.

Consumer Protections Proposals Will Face Great Frustrations

The perceived complexities of encountered problems are likely to continue to escalate. In turn, the complexity of the responses thereto will likely also increase. This is apt to have at least two identifiable impacts.

First, the **sheer complexity** of the responses will likely exacerbate the anti-governmental animus already so widely prevalent among the public generally. The task of overcoming political inertia will thus become ever more difficult. While proposed responses to various emerging problems may well be thoroughly thought through and intellectually coherent and honest, their sheer complexity will fan the flames of frustration for those subject to such directives.[28] Legislators already disinclined to intervene in markets can easily be expected to seize upon such complexity as grounds for ridicule and

---

[27]Indeed, representation of consumers' interests in such arenas has been institutionalized regarding regulation of selected industries (e.g., public utilities through CUBs, the Citizens' Utility Boards in a number of states, or insurance, through agencies such as the Office of the Public Advocate in Texas). Similarly, proposals are currently pending in a number of states to create similar organizations regarding consumer financial services.

[28]One need look no further than the health care reform debates of the Summer and Fall of 1994 for demonstration of this reaction.

even more pointed, focused opposition.[29] This will likely make achieving consumer protection structures more difficult and, as a result, less frequent, less comprehensive, or more likely, both.

Second, the **greater complexity** of the required remedies for emerging consumer problems can reasonably be expected to increase the time required to develop and enact those responses. Coupled with an accelerating, shortened time frame in which problems emerge and are identified, the increased time frame in which government can even attempt to respond will likely only further fuel the frustrations with governmental consumer protection efforts.

The Importance of Ongoing Relationships With Regulatory Agency Personnel

If, as suggested herein, more and more substantive consumer protection activity will be occurring within the regulatory agencies, consumerists will face additional problems in terms of the increased requirements for establishing, cultivating, and maintaining relationships with the personnel in such agencies. Commercial entities and organizations are increasingly organized and committed to an **ongoing presence** relating to regulatory agencies. As such, they will be working diligently to establish and maintain their relationships with agency personnel. Whether or not these efforts result in the "capture" of an agency is really only a difference in degree as regards the level of influence exercised on the actions of the agency. The fact remains that industry relations with agencies are not apt to decline, rather they will intensify.

These ongoing relationships can have important substantive results favorable to those parties which constantly maintain their presence and nurture their input into the agencies. Conversely, failure on the part of consumerists to maintain such a presence and provide steady countervailing input can result in dilution or prevention of whatever protection strictures are ultimately achieved. For consumerists to compete in these arenas, they will need to commit to comparable long-term efforts. Given their limited resources and frequent staff turnover, the already existent problems they face in this regard will likely become even more severe.

The Need for Different Tactics to Influence Regulatory Agency Personnel

The difficulties which consumerists will face in mobilizing effective political support for their efforts are qualitatively different in attempting to influence administrative agencies. Coupled with the anticipated complexities of both the problems identified and the solutions proposed, struggling within the regulatory framework will reduce or eliminate the effectiveness of many of the more traditional tactics aimed at organizing and mobilizing public opinion; for example, regulatory agencies are less likely to be influenced by media pressure.

---

[29]For the less scrupulous, it will also likely create an environment in which spurious allegations can more frequently be employed—both presumably by opponents of consumer protection initiatives and by consumerists—regarding various proposals, since it will be more technically complex, and thus more difficult, to refute such allegations effectively. Subsequent exposure of the inaccuracy of such charges will likely only further the public animus against governmental processes.

The Expanding Role of Information Provision as a Means for Consumer Protection

Ultimately, the confluence of these trends is likely to lead consumerists and those interested generally in consumer protection toward more frequent, complementary efforts outside governmental channels. Because of the **heightened hurdles** which activists will face in this new environment, there will be increased activity in the form of **comparative product information and education**. This tendency is likely to be strengthened by the natural preference of business for consumer information as a means of consumer protection as compared to what are widely seen as more intrusive legal mandates and prohibitions. The proliferation of comparative consumer information sources, along the lines of *Consumer Reports* magazine, has already begun. It is only likely to be accelerated by the trends noted above.

Such a shift will involve a major adjustment for consumerists. It will, to some extent, require them to retreat from their prevailing predilection for governmentally imposed mandates as a means for achieving consumer protection, and to embrace consumer education as a means for protection. It also will entail difficult implementation problems to reach those classes of consumers already difficult to reach effectively with information/education, such as the less educated, those lacking proficiency in English, and those lacking either the inclination or the access to seek, acquire, and use such comparative information. Notwithstanding these problems, such a shift seems inevitable.

Additionally, it is likely that consumerists and those wanting to promote the interests of consumers will also look to mechanisms which attempt to appeal to the competitive (e.g., economic) instincts of providers of goods and services. By designing structures which heighten the comparative advantages which specific competing sellers enjoy by behaving in given ways, the emphasis will likely shift to include both the "stick" and the "carrot." Whether this will (or even, can) ultimately result in greater protections and benefits for consumers will be one of the great questions of the next few decades.

AN EXAMPLE OF CONSUMER PROTECTION ACTIVITIES: ELECTRONIC BENEFITS TRANSFER

As suggested at the beginning of the chapter, no attempt has been made here to list all of the various entities acting in the current consumer protection milieu. This entire volume is a better source for such a comprehensive enumeration. However, a vivid example is offered which demonstrates generically a number of the **structural concepts** used to describe consumer protection activity by subject matter area throughout the volume. Among these concepts are such notions as the interrelationships involving:

- various competing economic implications;
- technological innovations;
- legislative/regulatory authority and goals;
- bureaucratic expertise;
- diverse levels of governmental oversight;
- conflicts between governmental goals;
- influence of private and public actors; and,

- systemic profitability, among many others.

In the early 1990s, various levels of government were seeking more cost-effective ways in which to distribute to differing populations various public financial benefits, such as welfare, disability benefits, food stamps, retirement, and public pension benefits, and the like. Financially pressed governments, both state and federal, sought to reduce distribution costs, to reduce fraud, replacement and misrouting losses, to speed receipt of benefits, to reduce complaint and dispute handling time, etc. The method of choice was the use of the technologies of **Electronic Benefits Transfer (EBT)**. By linking the use of telecommunications, computer-based data processing and other emerging technologies, various benefit programs hoped to improve the efficiency of the burgeoning public benefits systems.

Industry and Government Support for EFT and EBT

Since 1977, it has been national policy that consumers utilizing **Electronic Funds Transfer (EFT) Systems** to make routine financial transactions are entitled to certain specified consumer protections.[30] Several states have also superimposed additional substantive consumer protections in this area. The question thus arose as to whether or not—and if so, to what extent—the consumer protections of the EFT Act (as well as those of the several states) applied to the use of Electronic Benefits Transfer.

The banking industry, together with the various affiliated interested industries supplying supporting EFT services like hardware, software, encryption, etc., had an obvious financial interest in the emerging market for EBT services. Advocates for recipients, be they the elderly, the retired, the low-income, etc., were also concerned with the potentially significant consumer protection implications for their clientele under such systems.[31] The position of the various advocates for recipients was further complicated by their general recognition of the many potential benefits to recipients from the implementation of EBT systems.

Potential Fraud Liability Problems

Additionally, local and state governments, as **paying authority** for many of these benefits programs, were clearly interested, both in the possibilities for systemic improvements in efficiency, and in the possible ramifications of the application of various consumer protection norms. However, they feared that application of a few of the specific EFT Act standards would expose them to potentially ruinous fraud liability, by attaching enormous costs to the electronic distribution system.

In particular, they were very concerned with the standards under the EFT Act which limit, in some instances quite severely, a consumer's liability for unauthorized usages of EFT systems. They argued that, unlike banks which could discontinue a given consumer's

---

[30]The Electronic Funds Transfer Act, 15 USC 1691 et seq (hereinafter, the "EFTA"). Among these rights are strictures limiting liability for unauthorized transactions, requirements regarding receipts and periodic statements, error resolution procedures, standards regarding the issuance of access cards, etc.

[31]After all, the consumer protection implications regarding EFT Systems generally were sufficiently weak earlier to prompt enactment of substantial federal legislation, and extensive associated administrative rule-making. Presumably, many of the same considerations are present for consumers in EBT systems.

access to EFT services if they suspected fraud, paying governmental agencies could not discontinue the payment of benefits to recipients, where they suspected (or even where they could prove) fraud. They contended that the potential fraud losses would swamp the very cost-savings driving the examination of EBT systems.

Involvement of a Regulatory Agency: The Federal Reserve System

The **Federal Reserve System**, sometimes called the **Federal Reserve Board** (shorthand for the Board of Governors of the Federal Reserve System), as the administrative rulemaking agency with oversight responsibility under the EFT Act—with its considerable prestige by virtue of both its acknowledged technical competence and its reputation for evenhandedness—was asked to determine the scope of the applicability of the EFT Act protections to the potential users of EBT systems.

The Fed was under considerable public pressure to extend the consumer protection provisions of the EFT Act to benefit recipients. Already under substantial criticism for allegedly being too timid in addressing or remedying allegations of discriminatory lending practices, the Federal Reserve Board certainly could not relish being further criticized for acting so as to deny or limit to public benefit recipients[32] comparable consumer protections as received by other consumers. Yet, the various payer governmental agencies pushing for implementation of EBT technologies were contending that application of the existing consumer protection standards to EBT systems would quite literally preclude them from offering these systems at all, and thereby deprive benefit recipients of the numerous advantages of such systems.

Thus, the Board was, at the same time, under considerable countervailing pressure from both the banking industry and its allies—as the potential providers of the system—and from state and local governments—as the payers in such systems—to interpret the EFT Act so as to exclude EBT systems from its coverage.[33]

Balancing Competing Interests

The Federal Reserve Board was asked to balance the potential benefits to recipients in applying normative consumer protection standards against the possible cost implications to the delivery systems themselves, and, by extension, to the ultimate **payers of public benefits systems** (e.g., taxpayers). It was also compelled to consider that the potential systemic costs of applying those standards against the possibility that the imposition of such costs might cause the providers to forego implementing EBT systems altogether. This, in turn, might thereby deprive benefit recipients of the many, widely recognized and generally non-controversial advantages of EBT systems.[34]

---

[32]Many public benefit recipients were often the same persons victimized by discriminatory lending practices.

[33]The banking industry, of course, was already compelled to apply EFT Act standards in other EFT environments. As such, it was not necessarily substantively opposed to application of the EFT Act liability standard to EBT systems. However, with the paying governmental agencies threatening to abort the entire EBT system if the Act was applied to EBT—and thus eliminating an entire, potentially profitable market, they quite naturally aligned themselves with the paying governmental agencies in opposition.

[34]As of the writing of this chapter, the Federal Reserve was still wrestling with this question.

SUMMARY

The confluence of these factors in this instance demonstrates quite vividly the complexity of and the interactions involved in formulating consumer protection policy. It also is consistent with the interrelationships in such a process as demonstrated by the various substantive topics and examples discussed in more detail in the specific chapters in this book. Table 18.1 provides an overview of the regulatory aspects of contemporary consumer protection.

Table 18.1   A Summary of Contemporary Consumer Protection

Economics	
Ease of entry	Moderate
Number of firms	NA
Profits	NA
Technology	
Complexity	Moderate
Stability	High
Substitutes	Low
Subsystem	
Bureau control	Moderate
Industry coalition	Strong
Nonindustry coalition	Moderate
Bureaucratic resources:	
Expertise	High
Cohesion	Moderate
Leadership	Moderate
Legislative authority:	
Goals	Both general and specific
Coverage	Expansive, or industry-specific
Sanctions	Moderate
Procedures	Extensive
Impact of Macropolitical Actors	
Congress and state legislatures	Strong
President	Weak
Courts	Moderate

Chapter 19
Reforming Regulation

Kevin B. Smith[1]

Regulatory reform has been a fixture on the national agenda ever since the federal government created its first regulatory commission in 1887. Since the comparatively small beginnings of the Interstate Commerce Commission more than a century ago, regulation has grown "from a small and relatively noncontroversial part of the federal bureaucratic establishment to a large and controversial function" (Goodman and Wrightson, 1987: 45). From the New Deal to the Great Society, to the deregulation efforts of the late 1970s and 1980s, regulatory reform has never been far from the government's list of things to do. This continuing process of regulatory reform has several implications, among them that regulation has **shortcomings**. The implication of shortcomings suggests that existing regulation has failed to meet its goals and reform is necessary. This chapter examines regulatory reform within this context. First, the general goals of regulation are discussed. Second, regulation's failure to meet these goals is briefly examined. Third, a series of reforms designed to improve regulatory performance is evaluated.

REGULATORY GOALS

Regulation, like all other public policies, is **purposive** (Anderson, 1994:5). Regulatory agencies are created and regulations are issued to attain some **goal**. Although goals might be as vague as the "public interest, convenience, and necessity" or as specific as "fishable and swimmable waters by 1985," all programs have some goals. To integrate this discussion across numerous policy areas, we will treat the goals of regulation in general rather than the specific goals of any single policy. Regulation's goals can be divided at

---

[1]Kevin B. Smith is an assistant professor of political science and public policy at the University of Nebraska-Lincoln. He is the author of books on Congress and education policy, and has focused much of his research on the role of bureaucracy as a political actor. In addition to his academic career, he is also known as a newspaper columnist in southeastern Wisconsin, where he was recently featured in a series of promotional ads and billboards under the caption "witless blatherskite." He received his PhD from the University of Wisconsin-Milwaukee where he spent one year as a University Fellow and one year as an editorial assistant at the *American Journal of Political Science*.

a general level into two clusters—those dealing with **efficiency** and those dealing with **equity**.[2]

EFFICIENCY

The dominant goal of regulation as expressed in the literature is efficiency. After an analysis of government regulation's various goals, for example, Thompson and Jones (1982:232) conclude, "This leaves only one function for regulation to perform: promotion of the more efficient use of society's scarce resources." **Efficiency** is normally defined as the optimal allocation of resources such that total utility for a society is maximized.

Efficiency was the expressed goal driving the most notable general regulatory reform effort of the past two decades—the deregulation movement of the late 1970s and 1980s. Beginning as early as the 1960s some economists began to see **regulatory failure** as a counterpart to **market failure**. As government expanded its regulatory responsibilities, there was increasing concern that regulation was stifling the efficiencies of the market without promoting the public interests that justified government intervention (see McKie, 1989). Ideologically committed to the free market, both the Reagan and Bush administrations argued strongly in support of deregulation and sought to offer empirical backing for its efficiency-based benefits. In his introduction to an in-depth study of two decades of deregulatory activity, Vice President Dan Quayle stressed efficiency, writing that, "Overall, the evidence reveals that regulatory reform has increased the efficiency of our firms" (President's Council on Competitiveness, 1992).

While such arguments can be persuasive—especially from certain ideological perspectives—in practice efficiency is a slippery term; knowing when any allocation of resources is optimal is impossible simply because such perfect knowledge does not exist. In a practical situation, efficiency is generally used in a comparative sense; if firm A produces a good more cheaply than firm B, then firm A is more efficient than firm B. The comparative standard usually employed to evaluate regulation's efficiency is the theoretical distribution of goods resulting from perfect competition in microeconomic theory.[3]

Perfectly Competitive Markets

In a **perfectly competitive market system**, all goods are allocated to their optimal use. **Perfect competition** exists when six conditions are met (see Stokey and Zeckhauser, 1978:293, or any economics text).

---

[2]This discussion assumes that such specific goals as safe work places, fishable waters, safe consumer products, national transportation systems, and so on, can be generalized for comparison purposes.

[3]Although economists often compare the actions of government to this ideal, **perfectly competitive market**, they rarely compare the actions of individual private firms to the ideal. Such firms are given the benefit of the doubt; either they are efficient or they tolerate inefficiencies because they are maximizing other goals. Just as public organizations generally fail to meet this ideal standard, private organizations would probably also fail.

First, all participants in the market have **perfect information**; sellers know the quantity that will be demanded at various prices; buyers know the relevant performance information about the good offered for sale.

Second, all **exchanges** of goods are costless; that is, individuals can buy or sell goods in the marketplace without transaction costs.

Third, a **market** exists for all goods; if markets do not exist, the model does not hold because black markets impose transaction costs.

Fourth, the number of buyers and sellers is large so that no buyer can affect price by his or her decision to sell.

Fifth, consumption by one individual does not affect the consumption of others; that is, no **externalities exist**.

Sixth, the goods concerned are not common goods such as national defense; a **common good** is a good that must be provided for everyone if it is provided for anyone. Common goods create a **free rider problem** whereby individuals can enjoy the benefit of a good without paying for it. In a perfectly competitive market, prices are set by supply and demand, and prices allocate goods and services to their optimal uses.

The Reality of Markets

The market described by the microeconomist is a theoretical ideal to be used for comparison purposes.[4] No one argues that actual markets work like this although some markets approach this ideal more than others. For example, the market for farm products such as wheat and corn also approaches ideal. Other markets such as the market for medical care (with restrictions on practice) or the market for local phone service deviate greatly from the ideal.

Economists recognize that real markets do not operate the way the theoretical model works. They argue, however, that the theoretical model is superior to any alternative and failure to attain such an ideal in the real world may be justification for regulation. Four major deviations from the ideal model have been identified: (1) lack of competition, (2) externalities, (3) imperfect information, and (4) public goods. Collectively, these deviations are termed **market failures**, and each provides an **efficiency-related goal** for regulation. Although market failures can be used to justify regulation, regulation in this view should be undertaken only if regulation is superior to the unregulated market (that is, if the market is more efficient after regulation than before).

---

[4]Economists are generally not bothered by the criticism of political scientists that this model does not fit the real world (see Kelman, 1981a). For the most part, few argue that the real world ever meets the requirements of the model; usually, the argument is that the private sector better approaches the model than public sector interventions. A more serious criticism is that offered by Armentano. In his analysis of antitrust policy, Armentano (1982) argues that the model may be less efficient than some instance of monopoly markets in the real world. If the model is inappropriate (either because it produces inefficient outcomes or because efficiency is not a goal), then the prescriptions based on this model have little justification.

Lack of Competition

Regulation may be justified if lack of competition produces market failure (Daly and Brady, 1976:172; Thompson and Jones, 1982:232; Breyer, 1982:15; Meier, 1993:83-84). Competition is guaranteed in the ideal model by the requirement that the market have numerous sellers and buyers so that no one seller or buyer can determine the market price. In practice, a market may not be large enough to support numerous sellers (e.g., local markets for professional services), or capital investments might create large barriers to entry, thus limiting the number of firms that enter or are likely to enter (e.g., railroads).

MONOPOLY

The most extreme case of lack of competition is **monopoly**, dominance of the market by a single firm. If one firm controls 100 percent of the market, that firm can set prices by manipulating supply. Classic monopoly behavior is to restrict output, thus creating shortages that raise prices and allow the monopolist to make **economic profits** (e.g., profits greater than the normal return to capital). In strictly economic terms, monopoly is inefficient because fewer goods are produced at higher prices than in a perfectly competitive world.

NATURAL MONOPOLIES

In some cases, **natural monopolies** exist and may be more practical than a competitive market. Clearly, one would not expect the government to provide land grants so that five railroads would serve the same community, nor would one find value in having several local telephone companies if these companies were not interconnected. In cases of monopoly, regulation is justified in the theoretical model; the purpose of such regulation is efficiency, to set prices such that the monopolist's **marginal revenue** is equal to **marginal cost**. An option other than regulation in this situation is government operation of the enterprise; this option, however, is rarely considered in the United States.

OLIGOPOLY

In monopoly, the absence of competition is clear-cut; the monopoly firm has no competitors. Monopoly, however, is only a special case; absence of competition can occur anytime the number of firms is small and explicit or implicit **collusion** is permitted.[5] **Oligopoly** can create the same problems as monopoly (restricted output and higher prices) if the firms are permitted to meet and set prices such as merchant marine shippers do and as local professionals, trucking firms, and airlines once did. If collusion is evident, regulations can be used either to control prices or to prevent collusion (e.g., vigorous prosecution of antitrust laws).

---

[5]One type of collusion is not addressed here, collusion that is expressly granted by government. Governments from time to time sponsor **cartels** to eliminate competitive behavior. European industries are often formed into cartels. In recent years, the U.S. government has been hard on cartels opposing such practices by professional groups, truckers, airlines, railroads, and stockbrokers.

OPTIMUM REGULATORY INTERVENTION

Regulation in the absence of total monopoly is controversial even within the economics profession, and there is no agreement on what constitutes "**optimum regulatory intervention**" (McKie, 1989:45). Antitrust critics have argued that many of the famous trusts such as Standard Oil and the Sugar Trust never engaged in monopoly behavior and were actually opposed because they were ruthless competitors. Such large concentrations often resulted from large economies of scale in some facet of production.

Negative Externalities

When consumption by one person affects consumption by another person, an **externality** exists. Although externalities can be either positive or negative, we normally are concerned only with **negative externalities** (when consumption by one person harms the consumption of another; see Breyer, 1982:23; Daly and Brady, 1976:172; Thompson and Jones, 1982:232; Ripley and Franklin, 1987:124-144; Eisner, 1993:119). Pollution, workplace accidents, and communicable diseases are negative externalities.[6] In economic terms, externalities are inefficient because the cost of a good to an individual is less than the cost of the good to society. For example, if a firm manufacturing steel does not have to worry about air pollution, it will be able to produce steel more cheaply by polluting the air. This pollution affects **third parties** and imposes a cost on them. Because this cost is not incorporated into the price of steel, more steel than optimal will be demanded (which, of course, aggravates the externality).[7]

The solution to externalities is simple. If regulation is merited, then the regulatory agency's function is to make sure the good's **market price** is equal to its **social price**. As the debates over environmental policy illustrate (Goodman and Wrightson, 1987:113-146; Eisner, 1993:135-153), such regulation might take more than one form. The regulator could rule that the externality be eliminated (zero discharges in water pollution) or impose a tax on the manufacturer equal to the difference between the market price and the social cost (an **effluent tax**).

Imperfect Information

When buyers lack information about goods or services, they make decisions that misallocate resources (Daly and Brady, 1976:173; Thompson and Jones, 1982:232; Meier, 1993:84). In a variety of markets, consumers lack information to make rational decisions. In choosing the services of a lawyer or doctor, for example, the layperson usually has little information about the quality of service that individual practitioners provide or about

---

[6]**A positive externality** would exist if one person who appreciated art a great deal collected art in a gallery (and was willing to pay the full price of such a collection) and then opened the gallery to the public. Education is believed to have positive externalities in terms of civic contributions and quality of life.

[7]In a strict economic sense, consumption of every good creates some externalities, however small. Resources are not infinite; because they are scarce, the consumption of any good reduces the total supply of that good that can be consumed by others. Such externalities may be small, but they still exist and limit the strict application of the concept to regulatory problems because almost every act of consumption has externalities.

the optimal amount of service to purchase. Because consumers often rely on the seller for advice about such matters, they are likely to purchase more services than needed.

Lack of information also encompasses those situations when consumers purchase harmful products. Consumers would not normally eat foods that contain carcinogenic additives or purchase automobiles that are unsafe. At the very least, with **adequate consumer information**, the price of such goods would drop compared to the price of similar goods without the defects.

In a situation with information **asymmetry** (that is, where the seller's information is superior to the buyer's), two major regulatory options exist. The first and simplest remedy is to provide information to the consumer. Because consumers may be unwilling to consider such information (information consumption has costs, and without consuming the information, it is difficult to know what the costs of not consuming it are), a second alternative is to **ban** unsafe products.

Public Goods

The final market failure justification for regulation is public goods. A **public good** is a good that, if provided to one person, must be provided to all persons. Opening a public park in a city creates a public good that is available to all citizens. Because public goods once provided are often free, public goods can be overused, thus diminishing their value. For example, after the invention of radio, the public airways (a public good) were available to all who wished to broadcast. The result was overuse and chaos; the broadcast industry demanded federal regulation so that orderly broadcasting could be undertaken.

Creating a public good, therefore, requires regulation either to (1) limit access to the public good, or (2) to guarantee that the public good is paid for by the users. In general, the problem with most public goods is the latter. Citizens have an interest in such public goods as national defense, police protection, and pest control (Daly and Brady, 1976:172; Meier, 1993:84); but they have no interest in paying for them. The mandatory tax system is the normal solution for such situations, however, rather than regulation.[8]

EQUITY

According to Arthur Okun (1976), the major **trade-off** in public policy is between efficiency and equality. Market systems are designed to enhance efficiency but are unconcerned with the distribution of benefits in society. A concern with **equity** or the

---

[8]Daly and Brady (1976) list one additional economic justification for regulation, the **inefficient extraction of natural resources**. As an example they note the practice of flaring gas from oil fields before the invention of the seamless pipe. They argue that government regulation is justified to conserve such resources. Such an argument could be made to defend the federal automobile mileage requirements. This argument is not included here because it is not solely an economic argument. Gas in oil fields actually had no market value until it could be transported; without flaring, it was a hazard. Similarly, gasoline mileage regulation is more likely to be justified for political reasons (e.g., unstable foreign supplies, balance of payment problems, and so on) than for economic reasons.

justice of any distribution of goods falls outside the range of economic analysis based on the microeconomic model. Regulation has never been solely concerned with efficiency; as Schuck (1980:120) notes, "significant regulatory decisions are ineluctably political." Under a broad interpretation of equity, a variety of regulatory values can be subsumed, including fairness, justice, openness, and equality. Three specific **equity goals** that combine elements of all these values will be discussed: (1) equalizing the distribution of political and economic power, (2) altering the distribution of income, and (3) reducing uncertainty.

Equalizing Power

The history of regulation provides numerous examples of regulation designed to **neutralize the political or economic power** of other individuals (see Daly and Brady, 1976:174; Eisner, 1993:202-203). Legislative battles in collective bargaining followed such a pattern as first unions sought government intervention to support their collective bargaining position (the Wagner Act) and then business made a similar effort to limit the power of unions (the Taft-Hartley Act). The movement to regulate railroads can be attributed as much to efforts by farmers and shippers to limit the economic power of railroads and their ability to decide what towns would survive and prosper (see Kolko, 1965) as to any effort to limit monopoly pricing. In fact, railroad practices such as rebates, long-haul discounts, and volume discounts can be interpreted as competitive behavior.

The argument that regulation was established to alter power distributions can also be made for more recent regulatory efforts. Automobile safety advocates seek to impose the costs of safer vehicles on the manufacturers rather than let the market or a newly designed market determine safety. Support for, and opposition to, the Occupational Safety and Health Administration (OSHA) illustrate that OSHA regulation concerns workplace power relationships; organized labor opposed the repeal of the "Mickey Mouse" safety regulations in 1978 and used complaints to trigger inspections even though few violations were found.

Without a doubt, regulation has been used to alter power relationships in American society. Individuals in unfavorable economic situations often seek the aid of government. Farmers demanded subsidies, grangers wanted lower railroad rates, small businesses requested Robinson-Patman protection, and the financial industry supported a taxpayer bailout for the savings and loan crisis. Because economic advantages are not difficult to translate into political advantages, seeking political solutions to economic problems is a rational political action.[9]

---

[9]Thompson and Jones (1982) and others would reject the political and economic power goals as inappropriate for regulatory policy. Such a rejection is based on a normative argument that other mechanisms are better able to address such problems. The empirical reality is that regulation is used to alter the distribution of both economic and political power.

Unacceptable Income Distribution

Often regulation is an effort to alter the **distribution of income** within society. Regulations and market orders that limit farm production and subsidize the incomes of farmers redistribute income from urban to rural residents. Laws requiring equal pay for equal work were originally proposed to prevent a redistribution of income from men to women and later were used to seek a redistribution of income from men to women. The meager legislative history of the Sherman Act suggests that the lavish life-styles of the trust owners had as much to do with mobilizing public support for the Sherman Act as anything else.

Regulation may not be the most efficient way to **redistribute** income from one group to another; transfer payments such as Social Security can clearly redistribute greater amounts of money with fewer transaction costs. Regulation, however, is traditionally less visible than direct transfers of income and probably has fewer political obstacles to overcome. Efficient or not, some regulation is designed to redistribute income.

Reducing Uncertainty

Unfettered **free markets** contain a great deal of uncertainty for both business and consumers. Regulation can be used as a means to reduce this uncertainty. The system of bank regulation and deposit insurance was established to restore the confidence of consumers in the banking system and reduce their uncertainty about the safety of such institutions. Agricultural regulation is often justified in a similar manner; market orders were authorized, in part, to assure consumers a stable flow of food to market and, thus, reduce consumer uncertainty. Food and drug safety laws can be supported in a similar fashion.

Businesses also see certainty and regulation to provide it. One member of Congress quoted the pleas of the oil and gas industry in the late 1970s: "We would just like to get Congress to do something—regulate, deregulate, put on a tax—but let us know as soon as you can what it is so we can go out and make our plans" (Brown, 1980:72). Examples of business seeking protection from marketplace uncertainty include the radio industry requesting the Federal Communications Commission (FCC), the airline industry demanding a Civil Aeronautics Board (CAB), and the utility industry seeking state regulation (Anderson, 1980).

A final point about equity goals is in order. Although equity is a **value-neutral** term in that one could advocate more or less equity, equity arguments are rarely used to advocate greater inequality (and when regulation creates inequity as the Federal Maritime Commission does, the actions are usually wrapped in other values). Democratic nations such as the United States have a general bias favoring equity. Government action, therefore, is more easily justified if it is undertaken on behalf of the politically disadvantaged, the poor, or consumers. In fact, in a democratic society, little justification exists for marketplace interventions that exacerbate political inequality, increase the maldistribution of income, or protect the privileged from uncertainty. Accepting equity as a regulatory goal implies normative preferences about equity in society.

EFFICIENCY, EQUITY, AND REGULATION

Three points about the regulatory goals of efficiency and equity merit discussion.

Equity and Efficiency are Distinct Criteria

First, equity and efficiency are two distinct criteria for regulatory policy. Some equity goals clearly conflict with some efficiency goals. The equity goal of low utility prices conflicts with the efficiency goal of providing utilities with sufficient returns to attract investment; the equity goal of providing farmers with greater incomes conflicts with the efficiency goal of optimal allocation of resources across economic sectors. Equity and efficiency may also coincide; correcting imperfect information in consumer areas is consistent with reducing uncertainty; eliminating the externalities of workplace safety corresponds to adjustments in the political balance between management and labor.

Equity and Efficiency Are Normative Goals

Second, both equity and efficiency are **normative goals**; they are proposals for what regulatory goals should be. Of the two, equity is far more likely to be the actual goal of regulation than efficiency; that is, an analyst is more likely to be able to explain why regulation exists in an area by referring to equity than by referring to efficiency. The creation of the **Interstate Commerce Commission** (ICC) reflected the concerns of farmers and others about the economic power of the railroads; the creation of the FCC was at the request of the radio industry to reduce uncertainty; and the FDA was created to eliminate the dangers of unsanitary food.

The legislative history of regulation, including those areas discussed in this book, demonstrates that the United States regulates for **political reasons**. Business, consumers, or other groups organize politically and press for regulation (e.g., they seek to acquire the benefits of regulation for themselves). Efficiency concerns in regulation are a more recent phenomenon, dating from the post-World War II economic studies of regulation (Weiss, 1981:3). When such agencies as the Interstate Commerce Commission, the Food and Drug Administration, the Federal Trade Commission, and the New Deal regulatory agencies were created, efficiency was an underdeveloped concept in economics. Legislative justifications for action accordingly did not rely on efficiency. Therefore, to argue efficiency is the prime goal of regulatory agencies is to argue that the agencies should seek a goal different from the one that policymakers intended (Litan and Nordhaus, 1983:36).

Goals Are Not Always Clear

Third, the goal of a regulatory program is not always clear. The antitrust chapter discussed the multiple goals attributed to antitrust policy-protection of small business, reduction of uncertainty for large business, limiting the economic power of trusts, providing for consumer welfare, and so on. By viewing various parts of antitrust policy, one can argue for any of these goals. Similarly, economic regulation in agriculture is defended in terms of reducing uncertainty, ensuring adequate supplies, and redistributing incomes. Even at levels more specific than such general goals as equity and efficiency, regulatory agencies' goals are multiple; and often these goals conflict.

REGULATION'S SHORTCOMINGS

Regulatory policy is not perfect; no government policy is. Large-scale bureaucratic organizations, be they public or private, make mistakes and fail to attain goals (Goodsell, 1994:4). Regulatory agencies are not exceptions to this rule. This section details the criticisms of regulation. These shortcomings may be divided into (1) political shortcomings, and (2) economic second-order consequences. The first are considered direct failings of regulation; the second are indirect failings that may be unintended.

Political Shortcomings

This examination of the political shortcomings of regulation considers several factors: (1) lack of responsiveness, (2) unresponsiveness to political institutions, (3) ineffectiveness, (4) poor decisions, (5) lack of coordination, (6) delay, and (7) unfair procedures.

LACK OF RESPONSIVENESS

The core political criticism of regulation revolves around the beneficiaries of regulation. Regulation has long been justified as action in some vague public interest, which, in turn, has been interpreted as regulation in the interests of the nonregulated rather than the regulated. The charge that regulatory agencies are more responsive to the individuals that they regulate than to a more general public has a long scholarly tradition. Samuel Huntington (1952) first proposed this as a hypothesis based on a case study of the Interstate Commerce Commission. Marver Bernstein (1955) generalized it in his **life cycle theory of regulation** when he argued that all regulatory agencies eventually become **captives** of the industry that they regulate. George Stigler (1971), Richard Posner (1974), and Sam Peltzman (1976) formalized this theory in economic terms. Ralph Nader's early studies of regulation (e.g., Fellmuth, 1970) introduced this theory to the popular press, and the strategic use of regulation by business remains a theoretical touchstone for those who study the politics of regulation (see McCormick, 1989). Regulation that protects the regulated industry is perceived as a perversion of the regulatory process, as the use of regulation to protect the fortunate rather than the unfortunate.

Although some scholars would apply the capture criticism to all regulatory agencies (e.g., Lowi, 1969; McCormick, 1989), it clearly applies to some agencies more than to others. The chapters in this book illustrated that the relationship between the agency and the regulated varies a great deal. In some cases (occupational regulation), capture was an appropriate description; in others (consumer protection), it was not (see Quirk, 1981). Because all public bureaucracies are political institutions, they are responsive to their environments (see Salamon and Wamsley, 1975). When regulatory agencies respond to the regulated portion of the environment, intended or not, such responsiveness is perceived as a failure.

UNRESPONSIVENESS TO POLITICAL INSTITUTIONS

In the literature on bureaucratic politics, the **unresponsiveness** of bureaucratic institutions to elected public officials is seen as a major shortcoming (see Rourke, 1984; Redford, 1969; Meier, 1993). Because policymaking bureaucrats are not elected, the **responsiveness** of bureaus to democratic political institutions is essential. Only through the electoral process is public policy accorded legitimacy. Bureaucracies, including the regulatory bureaucracies, are criticized for being unresponsive to the president or to Congress. Congress, for example, frequently criticized the Federal Trade Commission in the late 1970s for aggressively regulating funeral directors, optometrists, and a variety of other businesses (Weingast and Moran, 1982). Many proposals to reorganize regulatory agencies and eliminate the commission form (e.g., the Ash Council Report) were designed to make regulatory agencies more responsive to the president (see also Ball, 1984).

Some recent studies indicate that the concerns about responsiveness may be exaggerated and that regulatory agencies are heavily influenced by the relevant political actors and institutions. From this perspective political actors are seen as **"principals"** that can do a good deal to influence the regulatory behavior of their bureaucratic **"agents,"** and there is a growing literature devoted to empirically studying this relationship (e.g., Chubb, 1985; Wood, 1992; Wood and Waterman, 1994).

Support for responsiveness to political institutions operates at two levels. First, at the most abstract level, responsiveness is supported for the democratic reasons mentioned earlier. Second, at a more specific level, responsiveness is supported because it affects the regulator's policy orientation. For example, one could advocate that the Environmental Protection Agency be more responsive to the president because under Republican presidents such responsiveness would mean a less active EPA. Similarly, many who advocate that the EPA be more responsive to Congress are individuals who seek such responsiveness because they favor more stringent regulation. The responsiveness of regulatory agencies to government's political institutions has been demonstrated to have policy implications (Wood, 1992; 1988; Moe, 1982; 1985; Weingast and Moran, 1983).

INEFFECTIVENESS

A regulatory agency can be considered **ineffective** when it fails to attain specific legislative goals. Although a judgment of ineffectiveness under the "public interest" goals normally used before 1970 was difficult, since 1970 regulatory goals have become more specific. OSHA has been criticized as ineffective in improving workplace safety (see Chapter 8); EPA has moved toward its goals of clean air and clean water only slowly. Regulatory policy in agriculture has been strikingly unsuccessful in reducing the overproduction of agricultural goods, and antitrust policy has been faulted for failing to reach any of its myriad goals. At a general level, sufficient evidence of ineffectiveness exists to designate it as a serious shortcoming.

A closer look at regulatory policy, however, reveals some difficulties with the term ineffective. The Clean Air Act Amendments of 1990, for example, have simultaneously been praised as a significant advancement of environmental quality control and an ineffective set of regulations that places undue and unnecessary burdens on business (Ringquist, 1993:50-52). Disputes over effectiveness may, in fact, be disputes over goals.

In addition, some regulatory agencies will never attain their legislative goals and, therefore, will be "ineffective" for two reasons. First, some regulatory goals are impossible to meet. The legislative history of the Clean Air and Clean Water Acts is strewn with requirements that could not be met because of unrealistic deadlines or unavailable technology (Eisner, 1994:135-152; Ringquist, 1993:43-59). Second, many regulatory agencies are not given the resources to attain the goals established by Congress. Regulation in occupational safety and health or environmental protection is characterized by a lack of resources (both personnel and money), inadequate sanctions, and a lack of political support for vigorous regulation. Drug enforcement has received considerable support and a high level of resources to achieve goals many believe to be unreachable or even irrational (see Meier, 1994). Many regulatory policies may well be ineffective, but the explanation for such failures can often be found at the political level, not at the bureaucratic level.[10]

POOR DECISIONS

Regulatory policy has long been criticized for simply making **bad decisions** (see Daly and Brady, 1976:181). Recent criticized decisions include the EPA's sale of emissions permits to utilities, OSHA's encouragement of business self-inspections, and the FCC's reregulation of the cable television industry. The charge of poor decisions, although clearly correct, also is problematic for three reasons.

First, whether or not a decision is a poor one is a function of the critic's perception. Emission permits have become valuable assets to some of the purchasers. OSHA's cooperative compliance approach of the early 1980s was uniformly popular with business. Reregulation of cable television was supported by consumer groups who viewed local cable franchises as monopolies. Few regulatory decisions will be universally condemned. If regulatory agencies had only a single goal, criticism might reflect poor decisions only. With **multiple goals**, however, many poor decisions can be viewed as maximizing one goal rather than another.

Second, some poor decisions can be explained, though not justified, by the limitations placed on the regulatory organization. Only a few regulatory agencies have their own research and information units. For the most part, regulatory agencies rely on industry for data. Because industry is not disinterested in the outcome of regulatory decisions, data from industry are suspect. When complex decisions are made with **questionable information**, less than optimal decisions will result.

Third, all large bureaucratic organizations make mistakes (Goodsell, 1994:4). To expect that regulatory agencies will be less prone to mistakes is unrealistic. Because the

---

[10]Legislative actions to create regulatory agencies always reflect compromises even if the compromise concerns only the level of funding. The creation of the Equal Employment Opportunity Commission (EEOC) illustrates the use of symbolic politics in establishing regulation. By creating the EEOC, the advocates of equal employment achieved some of their ends; by not giving the agency any real power, the opponents of equal employment also achieved some of their ends. The price of passage of any controversial regulatory legislation may be the limitation of agency resources; in such cases, regulatory agencies may be ineffective by design.

decisions made by public organizations are more visible than those made by private organizations, the general perception will be that public organizations make more mistakes. Given the nature of the problems faced by regulatory agencies and the resources at their disposal, an occasional error by regulators must be expected. If such errors are intolerable, the solution is either more realistic goals or greater resources committed to regulation.

LACK OF COORDINATION

Regulatory policy is charged with a **lack of coordination** resulting in policies that work at cross-purposes. In part, the absence of coordination results because different regulatory agencies attempt to maximize different goals. OSHA, for example, may require that an industrial firm vent emissions to protect workers from exposure whereas EPA prohibits such venting to protect individuals living nearby. Often **regulatory authority overlaps**. Exposure to carcinogens is regulated by EPA, OSHA, FDA, and CPSC with little effort to prevent duplication or conflict. Overlapping jurisdictions may result in inconsistent policy. Insurance companies, because they are "regulated" by state insurance commissions, moved rapidly into other financial services whereas banks regulated at the federal level entered slowly.

Even within agencies a lack of coordination is evident. The Environmental Protection Agency regulates air pollution separately from water pollution; this resulted in one Pittsburgh plant's cleaning its water emissions by increasing its air emissions. Many agencies regulate on a **case-by-case basis**, resulting in different levels of enforcement in different parts of the country. The Federal Communications Commission has been strongly criticized for the unplanned development of television because it decided to mix UHF and VHF television stations in the same market (see Krasnow, Langley, and Terry, 1982).

Absence of coordination is a serious problem, not just in regulation but in all policy areas at the national level. Failure to coordinate regulation means that regulation will work at cross-purposes (e.g., requiring greater fuel economy and lower emissions from automobiles). The result will be regulatory policy that is ineffective and confusing.

DELAY

In theory, bureaucracies are organizations capable of making a large number of decisions quickly. Several regulatory procedures, however, result in significant delays. The Magnuson-Moss Act required that the Federal Trade Commission adopt rules via a **formal rulemaking procedure**; the result was that rules took three times as long to promulgate as before the act (West, 1982; Breyer, 1982:347). The application to market a new drug takes the FDA eight to nine years to process (Grabowski and Vernon, 1983). The Nuclear Regulatory Commission, back in the days when new licenses to operate nuclear plants were granted, took 10 years to license a new plant (Daly and Brady, 1976:181). Even on trivial issues, the bureaucracy sometimes takes an inordinate amount of time; the FDA took 12 years, for example, to decide whether peanut butter should contain 87 percent or 90 percent peanuts (Stone, 1982:212).

Although regulatory bureaucracies can move quickly, in many cases they do not. One reason for slowness in regulatory procedures is that laws governing **participation** encourage processes that are slow and deliberate. In a sense, then, the ill-effects of delay must be traded off against the benefits of procedural fairness (Breyer, 1982:348; Goodsell, 1994:81-83).

UNFAIR PROCEDURES

Administrative procedures have been the subject of many reform efforts. Under the leadership of the American Bar Association, administrative procedures have come to resemble courtroom procedures to a significant degree. Although most agencies are subject to the requirements of the Administrative Procedure Act, an agency's enabling legislation often specifies **additional procedures**.

In terms of rulemaking, one distinction is between formal and informal rulemaking (West, 1995). **Informal rulemaking** is fairly brief, requiring notice and an opportunity to comment; it resembles the legislative process. Formal rulemaking has far more elaborate procedures, including extensive cross-examination of witnesses by other witnesses. Among the "**unfair administrative procedures**" are limiting verbal testimony, restricting cross-examination, and limiting who can participate (e.g., the FCC and the United Church of Christ).

Adjudicative procedures have also been criticized for denying rights to citizens. Administrative proceedings, for example, have no formal pleadings (the agency can change the subject of the hearing by giving adequate notice), use a lower standard of evidence than courts, have less formal rules of evidence (Cooper, 1983:147), and usually place the burden of proof on the citizen, not on the agency (Warren, 1982:294). In addition, regulatory agencies fuse powers that are normally kept separate in the American policy. The same agency often has the authority to establish regulations, inspect to enforce the regulations, try the individual for violations, and levy fines.

The literature normally defines **fair procedures** as those resembling courtroom procedures (Davis, 1972; but see Warren, 1982:289). Under such a definition, a clear trade-off exists between fair procedures and delays. More procedural safeguards require slower procedures (see Meier, 1993:87). To a proponent of regulation, delay may be a greater evil than the lack of court room procedures.

Economic Second-Order Failings

Economists have detailed a series of **second-order economic consequences** to regulation. In essence, these criticisms charge that regulation distorts the efficient operation of the marketplace. According to Stokey and Zeckhauser (1978), government policy (including regulation) should always be evaluated against the standard of doing nothing; that is, is regulation an improvement over the imperfect operations of the marketplace? Among the distortions attributed to regulation are (1) price-fixing, (2) subsidies, (3) limiting competition, (4) restricting choice, (5) retarding technology, and (6) acting as a drag on productivity (see Daly and Brady, 1976:177-179; MacAvoy, 1979; Stone, 1982; Swann, 1989:13-21; Meiners and Yandle, 1989).

PRICE-FIXING

Price-fixing in regulation is not inappropriate per se; after all, one economic justification for price-fixing is monopoly because monopolists set prices too high. Of concern to economic critics is price setting in areas that are not **natural monopolies** (e.g., agriculture, railroads, trucking, merchant marine shipping). If the regulatory agency sets the price too high, surpluses will result; if the price is set too low, more will be demanded than produced, and shortages will result. **Government-determined prices**, in general, are less flexible than those set by the market and will not fluctuate fast enough to prevent shortages and surpluses.

The criticism of inappropriate price-fixing was more telling in 1976 than it is today. Beginning with the Ford administration, the federal government has eliminated or partially eliminated regulatory price setting in areas such as natural gas, brokerage commissions, airline fares, railroad and truck rates, interest rates, and long-distance telephone rates. In addition, the federal government has taken a strong stand against price setting by professional associations and state occupational regulators.

Despite the federal government's general withdrawal from the price setting area (the one exception is health care), serious problems still exist. By setting price floors for agricultural products, the U.S. government has encouraged farmers to overproduce and generate large surpluses. Although many crops are not permanently overproduced, such goods as milk and peanuts are chronically in surplus. At the state level, price regulation of utilities has also created problems (Anderson, 1980; Gormley, 1983b). Some state regulators set prices too high, thus hurting consumers whereas others set prices too low, thus preventing the utilities from attracting capital to expand.

SUBSIDIES AND CROSS-SUBSIDIES

Another way that government regulation distorts the marketplace is by the use of regulation to create subsidies or cross-subsidies. With **subsidies**, the production of a good is partially underwritten by government so that more will be produced than the market demands. Under **cross-subsidies**, profits in one area of an industry's production are kept high to compensate for low profits in other areas.

In our regulatory history, subsidies have been used to create inefficiencies. By subsidizing shipping rates, the ICC permitted trucking companies to undercut railroads on their more efficient long hauls (see Daly and Brady, 1976:178). Subsidies as a component of regulation, however, have become less common. Some subsidies still exist in such programs as agriculture regulation, maritime regulation, and the EPA's waste water treatment grants.

Cross-subsidies were often used in regulation to expand service. Airline companies were granted highly profitable routes in exchange for flying unprofitable routes to smaller cities (Brown, 1987). Federal regulation permitted high profits from long-distance service to subsidize local telephone service to maximize the number of telephone users.

From a political-economic perspective, the exact criticism of subsidies and cross-subsidies is difficult to pin down. Economists have consistently urged that incentives (both taxes and subsidies) be used to encourage pollution control. The use of subsidies in the preceding areas reflects or reflected values other than efficiency that the political system wanted to attain. Universal telephone service, a national pattern of air transportation, elimination of food shortages, and a U.S. flag merchant marine fleet are all goals that subsidies were used to obtain. The legitimacy or illegitimacy of subsidies and cross-subsidies must rest on a political judgment about the merits of the programs.

LIMITING COMPETITION

Regulatory agencies are charged with **limiting competition**, and in many cases they are guilty. Before the federal deregulation movement of the 1970s, several examples of regulation limiting competition were evident—government-sponsored cartels were allowed to set trucking rates, marketing orders limited the amount of fruits and vegetables sent to market, financial institutions were not permitted to compete via interest rates paid to depositors, and the FCC restricted technology to prevent competition in the television industry. At the state level, many professions used occupational regulation to limit competition both from other professions (physicians v. osteopaths, chiropractors, podiatrists, midwives, and so on) and from within the profession (fee schedules, advertising limits).

Competitive industries can often provide more benefits to consumers. Whether or not limiting competition is an evil, however, should be judged on a case-by-case basis because competition is not always an unmitigated blessing. The highly competitive banking industry of the 1920s, for example, produced far fewer benefits to consumers than the uncompetitive system established in the 1930s. Similarly, the deregulated savings and loan industry of the 1980s produced more competition, but it resulted in widespread insolvency and required a taxpayer bailout estimated at $400 billion (Lindeen, 1994:136).

Price-fixing, subsidies, and limiting competition are the three **classic economic criticisms** of regulation. These criticisms were developed shortly after World War II in response to perceived problems of economic regulation. As emphasis changed from **economic regulation** to **social regulation**, these three classic criticisms were joined by three new ones—restrictions on choice, retarding technological development, and limiting productivity.

RESTRICTING CHOICE

The microeconomic model of perfect competition is based on voluntary choices by individuals; restrictions on such choices mean that the overall selection of goods and services will be less than optimal. **Regulation**, by definition, is governmental action designed to limit the choices of individuals, corporations, or other governments. Regulation, therefore, limits individual choice and correspondingly individual freedom (see Friedman and Friedman, 1980).

As with competition, however, **unlimited choice** is a mixed blessing. Without perfect information about products, their use, and their hazards, restrictions on choice can often be justified. No one, for example, believes that any valuable freedom is lost because pregnant women are denied thalidomide or because parents are denied the opportunity to purchase baby cribs with slats more than 2.375 inches apart.[11]

---

[11]Occasionally, one will see passionate defenses of an individual's right to choose dangerous or worthless

Some restrictions on individual choice, however, have little justification. Restrictions on individual practice by nurse practitioners and physicians' assistants deprive many individuals of low-cost, routine health care. Similar restrictions on the practice of law eliminate an individual's choice of low cost-low quality legal assistance.

Restricting choice via regulation may have second-order consequences. If the Environmental Protection Agency someday bans the use of leaded gasoline, the owners of pre-1974 vehicles will suffer engine damage. When NHTSA required air bags in all cars, those who already used seat belts began subsidizing those who did not. Passive restraint systems were imposed on all and paid for by seatbelt users, even though seatbelt users gained, at best, only a marginal increase in safety benefits.

Clearly, restrictions on choice must be challenged as deleterious second-order consequences on a case-by-case basis. Limiting individual choice is necessary for the operation of modern society. Because the nation has not adopted utilitarian political theory as the paramount rationale for society, some balancing of choice with the benefits received is necessary. Although no one should be denied the choice of a wide range of foodstuffs simply because many foods naturally contain small amounts of carcinogenic substances, no one should be free to drive while intoxicated.

RETARDING TECHNOLOGY

In some cases, regulation has restricted the development of new technology. The Federal Communications Commission originally limited the development of cable technology and did not encourage such new technologies as direct satellite broadcasting, low power television, and multipoint distribution systems until the late 1970s. The Interstate Commerce Commission refused to permit larger boxcars to avoid disturbing the relationship between railroads and trucks (Fellmuth, 1970), and AIDS activists have charged the Food and Drug Administration with restricting the development of new drugs and creating a drug lag.

Regulation may have had some success in **retarding technology**, but it is not omnipotent. Technological changes in financial services overwhelmed the elaborate network of banking regulation in the 1980s. New options in telecommunications forced the FCC to consider new technologies or risk the chance that commercial television would be damaged by nonregulated sources of entertainment. The FDA has increased the rate of new drug approval but is more comfortable trading off delays in introducing new drugs for higher guarantees of safety.

---

activities. The Food and Drug Administration was criticized by many for prohibiting the drug laetrile as a cancer treatment. Similarly, Congress responded to criticism of seat belt interlock systems by preventing the Department of Transportation from requiring them. Similar defenses can be found against motorcycle helmet laws and against laws that require medical treatment for severely ill children.

ACTING AS A DRAG ON PRODUCTIVITY

The most persistent economic criticism of regulation is that it limits industrial productivity. The growth in regulation of the 1970s corresponded with a decline in the growth rate of productivity for American industry and a sluggish economy. Productivity grew at the rate of 2.5 percent annually from 1948 to 1973 but only at the rate of 0.5 percent from 1973 to 1982 (Litan and Nordhaus, 1983:27). There was growth in the 1980s, but by the early 1990s this slowed and productivity posted an annual growth rate of 0.9 percent (Stewart, 1992). Social regulation of worker health and safety and the environment, according to the critics, has required industry to make investments that add little to productivity. With a limited amount of capital to invest, investments in regulation divert capital from productive investments.

Some argue that the decline in productivity is substantial; Thomas Hopkins, who served in the Office of Management and Budget, estimated that regulation imposes an annual cost on business and industry of nearly $400 billion (Bandow, 1992). By the early 1980s, direct and indirect regulatory costs were being charged with significantly reducing annual productivity gains (Weidenbaum, 1978; Denison, 1979; Litan and Nordhaus, 1983:31).

Before concluding that regulation is a major factor in the decline of the American economy, we should consider some additional information. First, the rise of regulation and decline in productivity occurred at the same time as three other important **trends**—the elimination of cheap energy, the rise of an inflation mentality, and the increase in foreign competition. Because the productivity studies rely heavily on correlational methods, accurately discerning the impact of several simultaneous trends is difficult.

Second, much of the analysis does not find significant results or is contradictory. Regulation of the airlines, for example, was argued to impose significant costs, and deregulation was estimated to save as much as $10 billion per year (President's Council on Competitiveness, 1992:v). Deregulation was also charged with promoting collusion, overcharging and industry losses totalling $7 billion in 1992 (Kuttner, 1993). Regulation has thus been portrayed as the savior and the destroyer of the economic fortunes of the airline industry. In other areas, the productivity of such capital-intensive industries as steel, automobiles, copper, aluminum, cement, and petroleum refining is affected far more by the general state of the economy and foreign competition than by regulation.

Third, precisely how regulation is placing burdens on industry is not clear. Pettus (1982) found that the average firm has a probability of 0.8 of seeing an OSHA inspector and will be fined about $400 for violations; certainly, this could hardly affect productivity, although changing corporate behavior to meet the regulations certainly has an impact. Downing (1984) notes that most environmental standards are negotiated favorably to the industry, and most investment in pollution controls is subject to highly favorable tax write-offs. The argument that regulation is placing an onerous burden on industry comes primarily from industry estimates of costs, estimates that in past experience demonstrate a strong bias toward **overestimation**.

REGULATORY REFORMS

Within each of the chapters specific substantive reforms were proposed and evaluated. In addition to **agency-specific reforms**, many analysts propose general reforms that can be undertaken in all areas of regulation. **General regulatory reforms** can be grouped into two categories. First, among those who perceive that regulation in general is a problem, the solution is usually less regulation. Second, among those who feel regulation is necessary but that the pattern of regulation is ineffective, better control mechanisms are advocated. In the latter case, regulation is perceived as responsive to the wrong groups, and changes need to be made so that regulation responds to different groups. The reforms of these two groups can be divided into those who seek to decentralize decision making, usually to the market, and those who wish to centralize regulation by vesting greater control in the political branches of government.

Market-Oriented Reforms

If correcting market failures is the goal of regulation and regulation often creates greater market distortions via subsidies, price-fixing, increasing costs, and so on, the solution is less regulation. Regulation is seen as a set of policies that on balance contributes less in benefits than it imposes in costs. As Stokey and Zeckhauser (1978:309-310) conclude, "the history of [government] interventions to deal with market failure is a history of disappointments. In a variety of areas, programs have accomplished much less than we had hoped, at a cost far greater than we expected."[12] Five general reforms are proposed by market advocates—(1) more vigorous prosecution of antitrust laws, (2) general deregulation, (3) cost-benefit analysis, (4) tax-based incentive systems, and (5) nontax incentive systems.

VIGOROUS ANTITRUST ACTION

If the problems facing government regulators stem from lack of competition in the marketplace, the obvious solution is to increase the amount of competition. A lack of competition is perceived as especially harmful when it has the sanction of the government (see Armentano, 1982). One mechanism proposed to increase competition is the vigorous use of the federal government's antitrust powers (see Kohlmeier, 1969).

The supporters of antitrust action might be termed **structural competition advocates** because they believe that competition is a function of the number of firms in the marketplace. By the use of antitrust laws to break up large firms into numerous smaller firms, the total number of firms increases; and competition should also increase. Advocates estimate that a costless and effective antitrust policy could increase the nation's gross national product by 5 to 12 percent (Schwartzman, 1964; Comanor and Leibenstein, 1969). Such a use of antitrust laws, of course, would require that the law be amended to

---

[12]The advocates of the following reforms show a general bias against all forms of government intervention. To receive a good sampling of opinion in this area, see any issue of *Regulation*. For more academic views on regulation with the same conclusions, see recent issues of the *Journal of Law and Economics*.

ban monopoly per se rather than the current ban on **monopolizing** because the lack of competitors per se is viewed as the problem.

In classical microeconomic theory, the relationship between the number of firms, the amount of competition, and the basic evils of marketplace failure are well known. If prices are set too high, competition will reduce prices because price-cutters will take market shares away from nonprice-cutters. If imperfect information is the problem, firms will compete to offer information about their products so that greater information is available to consumers. The only major market failure that competition does not address is externalities because firms in a competitive marketplace have even less incentive to consider externalities, for doing so will reduce already limited profits. In addition, structural competition advocates are not concerned with the political failings of regulation.

Vigorous antitrust prosecution as a regulatory reform has three problems that must be addressed before one concludes that antitrust can correct regulatory ills:

First, such a strategy is essentially untried. At no time in the nation's history could antitrust enforcement ever be characterized as vigorous. The market-oriented Reagan and Bush administrations showed little interest in vigorous structural antitrust; overall antitrust activity declined during the 1980s and early 1990s (Wood and Anderson, 1993).

Second, antitrust enforcement to date is slow, expensive, and uncertain. The famed IBM case took 13 years before the government dropped the case because it lacked merit. Numerous days of court time, hundreds of lawyers, and millions of dollars were spent for no gain. Except for increasing legal employment opportunities, no net benefits were produced in this process.

Third, even among economists, a large literature criticizing the use of structural antitrust has developed. Brozen (1982) and others have argued that no systematic relationship between the number of firms and the competitiveness of an industry has been found. Armentano (1982) argues that large-scale organizations usually develop because they achieve significant economies of scale. When a large firm loses these advantages, it loses its market share. In general, Armentano and others believe that vigorous antitrust enforcement would be devastating to the American economy and produce no benefits.

GENERAL DEREGULATION

If regulation results in a net loss to society, then one solution to regulatory problems is to eliminate regulation (Daly and Brady, 1976:182). As Alan Stone (1982:252) noted, **deregulation** and a return to the free market usually are defined as the elimination of restrictions on entry, exit, and prices. A strategy of general deregulation is designed to address the second-order economic consequences of regulation noted earlier. Deregulation should result in increased competition and, therefore, in lower prices and provision of as much product information as is efficient.

Advocates of deregulation have a pattern of successes to illustrate that deregulation works (Weiss, 1981:7-9; President's Council on Competitiveness, 1992; Meiners and Yandle, 1989). In the mid 1970s, brokerage fees were deregulated, with the result being an increase in competition and a decline in fees. The economic deregulation of airlines was mandated in 1978 and implemented by the early 1980s. Following in rapid succession were the deregulation of cable TV at the federal level (although this industry was reregulated in the early 1990s), the elimination of economic regulation for trucking with price flexibility for railroads, the deregulation of natural gaslines, and the easing of economic regulations on depository institutions. Each of these cases resulted in some gains and losses, but in general consumers benefitted from deregulation efforts.[13]

All the deregulation successes, however, have been in **economic regulation** rather than in newer areas of **social regulation**. The total benefits of deregulation, therefore, might be close to being exhausted because at the federal level only a few industries (e.g., parts of agriculture, the merchant marine, and possibly rail and truck common carriers) are still regulated economically. Most problems amenable to solution via general deregulation have already been addressed. Krier (1982:156) relates this to the basic difference between economic and social regulation: "[T]he theory underlying deregulation of the airlines, for example—that competition works simply does not apply to environmental problems—where competition does not work." Similar statements could be made about hazardous waste, occupational health, pure food and drugs, and other areas of social regulation.

COST-BENEFIT ANALYSIS

Cost-benefit analysis is perhaps the most intuitively attractive reform proposed for regulation. Nothing could make more sense than to issue regulations only if the regulation provided more benefits than costs. Cost-benefit analysis has been the cornerstone of regulatory reform efforts of several presidents.[14] Gerald Ford required **inflation impact analyses** that included cost considerations. Jimmy Carter used the Council of Economic Advisors and other staff to conduct regulatory analysis reviews that included costs and benefits. Ronald Reagan's and George Bush's OMB control mechanism stressed the use of cost-benefit analysis.

Cost-benefit analysis is applicable to both economic and social regulation. In fact, the most prominent use of cost-benefit analysis has been in social regulation areas such as environmental protection, occupational health, and consumer protection. Although cost-benefit analysis seeks to apply the principles of the market to government decision making (both costs and benefits are based either on market values or on hypothetical market values) and, therefore, in theory uses decentralized criteria for decisions, in practice cost-benefit analysis has been used to centralize regulatory decision making.

Although cost-benefit analysis appears simple (one merely adds up the benefits and costs), in reality cost-benefit analysis is difficult to do well. Thompson and Jones (1982:153) note this: "Costs and benefits are not easily defined; the relationships between

---

[13]As evidenced by the turmoil in the airline industry, deregulation preceded some economic shake outs. Braniff and Continental Airlines were the first bankruptcies among major airlines since the advent of regulation. Since then a good number of other carriers have shared their fate. Whether these difficulties were the result of deregulation or the result of economic downturns in the early and late 1980s is unclear. The more important question is whether or not these failures have adversely affected consumers; the evidence on this question is mixed.

[14]The exact methods used to estimate costs and benefits are not important from a reform perspective. A good example of the procedures used can be found in Eisner (1993:182-192).

direct and indirect costs often are not easily discernible; the estimate of costs is highly sensitive to assumptions; and the price of good staff work is high, and high-quality analysis typically requires a long time to perform." Discretion in the estimation of benefits and costs is widely recognized, and in the view of some, manipulable. When George Bush imposed a moratorium on new regulations in the early 1990s supporters of the freeze reported extensive savings with relatively few costs. Figures to support such claims, however, were questionable or unavailable, and citizen watchdog groups charged that the freeze was delaying important safety regulations and thus imposing significant—although hard to measure—social costs (Palmer and Veron, 1992).

If cost-benefit analysis were not limited by a series of technical problems, it might provide valuable information concerning regulatory programs. Even without valid techniques, the use of cost-benefit analysis often raises questions not considered by regulators. In the best of circumstances, however, cost-benefit analysis can play only a limited role because such analysis proceeds from the assumption that efficiency is the primary goal of regulation. In areas of regulation with other goals (that is, most of them), cost-benefit analysis is of only moderate value.

In operation, cost-benefit analysis has been of less value than its proponents suggest. Cost-benefit analysis has become politicized because it has been used to centralize regulatory power for the president and because it has been used primarily by advocates of less regulation (West, 1995; Eisner, 1993:188-201). Accordingly, its value as an analytical tool has dropped. Cost-benefit analysis in the Reagan and Bush administrations was oversold and underfunded. Although there are continued calls for greater use of cost-benefit analysis (see Lave, 1992), little evidence exists that the quality of regulation has improved with the introduction of the technique to regulatory analysis.

INCENTIVE SYSTEMS

Creating incentive systems is a reform proposed by those who feel that regulation is inefficient and creates a serious drag on the economy (see Poole, 1982). By using **command-and-control systems**, they argue, regulation in excess of what consumers would be willing to pay for is introduced. Government, they feel, should limit its role in regulation to creating incentives that eliminate market failures. Rather than specify how a plant should control its pollution emissions, for example, the tax system should be used to tax the firm based on the amount of pollution that it produces. Each plant then can make efficient decisions about how much pollution control equipment to install.

ADVANTAGES OF INCENTIVE SYSTEMS In contrast to command-and-control systems, **incentive systems** are credited with several advantages (Litan and Nordhaus, 1983:97). First, incentive systems stress the attainment of regulatory goals in the most efficient manner possible because decisions are made under the constraints of the marketplace. Second, incentive systems are more likely to encourage innovation; firms discovering more effective methods of pollution control may use them without penalty. Third, decisions regarding costs are decentralized so that each firm can decide the mix of controls and penalties that is optimum for it. Fourth, such systems can be used to avoid politically volatile questions about income redistribution—the market is heartless and has no compunction about eliminating inefficient industries.

INCENTIVE SYSTEMS ARE NOT NEW   Proposals for incentive systems rather than regulation are not new. The English economist A. C. Pigou proposed a smokestack emissions tax in the 1930s. Over the years, a variety of incentive systems have been suggested in social regulation. Robert S. Smith (1974) proposed an **injury tax** as an alternative to OSHA safety regulation. Dales (1968) suggested that water pollutants be taxed as an incentive for industries to clean up their effluents.

PROBLEMS WITH INCENTIVE SYSTEMS   Although economists, in general, are enthusiastic about incentives as a replacement for regulation, they recognize that incentives might have some problems:

First, the use of incentives such as pollution taxes requires **monitoring systems** that are far advanced over current systems. The advantage of engineering controls is that one can easily tell if such a system is installed and operating. With emissions, monitoring must be continual (see Krier, 1982:154, Hahn and Noll, 1982:127; Ringquist, 1993:93-94). Second, tax incentives in place of regulation might result in even larger federal bureaucracies. One can not imagine the implementation of an injury tax, which implies a staff of economic analysts to set rates, a group of auditors to guarantee data accuracy, and another agency to compensate victims being operated with a staff as small as that of OSHA.

Third, any attempt to create incentive systems will be hopelessly tied up in debates over **moral issues**. Environmentalists generally see emissions taxes as licenses to pollute; labor unions see an injury tax as permission to maim (see Kelman, 1981a). Cool, reasoned debate is not the norm in this area.

Ignored in the debate over incentives is the one area of federal regulation that relies heavily on incentives to operate—regulation of crop production. Agricultural regulation links benefits (subsidies) to compliance (reducing acreage). Individual farmers decide whether or not to accept regulation and benefits or to forego benefits and operate outside the regulatory system. Decisions on what land to idle are made on a decentralized basis. The record has been one of failure with high-program costs and chronic oversupply.

A MARKET FOR POLLUTION RIGHTS EXISTS NOW   As of 1990 there has been one other ongoing "empirical test of the feasibility of using economic incentives to regulate economic activity" (Anderson, 1994:223). As part of the Clean Air Act of 1990, a market for **pollution rights** was instituted in an attempt to combat sulfur dioxide emissions. Specific numbers of allowables—an allowable permits the discharge of a single ton of sulfur dioxide—were issued to 110 electric power plants. Utilities that reduce emissions below their allotment of allowables can sell their excess. In the first sale of this kind, the Tennessee Valley Authority paid Wisconsin Power and Light more than $2.5 million for the right to produce 10,000 tons of sulfur dioxide emissions (Ringquist, 1993:52). The ultimate effect of this experiment in using incentives to improve environmental quality has yet to be determined. Initial reaction, however, has been mixed.

NONTAX INCENTIVE SYSTEMS

Incentive systems have not been limited to proposals that use the federal tax system only. Other proposals seek to strengthen the incentives that already operate in the private sector. The three most often proposed **nontax incentive systems** are collective bargaining, providing product information, and greater use of private litigation under liability law.

COLLECTIVE BARGAINING   **Collective bargaining** has been proposed as a private sector alternative to workplace safety regulation (see Bacow, 1982). Rather than impose safety requirements from the outside by a regulatory agency, unions and management can negotiate safety requirements more acceptable to each other (a form of Lindblom's [1965] partisan mutual adjustment). Collective bargaining has some advantages over direct regulation. It can permit greater consideration of local conditions, it can be more flexible because contracts are renegotiated periodically, and it may be more enforceable via grievance procedures and job actions (Bacow, 1982:204).

Collective bargaining approaches, however, have some major limitations. Because safety benefits are long-term in nature, unions have a greater incentive to stress short-term benefits such as wages rather than use scarce bargaining capital on safety issues (Bacow, 1982:206). Effective collective bargaining also assumes that unions possess accurate information about job hazards; in cases such as exposure to hazardous substances, this may not be true. Finally, collective bargaining offers no protection to the large number of workers who do not work in unionized facilities (Bacow, 1982:218).

PROVIDING PRODUCT INFORMATION   Providing the buyer with product information about performance or safety is another alternative to direct regulation. Included as **product information** are guarantees, warranties, and sometimes insurance (e.g., some bonds are insured). The proposed advantages of information over regulation include lower costs, greater choice given to consumers, and allowing individual flexibility (O'Hare, 1982:227).

The major problem with information is that most consumers ignore it. Bardach and Kagan (1982), for example, note that one bank offered ATM customers $10 if they would write the words "Regulation E" on a postcard and send it to the bank. Of 115,000 customers who received this offer via the ATM disclosure statement, none made a claim. On the other hand, lack of use may simply be a rational decision on the part of a consumer that getting additional information has costs in excess of benefits.

GREATER USE OF PRIVATE LITIGATION   The traditional private remedy for injuries is litigation. **Lawsuits** can be used in worker safety cases, hazardous product cases, defective goods, and environmental damages among others. Sobel (1977) proposed this procedure as a solution to the dangers of exposure to toxic substances. Greater use of private litigation in place of regulation is proposed to have three advantages:

First, the legal penalties are larger and, therefore, provide a greater deterrent than regulatory fines (Heffron with McFeeley, 1983:384).

Second, private litigation provides incentives for companies to establish safety departments and quality control (Bardach and Kagan, 1982:272). And because litigation is expensive and injury awards and settlement costs potentially high, the incentives are significant.

Third, litigation punishes firms for actual damages rather than for potential damages.

The use of litigation is often linked to the use of **private insurance** (Ferreira, 1982; Meier, 1988:158). Insurance companies have an incentive to change the behavior of the insured and can often provide cheaper rates in the process. Insurance systems work best when risks are easy to assess, the parties are financially responsible, and sufficient information exists. In such cases, litigation resolves into insurance disputes.

Over time, states have made litigation easier by moving to a standard of strict liability (Heiners, 1982:298). **Strict liability** holds the maker of a product liable if the product is "unreasonably dangerous" even if the user was negligent. In fact, corporations—and an increasing number of politicians—feel the courts have gone too far. In the 1980s a number of states pursued tort reform efforts aimed at limiting liability, and there was an effort to preempt state liability laws with a uniform federal law.

Although litigation has some impact, it is clearly not a cure-all. Several limitations exist. The burden of proof rests with the injured party, and courts are notoriously slow and expensive (Bardach and Kagan, 1982:272). The delays inherent in the legal process are perceived to hurt meritorious claims the most (Ferreira, 1982:272). Litigation is also difficult to use when damages are remote in time, damages are collective in nature, and damages are hard to quantify (Bardach and Kagan, 1982:280). The ex post facto nature of litigation is also a problem; liability suits compensate victims or their heirs; they are not **preventative**.

Because litigation has weaknesses, several states have made efforts to facilitate product liability suits. Among the incentives that encourage the use of courts are laws that permit awarding attorneys' fees, treble damage awards, class actions, and legal assistance. Sobel (1977) proposes the use of administrative tribunals with eased burdens of proof to make litigation a more efficient check.

Responsiveness Reforms

Reforms that stress increased responsiveness must answer this question: Responsive to whom? In general, some consensus exists that regulation, as in all government programs, should be responsive to the general public; but the literature also recognizes that defining what being responsive to the general public entails is difficult (Gilbert, 1959). One argument presented by Ralph Nader and other populists is that regulatory agencies should be directly responsive to consumers. A second argument holds that regulatory agencies should be responsive to the major political institutions and that these institutions, in turn, should be responsive via elections to the general public (see Redford, 1969). As the following discussion will illustrate, arguments about responsiveness have substantive implications concerning who should benefit from regulation.

RESPONSIVENESS TO CONSUMERS

Among those who feel regulatory agencies are captured by the industries they regulate, an oft-advocated solution is to redesign agencies so that they are more responsive to consumers than they are to the industry. Such an argument is easy to justify normatively because reconciling democracy with responsiveness to vested interests is not easy. Two formal mechanisms proposed to increase the responsiveness of regulatory agencies to consumers are an **Agency for Consumer Advocacy** and the use of public funds to support consumer participation in agency procedures. Other proposals sometimes linked to consumer responsiveness are requirements that regulatory meetings be open to the public, requirements that citizens have access to agency information (the Freedom of

Information Act), and establishment of agency advisory committees (see Cooper, 1983:295 ff).

CREATE AN AGENCY FOR CONSUMER ADVOCACY   The proposal to create an agency whose function would be to represent the consumer viewpoint before other agencies was at one time an issue on the agenda. In 1976 both houses of Congress passed legislation creating an Agency for Consumer Advocacy. Despite earlier support by President Ford, the legislation was vetoed for political reasons. Ford at the time was locked in a heated battle for the Republican nomination with Ronald Reagan, and the move was seen as an effort to attract conservative votes. A similar bill was defeated by Congress in 1978, marking for some observers the end of the contemporary era of consumer protection (see Pertschuk, 1982). The Reagan and Bush administrations showed little interest in similar legislation. The short-term prospects for a consumer agency are not promising, especially since reviews of such ombudsman-like institutions reveal at best a minimal level of effectiveness (Meier, 1993:186-187).

USE PUBLIC FUNDS TO SUPPORT CONSUMER PARTICIPATION IN AGENCY PROCEEDINGS Another option for consumer representation is to allow individual consumers to represent themselves and to permit them to do so by providing federal funds to underwrite the costs. Without assistance, participation by regulated groups outnumbers that of public interest groups nine to one (Breyer, 1982:352). The Federal Trade Commission, for example, funded intervenors for a time during the 1970s. The program was intensely disliked by business, which perceived that the government was funding the other side and, therefore, was somewhat biased. Congress restricted **intervenor programs** by limiting funds and using riders to prevent spending for this purpose.

Efforts to create mechanisms to increase responsiveness to consumers face two fundamental problems. First, consumers as a group are similar to the general public; they are far too varied a group to be represented by a single viewpoint. Although a number of consumer organizations advocate concern for both value for money and equity for all consumers in marketplace transactions, issues of primary importance to the consumer interest take precedence. Interesting arguments have been presented by individuals such as James Miller that some consumers might actually prefer cheap quality (and possibly unsafe) goods. Representing the diversity of views that consumers have within a single agency might well be impossible.

Second, representation of consumer interests does not necessarily result in responsiveness to consumer viewpoints. During the 1980s, a wide variety of public interest groups existed on the Washington scene, but regulatory agencies, in general, were not overly responsive to their petitions. Perhaps formal representation of consumer interests is less important than appointing regulators who hold proconsumer values.

RESPONSIVENESS TO THE PRESIDENT

Proposals for making regulatory agencies more responsive to the president date back to Franklin Roosevelt's attempt to remove William Humphrey from the Federal Trade Commission. In light of recent evidence, however, some questions must be raised about whether or not presidents need additional authority to govern regulation. By using the powers of appointment and budget, both Presidents Carter and Reagan were able to redirect the activities of many regulatory agencies (Wood and Waterman, 1994; Meier 1993:232). Several examples of policy change in response to presidential initiatives can be noted. OSHA changed from a nitpicking enforcer of safety regulations to an organization concerned with health issues under Carter's administrator Eula Bingham; under Reagan's head, Thorne Auchter, the agency deemphasized its enforcement programs. Under Joan Claybrook (Carter), the National Highway Traffic Safety Administration was a strict regulator of automobile safety whereas under Raymond Peck and Diane Steed (Reagan), many safety rules were been relaxed. Similar contrasts under Carter and Reagan could be noted for the EEOC, the FTC, the ICC, etc. (Wood and Waterman, 1994).

Recent presidents have had little trouble in gaining control over the direction of regulation; Carter generally increased the intensity of social regulation while moving toward economic deregulation; Reagan decreased the intensity of regulation in all areas (except trucking). President Reagan was able to achieve major budget cuts in regulatory agencies and reduce the number of rules they promulgated by 25 percent (Eisner, 1993:190).

For those seeking to enhance further the president's control over regulatory agencies, three mechanisms are proposed. Advocates favor (1) decreased independence for regulatory commissions, (2) greater formal oversight by the president, or (3) a regulatory budget. Each of these is discussed in turn.

DECREASED INDEPENDENCE FOR REGULATORY COMMISSIONS Independent regulatory commissions have always concerned regulatory analysts. Because regulatory commissioners serve long, overlapping terms, commissioners appointed by previous presidents often continue to serve. In such a situation, the regulatory commission can operate independently from the president's wishes. Some independent commissions also have the authority to submit their budgets directly to Congress so that the budget control normally operated through OMB is absent.

Advocates of decreased independence fail to realize, however, that independence is a minor obstacle for the president. The president can designate the chairperson of all but a handful of independent commissions and with resignations can often control a majority of the board within a year or two. President Reagan, for example, had little trouble asserting control over the EEOC, the ICC, and the FTC. In the process, he was able to alter the direction of regulatory policy established by President Carter. Given the attachment of Congress to the independent commission structure, proposals to limit independence are likely to generate a great deal of political conflict for little potential gain.

GREATER FORMAL OVERSIGHT BY THE PRESIDENT Proposals for increased oversight involve establishing formal mechanisms for reviewing regulations issued by the agencies, and several recent presidents have done so. Gerald Ford had the inflation impact process, Carter had his Regulatory Analysis Review Group, and Ronald Reagan established a Presidential Task Force on Regulatory Relief supplemented by analysis performed by the Office of Management and Budget. The OMB played a reduced role in the Bush administration after the nominee for the agency's Office of Information and Regulatory Affairs failed the confirmation process. Instead the President's Council on

Competitiveness, headed by Vice President Dan Quayle, became the center of the administration's efforts to assert control over regulatory review (Eisner, 1993:191). Clinton continued the oversight process through OMB, although in a reduced and reshaped form.

Reagan's regulatory review mechanism provides a particularly good opportunity to examine the effectiveness of increased presidential oversight. President Reagan, on taking office, froze a series of **"midnight rules"** issued in the last days of the Carter administration. He then issued **executive order 12291**, subjecting regulations to cost-benefit standards with review based in OMB. Actions on the midnight rules suggested the direction of the new oversight procedure. Of the 172 frozen rules, 100 were eventually approved. Many of these rules were minor or were mandated by emergencies or court orders (Thompson and Jones, 1982:161). Thirty-five rules were withdrawn, and 37 more were held back for further study. The volume of regulation was clearly on the decline.

After two and one-half years of operation, the president announced that the President's Task Force on Regulatory Relief had achieved its goal and was being disbanded (Presidential Task Force, 1983). According to Vice-President Bush, the actions of the Task Force along with OMB would save the American public $150 billion over a ten-year period. Closer analysis, however, suggests that such savings were exaggerated. The largest saving, for example, was $40 billion in increased interest paid on deposits resulting from the Garn-St Germain Act, an action hardly the result of the Presidential Task Force. As the Garn-St Germain Act is widely held to have played a large role in precipitating the savings and loan crisis—a crisis that required a $400 billion taxpayer bailout—such purported savings are even more questionable. In addition, many other suggested gains such as reduced costs to the automobile industry were simply transferred costs because they imposed additional costs on insurance companies and consumers.

The review process had examined 6,701 regulations by June of 1983; of these rules, 89 final and 53 proposed rules were reviewed because they were defined as major (imposing costs of $100 million or more). A total of 59 impact analyses were performed (Presidential Task Force, 1983:56). An overwhelming proportion of the rules was approved. Some 86 percent were accepted as is, another 8 percent were accepted after only minor changes. Only 3 percent of all rules (182) were withdrawn or returned to the agencies. A closer examination of these rules suggests that they were primarily social regulations. The EPA had by far the greatest number of rules rejected (53); the Department of Commerce and the Department of Transportation (NHTSA rules on automobile safety) were the only other agencies in double figures. The reasons for rejecting rules were made fairly clear: "[T]he administration has made little effort to hide the fact that reviews of some rules have been designed primarily to provide relief to a troubled industry" (Litan and Nordhaus, 1983:122). As the Reagan administration exerted control over the regulatory agencies, the OMB review process in one sense became less important because fewer "controversial" rules were submitted by the agencies; accordingly, most of the rules withdrawn or rejected occurred early in the process.

In general, however, the review process was highly controversial, and critics accused the White House of using it to favor business interests and to circumvent the Administrative Procedure Act (Eisner, 1993:191; West, 1995). During Reagan's second term a series of scandals in several regulatory agencies made regulatory review and control increasingly politically expensive. Regulatory activity subsequently increased. Although Bush inherited the regulatory review mechanism instituted by Reagan—indeed, as head of the Task Force on Regulatory Relief he had a large hand in creating it—regulatory activity during his administration picked up considerably.

A REGULATORY BUDGET   A final reform to increase presidential control favored by a variety of regulatory analysts is the regulatory budget (see Thompson and Jones, 1982:180 ff; Litan and Nordhaus, 1983:133 ff). Originally proposed by economist Robert Crandall, the **regulatory budget** recognizes that agency budgets are only a small part of the costs of regulation and that a far larger cost is the cost of compliance. Under the regulatory budget, a government-wide budget for regulatory costs would be adopted, and each agency would be allocated a cost budget. The process would parallel the regular budget process through both the executive and Congress. The idea behind a regulatory budget is not only to limit private sector costs but also to force Congress and the president to make trade-offs between regulatory programs (e.g., should we require air bags at a cost of X or tighten exposure to benzene standards?—see Kosters, 1980:69).

Although the regulatory budget is intuitively attractive, it has four limitations that might prevent its achieving politically efficient trade-offs:

First, costs are often extremely difficult to measure (Litan and Nordhaus, 1983:82; Stone, 1982:265), and industry estimates are clearly biased. In the classic vinyl chloride case, industry estimated compliance costs at between $60 and $90 billion whereas actual compliance costs were only $250 million (see Chapter 8). The CPSC estimated compliance costs for flammable fabrics regulation in the furniture industry at $57 million to $87 million; the textile manufacturers' estimate was $1.3 billion (see Litan and Nordhaus, 1983:152).

Second, the regulatory budget would overemphasize costs relative to benefits. A high-cost program may well be preferred over a low-cost program if the former program yields greater benefits to society. Focusing on costs only encourages regulatory agencies to suboptimize (Thompson and Jones, 1982:184).

Third, the regulatory budget might have as a second-order consequence the creation of an even larger federal bureaucracy. To operate successfully, regulatory agencies as well as OMB and Congress would need more staff. Neither industry nor agency estimates could be taken as unbiased without further checks. The process would create numerous jobs for economists and auditors (see Stone, 1982:264).

Fourth, the regulatory budget does not appear to have any incentives for agency compliance. If the agency incorrectly estimates its costs, a regulatory budget provides no obvious penalty as there is in the regular budget process when the agency runs out of money (Litan and Nordhaus, 1983:135; L. J. White, 1981:227). Agency overruns could be deducted from the next year's budget as a penalty; however, such a process would not allow the trade-off that is the heart of the regulatory budget.

Although the regulatory budget may improve the regulatory process, it is no panacea. The likely impact of a regulatory budget would be to delay the regulatory process even more than it is delayed now. Such delays are not policy neutral; they benefit opponents of regulation and discourage regulatory agencies from action. According to Lawrence J.

White (1981:221), the Regulatory Analysis Review Group process in the Carter administration actually resulted in no major rules being issued for a six-month period in 1979.

RESPONSIVENESS TO CONGRESS

Regulatory agencies have been criticized as unresponsive to the wishes of Congress. Claims of unresponsiveness should not be unexpected given the vague goals established for most regulatory agencies and the passing interest most members of Congress have in regulation. In fact, regulatory agencies do respond to Congress (Weingast and Moran, 1983; Wood, 1992), but they do not respond as fast as Congress would like. In the late 1970s, the FTC was frequently criticized for being unresponsive to Congress when FTC programs vigorously regulated small business (see Pertschuk, 1982). The FTC, however, began these initiatives after urging from Congress in the early 1970s, a Congress more liberal than the one in the late 1970s (see Weingast and Moran, 1982). Regulators respond to Congress; they just do so slowly. The slow response is a function of two factors. First, regulatory agencies are fairly small and, thus, often get lost in the budget and oversight process; they may go years with little direction from Congress. Second, Congress speaks with many voices so that responsiveness to one member of Congress may result in actions unresponsive to another (Ripley and Franklin, 1991:125-144).

SUNSET LEGISLATION Sunset legislation is often proposed to make regulatory agencies more responsive to Congress. Under **sunset legislation**, an agency is authorized to operate for a fixed period of years. If Congress fails to reauthorize the agency, it will cease to exist. Sunset legislation forces the agency to justify itself periodically; by requiring **formal reauthorization**, the sunset concept makes the normal, incremental, decision-making processes work against retaining the agency.

Sunset legislation is fairly popular. Approximately 35 states and several federal statutes have sunset provisions. State-level evidence indicates that sunset legislation can be effective in eliminating obsolete or ineffective programs (Kearney, 1990), and a comprehensive sunset law has been proposed as a way to establish congressional control over administrative priorities (Meier, 1993:235-236).

Sunset provisions, however, have shortcomings. It is expensive (Stone, 1982:273; Avery, 1980:42). Funds must be spent to analyze agency missions and performance. In Colorado, the first sunset review abolished 3 of the 13 agencies reviewed (agencies that regulated boxing, sanitarians, and shorthand reporters); this saved $11,000, but the process itself cost $212,000 (Stone, 1982:273).

The minor agencies affected in Colorado suggests that the impact of the sunset process may be trivial. At the federal level, this has been true. The Commodity Futures Trading Commission had its law changed to have the chairman serve at the pleasure of the president rather than for a fixed term. The only impact of the CPSC sunset legislation was that the commission chairperson resigned (Avery, 1980:43). The sunset process appears to have a disproportionate impact on minor agencies too weak to defend themselves (Slaughter, 1986:242; Kearney, 1990:52). It was used, for example, to eliminate 800 advisory commissions during the Carter administration (Clark, Kosters, and

Miller, 1980:46). The example of Colorado has been repeated several times by other states (Heffron with McFeeley, 1983:388; Kearney, 1990).

Finally, failure to reauthorize an agency does not mean the agency's termination. The Federal Trade Commission has often operated via **continuing resolution** when its authorizing legislation lapsed. Most of the legislation supporting the Environmental Protection Agency had expired by 1984, but the agency continued to operate on a year to year basis.

LEGISLATIVE VETO   Another major reform designed to make regulatory agencies more responsive to Congress is the legislative veto. According to former Senator Harrison Schmitt (1980:53), "The **legislative veto** is a means to return legislative responsibility to elected representatives white at the same time improving the quality of necessary administrative action." Under the legislative veto, Congress authorizes an agency to act in a certain area, but all rules must be presented to Congress for action before they are finalized. Legislative vetoes were adopted in over 200 pieces of legislation although they varied in the exact procedure Congress must use to veto an administrative action.

The legislative veto was declared unconstitutional by the Supreme Court in *INS* v. *Chadha*. The Court objected to the veto because it violated separation of powers and eliminated the president (by preventing a veto) from the legislative process. The Court's ruling raised questions about hundreds of federal laws containing veto-like provisions (Craig, 1983), and prompted a concerted effort to create an alternative form of the veto that could withstand a court challenger. In the two years following the *Chadha* decision Congress passed 53 laws containing legislative veto provisions, all of them aimed at passing constitutional muster (Cooper, 1986:60; Fisher, 1984 and 1985).

The legislative veto is actually nothing more than a streamlined version of legislation that allows Congress to intervene in the regulatory process. In fact, legislation has resulted in far more interventions than has the legislative veto. Instances of legislation used to change regulatory decisions after the fact also exist; Congress prohibited NHTSA from requiring seat belt interlock ignition systems and restricted the FTC's regulation of cigarette advertising (Fritschler, 1975).

Because Congress via legislation can and has determined the direction of regulation, a new legislative veto offers little improvement over current methods. In addition, the veto suffers from three limitations:

First, literally thousands of regulations are proposed and issued every year. Unless some selection device was used (limited to major regulations), the volume of regulations would overwhelm Congress. As Meier (1993:235) says, "The veto essentially encourages broad general grants of authority and reduces Congress to a negative role of nitpicking administrative action."

Second, the veto by definition involves a case-by-case review of regulations. In terms of responsiveness to Congress, the problem is not a matter of individual deviations but rather of control over the general direction of regulatory policy.

Third, regulation was initially delegated to agencies so that some expertise could be applied to solving regulatory problems. Congress has shown little willingness to develop expertise on complex regulatory issues; the decision to require scrubbing all coal no matter how little sulfur content it contained is an excellent example. Given this lack of expertise, would case-by-case veto actions improve the overall quality of regulation? Arguing that FTC regulation was improved via the used-car veto is difficult. The veto offers little chance of improvement because it does not permit Congress to do anything it could not do via other mechanisms. As Supreme Court Justice Antonin Scalia (1980:60) once said, "The real problem is not congressional power to reverse the agencies. Congress has that power and has always had it. The question is congressional will or congressional capacity."

RESPONSIVENESS TO COURTS

The responsiveness of bureaucratic organizations to the rule of law is a hallowed tradition (Fried, 1976; West, 1995). To foster this responsiveness, regulatory agencies could be made more accountable to the courts, and during the 1970s and early 1980s there were a number of attempts to extend court control over regulatory agencies. The foremost advocate of this was Senator Dale Bumpers of Arkansas. Although the Bumpers proposal went through various changes, it essentially had three parts. First, the standard for an administrative decision on questions of fact would be increased from **"supported by the evidence"** to **"preponderance of the evidence."** In theory, this would make regulatory agencies use the stricter standard of the courts. Second, in determining questions of law, courts would no longer defer to **agency expertise**. Third, in disputes between citizens and agencies, the **burden of proof** would be on the agency rather than on the citizen. The 1980 Republican party platform had a plank supporting similar reforms. In 1982 the Bumpers proposal actually passed the Senate but never won approval in the House.

Other proposals suggest lengthening the time period for comments in rulemaking, expanding notice procedures, and requiring more impact analyses (Litan and Nordhaus, 1983:225). In essence, all attempts to make regulation more responsive to the courts seek to maximize procedural fairness and are willing to tolerate longer delays.

Suggestions to judicialize the regulatory process further go counter to much of the scholarship on regulation (see Warren, 1982:287). Regulation is an **administrative process** because administrative agencies have advantages of speed and expertise. To judicialize administrative procedures robs the administrative process of a major strength. In areas of regulation where decisions are made by the courts (equal employment policy, antitrust policy), the policy process operates at a leisurely pace; and the quality of policy is no better.

Recent critics of judicializing the administrative process have also been numerous. The Ash Council argued that judicial review often stressed legal values to the detriment of economic, technical, and social values (see Daly and Brady, 1976:183). The presidential adviser Lloyd Cutler suggested that the most effective regulatory reform might be to close the law schools; although said in jest, his criticism was over-legalized regulation (Cutler, 1980:154). A former EPA administrator, Douglas Costle, noted that the delay resulting from judicialized procedures and legal appeals has substantive implications in that "litigation often benefits the polluter more than it does the public. By dragging a suit through the courts as long as possible, a polluter can postpone necessary capital expenditures and delay using pollution controls long enough to gain a substantial financial advantage over complying competitors" (Costle, 1980:132).

CONCLUSION

Regulatory policy is far too varied for simple solutions to work in all areas of regulation. General reforms such as those discussed in this chapter are unlikely to produce the benefits that substantive reforms of specific regulatory policies can. Deregulation, the centerpiece of regulatory reform in the 1970s and 1980s, has shown to be beneficial in some instances, but has at best mixed success as a general policy. Under the Reagan and Bush administrations it was simply oversold and underfunded. Even while still in office, these administrations seemed to recognize that the reality of deregulation fell far short of its rhetorical promises. The deregulatory movement seemed to crest even before Bush; and his successor, Bill Clinton, did not bring a broad-based ideological antipathy toward regulation. Soon after Clinton's election many forecast increased regulatory activity in areas such as consumer protection and occupational health and safety, although further deregulation appeared to be an option under the right economic circumstances (Walsh, 1993). While still a tool to be considered, deregulation rightly is no longer viewed as a general restorative for a troubled regulatory process.

The generalizations that arose around the deregulatory banner provide a sharp lesson on the dangers of attributing uniform problems or prescribing **uniform cures** to the regulatory process. The regulatory policies of the United States continue to reflect political forces, economic constraints, legal imperatives, bureaucratic routines, and numerous other social forces. The exact combination of forces varies from area to area, limiting generalizations about regulation and making uniform reforms impossible.

Disagreements about the most effective reform proposals are often at heart disagreements about the goals that regulation should serve. Just as those who favor efficiency goals predictably favor deregulation or incentive systems, so those who favor equity goals are likely to call for greater regulation. Disagreements over regulatory reforms reflect disagreements over fundamental political goals.

Despite this variation and conflict, regulatory reform is possible. Breyer (1982) accurately notes that regulatory reform must be conducted on a case-by-case basis, focusing on substantive changes in regulation. The success of reform in the airline industry, trucking, occupational safety and health, and other areas has come as the result of substantive changes in the policies rather than as the result of general changes in the regulatory process. The potential areas of reform are numerous, and they can only be reformed by addressing each problem area one at a time.

References

"A Year of Crucial Decision: 25th Annual Environmental Quality Index." *National Wildlife* 31(2):34-41.

AARP. 1987. *Effective Physician Oversight: Prescription for Medical Licensing Board Reform.* Washington: AARP Health Advocacy Services Program Department. p10.

AARP. 1986. *Unreasonable Regulation = Unreasonable Prices; A Report on the Effect of Certain State Occupational Licensing Regulations on Consumers.* Washington: AARP Consumer Affairs Section.

Abrams, Robert and Lloyd Constantine. 1991. "Dual Antitrust Enforcement in the 1990s." 484-515, in *Revitalizing Antitrust in its Second Century,* ed. Harry First, Eleanor M. Fox and Robert Pitofsky, New York: Quorum Books.

Abramson, Paul R., John H. Aldrich, and David W. Rohde. 1983. *Continuity and Change in the 1980 Election.* Washington, D.C.: Congressional Quarterly Press.

Accident Facts. National Safety Council, 1994 edition.

Achtenberg, Emily P. 1973. "The Social Utility of Rent Control," in Jon Pynoos and others, ed, *Housing Urban America.* Chicago, IL: Aldine.

Ackerman, Bruce A., and William T. Hassler. 1981. *Clean Coal Dirty Air.* New Haven: Yale University Press.

Adler, Jonathan. 1992. "Clean Fuels, Dirty Air." In *Environmental Politics: Public Costs, Private Rewards*, ed. Michael Greve and Richard Smith. New York: Praeger.

Advisory Commission on Intergovernmental Relations. 1991. *Significant Features of Fiscal Federalism, Volume 2: Revenues and Expenditures.* Washington, D.C.: ACIR.

Agricultural Economics Report 768. 1994. *Food Marketing Review 1992-1993.* Washington, D.C.: The United States Department of Agriculture, Economic Research Service: April.

Akers, Ronald L. 1968. "The Professional Association and the Legal Regulation of Practice." *Law and Society Review* 2 (May) 463-482.

Albrecht, Virginia S. and Golode, Bernard N. 1994. "Wetland Regulation In The Real World," Washington, D.C. (February).

Alm, Alvin. 1992. "A Need for New Approaches." *EPA Journal* 18(2): 7-11.

Amel, Dean F., and J. Nellie Liang 1992. "The Relationship between Entry into Banking Markets and Changes in Legal Restrictions on Entry." *Antitrust Bulletin* 37(3): 631-649.

American Enterprise Institute. 1981. *Major Regulatory Initiatives During 1980.* Washington, D.C.: American Enterprise Institute.

Amy, Douglas. 1990. "Environmental Dispute Resolution: The Promise and the Pitfalls." In *Environmental Policy in the 1990s,* ed. Norman Vig and Michael Kraft. Washington, D.C.: Congressional Quarterly.

Anderson, Douglas D. 1980. "State Regulation of Electric Utilities." In *The Politics of Regulation,* ed. James Q. Wilson. New York: Basic Books, pp. 3-41.

Anderson, Harry, Rich Thomas, and Christopher Ma. 1983. "Rewriting Antitrust Rules." *Newsweek* (August 29), 50-52.

Anderson, James E. 1994. *Public Policymaking, 2nd ed.* Boston: Houghton Mifflin Company.

Anderson, James E. 1982. "Agricultural Marketing Orders and the Process and Politics of Self-Regulation." *Policy Studies Review* 2:97-111.

Anderson, James E., David W. Brady, and Charles S. Bullock. 1977. *Public Policy and Politics in America.* N. Scituate, MA: Duxbury Press.

Anderson, Joan and Bob Patterson. "Enforcement-Answers to Some Frequently Asked Questions." *Job Safety and Health Quarterly* 44:16-20.

Andrews, Richard. 1994. "Risk-Based Decisionmaking." In *Environmental Policy in the 1990s, second edition*, ed. Norman Vig and Michael Kraft. Washington, D.C.: Congressional Quarterly.

Andrews, Richard. 1992. "Heading Off Potential Problems." *EPA Journal* 18(2):40-45.

Andrews, Richard. 1976. *Environmental Policy and Administrative Change*. Lexington, MA: Lexington Books.

Anthan, George. 1980. "The Super Farm Policy." *Des Moines Register* (June 1).

Archea, J., B.L. Collins, and F.I. Stahl. 1979. *Guidelines for Stair Safety*. Washington, D.C.: Department of Commerce.

Areeda Phillip. 1984. "The State of the Law." *Regulation* 8 (January-February): 19-23.

Armentano, Dominick T. 1982. *Antitrust and Monopoly*. New York: Wiley.

Asch, Peter, and Joseph Seneca. 1978. "Some Evidence on the Distribution of Air Quality." *Land Economics* 54: 278-97.

Ashford, Nicholas A. 1976. *Crisis in the Workplace: Occupational Disease and Injury*. Cambridge, MA: MIT Press.

Association of State and Interstate Water Pollution Control Officials. 1984. *America's Clean Water: The State's Evaluation of Progress 1972-1982*. Washington, D.C.: ASIWPCA.

Audretsch, David B. 1983. *The Effectiveness of Antitrust Policy Toward Horizontal Mergers*. Ann Arbor, Mich.: UMI Research Press.

Avery, Dennis. 1980. "The Record on Sunset Review of Two Agencies." In *Reforming Regulations*. eds. Timothy B. Clark, Marvin H. Kosters, and James C. Miller. Washington, D.C.: American Enterprise Institute, pp. 41-45.

Azumi, Koya, and Jerald Hage. 1972. *Organizational Systems*. Lexington, MA: D. C. Heath.

Baby Walkers, Advance Notice of Proposed Rulemaking, 59 Fed. Reg. 39306, 1994.

Bacow, Lawrence S. 1982. "Private Bargaining and Public Regulation." In *Social Regulation*, Eugene Bardach and Robert A. Kagan, eds. San Francisco: ICS Press, pp. 201-220.

Bailey, Martin J. 1980. *Reducing Risks to Life*. Washington, D.C.: American Enterprise Institute.

Baldwin, Sidney. 1968. *Politics and Poverty*. Chapel Hill: University of North Carolina Press.

Ball, Howard. 1984. *Controlling Regulatory Sprawl*. Westport, CT: Greenwood Press.

Bandow, Doug. 1992. "Is Business Drowning in a New Regulatory Tide?" *Business and Society Review*. (Summer): 45-49.

Bardach, Eugene, and Robert A. Kagan. 1982. *Going by the Book*. Philadelphia: Temple University Press.

Bartel, Ann P. and Lacy Glenn Thomas. 1985. "Direct and Indirect Effects of Regulation: A New Look at OSHA"s Impact." *Journal of Law and Economics* 18: 1-25.

Barth, James R. 1991. *The Great Savings and Loan Debacle*. Washington, D.C.: American Enterprise Institute Press.

Barton, Weldon V. 1976. "Coalition-Building in the United States House of Representatives." In *Cases in Public Policy-making*, James E. Anderson, ed. New York: Praeger, pp. 141-161.

Battaile, Janet. 1992. "Bush Overrides Agency on Pollution Restrictions," *New York Times*, 17 May, sec. A.

Beales, J. Howard. 1980. "The Economics of Regulating the Professions." In *Regulating the Professions*, Roger D. Blair and Stephen Rubin, eds. Lexington, MA: Lexington Books, pp.125-142.

Belonzi, Arthur, Arthur D'Antonio, and Gary Helfand. 1977. *The Weary Watchdogs*. Wayne, N.J.: Avery Publishing Group.

Beng, Song Chong 1991. "The Effects of Interstate Banking on Commercial Banks' Risk and Profitability." *Review of Economics and Statistics* 73(1): 78-84.

Benham, Lee. 1972. "The Effects of Advertising on the Price of Eyeglasses." *Journal of Law and Economics* 15: 337-351.

Benham, Lee. 1980. "The Demand for Occupational Licensure." In *Occupational Licensing and Regulation*, ed. Simon Rottenberg. Washington, D.C.: American Enterprise Institute, pp. 13-25.

Benham, Lee and Alexandra Benham. 1975. "Regulating Through the Professions: A Perspective on Information Control." *Journal of Law and Economics* 18 (October), 421-447.

Bernstein, Marver H. 1955. *Regulating Business by Independent Commission.* Princeton: Princeton University Press.

Berry, Frances Stokes. 1982. "The States' Occupational Licensing Debate." *State Government News* 25 (May): 10-14.

Berry, Jeffrey M. 1977. *Lobbying for the People.* Princeton: Princeton University Press.

Berry, Jeffrey M. 1984. *The Interest Group Society.* Boston: Little, Brown.

Bianco, David P., ed. 1993. *Professional and Occupational Licensing Directory: A Descriptive Guide to State and Federal Licensing, Registration, and Certification Requirements.* Detroit: Gale Research.

Bicycle Helmets, Proposed Rule, 59 Fed. Reg. 41719, 1994.

Blair, Roger D., and David L. Kaserman. 1980. "Preservation of Quality and Sanctions Within the Professions." In *Regulating the Professions,* Roger D. Blair and Stephen Rubin, eds. Lexington, MA: Lexington Books, pp. 185-198.

Blumm, Michael. 1993. "Property Myths, Judicial Activism, and the Lucas Case." *Environmental Law* 23:907-17.

Board of Governors of the Federal Reserve System. 1994a. "Domestic Financial Statistics." *Federal Reserve Bulletin* 80: A36-A41.

Board of Governors of the Federal Reserve System. 1994b. "Monetary Policy Report to the Congress." *Federal Reserve Bulletin* 80: 199-219.

Board of Governors of the Federal Reserve System 1994c. "Recent Development in Credit Card Pricing." *Federal Reserve Bulletin* 80: 296-301.

Bollier, David and Joan Claybrook. 1986. *Freedom from Harm: The Civilizing Influence of Health, Safety and Environmental Regulation.* Washington: Public Citizen & Democracy Project.

Bork, Robert H. 1978. *The Antitrust Paradox.* New York: Basic Books.

Bosso, Christopher. 1994. "After the Movement: Environmental Activism in the 1990s." In *Environmental Policy in the 1990s, second edition,* ed. Norman Vig and Michael Kraft. Washington, D.C.: Congressional Quarterly.

Bosso, Christopher. 1987. *Pesticides and Politics: The Lifecycle of a Public Issue.* Pittsburgh, PA: University of Pittsburgh Press.

Boulier, Bryan D. 1980. "An Empirical Examination of the Influence of Licensure and Licensure Reform on the Geographical Distribution of Dentists." In *Occupational Licensing and Regulation,* Simon Rottenberg, ed. Washington, D.C.: American Enterprise Institute, pp. 73-97.

Bovard, James. 1989. "Farm Policy Follies." *The Public Interest* 95: 75-87.

Breyer, Stephen. 1982. *Regulation and Its Reform.* Cambridge, MA: Harvard University Press.

Brinegar, Pamela L., and Kara L. Schmitt. 1992. "State Occupational and Professional Licensure." *The Book of The States 1992-93.* Lexington, KY: The Council Of State Governments, 567-580.

Brobeck, Stephen. 1991. "Economic Deregulation and the Least Affluent: Consumer Protection Strategies." *Journal of Social Issues* 47:169-191.

Brobeck, Stephen and Anne C. Averyt. 1983. *The Product Safety Book.* New York: E.P. Dutton, Inc.

Broder, Ivy. N.d. "Ambient Particulate Levels and Capital Expenditures: An Empirical Analysis." Photocopy. Department of Economics, American University, Washington, D.C.

Brown, Anthony. 1987. *The Politics of Airline Deregulation.* Knoxville: University of Tennessee Press.

Brown, Clarence J. 1980. "Legislating a Regulatory Budget." In *Reforming Regulation,* Timothy B. Clark, Marvin H. Kosters, and James C. Miller, eds. Washington, D.C.: American Enterprise Institute, pp. 71-75.

Brown, Michael. 1981. *Laying Waste: The Poisoning of America by Toxic Chemicals.* New York: Washington Square Press.

Browne, William P. 1988. *Private Interests, Public Policy, and American Agriculture.* Lawrence, KS: University Press of Kansas.

Browne, William P., Jerry R. Skees, Louis E. Swanson, Paul B. Thompson, and Laurian J. Unnevehr. 1992. *Sacred Cows and Hot Potatoes: Agrarian Myths in Agricultural Policy.* Boulder, CO: Westview Press.

Browning, Graeme. 1992a. "A Nudge Toward Greener Pastures." *National Journal* 24: 1601.

Browning, Graeme. 1992b. "Sagging Aggies." *National Journal* 24:452-5.

Brownstein, Ronald. 1983. "Merger Wars-Congress, SEC Take Aim at Hostile Corporate Takeover Moves." *National Journal* 15:1538-1541.

Brozen, Yale. 1982. *Concentration, Mergers and Public Policy.* New York: Macmillan.

Brueggeman, W. B. and J.D. Fischer. 1993. *Real Estate Finance and Investments.* Homewood, IL: Irwin.

"BST Labeling Law Challenged in Vermont." 1994. *Food Chemical News* 36 #10 (May 2), 49.

Buchholz, Rogene A. 1982. *Business, Environment and Public Policy.* Englewood Cliffs, N.J.: Prentice-Hall.

Bullard, Robert. 1990. *Dumping in Dixie: Race, Class, and Environmental Quality.* Boulder, CO: Westview.

Burby, Raymond and Robert Patterson. 1992. "Improving Compliance With State Environmental Regulations." *Journal of Policy Analysis and Management* 12:753-72.

Bureau of the Census. 1987. *1987 Census of Manufacturers: Concentration Ratios in Manufacturing.* Washington D.C.: U.S. Department of Commerce.

Butler, Richard J. 1983. "Wage and Injury Rate Response to Shifting Levels of Workers' Compensation." In *Safety and the Workforce.* John D. Worrall, ed. Ithaca, N.Y.: ILR Press, pp. 61-86.

Butter, Irene. 1976. *A Comparative Study of State Licensure Policies.* Hyattsville, Maryland: National Center for Health Services Research.

Caldwell, Lynton. 1982. *Science and the National Environmental Policy Act.* University, AL.: University of Alabama Press, 1982.

Calvert, Jerry. 1989. "Party Politics and Environmental Policy." In *Environmental Politics and Policy: Theories and Evidence,* ed. James Lester. Durham, NC: Duke University Press.

Canner, G. B., and R. D. Kurtz. 1985. *Service Charges as a Source of Bank Income and their Impact on Consumers.* Staff study. Washington, D.C.: Board of Governors of the Federal Reserve System.

Canner, G. B. and C.A. Luckett. 1992. "Developments in the Pricing of Credit Card Services." *Federal Reserve Bulletin* 78: 652-666.

Canon, Bradley, and Micheal Giles. 1972. "Recurring Litigants: Federal Agencies Before the Supreme Court." *Western Political Quarterly* 25: 183-191.

Carey, John L., and William 0. Doherty. 1967. "State Regulation of Certified Public Accountants." *State Government* (Winter): 26-30.

Carney, Elizabeth. 1994. "Lobbying Flood on Clean Water Bills." *National Journal* 26:664.

Carney, Elizabeth. 1992. "Industry Plays the Grassroots Card." *National Journal* 24:281-82.

Carron, Andrew S. 1982. *The Plight of the Thrift Institutions.* Washington, D.C.: Brookings.

Carson, D.H. J.C. Archea. S.T. Margulis, and F.E. Carson. 1979. *Safety on Stairs.* Washington, D.C.: Department of Commerce.

Carson, Rachel. 1962. *Silent Spring.* Boston: Houghton Mifflin.

Catalina, Camia. 1994. "Congress Bracing to Renew 1972 Water Law." *Congressional Quarterly Weekly Reporter* 52:164-66.

CFAnews. various issues. Washington, D.C.: Consumer Federation of America.

Chamness, R. 1994. "RESPA's 'Coverage' Just Got Broader." *ABA Banking Journal* 86(5): 36-38.

Chesney, James D. 1984. "Citizen Participation on Regulatory Boards." *Journal of Health Politics, Policy and Law.* (Spring) 125-135.

Child Safety Protection Act, *Congressional Record*, November 20, 1993, S 16889.

Chubb, John E. 1985. "The Political Economy of Federalism." *American Political Science Review.* 79: 994-1015.

Claiborne, William. 1994. "Unfunded Mandates Occupy Center Stage." *Washington Post*, 18 May, sec. A.

Clark, Timothy B., Marvin H. Kosters, and James C. Miller. 1980. *Reforming Regulation.* Washington, D.C.: American Enterprise Institute.

Cleland-Hamnett, Wendy. 1993. "The Role of Comparative Risk Analysis." *EPA Journal* 19(1):19-23.

Cocheo, Steve. 1994a. "Justice Opens Fire on Fair-lending Issues." *ABA Banking Journal.* (March): 32-38.

Cocheo, Steve. 1994b. "'Ratio-less' Underwriting Slated for Expansion." *ABA Banking Journal* 86(9): 80-82.

Cochrane, Willard W., and Mary E. Ryan. 1976. *American Farm Policy, 1948-1973.* Minneapolis: University of Minnesota Press.

Cohen, Jeffrey E. 1992. *The Politics of Telecommunications Regulation.* Armonk, NY: M.E. Sharpe.

Cohen, Richard. 1994. "An Ominous Rumbling in the Ranks." *National Journal* 26:379.

Cohen, Steven and Gary Weiskopf. 1990. "Beyond Incrementalism: Cross Media Environmental Management in the Environmental Protection Agency." In *Regulatory Federalism, Natural Resources, and Environmental Management*, ed. Michael Hamilton. Washington, D.C.: ASPA.

Colford, Steven W. 1991. "FDA Getting Tougher." *Advertising Age* (April 29): 1,3.

Colwell, Peter F. and Abdullah Yavas. 1992. "The Value of Building Codes." *Journal of the American Real Estate and Urban Economics Association* 20(4):501-517.

Comanor, W. S., and Harvey Leibenstein. 1969. "Allocative Efficiency, X-Efficiency, and the Measurement of Welfare Losses." *Economica* (August): 304-309.

Commission for Racial Justice. 1987. *Toxic Wastes and Race in the United States.* New York: United Church of Christ.

Committee on Banking, Housing, and Urban Affairs. 1993a. *The Consumer Reporting Reform Act of 1994*, Report 103-209. Washington, D.C.: Government Printing Office.

Committee on Banking, Housing, and Urban Affairs. 1993b. *Community Development Financial Institutions Act of 1993-S.1275.* Washington, D.C.: Government Printing Office.

Committee on Banking, Housing, and Urban Affairs. 1993c. *Fair Lending Enforcement and The Data on The 1992 Home Mortgage Disclosure Act.* S. Hrg. 103-451. Washington, D.C.: Government Printing Office.

Commoner, Barry. 1972. *The Closing Circle.* New York: Bantam.

Congressional Record, October 21, 1988, S17179

Connors, Helen V. 1967. "Laws Regulating the Practice of Nursing." *State Government* (Winter): 30-34.

Conte, Christopher. 1979. "A Reluctant Congress Faces New Debate on Banking Laws." *Congressional Quarterly Weekly Report* (July 7): 1364-1369.

Cooper, Joseph. 1986. "Congress and the Legislative Veto: Choices since the Chadha Decision." In *Making Government Work,* Robert S. Hunter, Wayne L. Berman and John F. Kennedy, Eds. Boulder, CO: Westview Press.

Cooper, Phillip J. 1988. *Public Law and Public Administration.* 2nd ed. Englewood Cliffs: Prentice-Hall.

Cordes, Renée. 1993. "Medical Boards Found Lax on Doctor Discipline." *Trial* 29 (April): 87-88.

Corrigan, Richard. 1986. "Rekindling OSHA?" *National Journal* 18:1054-7.

Corrigan, Richard. 1984. "Oil: Hunting for Bargains." *National Journal* 16:598-602.

Costle, Douglas M. 1980. "The Environmental Protection Agency's Initiatives." In *Reforming Regulation.* Timothy B. Clark, Marvin H. Kosters, and James C. Miller, eds. Washington, D.C.: American Enterprise Institute, pp. 130-133.

Cox, Edward F., Robert C. Fellmeth, John E. Schulz. 1969. *"The Nader Report" on the Federal Trade Commission.* New York: Richard W. Baron Publishing Co.

CPSC Consumer Product Safety Alert, July 1993

CPSC Long Range Planning Committee, Second Paper: Implementing the Mission of the Consumer Product Safety Commission, January 6, 1992.

CPSC Press Release No. 94-117 and 94-119, August, 1994

CPSC Press Release No. 94-103, July 7, 1994 and Update, August 19, 1994

CPSC Window Falls Roundtable. 1994. *Hazard Sketch.* July 27.

Craig, Barbara Hinkson. 1983. *The Legislative Veto: Congressional Control of Regulation.* Boulder, CO: Westview Press.

Crandall, Robert W. 1983. *Controlling Industrial Pollution.* Washington, D.C.: Brookings.

Crenson, Mathew. 1971. *The Un-Politics of Air Pollution: A Study in Non-Decision Making in the Cities.* Baltimore, MD: Johns Hopkins Press.

Crovitz, L. Gordon. 1992. "Economic Rights: Guild Cuts Off Cornrows." *The Wall Street Journal* February 5: A11.

Crowfoot, James, and Julia Wondolleck. 1990. *Environmental Disputes: Community Involvement in Conflict Resolution.* Covelo, CA: Island Press.

Crowley, David W. 1987. "Judicial Review of Administrative Agencies." *Western Political Quarterly* 40:265-284.

Cushman, John. 1993. "States and Government Lag in Meeting Clean Air Law." *New York Times,* 16 November, sec. A.

Cushman, John. 1991. "EPA Proposes Rules on Utility Emission Trading," *New York Times,* 30 October, sec. A.

Cutler, Lloyd N. 1980. "Reforms in Procedure, Structure, Personnel, and Substance." In *Reforming Regulation,* Timothy B. Clark, Marvin H. Kosters, and James C. Miller, eds. Washington, D.C.: American Enterprise Institute, pp. 153-158.

Dales, J. H. 1968. *Pollution, Property and Prices.* Toronto: University of Toronto Press.

Daly, George, and David W. Brady. 1976. "Federal Regulation of Economic Activity." In *Economic Regulatory Policies,* James E. Anderson, ed. Lexington, MA: Lexington Books, pp. 171-186.

Daniels, Peggy Kneffel, and Carol A. Schwartz. 1993. *Encyclopedia of Associations: 1994 28th Edition.* Washington, D.C.: Gale Research Inc.

Davies, J. Clarence. 1984. "Environmental Institutions and the Reagan Administration." In *Environmental Policy in the 1980s*, ed. Norman J. Vig and Michael E. Kraft. Washington, D.C.: Congressional Quarterly Press.

Davies, J. Clarence and Barbara S. Davies. 1975. *The Politics of Pollution.* 2d ed. Indianapolis: Pegasus.

Davis, Charles. 1993. *The Politics of Hazardous Waste*. Englewood Cliffs, NJ: Prentice-Hall.

Davis, Charles and James Lester. 1989. "Federalism and Environmental Policy." In *Environmental Politics and Policy*, ed. James Lester. Durham, NC: Duke University Press.

Davis, David A., Geoffrey R. Norman, Arnaud Panvin, Elizabeth Lindsay, Mohan S. Ragbeer, and Darlyne Rath. 1990. "Attempting To Ensure Physician Competence." *Journal of the American Medical Association* 263:2041-2042.

Davis, Kenneth Culp. 1972. *Administrative Law Text*. 3d ed. St. Paul: West.

Day, Kathleen 1993. *S&L Hell: The People and the Politics behind the $1 Trillion Savings and Loan Scandal*. New York: W. W. Norton & Company.

Denison, Edward F. 1979. *Accounting for Slower Economic Growth.* Washington, D.C.: Brookings.

Dennis, W. L. 1984. *Brick and Mortar Branches in the Era of Merchandising Financial Services*. Cleveland, OH: Federal Reserve Bank of Cleveland.

DeVany, Arthur S., Wendy L. Gramm, Thomas R. Saving, and Charles W. Smith. 1982. "The Impact of Input Regulation: The Case of the U.S. Dental Industry." *Journal of Law and Economics* 25:367-381.

DeVries, Raymond G. 1986. "The Contest for Control: Regulating New and Expanding Health Occupations." *American Journal of Public Health* 76:1147-1150

Dickerson, F. Reed. 1968. *Product Safety in Household Goods*. Indianapolis: The Bobbs-Merrill Company.

DiLorenzo, Thomas J. and Jack C. High. 1988. "Antitrust and Competition, Historically Considered." *Economic Inquiry* 26: 423-433.

Dolan, Andrew K. 1980. "Occupational Licensure and Obstruction of Change in the Health Care Delivery System." In *Regulating the Professions,* Roger D. Blair and Stephen Rubin, eds. Lexington, MA: Lexington Books, 223-244.

Doniger, David D. 1978. *The Law and Policy of Toxic Substances* Control. Baltimore: Johns Hopkins University Press.

Donnelley Marketing. 1991. *13th Annual Survey of Promotional Practices.* Donnelley Marketing, Inc. 70 Seaview Avenue, Stamford, CT 06902.

Dorfman, Robert. 1982. "Lessons of Pesticide Regulation." In *Reform of Environmental Regulation*, ed. Wesley A. Magat. Cambridge, MA: Ballinger.

Dorsey, Stuart. 1980. "The Occupational Licensing Queue." *Journal of Human Resources* 15:424-434.

Dower, Roger. 1990. "Hazardous Waste Policy." In *Public Policies for Environmental Protection*, ed. Paul Portney. Washington, D.C.: Resources for the Future.

Downing, Paul B. 1984. *Environmental Economics and Policy.* Boston: Little, Brown.

Downing, Paul B., and James N. Kimball. 1982. "Enforcing Pollution Control Laws in the United States." *Policy Studies Journal* 1:55-65.

Downs, Anthony. 1972. "Up and Down With Ecology: The Issue-Attention Cycle" *The Public Interest* 28(3):38-50.

Downs, Anthony. 1967. *Inside Bureaucracy.* Boston: Little, Brown.

Drellick, E. B. and A. Emery. 1939. *Rent Control in War and Peace*. New York, NY: National Municipal League.

Dryzek, John. 1987. *Rational Ecology: Environment and Political Economy.* New York: Basil Blackwell.

Dunlap, Riley. 1989. "Public Opinion and Environmental Policy." In *Environmental Politics and Policy,* ed. James Lester. Durham, NC: Duke University Press.

Dunlap, Riley and Rik Scarce. 1991. "Environmental Problems and Protection." *Public Opinion Quarterly* 55:651-72.

Easterbrook, Frank. 1984. "Restricted Dealing is a Way to Compete." *Regulation* 8 (January-February), 23-27.

Economic Research Service. 1993. *Economic Indicators of the Farm Sector: National Financial Summary, 1991.* Washington: USDA.

Eisenhauer, Joseph G. 1994. "Household Use of Open-end Credit to Finance Risk." *Journal of Consumer Affairs* 28: 154-169.

Eisner, Marc Allen. 1993. *Regulatory Politics in Transition.* Baltimore: The Johns Hopkins University Press.

Eisner, Marc Allen. 1991. *Antitrust and the Triumph of Economics.* Chapel Hill, NC: University of North Carolina Press.

Eisner, Marc Allen and Kenneth J. Meier. 1990. "Presidential Control versus Bureaucratic Power: Explaining the Reagan Revolution in Antitrust." *American Journal of Political Science* 34: 269-87.

Elders, M. Joycelyn. 1994. U.S. Surgeon General, Speech before Lifesavers National Conference on Highway Safety Priorities, March.

Elzinga, Kenneth G. 1980. "The Compass of Competition for Professional Services." In *Regulating the Professions,* Roger D. Blair and Stephen Rubin, eds. Lexington, MA: Lexington Books, pp. 107-123.

Elzinga, Kenneth G. 1969. "The Antimerger Law: Pyrrhic Victories?" *Journal of Law and Economics* 12:43-78.

Ember, Lois. 1993. "EPA's Browner to Take Holistic Approach to Environmental Protection." *Chemical and Engineering News* 71(9):19-21.

Energy, Department of. "Energy Conservation Program for Consumer Products" Docket No. EE-RM-90-201.

EPA Administrator. 1991. *Environmental Investments: The Cost of a Clean Environment.* Covelo, CA: Island Press.

Epstein, Richard. 1985. *Takings: Private Property and the Power of Eminent Domain.* Cambridge: Harvard University Press.

Esposito, John C. 1970. *Vanishing Air.* New York: Grossman.

Fairris, David. 1992 "Compensating Payments and Hazardous Work in Union and Nonunion Settings" *Journal of Labor Research* 13(2):205-217.

FannieMae. 1993. *Housing Impact Report 1992-1993.* Washington, D.C.: author.

Farley, Dixie. 1993. "Making Sure Hype Doesn't Overwhelm Science." *FDA Consumer* (November), 9-13.

"FDA, FSIS Merger, User Fees Among Gore Recommendations." 1993. *Food Chemical News* 35 #29 (September 13): 3-6.

"FDA Internal Document Details FDA FY'93 Enforcement." 1994. *Food Chemical News* 36 #8 (April 18): 13-14.

"FDA Issues Guidance Document on Lead in Shellfish." 1993. *Food Chemical News* 35 #30 (September 20), 44.

Federal Deposit Insurance Corporation. 1993. *FDIC Consumer News.* Vol. 1, Issue 1 (Fall).

Federal Deposit Insurance Corporation. 1991. *Annual Report.* Washington, D.C.: author.

Federal Emergency Management Agency. 1992. Interagency Hazard Mitigation Team Report. Atlanta, GA.

Federal Reserve System. 1994. *Flow of Funds Accounts: Flows and Outstandings.* (4th Quarter). Washington, D.C.: Board of Governors of the Federal Reserve System.

Federal Reserve System. 1989. "Domestic Financial Statistics." *Federal Reserve Bulletin.* 75(7).

Fellmuth, Robert C. 1970. *The Interstate Commerce Ommission.* New York: Grossman.

Ferreira, Joseph. 1982. "Promoting Safety Through Insurance." In *Social Regulation,* Eugene Bardach and Robert A. Kagan, eds. San Francisco: ICS Press, pp. 267-283.

Fise, Mary Ellen R. 1987. *The CPSC: Guiding or Hiding From Product Safety?* Washington: Consumer Federation of America.

Fisher, Franklin M., James W. McKie, and Richard B. Mancke. 1983. *IBM and the Data Processing Industry.* New York: Praeger.

Fisher, Louis. 1985. "Judicial Misjudgments about the Lawmaking Process: The Legislative Veto Case." *Public Administration Review* 45:705-711.

Fisher, Louis. 1984. "One Year after *INS v Chadha*: Congressional and Judicial Developments." Washington, D.C.: Congressional Research Service.

Flexner, Abraham. 1910. *Medical Education in the United States and Canada.* New York: Carnegie Foundation.

Focus on Food Labeling. 1993. *FDA Consumer-Special Report.* Rockeville, MD: The Food and Drug Administration.

"Food & Water Criticizes Espy's Support for Irradiation." 1993. *Food Chemical News* 35 #31 (September 27): 10-11.

"Food and Beverages." 1993. *U.S. Industrial Outlook 1994-Other Consumer Nondurables* 34-11 -34-21.

Food and Drug Administration. 1993a. "Food Labeling Regulations Implementing the Nutrition Labeling and Education Act." *Federal Register* (January 6), 58:2174-2964.

Food and Drug Administration. 1993b. "Regulation of Dietary Supplements." *Federal Register* (January 19 #116) 58:33690-33751.

Food and Drug Administration. 1989. "Food Labeling: Advance Notice of Proposed Rulemaking." *Federal Register* (August 8), 54:32610-32615.

Food and Drug Administration. 1973. "Regulations for the Enforcement of the Food, Drug and Cosmetic Act and the Fair Packaging and Labeling Act; Nutritional Labeling." *Federal Register* (January 19), 38:2125-2132.

"Food, Beverages & Tobacco ASIC Analysis." 1993. *Standard & Poor's Industrial Surveys* 161 (34, Sec 1: August 26): F15-F23.

"Food Guide Pyramid Replaces the Basic 4 Circle." 1993. *Food Technology* (July): 64-67.

"Food Safety a Top Concern for 21st Century U.S. Food System." 1994. *Food Chemical News* 36 #10 (May 2): 47-48.

Forste, Robert H., and George E. Frick. 1979. "Dairy." In *Another Revolution in U.S. Farming?* Lyle P. Schertz and others, eds. Washington, D.C.: U.S. Department of Agriculture.

Foulke, Judith E. 1993. "Is Something Fishy Going On?" *FDA Consumer* (September) 12-17.

Frank, John N. 1981. "New Competitors Zero in on Savings Market." *Savings and Loan News* 102 (April): 36-41.

Frech, H. E. 1974. "Occupational Licensure and Health Care Productivity." In *Health Manpower and Productivity,* John Rafferty, ed. Lexington, MA: Lexington Books, pp. 119-139.

Freedman, Warren. 1987. *Federal Statutes on Environmental Protection.* Westport, CT: Quorum Books.

Freeman, A. Myrick. 1994. "Economics, Incentives, and Environmental Regulation." In *Environmental Policy in the 1990s, second edition*, ed. Norman Vig and Michael Kraft. Washington, D.C.: Congressional Quarterly.

Freeman, A. Myrick. 1990. "Water Pollution Policy." In *Public Policies for Environmental Protection*, ed. Paul Portney. Washington, D.C.: Resources for the Future.

Freeman, A. Myrick. 1982. *Air and Water Pollution Control: A Benefit-Cost Assessment*. New York: Wiley and Sons.

Freeman, J. Leiper. 1965. *The Political Process*. New York: Random House.

Freeman, Richard B. 1980. "The Effect of Occupational Licensure on Occupational Attainment." In *OccupationalLicensingand Regulation*. Simon Rottenberg, ed. Washington, D.C.: American Enterprise Institute, pp. 165-179.

Fried, Robert. 1976. *Performance in American Bureaucracy*. Boston: Little, Brown.

Friedman, David H. 1989. *Money and Banking*. Washington, D.C.: American Banking Association.

Friedman, Milton. 1962. *Capitalism and Freedom*. Chicago: University of Chicago Press.

Friedman, Milton, and Rose Friedman. 1980. *Free to Choose*. New York: Harcourt Brace Jovanovich.

Friedman, Milton, and Simon Kuznets. 1945. *Income from Independent Professional Practice*. New York: National Bureau of Economic Research.

Friedrich, Carl J. 1940. "Public Policy and the Nature of Administrative Responsibility." In *Public Policy*, Carl J. Friedrich and Edward S. Mason, eds. Vol. 1. Cambridge, MA: Harvard University Press.

Fritschler, A. Lee. 1975. *Smoking and Politics*. Englewood Cliffs, N.J.: Prentice-Hall.

"FSIS Should Include Microbial Testing in HACCP: GAO Report." 1994. *Food Chemical News* 36 #15 (June 6): 40-43.

Fuller, Gordon W. 1993. "Ingredients and 'Green' Labels." *Food Technology* 41 (August), 68-71.

Funk, William. 1993. "Revolution or Restatement? Awaiting Answers to Lucas' Unanswered Questions." *Environmental Law* 23:891-900.

Furash, Edward E. 1994. "Payments System Under Siege." *ABA Banking Journal* (June): 55-57.

Gallo, Anthony E. 1991. "The Food Marketing System." *Food Marketing Review* (August-September), 38-41.

"GAO: FDA Hampered by Too Few Funds, Enforcement Powers." 1994. *Food Chemical News* 36 #14 (May 30): 42.

"GAO Recommends Blue Ribbon Panel on New Food Technologies." 1993. *Food Chemical News* 35 #28 (September 6): 3-10.

Garcia, G. 1980. "Credit Cards: An Interdisciplinary Survey." *Journal of Consumer Research* 6:327-337.

Gardner, Bruce L. 1987. "Causes of U.S. Farm Commodity Programs." *Journal of Political Economy* 95:290-310.

Gardner, Bruce L. 1981a. *The Governing of Agriculture*. Lawrence: Regents Press of Kansas.

Gardner, Bruce L. 1981b. "Consequences of Farm Policies During the 1970s." In *Food and AgriculturalPolicyforthe 1980s*. D. Gale Johnson, ed. Washington, D.C.: American Enterprise Institute, pp. 48-72.

Garman, E. Thomas 1994. *Consumer Economic Issues in America*. (2.5 ed.). Houston, TX: Dame Publications.

Garman, E. Thomas 1994a. (December 1) Private correspondence from Diane M. Salva, Senior Attorney, Federal Deposit Insurance Corporation.

Garman, E. Thomas 1993. *Consumer Economic Issues in America*. (2nd ed.). Houston, TX: Dame Publications.

Geisel, Jerry. 1992. "OSHA Needs More Funds, Labor Organization Says." *Business Insurance* 26(18): 2,36.

Gellhorn, Walter. 1976. "The Abuse of Occupational Licensing." *University of Chicago Law Review* 44 (Fall), 6-27.

General Accounting Office. 1994a. *Air Pollution*. Washington, D.C. :author.

General Accounting Office. 1994b. *Occupational Safety and Health: Changes Needed in the Combined Federal-State Approach*. Washington: GAO/HEHS-94-10.

General Accounting Office. 1993. *Commodity Programs: Flex Acres Enhance Farm Operations and Market Orientation*. Washington: GAO/RCED-94-76.

General Accounting Office. 1991. *OSHA Action Needed to Improve Compliance with Hazard Communication Standard*. Washington: GAO/HRD-92-8.

General Accounting Office. 1988. *Assuring Accuracy in Employer Injury and Illness Records*. Washington: GAO/HRD-89-23.

General Accounting Office. 1987. *Superfund: Extent of Nation's Potential Hazardous Waste Problem Still Unknown*. Washington, D.C.: author.

General Accounting Office. 1986. *The Nations Water: Key Unanswered Questions About the Quality of Rivers and Streams*. Washington, D.C.: author.

General Accounting Office. 1980. *Indoor Air Pollution: An Emerging Health Problem*. Washington, D.C.: author

Gianessi, Leonard and Henry Peskin. 1981. "Analysis of National Water Pollution Control Policies." *Water Resources Research* 17:796-821.

Gilbert, Charles E. 1959. "The Framework for Administrative Responsibility." *Journal of Politics* 21:373-407.

Gillis, Jack. 1994. *The Car Book*. New York: Harper Perennial, A Division of Harper Collins Publishers.

Gillis, Jack and Mary Ellen R. Fise. 1993. *The Childwise Catalog: A Consumer Guide to Buying the Safest and Best Products for Your Children*, 3rd edition. New York: Harper Collins.

Gladwell, Malcolm. 1990. "Risk-Assessment Techniques Throw Researchers a Curve." *Washington Post National Weekly Edition* (April 2): 39.

Glater, Jonathan D. 1994. "Senate Passes Interstate Banking Bill." *Washington Post* (September 14) pp. F1-2.

Glen, Maxwell, and Cody Shearer. 1984. "Workers' Safety: Is It Better?" *Oklahoma Daily* (March 7), 9.

"GM Knew of Brake Problem Before Production?" 1983. *Norman Transcript* (September 25), 3.

Goldberg, Lawrence G.; Gerald A. Hanweck, and Timothy F. Sugrue 1992. "Differential Impact on Bank Valuation of Interstate Banking Law Changes." *Journal of Banking and Finance* 16(6): 1143-1158.

Goodman, Marshall R. and Margaret T. Wrightson. 1987. *Managing Regulatory Reform: The Reagan Strategy and Its Impact*. New York: Praeger.

Goodsell, Charles T. 1994. *The Case for Bureaucracy: A Public Administration Polemic*. Chatham, NJ: Chatham House Publishers, Inc.

Gordon, Dan. 1992. *Examination Policies and Procedures of Federal Regulators of Depository Institutions*. Washington, D.C.: National Credit Union Administration.

Gormley, William. 1986a. "Regulatory Issue Networks in a Federal System." *Polity* 18:595-620.

Gormley, William T. 1986b. "The Representation Revolution: Reforming State Regulation Through Public Representation." *Administration and Society* 18:179-196.

Gormley, William. 1983. *The Politics of Public Utility Regulation*. Pittsburgh: Pittsburgh University Press.

Gottron, Martha V., ed. 1982. *Regulation: Process and Politics*. Washington, D.C.: Congressional Quarterly Press.

Grabowski, Henry G., and John M. Vernon. 1983. *The Regulation of Pharmaceuticals.* Washington, D.C.: American Enterprise Institute.

Graddy, Elizabeth and Michael Nichol. 1990. "Structural Reforms and Licensing Board Performance." *American Politics Quarterly* 18:376-400.

Graddy, Elizabeth and Michael Nichol. 1989. "Public Members on Occupational Licensing Boards: Effects on Legislative Regulatory Reforms." *Southern Economic Journal* 55:610-25.

Graham, John D. 1989. *Auto Safety: Assessing America's Performance.* Dover, MA: Auburn House Publishing Company.

Graham, John D. 1988. *Preventing Automobile Injury: New Findings from Evaluation Research.* Dover, MA: Auburn House Publishing Company.

Gray, Wayne B. and Carol Adaire Jones. 1991. "Longitudinal Patterns of Compliance with Occupational Safety and Health Administration Heath and Safety Regulations in the Manufacturing Sector." *Journal of Human Resources* 26:623-49.

Greenspan, Alan 1994. "Statements to the Congress." *Federal Reserve Bulletin.* (May) 80:382-385.

Greenwald, Carol S. 1977. *Group Power.* New York: Praeger.

Greer, Douglas F. 1983. *Business, Government, and Society.* New York: Macmillan.

Greve, Michael. 1992. "Private Enforcement, Private Rewards." In *Environmental Politics: Public Costs, Private Rewards*, ed. Michael Greve and Fred Smith. New York: Praeger.

Greve, Michael and Fred Smith, Jr. 1992. *Environmental Politics: Public Costs, Private Rewards.* New York: Praeger.

Gruppen, L. D., F. M. Wolf, C. Van Voorhees, and Jeoffrey K. Stross. 1986. "The Motivation of Primary Care Physicians to Participate in Continuing Medical Education." *Evaluation and the Health Professions* 9:305-316.

Gunther, Jeffery W. 1992a. "The Movement Toward Nationwide Banking: Assessing the Role of Regional Banking Difficulties." *Federal Reserve Bank of Dallas Financial Industry Studies* 5:1-9.

Gunther, Jeffery W. 1992b. "Regional Capital Imbalances and the Removal of Interstate Banking Restrictions." *Federal Reserve Bank of Dallas Financial Industry Studies* 5:1-8.

Guth, James L. 1980. "Federal Dairy Programs." Presented at the Symposium on Farm Structure and Rural Policy, Ames, Iowa, October 20-22.

"HACCP, ISO 9000 on Codex Import/Export Committee's Agenda." 1993. *Food Chemical News* 35 #39 (November 22), 20-22.

Hadwiger, Don F. 1992. "Technology in A Fragmented Politics: The Case of Agricultural Research." *Technology in Society* 14:283-297.

Hadwiger, Don F. 1982. *The Politics of Agricultural Research.* Lincoln, NE: University of Nebraska Press.

Hadwiger, Don F. and Ross B. Talbot. 1965. *Pressures and Protests: The Kennedy Farm Program and the Wheat Referendum of 1963.* San Francisco: Chandler Publishers.

Hagstrom, Jerry. 1984. "Candidates Woo Farmers as Agricultural PACs Step Up Their Contributions." *National Journal* 16:420-424.

Hahn, Robert W., and Roger G. Noll. 1982. "Implementing Tradable Emissions Permits." In *Reforming Social Regulation,* LeRoy Graymer and Frederick Thompson, eds. Beverly Hills: Sage, pp. 125-150.

Hall, Bob and Mary Kay Kerr. 1991. *The Green Index.* Washington, D.C.: Institute for Southern Studies.

Hall, John R. and Arthur E. Cote. 1991. "America's Fire Problem and Fire Protection." *Fire Protection Handbook.* Quincy, MA: NFPA. pp. 1-24.

Hamilton, Joan. 1994. "Babbitt's Retreat." *Sierra* 79(4):52.

Hanf, Kenneth. 1982. "The Implementation of Regulatory Policy: Implementation as Bargaining." *The European Journal of Political Research*, 10:159-72.

Hanna, S. 1994. "An Economic Focus on...Usury Laws and the Supply and Demand for Consumer Credit." In Thomas Garman (1994), *Consumer Economics Issues In America* (pp. 559-560), Houston, TX: Dame Publication, Inc.

Hannan, Timothy H, and Stephen A. Rhoades. 1992. "Future U.S. Banking Structure: 1990 to 2010." *Antitrust Bulletin.* 37:737-798.

Hansen, Nancy Richardson, Hope Babcock, and Edwin Clark. 1988. *Controlling Nonpoint Source Water Pollution: A Citizen's Handbook.* Washington, D.C.: Conservation Foundation.

Hanson, David J. 1993. "Occupational Safety and Health Administration Reform Stranded." *Chemical and Engineering News* 71(46):52-53.

Hardy, Stuart B. 1990. "Assuring a Healthy Food Supply: A Case for Fundamental Reform of Regulatory Programs." *American Review of Public Administration* 20:227-243.

Harter, Philip J. 1977. "In Search of OSHA." *Regulation* 1 (September-October), 33-39.

Hartley, Mark. 1994. "Joe Dear"s First Days." *Occupational Health and Safety* 63(1):4.

Haug, Marie. 1980. 'The Sociological Approach to Self-Regulation." In *Regulating the Professions*, Roger D. Blair and Stephen Rubin, eds. Lexington: Lexington Books, pp. 61-80.

Hayes, Edward. 1993. "What's a City to Do?" *EPA Journal* 19(1):48-9.

Haynes, D. J. 1989. "Incorporating Credit in Demand Analysis." *Journal of Consumer Affairs* 23:1-20.

Heady, Earl 0. 1983. "Economic Policies and Variables." In *Farms in Transition,* David Brewster, Wayne Rasmussen, and Garth Youngberg, eds. Ames, Iowa: Iowa State University Press, 23-26.

Healey, Jon. 1994. "Critics Call for Better Way to Deal with Catastrophes." *Congressional Quarterly.* 52:167-169.

Health and Human Services, Department of. 1993. "Guideline for the Study and Evaluation of Gender Differences in the Clinical Evaluation of Drugs." *Federal Register* 58 (July 22):39406-39416.

Health and Human Services, Department of. 1992. "Investigational New Drug, Antibiotic, and Biological Drug Product Regulations; Accelerated Approval." *Federal Register* 57 (April 15):13234-13242.

Health and Human Services, Department of. 1988. "Investigational New Drug, Antibiotic, and Biological Drug Product Regulations; Procedures for Drugs Intended to Treat Life-Threatening and Severely Debilitating Illnesses." *Federal Register* 53 (October 21):41516-41524.

Health and Human Services, Department of. 1987. "Investigational New Drug, Antibiotic, and Biological Drug Product Regulations; Treatment Use and Sale." *Federal Register* 52 (May 22):19466-19477.

Heclo, Hugh. 1977 *Government of Strangers*. Washington, D.C.: Brookings.

Heclo, Hugh. 1978. "Issue Networks and the Executive Establishment." In *The New American Political System,* Anthony King, ed. Washington, D.C.: American Enterprise Institute.

Hedge, David M., Donald C. Menzel, and George H. Williams. 1988. "Regulatory Attitudes and Behavior." *Western Political Behavior* 41:323-340.

Heffron, Florence, with Neil McFeeley. 1983. *The Administrative Regulatory Process*. New York: Longman.

Heggstad, A. 1981. "Introduction" In A. Heggstad (ed.) *Regulation of Consumer Finances.* Cambridge, MA: Abt Books.

Helfand, Gloria, Brett House, and Douglas Larson. 1992. "Toxics Regulation Under California's Proposition 65: A State Law With National Effects." *Choices* (first quarter) 18-21.

Henderson, Jorika P. Winter 1994. "Radon Abatement." *Human Ecology Forum* 22(1), 13-14.

Hershey, Nathan. 1969. "An Alternative to Mandatory Licensure of Health Professionals." *Hospital Progress* 50 (March):71-74.

Hertzberg, D. 1984. "Smaller Customers Get Less Service at Banks and Pay More Charges." *Wall Street Journal*. (October 18) pp. 1ff.

Heslin, Mary M. 1994. Conversations with Mary M. Heslin, former Commissioner of Consumer Protection, State of Connecticut June 12-22.

Holen, Arlene S. 1977. "The Economics of Dental Licensing." Center for Naval Analysis. Mimeographed.

Hunter, Beatrice Trum. 1993. "What's Wrong with Nutritional Labeling?" *Consumers' Research* (February):10-14.

Huntington, Samuel P. 1952. "The Marasmus of the ICC." *Yale Law Journal* 61:467-509.

Huth, Tom. 1992. "The Incredible Shrinking Swamp." *Conde Nast Traveler* (September):134-38; 184-91.

Injury in America: A Continuing Public Health Problem. 1985. Washington, D.C.: National Research Council, National Academy Press.

Insurance Institute for Highway Safety. 1994. "Future of Crashworthiness Research Includes Frontal Offset Tests into a Deformable Barrier," *Status Report*, Vol. 29, No.7, June 25.

Insurance Institute for Highway Safety and Highway Loss Data Institute. 1994. "25 Years of Work", IIHS, Arlington, Virginia, April.

"It's the Ecosystem, Stupid! The 26th Annual Environmental Quality Index." *National Wildlife* 32(2):38-45.

IVHS Architecture Bulletin: An Update of the Intelligent Vehicle-Highway System Architecture Development Program. 1994. "What is IVHS?" January.

Janssen, Wallace F. 1981. "The Story of the Laws Behind the Labels." *FDA Consumer* 15 (June): 32-45.

Jennings, Dianne. 1994. "Dental Board's Demise Causes Gap in Regulation, Licensing." *Dallas Morning News* (September 1), 1A ff.

"Job Safety Inspectors Seldom Required to Get Warrants Despite Justices' Ruling." 1978. *Wall Street Journal* (July 17), 13.

John, DeWitt. 1994. *Civic Environmentalism.* Washington, D.C.: Congressional Quarterly.

Johnson, Arthur M. 1965. *Government Business Relations.* Columbus: Charles Merrill.

Johnson, Cathy M. 1993. *The Dynamics of Conflict Between Bureaucrats and Legislators.* Armonk, NY: 1992.

Johnson, D. Gale. 1981. "Agriculture Policy Alternatives for the 1980s." In *Food and Agricultural Policy for the 1980s.* D. Gale Johnson, ed. Washington, D.C.: American Enterprise Institute, pp. 183-209.

Jones A. 1912. "The Object of the Association as Defined by the New Constitution." *American Food Journal* (July 15).

Jones, Charles 0. 1975. *Clean Air.* Pittsburgh: University of Pittsburgh Press.

Jones, Charles O. 1961. "Representation in Congress: The Case of the House Agriculture Committee." *American Political Science Review* 55:358-367.

Julin, Joseph R. 1980. "The Legal Profession: Education and Entry." In *Regulating the Professions,* Roger D. Blair and Stephen Rubin, eds. Lexington, MA: Lexington Books, pp. 201-221.

"Justice Department Pledges Tough Enforcement of FFD&C." 1993. *Food Chemical News* 35 #30 (September 20), 34.

Kamieniecki, Sheldon, and Michael Ferrall. 1991. "Intergovernmental Relations and Clean Air Policy in Southern California." *Publius* 26:143-54.

Kapoor, J.R., L.R. Dlabay, and R.J. Hughes. 1994. *Personal Finance* (3rd ed.) Burr Ridge, IL: Richard Irwin, Inc.

Katzman, Robert A. 1980. *Regulatory Bureaucracy.* Cambridge, MA: MIT Press.

Kearney, Richard C. 1990. "Sunset: A Survey and Analysis of State Experience." *Public Administration Review* 50:49-57.

Keller, Bill. 1982. "Liberation of Bank Industry: This Year May be Thwarted by Fractured Finance Lobbies." *Congressional Quarterly Weekly Report* 40:187-191.

Kelman, Steven. 1981a. *What Price Incentives?* Boston: Auburn House.

Kelman, Steven. 1981b *Regulating Sweden, Regulating America.* Cambridge, MA: MIT Press.

Kelman, Steven. 1981c. "Cost-Benefit Analysis: An Ethical Critique." *Regulation* 5:33-40.

Kelman, Steven. 1980. "Occupational Safety and Health Administration." In *The Politics of Regulation,* James Q. Wilson, ed. New York: Basic Books, pp. 236-266.

Kemp, Kathleen A. 1983. "The Regulators: Partisanship and Public Policy." *Policy Studies Journal* 11:386-397.

Kemp, Kathleen A. 1982a. "Accidents and Political Support for Regulatory Agencies." Paper presented at the Midwest Political Science Association, Milwaukee.

Kemp, Kathleen A. 1982b. "Instability in Budgeting for Federal Regulatory Agencies." *Social Science Quarterly* 63:643-660.

Kenski, Henry C., and Margaret Corgan Kenski. 1984. "Congress Against the President: The Struggle over the Environment." In *Environmental Policy in the 1980s,* Norman J. Vig and Michael E. Kraft, eds. Washington, D.C.: Congressional Quarterly Press, pp. 97-120.

Kessel, Reuben A. 1970. "The AMA and the Supply of Physicians." *Law and Contemporary Problems.* 35:267-283.

Kessel, Reuben A. 1959. "Price Discrimination in Medicine." *Journal of Law and Economics* 1:20-51.

Kidwell, D.S., R.L. Peterson, and D.W. Blackwell. 1993. *Financial Institutions, Markets, and Money* (5th ed.). Fort Worth, TX: The Dryden Press.

Kintner, Earl W. 1964. *An Antitrust Primer.* New York: Macmillan.

Kirby, R. and O. Capps. 1994. "Impact of Consumer Installment Debt on Food Expenditures. *Journal of Consumer Affairs* 28:81-95.

Kirkendall, Richard S. 1980. "The New Deal for Agriculture: Recent Writings, 1971-76." In Trudy Huskamp Peterson, ed., *Farmers, Bureaucrats, and Middlemen.* Washington, D.C.: Howard University Press.

Kirst, Michael W. 1969. *Government Without Passing Laws.* Chapel Hill: University of North Carolina Press.

Kleiner, Morris M., Robert S. Gay, and Karen Greene. 1982. "Licensing, Migration, and Earnings: Some Empirical Insights." *Policy Studies Review* 1:510-522.

Washington Post. 1994. "Food Industry Says Label Law Costs Billions." (April 22), A7.

Kobliner, Beth 1993. "What Banks Don't Know Can Hurt You." *Money* (March):144-7.

Kohlmeier, Louis M. 1969. *The Regulators.* New York: Harper & Row.

Kolesar, David. 1992. "Cumulative Trauma Disorders: OSHA General Duty Clause and the Need for and Ergonomics Standard." *Michigan Law Review* 90:2079-2112.

Kolko, Gabriel. 1965. *Railroads and Regulation.* Princeton: Princeton University Press.

Kolko, Gabriel. 1963. *The Triumph of Conservatism.* New York: Free Press.

Kosters, Marvin H. 1982. *Major Regulatory Initiatives During 1981.* Washington, D.C.: American Enterprise Institute.

Kosters, Marvin H. 1980. "Introduction." In *Reforming Regulation*, Timothy B. Clark, Marvin H. Kosters, and James C. Miller, eds. Washington, D.C.: American Enterprise Institute, pp. 69-70.

Kovacic, William. 1991. "The Reagan Judiciary and Environmental Policy: The Impact of Appointments to the Federal Courts of Appeals." *Boston College Environmental Affairs Law Review* 18:669-713.

Krasnow, Erwin G., Lawrence D. Langley, and Herbert A. Terry. 1982. *The Politics of Broadcast Regulation*. 3d ed. New York: St. Martin's Press.

Krier, James E. 1982. "Marketlike Approaches." In *Reforming Social Regulation,* LeRoy Gramer and Frederick Thompson, eds. Beverly Hills: Sage, pp. 151-8.

Kriz, Margaret. 1994a. "Superfight." *National Journal* 26:224-29.

Kriz, Margaret. 1994b. "The Week That Was." *National Journal* 26:393.

Kriz, Margaret. 1994c. "What's the Point of Finger Pointing." *National Journal* 26:1097.

Kriz, Margaret. 1992a. "Poison Gamesmanship." *National Journal* 24:930-33.

Kriz, Margaret. 1992b. "The New Eco-Nomics." *National Journal* 24:1280-85.

Kriz, Margaret. 1988. "Pesticidal Pressures." *National Journal* 20:3125-27.

Krupnick, Alan, and Paul Portney. 1991. "Controlling Urban Air Pollution: A Benefit-Cost Assessment." *Science* 252:522-27.

Kurtzweil, Paula. 1993. "Good Reading for Good Eating." *FDA Consumer* (May), 7-13.

Kuttner, Robert. 1993. "Flying in the Face of Reason: Why the Skies Need Reregulating." *Business Week* (May 3).

La Barbera, Priscilla. 1977, *Consumers and the Federal Trade Commission: An Empirical Investigation.* East Lansing: The Board of Trustees of Michigan State University, 1977.

Lammers, William W. 1985. "Alternative Strategies for Expanding State Regulatory Protection for the Aging." Working Paper, University of Southern California, Los Angeles. (November).

Landy, Marc, and Mary Hague. 1992. "Private Interests and Superfund." *The Public Interest* 108:97-115.

Landy, Marc, Marc Roberts, and Steven Thomas. 1990. *The Environmental Protection Agency: Asking the Wrong Questions.* New York: Oxford University Press.

Langsley, Donald G. 1991. "Recredentialing." *Journal of the American Medical Association* 265:772.

Lash, N. A. 1987. *Banking Laws and Regulations: An Economic Perspective.* Englewood Cliffs, NJ: Prentice-Hall Inc.

Lassila, Katherin. 1992. "See You Later, Litigator: Regulatory Negotiation Toward Consensus." *Amicus Journal* 14(2):5-7.

Lasswell, Harold D. 1936. *Politics: Who Gets What, When, How.* New York: McGraw-Hill.

Lave, Lester B. 1992. "Risky Business: Thinking About the Benefits and Costs of Government Regulation." *The American Enterprise.* (November).

Layer, M. 1994. *Financial Responsibility. A Consumer Education Program from American Express Company.* New York: American Express Company.

LeClair, Mark S. 1991. "Regional Interstate Banking in New England: Its Effect upon Competition and Access to Banking Services." *Journal of Business and Economic Studies.* 1(1):45-54.

Leffler, Keith B. 1981. "Persuasion or Information?: The Economics of Prescription Drug Advertising." *Journal of Law and Economics* 24:45-74.

Leffler, Keith B. 1978. "Physician Licensure: Competition and Monopoly in American Medicine." *Journal of Law and Economics* 21:165-186.

Leigh, J. Paul. 1984. "Compensating Wages for Employment in Strike-Prone or Hazardous Industries." *Social Science Quarterly* 65:89-99.

Leigh, J. Paul. 1981. "Compensating Wages for Occupational Injuries and Diseases." *Social Science Quarterly* 62:773-778.

Leigh, J. Paul and Andrew M. Gill. 1991. "Do Women Receive Compensating Wages for Risks of Dying on the Job?" *Social Science Quarterly* 72:727-737.

Leland, Hayne E. 1980. "Minimum-Quality Standards and Licensing in Markets with Asymmetrical Information." In *Occupational Licensing and Regulation,* Simon Rottenberg, ed. Washington, D.C.: American Enterprise Institute, 265-284.

Leland, Hayne E. 1979. "Quacks, Lemons, and Licensing: A Theory of Minimum Quality Standards." *Journal of Political Economy* 87:1328-1348.

Lemov, Michael R. 1983. *Consumer Product Safety Commission.* New York: Shepard's/McGraw-Hill.

Leonard, K. and W. Banks. 1994. "Automating the Credit Decision Process." *Journal of Retail Banking* 16(1):39-44.

Lester, James. 1990. "A New Federalism? Environmental Policy in the States." In *Environmental Policy in the 1990s,* ed. Norman Vig and Michael Kraft. Washington, D.C.: Conservation Foundation.

Letson, David. 1992. "Point/Nonpoint Source Pollution Reduction Trading: An Interpretive Survey." *National Resources Journal* 32:219-32.

Lettenmaier, D.P., E.R. Hooper, C. Wagoner, and K.B. Ferris. 1991. "Trends in Stream Water Quality in the Continental United States." *Water Resources Research.*

Levine, Michael E. 1982. "Regulating the Auto Industry." In *Reforming Social Regulation,* LeRoy Gramer and Frederik Thompson, eds. Beverly Hills: Sage. 111-124.

Lewis-Beck, Michael S., and John R. Alford, "Can Government Regulate Safety? The Coal Mine Example." *American Political Science Review* 74:745-756.

Lieber, Harvey. 1983. *Federalism and Clean Waters.* Lexington, MA: Lexington Books.

Lin, William, Linda Calvin, and James Johnson. 1980. *Farm Commodity Programs: Who Participates and Who Gets the Benefits?* Washington, D.C.: U.S. Department of Agriculture.

Lindblom, Charles E. 1965. *The Intelligence of Democracy.* New York: Free Press.

Lindeen, James W. 1994. *Governing America's Economy.* Englewood Cliffs, NJ: Prentice Hall.

Lindsey, Lawrence B. 1994. "Statements to the Congress." *Federal Reserve Bulletin.* 80:10-19.

Liroff, Richard. 1986. *Reforming Air Pollution Regulation: The Toil and Trouble of EPA's Bubble.* Washington, D.C.: Conservation Foundation.

Litan, Robert E., and William D. Nordhaus. 1983. *Reforming Federal Regulation.* New Haven: Yale University Press.

Loaharanu, Paisan. 1994. "Status and Prospects of Food Radiation." *Food Technology* (May):124-131.

Locke, Anrienne C. 1991. "Court Ruling Challenges Broad OSHA Standards." *Business Insurance* 25(29):2,4.

Long, Norton. 1962. *The Polity.* Chicago: Rand McNally.

Lott, John R., Jr. 1987. "Licensing and Nontransferable Rents." *The American Economic Review.* 77:453-455.

Lowi, Theodore. 1969. *The End of Liberalism.* New York: Norton.

Lowry, William. 1992. *The Dimensions of Federalism: State Governments and Pollution Control Policies.* Durham: Duke University Press.

Luckett, C.A. and J.D. August. 1985. "The Growth of Consumer Debt." *Federal Reserve Bulletin* 71:389-402.

MacAvoy, Paul. 1987. "The Record of the EPA in Controlling Industrial Air Pollution." In *Energy, Markets, and Regulation,* ed. R.L. Gordon, H.D. Jacoby, and M.B. Zimmerman. Cambridge, MA: Ballinger.

MacAvoy, Paul W. 1979. *The Regulated Industries and the Economy.* New York: Norton.

MacAvoy, Paul W. 1977. *Federal Milk Marketing Orders and Price Supports.* Washington, D.C.: American Enterprise Institute.

MacAvoy, Paul W., and Kenneth Robinson. 1983. "Winning Buy Losing: The AT&T Settlement and Its Impact on Telecommunications." *Yale Journal on Regulation* 1 (No. 1), 1-42.

Magat, Wesley, and W. Kip Viscusi. 1990. "Effectiveness of the EPA's Regulatory Enforcement: The Case of Industrial Effluent Standards." *Journal of Law and Economics* 33: 331-60.

Maney, Ardith L., and Donald F. Hadwiger. 1980. "Taking 'Cides: The Controversy over Agricultural Chemicals." In *Farmers, Bureaucrats, and Middlemen*, ed. Trudy Huscamp Peterson. Washington, D.C.: Howard University Press.

Marcus, Alfred. 1980. *Promise and Performance: Choosing and Implementing an Environmental Policy.* Westport, CT: Greenwood Press.

Marcus, Ruth. 1992. "Justices Make it Harder to Press Environmental Enforcement Cases." *Washington Post*, June 13, sec. A.

Markham, Jesse W. 1955. "Survey of the Evidence and Findings on Mergers." In *Business Concentration and Public Policy.* Princeton: Princeton University Press.

Marsh, Barbara. 1994. "Workers at Risk: Chance of Getting Hurt is Generally Far Higher at Small Companies." *Wall Street Journal* 3 February, sec. A.

Martin, Donald L. 1980. "Will the Sun Set on Occupational Licensing?" In Simon Rottenberg, ed. *Occupational Licensing and Regulation.* Washington, D.C.: American Enterprise Institute, pp. 142-154.

Marvel, Mary K. 1983. "Safety Regulation: Industry Capture or State Competition." Paper presented at the American Political Science Association Meetings, Chicago.

Marvel, Mary K. 1982. "Implementation and Safety Regulations." *Administration and Society* 14:5-14.

Mashaw, Jerry L. and Harfst, David L. 1994. *The Struggle for Auto Safety.* Cambridge, MA: Harvard University Press.

Maslow, Abraham H. 1970. *Motivation and Personality.* 2d ed. New York: Harper and Row.

Mathur, A. and G. Moschis. 1994. "Use of Credit Cards by Older Americans." *Journal of Services Marketing* 8(1):27-36.

Matlack, Carol. 1988. "Tapping into Trouble?" *National Journal* 20:3070-3.

Matlack, Carol. 1987. "Worker Warnings Switch to Fast Track." *National Journal* 19:832-3.

Mattingly, Kimberly A. 1988. "Testing OSHA"s New Fast Track." *National Journal* 20:1872-3.

Maurizi, Alex R. 1980. "The Impact of Regulation on Quality: The Case of California Contractors." In *Occupational Licensing and Regulation.* Simon Rottenberg ed. Washington, D.C.: American Enterprise Institute, 26-35.

Maurizi, Alex R. 1974. "Occupational Licensing and the Public Interest." *Journal of Political Economy* 82:399-413.

Maurizi, Alex R., Ruth L. Moore, and Lawrence Shepard. 1981. "Competing for Professional Control: Professional Mix in the Eyeglasses Industry." *Journal of Law and Economics* 24:351-364.

Mayer, Martin. 1974. *The Bankers.* New York: Ballantine.

Mazmanian, Daniel, and David Morrell. 1992. *Beyond Superfailure: A Hazardous Waste Policy for the 1990s.* Boulder, CO: Westview.

Mazmanian, Daniel and Jeanne Nienaber. 1979. *Can Organizations Change? Environmental Protection, Citizen Participation, and the Corps of Engineers.* Washington, D.C.: Brookings Institution.

Mazmanian, Daniel A. and Paul A. Sabatier. 1983. *Implementation and Public Policy.* Glenview, Ill.: Scott, Foresman.

Mazmanian, Daniel A. and Paul A. Sabatier. 1980. "A Multivariate Model of Public Policy-Making." *American Journal of Political Science* 24:439-468.

McCarthy, J.E., and M.E. Reisch. 1987. *Hazardous Waste Fact Book.* Washington, D.C.: Congressional Research Service.

McCaull, Julian. 1976. "Discriminatory Air Pollution: If the Poor Don't Breathe." *Environment* 19:26-32.

McConnell, Grant. 1966. *Private Power and American Democracy.* New York: Knopf.

McCormick, Robert E. 1989. "A Review of the Economics of Regulation: The Political Process." In *Regulation and the Reagan Era,* Roger E. Meiners and Bruce Yandle, eds. New York: Holmes and Meier.

McCraw, Thomas K. 1981. "Rethinking the Trust Question." In *Regulation in Perspective,* Thomas K. McCraw, ed. Cambridge, MA: Harvard University Press, 1-55.

McCubbins, Mathew D., and Thomas Schwartz. 1984. "Congressional Oversight Overlooked: Police Patrols Versus Fire Alarms." *American Journal of Political Science* 28:165-179.

McFadyen, Richard E. 1981. "Thalidomide: Its Place in the History of Drug Regulation Since 1945." In *Drugs and Drug Regulation in the United States Historical Perspectives.* Chicago, IL: University of Illinois, pp. 15-27.

McGillan, James J., John E. Fiorini, III, Charles A. O'Connor, III, and Michael A. Brown. 1977. *Consumer Product Safety Law.* Washington: Government Institutes.

McGraw, Jack. 1992. "The Denver Airport: Pollution Prevention by Design." *EPA Journal* 18(2): 18-19.

McGregor, Eugene B. 1974. "Politics and Career Mobility of Civil Servants." *American Political Science Review* 68:18-26.

McGuire, Jack. 1994. Conversations with Jack McGuire, Director of the Food Division, State of Connecticut, Department of Consumer Protection, June 17.

McKie, James W. 1989. "US Regulatory Policy." In *The Age of Regulatory Reform,* Kenneth Button and Dennis Swann, eds. Oxford: Clarendon Press.

McWilliams, Joe. 1994. Conversation with Joe McWilliams, FSIS Personnel Director. June 13.

Meeks, Carol B. 1992. "Balancing Regulation and Affordability of Housing." *Journal of Family and Economic Issues* 13(4):373-382.

Meier, Kenneth J. 1994. *The Politics of Sin: Drugs, Alcohol and Public Policy.* Armonk, NY: M.E. Sharpe.

Meier, Kenneth J. 1993. *Politics and the Bureaucracy.* 3rd ed. Monterey, CA: Brooks/Cole.

Meier, Kenneth J. 1988. *The Political Economy of Regulation: The Case of Insurance.* Albany, NY: State University of New York Press.

Meier, Kenneth J. 1985. *Regulation: Politics, Bureaucracy, and Economics.* New York: St. Martins Press.

Meier, Kenneth J. 1984. "The Limits of Cost-Benefit Analysis." In Lloyd G. Nigro, ed., *Decisionmaking in Public Administration.* New York: Marcel Dekker, 43-63.

Meier, Kenneth J. 1983a. "Consumerism or Protectionism: State Regulation of Occupations." Paper presented at the annual meeting of the American Political Science Association, Chicago.

Meier, Kenneth J. 1980. "The Impact of Regulatory Agency Structure: IRCs or DRAS." *Southern Review of Public Administration* 3:427-443.

Meier, Kenneth J. and John P. Plumlee 1979. "The Impact of Organizational Structure on Regulatory Policy." Paper presented at the Symposium on Strategies for Change in Regulatory Policy, Chicago.

Meier, Kenneth J. and David R. Morgan. 1981. "Speed Kills: A Longitudinal Analysis of Traffic Fatalities and the 55 MPH Speed Limit." *Policy Studies Review* 1:157-167.

Meier, Kenneth J. and John P. Plumlee. 1978. "Regulatory Administration and Organizational Rigidity." *Western Political Quarterly* 31:80-95.

Meiners, Roger E. and Robert Crandall, eds. 1989. *Regulation and the Reagan Era.* New York: Holmes and Meier.

Melnick, R. Shep. 1983. *Regulation and the Courts.* Washington, D.C.: Brookings.

Mendeloff, John. 1979. *Regulating Safety.* Cambridge, MA: MIT Press.

Merkatz, Ruth B., Robert Temple, Solomon Sobel, Karyn Feiden, and David A. Kessler. 1993. "Women in Clinical Trials of New Drugs: A Change in Food and Drug Administration Policy." *The New England Journal of Medicine* 329:292-296.

Mermelstein, Neil H. 1993. "A New Era in Food Labeling." *Food Technology* (February): 81-86, 94-96.

Meyer, Henry Balthasar. 1906. "A History of the Northern Securities Case." *Wisconsin University Bulletins 1.*

Meyer, Lois S. 1982. "Consumer Protection." *Book of the States, 1982-83.* Lexington, Ky.: Council of State Governments, 540-545.

Milbrath, Lester. 1963. *The Washington Lobbyists.* Chicago: Rand McNally.

Mikulski, Barbara. 1993. Letter to, Chairman, Senate Subcommittee on VA, HUD and Independent Agencies, May 19.

Miller, James C. 1984. "An Analytical Framework." *Regulation* 8 (January-February): 31-32.

Miller, Sanford A. 1993. "Health, Safety, and Standards: Do We Need an International Food Regulatory Institution?" *Food Technology* (March): 125-130.

Mitnick, Barry M. 1980. *The Political Economy of Regulation.* New York: Columbia University Press.

Moe, Terry M. 1985. "Control and Feedback in Economic Regulation." *American Political Science Review.* 79:1094-1116.

Moe, Terry M. 1982. "Regulatory Performance and Presidential Administration." *American Journal of Political Science* 26:197-225.

Money Management Institute. 1988. *Managing Your Credit.* Prospect Heights: IL, Household Financial Services.

Moore, W. John. 1993a. "Antitrust Comeback" *National Journal* 25:2666-7.

Moore, W. John. 1993b. "Rough Ride." *National Journal* 25:2874-9.

Moore, W. John. 1993c. "Golden Rules." *National Journal* 20:1124-1128.

Moore, W. John. 1992. "Just Compensation." *National Journal* 24:1404-07.

"More Research Needed on Irradiation Plus Packaging: JFP." 1993. *Food Chemical News* 35 #35 (October 25):21-22.

Morgenstern, Richard. 1992. "A Market Approach at EPA." *EPA Journal* 18(2):27-9.

Morse, L. D. Richard. 1992a. "Truth in Savings Act: Accomplished, Yet Unfinished." *Advancing the Consumer Interest.* 4(2):36-36.

Morse, L.D. 1992b. *Truth in Savings with Centsible Interest and Morse Rate Tables.* Manhattan, Kansas: Family Economics Trust Press.

Morse, L.D. 1987. "Truth in Savings: Its Legislative History and Status." In Vickie Hampton ed. *Proceedings of the 33rd Annual Conference of American Council on Consumer Interests*, 95-101, Columbia, MO: ACCI.

Mosher, Lawrence. 1983a. "A Ticking Time Bomb -- Compensation for Victims of Hazardous Waste Dumps." *National Journal* 15:120-21.

Mosher, Lawrence. 1983b. "Ruckelshaus Is Seen as His Own Man in Battle to Renew Clean Water Act." *National Journal* 15:1497-1500.

Moyer, H. Wayne and Timothy E. Josling. 1990. *Agricultural Policy Reform*. Ames: Iowa State University Press.

Mueller, Willard F. 1979. *The Celler-Kefauver Act*. Washington, D.C.: U.S. House of Representatives, Committee on the judiciary, Subcommittee on Monopolies and Commercial Law. (November 7).

Muris, Timothy J., and Fred S. McChesney. 1979. "Advertising and the Price and Quality of Legal Services." *American Bar Foundation Research Journal* 1979 (Winter): 179-208.

Nadel, Mark V. 1971. *The Politics of Consumer Protection*. Indianapolis: Bobbs-Merrill.

Nader, Ralph. 1965. *Unsafe at Any Speed*. New York: Grossman Publishers.

National Association of Home Builders. 1994. *Low-Cost, Low-Flow Residential Fire Sprinkler Systems*. Mimeo. Washington, D.C.: author.

National Association of Home Builders. 1993. *Cost/Benefit Analysis of Change in Stair Geometry*. Mimeo. Washington, D.C.: author.

National Association of Home Builders. 1992. *The Future of Home Building 1992-1994 and Beyond*. Washington, D.C.: author.

National Commission on Consumer Finance. 1972. *Consumer Credit in the United States*. Washington, D.C.: Government Printing Office.

National Conference of States on Building Codes and Standards. *Manufactured Housing Statistics*. Herndon, VA. author.

National Highway Traffic Safety Administration, Office of Plans and Programs, "The Contributions of Automobile Regulation," December 1979.

Navarro, Peter. 1981. "The 1977 Clean Air Act Amendments: Energy, Environmental, Economic, and Distributional Impacts." *Public Policy* 29(2):121-46.

National Credit Union Administration. 1993. "Financial Trends in Federally Insured Credit Unions: January 1, 1992 to December 31, 1992." *Letter to Credit Unions*. No. 145 (March).

National Credit Union Administration. 1992. *Annual Report*. Washington, D.C.: author.

"NCUA's Hot Topics." 1994. *Credit Union Management*. 17(2) (February): 20-21.

Nelson, Ralph L. 1959. *Merger Movements in American Industry, 1895-1956*. Princeton: Princeton University Press.

"Newsline." 1992. *EPA Journal* 18(2):2.

Nichols, Albert, and Richard Zeckhauser. 1981. "OSHA After a Decade." In Leonard W. Weiss and Michael K. Klass, eds., *Case Studies in Regulation*. Boston: Little, Brown, 202-234.

Niskanen, William. 1971. *Bureaucracy and Representative Government*. Chicago: Aldine.

Norton, Clark F. 1976. *Congressional Review, Deferral and Disapproval of Executive Actions*. Washington, D.C.: Congressional Research Service.

Novak, Viveca. 1993. "The New Regulators." *National Journal*. 25:1801-4.

Nutrition Labeling and Education Act of 1990 P.L. 101-535

O'Hare, Michael. 1982. "Information Strategies as Regulatory Surrogates." In Eugene Bardach and Robert A. Kagan, eds., *Social Regulation*. San Francisco: ICS Press, 221-236.

Okun, Arthur. 1976. *Equality vs. Efficiency: The Big Tradeoff*. Washington, D.C.: Brookings.

Olempska-Beer, Zofia S., Paul M. Kuznersof, Michael DiNova, and Mitchell J. Smith. 1993. "Plant Biotechnology and Food Safety." *Food Technology* (December), 66-71.

Oliver, Dean O. 1993. "Research Needs in Food Safety." *Food Technology* (March), 10S-12S.

"Oraflex Linked to Cancer in Mice, Lilly Tells FDA." 1983. *Saturday Oklahoman and Times* (December 24): 26.

Ornstein, Norman J., and Shirley Elder. 1978. *Interest Groups, Lobbying and Policymaking*. Washington, D.C.: Congressional Quality Press.

Paarlberg, Don. 1980. *Farm and Food Policy*. Lincoln: University of Nebraska Press.

Pace, E. E. 1980. "The Practical Effects of Usury Laws." *The Journal of Commercial Bank Lending* (June): 24-33.

Page, Joseph, and Mary O'Brien. 1973. *Bitter Wages.* New York: Grossman.

"Panetta Criticizes Espy for Bypassing OMB on Safe Labels." 1993. *Food Chemical News* 35 #28 (September 6), 23-26.

Parsons, Donald O., and Edward J. Ray. 1975. "The United States Steel Consolidation." *Journal of Law and Economics* 18:181-220.

Pashigian, B. Peter. 1983. "How Large and Small Firms Fare Under Environmental Regulation." *Regulation* 7:19-23.

Pashigian, B. Peter. 1980. "Has Occupational Licensing Reduced Geographical Mobility and Raised Earnings?" In *Occupational Licensure and Regulation,* Simon Rottenberg, ed. Washington, D.C.: American Enterprise Institute, pp. 299-333.

Pashigian, B. Peter. 1979. "Occupational Licensing and Interstate Mobility of Professionals." *Journal of Law and Economics* 22:1-25.

Patterson, Samuel C. 1978. "The Semisovereign Congress." In Anthony King, ed., *The New American Political System.* Washington, D.C.: American Enterprise Institute, pp. 125-177.

Patton, Dorothy. 1993. "The ABCs of Risk Assessment." *EPA Journal* 19(1):10-15.

Pauls, Jake. 1993. "Notes on the Cost-Benefit Impact of The "7-11" Riser-Tread Geometry for Stairs in Dwellings." Maryland: author.

Pauly, David and Erik Ipsen. 1983. "The Saving of the Thrifts." *Newsweek* (April 18), 59.

Pearson, Cynthia. 1994. Interview. September 8, Program Director, National Women's Health Network, Washington, D.C.

Peltzman, Sam. 1976. "Toward a More General Theory of Regulation." *Journal of Law and Economics* 19:211-240.

Peltzman, Sam. 1975. "The Effects of Automobile Safety Regulation." *Journal of Political Economy* 83:667-735.

Penn, J. B. 1981. "Economic Development in U.S. Agriculture During the 1970s." In *Food and Agriculture Policy for the 1980s,* D. Gale Johnson, ed. Washington, D.C.: American Enterprise Institute, 3-47.

Penoyer, Ronald J. 1981. *Directory of Federal Regulatory Agencies.* St. Louis: Center for the Study of American Business, Washington University.

Perloff, Jeffrey M. 1980. "The Impact of Licensing Laws on Wage Changes in the Construction Industry." *Journal of Law and Economics* 23:409-428.

Pertschuk, Michael. 1982. *Revolt Against Regulation.* Berkeley: University of California Press.

Peters, John G. 1978. "The 1977 Farm Bill: Coalitions in Congress." In *The New Politics of Food,* Don F. Hadwiger and William P. Browne, eds. Lexington, MA: Lexington Books, pp. 23-36.

Peterson, R. L. 1980. "The Costs of Consumer Credit Regulation." Reprint No. 13. West Lafayette, IN: Credit Research Center, Purdue University.

Peterson, R. L. and G.A. Falls. 1981. "Impact of a Ten Percent Usury Ceiling: Empirical Evidence," Working Paper No. 40. West Lafayette, IN: Credit Research Center, Purdue University.

Pettus, Beryl E. 1982. "OSHA Inspection Costs, Compliance Costs, and Other Outcomes." *Policy Studies Review* 1:596-614.

Pfeffer, Jeffrey. 1974. "Some Evidence on Occupational Licensing and Occupational Incomes." *Social Forces* 53:102-111.

Phelan, Jack. 1974. *Regulation of the Television Repair Industry in Louisiana and California: A Case Study.* Washington, D.C.: Federal Trade Commission.

Pitofsky, Robert. 1984. "Why Dr. Miles Was Right." *Regulation* 8 (January-February), 27-30.

Plamer, Elizabeth A. and Ilyse J. Veron. 1992. "White House War on Red Tape: Success Hard to Gauge." *Congressional Quarterly Weekly Report.* (May 2).

Plott, Charles R. 1965. "Occupational Self-Regulation: A Case Study of the Oklahoma Dry Cleaners." *Journal of Law and Economics* 8:195-222.

Poole, Robert W. 1982. *Instead of Regulation.* Lexington, MA: Lexington Books.

Porter, Donna V. and Robert O. Earl, (eds.). 1992. *Food Labeling - Toward National Uniformity.* Washington, D.C.: National Academy Press.

Portney, Paul, ed. 1990. *Public Policies for Environmental Protection.* Washington, D.C.: Resources for the Future.

Portney, Paul, ed. 1981. *Environmental Regulation and the U.S. Economy.* Baltimore: Johns Hopkins Press.

Posner, Richard A. 1976. *Antitrust Law: An Economic Perspective.* Chicago: University of Chicago Press.

Posner, Richard A. 1970. "A Statistical Study of Antitrust Enforcement." *Journal of Law and Economics* 13:371-390.

President's Council on Competitiveness. 1992. *The Legacy of Regulatory Reform: Restoring America's Competitiveness.* Washington, D.C: U.S. Government Printing Office.

Presidential Task Force on Regulatory Relief. 1983. *Reagan Administration Regulatory Achievements.* Washington, D.C. (August 11).

Princeton Survey Research Associates. 1994. *Changes in Credit Card Practices and Perceptions: Findings from the Third Annual National Survey Conducted for American Express*, Princeton, NJ: Princeton Survey Research Associates.

Pszczola, Donald. 1993. "Irradiated poultry Makes U.S. Debut in Midwest and Florida Markets." *Food Technology* (November): 89-96.

Public Health Service. 1990. " Expanded Availability of Investigational New Drugs Through a Parallel Track Mechanism for People With AIDS and HIV-Related Diseases." *Federal Register* 55 (May 21): 20856-20860.

Shapo, Marshall S. 1980. *Public Regulation of Dangerous Products.* Mineola, NY: Foundation Press.

Puckett, Richard H. 1983. "Deregulation and the Principles of Regulation." *The Bankers Magazine* 166 (March-April): 86-88.

Quirk, Paul J. 1981. *Industry Influence in Federal Regulatory Agencies.* Princeton: Princeton University Press.

Quirk, Paul J. 1980. "The Food and Drug Administration." In *The Politics of Regulation,* James Q. Wilson, ed. New York: Basic Books, pp. 191-234.

Rabe, Barry. 1986. *Fragmentation and Integration in State Environmental Management.* Washington, D.C.: Conservation Foundation.

Rabe, Barry, and Janet Zimmerman. 1994. "An Empirical Examination of Innovations in Integrated Environmental Management: The Case of the Great Lakes Basin." Department of Public Health Policy and Administration, University of Michigan, Ann Arbor, MI. Mimeo.

Rabin, R. 1989. "Warnings Unheeded: A History of Childhood Lead Poisoning." *American Journal of Public Health.* 79:1668-1674.

Rausser, Gordon C. 1992. "Predatory Versus Productive Government: The Case of U.S. Agricultural Policies." *Journal of Economic Perspectives* 6:133-157.

Redford, Emmette S. 1969. *Democracy and the Administrative State.* New York: Oxford University Press.

"Reforming FDICA is Banking's Top Priority." 1993. *Bank Management.* (February) 69(2):22.

"Regulators Seek Comments on CRA Proposal." 1994. *FDIC Consumer News.* 1(2): 10.

"Reinventing Meat and Poultry Inspection: Building Public Health Based Program." 1993. Unpublished document distributed by the Safe Food Coalition, 1155 21st Street, NW, Suite 1000; Washington, D.C. 20036 (August 17).

Reynolds, Larry. 1993. "NSC"s Standards Could Become a Model for OSHA." *HR Focus* 70(12):2.

Rice, Dorothy P., and Ellen J. MacKenzie, and Associates, "Cost of Injury in the United States," A Report to Congress, 1989.

Richardson, Lee, "A Ten-Year Agenda for Consumer Advocates." In *Consumerism: New Challenges for Marketing*, Norman Kangun and Lee Richardson, eds. Chicago: American Marketing Association, 1976.

Ringquist, Evan J. 1993. *Environmental Protection at the State Level: Politics and Progress in Controlling Pollution*. Armonk, NY: M.E. Sharpe.

Ringquist, Evan J. N.d. "Evaluating Environmental Policy Outcomes." In *Environmental Politics and Policy: Theories and Evidence, second edition*, ed. James Lester. Durham, NC: Duke University Press (forthcoming).

Ripley, Randall B., and Grace A. Franklin. 1991. *Congress, the Bureaucracy, and Public Policy*. Homewood, Ill.: Dorsey Press.

Risen, James. 1994. "Redlining Revisited." *Financial World*. 163(2) (January 18): 16.

Rockett, James M. 1994. "Understanding Regulatory Enforcement Actions." *The Banker Magazine*. (January/February), 60-64.

Romzek, Barbara S., and J. Stephen Hendricks. 1982. "Organizational Involvement and Representative Bureaucracy." *American Political Science Review* 76:75-82.

Rosenbaum, Walter. 1994. "The Clenched Fist and the Open Hand: Into the 1990s at EPA." In *Environmental Policy in the 1990s, second edition*, ed. Norman Vig and Michael Kraft. Washington, D.C.: Congressional Quarterly.

Rosenbaum, Walter. 1991. *Environmental Politics and Policy, second edition*. Washington, D.C.; CQ Press.

Rosenbaum, Walter. 1989. "The Bureaucracy and Environmental Policy." *Environmental Politics and Policy: Theories and Evidence*, ed. James Lester. Durham, NC: Duke University Press.

Rosenbaum, Walter. 1973. *The Politics of Environmental Concern*. New York: Praeger.

Rottenberg, Simon. 1980. "Introduction." In *Occupational Licensing and Regulation*, Simon Rottenberg, ed. Washington, D.C.: American Enterprise Institute, 1-10.

Rourke, Francis E. 1984. *Bureaucracy, Politics, and Public Policy*. Boston: Little, Brown.

Rowland, C. K., and Roger Marz. 1982. "Gresham's Law: The Regulatory Analogy." *Policy Studies Review* 1:572-580.

Ruff, Larry E. 1981. "Federal Environmental Regulation." In *Case Studies in Regulation*, ed. Leonard W. Weiss and Michael W. Klass. Boston: Little, Brown.

Ruser, John W. and Robert S. Smith. 1990. "Reestimating OSHA"s Effects: Have the Data Changed?" *Journal of Human Resources* 26: 212-35.

Russell, Clifford. 1990. "Monitoring and Enforcement." In *Public Policies for Environmental Protection*, ed. Paul Portney. Washington, D.C.: Resources for the Future.

Russell, Clifford. 1983. *Pollution Monitoring Survey: Summary Report*. Washington D.C.: Resources for the Future.

Ruttan Vernon. 1982. *Agricultural Research Policy*. Minneapolis: University of Minnesota Press.

Rycroft, Robert, James Regens, and Thomas Dietz. 1988. "Incorporating Risk Assessment and Benefit-Cost Analysis in Environmental Management." *Risk Analysis* 8:415-420.

Sabatier, Paul A. 1988. "An Advocacy Coalition Framework of Policy Change and the Role of Policy-Oriented Learning Therein." *Policy Sciences* 21:129-168.

Sabatier, Paul A. 1977. "Regulatory Policy Making: Toward a Framework of Analysis." *National Resources Journal* 17:415-460.

Sabatier, Paul A. 1976. "Social Movements and Regulatory Agencies." *Policy Sciences*. 21:301-342.

Sabatier, Paul, and Hank Jenkins-Smith. 1993. *Policy Change and Learning: An Advocacy Coalition Approach*. Boulder, CO: Westview.

"Safe Handling Instructions." 1993. *Food Chemical News* 35 #37 (November 8), 5.

"Safe Handling labels Due in 60 Days for Ground Meat/Poultry." 1994. *Food Chemical News* 36 #5 (March 28), 64-67.

Salamon, Lester B., and Gary L. Wamsley. 1975. "The Federal Bureaucracy: Responsive to Whom." In Leroy N. Rieselbach, ed., *People vs. Government*. Bloomington: Indiana University Press.

"Sales Guidelines Set for Uninsured Products." 1994. *ABA Banking Journal*. (March): 51-54.

Saltos, Etta. 1993. "The Food Pyramid-Food Label Connection." FDA Consumer (May), 56-63.

Samuels, Sarah E. and Smith, Mark D. 1994. *The Pill: From Prescription To Over The Counter*. Menlo Park, CA: Fog Press.

Sapper, Arthur G. and Stephen C. Yohay. 1993. "OSHA's Egregious Penalty Policy: Recent Developments and Future Prospects." *Employee Relations Law Journal* 19(2):289-294.

Savage, Donald T. 1993. "Interstate Banking: A Status Report." *Federal Reserve Bulletin*. 79(12): 1075-1089.

Scalia, Antonin. 1980. "The Legislative Veto." In *Reforming Regulation*, Timothy B. Clark, Marvin H. Kosters, and James C. Miller, eds. Washington, D.C.: American Enterprise Institute, pp. 55-61.

Scheman, Carol R. 1994. "FDA Policy Options." In *The Pill: From Prescription To Over The Counter*, Sarah E. Samuels and Mark D. Smith, ed. Menlo Park, CA: Fog Press, 243-250.

Scher, Seymour. 1960. "Congressional Committee Members as Independent Agency Overseers." *American Political Science Review* 54:911-920.

Scherer, Robert F., Kaufman, Daniel J., Ainina, M. Fall. 1993a. "Resolution of Complaints by OSHA in Union and Non-union Manufacturing Organizations." *Journal of Applied Business Research*. 9(2):55-61.

Scherer, Robert F., Kaufman, Daniel J., Ainina, M. Fall. 1993b. "Complaint Resolution by OSHA in Small and Large Manufacturing firms." *Journal of Small Business Management* 31(1):73-82.

Schertz, Lyle P., and others. 1979. *Another Revolution in U.S. Farming?* Washington, D.C.: U.S. Department of Agriculture.

Schmitt, Harrison H. 1980. "Putting Democratic Controls on the Law of Bureaucrats." In *Reforming Regulation*, Timothy B. Clark, Marvin H. Kosters, and James C. Miller, eds. Washington, D.C.: American Enterprise Institute, 51-54.

Schneider, Keith. 1992. "Courthouse a Citadel No Longer," *New York Times*, 23 March, sec. B.

Schneider, Keith. 1991. "EPA Forces States to Adopt Toxic Pollutant Regs," *New York Times*, 7 October, sec. A.

Schneider, Saundra K. 1987. "Influences on State Professional Licensure Policy." *Public Administration Review* 47:479-84.

Scholz, John T. 1991. "Cooperative Regulatory Enforcement and the Politics of Administrative Effectiveness." *American Political Science Review* 85:115-36.

Scholz, John T. and Wayne B. Gray. 1990. "A Behavioral Approach to Compliance: OSHA Enforcement"s Impact on Workplace Accidents." *Journal of Risk and Uncertainty* 3:283-305.

Scholz, John T. and Feng Heng Wei. 1986. "Regulatory Enforcement in a Federalist System." *American Political Science Review* 80:1249-70.

Schubert, Glendon. 1960. *The Public Interest*. New York: Free Press.

Schuck, Peter R. 1980. "A Tool for Assessing Social Regulation." In *Reforming Regulation,* Timothy B. Clark, Marvin H. Kosters, and James C. Miller, eds. Washington, D.C.: American Enterprise Institute, pp. 117-122.

Schultze, Charles L. 1971. *The Distribution of Farm Subsidies: Who Gets the Benefits?* Washington, D.C.: Brookings.

Schutz, Howard G. 1983. "Effects of Increased Citizen Membership on Occupational Licensing Boards in California." *Policy Studies Journal* 11:504-516.

Schwade, John. 1994. Conversation with John Schwade, Director of Federal and State Services, FDA - New York, June 19.

Schwartz, Warren F. 1981. *Private Enforcement of the Antitrust Laws.* Washington, D.C.: American Enterprise Institute.

Schwartzman, David. 1964. "The Effect of Monopoly on Price." *Journal of Political Economy* 72:352-361.

Segal, Marion. 1991. "Rx To OTC: The Switch Is On." *FDA Consumer* (March), 9-11.

Seidman, Harold and Robert Gilmour. 1986. *Politics, Position and Power.* 4th ed. New York: Oxford University Press.

Shaffer, Helen B. 1977. "Job Health and Safety." In *Earth, Energy and Environment.* Washington, D.C.: Congressional Quarterly, pp. 189-208.

Shanley, Robert. 1992. *Presidential Influence and Environmental Policy.* Westport, CT: Greenwood.

Shapiro, Carl. 1986. "Investment, Moral Hazard, and Occupational Licensing." *Review of Economic Studies* 53:843-862.

Shapiro, Martin. 1982. "On Predicting the Future of Administrative Law." *Regulation* 6 (May/June), 18-25.

Shapiro, Michael. 1990. "Toxic Substances Policy." In *Public Policies for Environmental Protection,* ed. Paul Portney. Washington, D.C.: Resources for the Future.

Shapiro, Sidney A. and Thomas O. McGarity. 1989. "Reorienting OSHA: Regulatory Alternatives and Legislative Reform." *Yale Journal on Regulation* 6:1-64.

Sheehan, Reginald S. 1990. "Administrative Agencies and the Court." *Western Political Quarterly* 43:875-886.

Shepard, Lawrence E. 1978. "Licensing Restrictions and the Cost of Dental Care." *Journal of Law and Economics* 21:187-201.

Shimberg, Benjamin. 1982. *Occupational Licensing: A Public Perspective.* Princeton, NJ: Educational Testing Service.

Shimberg, Benjamin, Barbara F. Esser, and Daniel H. Kruger. 1973. *Occupational Licensing: Practices and Policies.* Washington, D.C.: Public Affairs Press.

Shinkel, B. A. 1976. *The Effects of Limiting Information in the Granting of Consumer Credit.* Unpublished doctoral dissertation, Purdue University, West Lafayette.

"Should You Buy Mutual Funds from your Bank?" 1994. *Consumer Reports.* (March) 148-150.

Shryock, Richard Harrison. 1967. *Medical Licensing in America, 1650-1965.* Baltimore: Johns Hopkins Press.

Simon, Herbert A. 1969. *The Science of the Artificial.* Cambridge, MA: MIT Press.

Simon, Herbert A. 1957. *Administrative Behavior.* New York: Free Press.

Singer, James W. 1976. "New OSHA Task Force." *National Journal* 8:973-975.

Slaughter, Cynthia. 1986. "Sunset and Occupational Regulation: A Case Study." *Public Administration Review.* 46: 241-245.

Smith, Adam. 1937. *Wealth of Nations.* New York: Random House.

Smith, Blake R. 1991. "1991 a Year of Major Changes in Occupational Health and Safety." *Occupational Health and Safety* 60(10): 33-36.

Smith, Daniel R. 1994. "Three Issues to (Really) Watch." *ABA Banking Journal*. (April), 16.

Smith, Robert S. 1979. "The Impact of OSHA Inspections on Manufacturing Injury Rates." *Journal of Human Resources* 14:145-170.

Smith, Robert S. 1976. *The Occupational Safety and Health Act*. Washington, D.C.: American Enterprise Institute.

Smith, Robert S. 1974. "The Feasibility of an 'Injury Tax' Approach to Occupational Safety." *Law and Contemporary Problems* 38:730-744.

Smith, Zachary. 1992. *The Environmental Policy Paradox*. Englewood Cliffs, NJ: Prentice Hall.

Sniderman, M. 1994. *Issues in CRA Reform*. Cleveland, OH: Federal Reserve Bank of Cleveland.

Sobel, Stephen. 1977. "A Proposal for the Administrative Compensation of Victims of Toxic Substances Pollution." *Harvard Journal of Legislation* 14:683-824.

Spellman, Lewis J. 1982. *The Depository Firms and Industry*. New York: Academic Press.

Spix, M. (1986). *Study on New Redlining of Bank Branch Closings in New York, 1977-84*. New York: Community Training and Resource Center.

Sprecher, Robert A. 1967. "Admission to Practice Law." *State Government* (Winter), 21-25.

Stanfield, Rochelle. 1988. "Out-Standing in Court." *National Journal*, 20:388-91.

Stanfield, Rochelle. 1984. "Ruckleshaus Casts EPA as 'Gorilla' in State's Enforcement Closet." *National Journal*, 16:1024-38.

Stewart, David. 1992. "Green Law: Supreme Court's Environmental Law Docket Blossoms." *ABA Journal* 78(2):46.

Stewart, Joseph, James E. Anderson, and Zona Taylor. 1982. "Presidential and Congressional Support for Independent Regulatory Commissions." *Western Political Quarterly* 35:318-326.

Stewart, Richard. 1975. "The Reformation of American Administrative Law." *Harvard Law Review* 88:1667-813.

Stewart, Thomas A. 1992. "U.S. Productivity: First but Fading." *Fortune* 126: 54.

Stigler, George J. 1971. "The Theory of Economic Regulation." *Bell Journal of Economics and Management Science* 2:3-21.

Stokey, Edith, and Richard Zeckhauser. 1978. *A Primer for Policy Analysis*. New York: Norton.

Stone, Alan. 1982. *Regulation and Its Alternatives*. Washington, D.C.: Congressional Quarterly Press.

Stone, Alan. 1979. "New Directions in Banking and Its Regulation." Paper presented at the Symposium on Regulatory Policy, Chicago.

Stone, Peter H. 1994. "Learning from Nader," *National Journal*, June 11, 1994.

Strelnick, Hal. 1983. "An Empirical Analysis of Institutional Patterns of Affirmative Action in American Medical Schools." Paper presented at the Hendricks Symposium on Affirmative Action, Lincoln, Nebraska.

Strelnick, Hal and Richard Young. 1980. *Double Indemnity*. New York: Health Policy Advisory Center.

Strickland, Allyn Douglas. 1980. *Government Regulation and Business*. Boston: Houghton Mifflin.

Strong, Thomas. 1994. "EPA Unveils Ethanol Rules." *Tallahassee Democrat* 30 June, sec. A.

Stross, Jeoffrey K. and Thomas J. DeKornfeld. 1990. "A Formal Audit of Continuing Medical Education Activity for License Renewal." *Journal of the American Medical Association* 264:2421-2423.

Sudduth, Mary Alice. 1993. "Genetically Engineered Foods: Fears & Facts." *FDA Consumer* (January-February): 11-13.

Sullivan, A. C. 1980. "The Response of Commercial Banks to Rate Ceilings and Restrictions on Remedies on Consumer Credit Contracts." Working Paper No.32, West Lafayette, IN: Credit Research Center, Purdue University.

Sullivan, Edward. 1993. "Lucas and Creative Constitutional Interpretation." *Environmental Law* 23:919-23.

"Supplement Industry in 'Desperate Need' of GMPs, FDA Told." 1993. *Food Chemical News* 35 #33 (October 11), 41-45.

"Survey: Variance Between Food Safety, Consumer Perceptions." 1993. *Food Chemical News* 35 #30 (September 20), 48-49.

Svorny, Shirley N. 1987. "Physician Licensure: A New Approach To Examining the Role of Professional Interests." *Economic Inquiry* 25:497-509.

Swann, Dennis. 1989. "The Regulatory Scene: An Overview." In *The Age of Regulatory Reform,* Kenneth Button and Dennis Swann, eds. Oxford: Clarendon Press.

Swann, John. 1992. *40 Years of Consumer Education: 1952-1992.* Washington, D.C.: U.S. Government Printing Office.

Talbot, Ross B., and Don F. Hadwiger. 1968. *The Policy Process in American Agriculture.* San Francisco: Chandler.

Tarbell, Ida. 1950. *History of Standard Oil Company.* New York: Peter Smith.

Taylor, Carl C. 1953. *The Farmer's Movement, 1620-1920.* New York: American Book Company.

Templer, J.A. 1975. *Stair Shape and Human Movement.* Doctoral dissertation. New York, NY: Columbia University.

Templer. J., Archea, J. and H.H. Cohen. 1985. "Study of Factors Associated with Risk of Work-Related Stairway Falls." *Journal of Safety Research.* 16: 193-196.

The Boston Company Economic Advisors, Inc. 1992. *Debt, Credit Card Borrowing and the Economy.* Boston: MA: author.

The Nation's Health and Safety: A Status Report. 1994. Coalition for Consumer Health & Safety.

Thompson, Frank J. 1982. "Deregulation by the Bureaucracy: OSHA and the Augean Quest for Error Correction." *Public Administration Review* 42:202-212.

Thompson, Frank J. and Michael J. Scicchitano. 1987. "State Implementation and Federal Enforcement Priorities: Safety Versus Health in OSHA and the States." *Administration and Society* 19:95-124.

Thompson, Fred, and L. R. Jones. 1982. *Regulatory Policy and Practices.* New York: Praeger.

Thompson, Mark S. 1980. *Benefit-Cost Analysis for Program Evaluation.* Beverly Hills: Sage.

Thorelli, Hans B. 1955. *The Federal Antitrust Policy.* Baltimore: Johns Hopkins Press.

Tobin, Richard J. 1982. "Recalls and the Remediation of Hazardous or Defective Consumer Products." *Journal of Consumer Affairs* 16:278-306.

Toy Choking Hazards, Proposed Rules, 59 Fed.Reg.33932 and 59 Fed.Reg. 33925, 1994.

"Trading Protects Liquid Assets." 1992. *ENR* 229(25):33.

Tweeten, Luther. 1981. "Prospective Changes in U.S. Agricultural Structure." In *Food and Agricultural Policy for the 1980s,* D. Gale Johnson, ed. Washington, D.C.: American Enterprise Institute, 113-146.

Tweeten, Luther. 1979a. *Foundations of Farm Policy.* Lincoln: University of Nebraska Press.

Tweeten, Luther. 1979b. "Structure of Agriculture and Policy Alternatives to Preserve the Family Farm." Presented at the Farmer's Agricultural Policy Conference, Stillwater, Okla.

Tyson, Patrick R. 1992. "Court Favors Huge OSHA Penalties." *Safety & Health* 146(5): 19-26.

U.S. Congressional Budget Office. 1988. "Environmental Federalism: Allocating Responsibilities for Environmental Protection." Staff Working Paper: September, 1988.

U.S. Congressional Budget Office. 1985. *Environmental Regulation and Economic Efficiency.* Washington, D.C.: CBO.

U.S. Council on Environmental Quality. 1993. *Environmental Quality 1993: 24th Annual Report of the Council on Environmental Quality.* Washington, D.C.: GPO.

U.S. Council on Environmental Quality. 1989. *Environmental Trends*. Washington, D.C.: GPO.

U.S. Department of Agriculture. 1993. Mandatory safe handling statements on labeling of raw meat and poultry products; Interim rule. Food Safety and Inspection Service. U.S. Dept. of Agriculture *Federal Register* 58(156:43477-43489.

U.S. Department of Commerce. 1993. *Statistical Abstract of the United States 1993*. Washington, D.C.: GPO.

U.S. Environmental Protection Agency. 1994. *The 1992 Toxics Release Inventory National Report*. Washington, D.C.: EPA, Office of Pollution Prevention and Toxic Substances.

U.S. Environmental Protection Agency. 1993. *RCRIS National Oversight Database*. Washington, D.C.: EPA Office of Solid Waste and Emergency Response.

U.S. Environmental Protection Agency. 1992. *National Air Quality and Emissions Trends Report, 1991*. Research Triangle Park, NC: EPA, Office of Air Quality Planning and Standards.

U.S. Environmental Protection Agency. 1991. *Managing Environmental Results: A Status Report on EPA's Environmental Indicator Program*. Washington D.C.: EPA.

U.S. Environmental Protection Agency. 1990. *National Water Quality Inventory: 1988 Report to Congress* Washington, D.C.: EPA Office of Water.

U.S. Environmental Protection Agency. 1989. "Briefing on NMP Effectiveness Study." Staff Briefing Paper, Office of Water Enforcement and Permits.

U.S. Environmental Protection Agency. 1988. *Environmental Progress and Challenges: EPA's Update*. Washington, D.C.: U.S. GPO.

U.S. Environmental Protection Agency. 1987. *Unfinished Business: A Comparative Assessment of Environmental Problems*. Washington, D.C.: EPA.

U.S. Environmental Protection Agency, Science Advisory Board. 1990. *Reducing Risk: Setting Priorities for Environmental Protection*. Washington, D.C.: EPA.

U.S. Government. 1994. *Budget of the U.S. Government*. Washington, D.C.

U.S. Department of Housing and Urban Development. 1993. *Manufactured Housing*. Rockville, MD: HUD USER.

U. S. Department of Labor. 1993. *Report of the President to the Congress on Occupational Safety and Health for Fiscal Year 1991*. Washington D.C. Department of Labor.

Upholstered Furniture, Advance Notice of Proposed Rulemaking, 59 Fed. Reg. 30735, 1994.

"USDA FDA HACCP Plans More Similar than Different: Speller." 1993. *Food Chemical News* 35 #28 (September 6), 19-22.

Van Cise, Jerrold G. 1982. *The Federal Antitrust Laws*. Washington, D.C.: American Enterprise Institute.

Van Horn, Carl E., ed. 1992. *The State of the States, second edition*. Washington, D.C.: CQ Press.

Vaughn, William and Clifford Russell. 1982. *Recreational Freshwater Fishing: The National Benefits of Water Pollution Control*. Washington, D.C.: Resources for the Future.

Verba, Sidney, and Norman H. Nie. 1972. *Participation in America*. New York: Harper and Row.

Victor, Kirk. 1994. "Sparring over Safety." *National Journal* 10:835-838.

Victor, Kirk. 1992. "Bashing OSHA Didn't Rescue a Campaign." *National Journal* 24:1123-4.

Victor, Kirk. 1990a. "Explosions on the Job." *National Journal* 22: 1941-5.

Victor, Kirk. 1990b. "Activating OSHA." *National Journal* 22:1257.

Victor, Kirk. 1990c. "State-Style Safety." *National Journal* 22:440-3.

Victor, Kirk. 1989a. "OSHA"s Turnabout." *National Journal* 21:2889-92.

Vig, Norman J., and Michael E. Kraft. 1984. "Environmental Policy from the Seventies to the Eighties." In *Environmental Policy in the 1980s*, ed. Norman J. Vig and Michael E. Kraft. Washington, D.C.: Congressional Quarterly.

Viscusi, W. Kip. 1986. "The Impact of Occupational Safety and Health Regulation, 1973-1983." *Rand Journal of Economics* 17:567-580.

Viscusi, W. Kip. 1985. "Cotton Dust Regulation: An OSHA Success Story?" *Journal of Political Analysis and Management* 4:325-43.

Viscusi, W. Kip. 1983. *Risk By Choice*. Cambridge, MA: Harvard University Press.

Viscusi, W. Kip. 1982. "Health and Safety." *Regulation* 6 (January-February), 34-37.

Vogel, David. 1992. "When Consumers Oppose Consumer Protection: The Politics of Regulatory Backlash." *Journal of Public Policy* 10:449-470.

Wald, Mathew. 1992a. "Utility is Selling Right to Pollute," *New York Times*, 12 May, sec. A.

Wald, Mathew. 1992b. "States Sue EPA Over Lack of Clean Air Rules," *New York Times*, 14 April, sec. B.

Waldman, Steven. 1989. "Danger on the Job." *Newsweek* (December 11), 42-6.

Wallace, A. W. 1992. "Industry and Consumers Profit from Privacy Protection." *MOBIUS* 11(1): 12-13.

Waller, Julian A. 1994. "Reflections on a Half Century of Injury Control," *American Journal of Public Health* 84:664-70.

Wallis, Claudia. 1986. "Weeding Out the Incompetents." *Time*. 127 (May 26) 57-58.

Walsh, Kenneth T. 1992. "Regulation Returns." *U.S. News & World Report*. 113: 52 (Dec. 28).

Walton, Clarence C. and Frederick W. Cleveland, Jr. 1964. *Corporations on Trial: The Electric Cases*. Belmont, CA: Wadsworth.

Warren, Kenneth F. 1982. *Administrative Law in the American Political System*. St. Paul: West.

Waxman, Henry. 1992. "The Environmental Pollution President," *New York Times*, 29 April, sec. A.

Wayland, Robert. 1993. "What Progress In Improving Water Quality?" *Journal of Soil and Water Conservation* 48(4):261-66.

Weaver, Suzanne. 1977. *Decision to Prosecute*. Cambridge, MA: MIT Press.

Weidenbaum, Murray L. 1981. *Business, Government, and the Public, second edition*. Englewood Cliffs, NJ: Prentice-Hall.

Weidenbaum, Murray L. 1978. "On Estimating Regulatory Costs." *Regulation*. 2: 14-17.

Weil, David. 1992. "Building Safety: The Role of Construction Unions in the Enforcement of OSHA." *Journal of Labor Research* 13(1):121-132.

Weingast, Barry R. 1980. "Physicians, DNA Research, Scientists and the Market for Lemons." In *Regulating the Professions*. Roger D. Blair and Stephen Rubin, eds. Lexington: Lexington Books, 81-96.

Weingast, Barry R. and Mark J. Moran. 1983. "Bureaucratic Discretion or Congressional Control? Regulatory Policymaking by the Federal Trade Commission." *Journal of Political Economy* 91:765-800.

Weingast, Barry R. and Mark J. Moran. 1982. "The Myth of the Runaway Bureaucracy: The Case of the FTC." *Regulation* 6 (May-June), 33-38.

Weintraub, Michael. 1994. Interview. September 12, Director, Office of OTC Drug Evaluation, Center for Drug Evaluation, Food and Drug Administration, Rockville, MD.

Weiss, Leonard W. 1981. "Introduction: The Regulatory Reform Movement." In *Case Studies in Regulation*, Leonard W. Weiss and Michael W. Klass, eds. Boston: Little, Brown, 1-11.

Weizovick, Jack. 1993. "The Effects of Government Regulations on Major Home Appliances." Association of Home Equipment Education. National Technical Conference Proceedings. Columbus, Ohio: The Ohio State University.

Welborn, David M. 1977. *The Governance of Federal Regulatory Agencies*. Knoxville: University of Tennessee Press.

Welsh, Susan, Carole Davis, and Anne Shaw. 1992. "Development of the Food Guide Pyramid." *Nutrition Today*. (November-December), 12-22.

Wenner, Lettie. 1994. "Environmental Policy in the Courts." In *Environmental Policy in the 1990s, second edition*, ed. Norman Vig and Michael Kraft. Washington, D.C.: Congressional Quarterly.

West, William F. 1995. *Controlling the Bureaucracy: The Theory and Practice of Institutional Constraints*. New York: M.E. Sharpe.

West, William F. 1985. *Administrative Rulemaking: Politics and Processes*. Westport, CT: Greenwood Press.

West, William F. 1982. "The Politics of Administrative Rulemaking." *Public Administration Review* 42:420-426.

Westin, A. F. 1992. "Consumer Privacy Protection: Ten Predictions." *MOBIUS* 11(1): 5-12.

White, Lawrence. 1983. *Human Debris: The Injured Worker in America*. New York: Seaview/Putnam.

White, Lawrence J. 1981. *Reforming Regulation: Processes and Problems*. Englewood Cliffs, NJ: Prentice-Hall.

White, Lawrence J. 1991. *The S&L Debacle: Public Policy Lessons for Bank and Thrift Regulation*. New York: Oxford University Press.

White, Lawrence J. 1982. *The Regulation of Air Pollutant Emissions for Motor Vehicles*. Washington, D.C.: American Enterprise Institute.

White, Lawrence J. 1981. *Reforming Regulation: Processes and Problems*. Englewood Cliffs, N.J.: Prentice-Hall.

"White Paper - FDA/State Relations in the Year 2000: FDA Limits and Requirements for Reaching What Some People See as the Ideal." 1994. AFDO Final Committee Reports 1993-1994.

White, William D. 1980. "Mandatory Licensure of Registered Nurses: Introduction and Impact." In *Occupational Licensing and Regulation*, Simon Rottenberg, ed. Washington, D.C.: American Enterprise Institute, 47-72.

White, William D. 1978. "The Impact of Occupational Licensure on Clinical Laboratory Personnel." *Journal of Human Resources* 13:91-102.

Wierenga, D.E., and C.R. Easton. 1993. "The Drug Development and Approval Process." In *Development: New Medicines for Older Americans*. Washington, D.C.: Pharmaceutical Manufactures Association.

Williams, Marcia. 1992. "Pesticides: The Potential for Change." *EPA Journal* 18(2): 15-16.

Willis, J. W. "A Short History of Rent Control Laws." *Cornell Law Quarterly* 36 (Fall 1960), 54-94;

Wilson, David L. 1988. "On-the-Job Safety in the United States." *National Journal* 20:2430.

Wilson, James Q. 1980. *The Politics of Regulation*. New York: Basic Books.

Wines, Michael. 1984. "Steel: Managing the Decline." *National Journal* 16:603-7.

Wines, Michael. 1983a. "Auchter's Record at OSHA Leaves Labor Outraged, Business Satisfied." *National Journal* 15:2008-13.

Wines, Michael. 1983b. "Scandals at EPA May Have Done in Reagan's Move to Ease Cancer Controls." *National Journal* 15:1264-69.

Wines, Michael. 1983c. "Auchter's Record at OSHA Leaves Labor Outraged, Business Satisfied." *National Journal* 15:2008-13.

Wines, Michael. 1983d. "Less Milk Could Mean More Money for Dairy Farmers, Higher Federal Costs." *National Journal* 15:2666-2669.

Wines, Michael. 1982a. "Reagan's Antitrust Line-Common Sense or Invitation to Corporate Abuse?" *National Journal* 14:1204-9.

Wines, Michael. 1982b. "Banks, S&Ls, and the Securities Industry Scramble for Congressional Goodies." *National Journal* 14:1498-502.

Winger, B. and R. Frasca. 1993. *Personal Finance: An Integrated Planning Approach* (3rd ed.). New York: Macmillan.

Winter, Carl K. 1993. "Pesticide Residues and the Delaney Clause." *Food Technology* 41 (July): 81-88.

Wolf, H. A. 1989. *Personal Financial Planning*. Boston, MA: Allyn and Bacon.

Wood, B. Dan. 1992. "Modeling Federal Implementation as a System: The Clean Air Case. *American Journal of Political Science* 36:40-67.

Wood, B. Dan. 1990. "Does Politics Make a Difference at the EEOC?" *American Journal of Political Science* 34:503-530.

Wood, B. Dan. 1988. "Principles, Bureaucrats, and Responsiveness in Clean Air Enforcements." *American Political Science Review* 82:213-234.

Wood, B. Dan and James E. Anderson. 1993. "The Politics of U.S. Antitrust Regulation." *American Journal of Political Science.* 37:1-39.

Wood, B. Dan and Richard Waterman. 1994. *Bureaucratic Dynamics: The Role of a Bureaucracy in a Democracy*. Boulder, CO: Westview Press.

Wood, B. Dan, and Richard Waterman. 1993. "The Dynamics of Political-Bureaucratic Adaptation." *American Journal of Political Science* 37:497-528.

Wood, William C. 1978. "Pricing Behavior of Attorneys in Northern Virginia After *Goldfarb*." *The American Economist* 22:56-68.

Wright, Patrick J. 1978. *On a Clear Day You Can See General Motors*. New York: Avon.

Yandle, Bruce. 1989. *The Political Limits of Environmental Regulation*. Westport, CT: Quorum.

Yantek, Thom and Kenneth D. Bartrell. 1988. "Political Climate and Corporate Mergers: When Politics Affects Economics" *Western Political Quarterly* 41: 309-22.

Young, David S. 1988. "The Economic Theory of Regulation: Evidence from the Uniform CPA Exam." *The Accounting Review* 63:283-291.

Youngberg, Garth. 1976. "U.S. Agriculture in the 1970s: Policy and Politics." In *Economic Regulatory Policies,* James E. Anderson, ed. Lexington, MA: Lexington Books, pp. 51-68.

Zeiger, L. Harmon, and G. Wayne Peak. 1972. *Interest Groups in American Society*. Englewood Cliffs, N.J.: Prentice-Hall.

Zwick, David, and Marcy Benstock. 1971. *Water Wasteland*. New York: Grossman.

Court Cases Cited

AFL-CIO v. *Occupational Health and Safety Administration* 965 F.2d 962 (11th cir. 1992).

Addyston *Pipe and Steel Co.* v. *United States*, 175 U.S. 211 (1899).

American Bankers Association v. *Connell*, 194 U.S. App. D.C. 80 (1980).

American Column and Lumber Co. v. *United States*, 257 U.S. 377 (1921).

American Medical Association v. *Federal Trade Commission*, 50 L.W. 4313 (1982).

American Textile Manufacturers v. *Donavan*, 452 U.S. 490 (1981).

Atlas Roofing v. *Occupational Safety and Health Review Commission*, 430 U.S. 442 (1977).

Baker v. *Carr*, 369 U.S. 186 (1962).

Bates v. *State Bar of Arizona*, 433 U.S. 350 (1977).

Brown Shoe Company v. *United States*, 370 U.S. 294 (1962).

California v. *ARC America Corporation*, 490 U.S. 93 (1989)

Continental TV v. *GTE Sylvania,* 433 U.S. 365 (1977).

Federal Trade Commission v. *Consolidated Foods*, 360 U.S. 592 (1965).

Federal Trade Commission v. *Morton Salt*, 334 U.S. 37 (1948).

Federal Trade Commission v. *Procter & Gamble*, 386 U.S. 568 (1967).

Federal Trade Commission v. *Sperry and Hutchinson*, 405 U.S. 233 (1972).

Gade v. National Solid Wastes Managment Association 505 US-,120 LEd 2nd 73, 112 S Ct (1992)

Goldfarb v. *Virginia State Bar*, 421 U.S. 733 (1975).

Humphrey's Executor v. *United States*, 295 U.S. 602 (1935).

Illinois Brick Co. v. *Illinois,* 431 U.S. 720 (1977).

Immigration and Naturalization Service v. *Chadha*, 77 L. Ed. 2d 317 (1983).

Industrial Union Department, AFL-CIO v. *American Petroleum Institute*, 448 U.S. 607 (1981).

International Harvester v. *Ruckelshaus*, 478 F. 2d 615 (D.C. Cir. 1973).

International Salt Co. v. *United States*, 332 U.S. 392 (1947).

International Union, UAW v. *Occupational Safety and Health Administration* 938 F.2d 1310 (D.C. Cir. 1991)

Loewe v. *Lawler*, 208 U.S. 274 (1908).

Marshall v. *Barlow's*, 436 U.S. 307 (1978).

Miles Medical Co. v. *John Park,* 220 U.S. 373 (1911).

Motor Vehicle Manufacturers Association v. *State Farm Mutual Automobile Insurance,* 77 L. Ed. 2d 443 (1983).

Northern Securities v. *United States*, 193 U.S. 197 (1904).

Packard Motor Co. v. *Webster, 355* U.S. 822 (1957).

Philadelphia v. *Westinghouse Electric*, 210 F. Supp. 483 (1961).

Raladam v. *Federal Trade Commission*, 42 F.2d 430 (1930).

Reich v. *Simpson, Gumpertz and Heger, Inc.* 3 F.3d 1 (1993).

Siegal v. *Chicken Delight*, 448 F.2d 653 (1971).

Sierra Club v. *Ruckelshaus*, 489 F.2d 390 (5th Cir. 1974).

Standard Oil of California v. *United States*, 337 U.S. 293 (1949).

Standard Oil Company of New Jersey v. *United States*, 21 1 U.S. 1 (1 91 1).

Tampa Electric Co. v. *Nashville Coal Co.,* 365 U.S. 320 (1961).

Times-Picayune Publishing Co. v. *United States*, 354 U.S. 594 (1953).

United Cburch of Christ v. *Federal Communications Commission*, 359 F.2d 994 (1966).

United States v. *Aluminum Company of America*, 148 F.2d 416 (2d Cir., 1945).

United States v. *American Tobacco Company*, 221 U.S. 106 (191 1).

United States v. *Arnold, Scbwinn and Co.*, 388 U.S. 365 (1949).

United States v. *Bethlehem Steel Corp.*, 168 F. Supp. 576 (1958).

United States v. *Butler,* 297 U.S. 1 (1936).

United States v. *Container Corporation of America*, 393 U.S. 333 (1969).

United States v. *E. C. Knight*, 156 U.S. 1 (1895).

United States v. *General Dynamics*, 415 U.S. 486 (1974).

United States v. *International Telephone and Telegraph,* 324 F. Supp. 19 (D. Conn., 1970).

United States v. *Jerrold Electronics*, 365 U.S. 567 (1961).

United States v. *Loew's Inc.,* 371 U.S. 38 (1962).

United States v. *Philadelphia National Bank*, 374 U.S. 321 (1963).

United States v. *Socony-Vacuum Oil Company*, 310 U.S. 150 (1940).

United States v. *United States Steel Corp.*, 251 U.S. 417 (1920).

United States v. *Trenton Potteries Co.*, 273 U.S. 392 (1927).

United States v. *Von's Grocery*, 384 U.S. 270 (1966).

Utah Pie v. *Continential Baking*, 386 U.S. 685 (1967).

Index